series7

STOCKBROKER NASD EXAM

fifth edition

ARCO

series7
STOCKBROKER NASD EXAM
fifth edition

PHILIP MEYERS • PETER SOLOMON

MACMILLAN • USA

Tables on pages 93 copyright © 1999, 1995, 1994, 1993, 1991 by The New York Times Company. Reprinted by permission.

Fifth Edition

Macmillan Reference USA
A Simon & Schuster Macmillan Company
1633 Broadway
New York, NY 10019-6785

An Arco Book

Macmillan is a registered trademark of Macmillan, Inc.
Arco is a registered trademark of Simon & Schuster Inc.

Library of Congress Cataloging-in-Publication

ISBN: 0-02-862196-4

Manufactured in the United States of America

1 2 3 4 5 6 7 8 9 10

foreword

This fifth edition of Arco's *Series 7 / Stockbroker Exam* should prove just as successful as the first four editions due to two important factors. The first is the clear, precise way that the authors explain the complex subjects that prospective stockbrokers must master in order to pass the Series 7 Exam. In all of the twenty-four subject areas covered on the test, this book is right on target both with the information test-takers need to know and with the way that information is addressed on the exam.

The second factor that will surely contribute to the book's success is its low price. In a market where some study materials can cost up to $150, this information-packed book is, quite simply, a great value. Because its price is so economical, it makes not only an ideal single-volume guide to the test, but also a natural supplement to a larger-scale preparation program. In addition, for readers who are not necessarily preparing for the Series 7 Exam but who are interested in the securities industry in general, this book makes an excellent, concise introduction to the day-to-day workings of Wall Street.

For this new edition, Philip Meyers and Peter Solomon have judiciously expanded the original text, providing the reader with additional information on those areas that now receive more emphasis on the Series 7 Exam. They have also updated all of the instructional and review sections to reflect the most recent industry regulations—and today's most popular investment instruments and strategies. Furthermore, the practice tests have been similarly updated so that the amount of coverage given to each topic accurately reflects the actual makeup of today's Series 7 Exam.

To derive the most benefit from this book, the reader will need to be both diligent and conscientious. Just as the authors have taken no shortcuts in presenting the information, the reader should take no shortcuts in studying the material. Furthermore, it pays to remember that the Series 7 Exam is not static. The pool of several thousand questions is constantly being revised and updated, and most recently there has been a decreasing emphasis on simply memorizing facts—and an increasing emphasis on understanding basic principles. For the prospective stockbroker, this means a more difficult examination. This book is a good place to begin not only your preparation for the Series 7 Exam but also your career in the securities industry.

ALVIN D. HALL
Faculty Member
New York Institute of Finance

WILLIAM A. RINI
Senior Vice President
New York Institute of Finance

contents

FOREWORD   by the New York Institute of Finance   v

PART ONE   1
About the Series 7 Examination

INTRODUCTION   3

General Examination Information and   3
Preparation for the Series 7 Test

PART TWO   9
Subject Review

CHAPTER ONE: STOCKS   11

Stock Terms   12

Types of Stock   13

Ownership   14

Rights of Ownership—Voting   15

Rights of Ownership—Dividends   17

Other Rights   18

Preferred Stock   20

ADRs and Warrants   21

Terms   21

Review Questions   23

Answers to Review Questions   26

CHAPTER TWO: BONDS   29

PART ONE: Basics of Debt Securities   30

Forms of Bonds   30

Other Bond Types and Terms   31

Callability   32

Putability   33

Bond Trading, Pricing and Yields   33

PART TWO: Corporates   37

Trust Indenture   38

Secured Bonds   39

Unsecured Bonds   40

Other Types of Bonds   40

Convertibility   40

Bond Ratings   45

Eurobonds   46

PART THREE: United States Government Issues   46

Negotiable Securities   46

Non-Negotiable U.S. Government Obligations   49

Other Government Agency Obligations   50

U.S. Government—Owned Agency Obligations   52

Mortgage Backed Securities   52

Other Bond Issuing Agencies   54

Rules on Delivery of U.S. Government Instruments   54

PART FOUR: Municipal Bonds   55

Types of Municipals   56

Types of Municipal Issues   59

Legal Opinion   59

Indenture   60

Interest and Principal Payment   60

Tender, Call and Put   61

Municipal Bond Insurance   62

Yields and Taxation   62

Trading in Municipals   64

Judging Municipals   66

Terms   67

Review Questions 74

Answers to Review Questions 78

CHAPTER THREE: Money Market Instruments 81

Federal Funds 82

Repurchase Agreements 82

Banker's Acceptances 82

Commercial Paper 83

Negotiable Certificates of Deposit 83

Broker's Loans (Call Loans) 84

Eurodollars 84

Terms 84

Review Questions 85

Answers to Review Questions 85

CHAPTER FOUR: INVESTMENT COMPANIES—MUTUAL FUNDS **87**

Forms of Management Companies 88

Earnings 90

Features of Mutual Funds 91

Management Company Structure 92

Calculating Mutual Fund Yields 93

Pricing of Shares 93

Calculating Sales Charges and Redemption Fees 94

Breakpoints 95

Dollar Cost Averaging 96

Redeeming Shares 96

Rules Governing Open-End Investment Companies 97

Ownership 98

Taxation 98

Closed- and Open-End Investment Companies 99

Investor Accounts 100

Withdrawal Plans   102

The Investment Company Act of 1940   102

NASD Rules on Mutual Funds   104

Terms   106

Review Questions   108

Answers to Review Questions   111

CHAPTER FIVE: Tax-Advantaged Investments, Annuities   115
and Retirement Plans

PART ONE: Tax-Advantaged Investments   115

Tax Shelters Today   116

Direct Participation Programs   116

Evaluating a Limited Partnership   118

Methods of Funding a Limited Partnership   119

Types of Offerings   119

The Subscription Agreement   120

Real Estate Programs   120

Oil and Gas Programs   123

Equipment-Leasing Programs   125

Taxation and Accounting Practices   125

Dissolving a Limited Partnership   126

PART TWO: Annuities   126

Fixed Annuity   126

Variable Annuity   127

Annuity Purchase Options   129

Annuity Payout Options   130

Other Features   131

Taxation of Annuities   131

PART THREE: Retirement Plans   131

Employer Pension Plans   132

Retirement Plans for Small Employers and Self-Employed   133

Terms   136

Review Questions   139

Answers to Review Questions   142

CHAPTER SIX: New Issues   145

The Investment Banker   145

Types of Offerings   146

Private Placements   146

Negotiated Offering   146

The Underwriting Agreement   147

Types of Underwriter Commitments   148

Formation of Underwriters' Syndicate   149

Types of Underwriters' Agreements   149

The Selling Group   150

Preparation of New Issues   150

Sale of New Issues   152

Compensation   154

New Issues of Municipals   155

Municipals: Bidding and Selling Procedures   156

Terms   158

Review Questions   161

Answers to Review Questions   164

CHAPTER SEVEN: Over-the-Counter Market (OTC)   167

The Four Markets   167

Over-the-Counter Trading   168

The Market Maker   169

Broker or Dealer   169

Confirmation   169

Types of Quotes   170

Types of Orders   170

Wholesale and Retail Trading   171

The NASDAQ System   171

Other Sources of OTC Information   172

NASD Markup Policy   173

OTC Municipal Bond Trading   175

Terms   175

Review Questions   177

Answers to Review Questions   179

CHAPTER EIGHT: Exchange Markets   181

Membership   182

Operation of the Exchange   183

Types of Orders   184

Block Trades   187

The Specialist   189

Odd-Lot Trading   192

Bond Trading   194

Reading the Tape   195

Terms   196

Review Questions   199

Answers to Review Questions   202

CHAPTER NINE: Options   205

Forms of Options   206

Terminology   207

Basic Options Possibilities   208

Premiums   210

Covered vs. Uncovered Options   212

Break-Even Points   213

Strategies: Hedges, Straddles, Combinations, and Spreads   213

Objectives of Options Traders   216

Margins   217

Option Transaction Procedures   219

Options Pricing   222

OCC Rules and Regulations   222

Position Limits   224

Exchanges   224

Tax on Options   225

Suitability   226

Stock Index Options   226

Interest Rate Options   229

Foreign Currency Options   232

Terms   237

Review Questions   242

Answers to Review Questions   246

CHAPTER TEN: Client Accounts   249

Opening a New Account   249

Types of Customer Accounts   252

Custodian Accounts for Minors   254

Restrictions on New Accounts   256

Requirements in Dealing with Deceased Persons' Accounts   257

Order Procedures for Client Accounts   258

Terms   261

Review Questions   263

Answers to Review Questions   265

CHAPTER ELEVEN: Margins and Short Sales   267

PART ONE: Margins   267

Regulation of Margin Accounts   268

Characteristics of Margin Accounts   269

Reg T Initial Margin Requirement   271

Calculations Involving Margin Accounts   271

Restricted Accounts   274

Industry Requirements   277

Special Memorandum Account (SMA)   281

PART TWO: Short Sales 285

Purpose of Short Sales 286

Rights of Lenders 287

Closing Out a Short Sale 288

Margin Requirements for Short Sales 288

Regulation of Short Sales 289

Calculations in Short Sales Accounts 290

Terms 293

Review Questions 298

Answers to Review Questions 301

CHAPTER TWELVE: Analyses 303

PART ONE: Economic Analysis 303

National Income and GNP 303

Business Cycles 304

Controlling the Cycles—The Monetary Approach 307

Controlling the Cycles—Fiscal Policies 310

International Factors 311

PART TWO: Technical and Fundamental Analysis 313

Technical Analysis 313

Fundamental Analysis 318

PART THREE: Securities Analysis 319

The Balance Sheet 320

The Income Statement 322

Statement of Changes in Financial Condition 324

Valuation Practices 325

Effects of Corporate Changes 326

PART FOUR: Financial Ratios and Investment Policies 328

Liquidity Ratios 328

Debt Ratios 329

Capitalization Ratios 329

Asset Utilization Ratios 330

Profitability Ratios 330

Cash Flow 331

Valuation Ratios 331

Earnings Ratios 332

PART FIVE: Investment Risks 333

Portfolio Policies 334

PART SIX: Portfolio Theory 335

Terms 338

Review Questions 342

Answers to Review Questions 345

CHAPTER THIRTEEN: Taxation 349

General Information 349

Treatment of Income from Securities 351

Treatment of Debt Instruments 353

Mutual Funds 354

Options 354

Gifts and Estates 354

Tax-Advantaged Investments 354

Terms 355

Review Questions 356

Answers to Review Questions 359

CHAPTER FOURTEEN: Reading the Financial News 361

New York Stock Exchange Issues 361

NYSE Bond Trading 363

Over-the-Counter Quotations (NASDAQ National Market) 363

Treasury Bills, Bonds, and Notes 364

Government Agency Bonds 365

Stock Options 365

Mutual Funds   365

Corporate Sales and Earnings Reports   367

Corporate Dividend Reports   369

Tombstone Announcements   369

Blue List (Secondary Market for Municipals)   369

Municipal Bond Official Notice of Sale   370

Municipal Bond Buyer Index   372

Visible Supply of Munis   373

Municipal Bonds Tombstone   373

Standard & Poor's Stock Guide   374

CHAPTER FIFTEEN: Federal and State Regulations   377

PART ONE: The Securities Act of 1933   377

Registration Requirements   378

Exempt Securities   380

Exempt Transactions   381

Private Placement (Regulation D)   381

Sale of Restricted and Control Securities (Rule 144)   382

Intrastate Transactions (Rule 147)   383

Regulation A Offerings   384

Advertising   384

PART TWO: The Securities Exchange Act of 1934   385

Rules Governing Registration   386

Credit Regulations   386

Hypothecation and Commingling of Customers' Securities   386

Manipulation and Deception   387

Stabilization   388

Insider Rules   388

Proxies   389

Record-Keeping and Report-Filing Requirements   389

OTC Regulations   389

Capital Requirements   390

PART THREE: Other Regulations — 391

  Investment Company Act of 1940 (ICA 1940) — 391

  Federal Reserve Board Regulations — 391

  Securities Investor Protection Corporation (SIPC) — 392

  Trust Indenture Act of 1939 — 393

  State Regulations — 393

CHAPTER SIXTEEN: Industry Regulations — 395

  PART ONE: NASD Regulations — 395

    Purposes — 396

    Bylaws: Membership — 396

    Rules of Fair Practice — 398

    The Uniform Practice Code — 406

    Code of Procedure — 407

    Code of Arbitration — 407

  PART TWO: NYSE Regulations — 407

    The Registered Representative — 407

    Public Communications (Advertising and Speaking) — 409

    Conduct of Accounts — 410

    Arbitration — 412

    Listing — 412

  PART THREE: MSRB Regulations — 413

    Rules — 414

    Terms — 418

    Review Questions — 424

    Answers to Review Questions — 426

PART THREE
Three Practice Examinations — 429

  PRACTICE EXAMINATION ONE — 431

    Part One — 435

    Part Two — 449

    Answer Key, Part One — 463

Answer Key, Part Two   464

Answer Explanations, Part One   465

Answer Explanations, Part Two   493

PRACTICE EXAMINATION TWO   521

Part One   525

Part Two   539

Answer Key, Part One   554

Answer Key, Part Two   555

Answer Explanations, Part One   556

Answer Explanations, Part Two   585

PRACTICE EXAMINATION THREE   613

Part One   617

Part Two   632

Answer Key, Part One   645

Answer Key, Part Two   646

Answer Explanations, Part One   647

Answer Explanations, Part Two   675

INDEX   703

ABOUT THE
SERIES 7 EXAMINATION

introduction

GENERAL EXAMINATION INFORMATION AND PREPARATION FOR THE SERIES 7 TEST

This book is intended for those people who plan to become stockbrokers—licensed registered representatives or account executives employed by brokerage firms. These professionals must be able to call on an extraordinary amount of knowledge in their day-to-day dealings with the investing public and with colleagues in the investment industry. To ensure that they have command of the needed information, they must pass the Qualification Examination for General Securities Registered Representative ("Test Series 7"). This comprehensive test consists of 250 questions on every aspect of the industry and is formulated and administered by the National Association of Securities Dealers (NASD).

Anyone who masters the material in these pages should be able to pass the test.

The comprehensive focus should also make this book useful to the serious investor or to anyone who is considering becoming an investor—in fact, to anyone curious about just what a stockbroker knows. Because it contains so much information in such a clearly organized fashion, it can also be a convenient general reference source for anyone who needs to know (or be reminded of) details about various facets of the investment industry.

In short, while our principal audience is the potential registered representative, this is not simply a test preparation manual. Although some knowledge of general business practice and terminology is helpful, every effort has been made to present the material in a way that is accessible to any reader. All technical terms are thoroughly defined; industry practices, rules, and regulations are not simply described but are explained in terms of their rationale in the context of actual operations. Wherever possible, we provide illustrations and examples and avoid long lists of facts.

This approach should also serve those whose main interest is in taking the examination, as many of the questions require more than recalling the pertinent term or formula. Rather, candidates are asked to apply their understanding of the industry in making judgments and comprehending and analyzing unfamiliar material.

Note that these pages contain more information than any single test will cover; we have tried to be as complete as space allows, offering more detail than strictly necessary. At the same time, it is not possible to cover every item on every test in any one book. The work of the registered representative is not based on a fixed code; products, practices, laws, and regulations are all subject to change, and the test along with them.

Plan of the book

We begin the book with five chapters of basic information on the "products" that a registered representative can offer a customer, the basic elements of the securities industry: common and preferred stocks, bonds and other debt instruments, mutual funds, and investments designed to present tax advantages.

In the following four chapters, we examine the operation and role of the various securities markets, tracing the steps involved in a new issue of each of several types of instruments and describing in detail the workings of over-the-counter markets, the national exchanges, and options markets.

In Chapters 10 and 11, we describe the procedures followed in handling customer accounts and orders, both regular brokerage office practices and the special treatment required in dealing with margin accounts and short sales.

Chapter 12 presents an extended review of the elements involved in analyzing and selecting investments or investment strategies for a particular individual. There are separate sections on broad economic analysis, the "technical" and "fundamental" approaches, ways to assess a particular firm and its securities, and mathematical techniques.

Chapter 13 sketches out the tax consequences of investment moves and positions. This has become a volatile area in recent years, with major changes in thinking about taxation on investments, but we provide the essential general information needed to guide registered representatives and their customers.

Chapter 14 follows with a guide to reading published financial news.

Chapters 15 and 16 cover the rules that affect all securities transactions: federal and state laws, regulations imposed by the National Association of Securities Dealers, rules of the national exchanges, and the special rules governing municipal issues.

Special features of the book

In addition to the text, with its many examples and clearly defined subsections, each chapter is followed by a brief glossary of key terms. These, along with the index, should serve as a helpful "refresher" both while studying for the test and in years to come.

Review questions at the end of each chapter are designed to help strengthen your comprehension of the material in that chapter. These questions should be approached not so much as a challenge, but as a way of highlighting and reinforcing information. In effect, they help teach the material: many of the questions describe a fact or condition that is not explicit in the text but must be inferred, so becoming thoroughly familiar with the answers is essential to mastering the material.

Practice tests

Finally, there are three complete tests, chances for a trial run. It is impossible to overemphasize their importance. The Series 7 Exam includes 250 questions; this means, on average, you will have less than a minute and a half to choose the correct answer. As each question offers four possible answers, it is essential that you become thoroughly familiar with the *form* of the questions. With 1,000 answers to choose from, there is no time during the test to do more than remember the correct information.

These practice tests simulate the actual exam in length, form, and content (that is, in the mix of questions). It cannot simulate the presentation precisely, as the test is now offered on the PROCTOR™ system. This involves a video terminal which displays questions much as they are on these pages, but to answer, one touches an indicated point on the screen. PROCTOR draws questions randomly from a central question bank.

Although randomly selected, the questions are chosen in the proportions shown below. The questions are distributed so that more difficult ones occur in the middle of the test with easier ones at the beginning and end of the exam. The system allows individual testing and immediate grading.

Distribution of questions

Responsibility	Number of Questions
Providing customers and prospective customers with information on investments and making suitable recommendations	123
Explaining the organization, participants, and functions of various securities markets and the principal factors that affect them	53

Responsibility	Number of Questions
Opening, transferring, and closing customer accounts and maintaining appropriate account records	27
Monitoring the customers' portfolios and making recommendations consistent with changes in economic and financial conditions, as well as the customers' needs and objectives	21
Obtaining and verifying the customers' purchase and sale instructions, entering orders, and following up on completion of transactions	13
Seeking business for the broker-dealer through customers and potential customers	9
Evaluating customers in terms of financial needs, current holdings, and available investment capital and helping them identify their investment objectives	4

The best possible preparation involves working within the real time limits imposed by the examiners. Try to complete each practice exam in two three-hour sessions, with a one-hour break.

In grading yourself, remember that the exam is designed only to gauge your knowledge of the duties of a registered representative. You are not competing with others taking the test; anyone who correctly answers 70 percent (175) of the 250 questions is considered qualified.

Question format

All questions asked, on the test and in this book, are in one of six formats:

1. A simple question.

   Which of the following is true of T-bonds?

   (A) They have little inflation risk.
   (B) They have little interest rate risk.

(C) They have little credit risk.
(D) They are not widely available.

2. An incomplete statement; you must find the answer that logically completes it.

A trade between an investment company and a bank is a:

(A) first market trade
(B) second market trade
(C) third market trade
(D) fourth market trade

3. An incomplete statement; you must choose which answer is incorrect. To differentiate this sort of question, the word "EXCEPT" is always used in capitals.

All of the following are acceptable investments for an IRA EXCEPT:

(A) unlisted stocks
(B) non-investment grade bonds
(C) diamonds
(D) junk bond funds

4. Multiple-answer questions; here, two or more (sometimes all) responses are correct. The possible responses are identified by Roman numerals.

Option allocation assignments notices to customers may use which of the following methods?

  I.   random selection
 II.   FIFO
III.   LIFO
IV.   equitable allocation

(A) I, II, and IV only
(B) II, III, and IV only
(C) I and II only
(D) II and IV only

5. Matching one or more offered answers with its appropriate description, usually offered in a series of questions. Note that more than one, or none, of the choices may apply.

Questions 37–39 refer to the following choices:
(A) spread
(B) takedown concession
(C) reallowance
(D) manager's expense

Which choice is described in the following questions?

37. The portion of a municipal bond offering that is the difference between the public offering price and what the issuer receives.

38. The amount that a member of the syndicate receives.

39. The amount that a member of the selling group receives.

6. Questions based on an exhibit, such as a tombstone ad, a stock table, or a rule; the questions themselves are usually of the type described in (1) or (2) above.

PART TWO

SUBJECT REVIEW

CHAPTER ONE
stocks

The predominant form of business in the United States today is the corporation. All corporations must issue common stock; each share of stock represents a unit of ownership in (a "share of") the corporation.

All U.S. corporations must be chartered in some state under the laws of that state. This charter, filed with the secretary of state, is also called the Articles of Incorporation. It includes the:

- name, purpose, and nature of the business

- number and type of shares of stock being offered ("authorized stock")

- duties of corporate officers

- names and addresses of the corporation's original directors

Those who hold common stock have certain rights (enumerated below), but only a limited liability. That is, they are liable only for the amount they paid for their stock, not for any of the debt of the corporation.

Before going further, let us define some terms used in connection with stocks.

STOCK TERMS

Authorized stock (authorized shares)

As noted above, a corporation's charter limits the number of shares it may issue. This allowed amount is referred to as "authorized stock."

Unissued stock

This is stock authorized but not yet issued by the corporation. Most firms issue less stock than has been authorized and hold the remainder for future use.

Issued stock

The portion of the issued stock sold to investors.

Outstanding stock

Issued shares currently in public hands. Note that this is not necessarily identical with issued stock because some issued stock is considered treasury stock (see below).

Treasury stock

Outstanding stock that has been reacquired by the corporation, through purchase in the open market or by other means, is called treasury stock. Treasury stock can be held, reissued, or retired. It is not considered outstanding stock.

Treasury stock carries no right to vote or to collect dividends, nor is it used in calculating earnings per share. It is generally not considered part of the capitalization of the company.

Par value

An arbitrary value assigned when the stock is issued and printed on the stock certificate. Historically, par value has been used as a corporate bookkeeping entry. It has been traditionally set at a low price, partly because some states' taxes are based on it. This value has no relationship to any other valuation of the stock.

For stock issued at a price above par value, the difference is carried on the books as paid-in surplus. Sometimes stock is issued with no par value.

Book value

Unlike par value, the book value of a share reflects the net worth of the corporation, as determined by generally accepted accounting principles, divided by the number of shares outstanding. (See Balance Sheet, pages 320–322.)

Market value

This is simply the value assigned to a share in the marketplace, for example, the currently quoted price of a share.

TYPES OF STOCK

Stocks are often classified in terms of the differing objectives of investors or investment plans. These categories are somewhat fluid, but the vocabulary is widely used to describe stocks or groups of stocks.

Blue chips

These are stocks in large, well-established corporations with long histories of adequate earnings and regular dividend payments. They are considered among the least risky of investments and appeal to those seeking both current income and long-term gains.

Growth

Stock in firms which have shown the ability to grow at a faster pace than other, comparable firms. Because they are most concerned with growth, these companies often reinvest most or all of their yearly earnings, so dividends may be small or nonexistent. They are suitable for investors primarily seeking capital gain over the long term rather than income. They tend to be more volatile, and hence riskier, than most stocks.

Income

Shares of companies in "mature" industries which tend to pay a significant portion of their income in dividends—utilities are a prime example. They are suited for those investors, mostly older, whose main interest is in current income rather than in capital gains.

Defensive

Stocks in companies thought to be generally unaffected by the business cycle so that their earnings continue even when the economy is faltering. An extreme example would be stock in a firm known to thrive on hard times—perhaps a chain of pawnbrokers.

Cyclical

These are holdings in companies whose returns mirror those of the economy as a whole: thriving when the economy is thriving, slowing when it falters. The automobile industry behaves this way at times. These stocks are of interest to investors who feel they can divine an upcoming surge in the economy.

Speculative

Stocks with poor or nonexistent current earnings but with the possibility of large capital gains. Examples would include a biotechnology firm with a new drug or a mining company reporting a big find. These are risky investments and are likely to be losing propositions if the firm does not realize its potential.

OWNERSHIP

The stock certificate

This document provides evidence of ownership of stock. The stock certificate is negotiable. It shows:

- name of the corporation
- number of shares represented by the certificate
- name or names of the registered owner(s)
- name of the transfer agent
- name of the registrar
- signatures of authorized corporate officers

Transfer of ownership

A stockholder has the right to transfer ownership of his or her shares except in the case of certain "restricted stocks" where this right is specifically withheld. The issuing corporation must record the name of any purchaser of its stock. When stock changes hands, the new owner is entitled to stockholder's rights only after a record of the transfer of ownership is made.

To transfer a stock, the stockholder endorses the back of the certificate. Such a transfer involves two vital steps:

Transfer agents   A transfer agent records the name, address, social security number, and number of shares held by each registered shareholder. The transfer agent also assures that properly endorsed old certificates are canceled and that new certificates in the name(s) of the new owner(s) of record are signed (by the responsible corporate officer), sealed (with the corporate seal), and delivered (to the new shareholder(s)).

Transfer agents are often responsible for sending dividend payments, proxy votes, and notices of annual meetings. In the case of securities held in "street name," *i.e.,* in the name of the broker-dealer who is carrying the account, the firm is then responsible for forwarding these to the beneficial owner.

Registrars   The registrar must always be independent of the corporation. The registrar gets both old and new certificates, determines that the corporation has not issued more stock than authorized under its charter, and that all outstanding shares are accounted for (as to ownership) on the corporation's books.

Figure 1.1   Stock Certificate (front)

Assignment

Stocks may also be "assigned." This requires a form called a "stock power." Assigned changes of ownership are not recorded on a corporation's books.

RIGHTS OF OWNERSHIP—VOTING

The principal rights of ownership are voting rights, the right to share in the profits of the corporation by receiving dividends, and residual rights when a company is liquidated.

Voting rights

Most common stock entitles the owner to attend annual meetings and to vote on all important matters affecting shareholders. These include:

- alterations to the corporate charter

- mergers and acquisitions

- recapitalization (an exchange of one form of security—stock, preferred stock or bond—for another)

- financial reorganization

- election of the board of directors of the corporation (the choice shareholders face most frequently)

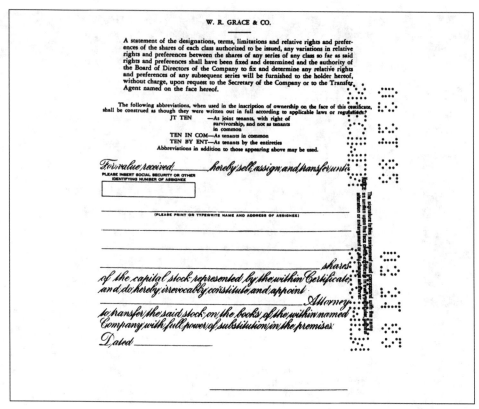

Figure 1.2   Stock Certificate (back)

Voting for directors follows one of two procedures:

Regulatory (statutory) voting
Each share has one vote for each position on the board of directors. For example, if there are seven positions to be filled on the board of directors, a shareholder owning 100 shares may cast up to 100 votes for each of seven different candidates. Under this system, a majority of the shareholders can determine the composition of the board.

Cumulative voting
Each share controls as many votes as there are members of the board. For example, if there are seven positions to be filled, a shareholder with 100 shares can cast 700 votes and may cast them all for a single board member if he or she so desires. This method of voting allows a minority—by cumulating votes for one candidate—to assure itself of representation on the board.

Proxies

As it is not possible for most shareholders to actually attend corporate meetings, corporations are required to send all shareholders a "proxy," or power of attorney, authorizing the holder to vote on the shareholder's behalf either according to specific instructions or at the proxyholder's discretion. When an outside management group or firm attempts to take control of a corporation, it must persuade shareholders to vote out current directors. These efforts usually involve soliciting of proxies and are called "proxy contests."

The proxy form also includes all pertinent information on matters to be voted on at the meeting. Organized exchanges like the NYSE are required to de-list firms that fail to provide the proxy form.

RIGHTS OF OWNERSHIP—DIVIDENDS

The principal financial rewards of owning common stock are the opportunity for capital appreciation—the chance that the price of the stock will rise—and dividend income. Dividends are paid to common shareholders at the discretion of the company's directors (that is, if they choose to do so). Common stock dividends may be paid only after all taxes, interest on bonds, and preferred stock dividends (if any) have been paid. *They must come from current earnings or from retained earnings from prior years.*

When a cash dividend is declared, it is recorded immediately on the corporation's books as a current liability. Actual payment of the dividend causes a reduction in the working capital of the company.

Directors must officially declare the dividend, including the size, date of record, and the date payable. Thus the stockholder has a right to the dividend "when, as and if declared." Shareholders have rights to dividends in proportion to their holdings of the outstanding stock. Someone holding 5% of the outstanding stock is entitled to 5% of the total declared dividend, whether paid in cash or in stock.

Owners of the stock before the date determined by the board of directors as the "record date" for dividends are entitled to the dividends. This is true until two business days before the record date (since the transactions are settled in three business days). From then on the stock sells "ex-dividend," and the market price declines to reflect that loss of dividend.

Example

Amalgamated Consolidated Inc. is selling at $50, and a $2.50 dividend is declared for owners of record date of Friday, March 15th. Assuming no other changes, we can expect the stock to have an opening price on March 13th of $47.50.

Cash dividends

Most often, dividends are paid quarterly in cash and are declared as dollars per share rather than as total dollars of dividend. If XYZ Corp. declared a dividend of $2.40 per share, a person owning 200 shares of XYZ stock would receive a check for $480.

Stock dividends

Corporations sometimes declare "stock dividends" as opposed to cash dividends. These are expressed in percentage terms. For example, if XYZ Corp. declares a 5% stock dividend, a holder of 200 shares would receive a stock certificate for 10 additional shares.

This can sometimes lead to the creation of fractional shares. A 5% stock dividend on 50 shares would generate $.05 \times 50$ or 2.5 additional shares. Most often, firms redeem fractional shares for cash or allow them to be bought and sold through a broker at no commission. Increases beyond 25% are generally called stock splits.

Property dividends

A corporation may declare a property dividend. This is often in the form of securities. For instance, a corporation wishing to divest itself of a subsidiary might do so by distributing stock in that subsidiary to its own shareholders.

Stock splits

A firm will sometimes declare a stock split, i.e., a declaration that each old share is now equal to some number of new shares. This does not change the value of the underlying corporation, and so the other values are changed proportionately. Stock splits that do increase the number of authorized shares or change the par value must be approved by the shareholders.

Example

A stock with a par value of $1.00 and a market value of $20.00 per share which had a 2-for-1 stock split would now have twice as many authorized shares, each with a par value of $.50. Each outstanding share would now have a market value of $10.00.

Reverse splits

A reverse split declares that each old share is now equal to some fraction of a new share.

Example

In a 1-for-3 reverse split, 300 shares of old stock would now be 100 shares of the new stock. Both the par and market values would be tripled.

OTHER RIGHTS

Pre-emptive right

The right of a shareholder to maintain a proportionate share of ownership of the corporation. When this right exists, a current shareholder has the right to purchase any newly-issued stock in proportion to his or her original holdings in the company.

Example

A person owning 10% of the outstanding shares of a particular stock would have the right to purchase 10% of any new issue of this stock. If 50,000 new shares are issued, this person would have the right to purchase 10% of 50,000 or 5,000 of the shares.

Value of rights

The subscription price of a new issue is usually lower than the market price of already-issued stock. Hence, the right to purchase this new issue has some value and may be traded in the marketplace.

As with dividends, those who buy the stock before the date determined by the board of directors as the "record date" for "subscription rights" get the rights as well. The stock is said to sell "cum rights" or "with rights."

Again, this holds until two business days before the record date. From then on the stock sells "ex-rights," and the market price declines to reflect that loss of rights.

One can compute the theoretical value of a right as follows:

For stock selling "cum rights," the value is given by the formula:

$$\frac{\textbf{Market Price} - \textbf{Subscription Price}}{\textbf{Number of Rights Required} + 1}$$

or

$$\frac{\textbf{M} - \textbf{S}}{\textbf{N} + 1} = \textbf{Value}$$

Note that the market price of the stock M includes the value of the right in this case.

Example

If a stock is selling for $60 and two (2) rights are required to purchase a single share at the subscription price of $51, the value of a single right would be:

$$\frac{\$60 - \$51}{2 + 1} = \frac{\$9}{3} = \$3$$

For a stock selling "ex-rights," the theoretical value for a right is given by the formula:

$$\frac{\textbf{Market Value} - \textbf{Subscription Value}}{\textbf{Number of Rights Required}} = \frac{\textbf{M} - \textbf{S}}{\textbf{N}} = \textbf{Value}$$

Example

If the stock in the example above is now "ex-rights," its market value should reflect that and be $60 − $3 or $57. Thus we have

$$\frac{\$57 - \$51}{2} = \frac{\$6}{2} = \$3$$

Note that both formulae give the same theoretical value for the right.

Rights to inspection

Shareholders have the right to inspect certain corporate records, for example, the list of shareholders, minutes of shareholders' meetings, and certain corporate books.

Rights in liquidation or dissolution

When a company is liquidated or dissolved, the shareholders have residual rights to the assets of the company after bonds, other liabilities, and preferred stockholders are satisfied.

PREFERRED STOCK

Like common stock, preferred stock is an equity security, representing ownership in the company. It differs from common stock in the following ways:

- the dividend for preferred stock is fixed at some rate

- par value is usually set at $100 and the dividend is quoted, for example, "7% preferred" or, especially if the stock has no par value, as some dollar amount, *e.g.*, $6.50 "preferred"

- the preferred dividend must be paid before any common stock dividend can be paid

- preferred stock has prior claim in the event of liquidation

- in general, preferred stock holders do not have preemptive rights

Types of preferred stocks

There are several varieties of preferred stock, each differing in the method of payment and privileges.

Cumulative   Any dividend due that is not declared accumulates and must be paid before any common stock dividend can be declared.

Non-cumulative   By contrast, holders of non-cumulative preferred lose their dividend for any period when directors do not declare one.

Participating   Here an additional dividend is paid over and above the stated dividend if the common stock dividend exceeds a stated amount.

Convertible   These shares can be exchanged for (converted into) a designated number of shares of common stock at a specified rate. For obvious reasons, the value of these shares tends to rise and fall with the price of the common stock.

The term "parity price" applies to common stock delivered in exchange for convertible preferred. It is the price at which the shares of common are equal in value to the preferred. Given a preferred convertible into two shares of common, the parity price of the common is $\frac{1}{2}$ the price of the preferred. In general, the parity price of common is equal to the market price of the preferred divided by the conversion rate of preferred to common.

Callable   These are shares that the corporation reserves the right to "call," *i.e.*, to buy back at some (premium to the issued) price.

These features can be combined. For example, one might have a convertible, cumulative, participating preferred.

If a company issues several classes of preferred, they would be called Class A and Class B preferred, with the A having precedence as to dividends and at liquidation.

ADRS AND WARRANTS

Two other equity securities deserve brief mention here.

ADRs   An American Depository Receipt (ADR) is a security which represents shares of a foreign company. It is issued and traded in the United States. By issuing ADRs, foreign companies gain access to American investors.

The ADRs are usually issued by large commercial banks which have the underlying stock in their vaults. ADRs are registered on the bank's books, and any dividends, as well as proceeds from other rights sold overseas, are passed through to the ADR holders. While foreign stocks themselves are not subject to SEC regulation, ADRs are covered; in particular, they are subject to the rules on disclosure of the 1934 Securities Act.

Warrants   Warrants are securities, like rights, but they usually have a much longer life. They are sometimes attached to issues of bonds or preferred stock. They are also sometimes attached to speculative stock offerings and awarded to underwriters of these offerings as incentives. A warrant gives its owner the right to buy a share of common stock at some fixed price, called the exercise price. Warrants are considered an attractive feature since they provide the investor with the opportunity to participate in appreciation of the common stock. Some can be detached and traded; these have an intrinsic value equal to the difference between the market price of the stock and the exercise price. The warrant may be detachable immediately on issue, or at some later date; if the warrant is not detachable, it has no market value of its own.

The warrant and the right to buy typically expire after a number of years. When a warrant is exercised, its owner relinquishes it and pays the exercise price in return for the share of common stock.

TERMS

Stock   Units of ownership in a corporation

Authorized stock   Number of shares a corporation may issue

Unissued stock   Stock authorized but not issued

Issued stock   Shares of authorized stock actually issued

Outstanding stock   Stock issued to the public

Treasury stock   Stock issued but reacquired

Par value   Arbitrarily assigned at issue; not book value or market value

Types of stock   Often grouped in terms of investment objectives (*e.g.,* income or growth) and relative risk/safety

Stock certificate   Documentary proof of ownership

Transfers   Owners have right to transfer ownership; transfers involve transfer agent and registrar; must be recorded on the issuing corporation's books

Assignment   Owners may assign stock without transferring ownership through a stock power

Rights of ownership—voting

Statutory method   Each share = one vote for each position on the board of directors

Cumulative method   Each share = as many votes as there are directors

Proxies   Authorize holder to vote for shareholder; corporations must send proxies to all shareholders

Dividend rights   Dividends declared at directors' discretion; must come from earnings; must be paid in proportion to holdings; can be in cash or in stock

Splits   Corporation may declare that each share is now split into several shares, *e.g.,* a 3-for-1 split with each old share equal to 3 new shares

Pre-emptive rights   Shareholders keep their proportion of outstanding shares if new shares are issued; rights have value and may be traded

Theoretical Value for stock selling with rights

$$\frac{\text{Market Price} - \text{Subscription Price}}{\text{Number of Rights Required} + 1} = \text{Value}$$

for a stock selling "ex-rights"

$$\frac{\text{Market Price} - \text{Subscription Price}}{\text{Number of Rights Required}} = \text{Value}$$

Other rights   Right to inspect corporate records; right to assets of a firm in liquidation (after bondholders, other creditors, preferred shareholders)

Preferred stock   Represents ownership, pays fixed dollar or percentage dividend; par usually at $100; preferential treatment when dividends declared or in liquidation

Kinds of preferred

Cumulative   Undeclared dividends accumulate

Non-cumulative   Undeclared dividends not payable

Participating   Can pay more than the stated dividend

Convertible   Can be exchanged for common stock at stated rate

Callable   Must be sold back to issuer at its request (several features may be combined in one type of preferred)

Other equity securities

ADRs   American Depository Receipts, represent shares of a foreign company; usually issued by banks; subject to SEC regulation

Warrants Attached to some bonds or preferred; carry right to buy common at fixed price ("exercise price"); if detachable, can be traded; typically expire after a number of years

REVIEW QUESTIONS

1. The record and payable dates for stock dividends are chosen by:

   (A) the SEC
   (B) the corporation's transfer agent
   (C) the corporation's board of directors
   (D) a majority of the stockholders

2. If a $.20 dividend is declared with a record date of Monday, June 12, the stock goes "ex-dividend" on:

   (A) June 5
   (B) June 6
   (C) June 8
   (D) June 12

3. In the event of a corporate liquidation, which of the following would be last in claiming assets?

   (A) common stock
   (B) preferred stock
   (C) Internal Revenue Service
   (D) convertible debentures

4. If ACI has a 7% participating preferred, then 7% represents the:

   (A) maximum dividend
   (B) minimum dividend
   (C) maximum dividend but not the minimum
   (D) minimum dividend but not the maximum

   Questions 5–7 are based on the following information:
   The XYZ Corp. has authorized 10,000,000 shares of stock. It has issued 9,500,000 shares and has since repurchased 300,000 shares.

5. The number of unissued shares is:

   (A) 200,000
   (B) 500,000

   (C) 700,000
   (D) 800,000

6. The number of outstanding shares is:

   (A) 10,000,000
   (B) 9,800,000
   (C) 9,500,000
   (D) 9,200,000

7. The amount of treasury stock is:

   (A) 200,000
   (B) 300,000
   (C) 700,000
   (D) 800,000

8. Voting stock is the same as:

   (A) treasury stock
   (B) outstanding stock
   (C) authorized stock
   (D) issued stock

9. If three directors are to be elected under statutory voting rules, which of the following is permitted to an owner of 200 shares of common stock?

   (A) 200 votes for each of three candidates
   (B) 300 votes for one candidate
   (C) 600 votes for each of two candidates
   (D) all are permitted

10. Under cumulative voting rules, an owner of 200 shares voting for three directors could cast:

    (A) 300 votes for each of two directors
    (B) 600 votes for one director
    (C) up to 200 votes for each of three directors
    (D) all of the above

11. A woman owning 3,000 shares of common of a firm with 300,000 shares outstanding would be entitled to what portion of a $100,000 total declared dividend?

    (A) 1% of the dividend
    (B) $1,000
    (C) $.33$\frac{1}{3}$ per share
    (D) all of the above

12. If the company in question 11 subsequently declared a 5% stock dividend, she would receive:

    (A) 150 shares
    (B) 500 shares
    (C) 750 shares
    (D) 15,000 shares

13. The pre-emptive rights of stockholders include the right to:

    (A) continue proportionate ownership
    (B) vote on stock dividends
    (C) treasury stock
    (D) inspect records

14. A corporation offers a new issue of stock at $55. The market price of existing common is $60. If four rights are required to purchase each share of new stock, the theoretical value of a right is:

    (A) $1.00
    (B) $1.25
    (C) $5.00
    (D) $20.00

15. Amalgamated Consolidated, Inc., has not paid dividends for the past three years. Before a common stock dividend could be paid, dividends for the past three years must be paid to:

    (A) all common stockholders
    (B) all preferred stockholders

    (C) all cumulative preferred stockholders
    (D) all of the above

16. A firm with 1,000,000 shares outstanding is to issue 200,000 new shares. A shareholder owning 1,000 shares would receive how many rights?

    (A) 40
    (B) 200
    (C) 5,000
    (D) 1,000

17. In the case in question 16, how many rights would be needed to buy 100 shares?

    (A) 100
    (B) 200
    (C) 500
    (D) 1,000

18. A 5.5% preferred stock with par value of $100 would pay someone owning 300 shares:

    (A) 5.5% of $300
    (B) 16.5 shares
    (C) $550
    (D) $1,650

19. If a preferred stock is convertible into 2 shares of common for each share of preferred, the parity price for the common on a preferred selling at $105 is:

    (A) $50
    (B) $52.50
    (C) $100
    (D) $105

20. Election of the board of directors is the responsibility of:

    (A) common stockholders
    (B) preferred stockholders
    (C) officers of the corporation
    (D) all of the above

21. If a firm is liquidated, which is the correct order for claimants?

    I. common stockholders
    II. bond holders
    III. unpaid employees
    IV. preferred stockholders

    (A) I, II, III, and IV
    (B) III, II, I, and IV
    (C) III, II, IV, and I
    (D) IV, III, II, and I

22. Every U.S. corporation has a charter filed with the:

    (A) Securities and Exchange Commission
    (B) U.S. Attorney General's office
    (C) attorney general of its charter state
    (D) secretary of state of its charter state

23. The registrar for the stock of XYZ Corp.:

    (A) must be independent of the corporation
    (B) is the same as the transfer agent
    (C) cancels old stock certificates
    (D) all of the above

24. The transfer agent for XYZ Corp.:

    (A) may be from part of XYZ
    (B) records vital data on shareholders
    (C) assures that properly endorsed stock is canceled
    (D) all of the above

25. CAI declares a dividend of $1.75. The stock is selling at $40 and goes "ex-dividend" tomorrow. Assuming no other changes, we can expect tomorrow's opening price to be:

    (A) $38.25
    (B) $40.00

(C) $41.75
(D) cannot be determined

26. A company has $150 million of outstanding 6% convertible preferred. If the conversion ratio is 40 to 1 and the company also redeems $50 million of this preferred for cash, how many new shares will be created if the rest of the preferred is converted?

    (A) 2 million shares
    (B) 4 million shares
    (C) 6 million shares
    (D) 8 million shares

27. An investor owns 300 shares of ACI. In a rights offering, ACI plans to issue 400,000 new shares to bring the total outstanding to 2,400,000. How many new shares can the investor buy with his rights?

    (A) 20 shares
    (B) 30 shares
    (C) 60 shares
    (D) 300 shares

28. CAI $5 preferred has failed to pay a dividend for the past two years. If this were cumulative preferred and the company plans to pay a common dividend this year, how much dividend will a preferred stockholder receive this year?

    (A) Depends on the common dividend
    (B) $5
    (C) $10
    (D) $15

29. Choose the statements that hold for treasury stock.

    I. dividends for treasury stock are added to paid in surplus
    II. management votes treasury stock

III. it is part of issued shares
IV. it has no voting rights

(A) I and III
(B) II and III
(C) I, III, and IV
(D) III and IV

(A) his interest is increased
(B) the number of shares out-
standing is likely to increase
(C) his interest is decreased
(D) he may sell these rights

30. If an investor chooses not to subscribe to a rights offering, all of the
following are true EXCEPT:

ANSWERS TO REVIEW QUESTIONS

1. **(C)** These are all part of the board's responsibility when they vote to declare a dividend.

2. **(C)** Since settlement is in three business days, the stock goes "ex-dividend" two business days before the record date.

3. **(A)** The common stock holder is the residual owner after all of the other claims have been satisfied.

4. **(D)** The 7% represents the payable dividend; however, since it is partici-pating preferred it may participate in additional dividends. Hence, it is the minimum but not the maximum.

5. **(B)** 10,000,000 authorized – 9,500,000 issued = 500,000 unissued.

6. **(D)** 9,500,000 issued – 300,000 repurchased = 9,200,000 outstanding.

7. **(B)** Treasury stock is stock issued and repurchased.

8. **(B)** Only outstanding stock can be voted. In particular, treasury stock cannot be voted.

9. **(A)** With statutory voting, votes may not be accumulated. Therefore, no more than 200 votes (for 200 shares of stock) can be cast for any one director.

10. **(D)** The point of cumulative voting is precisely to allow the accumula-tion of votes for any one or group of directors.

11. **(D)** These are all the same.

12. **(A)** Five percent of 3,000 is 150.

13. **(A)** This is what is meant by pre-emptive right.

14. **(A)** The formula is (market price – subscription price) ÷ (number of rights required + 1). Here ($60 – $55) ÷ (4 + 1) = $1.

15. **(C)** The right to unpaid dividends belongs to those holding cumulative preferred. Those dividends accumulate and must be paid before any common stock dividend can be paid.

16. **(D)** Each original share is entitled to one right.

17. **(C)** Since 1,000,000 rights are issued to purchase 200,000 shares, each share requires 5 rights.

18. **(D)** 5.5% of $100 × 300 shares.

19. **(B)** For parity to exist, 2 shares of common must be worth $105. Therefore, each share is worth $105 ÷ 2.

20. **(A)** The common stockholders elect the board of directors.

21. **(C)** The important idea is that bonds come before preferred stock which come before common stock.

22. **(D)** The charter, called the Articles of Incorporation, must be filed under the laws of that state. The filing is with the Secretary of State.

23. **(A)** Choices (B) and (C) are the responsibility of the transfer agent.

24. **(D)** By definition.

25. **(A)** When it goes "ex-dividend," it loses the value of the dividend. So with no further changes, we have $40 − $1.75 = $38.25.

26. **(B)** If $50 million are redeemed, then $100 million or 100,000 bonds are available to be converted. At a conversion rate of 40 to 1, this gives 4,000,000 new shares.

27. **(C)** A total of 2,400,000 shares including 400,000 new ones means that 2,000,000 rights are issued. Since these can purchase 400,000 shares, it follows that 5 rights (2,000,000 ÷ 400,000) are required for one new share. A holding of 300 shares would allow an investor to subscribe to 60 new shares.

28. **(D)** All cumulative preferred must be paid before any common stock dividends can be paid. Since the company missed two years of payments, it would have to pay $15 to preferred stockholders.

29. **(D)** Treasury stock is stock that has been issued and then repurchased. It has no voting rights and does not pay dividends. Note that authorized but unissued stock is not part of treasury stock.

30. **(A)** If the investor does not exercise his rights, his interest is decreased since he now owns a smaller proportion of the outstanding stock.

bonds

Bonds are long-term, fixed interest debt obligations. As such, they are a second major category of investment securities. They are called debt securities, as distinguished from equity securities, or shares, because they involve money borrowed from investors, not ownership. In recent years, debt instruments have become increasingly complicated, and in fact have sometimes been "engineered" to have some characteristics of stock, but for the Series 7 examination, it is most important to be thoroughly familiar with the basic features of plain bonds.

We begin with a discussion of terms and concepts that apply to all forms and types of bonds, such as maturity, pricing, yields, and the relationship of price to interest rates. The following sections consider the specific characteristics of each of the three broad classes of bonds: corporate, federal government, and state and local government or municipal bonds.

PART ONE
Basics of debt securities

The bond is a contract between the issuer and the investor. Under this contract, the issuer promises to pay back a given amount at a given date and to pay interest, at a fixed and stated rate, throughout the life of the bond. This rate, called the "nominal" or "coupon" rate of the bond, remains constant even if the general level of interest rates in the economy (for example, mortgage interest rates or savings account rates) changes over time. This fixed-rate characteristic has important consequences for the price of an issued bond as interest rates change. For instance, if interest rates go up, the existing bond is "less attractive" and hence worth less to potential investors than new bonds paying the higher rate.

Bond issuers seek to obtain capital for relatively long-term use (short-term needs are usually met by bank loans and by the money market instruments discussed in the next chapter). This is often called "funded debt" and is borrowed for a minimum of five years, though 20 to 30 year terms are most common.

The date on which the issuer promises to repay the entire amount borrowed is the "maturity date"; and when that day is reached, the bonds themselves are said to "mature." The amount to be repaid on each individual bond is called the "par value" or "face value" (as the amount is printed on the face of the bond certificate). Most bonds issued have a par value of $1,000, and this is assumed to be the case in all of the examples given here.

Example

ACI issues a 20-year 8% bond. This means that ACI promises to pay the lender (bondholder) $80 per year (8% of $1,000) for the next 20 years, at which time it will repay the principal $1,000.

In practice, interest payments are almost always made at six-month intervals, so there would actually be two $40 payments each year. The actual date of maturity is declared on the bond, *e.g.,* March 15, 2020, and interest payments would be made on March 15 and September 15 each year.

Failure to pay interest when due or to repay principal at maturity can lead to bankruptcy. (Technically this failure to pay cannot occur for federal bonds.) Payment must be in "legal tender," though with some U.S. bonds issued abroad, payment can be in U.S. dollars and/or one or more foreign currencies. These are called multiple currency bonds.

The bond certificate shows the name of the issuing entity, the face value of the bond, and the rate of interest and gives the name of a "paying agent" for both interest and principal. The paying agent can be the issuer itself or an outside agent like a bank. The certificate also shows the dates interest will be paid, the maturity date, and any special features.

FORMS OF BONDS

Coupon or bearer bonds

These bonds have actual coupons attached to them that must be clipped twice a year and mailed or presented to the paying agent for interest payments. The coupon is, in effect, a promissory note to the bearer.

Such bonds are negotiable and should be kept in a secure place, such as a safe deposit box. The coupon and the certificate are proof of ownership; the issuer keeps no record of ownership. Bearer bonds have not been issued since the early 1980s, and while many are still in circulation, their number diminishes each year as those outstanding reach maturity.

Registered bonds

Most bonds are registered in the owner's name on the issuer's books. Such bonds are usually "fully registered," that is, registered as to both principal and interest. (Bonds registered as to principal only have coupons attached which the owner "clips" and forwards to the paying agent. Because of the additional work required to process these instruments, they are now virtually non-existent.)

The certificates carry no coupons. Interest payments are mailed on schedule by the paying agent. When registered bonds are sold or otherwise exchanged, the certificate goes to a transfer agent, who cancels the old certificate and issues a new one.

As with stocks, to effect a transfer, the seller must endorse the certificate or fill out a "bond power." The transfer is complete only when the new name is recorded. At maturity, the certificate is surrendered to the transfer agent who issues payment to the registered holder.

Book-entry bonds

With this type of bond, no certificate is issued, but a computerized record of ownership is kept. As this avoids the costs of printing and handling documents, these are becoming more common. All marketable U.S. Treasury securities are now issued in book-entry form.

For more information on new issues of bonds, see Chapter 6.

OTHER BOND TYPES AND TERMS

Serial bond

Most municipal and some corporate bonds are issued in this fashion. With serial bonds, one offering is made with maturity coming over a period of years: for example, 2,000 bonds issued in 1999 with 500 coming due each year from 2019 to 2022.

Serial bonds can be issued at one rate for the early-maturing bonds, with a higher rate for the later-maturing bonds, or with the longer-term bonds sold at a discount.

If the issuer defaults at any time, the entire issue is considered in default. Serial bonds are quoted in terms of yield rather than price (see below).

Series bonds

Securities of the same class issued over a period of years but with the same maturity date.

Sinking fund

As part of the trust indenture (see p. 38), the issuer may be required to set money aside regularly into a "sinking fund" to assure it will be able to redeem the bonds at maturity. This is the most usual method of retiring issues (it can be used to buy bonds in the market), and allows the issuer to avoid the burden of having to raise a large sum at one time.

Balloon maturity

These are serial bonds, but most mature in one year. For example, a corporation might issue $20 million of bonds with $1 million maturing every year from years 15 to 19 and the remaining $15 million maturing in the 20th year.

CALLABILITY

Issuers sometimes desire to redeem outstanding bonds, "retire" them, before they reach maturity. They may do so by buying the bonds in the marketplace, by offering a new bond issue and using the proceeds of that issue to retire outstanding debt (this is known as "refunding") or, where possible, by "calling" the bond—that is, redeem the bond before the maturity date.

Bonds issued with a "callability" feature must spell out, in the bond indenture (see p. 40), the "call provisions" as to the date when the issuer has the option of calling the bond, and as to what price the issuer must pay. The date on which this option is first available to the issuer is called the "Call Date." The redemption price offered in a call is usually at a slight premium to par value, with that premium declining as the bond approaches maturity.

Reasons for calling

Issuers usually call a bond when interest rates drop significantly below the rate being paid on outstanding bonds, or to change the date of maturity of the debt.

Refunding   When the call is accompanied by the issuance of a new offering of bonds at a more favorable interest rate or longer maturity, the process is described as "refunding."

One particular type of refunding, usually seen with municipal bonds, is called "prerefunding" or "advanced refunding." Here the proceeds of a new offering are used to pay off an older debt at maturity; the old issue is "escrowed to maturity," that is, the proceeds of the new issue are used to buy treasury securities which are held in escrow and serve to guarantee interest and principal and any call premium of the old issue. If prerefunding occurs, the old issue is called "prerefunded" to the call. Since the old issue is now secure and the responsibility of the escrow agent, the original obligations of both borrower and lender are terminated. This is called "defeasance."

Sinking fund call   A call does not necessarily involve refunding. When a sinking fund has been established, the issuer may make a call to meet the requirements of retiring debt set forth under that provision. These can be mandatory or optional.

Another reason for calling a bond is to get out of an indenture agreement that has proven unfavorable.

Call procedures

These are spelled out in the indenture, and usually include "call protection" for investors, prohibiting any call for an initial period. They often stipulate a higher call premium if the call comes early in the term of the bond.

Bondholders are notified before the actual call date, directly (for owners of registered securities) or through a newspaper announcement. It is the investor's responsibility to know about the call and, since no interest is paid on the bond beyond the call date, there is a need to respond quickly.

A call may involve an entire issue, only part of one, or a given portion each year. In partial calls, the actual bonds to be recalled are chosen by lot.

Sometimes an issuer "calls" a convertible bond when the conversion value of the stock to which it can be converted is higher than the redemption price of the debt issue, thereby "forcing conversion." (See Convertibility, below.)

PUTABILITY

Just as callability gives the issuer the right to redeem a bond before maturity, so putability gives the investor the right to "put" or have the issuer redeem a bond before maturity. This gives the investor some insurance against rising interest rates during the life of the bond.

Typically this right is combined with the right of the issuer to change the nominal rate of the bond. The effect is to give the investor a choice—accepting the new rate or getting his money back. This choice is usually available once a year beginning some years after the issuance of the bond.

Put procedures

These are spelled out in the indenture. The issuer announces a new nominal rate effective some 30 to 60 days in the future. For some period after the effective date, the investor then has the right to put the bond back to the issuer at the announced price. If he doesn't exercise that right, he is assumed to have agreed to accept the new rate.

BOND TRADING, PRICING AND YIELDS

Bonds are negotiable. They can be bought and sold. Some are traded on the New York Stock Exchange Bond Division, but most transactions are over the counter. Trading is usually far less active than with stocks.

Pricing

Like stocks, bonds have both a par value which is fixed and a market value that fluctuates. But with bonds, since par value represents an actual future payment, bond prices are always quoted as a percentage of par, which is assumed to be $1,000. Thus a $1,000 bond selling "at 97" sells for 97% of par or $970.

Corporate bonds are quoted in $\frac{1}{8}$ths of 1%; Treasury Notes and Bonds in $\frac{1}{32}$nds of 1% (written with a colon, *e.g.,* 102:12 for 102 and $\frac{12}{32}$), and municipals in $\frac{1}{100}$ of 1%. Thus a corporate bond selling at $97\frac{1}{8}$ will cost $971.25 while the treasury instrument at 102:12 will cost $1,023.75.

Each 1% of par is called a point, and so a change in price of two points, *e.g.,* from 97 to 95 would mean a change from 97% to 95% and a price drop of $20 from $970 to $950. Each point or 1% is in turn subdivided into 100 basis points, so a change of $\frac{1}{2}$ a point or $\frac{1}{2}$ of 1% is also called a change of 50 basis points.

Prices and interest rates

As noted above, the price of an already-issued bond changes as interest rates change. The change in price is inverse to the rate change—in other words, if one goes up, the other goes down. If interest rates rise, then newly issued bonds will pay a higher rate per $1,000 of borrowed money than previously issued bonds. Potential investors will then balk at buying the old bonds at par, so the price of existing bonds drops (they are at a discount) to bring the total return close to that of new issues. Conversely, if rates fall, then newly issued bonds will pay a lower rate per $1,000 of borrowed money than those issued earlier, and the older bonds become more valuable thus causing their price to rise (they are at a premium). See Figure 2.1.

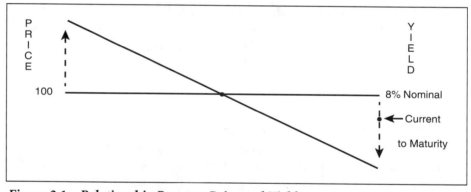

Figure 2.1   Relationship Between Price and Yield

There are several other relationships between bond rates and prices. The most important of these is that, for any given change in interest rates, the change in price of bonds with longer maturities is greater than the change in price of bonds with shorter maturities. See Figure 2.2.

Yields

A basic consideration in discussing any investment is its return. For bonds, this return is called the yield, and we speak of three different types of yields:

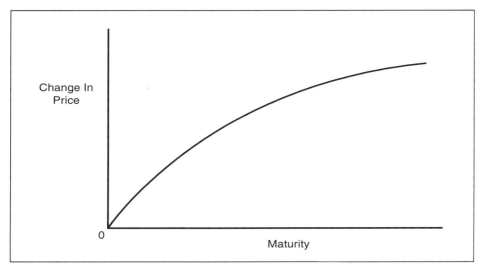

Figure 2.2   Relationship of Price Change to Maturity

Nominal yield (or the coupon rate)   This is the rate proclaimed on the bond. It is the interest rate that one receives when the bond is selling at par. For example, a $1,000 par value bond with a stated rate of 10% would return $100 per year. We say its nominal yield is 10%.

Current yield   This is the actual rate of return based on the current price of the bond.

Example

If a bond with 10% nominal yield is selling at $1,250, the actual interest payment of $100 represents a return of 8% on the purchase price of $1,250. This would be the current yield of the bond. If it were selling for $800, the current yield would be 12.5%.

This example also demonstrates the potentially confusing inverse relationship between bond prices and bond yields. That is, bond prices rise when yields go down and vice versa. If comparable bonds being issued currently carry a nominal yield of 12.5%, those who purchase older bonds with a nominal yield of 10% will demand a discount to $800 so they can receive the 12.5% available on new issues.

Yield to maturity   This is the return on a bond if it is held to maturity. If the bond is selling at par, this is the same as the nominal yield (and the current yield); however, if it is selling at a discount, at maturity the investor will receive, in addition, the difference between the discount and par. Similarly, if it is currently at a premium, the investor loses the difference between the premium and par at redemption.

Example

If the $1,000, 10% bond of the previous example is selling at $800 and matures in 5 years, then, at maturity, the investor will receive $200 in addition to the $100 per year for the five years, a total of $700.

An exact computation of the yield to maturity is complex and is usually left to bond tables or to specially designed calculators. However, a useful and fairly accurate approximation can be computed as follows:

1. Compute the average annual increase in price between the purchase price and par: ($1,000 − $800) ÷ 5 = $40

2. Find the return as the sum of this and the annual return: $100 + $40 = $140

3. Find the average cost of the bond as the average of the first and last prices: $800 + $1,000 ÷ 2 = $900

4. Find the yield to maturity as the return divided by the average cost: $140 ÷ $900 = 15.55%

In summary, this bond with a nominal yield of 10%, if selling for $800, has a current yield of 12.5% and a yield to maturity (approximate) of 15.55%. If this bond were currently selling for $1,250, the yield to maturity would be approximately:

1. ($1,000 − $1,250) ÷ 5 = −$50

2. $100 − $50 = $50

3. ($1,000 + $1,250) ÷ 2 = $1,125

4. $50 ÷ $1,125 = 4.44%

Yield to maturity is a way of accounting for the money received over the cost of the bond. It considers both the purchase price of the bond and also the gain to a bond bought at a discount (or the loss on one bought at a premium) when redeemed at par at maturity.

Yield to call   is calculated like yield to maturity, with the call date substituted for the maturity date and the call price for the maturity price. One general rule is that for bonds at a discount, yield to call is higher than yield to maturity; for bonds at a premium the reverse is true. These yields are discussed again in the section on municipal bonds.

Formulae for these two yields are:

$$YTM = \frac{\textbf{Coupon} + \textbf{(Net Change in Price)} \div \textbf{(Years to Maturity)}}{\textbf{(Purchase Price} + \textbf{Par Value)} \div 2}$$

$$YTC = \frac{\textbf{Coupon} + \textbf{(Net Change in Price)} \div \textbf{(Years to Call)}}{\textbf{(Purchase Price} + \textbf{Par Value)} \div 2}$$

Quotations

Bonds are generally quoted on the basis of yield to maturity since it is easier to compare bonds of the same maturity on the basis of yield than on price. Translating price to yield can be complicated. For this reason, bond traders often refer to a "basis book," a book of tables showing the results of this conversion for various combinations of coupon rate, maturity and yield to maturity (see sample page below). Bond traders often use special calculators programmed to do this conversion.

SAMPLE BASIS BOOK PAGE

Coupon 4%

YTM	9 Yrs.	10 Yrs.	11 Yrs.	12 Yrs.
3.80	101.51	101.65	101.78	101.91
3.90	100.75	100.82	100.89	100.96
4.00	100.00	100.00	100.00	100.00
4.10	99.25	99.19	99.12	99.05
4.20	98.51	98.38	98.25	98.12

For example, a 4% coupon with a 4.10% YTM which had 11 years to maturity would have a price of 99.12 or $991.20. Naturally, a 4% YTM would yield a price of $100.00 for any maturity.

In using the basis book, one often needs to find the price for a yield not listed in the book. Assume, for example, we have a 4% coupon with a yield of 3.95 and a maturity of ten years. Obviously, it has a price between 100 (the price for a 4% YTM) and 100.82 (the price for a 3.90 YTM). Since 3.95 is approximately halfway between 4.00 and 3.90, the price for this security would be $100.41, halfway between the corresponding prices.

This process, called "arithmetic interpolation," can be formalized as follows: To find the price for a YTM not given in the basis book, choose the next highest and next lowest YTMs (with the same coupon and years to maturity) that do appear in the book. Then find a price that is at the same relative distance from those neighboring prices.

Example

A yield of 3.96 is 60% (or .6) of the way from 3.90 to 4.00. The corresponding price is computed by subtracting 60% of the difference between the yields (.6 × [100.82 – 100]) from the price of the 3.90 YTM. Thus, 100.82 – .492 = 100.328, or $1,003.28—the price for a 3.96 YTM.

PART TWO
Corporates

Corporations issue bonds to obtain capital for relatively long-term use. Corporate bonds represent debts of the corporation. Like stocks, they are securities, but "debt securities," not equity securities. Bondholders are creditors, not owners. They have no voting rights or other say in the management of the issuing company.

Bondholders do have rights as creditors that are not accorded to shareholders, however. In particular, the issuing company is bound to pay interest on bonds, whereas with stock, even preferred, there is no comparable obligation with respect to dividends. Interest on bonds must be paid before stock dividends are considered. Similarly, at liquidation, bondholders' claims are honored before those of shareholders. For this reason, bonds are sometimes called "senior securities."

The bond is a contract between the issuing firm and the investor. Under this contract, the corporation promises to repay the amount it has borrowed on a given date, the "maturity date," and to pay interest at a stated rate for the life of the bond. The bond certificate shows the name of the issuing firm, the face value of the bond, and the rate of interest and gives the name of a "paying agent" for both interest and principal. This can be the issuing corporation itself or an outside agent like a bank. The certificate also shows the interest dates, the maturity date, and any call features.

TRUST INDENTURE

An essential part of every bond issue is the "trust indenture," also called a "deed of trust." This contract supplements the bond contract itself and is required under the Trust Indenture Act of 1939 for all issues registered under the Securities Act of 1933 (which exempts certain securities, including issues of under $5,000,000, government and municipal bonds, and those issued by foreign governments). A copy must be filed with the SEC.

While designed to protect bondholders' rights, the trust indenture is really an agreement between the issuer and the trustee who is acting as a fiduciary administering the property and funds. Basically, it sets forth the terms between corporation and creditors. It describes both bondholders' rights and issuer's obligations and appoints a trustee—usually a commercial bank or trust company with expertise in this area—to see that these obligations are carried out.

Typical provisions not only oblige the issuer to pay interest and repay principal when due, but also stipulate locations where coupons or bonds can be presented for payment. Other items may cover protecting properties pledged as security for the bond (for example, requiring the trustee to hold adequate insurance; in case of loss, the trustee is paid and pays for repairs). Still others may call for keeping equipment in good repair and, more generally, pledge that the issuer continue doing business, etc. These and many other promises are called "protective covenants."

If the trust indenture is abrogated, the corporation can be considered in default and can be compelled to immediately repay the principal amount of the bonds. Thus, the indenture can give the trustee the right to take over the business and operate it for the bondholders' benefit or to sell pledged property to the highest bidder, etc. The rationale underlying many of these rights is the attempt to preserve the seniority of bondholders when a corporation faces reorganization, liquidation, or bankruptcy.

Changes in the trust indenture require the consent of the bondholders. Typically, bondholders will give their consent by depositing their bonds with a committee appointed to oversee the changes. Usually, the changes are made only if a sufficient number of bonds—at least a majority—are deposited. In some circumstances, changes are made only on those bonds voting their consent; these bonds are duly stamped and trade separately.

SECURED BONDS

Bonds can be considered in two broad groups: "secured," those backed by real assets, and "unsecured," where backing is less tangible. There are several types in each group.

First mortgage bonds or senior lien bonds

These give the bondholder claim against the corporation's fixed assets, that is, assets secured by real property. In fact, these issues involve two instruments: the bond itself and a mortgage. First mortgage bondholders have priority of claim in reorganization or liquidation. This is the most secure type of corporate bond available.

Second mortgage bonds or general, consolidated or refunding bonds or junior liens

These bonds are also backed by real property, but are second in priority. Mortgage bonds of any class may be "open-end" or "closed-end" issues.

Open-end   The corporation may issue more bonds of the same class under the same indenture. There are usually restrictions in the indenture of an open-end issue to protect creditors. For example, the value of the property pledged must provide adequate collateral for the new bonds.

Some open-end issues are limited, with a maximum dollar amount set for bonds issued under this priority.

Closed-end   No additional bonds may be issued beyond a maximum number authorized in the indenture as first mortgage bonds; all others are second, or third, etc.

Collateral trust bonds

These bonds are backed by marketable securities deposited with the trustees. These must be securities in a company other than the issuing company (it can be a subsidiary). Rarely are they intangible assets, like a patent. In the case of default, the trustees have the right to sell these securities.

The collateral pledged can be stocks or bonds, but not real estate. Either the trustee or the debtor can hold actual title, but the trustee always has the power to transfer property in a default.

Equipment trust certificates or equipment trusts, notes or bonds

These are issued generally by corporations engaged in transportation, like railroads or airlines, with a specific piece of equipment pledged as collateral. The trustee holds title to the equipment—say an airplane or locomotive—until the certificate is paid.

ETCs are considered a high-grade security, since transportation equipment is generally salable in case of default. Such issues have a good record and pay relatively low yields.

UNSECURED BONDS

These bonds are not backed by any specific assets. If default should occur, bondholders have no direct claim on any real property.

Debentures

These are backed by the issuing corporation's "good faith and credit," *i.e.*, by its promise to pay. For investors, these are inferior to secured instruments, but they are superior to stocks in liquidation because debentures must be honored first before any payment to holders of equity securities.

Because they are unsecured, the protective covenants of the trust indenture are particularly important with debentures, as is the credit-worthiness of the issuing corporation. Debentures usually pay higher interest than secured bonds and are often "convertible" (see below).

Subordinated debentures

The issuer is obliged to pay principal and interest on these instruments, but they are "subordinate" in the sense that they are honored after debentures in the case of liquidation or reorganization (though still before stocks). Subordinated debentures tend to pay relatively high interest, to be relatively short-term, and to be convertible.

OTHER TYPES OF BONDS

Income or adjustment bonds

These may be secured issues or debentures. They include a promise to repay the principal at maturity, but no interest is guaranteed in the trust indenture. Interest is contingent on the company's earnings, must be declared by the board of directors, and can be skipped entirely.

These bonds are usually issued when a company is in reorganization or receivership. Again, they are less safe, but pay relatively high interest when they do pay interest. Income bonds are traded "flat," that is without interest (see page 44).

Guaranteed bonds

These are guaranteed by a corporation or corporations other than the issuer. Most often, the guarantor is the stronger of the two, and the issue thus enjoys a lower rate. These bonds are usually unsecured, though collateral may be pledged. Indeed, they are often used when the issuing firm leases property to the guarantor. As the name implies, the guarantor pays in case of default. The guarantee may cover interest only or both interest and principal.

Zero-coupon bonds

These pay no regular interest. Instead, the bonds are purchased at a discount and are paid off at par on maturity. The difference between the purchase and redemption price and the time to maturity determine the annual return. An important tax aspect of these bonds is that interest is taxable annually even though the "phantom income" has not been received.

Below investment grade

Bond issues that are rated below BBB or the equivalent by one of the rating firms (see page 45) are sometimes called "junk bonds." When perceptions of creditworthiness change, they often experience dramatic price changes.

CONVERTIBILITY

Many debentures and some other types of issues include the right to "convert" holdings into common or preferred stock. The trust indenture usually spells out the conditions and terms of conversions. This feature merits a separate discussion.

Advantages and disadvantages of convertibility

Offering convertibility presents a number of advantages to the issuer:

- Convertible issues can usually be offered at a somewhat lower interest rate, as buyers expect the issue to grow in value as the common stock rises.

- These issues do not dilute ownership immediately as a stock issue would, and they offer the potential for reducing debt when conversion occurs.

- As bondholders only convert when stock has risen in value, the issuer in effect gets a good price for stock purchased through conversion. Thus the bond offering does not tend to depress the stock's market price as a new stock issue does.

There are also disadvantages:

- When conversion does take place, existing stockholders' equity is diluted. In addition, the total declared dividend is now divided by a larger number of shares so dividends per share can go down, making the stock less attractive. This is why convertible issues are often offered to current shareholders like stock rights on a new issue.

- Conversion on a significant scale could lead to a change in the controlling interest in the company.

- Since bond interest is tax-deductible for the issuer but stock dividend payments are not, issuing debt securities can result in greater retained earnings for the company than issuing stocks; any such advantage is lost when investors convert their bonds to stock.

- Finally, issuing convertible instruments can cause doubts about the corporation's financial structure, as there is no way to know how many bonds will be converted.

For investors, too, convertible issues have both advantages and disadvantages. Chief among the advantages is that they offer, in theory, both the safety associated with bonds and the possibility of rising in value like stocks. A convertible debenture will tend to hold its value more firmly than a stock because it pays fixed interest and may rise in price as the stock price rises, giving the investor a profit even without conversion if he or she trades the debenture.

Investors or institutions barred by law from owning significant amounts of common stock often turn to convertibles to try to capture some of the advantages of common stocks.

Among the disadvantages to investors are: that convertibles tend to offer lower rates than non-convertible issues, that convertibles are sometimes issued when a company is in a relatively weak financial position or when the market is not strong, and that a large outstanding convertible issue can depress stock prices.

Mechanics of conversion

The terms of conversion set forth in the indenture can be stated in terms of conversion ratio (sometimes called conversion rate) or conversion price.

Conversion ratio   The conversion ratio (or rate) indicates the number of shares of stock that one would receive in exchange for a bond. For example, a conversion rate of 20:1 would mean that one receives 20 shares of common when converting a bond. If the bond were convertible into 25 shares, the conversion ratio would be 25 to 1.

Conversion price   In many cases, the indenture will express convertibility in terms of price—the price per share at which the corporation offers stock when the bond is converted. This calculation is based not on the current market price of the bond, but on its par value of $1,000. Thus, to calculate how many shares the bond could be converted into, one divides the par value by the conversion price: a bond with conversion price of $50 per share is convertible to 20 shares since $1,000 ÷ $50 = 20 shares.

Remember, the conversion price is set when the bond is issued. A bond issued at 100 ($1,000), now selling at 110 ($1,100) with a conversion price of $100 would bring only 10 shares, not 11 shares.

Note that the indenture sometimes provides for a change in the conversion ratio or price at intervals over the life of the bond. Thus, a bond could have a conversion price of $20 for the first five years after issue, $25 for the next five years, and so forth. Stock splits or stock dividends can also lead to a change in the conversion price. For example, if a stock splits 2 for 1, the conversion rate would be doubled, and the conversion price would be halved.

Parity

As the conversion price or conversion ratio are fixed, bondholders' decisions on whether or not to convert depend on the market value of the common stock. When the number of shares received at conversion is equal to the market value of the bond, the situation is said to be one of "parity." For example, if a $1,000 bond has a conversion ratio of 40, the stocks are at parity at $25—the price of the bond is at parity with the price of the common stock. In practice, the stock usually trades at somewhat less than parity to reflect the fact that the bond has investment value in its own right.

Example

A convertible bond quoted at 104 has a conversion price of $40. To discover the parity price, we must first know the number of shares to be received.

$$\$1,000 \div \$40 = 25 \text{ shares}$$

Then to determine the parity price per share we divide the market value of the bond by the number of shares received; the parity price involves market values:

$$\$1,040 \div 25 = \$41.60$$

Thus, if the shares are selling for less than $41.60, they are "below parity" (and the bond is "above parity"); if they are trading for more than $41.60, they are above parity (and the bond is below parity).

Arbitrage

When the stock is selling above parity, an "arbitrage" situation exists—that is, it is possible to make a profit by buying and selling two similar securities at one time. For example, if the shares in the example above are selling at $45, an arbitrageur could buy bonds for $1,040 and immediately convert them to $1,125 worth of stock (26 shares at $45 a share), for a profit of $85 per bond.

At the time of issue, the conversion price is usually set above parity in order to discourage quick conversion.

Duration

In most cases, conversion is allowed over the life of the bond, but often at terms that become less favorable as time goes on. With some issues, convertibility is not allowed for a certain time after issue or for a short period before maturity.

Rights

As noted, stockholders can have pre-emptive rights to purchase convertible shares and these have value like pre-emptive rights with stocks (see page 18).

Forced conversion   Under some circumstances, a corporation may wish to compel bondholders to convert to stocks. These "forced conversions" are discussed above.

Other safeguards   A number of protections are included in the indenture for holders of convertible issues. Many are directed at preventing dilution, that is, the danger of lowering the value of existing shares by having too many shares on the market. These cover such matters as stock splits and stock dividends, both of which increase the number of shares outstanding, so the conversion rate must be adjusted accordingly. Similar nondilutive provisions limit the number of shares the corporation can issue.

Accrued interest

Almost all bonds trade "with interest" or "and interest." Any transaction completed between the regular semi-annual payment dates must include interest accrued, and the buyer must pay this amount to the seller.

The rules for calculating this are very specific. Each month is considered to have 30 days (except for U.S. government bonds); the year has 360 days. Accrued interest is found by multiplying:

$$principal \times rate \times time = interest$$

Time is calculated to begin on the morning of the last interest payment and extending to, *but not including*, the settlement date. That date is usually 3 business days after trade, but can vary. (The only exception to the accrued interest rule is with bonds where interest is in default, on income bonds, or on zero-coupon bonds; such bonds trade "flat," *i.e.,* without accrued interest.)

Example

If the 10% bonds cited above were purchased at par on July 14 for settlement on July 17, and the payable dates are February 15 and August 15, accrued interest up to but not including the settlement date would be:

February 15–30 [sic]	16 days
March	30 days
April	30 days
May	30 days
June	30 days
July	<u>16 days</u>
	152 days

Thus, the accrued interest would be:

$$\$1,000 \times 10\% \times \left(\tfrac{152}{360}\right) = \$42.22$$

Types of transactions

A bond trade can be completed in one of several ways:

Regular way   Almost all transactions fall into this category. Settlement is on the third business day after the day of the trade, which is also called the "settlement date."

Seller's or buyer's option   When either party wishes to postpone delivery, the date can be delayed. Under NYSE rules, such transactions can take no less than six business days nor more than 60 calendar days. Most often, if the delay is at the seller's request, the bond goes at a discount; if at the buyer's request, at a premium.

Cash transactions   If cash or the bond certificate are needed urgently, or if either party has failed to satisfactorily complete a transaction in the past, cash terms can be agreed to. Under these terms, the security must be delivered "same day," which is defined as no later than 2:30 P.M. Eastern Time. If the trade takes place after 2:00 P.M., then delivery must take place within 30 minutes.

When issued   Some new issues are traded on the NYSE (or, if unlisted, through NASD) for delivery when the corporation schedules delivery of the actual certificates. As soon as the physical bond appears, when-issued transactions must be reconfirmed.

BOND RATINGS

Most corporate bonds carry "ratings" made by an independent firm, usually Standard & Poor's, Moody's, or Fitches Investors' Service.

Ratings of BBB to AAA for S & P (Baa to Aaa for Moody's) are called "investment grade." Those below these ratings are considered speculative, with increasing risk of default as the rating goes down. Additional refinements in these ratings are (+) and (–) for S & P (e.g., A, A+, AA–, AA are increasingly higher ratings); and 1 for Moody's (e.g., A, Al, Aa are increasing ratings).

These ratings reflect the raters' best judgment of the issuing corporation's ability to pay both interest and principal. In making this assessment, they use a number of standardized approaches to examine the corporation's earnings potential with particular attention to income stability and predictability, as well as gauging the value of corporate assets.

In general, the higher the rating, the lower the yield.

ILLUSTRATION OF RATINGS

S & P	Moody's
AAA	Aaa
AA	Aa
A	A
BBB	Baa
BB	Ba
B	B
CCC	Caa
CC	Ca
C	C
D	

EUROBONDS

Bonds sold in one country but denominated in the currency of another country are called "Eurobonds." This designation is not restricted to bonds issued by European countries; rather, it reflects the fact that these bonds first appeared in Europe, and they are still more common there than elsewhere.

An investor purchasing such a bond must take into account the extra risk associated with being paid in the currency of a foreign country, which might fluctuate with respect to his or her own currency (for U.S. investors, with respect to the U.S. dollar).

A Eurodollar bond, then, is issued outside the United States and pays interest and principal in U.S. dollars. Eurobonds are not registered in this country, but may be traded here after issue. These bonds are of use to countries, international agencies, and multinational corporations with a need to borrow dollars. (A dollar-denominated bond issued in the United States by a foreign entity is called a Yankee bond.)

The characteristics of Eurobonds vary, but they usually pay interest annually. They can have a fixed or floating (variable) rate, can be convertible, and can be zero-coupon.

PART THREE
United States Government Issues

Because it borrows more money than any organization or institution in the world, the U.S. government must seek funds regularly and often. To do this, it issues a variety of debt instruments, most of them marketable, with maturities ranging from 3 months to 30 years.

These securities—called "government obligations," "government issues," or just "governments"—are considered the safest offered in any market. There has never been a default, and these issues are backed by the full faith and credit of the U.S. government and by its power to tax its citizens.

This section will discuss both negotiable and non-negotiable securities issued directly by the government and instruments issued by government agencies or government-sponsored agencies. Material on trading will focus on the differences between government and corporate issues.

NEGOTIABLE SECURITIES

These securities are traded continuously. There is a vigorous market with relatively narrow changes in price. Among the reasons for this high level of activity is the fact that these are the most liquid issues traded on any market, are extremely safe, have some tax advantages (returns are not usually subject to state or local taxes), and can be used as loan collateral.

Treasury bills

These are short-term instruments; sold at auction, that is, by competitive bidding. They are sold at a discount (the only federal debt security issue sold in this way) and mature at their face value. For tax purposes, the difference between selling price and face is considered interest income, not a capital gain.

"T-bills" are book-entry instruments; no certificates are issued. Instead, banks that are members of the Federal Reserve System hold securities accounts at the Federal Reserve, which maintains a computerized record. They are issued with maturities of 3 months (91 days), 6 months (182 days), or one year, although they are sold in the secondary over-the-counter market with all maturities from 1 day to 1 year. Minimum denomination is $10,000, with larger bills usually in increments of $5,000. T-bills are highly liquid and essentially risk-free.

Auctions for the 3- and 6-month issues are held weekly; those for 12-month issues take place monthly. Individual investors can participate directly in these auctions though most prefer to buy through a bank or broker, usually paying a service charge.

Because these are discounted notes, the winners of the auction are the bidders who offer the highest dollar prices. This is equivalent to the lowest interest cost for the U.S. government, since the difference between the dollar price and the face value is the cost to the United States. Some bidders enter noncompetitive bids. The amount of these bids is subtracted from the total offering, and the remainder of the offering is awarded competitively. The noncompetitive bidders are then awarded their T-bills at the average price of the winning competitive bid. This is the method open to individual investors.

Return on T-bills

To calculate the current return—called "bond equivalent yield"—use the formula:

$$\frac{\text{appreciation}}{\text{purchase price}} \times \frac{365}{\text{days to maturity}} = \text{bond equivalent yield}$$

Example

For a 1-year $10,000 bill selling at $9,200, the current return is found by dividing the appreciation (from $9,200 to $10,000) by the purchase price. So we have:

$$\frac{\$800}{\$9,200} = 8.70\%$$

Yields and quotes

Although they can only be redeemed at maturity, T-bills are marketable until that time. Alone among government securities, they are quoted on the basis of yield. This is called the "discount yield." It is calculated as follows:

$$\text{Discount yield} = \frac{(\text{par} - \text{purchase price}) \times 365}{\text{days to maturity}}$$

So, for a 6 month bond selling at 94 we have:

$$\text{Discount yield} = \frac{(100 - 94.00) \times 365}{182} = 12.04\%$$

(It is possible to determine the price from the discount yield by inverting this formula):

$$\text{Purchase price} = 100 - \frac{(12.04 \times 182)}{365} = 94.00$$

Changes in price are quoted in terms of "basis points," or $\frac{1}{100}$ of 1% (.01%) of the yield. Thus, a typical quote might be:

"March 4, bid 4.30%, asked 4.20%"

This describes the maturity as March 4, and says that someone is offering to buy this bill at $95.70 (the bid) and offering to sell this bill at $95.80 (the asked price).

Treasury notes

These are interest-bearing with payments made semi-annually and are issued in book-entry form; that is, the purchaser receives a receipt but no certificate.

Treasury notes are redeemable at maturity; they are not callable. Payment at maturity can be in cash, or the notes can be refunded at that point, *i.e.*, investors are given the option of buying a new security with a new maturity.

Maturities range from 2 to 10 years; denominations range from $1,000 to $1,000,000. Treasury notes are most appealing to large investors such as banks and major corporations seeking highly liquid assets.

Like T-bills, T-notes are sold at auction, but the notes are offered at a fixed interest rate so the auction involves bids that are equal to, above (at a premium to), or below (at a discount from), par. They are quoted in $\frac{1}{32}$s of a percentage point, written with a colon (:). For example:

"Maturing 11/10/90—Bid: 99:16; Ask: 99:24"

means bid at $99\frac{16}{32}$ or $99\frac{1}{2}$ or $995; ask at $99\frac{24}{32}$ or $99\frac{3}{4}$ or $997.50. (Note the convention of :16 for $\frac{16}{32}$.)

Treasury bonds

These are interest-bearing with semi-annual payments and come in bearer, registered, and book-entry form. They are issued only in book-entry form now.

Maturities generally range from 10 to 30 years although only a 30-year bond is now issued. Some have optional call dates, usually 5 years before the stated maturity. These are listed, for example, as "Due 6/30 2002/07" where the first date shown is the call date and the second the maturity date.

If the Treasury decides to issue a call, it must give four months' notice. For obvious reasons, no call is issued when bonds are selling at a discount.

Treasury bond denominations range from $1,000 to $1,000,000; the most usual instrument is a $10,000 bond. They are sold at auction. Like T-notes, they are quoted with variations of $\frac{1}{32}$ of a percentage point and with the same notation, *e.g.*, 104.03 means 104 and $\frac{3}{32}$ percent of par.

("Flower bonds" is the term used to describe certain T-bond issues customarily used to pay estate taxes. They carry a low [less than 4.5%] coupon rate so they can be purchased at a discount. Their special distinction is that they are accepted at face value in settlement of estate taxes. The last flower bonds matured in 1998.)

Under the doctrine of reciprocal immunity, federal obligations are exempt from state and local taxes just as municipal obligations are exempt from federal taxes.

Zero-coupon securities ("zeroes")

Zeroes are fixed-income securities on which no interest payments are made (see "Strips" in next section). Rather, they are sold at a discount and redeemed at par; the difference generates the yield. Conversely, a given yield determines the discount. Since zeroes make no interim interest payments, changes in the yield produce dramatic changes in price.

Strips (Treasury receipts)

In 1982 when interest payments on Treasury bonds were separated from the principal, a new type of security was created. The coupons representing interest payments due were removed ("stripped") from bonds; coupons from many bonds with the same payment date were then bundled together in units and were marketed as independent items called "strips." Each unit trades as a zero-coupon on its own. These are sold directly by the U.S. Treasury. In addition, brokerage firms offer bundles of these (variously called CATS, TIGRS, etc.) For example, a dealer might bunch coupons from twenty-five bonds each paying $40 into a single unit with a value of $1,000 to be sold at a discount. These are not government securities, but instruments issued by brokerage houses. Nevertheless, the inherent safety of the underlying collateral makes them a very safe investment.

NON-NEGOTIABLE U.S. GOVERNMENT OBLIGATIONS

These are non-transferable instruments. They can be redeemed only by the purchaser and can be neither marketed nor used as collateral for loans. In other words, securities firms have little to do with them. However, as these bonds are probably held by more individuals than any other single debt instrument, a few details about them might prove helpful.

Series EE bonds or savings bonds

These issues are sold at a discount and mature at their face value. The difference represents compound interest. Available only in registered form, EE bonds can have one owner, or two co-owners, or an owner and a named beneficiary in case of death. Commercial banks cannot buy them.

There is a legal maximum to purchases by individuals in one year of $15,000, which represents a face value of $30,000 since Series EE bonds are always sold at a 50% discount. The bonds come in denominations from $50 to $10,000.

Maturity has varied over time (it was 12 years for bonds issued in 1992), but EE bonds can be redeemed at any time after they have been held for six months. To discourage early redemption, the bonds pay on a sliding scale, offering lower returns in earlier years.

Proceeds are treated as ordinary income and may be deferred until redemption for federal tax purposes. They may be further deferred if on redemption they are traded for HH bonds instead of cash.

Since November, 1982, government regulations have provided that EE bonds held five years or more pay a varying rate. This is pegged at 85% of the five-year average for Treasury notes over that time, with a guaranteed minimum of 6% if held to maturity.

For bonds issued in May 1997 or later, the rate is pegged at 90% of average yields of Treasury securities in the preceding six months.

HH Series bonds

These are issued at par, with interest paid semi-annually direct to the holder by Treasury check. They are available in registered form only.

These bonds mature in 20 years. If held to maturity they yield 7.5% annually (8.5% for those issued before 11/1/82). As with EE bonds, payoff is less than face value for bonds redeemed before maturity. They must be held for at least six months and are redeemable only on the first of the month. Redemption requires one month's notice in writing.

Four denominations are available from $500 to $10,000. Maximum purchase in one year is $20,000 face or maturity value for one individual (commercial banks are excluded) or $40,000 for two co-owners.

HH bonds may be purchased from Federal Reserve Banks or U.S. Treasury offices. However, they cannot be purchased for cash, but only by trading EE (or E) bonds with a minimum face value of $500, held a minimum of 6 months.

Interest on HH Series bonds is taxable each year. However, as mentioned above, an investor who exchanges EE bonds for HH bonds can defer taxes due on the former at their maturity.

OTHER GOVERNMENT AGENCY OBLIGATIONS

With one exception, noted below, these are not direct obligations of the U.S. government, but are generally issued and backed by agencies—some of them privately owned—sponsored by the government. These securities are considered very safe since the issuers usually show considerable strength in both income and assets, and it is generally assumed the government would not allow any of them to default. Yields on these securities tend to be somewhat higher than on direct government obligations but lower than on corporate instruments.

There is considerable variety available in terms of both maturities and types of issues, and an active secondary market exists.

Federal Farm Credit Banks

A system of Federal Farm Credit Banks supplies credit to farmers through the Federal Farm Credit Agency, the Federal Intermediate Credit Banks, and the Central Banks for Cooperatives. This system issues securities called Federal Farm Credit Consolidated Systemwide Obligations. They are the joint obligation of the 37 banks in the system.

Bonds are issued in book-entry form only, through a network of banks and brokers. Once issued, they are traded over the counter.

Federal Home Loan Banks

There are 12 of these banks, owned by nearly 5,000 institutions (such as savings and loan associations). The Home Loan Banks provide capital to those institutions up to a limit authorized by the U.S. Treasury. They do so by buying mortgages from those institutions, thereby providing them with new capital to lend. These guaranteed residential mortgages (along with cash, government securities and bank assets) are the collateral for instruments issued by the Home Loan Banks. These include short-term discount notes (30 to 270 days), interest-bearing notes that mature in less than a year, and bonds with 1- to 20-year maturities. Minimum denomination for the notes is $100,000. Bonds are issued in $10,000, $25,000, $100,000 and $1,000,000 denominations. Interest is paid semi-annually.

Federal Home Loan Mortgage Corporation (Freddie Mac)

This corporation buys residential mortgages from federally-insured savings institutions, and issues mortgage-backed bonds, participation certificates, and mortgage certificates.

The bonds have maturities ranging from 12 to 25 years, and are backed by GNMA (see below). Issued in registered form, they are available in denominations of $25,000, $500,000, and $1,000,000.

Participation certificates are backed by pools of mortgages (but not Veterans Administration [VA] or Federal Housing Administration [FHA] mortgages), with payments passed through monthly (see next section). These certificates usually mature more quickly than the mortgages in the pool. Minimum denomination is $100,000.

Guaranteed mortgage certificates pay interest and a portion of the principal semi-annually. They are available only in registered form, with a minimum value of $100,000.

Federal National Mortgage Association (also called FNMA or Fannie Mae)

This is a publicly held corporation, traded on the NYSE. It buys and sells conventional residential mortgages—insured or guaranteed by FHA, VA, and Farmer's Home Administration—from savings institutions, thus freeing their funds so they can grant new mortgages.

FNMA issues debentures in book-entry form that mature in periods ranging from 3 to 25 years. These are generally non-callable. Denominations range from $10,000 to $1,000,000. FNMA also issues short-term discount notes denominated in multiples of $5,000 up to $50,000. These are bearer notes with maturities ranging from 30 to 270 days. FNMA securities are subject to state, federal, and local taxes and tend to pay rates similar to, but higher than, comparable maturity treasury debt.

Student Loan Marketing Association (SLMA or Sallie Mae)

This provides financing for state agencies and others making loans to students. Some, but not all, of these loans are insured by the federal Guaranteed Student Loan Program.

U.S. GOVERNMENT-OWNED AGENCY OBLIGATIONS

Government National Mortgage Association (GNMA or Ginnie Mae)

Securities are backed by the U.S. government, but proceeds are not tax exempt in any way. GNMA pools mortgages insured by the VA and FHA and issues certificates that represent a stated share of a mortgage pool. These are called "pass-through" certificates, because the monthly payments on the underlying mortgages are literally passed through to GNMA certificate holders. Pass-through payments are partly a return of capital (which is not subject to income tax) and partly interest income (which is taxable).

Selling at a minimum denomination of $25,000, the "pass-through" certificates mature like mortgages over a period of 12 to 40 years, but usually more quickly than the underlying mortgages as mortgage-holders tend to prepay. If the particular pool has many high-interest mortgages, prepayment will be more likely to occur, and yields will therefore be lower than anticipated. Note, however, that the interest payments to investors are determined by the coupon rate of the security, not by the interest rate of the underlying mortgages.

MORTGAGE BACKED SECURITIES

Collateralized Mortgage Obligations (CMOs)

CMOs are debt securities backed (collateralized) by fixed rate GNMA, FNMA, and other mortgages or by securities backed by such mortgages. These, too, are "pass through" certificates, like those described above, involving a pool, but there is an important difference between CMOs and other pass-through instruments: CMOs are bonds, with a stated maturity—some mature relatively early, some later; and some are long-term. So while an ordinary pass-through certificate offers some return of principal each month, and matures when the last mortgage is paid off, the components of a CMO pool are arranged in different maturities called "tranches" ("tranche" is the French word for "slice"), each with its own rate of interest and payment schedule.

As with GNMA securities, CMO investors are subject to the risk presented by early repayment of mortgages which can reduce the return. To help estimate returns, the Public Securities Association (PSA) has constructed a model of the expected prepayment rate based on historical data, which reflects the fact that the percentage of prepayments is lowest in the first few months after the mortgage is issued. Such estimates may be used in advertising CMOs, but the NASD has ruled that such advertisements must make it clear that these are only estimates and may differ from actual yields. (This is one of several special rules governing CMO advertising.)

Structure of CMOs

CMOs can be set up in a variety of ways. In the simplest form, as mortgage holders pay off the principal, these funds are used to retire the next tranche to mature. Thus, only when the first tranche is paid off does retirement of the second tranche begin, and so on until each maturity has been paid off. This sequence is called a "plain vanilla" CMO.

Other structures are designed to reduce the effects of prepayment—in effect to spread the risk that the underlying mortgages will be paid off much sooner than anticipated, often by establishing a sort of sinking fund or special tranches to absorb prepayments.

Both "interest only" and "principal only" mortgage bonds have been created. With interest only instruments, the bondholder receives the interest payment (or a percentage of the interest payment) of the underlying mortgage and little or no principal. As the principal is repaid, the interest payment drops accordingly. If prepayment is common, the interest only bondholder may suffer a loss; if payments are slow, on the other hand, such bonds will increase in value.

With principal only bonds, interest is stripped from the underlying instrument, and the bond is sold at a discount to its face value. Eventually, investors are paid the face value; if prepayment becomes more common, they will receive a higher yield.

The quality of the underlying securities is such that most CMOs have AAA ratings. CMOs are issued by both private firms and the Federal Home Loan Mortgage Corporation (Freddie Mac). Returns are usually lower than for other pass-through instruments, but they do offer greater certainty that returns on the investment will continue for a given term.

REMICs

One particular kind of collateralized mortgage obligation is the Real Estate Mortgage Investment Conduit (REMIC). The REMIC is formed for the purpose of holding a fixed pool of mortgages, again secured by interests in real property. A REMIC issues classes of interest, including "regular interests" and "residual interests," to investors.

Regular interests A REMIC can have several classes (again, also known as "tranches") of regular interests, but any regular interest unconditionally entitles the holder to receipt of a specified principal amount. The timing (but not the amount) of principal payments can be made contingent on the extent of prepayments on mortgages in the pool and on income from investments of a REMIC.

Any interest payments to holders of regular interests must be payable based upon a fixed or stated variable rate or consist of a specified portion of the interest payments on qualified mortgages—a portion that cannot vary during the period.

A residual interest is defined as an interest in a REMIC that is not a regular interest and is so designated by the REMIC.

Tax Treatment of CMOs

For income tax purposes, the CMO is considered a debt instrument, and all the rules that apply to bonds and other debt instruments apply. This includes REMIC regular interest—all the income reporting rules that apply to bonds and other debt instruments apply, with certain modifications.

For tax purposes, REMIC residual interest holders are generally treated as partners in a partnership. Gains and losses by either regular or residual interest holders of REMICs are treated like gains or losses from a portfolio.

OTHER BOND ISSUING AGENCIES

Inter-American Development Bank

This agency issues securities in varying currencies and in many parts of the world to finance projects in Latin America. Earnings on IADB issues are fully taxable.

World Bank or International Bank for Reconstruction and Development

Issues securities, including capital stock in various forms (and currencies), to make loans to developing countries.

Tennessee Valley Authority (TVA)

Not guaranteed, but backed by power sales and issued with Treasury authorization, TVA instruments include short-term discount notes with a minimum denomination of $1,000,000 and relatively small denomination bonds (minimum $1,000) that are sold like corporate utility bonds.

RULES ON DELIVERY OF U.S. GOVERNMENT INSTRUMENTS

Accrued interest

All government securities are traded "and interest" or "with interest" except T-bills, which are sold at a discount. In calculating interest accrued with these securities, unlike the method with corporate securities, one considers the actual number of days in a month and a 365-day year.

Example

A bond sold for settlement on August 10 with interest last paid on April 15 would have accrued the following interest:

April	16 days
May	31 days
June	30 days
July	31 days
August	11 <u>days</u>
	119 days

A bond sold for cash on June 10 with a last interest payment on April 15 would accrue the following:

April	16 days
May	31 days
June	9 <u>days</u>
	56 days

Delivery

As with corporate bonds, contracts for delivery can call for a cash, "regular way" or seller's (buyer's) option. *A cash contract requires same day delivery* by 2:30 P.M. Eastern time. *Regular way transactions with government issues call for delivery the first business day after trade.* (Transactions completed on the second business day are called "skip day.")

Seller's (or buyer's) option contracts call for delivery sometime from the second business day to no more than 60 calendar days after the trade date. Such transactions may be completed ahead of schedule with one day's written notice.

PART FOUR
MUNICIPAL BONDS

This section concerns debt obligations (bonds, notes, etc.) issued by states of the United States, by U.S. territories such as Puerto Rico, by U.S. possessions, or by any political subdivision or public agency that is not federal—a city, school district, airport authority, etc.

These instruments, usually called "municipals," are considered safer than any debt instruments but those of the U.S. government. Nevertheless, their safety depends on the source of revenue backing them and therefore this source is an important consideration. City and county issues, for example, are usually backed by real estate taxes, a steady and predictable source of income. State issues are often predicated on sales or other taxes that can fluctuate. In default, investors have the right to sue a municipality, but not the state.

Like all debt obligations, municipals are issued to raise funds—to build or repair public facilities such as roads, waterworks, bridges, etc. To raise money, government agencies must issue debt instruments; they may not issue equity securities.

Default is quite rare and is more likely to affect interest payments than the principal. With most municipals, interest is paid semi-annually, with principal paid at maturity.

For investors, a principal attraction of these issues is that proceeds are exempt from federal tax. (*This status has been upheld by the U.S. Supreme Court.*) Obviously, this feature is less attractive to investors in low tax brackets, since a tax break is not so important to them. This tax-free status benefits the issuers as well. It allows them to issue instruments at a lower yield, in effect lowering the cost of the issue.

In effect, the tax status is the reverse of the one that obtains for federal obligations, as municipals are subject to state and local taxes. Some issues, however, are exempt from all taxes and are termed "triple exempt." This is true primarily for instruments issued by territories or possessions. Bonds issued by a state and purchased by residents of that state (intrastate) are also usually triple exempt.

TYPES OF MUNICIPALS

Municipal issues include short-term notes, with terms of one month to one year, and bonds described as short term (1 to 6 years), intermediate term (6 to 19 years) and long term (20 years and more). At issue, they are sold at auction, that is, by competitive or negotiated bidding.

General obligation (G.O.) bonds

These are backed by the full faith and credit (and by the taxing power) of the issuer. In most cases, no particular property or revenues are pledged, but there is a promise to use taxes—usually income, sales, or gas taxes in a state issue; usually real estate (*ad valorem*) taxes for those issued by local governments and smaller agencies. G.O. bonds are used to finance projects that do not produce revenue. They are usually issued under competitive bidding.

The safest G.O. bonds are "unlimited tax G.O. bonds," which are backed by the issuer's unlimited taxing power. If that taxing power is limited by law to a specified maximum, these are called "limited tax G.O. bonds." Such limits can take several forms. For example, voter approval may be required past a certain point, or a state constitution may have statutory ceilings or limits. The "limited" bonds usually offer a somewhat higher yield to compensate for the increased risk.

One other possible limitation on taxing power is the existence of "overlapping" tax jurisdictions, where more than one entity may be able to tax the same set of taxpayers (for example, residents of a city within a county).

Investors need to consider both direct limitations and the possibility of overlapping jurisdictions in evaluating a bond.

Revenue bonds

The most common type of municipal bond is a revenue bond. These are not backed by the issuer's full faith and credit, but are repayable with proceeds from tolls, user fees, rental payments, etc., generated by the facility or facilities built with the proceeds of the bond issue. Since taxes are not involved, revenue bonds are not subject to statutory limits, nor, in general, does their issue dilute the debt standing of the issuer.

Revenue bonds are supposed to be "self-supporting" or "self-liquidating." The issuer can be a state or subdivision, or an interstate, or intrastate authority. Revenue bonds are usually underwritten using a negotiated price.

If revenues do not meet expectations, interest payments are sometimes deferred. These issues generally deliver a higher yield than G.O. bonds. In many cases, local law requires that an independent agency conduct a feasibility study of the project(s) to be financed. Such a study usually includes a projection of the scheduled flow of funds.

Revenue bonds can have serial, term, or balloon maturity provisions, with serial maturity usually in reverse order. Most are callable under provisions detailed in the Official Statement.

"Net revenues," *i.e.*, any proceeds that remain after providing for operation and maintenance of the facility(ies) built with the bond issue, are pledged for paying off the bonds. They are typically disbursed as follows:

1. Current interest and principal of bond due to mature next.

2. Reserve fund for the next two years of principal and interest.

3. Reserve fund for maintenance and replacement of facility(ies).

4. Surplus, for such purposes as expansion or to retire bonds.

Special tax bonds

These instruments are repayable from the proceeds of a special tax. An example would be a gas tax imposed to repay bonds issued to fund highway construction. (Some of these bonds are backed by the full faith and credit of the issuer as well; they are then considered general obligation bonds.)

Three types of taxation are used:

1. Excise taxes—taxes imposed on liquor or gasoline, etc., or license fees.

2. Special assessments—those who benefit directly from the funds expended (for example, those who live on a street being repaired or where a new sewer system is installed) pay a special tax.

3. *Ad valorem*—in some cases, general property taxes are pledged to pay off these bonds.

Double-barreled bonds

When a bond is backed by two sources of revenue, it is called "double-barreled" or "self-supporting." The two sources may be two different agencies or two different sorts of commitment: for example, a special tax bond which is also backed by the full faith and credit of the issuer is double-barreled.

New Housing Authority (NHA) bonds are representative. These were issued by local housing authorities and were payable with proceeds from rentals paid to the authority and by an annual contract with the U.S. Public Housing Authority (PHA). The bonds were unconditionally guaranteed by the PHA, which was in turn backed by the government, and were considered very safe. They are no longer being issued, but some are still traded.

Note

Other, less common types of municipal bonds include:

Moral obligation bonds

These bonds are backed by the revenue of some project. If the project does not generate funds sufficient to cover the debt service, the issuer is morally, but not legally, bound to repay these bonds.

Industrial revenue (or industrial development) bonds

Issued to acquire funds to build an industrial plant which is then leased to a corporation. These are a primary obligation of the corporation; that is, they are not backed by the municipality, and their safety is judged in terms of the corporation. (But note that a corporation can have a higher credit rating than a municipal agency.)

Pollution control bonds

Usually backed by a corporation that leases the equipment built with the proceeds of the bond. Lease payments cover the bond payments. (Some of these could also be double-barreled.)

Both industrial revenue bonds and pollution control bonds are used as incentives to industry since they allow corporations to borrow money at below-market rates.

Note

The Tax Reform Act of 1986 limits the tax-exempt status of some municipal bonds. Where 10% or more of the proceeds are used for a project run by a non-government entity, and 10% of the proceeds from the bond will be secured by property used in that entity's business, the definition "private activity bonds" applies.

Bonds so categorized must be "qualified" before the interest payments can be considered tax-exempt. This involves meeting certain technical requirements, as well as certain purposes, *e.g.*, to build major public works or to benefit homeowners, veterans, students, hospitals, and universities. Each category has its own specific requirements.

Short-term municipal notes

These are offered so work on a project can begin while the issuer awaits proceeds from a bond sale or the like (which can take up to a year), taxes, or revenues. They are often called "anticipation notes."

1. **Tax Anticipation Notes (TAN)** —issued in anticipation of future tax receipts, often property taxes. These are also usually G.O. securities.

2. **Bond Anticipation Notes (BAN)**— issued in anticipation of proceeds from a bond not yet issued.

3. **Revenue Anticipation Notes (RAN)**—issued in anticipation of revenues to be received from federal and state governments.

Other short-term instruments issued by municipalities include tax-exempt commercial paper (see page 83) and variable rate demand notes.

TYPES OF MUNICIPAL ISSUES

Registered to principal and interest

The owner's name is registered on the books of the issuing agency; there are no coupons. Interest is paid by check mailed semi-annually. They must be endorsed to be negotiable. Issued in denominations of $1,000 or multiples to $100,000.

Registered to principal only

The owner's name is registered as above, but the bond coupon (which shows the rate of return) must be received before interest is paid. Principal is paid to the registered owner at maturity. Also offered in denominations of $1,000 and multiples to $100,000.

Coupon, bearer, unregistered, or owner bonds

These are negotiable instruments; the holder of the bond is the owner. Since July 1, 1983, all tax-exempt issues of over one year must be registered, but many bearer bonds are still outstanding. If the bond is in default, *i.e.*, if interest payments have been missed, these bonds can be delivered only if all past due and future coupons are attached.

LEGAL OPINION

Unlike corporate securities, municipals are not subject to the filing provisions of the Securities Acts of 1933 or 1934 (though the fraud provisions apply) nor to the Trust Indenture Act of 1939. For this reason, investors consider it vital to have an opinion by a municipal bond attorney, an independent attorney who specializes in acting as bond counsel to municipalities. This has become more important since passage of the Tax Reform Act of 1986, which distinguishes among classes of municipal bonds giving some more favorable tax treatment than others. The legal opinion is the basis for these distinctions. This opinion does not provide any estimate of the worth of the issue, but says the attorney thinks it is both exempt from taxes and a binding debt of the issuer. The opinion may be qualified if some aspect of it is questioned.

Customarily, the issuing agency or municipality employs the bond attorney to ensure that its bonds will enjoy tax-free status, that they do not exceed any statutory debt limit, and that the issue is otherwise legally sound. Once these three matters have been decided, the attorney issues an opinion as to the "validity, legality, and tax-exempt status" of the issue. In addition, the legal opinion includes terms of the offering and call provisions and makes note of any limitations on the issuer's taxing power. This opinion must be on the face of the bond. If no attorney has been retained, the bond must be stamped "EX-LEGAL."

INDENTURE

Although an indenture is not required, as it is with corporate bonds, the issuer's obligations are often spelled out on the face of the bond in a series of "covenants," also called a "bond resolution." Almost all revenue bonds have these. Among the most likely covenants are those concerning:

- rates—under this heading, the issuer promises to maintain rates sufficient to meet expenses and service the debt

- redemption—the call privilege

- insurance—a pledge to insure facilities built with proceeds of the bond

- maintenance—a pledge to maintain those facilities

- nondiscrimination in hiring

- feasibility—pledging to ensure the project will be self-sustaining

- financial reports and auditing—a promise to issue regular financial reports and to retain an outside auditor

- additional bonds—like corporates, revenue bond issues can be "open" or "closed"

INTEREST AND PRINCIPAL PAYMENT

Municipal bonds show on their face the interest or coupon rate applied to par. For example, an 8% $1,000 bond will pay $80 a year. Interest is usually paid semi-annually on the dates shown on the face. The principal is paid at maturity.

Municipals come in a wide range of maturities, ranging from one month to more than 50 years. They can be issued in term or serial form.

Term bonds

All bonds in the issue mature at the same time, for example 20 years after issue. These are often used when revenues are estimated, and not for short terms because such estimates can be uncertain. Also called "dollar bonds," they are quoted as a percent of par, thus $97\frac{1}{4} = \$972.50$. Many term bonds are callable.

Serial bonds

As with corporates, these mature over a series of years. Typically, they are used when revenues are stable, for example, with a waterworks, and are scheduled to mature when income peaks. But they can be issued on a "level debt service" basis, with equal payments (for combined principal and interest) over the life of the bond, like a conventional home mortgage. They are usually quoted on a yield-to-maturity basis.

Balloon serials

A serial issue where most bonds mature in one year, usually with fewer bonds coming due in early years. These are also usually callable.

TENDER, CALL AND PUT

Most revenue bonds include a call provision. When this is not the case, but issuers wish to retire the debt early, they can ask for a "tender offer." This is published in a newspaper and invites holders to "tender" their bonds to the issuer at a stated price.

When call provisions do exist, they usually resemble those in corporate issues. They can be at par or at a premium, usually declining over the life of the bond, can be optional or mandatory, and are usually delayed for some time after issue. Most require a published notice 30 days in advance of the call date.

With serial issues, bonds are usually called in inverse order; *i.e.,* bonds with the most remaining life are called first. Calls of term issues customarily proceed by lot. Calls can be partial (this usually occurs when revenues exceed expectations), or total, as in a refunding.

Recently, in an attempt to attract more investors, some municipal bonds have been issued with a "put" provision. While not truly a Put, as it cannot be traded separately, such a provision does allow the investor to "put" the bonds back to the issuer, *i.e.,* to compel the issuer to redeem the bonds. This opportunity is available only at specified times and usually not for some time after the bonds are issued.

In effect, the put provision gives the investor some protection against changes in rates. If rates rise and investors have the right to return the bonds, the issuer can either redeem the bonds or offer to adjust the rate on them.

Trade confirmations for bonds with a call provision have to consider this feature in computing the yields that must be declared on all callable bonds.

MUNICIPAL BOND INSURANCE

Insurance on municipal bonds is available to both issuers and to investors. If issuers buy insurance, it has the effect of increasing the bond's rating and therefore lowering the rate at which it sells.

Investors with portfolios of at least $50,000 in at least three different issues can also purchase insurance, for example, from the Municipal Guarantee Insurance Corporation (MGIC), a division of American Municipal Bond Assurance Corporation (AMBAC), one of several firms which offer such insurance. Others are Bond Investors Guaranty Insurance Company (BIG) and Municipal Bond Investors Assurance Corp. (MBIAC).

YIELDS AND TAXATION

The yield to maturity, or any other yield, is computed as for any bond; however, the special tax status of a municipal bond does create some changes.

Tax treatment of municipal yields

While interest income from municipal bonds is free from federal taxes, any capital gain realized in the purchase and sale of a municipal bond is subject to capital gains tax.

This last must be modified when, as sometimes occurs, municipals are issued at a discount. Then the difference between the discount and par is considered as interest income which accrues over time and is not subject to federal tax.

Example

For a 5% coupon 20-year $1,000 bond issued at $800, the $200 appreciation to par would be considered as accruing at the rate the interest is paid—that is, not at $10 per year for 20 years, but at the compound interest rate. If, for example, after some time, $50 of interest had accrued and the bond was sold for $925, then $50 of the $125 increase over the issue price is not considered a capital gain but the other $75 is.

For bonds issued at a premium, the same considerations hold. Thus, a bond purchased at $1,050 which matures in ten years has its cost basis adjusted downward to reflect the dissipation of the premium as the bond nears maturity. If the adjustment was $9 after two years, and the bond was sold for $1,030, the investor realized an $11 capital loss, since the basis was $1,050 − $9 = $1,041, or $11 higher than the $1,030 sales price.

If the bond is held to maturity and redeemed at $1,000, the investor experiences neither a loss nor a gain but has benefited from the tax-free interest income for the life of the bond.

Equivalent yield

Though municipal yields are computed in the same way as are yields for taxable instruments, to compare the two, one must compute the equivalent yields, *i.e.,* take into account the marginal tax rate (tax bracket) for the investor's income.

The equivalent municipal rate (to a taxable rate) is found by multiplying the latter by (1 − marginal rate).

Example

A 12% taxable instrument for someone in the 28% bracket is equivalent to an 8.64% municipal rate:

$$12\% \times (1 - .28) = 8.64\%$$

For a person in the 33% bracket the equivalent municipal rate would be 8.04%:

$$12\% \times (1 - .33) = 8.04\%$$

In other words, the higher the tax bracket, the more attractive any specific municipal bond is.

To find the equivalent taxable rate for a given municipal rate, simply reverse the algebra: divide the municipal rate by (1 − marginal rate).

Example

For someone in the 15% tax bracket, an 8% municipal is equivalent to a bond with a taxable yield of

$$8\% \div (1 - .15) = 9.41\%$$

In general, to compare two bonds—one taxable, the other tax-free—an investor should convert both to the taxable equivalent for his or her own tax bracket and determine which has a higher yield. Alternatively, an investor could convert both to the tax-free equivalent rate and again find the higher rate. Both methods always yield the same result.

Yield to maturity

As with corporate issues, YTM is approximated by the formula:

$$\frac{\textbf{Coupon} + (\textbf{change in price} \div \textbf{years to maturity})}{(\textbf{purchase price} + \textbf{maturity price}) \div 2} = \textbf{YTM}$$

Note that the change in price may be negative, for instance, with a bond purchased at a premium, where the premium would be amortized over the remaining life of the bond.

Example

A 6% coupon $1,000 bond maturing in 10 years that sold at $1,200 would have the following YTM:

$$\frac{\$60 + (-\$200 \div 10 \text{ years})}{(\$1,200 + \$1,000) \div 2} = \frac{\$60 - \$20}{\$1,100} = 3.636\%$$

Yield to Call or Put

These yields are similar to the yield to maturity and can be computed by replacing the years to maturity with the years to call or put. Thus YTC can be found as:

$$\frac{\text{Coupon} + (\text{net change in price} \div \text{years to call})}{(\text{purchase price} + \text{call price}) \div 2} = \text{YTC}$$

Example

A 6% coupon $1,000 bond callable in 6 years at 130 would have the following YTC:

$$\frac{\$60 + (\$100 \div 6)}{(\$1,200 + \$1,300) \div 2} = \frac{\$76.66}{\$1,250} + 6.1328\%$$

TRADING IN MUNICIPALS

There is a steady market for municipals—both a primary and a secondary market—because of their reputation for safety and because they can be used as collateral. Traditionally, banks and insurance companies have held these instruments, but not charitable organizations or pension funds that have no need of tax benefits.

The major figures in the municipal market are dealers who specialize in municipal bonds, large banks, and those large brokerage firms with separate municipal bond departments. Banks are allowed to make a market in general obligation bonds but not in revenue bonds. They can also act as brokers for revenue bonds, but a bank may not act in this capacity for its own trust department when it buys or sells for client trust accounts.

Although some firms act solely as brokers for other dealers, traders in municipals typically act as principals (see Chapter 8). That is, they maintain an inventory of such bonds and sell from that inventory to investors wishing to purchase municipal bonds. If the broker does not hold the bond, he or she will consult the *Blue List* to find such bonds, purchase them, and then resell them to the client.

The usual face value for a municipal obligation is $5,000, though some come in $1,000 or $10,000 denominations. This is intended to make trade and payment more efficient. A "round lot" usually refers to $100,000 in bonds.

When issued, municipals trade like corporates. Most trading is over-the-counter through brokers, specialist dealers, and major banks. Available issues are shown in the *Blue List*, a daily publication which describes the issues, showing the quantity available and the yield to maturity. The *Blue List* also has a computer service and a news ticker called Munifacts.

Another publication, called the *Daily Bond Buyer*, shows average yields, but not average prices, and publishes a weekly *Index*. It also gives figures on the proportion of offered issues that have been placed. Another publication, *Moody's Manual*, is used mostly for background information.

Trading in municipal securities is subject to the governance of the Municipal Securities Rulemaking Board (MSRB). These rules are discussed in Chapter 16.

Terminology

Some special language is used in municipal bond transactions. For example, dealer Smith calls and requests a firm offer from dealer Brown. Brown responds

"7.20 basis firm for two hours with five." Smith understands this to mean:

- The bonds are offered at a yield to maturity of 7.20%.

- The offer is firm.

- The offer is good for two hours—that is, Smith has two hours to decide if she wishes to buy the bonds at the offered yield of 7.20%.

- If a third broker wants to buy these bonds and makes a firm bid to dealer Brown, Brown must call Smith and give her five minutes to decide. After five minutes, Brown can sell the bonds to the third broker. (This is the meaning of "with five.")

"Workable quote" The price at which a dealer is willing to buy a municipal bond. It is firm at the moment it is given, but the buying dealer cannot be held to that figure if the selling dealer must first consult a client to see if he wishes to sell the bond at that price.

"Concession" In this context, a discount from the quoted yield on an interdealer transaction. For instance, a transaction at "$8\frac{1}{4}$ less $\frac{3}{8}$" means that a bond was sold to yield $8\frac{1}{4}$% minus a concession of $\frac{3}{8}$, or $3.75 for each $1,000 bond.

A concession is usually available on bonds quoted by yield. Dealers purchase term bonds, which are offered at a price in dollars, at the quoted price with no discount, *e.g.,* a bond quoted at $102\frac{1}{4}$ would be bought at $1,022.50.

Accrued interest

The purchaser of a municipal bond must pay the interest which has accrued since the last coupon payment. Recall that interest on municipals is computed on the basis of 12 months, each 30 days long. Accrued interest is computed by counting from the last coupon date up to, but not including, the settlement date. If the transaction is "for cash," which means same-day settlement, interest is computed up to the day before the sale.

Example

A bond with April 15 and October 15 coupon dates is sold on June 16 for settlement on June 19. Accrued interest would total:

April 15-30	16 days
May	30 [sic] days
June	<u>18 days</u>
	64 days

This accrued interest would be included in the price the buyer paid and would appear on the trade confirmations to both parties.

Bond swaps

If interest rates rise, the market value of a bond portfolio will fall. An investor holding a portfolio of tax-free bonds could take advantage of this situation with a "bond swap." This involves the following steps:

The investor sells the bonds, thereby incurring a capital loss which can be used to offset other income. At the same time, the investor buys a similar portfolio of municipal bonds at a comparable discount, thereby setting up a potential capital gain in the future. The effect is to defer taxes, which can be of advantage in some situations.

A bond swap is especially attractive to banks, which must treat all proceeds from municipal bond investments as ordinary income and therefore not subject to the limitations on capital losses.

To avoid violating the restrictions on "wash sales" in the tax code, the swap should involve bonds from different issuers or, if that is not possible, bonds that differ substantially in coupon and/or maturity.

JUDGING MUNICIPALS

Like corporate issues, most municipal bonds of sizable issue carry quality ratings from an independent firm. For example, Moody's rates municipal notes as (in decreasing order) Investment Grade 1, 2, 3, 4; Standard and Poor's has SP-1, SP-2, SP-3. Fitches and Dun & Bradstreet also offer such services. These represent a measure of the relative risk of an issue, based on an examination of its legality, the issuer's past record, and, most importantly, on the ability to pay.

Beyond the ratings, it is possible to examine individual offerings in a number of ways. The issuer's current debt level should be assessed. As a rule of thumb, no more than 25% of the issuer's budget should be devoted to debt service. With revenue bonds, it is advisable to think in terms of a 20% cushion; *i.e.,* expected revenues should be about 120% of requirements with a revenue bond; with a general obligation bond, a cushion of 10% (of applicable taxes) is advised.

Evaluating general obligation bonds

Here are some questions to ask in judging the strength of a general obligation municipal issue:

- What is the issuer's history—has there ever been a default in the past?

- How economically healthy is the issuing community? Answering this can involve looking at overall wealth, for example, property values, retail sales, bank holdings, and bank activity. Other indications may come from examining the mix of economic activity: is it diverse, or over-reliant on one firm or one type of activity? Is the community growing?

- What is the character of city officials—have there been cases of malfeasance or corruption?

- Is the issuer in sound financial shape? For example, what is the current ratio of debt to property values (remember, G.O. bonds are backed by property taxes) or to overall annual revenues? Are any of the issuer's other debt service obligations about to come due?

- Is there "overlapping debt"? This term refers to obligations of other government entities which overlap the issuing body—a simple example would involve a city that bears some obligations as part of the surrounding county.

- Other related questions involve finding the issuer's direct debt—*i.e.*, debt that is not self-liquidating (for example, a revenue bond), especially in relation to the value of real property.

- Does the issuer show a likely ability to pay? Under this broad heading, one could see whether there are any legal limits on taxation, whether an outstanding issue has prior claim on taxes, and how great a percentage of taxes is actually collected.

Evaluating revenue bonds

Many of the questions about the worth of revenue bonds should be answered in the feasibility study. Chief concerns are:

- Is the proposed project justifiable on economic grounds?

- Will earnings be adequate to meet the debt obligation?

- Are there existing or proposed facilities that might compete with the facility funded by this issue?

- Are the covenants and the "flow of funds" arrangements adequate?

Default

Technically, if a bond issued by a state is in default, the investor has no direct legal redress since the sovereign states cannot be sued without their consent. This is not the case for municipalities or subdivisions of a state, which are subject to court action in case of default.

TERMS

Bonds   Long-term debt obligations offering fixed interest; do not represent ownership

Contract between issuer and investor   Issued to raise long-term capital or "funded debt." Minimum 5 years; 20-30 year terms most common

Par value or face value   Amount to be repaid on individual bond. Usually $1,000

Nominal rate or coupon rate   Fixed rate of interest issuer promises to pay for life of bond; usually paid semi-annually

Maturity date   Date when issuer guarantees repayment of amount borrowed

Bond certificate   Shows issuer's name, face value, interest rate, name of "paying agent," dates interest paid, maturity date

Forms of bonds

Bearer bonds   Negotiable; interest paid when coupon submitted; issuer keeps no record of ownership

Registered   Issuer's books show owner's name; transfer procedure as with stocks

Book-entry   Computerized record only; no certificate

Bond types and terms

Serial bond   One offering with maturity over a range of years

Series bonds   Issued over several years, maturing in the same year

Sinking fund   Separate fund to assure redemption; required in some indentures

Balloon maturity   Serial bonds with most maturing in one year

Callability

Call provisions   Some issues give issuer right to redeem bond before maturity, after given date (call date), at specified price, usually at premium to par

Refunding   New bonds issued to pay off called bonds

Prerefunding or advanced refunding   Proceeds of a new offering used to pay off older debt at maturity

Sinking fund call   Call to meet requirements of sinking fund

Call procedures   Spelled out in indenture

Put provisions   Investor can demand redemption of bonds

Bond trading, pricing and yields

Prices   Quoted as percentage of par, assumed to be $1000. Fractions in $\frac{1}{8}$ths of a percentage point for corporates; in $\frac{1}{32}$ of 1% for Treasury notes and bonds; in $\frac{1}{100}$ of 1% for munis. Above par is "at a premium"; below par "at a discount".

Points   Each 1% of par ($10) = one point. Each point = 100 basis points (so $\frac{1}{2}$ point change = 50 basis points)

Prices and interest rates   Change in inverse relation

Yields

Nominal yield   Rate of return at par

Current yield   Rate of return at current market price. Note: current yield is in inverse relationship to price.

Yield to maturity   Return actually received at maturity date

Yield to call   Like yield to maturity, using call date instead of maturity date

Quotations   Usually in terms of yield to maturity, translated into dollar price by basis book; changes in "points" (10 cents)

Corporate bonds

Debt securities   Not equity securities: no voting rights. Bondholders creditors, not owners

Bondholders' rights   Issuer bound to pay interest on bonds before dividends on stock.

Trust indenture   Contract required by law for most bonds stipulating rights and obligations of issuer and creditors

Secured bonds

Mortgage bonds   Backed by corporation's fixed assets; can be open-end (may issue more bonds of this class) or closed-end

Collateral trust bonds   Backed by negotiable securities

Equipment Trust Certificates (ETCs)   Backed by specific piece of equipment; usually issued by transportation companies

Unsecured

Debentures   Backed by issuer's good faith and credit (if "subordinated," honored after debentures in liquidation)

Other types

Income (adjustment) bonds   Pay principal at maturity, but interest only if declared

Guaranteed bonds   Backed by corporation(s) other than issuer

Zero-coupon   Pay no interest, but sell at discount, redeemed at par on maturity

Below investment grade   Rated low; sometimes called "junk bonds"

Convertibility   Debt instruments (usually debentures) can include right to convert to stock shares, sometimes with rights, at a stated rate of exchange

Conversion ratio (rate)   Number of shares received in exchange for a bond on conversion

Conversion price   Price per share for stock on conversion

Parity   When shares received from conversion exactly equal market value of bond

Conditions of conversion   Time usually limited; terms change over time

Accrued interest   Bonds sold after interest payment date; must include interest due calculated:

$$\textbf{principal} \times \textbf{rate} \times \textbf{time} = \textbf{accrued interest}$$

time begins morning of last interest payment and ends day before settlement; every month calculated at 30 days

Types of transactions

Regular way   Settlement on third business day

Seller's or buyer's option   Settlement delayed, but no more than 60 calendar days

Cash   Settled same day when issued

Bond ratings   Offered by investment services; reflected in yields

Eurodollar bonds   Sold in one country, denominated in currency of another

U.S. government issues

Exempt   From state and local taxes; very safe

Negotiable   Highly liquid, heavily traded

Treasury bills (T-bills)   Short term (3-, 6-, 12-month); sold at discount; book-entry; min. $10,000 denomination; sold at auction

Current return (bond equivalent yield):

$$\frac{\textbf{annualized appreciation}}{\textbf{purchase price}} \times \frac{\textbf{360}}{\textbf{days to maturity}} = \textbf{bond equivalent yield}$$

Only governments quoted on basis of yield ("discount yield"):

$$\text{Discount yield} = \frac{(\text{par} - \text{purchase price}) \times 360}{\text{days to maturity}}$$

Treasury notes Medium term (2- to 10-year) interest-bearing notes; book entry; $1,000 to $1,000,000 denominations; sold at auction; offered at fixed interest rate; sold at percentage of par; quoted in $\frac{1}{32}$nds of a percentage point

Treasury bonds Long-term (10- to 30-year) interest-bearing; come in any form (no longer issued in bearer form); $1,000 to $1,000,000 denominations; sold at auction; can be callable; quoted and sold like T-notes

"Flower bonds" Low-rate T-bonds sold at deep discount; no longer issued

Zero-Coupon Securities ("Zeros") No interest paid, but sold at discount and redeemed at par

Strips T-bond interest separated from principal placed in trusts; securities representing shares in the trusts are marketed. U.S. Treasury version called Strips or treasury receipts

Non-negotiable government issues Non-transferable; no loan value

Series EE ("savings") Sold at discount; mature at face; registered form only; $50 to $10,000 denominations

Series HH Issued at par; interest paid semiannually; registered form only; $50 to $10,000 denominations

Obligations of other government agencies

Federal Farm Credit Banks Issues Federal Farm Credit Consolidated Systemwide Obligations

Federal Home Loan Banks Short-term notes (minimum denomination $100,000) and bonds (1- to 2-year maturities; $10,000 to $1,000,000 denominations)

Federal Home Loan Mortgage Corporation (Freddie Mac) Mortgage-backed bonds (12 to 25 years), registered, $25,000 to $1,000,000 denominations; participation certificates (min. $100,000); registered mortgage certificates (min. $100,000)

Federal National Mortgage (FNMA; Fannie Mae) Publicly held corporation, issues debentures (3- to 25-year maturity), $10,000 to $1,000,000; short-term discount bearer notes ($5,000 to $50,000), maturing in 30 to 170 days

Obligations of U.S. government-owned agencies

Government National Mortgage (GNMA; Ginnie Mae) "Pass-through" certificates, shares of a mortgage pool; min. $25,000; maturities 12 to 40 years

Mortgage backed securities

Collateralized Mortgage Obligations (CMOs)   Debt securities backed by fixed rate mortgages; pass-through instruments but with mortgages arrange in "tranches" of different maturities and rates

CMS structure   Various arrangements—simplest ("plain vanilla"), next to mature paid first

REMICS (Real Estate Mortgage Investment Conduit (REMIC)   Type of CMS with "regular interests" and "residual interests" to investors.

Other bond issuing agencies

Inter-American Development Bank

World Bank or International Bank for Reconstruction and Development

Tennessee Valley Authority (TVA)

Delivery of governments

Accrued interest   Calculated in terms of actual calendar days, 365-day year

Delivery   Regular way = first business day after trade; seller's (buyer's) option (from second day to 60 calendar days); cash

Municipal bonds

Debt obligations of non-federal governmental entities   Exempt from federal tax; short-term notes and bonds of all terms; sold at auction when issued

General Obligation (G.O.)   Bonds backed by issuer's full faith and credit; based on taxing power ("limited" if that power is limited)

Revenue bonds   Repaid by fees from users of facility(ies) built with proceeds; may require feasibility study

Special tax bonds   Repaid from proceeds of special tax; can be G.O. bonds as well

New Housing Authority (NHA) Bonds   Repaid by rent on housing built by authority; guaranteed by federal agency

"Double-barreled bond"   Backed by two sources of income

Moral obligation bonds   Issuer not legally bound to repay

Industrial revenue and pollution control bonds   Funds used to build a plant leased to corporation; usually mortgage-backed. To earn tax exemption, must meet test as "private activity bonds"

Municipal notes   Short-term notes issued while awaiting proceeds from bond sale; called "anticipation notes"

Forms of municipals

Registered   To principal and interest, or to principal only (with coupon); in multiples of $1,000 to $100,000

Bearer bonds   No longer issued, but many outstanding

Legal opinion   On bond face; legal, tax-exempt; appears on bond face; if no opinion, bond is "Ex-legal"

Delivery   Regular way = third business day after trade

Indenture   Not required; covenants on face of bond cover issuer's obligations

Flow of funds   How receipts will be applied on some revenue bonds

Payment   At stated interest rate; principal paid at maturity

Term bonds   All mature at one time; quoted at percent of par

Serial bonds   Mature over a series of years; usually quoted on yield-to-maturity

Tender, call and put   Revenue bonds usually callable; if not, issuer can make "tender offer" to retire issue early; some have put provision

Insurance   Available to both issuers and to investors

Taxation   Interest income tax-exempt, but gains realized in trading are taxable; if issued at discount or premium, difference from par is tax-exempt

Equivalent yield   After-tax yield on municipal compared with corporate yield:

corporate yield rate × (1 − tax rate) = equivalent municipal rate

Yield to maturity

$$\frac{\textbf{coupon} + (\textbf{change in price} \div \textbf{years to maturity})}{(\textbf{purchase price} + \textbf{maturity price}) \div \textbf{2}} = \textbf{YTM}$$

Trading in municipals

Over the counter   Mostly involving specialist dealers, banks, and brokerage firms; banks cannot make a market in revenue bonds; traders typically maintain inventory

"Workable quote"   Price at which dealer is willing to buy municipal bond

"Concession"   In this context, the discount from quoted yield on inter-dealer transaction

Accrued interest   Purchaser must pay interest accrued since last coupon payment, computed on basis of twelve 30-day months

Evaluation

Ratings   Offered, as with corporates

REVIEW QUESTIONS

1. A general obligation bond would be backed by which of the following?

   (A) taxes
   (B) the full faith and credit of the issuer
   (C) general revenues
   (D) obligations on equipment

2. A capital gain could not be registered on:

   (A) T-notes
   (B) T-bills
   (C) T-bonds
   (D) corporate bonds

3. Which of the following would be most unattractive to the purchaser of a corporate bond?

   (A) high interest rate
   (B) convertibility
   (C) callability
   (D) sinking fund requirement

4. Bonds that mature in a sequence of years are called:

   (A) convertible
   (B) serial
   (C) series
   (D) balloon

5. A basis point is what percentage of yield?

   (A) 10%
   (B) 1.00%
   (C) 0.1%
   (D) 0.01%

6. Par value for most corporate bonds is:

   (A) $100
   (B) $1,000
   (C) $10,000
   (D) $100,000

7. A one-year T-bill with a discount yield of 5.00% would sell at approximately:

   (A) 94.50
   (B) 95.00
   (C) 95.25
   (D) 95.75

8. If interest rates fall, the price of previously-issued government bonds will generally:

   (A) fall
   (B) rise
   (C) be unaffected
   (D) vary

Questions 9–11 refer to a 7% corporate bond with par at $1,000 due to mature in 10 years which is bought at $700.

9. The nominal yield on this bond is:

   (A) 6.5%
   (B) 7.0%
   (C) 10%
   (D) 14.28%

10. The current yield is:

    (A) 6.5%
    (B) 7.0%
    (C) 10%
    (D) 14.28%

11. The yield to maturity is approximately:

    (A) 6.5%
    (B) 7.0%
    (C) 11.8%
    (D) 14.28%

12. An issue of bonds that mature at different times with a smaller amount maturing early and most late is:

(A) term

(B) serial

(C) series

(D) balloon

13. Debentures are backed by:

(A) the benchmark for revenues

(B) equipment

(C) real estate

(D) general credit

14. A $10,000 government bond priced at $104.04 would sell for:

(A) $10,400.04

(B) $10,404.00

(C) $10,412.50

(D) $10,440.00

15. The interest on corporates is computed on the basis of:

(A) actual days of the month and a 360-day year

(B) actual days of the month and a 365-day year

(C) 30-day months and a 360-day year

(D) 30-day months and a 365-day year

16. The interest on government bonds is computed on the basis of:

(A) actual days of the month and a 360-day year

(B) actual days of the month and a 365-day year

(C) 30-day months and a 360-day year

(D) 30-day months and a 365-day year

17. A purchase of $10,000 worth of T-bonds for cash on May 18 would settle on:

(A) May 18

(B) May 19

(C) May 24

(D) May 25

18. Which of the following is "triple exempt"?

(A) U.S. bonds

(B) U.S. Treasury bills

(C) GNMAs

(D) Puerto Rico bonds

19. A corporate bond quoted at $98.25 would normally cost:

(A) $98.25

(B) $980 and $\frac{25}{32}$ dollars

(C) $982.50

(D) $9,825.00

20. Bonds callable at 104 are currently selling at $105 \frac{25}{32}$. If the bonds were called, an investor who owned $30,000 face of these bonds would receive:

(A) $30,000

(B) $31,200

(C) $34,000

(D) $35,500

21. The yield to maturity is the yield an investor would earn if the security is held to maturity. It is arrived at by:

(A) taking account of the difference between purchase price and par

(B) considering the difference between coupon and current yield

(C) considering the difference between nominal and current yield

(D) averaging the discount and the premium on the bond ·

22. Which S&P rating is highest?

(A) Aaa

(B) AAA

(C) A+

(D) Al

23. The *Blue List* quotes:

    (A) corporate bonds
    (B) U.S. Government Agency obligations
    (C) municipal bonds
    (D) Treasury bills

24. A bond with a conversion rate of 20:1 selling at par would be convertible into:

    (A) 20 shares of common at $20
    (B) 50 shares of common at $20
    (C) 20 shares of common at $50
    (D) 50 shares of common at $50

25. The *Bond Buyer Index* measures on a weekly basis an average of:

    (A) 20-year Treasury bond yields
    (B) 20-year Treasury bond prices
    (C) 20-year municipal bond yields
    (D) 20-year municipal bond prices

26. The maximum amount (face value) of Series EE that an individual can purchase in any year is:

    (A) $7,500
    (B) $15,000
    (C) $22,500
    (D) $30,000

27. A municipal bond is purchased for delivery on November 26. It is a March 15–September 15 bond. How many days of accrued interest will the purchaser of the bond have to pay?

    (A) 66 days
    (B) 68 days
    (C) 72 days
    (D) 74 days

28. In evaluating a Water and Sewer Revenue Bond, which of the following would be taken into account?

    I. size of the customer base
    II. rate covenants
    III. the issuing authority's past performance

IV. the state in which the municipality is located

    (A) I only
    (B) I and II
    (C) I, II, and III
    (D) III and IV

29. A feasibility study is required for:

    (A) revenue bonds
    (B) general obligation bonds
    (C) school bonds
    (D) special assessment bonds

30. The lowest rating for bonds which are considered investment grade is:

    (A) A+ or A1
    (B) A or A
    (C) BBB or Baa
    (D) BB or Ba

31. Municipal bonds which are in bearer form and in default are traded:

    (A) flat and stripped of coupons
    (B) with accrued interest from the time of default
    (C) flat with all unpaid coupons attached
    (D) with accrued interest and a default penalty

32. Over a period of years, T-bill investments will have which of the following characteristics?

    I. stable interest rates
    II. varying interest rates
    III. stable principal
    IV. varying principal

    (A) I and III
    (B) I and IV
    (C) II and III
    (D) II and IV

33. An investor owns 10 corporate bonds with face value of $1,000 callable at a 5% premium. If the bonds are held to maturity the investor will receive:

(A) $10,000
(B) $10,050
(C) $100,000
(D) $100,500

34. A corporation which does not show a profit will still pay interest to holders of all of the following EXCEPT:

    (A) convertible bonds
    (B) callable bonds
    (C) debentures
    (D) adjustment bonds

35. An investor buys $20,000 face value corporate bonds at a price of 92 in the secondary market. If he sells them three years later at 96 he will realize:

    (A) a capital gain of $400
    (B) a capital gain of $800
    (C) interest income of $400
    (D) interest income of $800 with 60% long term

36. Which of the following is true of U.S. T-bonds?

    (A) they are issued at a discount
    (B) interest is not subject to federal income tax
    (C) maturity at issue is at least 10 years
    (D) the price will not fluctuate much over time

37. A bond selling at a premium with a coupon of 5% if held to maturity would have a yield:

    (A) lower than 5%
    (B) at 5%
    (C) higher than 5%
    (D) cannot be determined

38. None of the following is guaranteed by the U.S. government EXCEPT:

    (A) revenue bonds
    (B) Fannie Mae bonds

(C) GNMA certificates
(D) Tax Anticipation Notes (TANs)

39. If a legal opinion on a municipal bond was "qualified," it would mean:

    (A) the municipality is able to issue the bond
    (B) the bond counsel is in a position to offer an opinion
    (C) there are some conditions on the legal opinion
    (D) there is a debt ceiling on the issue

40. The information on municipal issues scheduled to be offered would be found in:

    (A) *Blue List*
    (B) 30-day visible supply
    (C) *Bond Buyer's Guide*
    (D) pink sheets

41. For Eurodollar bonds, all of the following are false EXCEPT:

    (A) They must be registered in the United States.
    (B) They are issued in Europe.
    (C) They never trade in the U.S.
    (D) They pay interest in the European currency.

42. A quote of 5.80–5.70 would apply to which of the following:

    (A) corporate bond
    (B) debenture
    (C) Treasury bond
    (D) Treasury bill

43. All of the following are true of CMOs EXCEPT:

    (A) They pay interest monthly.
    (B) They are high risk securities.
    (C) They have minimum denomination of $1,000.
    (D) They can be secured by GNMA or FNMA.

44. A municipal is purchased at a premium. If the bond is called, the yield to call is:

    (A) greater than the current yield
    (B) greater than the yield to maturity
    (C) less than the yield to maturity
    (D) cannot be determined

45. The dated date of a new municipal security is March 1, 1998. The coupon dates begin on October 1, 1998. The number of months of interest paid with the first coupon is:

    (A) 1 month
    (B) 6 months
    (C) 7 months
    (D) 9 months

46. If New York state issues a bond, all of the following are revenue streams that can be used to pay off the bonds EXCEPT:

    (A) *ad valorem* taxes
    (B) income taxes
    (C) sales taxes
    (D) corporate taxes

47. A municipal bond that is in default will be sold with:

    (A) defaulted coupons attached
    (B) no coupons attached
    (C) all coupons attached
    (D) only coupons for future payments attached

48. If a municipal revenue bond has a net revenue pledge, which of the following will be paid first?

    (A) sinking fund
    (B) operating costs
    (C) interest payments
    (D) reserves for future maintenance

The following list has answers for 49 and 50.
    (A) Visible Supply
    (B) Bond Buyer 20 Bond Index
    (C) Bond Buyer 30 Bond Index
    (D) placement ratio

49. The dollar amount of new bonds expected to reach the market in the next month.

50. The yield on A rated General Obligation bonds.

ANSWERS TO REVIEW QUESTIONS

1. **(B)** A general obligation bond is backed by all of the resources of the issuer, hence full faith and credit.

2. **(B)** The difference between the purchase and sale prices of a T-bill is always considered as interest.

3. **(C)** This is unattractive because it potentially reduces the time period over which the investor will receive the agreed-upon return.

4. **(B)** By definition. Not to be confused with series, which are bonds issued over a series of years all maturing in the same year.

5. **(D)** By definition. It can also be .01% of the yield.

6. **(B)** This is typical for corporates, not for governments.

7. **(B)** Discount yield of 5% means price is $100 − 5 = $95.00.

8. **(B)** Since they were issued before rates fell, they pay a higher rate and therefore are more valuable than current issues. Hence the higher price.

9. **(B)** A 7% bond means the nominal yield is 7%.

10. **(C)** The current yield is $70 (interest) ÷ $700 (price) = 10%.

11. **(C)** Since it will mature in ten years and pay $1,000, we approximate the yield to maturity by amortizing the $300 over this period. Hence we say that the gain is $70 + $30 = $100 per year, and this divided by the average of the purchase and redemption prices $700 and $1,000 yields $100 ÷ $850 = 11.8%.

12. **(D)** The word *balloon* refers to the large later payment.

13. **(D)** Debentures are not backed by any specific assets.

14. **(C)** The .04 is $\frac{4}{32}$ and, since each whole point is $100, $\frac{4}{32}$ is $12.50. $104\frac{4}{32}$ is $10,412.50.

15. **(C)** This is different from government bonds which are computed on actual days and a 365-day year.

16. **(B)** By definition.

17. **(A)** Cash settlement for U.S. securities is same day.

18. **(D)** In fact, all of the others are subject to federal tax.

19. **(C)** The usual par value for corporates is $1,000.

20. **(B)** The investor receives $104 for every $100 of bonds. If possible, the investor would have sold these bonds and received $105.50 for every $100 worth of bonds.

21. **(A)** The formula is

$$\text{YTM} = \frac{\text{Annual interest} + \text{prorated difference between purchase price} + \text{par}}{(\text{purchase price} + \text{par}) \div 2}$$

22. **(B)** Moody's highest rating is Aaa.

23. **(C)** *The Blue List* shows quantity available and the yield to maturity.

24. **(C)** The 20:1 means 20 shares of common to 1 bond. If selling at par, we have 20 × $50 = $1,000.

25. **(C)** The *Index* measures on a weekly basis an average of 20-year municipal bond yields.

26. **(D)** These are sold at 50% discount to mature at face so an investor can put $15,000 into these bonds each year.

27. **(D)** Accrued interest would be 16 days in September, 30 days in October, and 28 days (up to, but not including, delivery day) in November = 74 days.

28. **(C)** The state would have no direct obligation here.

29. **(A)** Since the payments depend on these revenues rather than any taxing ability, a feasibility study is required.

30. **(C)** Ratings below this are considered speculative.

31. **(C)** Since they are in default, there is no accrued interest, and they are traded flat. Naturally those coupons which have not been paid yet should be attached.

32. **(C)** The interest rates of T-bills vary with time, but since they are short term instruments, the principal is not subject to great variation.

33. **(A)** If they are held to maturity, the call option has not been exercised and there is no reason for paying a premium.

34. **(D)** Income or adjustment bonds include a promise to repay the principal at maturity, but interest is contingent on the company's earnings and must be declared by the board of directors.

35. **(B)** The purchase price of 92 means he paid $18,400 for $20,000 of face value bonds. The sale is at $19,200.

36. **(C)** T-bills have maturities up to 1 year and T-notes have maturities up to 10 years.

37. **(A)** If held to maturity, the investor receives face value and hence loses the amount of the premium. This reduces the yield.

38. **(C)** All of the others are issued by agencies or other entities and are not directly guaranteed by the U.S. government.

39. **(C)** If the opinion is "qualified," there are some conditions on it.

40. **(B)** This is a daily compilation of the total dollar value of municipal securities scheduled to come out within the next 30 days.

41. **(B)** Eurobonds are issued in Europe. While they do not require registration in the U.S., they can trade here. Since these are Eurodollar bonds, they pay interest and principal in dollars.

42. **(D)** Treasury bills are quoted as a discount yield with the bid before the offer. All of the others are quoted as a percentage of par.

43. **(B)** Since they are backed by pass-through obligations like GNMAs, they are generally AAA rated. They are issued in denominations of $1,000 and pay monthly interest like payments on the mortgages that back them.

44. **(C)** Since the premium is amortized over a shorter period if the bond is called, the yield to call is less than the yield to maturity.

45. **(C)** The first coupon pays interest from the dated date which in this case is 7 months earlier. All other coupons then follow the six-month schedule.

46. **(A)** *Ad valorem* taxes are local taxes and hence would not be available to the state to use.

47. **(D)** A bond in default will only have future coupons attached.

48. **(B)** A net revenue bond means that the bond will only pay interest and principal after operating expenses have been paid.

49. **(A).** The *Visible Supply* is published daily in the *Bond Buyer*. It is an estimate of the amount of new bonds due in the next thirty days.

50. **(B)** This index is made up of General Obligation bonds with an average rating of A and an average maturity of 20 years.

money market instruments

Money market instruments are very secure debt obligations which have maturities of less than one year. This category includes all short-term U.S. government and U.S. government agency obligations discussed in Chapter 2: Treasury bills; Treasury and agency-issued notes; and bonds maturing in less than one year. It also includes Federal Funds and non-governmental debt obligations like certificates of deposit, bankers' acceptances, and commercial paper, which are described in this chapter. These highly liquid instruments come in a number of forms. Individual investors are most likely to encounter these in the form of money market funds (see Chapter 4).

FEDERAL FUNDS

The Federal Reserve System requires each bank to hold a specified proportion of its funds in reserve. To meet these requirements, banks at times borrow from other banks which have a surplus or from the Fed itself. These are usually unsecured "overnight" borrowings in amounts of $1 million and up. Interest, usually one day, is calculated on the basis of a 360-day year.

The interest rate, called the "federal funds rate," is extremely volatile, changing from day to day depending on the demand for money. The Federal Reserve changes this rate when it wishes to tighten or ease credit.

REPURCHASE AGREEMENTS

Repurchase agreements, or "repos," occur when a security is sold with an agreement to buy it back, often the next day, at a higher price. Both the time and price of this repurchase are fixed, and these together determine the interest charge in the transaction.

These agreements are typically used by dealers in government securities. Dealers often require large amounts of cash in order to hold the large inventories of government securities which they need to conduct business. For this reason, they will, at times, sell some portion of their holdings to the Federal Reserve Bank or to a cash-rich corporate lender under an arrangement which includes a pledge to repurchase (repossess or "repo") those securities, at the selling price plus interest, in the future. (Dealers also raise cash using government issues as collateral for demand loans; see page 84.)

Under these agreements, funds can be borrowed overnight, for some days, or even longer. The Federal Reserve Bank participates directly in these arrangements in part because dealers play a vital role in maintaining an active market in government securities, especially when new issues are placed.

If the market price of the instrument rises more than the interest paid, dealers can realize a profit when securities are sold to a lender under a repurchase agreement. Similarly, if the price of these securities declines, dealers can suffer a loss.

The minimum denomination of repurchase agreements is $1,000,000. Interest, paid at repurchase, is calculated in terms of actual days on the basis of a 360-day year.

This procedure works in the opposite direction with a reverse repo: a dealer buys securities and agrees to sell them back at a specified later date. The dealer is effectively lending money, using very secure collateral.

Repos of either type have no secondary market since they represent contracts between a specified buyer and seller.

BANKER'S ACCEPTANCES

Used in international trade, a banker's acceptance can be thought of as a postdated certified check. A banker's acceptance is basically a commercial bank draft, ordering the bank to pay a specified amount to the holder on a specified date (usually 90 days from date of issue). The term "acceptance" comes into play when the bank accepts responsibility—gives its promise—to repay.

Once the bank does guarantee payment at maturity, a banker's acceptance becomes a money-market instrument and is traded between banks and in security markets, usually at a discount, with the discount tied to the time until maturity. (They are also discounted if presented for payment before they mature.) Holders of acceptances receive full payment from the bank at maturity. One way to understand the use of banker's acceptances is through an example:

Suppose a Baltimore wholesaler wishes to import mangoes from Malaysia. The wholesaler does not want to pay cash, and the Malaysian Mango Monopoly will not extend credit. The wholesaler then gets a "letter of credit" from his bank and presents it to the Malaysians. The Malaysians ship the mangoes and present the shipping documents and letter of credit to a Malaysian bank. This bank, in turn, draws a draft on a U.S. bank; when the U.S. bank gets and "accepts" this draft, it becomes a banker's acceptance.

Note that this does not involve financing, which is separate. The bank is only guaranteeing payment at maturity. The discount at which it is sold determines the interest rate.

Maturities can range from 1 to 270 days, though 90 days is usual.

COMMERCIAL PAPER

This term covers unsecured promissory notes, in bearer form, for a fixed amount at a fixed date. They are issued only by the most credit-worthy corporations. Issuance is at a discount and redemption at face value. Such notes have become a substitute for bank borrowing for those corporations that can issue them. Purchasers are mostly corporations, commercial banks, insurance companies, and mutual funds.

Commercial paper is sometimes sold directly to investors ("direct paper") and sometimes to dealers ("dealer paper"). Dealers can act as agents, selling to investors and collecting a commission, although dealers sometimes buy the paper directly and then resell it to investors. Maturities are up to 270 days. Denominations start at $100,000. Interest (in this case, the difference between the discounted price and payment at maturity) is calculated on the basis of a 360-day year.

NEGOTIABLE CERTIFICATES OF DEPOSIT

Negotiable Certificates of Deposit are tradeable certificates issued by commercial banks in exchange for time deposits. They are quoted on the basis of yield. They usually mature in one year, but can be for shorter periods (but no less than seven days) if the depositor agrees.

Units of $1 million or more are the rule for these "jumbo CDs," the minimum denomination is $100,000. Interest calculated in terms of actual days on the basis of a 360-day year is paid at maturity.

BROKER'S LOANS (CALL LOANS)

A broker's loan is made to a broker by a commercial bank to finance security purchases made by the broker's customers (margin purchases). The effect of this practice is that funds borrowed from brokers by individuals actually come from banks. As collateral, the broker pledges securities purchased in a "street name."

Broker's loans can be in the form of time notes or demand notes. Time notes pay a fixed interest rate and have varying maturities, usually up to six months. In contrast, interest on demand notes, or "call loans," varies daily. Basically, the call loan is payable on demand the day after it is made; if no demand is made, the note is renewed for another day at that day's interest rate. Such loans can last up to 90 days.

Note that brokers who make a market often use U.S. government bonds and bills as collateral for demand loans needed to pay for their inventories and that interest on these loans governs the interest charges on margin accounts. Like the "prime rate," the broker's loan rate is fixed by each bank individually; however, competitive conditions force rates to be comparable.

EURODOLLARS

A Eurodollar is a dollar deposited in a bank outside the United States. Since these banks have fewer restrictions than do banks in this country, the risk associated with such deposits is slightly higher. Eurodollar interest rates are the interbank interest rates for these monies. The London Interbank Offer Rate, LIBOR, is a 3-month rate usually slightly higher than that of 3-month T-Bills.

TERMS

Money Market Instruments   Short-term debt obligations, usually very secure, including T-bills, notes, and bonds

Federal funds   Overnight borrowings, $1,000,000 and up, by banks from Federal Reserve; rate changes daily

Repurchase agreements (repos)   Security sold with agreement to repurchase, usually at fixed time and price; minimum of $1,000,000

Banker's Acceptances   Commercial bank drafts agreeing to payment on a specified date; used in international trade

Commercial paper

Unsecured promissory notes of $100,000 and up; issued at discount; can be sold to dealers or investors

Negotiable certificates of deposit

Broker's Loans (Call Loans)   Notes covering commercial bank loans to brokers to finance margin purchases

REVIEW QUESTIONS

1. All of the following are money market instruments EXCEPT:

   (A) CDs
   (B) Banker's Acceptances
   (C) ADRs
   (D) Fed Funds

2. If the yield on a T-bill is in-creased by .10, it has increased by:

   (A) 20 basis points
   (B) 0.1 basis points
   (C) 10 basis points
   (D) 100 basis points

3. The instrument with the least active secondary market is the one for:

   (A) T-bills
   (B) negotiable CDs
   (C) commercial paper
   (D) banker's acceptances

4. Which of the following is used to finance foreign trade?

   (A) ADRs
   (B) Fed Funds
   (C) Banker's Acceptances
   (D) CDs

5. Federal funds are generated if:

   (A) the Federal Reserve does repos
   (B) a federal bank sells securities
   (C) a bank has excess reserves to lend
   (D) a non-federal bank buys T-bills

6. Which of the following is the most volatile?

   (A) federal funds rate
   (B) prime rate
   (C) T-bill rate
   (D) broker loan rate

7. Auctions for 3- and 6-month T-bills take place:

   (A) daily
   (B) weekly
   (C) bi-weekly
   (D) monthly

8. The maximum maturity on com-mercial paper is ordinarily:

   (A) 90 days
   (B) 180 days
   (C) 270 days
   (D) 1 year

9. If the rate on Treasury bills dropped, this would mean:

   (A) the Fed had tightened
   (B) the cost of bills had risen
   (C) the cost of bills had dropped
   (D) interest rates had risen

10. The money market instrument which most closely resembles a time deposit is:

    (A) negotiable CD
    (B) banker's acceptance
    (C) T-bill
    (D) federal funds

ANSWERS TO REVIEW QUESTIONS

1. (**C**) American Depository Receipts are certificates that represent owner-ship of stock in foreign companies.

2. (**C**) 100 basis points represent 1 point of yield, *e.g.*, from 6.00 to 7.00.

3. (**C**) Commercial paper is for the most part not bought and sold.

4. (**C**) Banker's acceptances are time drafts usually used for collections of payments on foreign trade.

5. **(C)** These are the funds that the Federal Reserve requires a bank to set aside. When too much has been set aside, fed funds are created.

6. **(A)** This changes rapidly, often several times within a single day.

7. **(B)** The 12-month bills are auctioned monthly.

8. **(C)** This allows them to be issued without going through registration as securities.

9. **(B)** If the rate went from 6.50 to 6.00 the price would go from 93.50 to 94.00.

10. **(A)** In fact, it is a time deposit with the additional proviso that it is negotiable.

CHAPTER FOUR

investment companies— mutual funds

This chapter describes a class of securities very different from those discussed in the first three chapters. These are not individual securities, but are securities issued by companies whose primary purpose is to invest their capital in the securities of other entities. Not unreasonably, these companies are called investment companies. The most important type of investment company is the mutual fund, and most of this chapter will be devoted to that subject.

Investment companies acquire funds by selling shares to shareholders, and they invest those funds in a portfolio of securities. Owning shares in an investment company means owning some part of this portfolio. The company income is the stream of dividends and interest payments that it receives from its portfolio of stocks and bonds. Similarly, the value of the company, as reflected in the worth of its shares, rises and falls with the rise and fall of the value of the portfolio of securities.

There are some advantages to such an investment. It enables an investor to diversify holdings even with a small investment; it helps to reduce record-keeping (one need only keep the records pertaining to the investment company); and it provides the benefits of having one's investment decisions made by professional investment managers. Naturally, these benefits have a price: this is reflected in fees charged by the company and sales commissions charged for buying shares.

There are three kinds of investment companies: unit investment trusts (UITs), face-amount certificate companies, and management companies (the most common form of which is known as mutual funds). We begin by discussing the first two kinds.

Unit Investment Trusts

Unit Investment Trusts invest in an identified portfolio of securities. Units (shares) of the trust represent ownership of some percentage of this portfolio. There are two types of UITs, fixed and non-fixed.

Fixed UITs typically buy a portfolio of bonds, collect the interest and repayments on those bonds, and cease to exist when the last bond matures. In other words, they last for the life of the bonds. The original portfolio is never changed, and thus there are no expenses related to trading.

Non-fixed UITs also invest in an identified portfolio, but this consists of shares in a professionally managed pool of funds. Investors contract to buy shares in the UIT over time, and, as these funds flow in, the trust buys more shares in the pool.

The important distinction here is that while the non-fixed UIT portfolio consists solely of shares in the pool, the pool itself is professionally managed, and the holdings in the pool (called the portfolio) vary over time.

Face-amount certificate companies

Face-amount certificate companies issue securities that require the company to pay the holder the "face amount" at some specified date. They are generally guaranteed as to principal and interest and are backed by identified securities such as corporate bonds, preferred stock, or U.S. government-backed securities. Face-amount certificates can be purchased either with a single payment or through some installment plan.

FORMS OF MANAGEMENT COMPANIES

There are two general formats for management companies: closed-end and open-end (or mutual funds).

Closed-End Funds

FRIDAY, NOV. 5, 1993

Fund Name	Stock Exch	NAV	Mkt Price	Pct. Diff.
General Equity Funds				
AdamsExpCo	N	20.80	19⅛	− 8.05
ChasAllmon	N	10.80	10¼	− 5.09
BakerFent	N	22.64	18¾	− 17.18
BergstCap	A	92.36	97	+ 5.02
BlueChipVl	N	7.79	7⅞	+ 1.09
CentSecCor	A	17.79	17¼	− 3.04
EngexInc	A	13.61	11¼	− 17.34
EquusII	A	21.31	14⅛	− 33.72
GabelliEq	N	11.42	11⅞	+ 3.98
GenAmerInv	N	26.05	24¼	− 6.91
IneffMktFd	A	12.10	10⅜	− 14.26
JundtGrow	N	15.19	14	− 7.83
LibAllStar	N	10.64	11	+ 3.38
MorGrSmCap	N	12.86	11⅜	− 11.55
RoyceValTr	N	14.23	13¾	− 3.37
SalomonSBF	N	16.00	13⅞	− 13.28
SourceCap	N	41.97	46⅝	+ 11.09
SpectraFd	O	21.40	18	− 15.89
TriCont	N	28.88	24¾	− 14.30
Z-SevenFd	O	16.56	17¼	+ 4.17
ZweigFund	N	11.63	13⅜	+ 15.00
Specialized Equity Funds				
AlliGlbEnv	N	10.88	9¼	− 14.98
ASALtd	N cv	46.06	48	+ 4.21
BGR PrMets	T cy	14.87	13½	− 9.21
CentCanada	A c	4.53	4 15/16	+ 8.98
C&SRltyInc	A	9.06	9¾	+ 7.62
C&STotRet	N	13.87	14½	+ 4.54
CounsTandm	N	17.38	15¼	− 12.26
DelaGrDiv	N	14.86	14⅝	− 1.58
Duf&PheUtl	N	9.70	10	+ 3.09
EmMktTele	N	19.65	22⅜	+ 13.87
1stFinanFd	N	19.42	17⅜	− 10.53
GlbHealSci	N	11.93	11¾	− 1.51
NewAgeMed	N	13.66	15¼	+ 11.64
PatGlblDiv	N a	14.79	15	+ 1.42
PatPrefDiv	N a	13.55	13⅞	+ 2.40
PatPremDiv	N	10.48	10¼	− 2.19
PatPrDivII	N	12.84	12	− 6.54
CorpHiYld	N	14.56	14⅞	+ 2.16
CurrentInc	N	14.33	13½	− 5.79
DnWitGovIn	N a	9.41	9	− 4.36
DreyStrGov	N a	10.93	11	+ 0.64
DuffUtCorp	N	15.11	14¾	− 2.38
1838Bd-Deb	N	22.65	23¼	+ 2.65
Excelsior	N c	19.51	18⅛	− 7.10
FstBstnInc	N	8.85	9⅛	+ 3.11
FstBstnStr	N	10.25	10¼	+ 0.00
FtDearInco	N	17.50	17⅜	− 0.71
FortisSecs	N	10.12	11¼	+ 11.17
FrankMuIln	N c	11.31	10¾	− 4.95
FrankPrin	N c	9.67	8¾	− 9.51
FrankUniv	N c	9.73	9⅛	− 6.22
JHncockInc	N	17.25	17¼	+ 0.00
JHncockInv	N	22.89	24	+ 4.85
HatterasIn	N	17.01	18¼	+ 7.29
HilnAdv	N a	6.06	6⅛	+ 1.07
HilnAdvII	N a	6.75	6⅝	− 1.85
HilnAdvIII	N a	7.27	7⅝	+ 4.88
HiYldInco	N	7.85	8⅜	+ 6.69
HiYldPlus	N	8.97	8⅝	− 3.85
Hyper1997	N c	8.46	8⅛	− 3.96
Hyper1999	N c	7.10	7	− 1.41
Hyper2002	N c	8.49	7¾	− 8.72
Hyper2005	N c	9.48	8¾	− 7.70
HyperToRet	N ac	10.60	10⅛	− 4.48
INAInvstmt	N	20.01	18½	− 7.55
IncOpp1999	N	9.40	9⅜	− 0.27
IncOpp2000	N	10.07	9⅝	− 4.42
IndependSq	O	18.74	17⅞	− 4.62
IntCapInc	N a	18.73	20⅝	+ 10.12
KemperHiln	N	9.40	9½	+ 1.06
KemperInGv	N	8.73	8½	− 2.63
KemperMult	N	11.28	11⅛	− 1.37
LibertyTm	N	9.09	10	+ 10.01
LincNatInc	N c	15.59	16⅜	+ 5.04
MgdHighInc	N	12.37	12⅜	+ 0.04
MentorInc	N c	11.23	10½	− 6.50
MontgmrySt	N	20.35	20¼	− 0.49
MutualOmah	N	14.44	14⅝	+ 1.28
NationGovt	N	9.04	10	+ 10.62
NuvSelTF4	N	14.93	14⅝	− 2.04
PWPremIns	N	15.08	15¼	+ 1.13
PWPreIntTF	A	14.70	14⅛	− 3.91
PWPremTxFr	N	16.62	16¼	− 2.23
PutHiYld	N	9.68	10⅝	+ 9.76
PutInvGrII	N	15.48	15⅛	− 2.29
PutInvGr	N	13.45	14½	+ 7.81
PutInGrInt	A	14.40	13⅞	− 3.65
PutMgdInc	N	10.74	11¼	+ 4.75
PutMunOpp	N	14.48	14¼	− 1.59
PutTFHlth	N	15.17	15½	+ 2.18
SeligQual	N	16.16	15	− 7.18
SeligSel	N	13.14	13½	+ 2.74
SmBarIntMu	A	10.75	10⅞	+ 1.16
SmBarMuni	A	15.64	15½	− 0.90
VKMAdvInII	A	14.83	14⅝	− 1.38
VKMAdvIn	N	16.89	15¾	− 6.75
VKMInvGr	N	11.96	13⅞	+ 16.01
VKMMunInc	N	11.19	12¼	+ 9.47
VKMMunOp	N	17.16	16¼	− 5.30
VKMMunOpII	N	15.12	14¾	− 2.45
VKMMuniTr	N	16.95	16⅝	− 1.92
VKMStrat	N	14.97	14½	− 3.14
VKMTrIns	N	17.85	16⅞	− 5.46
VKMTrInvMu	N	17.66	16¾	− 5.15
VKMValMun	N	15.96	15	− 6.02
Single State Municipal Bond Funds				
BlckCA2008	N	15.56	15½	− 0.39
BlckCAInv	A	14.13	13⅞	− 1.80
BlckFL2008	N	15.56	15⅝	+ 0.42
BlckFLInv	A	14.20	14½	+ 2.11
BlckNJInv	A	14.13	14	− 0.92
BlckNY2008	N	15.69	15⅛	− 3.60
BlckNYInv	A	14.14	13½	− 4.53
DreyCaMun	A a	9.70	10¼	+ 5.67
DreyNYMun	A	10.46	11½	+ 9.94
IntCapCAIn	N a	14.14	15⅛	+ 6.97
IntCapCAMu	N	13.70	15⅛	+ 10.40
IntCapNYMu	N	13.86	15¼	+ 10.03
MAHlthEduc	A	14.15	15⅝	+ 10.42

NAV — Net asset value. a — Ex-dividend. b — Fully diluted. c — As of Thursday's close. d — As of Wednesday's close. e — Assumes rights offering fully subscribed. v — Converted at the commercial Rand rate. Stock exchanges: N — New York. A — American. O — NASDAQ.
M — Midwest.
Source: Lipper Analytical Services

Figure 4.1 Closed-End Funds

Closed-end companies

These authorize and issue stock at their inception, after which no more shares are sold. The company does not redeem its shares; they are, however, traded on the open market. This form of investment company was much more popular before 1940.

Value of shares The shares of the company represent ownership of its assets. These assets, minus the liabilities, constitute the *net asset value;* when divided by the number of shares outstanding, this becomes *net asset value per share,* NAV.

Pricing of shares There is obviously a relationship between the NAV and the cost of these shares on the open market. However, since the company does not redeem these shares, there is no direct exchange between asset value and the price of shares. As a result, the price of shares in a closed-end company is not the same as the NAV. They are traded on exchanges, as well as over the counter.

In fact, shares tend to sell at a discount to NAV, although not always. The relationship between share price and NAV is dictated partly by tax considerations and partly by past performance of the investment company.

Offerings of shares
Although closed-end funds issue shares only at their inception, they can raise additional funds by issuing preferred stock or bonds.

The original offering of a fixed number of shares is made through a prospectus, similar to the one described in discussing common stocks. (See Chapter 6.) After this initial offering, there is no longer any need for this prospectus. This, and the fact that they do not redeem their shares (remember these are bought and sold through a broker and for a commission on the open market for whatever price they can bring), distinguishes closed-end from open-end companies (see chart, page 99).

Open-end investment companies (mutual funds)

These companies do redeem their shares. By law, they may only issue *common stock*. Since they do this continually, they must always have an appropriately revised prospectus on offer. The prospectus must describe the investment objectives of the mutual fund as well as the strategy that it plans to use to meet those objectives. By now, there are many kinds of mutual funds with varied objectives.

EARNINGS

Dividends

From time to time, mutual funds declare and pay dividends on net income. These represent:

- all the fund's dividend earnings on stocks, plus

- interest income from debt obligations, less

- operating fees and costs (management fees, commissions paid to brokers for buying or selling stocks, custodial fees, legal and accounting fees, and the costs of producing prospectuses and reports, and, in some cases, advertising expenses)

Rules for dividends

1. There is no fixed term for dividends; some funds declare dividends daily.

2. By law, to avoid taxation, the investment company must pay as dividend at least 90% of the net earnings from dividends (see page 98).

Gains

Any net gains realized by the fund from the sale of securities can also be distributed to investors in proportion to shares held. Short-term gains are often distributed along with dividend income. Long-term distributions usually take place once a year and are paid separately from dividends.

Tax treatment of earnings

The dividends that an investor receives from a mutual fund are exactly like those received from any other company and are treated as such for tax purposes.

Capital gains dividends are treated as long-term capital gains for the investor, regardless of how long the investor has held the shares.

FEATURES OF MUTUAL FUNDS

Advantages to investors

Individual investors find mutual funds attractive because they offer:

- the services of full-time professional managers
- safekeeping of securities
- the chance to invest in terms of dollar amounts, as funds offer both full and fractional shares
- the ability to reduce the amount invested without reducing diversity
- shares that can be used as collateral

Some funds also offer automatic reinvestment and/or the right to convert to other funds in a "family of funds."

Types of mutual funds

Mutual funds diversify their holdings in a variety of ways among different companies, or among different industries, or by mixing various instruments. Their objectives are often described broadly as "growth," "income," or "safety" funds. An investor should choose the fund that best meets his or her investment objectives.

Diversified common stock Mostly common stocks. If the objective is income, then the portfolio contains stocks that pay high dividends. If the objective is growth, the fund will concentrate on companies reinvesting their profits for research or expansion. A fund that buys highly volatile growth stocks is called an aggressive growth fund.

Specialized funds Common stock in one industry (for example, oil), or a group of related industries (such as energy companies), or in one geographical area in the U.S. or overseas. Such funds will subdivide again into growth, income, or safety.

Balanced funds   Usually a varying mix of bonds, common, and preferred stocks. These tend to be more conservatively managed than common stock funds and less subject to fluctuation. Their objective is often to preserve capital while producing a moderate income.

Bond and preferred stock funds   These offer safety, and, customarily, a fixed income.

Municipal bond funds   Usually only investment-grade municipal issues (BBB or above).

Money market funds   Invest in liquid, short-term debt securities; hence they are often called liquid asset or cash funds. Money market funds usually calculate and reinvest interest on outstanding shares daily and credit it to shareholders periodically. They also often provide limited "check writing" privileges as a convenient method for redeeming shares.

U.S. Government securities   These are government instruments, keeping principal well protected.

Hedge funds   Engage in aggressive trading practices, including short selling, and usually can hold any type of security.

Dual-purpose funds   Issue two classes of shares: dividend and capital gains. The former receive all income distributions but no gains; the latter all gains but no income. Investors choose one class and receive the stream of funds generated by that class.

MANAGEMENT COMPANY STRUCTURE

All mutual funds, of whatever type, share certain structural features. The mutual fund is a corporation that uses its capital to invest in securities. It raises that capital by issuing common stock. Although the fund has some stated objectives, day-to-day decisions about investment are made by a professional money manager or professional fund manager

This manager is actually a "management company" or "investment advisor." It is usually a corporation that is in the business of providing advice to institutions on their holdings and, in this capacity, contracts with the fund for these purposes. The management company can consist of a subcommittee of the fund's board of directors or of its corporate officers. However, the Investment Company Act of 1940 requires that at least 40% of the fund's directors be outsiders, unaffiliated with the management company or the fund. The initial contract must be for two years and must be approved by both a majority of the shareholders AND the board of directors. The contract must be renewed annually; for renewal, the approval of either directors or shareholders is sufficient.

Basically, the management company is charged with meeting the fund's goals as spelled out in the prospectus, maintaining an appropriate mix of investments, deciding when to buy or sell or hold, monitoring the tax status of fund holdings, and conducting business efficiently.

Usually, the management company has complete administrative powers: it pays salaries of fund officers and employees and other costs of running the corporation. In return, the fund pays a fee, typically, between 0.5% and 1% of average net assets; in some cases, the percentage declines as assets rise.

Management fees *cannot* be based on increases in value of the fund's portfolio (realized or unrealized). All management fees must be stated clearly in the prospectus.

CALCULATING MUTUAL FUND YIELDS

Under SEC regulations, the only mutual fund yields that may be discussed are those arising from income, dividends, and interest. Within these restrictions, yield may be calculated in any way that is not misleading. For instance, current yield could be calculated with or without including the past year's capital gains in the denominator.

Since including capital gains would make yield lower, investors must be alert to the different methods of calculating yields in comparing different funds.

$$\text{current yield} = \frac{\text{annual dividends paid over the past year}}{\text{today's price } + \text{ any capital gains paid}}$$

and

$$\text{historic yield} = \frac{\text{average annual dividends}}{\text{average annual price}}$$

PRICING OF SHARES

"Bid" and "ask" prices

Mutual fund prices are often quoted as "bid" and "ask." The bid is the price at which the fund will redeem its shares. It is the same as the NAV (a redemption fee may reduce the amount actually received). The ask or "offer" is the price that an investor must pay to purchase the shares.

MUTUAL FUNDS

Fund Family / Fund Name	NAV	Dly %Ret.	YTD %Ret.	Sales Chg.
AAL				
Bond m	9.99	−0.1	+13.6	4.75
CapGrow m	17.81	−0.8	+28.0	4.75
MuniBond m	11.17	−0.1	+15.2	4.75
SmCoStk m	14.40	−2.0	+39.3	4.75
Utilities m	10.75	−0.4	+21.8	4.75
AARP Investment				
BalStkBd	16.67	−0.2	+19.7	NL
CapGrow	38.74	−0.8	+28.5	NL
GNMAUSTrs	15.23		+10.9	NL
GrowInc	39.15	−0.3	+26.2	NL
HiQBond	16.18	−0.1	+14.3	NL
InsTaxFBd	18.05		+13.9	NL
AHA				
Balanced	13.38	−0.3	+21.0	NL
DivrEq	16.17	−0.4	+29.1	NL
FullMatFl	10.01	−0.1	+14.7	NL
LtdMatFl	10.28		+9.8	NL
CapWldGrl m	20.06	+0.3	+17.8	5.75
EurPacGr m	23.06	+0.5	+9.8	5.75
Fundminv m	22.24	−0.2	+30.5	5.75
GrowAmer m	32.92	−0.8	+28.9	5.75
HiInc m	14.42	+0.1	+19.0	4.75
HiIncMu m	15.51		+16.5	4.75
IncAmer m	15.75	−0.1	+24.9	5.75
IntBdAm m	13.65		+12.2	4.75
InvCoAm m	21.94	−0.2	+26.4	5.75
LtdTmTxE m	14.48	−0.1	+11.3	4.75
Mutual m	24.75	−0.2	+26.5	5.75
NewEcono m	16.51	−0.4	+20.6	5.75
NewPersp m	16.98	+0.2	+18.8	5.75
SmCpWorl m	25.29	−0.2	+18.4	5.75
TaxEBdAm m	12.15		+15.1	4.75
TaxECA m	16.00		+15.2	4.75
TaxEMD m	15.62		+14.3	4.75
TaxEVA xm	16.02		+13.9	4.75
USGovSec m	13.43	−0.1	+13.2	4.75
WAMutinv m	22.09	−0.3	+34.1	5.75

Figure 4.2 Quotation of Mutual Funds

"Load" and "no load"

Mutual funds can be divided into two broad classes: "load" and "no load." The latter do not have any sales charges and therefore have identical bid and ask prices. This can be seen in Figure 4.2 where some funds have "NL" in the sales charge column. For those funds in which the offer price differs from the bid, the difference is the load or sales charge that is being levied.

Determining NAV

The net asset value per share must be determined at the close of each business day on the basis of closing prices. The actual price paid by a buyer is the NAV for the day of purchase, that is, the price listed on the day after the order is executed. However, when shares are sold, the seller receives the *NAV next calculated after the order was received.*

CALCULATING SALES CHARGES AND REDEMPTION FEES

Sales charges are regulated by the Investment Company Act of 1940 and Investment Company Amendment Act of 1975. These Acts limit the maximum sales charge to 8.5% of the offering price and further hold that this charge can be imposed only if certain benefits are provided to the public. These benefits include discounts for lump-sum purchases, the chance to reinvest dividends, and "rights of accumulation"; *i.e.,* the right to include previous purchases in determining whether or not an investor qualifies for a sales charge discount. If these are not provided, the maximum sales charge is correspondingly reduced.

Sales charges

Sales charges are imposed only when mutual fund shares are sold to an investor. The charge is based on the *asking price*, not NAV.

Example

If the bid price (or NAV) is $15.00 and the ask is $16.00, the sales charge (or load) is $1.00 and the rate is $1.00 ÷ $16.00 = 6.25%.

This can be deceptive if one is provided with a quote of "NAV = $14.49, sales charge 8%." The actual sales charge is 8% of the ask price which is computed as follows: Ask price × (100% − 8%) = $14.49, or $14.49 ÷ 92% = $15.75. Thus the sales charge is $15.75 − $14.49 = $1.26, and not 8% of $14.49 which would be $1.16.

Mutual fund shares cannot be sold for less than the public offering price, and that price cannot include a sales charge of more than 9% (see page 100).

Redemption fees

When a redemption fee is imposed, it is usually 1% or less and is based on NAV.

Example

Bid $20; Ask $21. Redemption fee $\frac{3}{4}$%. An investor selling 1,000 shares would be charged $20,000 × .0075 = $150 and would therefore receive $20,000 − $150 = $19,850.

Sales charges and redemption fees must be shown in the prospectus.

BREAKPOINTS

Many funds offer reduced sales charges on large purchases, for example, at $10,000, $25,000, etc. These are called "breakpoints."

The Investment Company Act of 1940 allows reductions to any person who buys at the specified levels either at one time ("lump sum") or over a period of time, through "rights of accumulation" or by signing a "letter of intent."

Note that the Act limits the definition of "person" to:

- an individual

- an individual, spouse, and children under 21 purchasing for one or all of their number

- a trustee or fiduciary purchasing for a single estate or account

Groups such as "investment clubs" are specifically excluded.

Rights of accumulation

Investors are entitled to reduced sales charges when the total market value of their purchases accumulates to the breakpoints.

For instance, a fund cuts its sales charge from 8% to 6% for purchases of over $10,000. A buyer who puts $1,000 a month into the fund with rights of accumulation will pay 8% per month until the value of the account, including the next purchase, equals $10,000. From that next purchase on, the investor will pay 6%. Shares added to an account through reinvestment are included in the total.

Letter of intent

An investor announces the intention to make purchases at breakpoint levels over a period of *13 months*. Such letters can be *backdated as much as 90 days* to include an earlier purchase.

This is not a contract, as the investor is not bound to fulfill the plan. It is, however, binding on the fund: if the sales charge rises, rates stated in the letter hold; if they fall, the investor gets the lower rate. If purchases do not reach breakpoint volume, the higher sales charge is imposed. The fund can hold some of the shares purchased under the letter in escrow and redeem them to pay those added charges.

Note that such a plan, unlike rights of accumulation, allows lower sales charges on all shares purchased.

Example

On April 1, a customer signs a letter of intent backdated to the beginning of the year agreeing to purchase a total of $10,000 worth of ABC Fund within the next ten months. If he had already purchased $2,000 during that year and purchased $800 more in each of the following ten months, then he would pay the reduced sales commission on the entire $10,000 purchase (assuming $10,000 is a break-point).

DOLLAR COST AVERAGING

This plan involves investing a specific sum at regular intervals. As share prices fluctuate, the number of shares purchased will vary.

The attraction of this approach is that the buyer acquires more shares when the price is low; so as long as the share price does go up and down, the buyer will be paying less per share than the average price computed by buying the same number of shares in each purchase period.

Example

If the prices of a mutual fund in four successive quarters were $20, $15, $12, and $25, respectively, then the average price for these periods would be $72 ÷ 4 = $18. An investor who used a dollar cost averaging program of $300 for each period would accumulate 15, 20, 25, 12—or 72 shares for which he or she would have paid $1,200 for an average cost of $16.67 ($1,200 ÷ 72 = $16.67) in contrast to the average of $18 if equal numbers of shares were purchased each period.

Such a method requires patience and persistence and cannot offer protection against loss if shares continue to fall or if the investor must sell when the share price is below his or her average cost.

This approach is also called "cost averaging," "dollar averaging," etc., but mutual fund sales literature must use the word "cost" in describing these plans.

REDEEMING SHARES

The mutual fund must honor a request to redeem shares. The request can be executed in any of several ways:

If shares are held by a custodian or transfer agent (usually a commercial bank), the investor must write to the mutual fund, in care of the transfer agent. The letter must include the investor's account number and a signed stock power with the signature guaranteed (usually by an NASD member or a national bank).

If the investor holds the share certificates, he or she writes the mutual fund directly or informs the dealer (some funds redeem shares only through a dealer), presenting the certificate or a stock power with a guaranteed signature.

With no-load funds, all transactions are often made through the mails, including redemptions.

The redemption price is the next NAV per share computed after the fund (or transfer agent) receives a properly executed order. Under the Investment

Company Act of 1940, the net amount due (less redemption fees, if any) must be remitted to the investor within 7 days.

The 7-day requirement can be avoided only if NYSE trading is restricted or halted for some extraordinary reason, if the SEC has allowed the fund to stop redeeming shares to protect shareholders, or if some emergency makes it impractical to find the NAV or to dispose of shares.

RULES GOVERNING OPEN-END INVESTMENT COMPANIES

Registration requirements

All open end investment companies must be registered under the Investment Company Act of 1940. Under the Act such firms:

* must have a net worth of at least $100,000 before making a public offering of their shares

* can issue only common stock, not preferred stock or bonds

* can borrow from banks

Rights of shareholders

Like common stock shareholders, holders of mutual fund shares have the right to vote on directors and on matters that could affect their holdings. Proposed changes in the fund's objectives or investment practices, in the way NAV is calculated, in management or other fees, or in redemption privileges, all require a vote of more than 50% of all outstanding shares. Shareholders must be sent proxy forms that describe the fund's contract with its investment advisors and the connections between those advisors and fund officers.

Shareholders also have the right to receive a complete financial statement *semi-annually*.

Custodian

The Investment Company Act of 1940 states that open-end investment companies must employ a custodian. The custodian is usually an institution like a trust company or a national bank. The custodian is charged with safeguarding the company's physical assets, disburses funds needed to purchase securities, and receives funds realized from the sale of securities.

In some instances, the custodian also acts as transfer agent and registrar and issues new shares, cancels redeemed shares, distributes dividends and capital gains to investors, and performs clerical tasks—preparing reports, handling proxies, and keeping the books.

The custodian cannot take any part in share selling or offer any protection against depreciation of the company's assets.

OWNERSHIP

In addition to individual ownership, mutual fund shares can be owned in any of several ways:

- in a joint tenancy with rights of survivorship; if one owner dies, the shares go to the other owner

- under tenancy in common, where each owner holds a specified proportion of the shares; should one die, that person's heirs receive that portion

- held in trust for a minor, *e.g.*, under the Uniform Gifts to Minors Act, which may have tax advantages for some investors

- in trust accounts

To decide on form of ownership, the investor should consult an attorney. Registered representatives cannot recommend any form, as that is construed as practicing law.

TAXATION

Taxation of mutual fund companies

Under the Internal Revenue Code (Section M), a mutual fund does not have to pay tax on income from equities it holds or on any capital gains realized from sale of those equities *provided* (a) those gains are distributed to shareholders and (b) the fund meets the definition of a "regulated investment company." The theory is that these companies are simply a "pipeline" or "conduit" between corporations and investors.

A company is considered regulated under the Code if it is a domestic corporation registered (as a management company or a unit investment trust; see pages 102–103) with the SEC for the tax year. Further:

- *At least 90% of the firm's gross income must be from dividends, interest, and capital gains.*

- *At least 97% of the firm's net investment income and at least 90% of its capital gains net income in each calendar year must be distributed to shareholders as taxable dividends.* Any amounts held in excess of the required distribution are subject to a non-deductible 4% excise tax.

- Less than 30% of the firm's income can be derived from the sale of securities held less than 3 months.

Taxation of mutual fund shareholders

Shareholders must report dividend earnings and capital gains to the IRS even if they are reinvested. The former are taxed as regular income. Capital gains distributions are also treated as income, though some can be designated "long-term capital gains," a category of income which may be subject to a lower tax rate.

Individual investors can deduct as a business expense the management fees they pay as mutual fund shareholders, but only if all their business expenses exceed 2% of gross income. Mutual funds will show management expenses as a separate component of income on annual 1099 statements.

If a shareholder liquidates holdings, capital gain or loss is treated like gain or loss from any capital asset for tax purposes. Losses on mutual fund shares held less than six months cannot be claimed if the shareholder received tax-exempt dividends on those shares (*i.e.*, from municipal bond funds).

CLOSED- AND OPEN-END INVESTMENT COMPANIES

The most convenient way to discuss closed-end investment companies is to compare them with open-end.

OPEN	CLOSED
Always sells with a prospectus.	Can sell without prospectus after initial issue.
Can issue only common stock —no bonds or preferred stock.	Can issue bonds or preferred stock to raise additional funds and to buy more securities.
Shares continuously offered— as new investors come in, the company adds to its portfolio.	Fixed capitalization. Fixed number of shares outstanding; no continuing offer of shares.
Sells and redeems (sometimes through intermediaries) its own shares; no exchange market is involved. Redeems share at NAV—never less. May borrow from bank up to $\frac{1}{3}$ of its assets. Value computed daily.	Issuer does not redeem shares. Traded on exchange or over-the-counter after initial public offering. Price determined by supply and demand; could be below NAV.
Investors may pay a sales charge.	Investors pay market price plus commission or normal brokerage fees.
Can charge redemption fee.	No redemption fee.

INVESTOR ACCOUNTS

Types of accounts

Typically, mutual funds offer investors several types of accounts:

Regular or open account
Involves no periodic purchase; all investments are purely voluntary.

Periodic payment plan
An investor agrees to invest a minimum amount, say $100, at certain intervals, at least four times a year.

Voluntary accumulation plan
The investor decides when and how much to invest, but may reach breakpoints under rights of accumulation.

Contractual plan

In this form of periodic payment plan, the investor agrees to invest a specified amount over a specified time by making payments at regular intervals, for example, $48,000 over 20 years by buying $200 in shares each month.

The prospectus for a contractual plan must describe both the plan itself and the fund. These plans are actually a form of unit investment trust, with each share representing an undivided interest in the underlying mutual fund.

In a contractual plan, a custodian holds both money and securities for investors and issues "plan certificates" as evidence of the investor's holdings. In addition, the custodian acts as registrar and transfer agent and must be notified if the investor wishes to assign or transfer shares.

Many plans offer "plan completion insurance," which completes the plan by making payments to reach face value if the investor dies before the end of the designated period. This is like decreasing term life insurance and has no cash value. The policy names the plan custodian as beneficiary, but proceeds are considered part of the deceased's estate for tax purposes.

Example

If a customer contracts to buy $200 per month for ten years and dies after five years, the insurance will pay the custodian $200 per month for the remaining five years.

Sales charges on contractual plans

While the sales charge on mutual funds cannot exceed 8.5%, the sales charge on any contractual plan can reach 9% of the amount invested. On long-term acquisition plans, the Investment Company Amendments Act of 1975 allows accelerated collection of sales charges under one of two plans: "front-end load" or "spread load." The prospectus must say which is in use.

With either method, the plan custodian is required to send investors a statement of total charges within 60 days after the plan certificate is issued and to inform the investor of the *right to withdraw within 45 days* from the date the notice is mailed. An investor who leaves the plan within that time receives the current value of the shares, plus all sales charges, custodial fees, and insurance payments.

Front-end load   Up to 50% of the sales charges may be deducted, in equal amounts, from the first 12 monthly payments. Remaining sales charges are deducted proportionately over the life of the plan. If the plan is liquidated within 18 months of the date the certificate is issued, the investor receives a refund of sales charges paid in excess of 15% of the total invested in addition to the current value of all shares.

Example

An investor agrees to a 10-year $100-per-month front-end load plan with a 6% cumulative sales charge. If he chooses to terminate the plan after 40 days, during which time he has accumulated 30 shares, he would receive 30 × NAV less any redemption fee. If he did not terminate until after his 15th payment, the sales charge would be computed as follows:

Total sales charge = 6% × $1,200 per year × 10 years = $720

Front-end load = 50% × $720 = $360

Balance of sales charge = $360/9 years = $40 per year, or $3.33 per month

Total sales charge for 15 months = $360 + (3 × $3.33) = $370

Allowable sales charge = 15% of $1,500 = $225

Sales charges refunded = $370 − $225 = $145

After the 18th month, an investor can receive only the existing share value.

Spread-load plan   Up to 64% of the investment over the first four years can be deducted for sales charges, but no more than 20% in any one year. The allowed 64% may be divided to average 16% a year. With a spread-load plan, investors have only the 45-day grace period in which to withdraw, after which time they receive only the value of their shares.

Example

If the investor of the previous example had chosen a spread-load plan with a 16% average per year, his sales charges would have been computed as follows:

Total sales charges = $720 as above

Spread-load for 4 years = 64% × $720 = $460.80

Sales charge for 15 months = 15/48 × $460.80 = $144

Note that the entire $144 would have been deducted from his investment. With both plans, fund sponsors are required to have reserves to allow them to refund sales charges if necessary.

WITHDRAWAL PLANS

Many mutual funds provide plans for systematic withdrawal of funds, *i.e.*, for periodic payment to the investor. These usually require a minimum investment of $10,000.

Plans can be for a fixed dollar amount (*e.g.*, $100 per month), or a fixed percentage (*e.g.*, 6% a year), or a fixed number of shares (*e.g.*, 15 shares a month); or they can call for liquidation over a fixed time (*e.g.*, all shares over 10 years). Shareholders must approve such a plan in writing, usually to the custodian, authorizing the custodian to redeem shares to meet planned withdrawals if dividend payments will not suffice, or to reinvest dividends in additional shares if they exceed the withdrawal amount.

If shares must be sold to meet the planned withdrawals, the investor's principal could be eroded. Once begun, such a process could accelerate, especially in a falling market, and wipe out the principal entirely.

THE INVESTMENT COMPANY ACT OF 1940

This act is intended to ensure that investors are fully informed and fairly treated. (Note that these securities are all subject to SEC regulations [see Chapter 14].) It defines three specific categories of investment companies:

Face amount certificate company

These issue installment-type certificates. The holder makes regular, periodic payments to the issuer who promises to pay the face value at maturity or a surrender value if redeemed in advance.

Unit investment trust

These issue redeemable securities, each representing an undivided interest in a unit of a specified security, which can be a mutual fund portfolio. Most contractual plans are in fact unit investment trusts. Other examples are investment companies which pay *no management fee*, have a low sales charge, and hold a *fixed portfolio of municipal or corporate instruments*. Some of these are closed-end companies.

Management company

Under the Act, any investment company other than those defined above is considered a management company. A management company can be open- or closed-end and must manage a diversified portfolio of securities according to specific stated objectives.

These firms are divided into non-diversified and diversified companies. To be considered diversified, a firm must:

• have at least 75% of its total asset value in cash and securities but

- no more than 5% of assets may be invested in any one issuer's security, and

- cannot own more than 10% of the voting stock of any corporation.

The Act also requires that any investment company operating interstate must register with the SEC and that the company's objectives, practices, and policies must be announced in detail in regular statements to shareholders.

Requirements of ICA 1940

Many of the requirements of the act have been mentioned in this chapter, but a summary should be helpful:

1. Sponsor(s) must invest at least $100,000 of their own funds before offering securities to the public.

2. Open-end companies may issue only common stock. Closed-end companies may issue bonds (but only to $\frac{1}{3}$ the value of company assets) and preferred stock (but only to $\frac{1}{2}$ the value of assets). They can issue only one class of bonds or preferred stock.

3. Face Amount Certificate companies must have a minimum capitalization of $250,000. They cannot issue preferred stock.

4. At least 40% of the company's directors must be "outsiders," that is, neither an officer nor employee of the company or of its investment advisor.

5. A majority of the directors must be independent of the fund underwriter, and a majority may not be persons who are officers or directors of the fund's investment bank.

6. Directors must be elected by holders of outstanding shares.

Other elements of the Act include:

- cannot borrow more than $\frac{1}{3}$ of assets

- must compute NAV once each business day

- cannot buy on margin or sell short without SEC permission ("hedge" funds routinely get such permission)

- must have a written contract with the management company approved by the board of directors or a majority of shareholders; fees paid the management company must be based on a percentage of assets and must be set forth in the prospectus

- must use custodian banks

- shareholders must approve any change in the fund's objectives

- redemption of shares must be made within seven business days

ICA says sales literature, broadly defined (the rule includes not just advertising but also, for example, financial statements), cannot be untrue or misleading. Most of the specific prohibitions have been discussed in this chapter in one connection or another: such literature cannot state or imply any assured return, discuss returns without advising of risk, etc.

Open-end investment companies, like other issuers of securities, must be registered with the SEC under the Securities Act of 1933 (see Chapter 15) and must issue a prospectus.

Because they continually issue new shares, all mutual fund offerings must be accompanied by a prospectus. This must include all the essential information in the registration statement (see page 380), and, as noted above, must: describe the type of investment company, its objectives and policies; explain how the offering price is computed; include information about breakpoints, rights of accumulation, etc., and set out rights of transfer (if there is a "family" of funds), redemption procedures, etc. The fund must also *issue a financial statement semi-annually.*

NASD RULES ON MUTUAL FUNDS

The SEC imposed stringent rules on the sale of mutual fund shares in a 1950 Statement of Policy extending the Securities Act of 1935. That Statement is now incorporated into the NASD Rules of Fair Practice. Among the most important of these rules is a limit of $8\frac{1}{2}\%$ on sales charges instead of the 9% allowed under ICA 1940. Note, however, that 9% is still valid for contractual plans. The following are also worth noting:

Prohibitions on RR activity

Representatives *cannot:*

- combine profits and dividends. If a fund has paid $1.25 from capital gains and $.50 from income, these cannot be combined as "earnings" or "return," or the like

- "sell" dividends. This is the practice of urging an investor to buy shares in a fund in time to profit from a just-declared dividend. Net assets decline after a dividend is paid, so this is already figured into the price

- make unfair comparisons—such as with a fixed investment or a non-managed investment, like the Dow Jones average—without pointing out the differences

- promise future earnings on the basis of past earnings

- fail to mention that risk is involved (although they can say risk may be reduced in a particular plan)

- say that custodian banks safeguard the investment

- say that mutual funds provide capital for new companies

- make loans for mutual fund purchases (no margin sales)

- make any claims about the ability of fund managers, particularly guaranteeing against loss or guaranteeing a return

Requirements for RRs

Representatives *must*:

- say the redemption value of shares may be higher or lower than the purchase price

- file all mutual fund sales literature (including a statement of sales charges) with NASD 10 days *after* it is used

- send a prospectus before, or with, sales literature. This is true whether or not a sale is made. Simply intending to make a sale requires a prospectus. The only exception is when a customer asks for general information on mutual funds.

- sell to customers at the next calculated price; not at an earlier price, nor waiting longer, though specific limit orders are allowed

- inform a customer wishing to switch funds, in writing, that he or she will pay a new service charge, as trading in mutual fund shares is prohibited

Other rules

- Performance charts must cover at least 10 years, or the life of the fund, and must show the maximum sales charge, capital gains as reinvested, and dividends as taken in cash.

- There can be no "special deals" between a fund sponsor and NASD member to favor one fund. Specifically, underwriters or their associates or affiliates cannot offer, and registered representatives or their affiliates cannot accept, anything of "material value," *e.g.*, gifts or advertising of over $50 per person per year (exceptions are an occasional dinner or tickets to a reception or the like that is part of a genuine business meeting).

- Dealers must pay the underwriter (or custodian) for shares within 10 days or underwriter must notify NASD.

- A registered representative may earn continuing commissions on contractual plans after leaving his or her firm if prior agreement exists.

- A NASD underwriter cannot sell open-end investment company shares to a NASD member for less than NAV.

- Dealers may buy open-end investment company shares from an underwriter only to cover a customer's order or for personal investment.

TERMS

Investment companies   Invest in securities of other entities; acquire funds by selling shares

Advantages to investors   Can diversify holdings, simplify record-keeping, have decisions made by professional managers

Kinds of investment companies

Unit Investment Trusts   Invest in an identified portfolio; if "fixed," hold bonds and cease to exist when bonds mature; if "non-fixed," hold portfolio of shares in professionally managed pool; holdings vary over time

Face-amount certificate companies   Issue securities that pay "face-amount" at some specified date

Closed-end investment companies   Issue stock at inception and not after; do not redeem shares; shares represent ownership of company's assets; trade on open market

NAV   Assets divided by the number of shares outstanding

Open-end investment companies (mutual funds)   Redeem their own shares; may issue only common stock; shares always accompanied by a current prospectus

Dividends   Can be declared and paid on net income for any term

Types of funds   Growth or income, stock, bond, municipals, etc.

Structural features   Fund is a corporation that invests in securities; day-to-day decisions about investments made by a professional manager. Manager is a management company.

Management company   Usually a corporation in the business of advising institutions; can consist of fund's directors or officers, but at least 40% of directors must be unaffiliated with management company or fund. Usually has complete administrative powers; earns fee based on net assets not on increases in value of fund portfolio.

Yields   Under SEC rules, only mutual fund yields arising from income, dividends, and interest may be discussed

$$\text{current yield} = \frac{\text{annual dividends paid over past year}}{\text{today's price} + \text{any capital gains paid}}$$

and

$$\text{historic yield} = \frac{\text{average annual dividends}}{\text{average annual price}}$$

Bid   Price at which fund will redeem shares; same as NAV

Ask or offer   Price to investor

No-load   No sales charges; bid and ask prices are identical

Load   Sales charge; shows as difference between offer and bid

NAV   Determined by price at the close of each business day

Price to buyer   NAV for day of sale

Seller   Receives next calculated NAV after order was received

Sales charges   Imposed when shares are sold; based on asking price, not NAV; cannot exceed 8.5% except 9% on contractual plans

Redemption fees   Usually 1% or less, based on NAV

Breakpoints   Specified quantities at which sales charges may be reduced; only to an individual, family, or trustee, not a group; can be one-time purchase or over a period through:

Rights of accumulation   Sales charges reduced when purchases accumulate to breakpoints, or

Letter of intent   To purchase given amount; can stretch over 13 months; can be backdated 90 days; not binding on investor; binding on fund

Redeeming shares   Fund must honor request to redeem shares and remit amount due within 7 days, except in extraordinary circumstances

To register under ICA 1940   A fund must have minimum net worth of $100,000 before public offering made; can issue only common stock; can borrow from banks; 40% of the directors must be "outsiders"

Shareholder rights   Voting

Custodian   Fund must employ custodian (usually financial institution) which can also act as transfer agent and registrar and perform clerical tasks; cannot sell shares or offer any protection against depreciation of the company's assets

Forms of ownership   Individual, joint tenancy with rights of survivorship, tenancy in common, in trust for a minor under UGMA, in-trust accounts

Taxation of fund   To avoid tax, fund must pay out at least 90% of net earnings as dividends and meet requirements of regulated investment company

Taxation of investors   Dividend earnings and capital gains are considered income even if reinvested; management fees can be a business expense

See chart comparing closed-end and open-end investment companies on page 99.

Types of accounts

Regular or open account   No periodic purchase

Voluntary accumulation plan

Periodic payment plan   Can be a contractual plan

Contractual plan Agreement to invest specified amount over specified time; unit investment trusts; custodian holds money and securities, issues plan certificates, and acts as registrar and transfer agent

Sales charges Accelerated collection allowed, "front-end load" or "spread load" plans; limited right to withdraw

Withdrawal plans Can be for fixed dollar amount, percentage, number of shares, or time; shareholder must approve in writing

Categories of investment companies

Face Amount Certificate Company Issues installment-type certificates; holder makes regular payments; issuer promises to pay face value at maturity

Unit Investment Trust Issues redeemable securities each of which represents an undivided interest in a unit of a specified security

Management Company Any other investment company

NASD rules of fair practice

Limit sales charges; restrict RR

RR cannot Combine profits and dividends into "earnings" or "return," sell dividends, make unfair comparisons, fail to mention risk, sell mutual fund shares on margin, or guarantee against loss

RR must Disclose that shares may be above or below purchase price at redemption, file all fund sales literature with NASD 10 days after it is used, send a prospectus before or with sales literature, and sell to customers at next calculated price

Other rules See Chapter 16.

REVIEW QUESTIONS

1. When an investor sells her shares back to a mutual fund, the amount she receives is the:

   (A) NAV
   (B) offer
   (C) bid less commissions
   (D) asked price

2. The primary difference between open-end and closed-end funds is:

   (A) their capitalization
   (B) their investment objectives
   (C) diversification
   (D) their tax status

3. Capital gains distributions from investment companies are taxed:

   (A) as ordinary income
   (B) as long-term capital gains
   (C) only if not reinvested
   (D) when the shares are sold

4. Shareholders must receive financial statements from investment companies:

(A) monthly
(B) quarterly
(C) semi-annually
(D) annually

5. An investor in a contractual plan has completion insurance. In case of his death, the proceeds would go to the:

   (A) investment company
   (B) estate
   (C) beneficiary of the estate
   (D) custodian

6. This completion insurance would pay:

   (A) 100% of the contracted amount of the plan
   (B) 50% of the contracted amount of the plan
   (C) 50% of the unpaid amount in the plan
   (D) 100% of the unpaid amount in the plan

7. In a spread-load plan, the maximum that can be deducted from contributions in any of the first four years is:

   (A) 9%
   (B) 16%
   (C) 20%
   (D) 50%

8. In a front-end load plan, the maximum sales charge that can be deducted from contributions in the first year is:

   (A) 9%
   (B) 16%
   (C) 20%
   (D) 50%

9. If one purchases an open-end fund on Tuesday, the price paid is:

   (A) Monday's closing NAV
   (B) Tuesday's NAV
   (C) the next NAV after the order is entered

(D) the average of Monday and Tuesday closing NAV

10. If the shares of a mutual fund can be purchased at Net Asset Value (NAV), it is a:

    (A) no-load fund
    (B) dual purpose fund
    (C) closed-end fund
    (D) low cost fund

11. All of the following are purchased at or above NAV EXCEPT:

    (A) open-end funds
    (B) closed-end funds
    (C) no-load funds
    (D) funds that issue only common stock

12. An investor pays a 7.5% selling charge on the purchase of 1,000 shares of a mutual fund offered at $15. If he must pay a .5% redemption fee and the fund has not changed in value at redemption, he will receive approximately:

    (A) $13,730
    (B) $13,800
    (C) $14,925
    (D) $15,000

13. The NAV of a mutual fund is $14.80. If the maximum sales commission is $7\frac{1}{2}$%, what price is it offered at?

    (A) $14.80
    (B) $15.86
    (C) $16.00
    (D) $16.20

14. How long after the plan custodian mails notice of charges does the customer have to cancel a front-end load and still receive a full refund?

    (A) within 30 days
    (B) within 45 days
    (C) within 60 days
    (D) within 90 days

15. To qualify as a regulated investment company, a mutual fund must pay out as dividends at least:

    (A) 75% of investment income
    (B) 80% of investment income
    (C) 90% of investment income
    (D) 97% of investment income

16. An investment company has had an average price of $15.00 over the past year. If the year-end price is $14.50 and it had a $.75 income distribution and a $.70 capital gains distribution for the year, its (historical) yield can be described as:

    (A) 4%
    (B) 4.66%
    (C) 5%
    (D) 9.66%

17. The "conduit theory" for a regulated investment company says that:

    (A) the flow of revenues should be unimpeded by redemptions
    (B) investment income flows to the investor after taxes
    (C) the investor and the fund are taxed as a single entity
    (D) the investment income is taxable to the investor only

18. The responsibility for safeguarding the securities of a mutual fund belongs to the:

    (A) fund manager
    (B) investor
    (C) NASD
    (D) custodian bank

19. The "breakpoint" for a mutual fund is the:

    (A) point where sales break even
    (B) minimum investment at which one gets a volume discount
    (C) minimum number of shares for a volume discount
    (D) point at which one gets a break on a letter of intent

20. An investor interested in capital appreciation would most likely buy which of the following?

    (A) an income fund
    (B) a growth fund
    (C) a closed-end fund
    (D) a specialized fund

21. With respect to a letter of intent, all of the following hold EXCEPT:

    (A) it is good for 13 months
    (B) it may be backdated for 90 days
    (C) shares purchased under it can be held in escrow
    (D) the investor may not redeem shares while the letter is in effect

22. Under the Investment Company Act of 1940, a mutual fund must:

    (A) have minimum net worth of $100,000 before going public
    (B) not suddenly change its investment objectives
    (C) have at least 40% of its board made up of outside directors
    (D) all of the above

23. If a registered representative uses a chart to compare mutual funds, all of the following are true EXCEPT:

    (A) comparison must be based on maximum sales charge
    (B) comparison must be based on minimum investment
    (C) comparison must be based on lesser of ten years or the life of the fund
    (D) comparison must be based only on dividend yield

24. A money market mutual fund will:

    (A) declare and pay dividends daily
    (B) declare and pay dividends monthly
    (C) declare dividends daily and pay them monthly
    (D) declare dividends monthly and pay them quarterly

25. An investor might by a REIT achieve all of the following EXCEPT:

    (A) income from rentals
    (B) diversification from common stocks
    (C) capital gains
    (D) write-offs from depreciation

26. A mutual fund has an investment portfolio made up of Dow Jones Industrial stocks. It could best be classified as a(n):

    (A) index fund
    (B) growth fund
    (C) specialty fund
    (D) income fund

27. All of the following are taxable to owners of mutual funds EXCEPT:

    (A) capital gains that are reinvested in a new fund from the same family
    (B) cash dividends that are reinvested before distribution
    (C) capital gains reinvested at NAV
    (D) stock dividends that are distributed

28. A custodian bank for a mutual fund performs which of the following functions?

    (A) guarantees management fulfillment of its obligations
    (B) oversees investment decisions
    (C) insures investments
    (D) safeguards the fund's cash

The following information about closed-end funds is for use with questions 29 and 30.

	NAV	Market Price
Chaebol Fund	20.50	19.50
Keiratsu Fund	33.75	33.75

29 To buy Chaebol Fund, an investor would pay:

    (A) $19.50 + $1.00 sales charge
    (B) NAV + commission
    (C) market price
    (D) $19.50 + commission

30. Keiratsu fund is selling at:

    (A) NAV
    (B) premium
    (C) a discount
    (D) depends on whether or not it is a load fund

ANSWERS TO REVIEW QUESTIONS

1. (**C**) The bid is the same as the NAV.

2. (**A**) Closed-end funds issue shares once when they are formed and never redeem shares. Open-end funds are continually issuing and redeeming shares.

3. (**B**) Current tax law makes a distinction between long- and short-term gains.

4. (**C**) They also receive monthly statements about trading in their own accounts.

5. (**D**) The custodian also receives payments from the investor and holds securities for him.

6. (**D**) Hence the name "completion."

7. **(C)** Up to 64% of the first four year's investment may be deducted but no more than 20% in any one year.

8. **(D)** This may be deducted from each monthly payment.

9. **(B)** If one *sold*, then one would receive the next NAV after the order was entered.

10. **(A)** The bid is always at NAV. If the offer is, too, it is a no-load fund.

11. **(B)** Closed-end funds are not redeemed by the fund, and hence their price is not directly related to NAV. They often sell at a discount and sometimes at a premium.

12. **(B)** $15 × (1 − .075) × $1,000 = Bid = $13,875. A .05% redemption fee would be $69.38, leaving the investor with about $13,800.

13. **(C)** $14.80 ÷ (1 − .075) = $16.00.

14. **(B)** The notice of changes must be sent within 60 days after the plan certificate is issued.

15. **(D)** It must also distribute at least 90% of its capital gains income.

16. **(C)** $.75 ÷ $15.00 = 5%. Only investment income may be used to describe yield.

17. **(D)** The investment company merely acts as a conduit for the flow of income to the investor.

18. **(D)** In addition, the custodian collects and disburses funds from the purchase and sale of securities for the fund.

19. **(B)** The breakpoint is a fixed dollar value rather than a fixed number of shares. The latter would commit the investor to an indeterminate dollar sum.

20. **(B)** These funds invest in companies that pay little if any dividends, instead using the money to invest in company growth.

21. **(D)** The letter of intent would no longer be in effect if the shares were redeemed.

22. **(D)** All of these are requirements. The outside directors may not be affiliated with the management company in any way.

23. **(D)** Both income and capital gains may be used in this comparison.

24. **(C)** Money market funds generally declare daily dividends since their short-term portfolios change frequently. They pay dividends on a monthly basis.

25. **(D)** The REIT can take advantage of the depreciation. Only the income flows through to the investors.

26. **(A)** The D-J is an index. Most index funds do use broader indexes like the S&P.

27. **(D)** Stock dividends are not taxable.

28. **(D)** The custodian is responsible for safeguarding both the cash and the securities of the fund.

29. **(D)** The NAV is irrelevant since the shares trade in the market. Thus, an investor would pay the market price plus a commission.

30. **(A)** Since the market price is equal to the NAV, these shares are at par.

CHAPTER FIVE

tax-advantaged investments, annuities and retirement plans

PART ONE
Tax-Advantaged Investments

This chapter begins with a discussion of certain specialized investment plans known as "tax shelters." In general, these were originally devised for individuals in high tax brackets—those paying 50% or more. As designed, tax shelters allowed investors to defer taxes, or to incur certain losses that they could write off against other income, while still enjoying both current and potential net income. A good example would be a real estate investment in which year-by-year depreciation produced a loss on paper that could be charged off against income from other sources. Investments that have no economic function other than tax avoidance are labeled abusive and are illegal.

TAX SHELTERS TODAY

The Tax Reform Act of 1986 essentially decrees that losses from tax shelters can no longer be used to shelter other income, such as wages, interest or dividend income, or profits on securities trading. There are some specific exceptions: losses from tax shelters can be used to offset income from the same or other tax-sheltered investments. Certain types of real estate still offer tax advantages.

Note that the new law affects only so-called "passive losses." Individuals actively involved in running a business can still have expenses that exceed their income. Real estate developers are specifically excluded, but an investor actively managing rental property still receives some limited special treatment: landlords with an adjusted gross income of less than $100,000 can take up to $25,000 in tax losses. This allowance declines as income rises, disappearing completely at an income of $150,000.

Despite these new restrictions, some analysts think there is still a role for tax shelter programs, except that they will now be structured for profitability, to offset losses in shelters set up under the old law.

DIRECT PARTICIPATION PROGRAMS

As the name implies, direct participation programs (DPP) allow investors to participate directly in the benefits of the investment. That participation involves both economic gain or loss and tax consequences.

One type of DPP is a "subchapter S" corporation. This DPP gives investors the benefits of a corporate shield (that is, they do not have personal responsibility for corporate debt) while allowing all profits and expenses to flow directly to investors as income (or loss). Investors pay taxes on this income, but the corporation does not, so the program avoids double taxation.

The most important type of DPP is a limited partnership, and the remainder of this section will be devoted to limited partnerships.

Qualifications for limited partnership

To qualify for the tax treatment afforded a limited partnership, it must differ from a corporation in at least two of these six fundamental characteristics:

- being a profit-directed business

- providing limited liability

- being an association of individuals

- having central management

- having perpetual life

- being freely transferable

The last two ways are most commonly used to differentiate limited partnerships from corporations: to provide that the partnership has a limited life and to place some restriction on the ability to transfer ownership.

Note

The investor interested in a partnership is well advised to seek a tax opinion from an independent attorney as to whether the proposed partnership meets IRS requirements; if not, it will be taxed as a corporation.

Types of partners

A limited partnership has two kinds of partners: a general partner, who has unlimited liability with respect to the obligations of the partnership and is usually active in management; and one or more limited partners, who provide most of the capital, share any profits or losses, and who are not actively involved in management. These investor-partners have limited liability, *i.e.*, their potential loss is limited to the amount of their investment.

Formation of limited partnership

To form a limited partnership, a certificate must be filed in the state of origin, generally (*i.e.* in most states) under the Uniform Limited Partnership Act, which governs the interrelationships of the partners among themselves and the partnership's relationships to creditors. A sponsor (or syndicator), who is often the general partner, organizes and registers the partnership with state and federal authorities. This person may also serve as the partnership manager, who is charged with choosing investments and for overall management.

The certificate includes the following information:

- the name of the partnership, the names of each of the general and limited partners, and the business purpose for which it was formed

- the degree of participation of each partner as to both contribution and the allocation of profits and expenses

- the methods of changing membership, if any, including new partners, the transfer of partnership rights, and provision for dissolution in case of the death of the general partner

- the life-span of the partnership

In addition to the Certificate of Limited Partnership, there is an Agreement of Limited Partnership that describes the rights and responsibilities of both the limited and general partners. This contract between the partners is not a public document. The agreement can be modified with the written consent of the partners. This consent is often called "partnership democracy."

EVALUATING A LIMITED PARTNERSHIP

Under NASD rules, the managing underwriter of a DPP must exercise due diligence. In addition, a registered representative should evaluate the suitability of such an investment for any client. Nevertheless, it behooves each investor to take particular care to examine the proposed program in light of his or her own needs and resources. Especially under the new law, this means assessing the soundness of the projected activity(ies) in terms of both stated objectives and general economic validity.

In addition, prospective investors should investigate the sponsor's earlier offerings in the same area to get some indication of ability and knowledge. Another important consideration is whether the type of investment proposed fits the investor's ability and/or willingness to deal with risks (*e.g.,* oil and gas limited partnerships often bring no return, but pay off handsomely when they do succeed; real estate programs fail far less often, but pay far lower returns).

Potential conflicts of interest should also be a focus. Is the sponsor or the general partner involved with other programs that might conflict with the one proposed? One common example involves "adjacent leases," where the sponsor is raising funds to drill on a plot adjacent to one where a producing well has already been located under the same sponsor.

Other warning signs of potential conflict would include plans that do not strictly control the use of funds (for example, allowing them to be mixed with other offerings) and those that do not limit the sponsor's use of funds or compensation for sponsor's services.

In short, potential investors should be assured that the sponsor is committed to giving the limited partners a fair chance to protect their investment. If the program involves purchasing real property, investors should ascertain the basis on which it is appraised and should see whether the expected gain in value is reasonable. If the plan involves oil and gas production, the geological analysis is crucial.

Of particular concern in evaluating returns in these programs is the fact that they are often stretched over a long period of time. Thus, straightforward evaluations that do not take into account the time value of money can be misleading. For example, a dollar received in eight years would be worth $.50 if interest rates were at 9% throughout that period.

In addition to looking at potential returns, it is, of course, necessary to examine the risks of the venture. Two general risks are inherent in all such offerings: a limited partner can lose the entire amount invested, and there is no guaranteed return.

Other risks include the fact that these investments are relatively illiquid; these agreements also usually make it difficult to transfer interests (see page 116). Investors should also be confident that the IRS will approve the deductions taken by the partnership, that the level of leverage is not too great, and that cost projections are sufficiently realistic. Especially with the new restrictions on tax losses, it is necessary to look at projected returns from the project in light of one's own tax situation.

Finally, most programs have a considerable front-end load: expenses for organizing the partnership, fees involved in acquiring property, sales and other expenses, are all deducted from invested funds. An inordinately high front-end load reduces the amount actually invested, which means that returns on the net investment must be significantly higher.

METHODS OF FUNDING A LIMITED PARTNERSHIP

- Letter of credit—partners sign a letter that guarantees obligations of the partnership

- Installment payments—also called "staged payments"; partners make their contributions in designated amounts over a specified time

- Subscription amounts—these include both all initial investments and installments

- Capital contributions—cash or property

- Assessments—in such schemes, the general partner can assess the limited partners an additional amount

- Loans to the partnership—tax shelters may borrow money. These are called "recourse loans," as the lender has recourse in the sense that the limited partner is personally liable for payment of the loan. As we shall see, real estate tax shelters (and only real estate shelters) can incur non-recourse loans, under which the lender has no such claim.

TYPES OF OFFERINGS

Many of the terms and practices connected with other types of underwriting apply with these programs (see page 148). An important distinction is that between managed and non-managed offerings; the latter are more common with DPPs.

Managed offerings

Direct participation programs, usually limited partnerships, can be sold by underwriters in "managed offerings." The procedures resemble those with mutual funds (see Chapter 6): the issue can be purchased on a firm commitment basis or sold ("best efforts") on commission.

Non-managed offerings

The issuer can sell directly through registered representatives at various firms or through a "wholesaler" who hires representatives to work on commission. The wholesaler is usually hired by the sponsor of the offering—the general partner or an affiliate—or can be an affiliate of the sponsor.

For both managed and non-managed offerings, those participating are subject to the NASD Rules of Fair Practice as applied to underwriting compensation, which includes a limit on compensation payable to broker/dealers, underwriters, and affiliated persons to 10% of the total amount raised.

In addition, NASD policy restricts activity connected with seeking or paying for referrals. A registered representative cannot deliver unsolicited copies of an offer to "centers of influence"—accountants, attorneys, investment counselors, etc.—nor can they offer compensation for referrals from such persons unless they are registered representatives, licensed and associated with an NASD firm.

Note that the SEC offers guides particularly directed at DPPs: SEC Guide 4 for oil and gas offerings; SEC Guide 5 for real estate.

THE SUBSCRIPTION AGREEMENT

Investors in a direct participation offering are considered "subscribers"; they enter into a subscription agreement with the general partner or sponsor. In this, limited partners accept the terms of the agreement and attest to their ability to satisfy net worth and income requirements and to their ability to analyze the investment. No sales are completed until the general partner accepts the subscribers as limited partners.

It is the registered representative's responsibility to make reasonable inquiry about those parts of the agreement that attest to the participant's reading of the prospectus, understanding of the risks involved, income, net worth and suitability, state of residence, tax identification number, nature of ownership, and powers of attorney, if any.

As the general partner can refuse to admit an investor who does not meet certain requirements—for example, in terms of net worth, ability to absorb the potential loss, etc.—he or she must also assess the information shown in the individual's subscription agreement.

Before investing, the individual should consider the amount of liability and risk, tax effects, the difficulty in getting out of the program, and the fact that there is little governmental protection or regulation compared to what is provided with other investment plans.

The most popular types of programs are real estate, oil and gas, and equipment leasing. Programs involving cattle, movies, and other industries have been cut back substantially by the new tax laws.

REAL ESTATE PROGRAMS

In a real estate program, investors usually have a completely passive role. A partnership manager selects and arranges to buy or lease properties, and a property manager is in charge of daily operations. Both are appointed by the general partner.

The basic incentives in such programs are fourfold. They are: income, capital appreciation, diversification, and the opportunity to participate in an investment that requires substantial expertise and provides some tax relief. Tax relief comes because the investor is able to deduct expenses, mortgage interest, and depreciation. With depreciation, it is possible to create income losses while still enjoying cash flow from the investment. While this benefit has been curtailed somewhat by the 1986 Tax Reform Act, it remains a significant factor in real estate investment.

Real estate programs have an additional advantage. In most limited partnerships, the maximum deduction available is the amount involved or "at risk," including loans for which the limited partners are personally liable ("recourse loans"). But the law allows real estate investors to write off nonrecourse loans as well. With these loans, the lender may foreclose, but cannot hold limited partners liable for any balances due. This increase in allowable write-offs means that investors in real estate programs may enjoy greater potential tax benefits.

This advantage does not come without costs, however. Holding greater debt means that a larger percentage of revenues must be used for debt service. If rental income does not cover this debt service, partners may have to make additional contributions or face foreclosure.

A second concern is that any cash distributions in such a plan are treated as return of capital. At some point, when depreciation and other expenses wane, income rises. The limited partners' cash contribution may then be smaller than the taxable income attributable to that partner. This creates "phantom" income, which is taxable. Typically, a partnership will arrange to sell or refinance the property before this "crossover point" is reached.

There are several different types of real estate programs:

New construction

These programs are primarily vehicles for capital gains as opposed to income. The risks of such programs are all those inherent in building something: cost overruns, delays, inability to sell the finished product. They do however have the potential for enormous capital gains.

Government-aided housing

These programs were significantly changed by the 1986 tax bill, but do still provide some opportunities for tax relief and for very modest income and capital gains. The same is true for programs that focus on the rehabilitation of historic structures.

Existing properties

Investment in existing property is designed for those willing to give up some capital appreciation in favor of cash distributions and a diminution of risk. Most real estate syndicates try to purchase existing properties, improve them, and sell at a profit. Because this happens so often, it is possible to predict cash flows with some certainty and to receive accurate valuations from independent appraisers. However, it is still essential to be sure that the sponsor's projections are realistic. Two areas to look at are lease restrictions (which may severely limit needed changes) and tenant stability (tenants' leases should not be so loose that continued income is endangered nor so tight or long-lasting that they threaten returns once improvements are made).

Land

Undeveloped or "raw" land offers the potential for appreciation if there is change in land use or even when it remains unused, but there is population growth nearby. These ventures usually involve experienced, professional developers.

Because there is no income until the land is used, investors must be able to deal with a long-term cash outflow and consistent repeated costs, including taxes and interest. At times, the general partner may assess investors for additional funds to avoid foreclosure. These investments also face certain external risks as, for example, when development plans are vigorously opposed by local agencies or environmental groups. Finally, there is no depreciation on land, making such investments less attractive to those who need a tax shelter.

Condominium securities

A condominium may be a security under certain conditions, specifically if there is evidence of investment intent or if management is by a third party. If a condominium is classified as a rental pool, *i.e.*, is operated as a management company like a hotel, then all of the condominiums in the pool are securities. The benefits of such a program are primarily the potential for capital gains and significant tax advantages. A key element to be considered in calculating potential tax advantages is that the owner may not personally use the property for more than two weeks, or 10% of the rental days, without running the risk of losing the privileged tax status with respect to depreciation, fees and expenses, and interest. The tax benefits of a condominium include the possibility of deducting real estate taxes for the unit itself and for the unit's proportional share of taxes on common grounds. Interest payments are also deductible.

A limited partnership can buy a property and then lease it back to the seller. This is called a "sale-leaseback." Its primary advantages are the tax benefits of depreciation and the ability to deduct interest expense. Typically, a sale-leaseback involves a long-term lease in which the seller-tenant agrees to pay maintenance costs, property taxes, and insurance premiums along with the rent. These are called "triple net leases" because they are net of those three charges. The principal risk arises when the lessee cannot make the payments, as the partnership must then find a suitable replacement tenant.

REITs

Another type of real estate investment is called a Real Estate Investment Trust or REIT.

Purpose of REITs
These trusts invest in income property or mortgage loans and pay dividends from interest income or realized gains, or both. For investors, Real Estate Investment Trusts offer the possibility of buying shares in a mix of real estate holdings. For the real estate industry, REITs offer a chance to attract capital investment from individuals who are not customarily involved in direct real estate investment.

REIT shares are sold on stock exchanges and over the counter. Market price tends to reflect current yield because they are required to distribute 95% of their earnings from interest or rents or both. The Tax Reform Act of 1986 allows the REIT to act much more like a real estate operator in that it substantially liberalizes the amount that the trust can hold in reserve for both ongoing and future investment in the property, *e.g.*, maintenance and improvements.

The REIT Act   Under the REIT Act of 1960, qualified REITs are offered special tax treatment: only the retained earnings are subject to federal income tax.

Qualifications for REITs

To deserve the special tax treatment, a REIT must meet a number of requirements in addition to distributing at least 95% of its earnings:

Organization   The trust must be legally unincorporated. This could mean shareholders face some liability, but as the trust indenture states that they are not responsible for debts of the trust, there is no real risk, practically speaking.

Trust indenture   A trust indenture must be established. Shareholders elect the trustees, who are responsible for managing the trust; most often they contract with an adviser (usually a bank or insurance company or other financial institution with real estate expertise) to handle daily operations and to investigate and recommend investments.

Ownership   REITs must issue certificates of beneficial ownership as evidence of shareholding, and these shares must be transferable. REITs operate like closed-end investment companies (see page 89): they market a fixed number of shares and do not redeem them on request. Those who wish to liquidate their holdings must do so in the market, so shares may sell for more or less than their net asset value. The trust must have at least 100 beneficial owners; no five (or fewer) can own more than 50% of the stock.

Assets   At least 75% of the trust's total assets at the end of every quarter must be in real property. Real property is defined as mortgages, shares of other REITs, cash, or government securities.

Income   At least 75% of gross income must be from activities related to real estate, for example, rents, interest on mortgage-secured property, gains from property sales, etc. Another 15% must come from such sources or from the sale of securities, including other REITs. Only 10% may come from such items as clients' fees or other business income.

OIL AND GAS PROGRAMS

The law provides certain specific incentives to make exploration for, and production of, gas and oil more attractive. These include:

The chance to deduct "intangible drilling costs"   Basically, these are the expenses involved in getting the oil or gas—preparing the site, wages and supplies for the exploratory team, testing samples, etc.; in other words, items that are used up in the process, which have no residual value—as distinguished from capital expenses for equipment which would last a year or more.

A "depletion allowance"   This is a form of depreciation that reflects the using up of estimated reserves. This is computed in one of two ways: the percentage depletion method, in which a flat percentage of gross income is deductible each year; or the cost depletion method, in which the adjusted cost of the property is assumed to be reduced by the percentage of the recoverable oil which is actually sold in that year. The next year, the cost is adjusted by subtracting the previous year's depletion to get a new adjusted cost basis. For example, if the property costs $1,000,000 and includes an estimated 100,000 barrels (or $10 a barrel), and 20,000 barrels are sold in one year, then $200,000 can be deducted, and the following year the cost basis is $800,000.

"Sharing arrangements"

On oil and gas programs, the costs and revenues involved can be allocated in one of four ways:

Overriding royalty interest   The sponsor takes a share of revenues from the time the well starts to produce, but does not contribute to costs. As this tends to encourage drilling wells without concern for their overall profitability, it is generally not considered an ideal choice for investors.

Reversionary (or subordinate) working interest   Again, the sponsor does not contribute to the cost, but also does not share in any revenues until investors have recovered their investment.

Functional allocation   Investors contribute all deductible costs, the sponsor all non-deductible costs. The sponsor contributes capital only for the development of productive wells.

Disproportionate sharing arrangement   The sponsor does share in the program's cost, but disproportionately. Typically, the sponsor would pay 25% of the costs and be entitled to 50% of the revenues.

Types of oil and gas programs

Oil and gas programs are conventionally divided into two types, "drilling programs" and "income programs." The first of these drills wells in hopes of finding new sources of oil and gas, and the second type buys productive wells.

Drilling programs   are further subdivided into exploratory and development programs:

1. Exploratory ("wildcatting") involves drilling wells in an unproved area. The risk of no return (a dry hole) is high, but potential return is also high. The principal benefits of such a program are tax advantages and the opportunity for high return.

2. Development programs involve drilling in or near proven fields. This is less risky than an exploratory program, but also offers less potential for really spectacular return. These fields are generally costlier to lease and are often on land which other drillers have chosen not to try. These also provide tax benefits and the opportunity for income partially sheltered by the depletion allowance.

Income programs   Acquiring producing properties. The purchase price is based on a geologist's estimate of the reserves discounted to present value and allowing for risk factors. The benefit here is in sheltering income since with no drilling they offer little in the way of tax relief.

Combinations of the above   Often designed to combine these types of programs in ways that provide some or all of their potential benefits.

EQUIPMENT-LEASING PROGRAMS

Major capital equipment is very expensive. At times, a user of such equipment may prefer to lease rather than purchase to avoid a major capital outlay. This has led to creation of another type of direct participation program in which a partnership buys equipment (using its own capital and borrowed funds) from a manufacturer and leases it to a user. The lease payments provide revenue and the partners get the benefit of the depreciation on the equipment. By using accelerated depreciation, they get substantial write-offs early in the program.

If the lease arrangement provides rentals which cover the entire life of the equipment (a "full-payout lease"), the investment is less risky. However, because of depreciation, such a situation is likely to generate phantom income.

To avoid this, the partnership can sell the equipment before the crossover point is reached. This may generate a capital gain because of the recapture of depreciation expenses.

Lease arrangements that do not cover the entire purchase price are called operating leases. These run the risk that the equipment will be worth less than anticipated when the lease is up. They also have the potential for creating additional gain if the equipment is worth more than anticipated.

TAXATION AND ACCOUNTING PRACTICES

An accounting method called Accelerated Cost Recovery System (ACRS) applies to both new and used assets and does not consider salvage value in computing depreciation.

For tax purposes, expenses such as organization and syndication costs are capitalized and must be amortized over the life of the partnership. All depreciation and depletion deductions are recaptured when the asset is sold for a gain.

The partnership basis (*i.e.*, the cost of the property) is adjusted upward to reflect income, capital gain, new contributions, and new debt for which the partner is personally liable; it is adjusted downward to reflect distributions, losses, depreciation, and partial sales.

The alternative minimum tax affects many items of tax preference resulting from DPPs.

DISSOLVING A LIMITED PARTNERSHIP

There are several situations in which a limited partnership might be dissolved before the date specified in the partnership agreement. These include:

- retirement, insanity or death of general partner
- the sale of all partnership assets
- a vote by a majority of the ownership to dissolve

In any case, the general partner has the obligation of canceling the certificate of limited partnership; otherwise, partners can lose their limited liability protection.

On dissolution, creditors have first call on the assets of the partnership; the general partner is liable for any remaining debt. After creditors are satisfied, assets go to reimburse limited partners and then general partners, but the agreement can modify this.

PART TWO
Annuities

Some types of investment instruments are expressly designed for individuals who want future income, particularly at retirement. These include annuities and other plans discussed in Part Three of this chapter.

An annuity is a contract between an insurance company and an individual investor. The insurance company agrees to pay a stipulated amount to the investor (the "annuitant"), for life or for some specified period in return for a single payment or a series of payments; benefits may begin immediately or at some later date. The major types are fixed and variable annuities.

FIXED ANNUITY

With a fixed annuity, the insurance company guarantees to pay a fixed dollar amount at each specified period for the term of the contract, typically the life of the annuitant.

This means that the insurer assumes the "mortality risk," the possibility that the annuitant will survive beyond the actuarially expected life span. The insurer also assumes the investment risk, since it guarantees the rate of return on invested principal. Even if the insurer's investment return is lower than this guaranteed rate, the insurance company still must pay the guaranteed rate. Indeed, in many contracts, the annuitant receives additional payouts for those periods where the insurer's return is higher than anticipated.

The annuitants, on their part, assume the risk that inflation will lower the real value of the payout.

VARIABLE ANNUITY

The variable annuity attempts to deal with this inflation risk. It is designed to keep pace with inflation. However, neither the amount of payout nor the interest rate is guaranteed. Payments vary according to the market value of the portfolio used to fund the annuity. In other words, the annuitant assumes the investment risk.

In 1959, the U.S. Supreme Court ruled that because the investment risk was borne by the purchaser, these contracts were subject to regulation as securities. Therefore, they must be registered with the SEC and under the Investment Company Act of 1940 as open-end investment companies.

Because no fixed payment is involved, the variable annuity is valued in units, not in dollars (see below).

Note the resemblance to mutual funds—both involve participation in a portfolio of securities, and both are subject to federal regulation. But mutual fund participation is measured in shares, not in units, and while holders of mutual funds may seek income or growth in a long-term investment, the primary objective of variable annuity is retirement income. The most important difference, however, is that earnings on a variable annuity are tax deferred while mutual funds are taxed on distributions and gains each year.

Separate account

The insurance company puts moneys paid to it for variable annuities into a "separate" or "segregated" account. This serves the dual purposes of shielding the insurer's other assets (*e.g.*, from life insurance or fixed-rate annuities) and allowing the insurer to invest in securities that may not be appropriate for the insurer's regular business. Funds are usually invested in a portfolio including common stocks and often in the shares of mutual funds to avoid the costs of managing a portfolio.

Over time, this account grows, as dividends and interest are paid in, and changes, with gains and losses from the sale of securities. It also fluctuates daily, reflecting market ups and downs in the securities portfolio.

A professional investment advisor manages the fund under the supervision of a board of managers. As with mutual funds, firms that offer variable annuities are prohibited from making any statement implying that their management skills or investment policies guarantee against loss.

Regulations affecting variable annuities

Variable annuities are subject to regulation at two levels: first, all insurance companies must comply with the rules set by the state insurance commission in their state; second, at the federal level, three laws apply:

1. The separate account is considered an investment company, so all accounts that represent a pooling of variable annuity funds must be registered under the Investment Company Act of 1940.

2. A variable annuity contract is a security and is subject to registration under the Securities Act of 1933.

3. Any firm selling variable annuities is considered a broker/dealer and must register under the Securities and Exchange Act of 1934.

Value of variable annuity contract

The value of a variable annuity is expressed in "units" of two kinds: "accumulation" units while the annuitant is paying in and "annuity" units during distribution.

Accumulation units
These are an accounting measure of the contract owner's proportionate interest in the separate account during the accumulation period. The units vary in value daily as the investment portfolio varies in value. Thus, on any given day, one accumulation unit equals the value of the separate account portfolio divided by the number of accumulation units outstanding.

This is just like net asset value per share with mutual funds. The value of a contract at any point in time is thus the value of a single accumulation unit times the number of units. If a contract currently has 2,000 units and each unit has a value of $7.50, then the value of the contract is $15,000.

The contract usually specifies the date at which accumulation ends and payout begins. At that point, the annuitant will receive a lump sum payment or (by "annuitizing" the accumulation) regular monthly payments for some fixed period or for the length of his life, depending on the contractual agreement entered into earlier.

Annuity unit
This is the accounting measure used to determine how much the annuitant will receive during the payout period if a monthly payment plan was chosen.

The *first* month amount is fixed by the contract as follows:

When payout begins (usually at retirement), the value of the contract is determined by multiplying the number of units accumulated by the value of one accumulation unit at that point.

The first monthly payment is then calculated on the basis of the insurance company's annuity tables. These are actuarial tables showing monthly payment-per-$1,000 of value. They take into account the annuitant's age, the payout option chosen, any charges, and the "assumed interest rate" (AIR) of the portfolio. The AIR is the rate at which the issuer of the annuity assumes the separate account will grow. The actual rate of growth—whether more or less—will determine the value of each annuity unit.

This first payment is then divided by the current value of an accumulation unit to determine the total number of annuity units required to make that first payment. The number of annuity units remains fixed. Every month the annuitant receives the dollar amount of that fixed number of units times the *current* value of a unit.

Example

If at retirement an annuitant had 20,000 accumulation units and each had a value of $6, the value of the contract would be $120,000. Suppose that for this annuitant, actuarial tables show a monthly payment per $1,000 of $8.50; so the first month's payment was: $120 \times \$8.50 = \$1,020$.

Then $\$1,020 \div \$6 = 170$ units would have to be sold in order to make this payment. From then on, the contract-holder would get 170 units' worth of payment for each succeeding month. If for some later month, units were worth $7 (rather than the $6 value at the time of retirement), that month's check would be for $170 \times \$7 = \$1,190$.

The annuitant hopes that these payments would increase at least at the same rate as inflation; however, that is not at all certain: the annuitant assumes the investment risk.

Two final notes:

If the annuitant dies before the units are exhausted there is often provision for the unspent units to be transferred to the estate or to some beneficiary.

If the annuitant outlives the time required to use up all of the units, he or she still continues to receive the annuity. Thus, the insurer is still accepting the insurance risk.

ANNUITY PURCHASE OPTIONS

As noted above, an annuity can be purchased in one payment or in installments, and payout can begin at once or at a set future date. The possible combinations are:

Single payment immediate annuity

The value of the account is simply that of the initial lump-sum purchase, less any sales and administration charges, so payout is determined immediately and begins "one full payment period" after purchase. Any capital gains or investment income is reinvested in the separate account.

Single payment deferred annuity

Again, there is a lump-sum purchase, but payout begins only after an agreed waiting period (usually a set number of years) or at some occurrence (*e.g.*, retirement or death). Until payout begins, income and gains accumulate tax deferred.

Periodic (or installment) payment deferred annuity

The annuitant makes a series of payments, usually at regular intervals. During this accumulation period, any net income and gains are added to the value of the account. Once payout begins, this continues as "reinvestment."

ANNUITY PAYOUT OPTIONS

The possible forms of payout (or "resettlement") are:

Life annuity

Provides monthly (or other periodic) payment for life of annuitant, however long. This option offers the highest regular payments. The insurance company's obligation ends at death.

Life annuity, joint and survivor

Payments go to both the annuitant and a second person. If one should die, benefits go to the survivor. The insurance company's obligation ends with the death of both.

Life annuity, period certain

Payments continue for a specified period (usually 10, 15 or 20 years). If the annuitant dies, payment goes to the beneficiary.

Life annuity, unit refund

Regular payments are made during the annuitant's life. At death, a named beneficiary receives a payment, usually in a lump sum, for the remaining value of the account.

Installment for designated period (also called limited installment, fixed period)

Payments to the annuitant continue only for a specified period.

Installment for designated amount

Payments continue until the account is exhausted.

Investment income

Pays only from income, leaving the principal untouched.

Note that many of these payout options are available with either fixed or variable annuities or a "combined annuity," with a fixed portion paying a stated dollar amount, the variable in units.

OTHER FEATURES

Contract terms

The insurance company usually guarantees payment as long as the annuitant lives (payment for this risk is built into the annuity tables). In addition, the company guarantees it will not reduce payments because its expenses go up. A "termination provision" grants the investor the right to terminate the annuity any time before payouts begin; that is, the issuing company has no right to sue for the payments that remain.

If the annuitant should die before payout begins, a "death benefit" provision states that the value of the account goes to the beneficiary. If the investor stops paying for any other reason, a "non-forfeiture" provision ensures that he or she retains the accumulated units purchased and can redeem them at current value. Finally, some contracts include loan privileges, allowing the annuitant to borrow on units in the account.

Sales charges (and management and administrative fees)

As with mutual funds, the maximum sales charge is 8.5%. There may be other expenses described in the prospectus which are not part of the sales charge.

Some plans deduct most sales charges in the first year ("front-end load"). These have rights like those with mutual funds (full refund of sales charges if withdrawn in 45 days; if the front-end load is 50%, the purchaser can withdraw in up to 18 months with a refund of any charges over 15% of all payments).

TAXATION OF ANNUITIES

Tax treatment of annuities requires a number of distinctions. All interest, dividends, and capital gains accumulate on a tax-free (actually tax-deferred) basis; however, once payout begins, some part of the money received is taxable. The distinction here is between contributions made on a before-tax basis and those made after-tax.

Thus, that portion of the payout that represents the original contribution is considered a recovery of money paid in (this is determined by IRS-approved actuarial formulas for the cost basis) and is not taxed. The remainder—any gains in the separate accounts—is taxed as ordinary income; of course, this rate is usually somewhat lower for retirees.

PART THREE
Retirement Plans

Many individuals are covered by retirement plans. Some of these are employer-sponsored; others are individual plans. This section provides an overview of the various types of plans.

A key element here is the concept of "tax-qualified" plans. Only plans that meet certain requirements set forth by the Internal Revenue Code in compliance with ERISA (the Employee Retirement and Income Security Act) are considered qualified, and only under such plans are contributions deductible from income—either the income of an individual taxpayer or of a corporation sponsoring the plan.

ERISA basically sets standards for fair treatment of all those who participate in a plan: they concern what percentage of a firm's employees must be able to participate; the way benefits are distributed; when "vesting" occurs; how much each employee must contribute; and how the plan is funded.

With a tax-qualified plan, funds that go into the retirement account are deducted from income at that time and then are taxed (according to rules outlined below) when they are distributed. In non-qualified plans, funds deposited cannot be deducted from income; at distribution, this original contribution is not taxed again, though any accumulated investment income is.

EMPLOYER PENSION PLANS

Approximately half of all employees in the country are covered by employer plans. The employee is liable for taxes on the money in these plans only when he or she begins to receive it at retirement. Employer contributions are a deductible expense if the plan is "qualified." To be considered qualified, a pension plan must meet certain standards set by IRS and by ERISA, the Employment Retirement Income Security Act. These standards deal with reporting and fiduciary responsibilities and, most importantly, with vesting rights, eligibility, and fairness.

Vesting
To be "vested" in some property is to have the right of ultimate ownership to that property. Under the 1986 Tax Reform Act, private-sector employer-sponsored plans must vest eligible employees in one of two ways: either they are fully (100%) vested after five years or 20% vested after three years and 20% in each succeeding year to become fully (100%) vested after seven years. Government employers are permitted to withhold vesting until the public-sector employee has been employed for ten years.

Eligibility
Eligibility requirements vary, but must include the following minimum standards. For employees aged twenty-one or older, eligibility cannot be delayed for more than one year. Regardless of the vesting schedule (even if the employee is fully vested at once), participation may not be delayed for more than two years and must be within three years. (Employees include all who work more than 1,000 hours during the year.)

Fairness
The act requires that coverage be available to employees other than those who are highly paid. One criterion is that at least 70% of all non-highly compensated employees are covered.

Benefit plans

Benefit plans are labeled as either "defined contribution" or "defined benefit." In a defined contribution plan, a specified amount is contributed each year. The funds accumulate, including any interest earned, and are available for distribution at retirement very much like an annuity.

In a defined benefit plan, the benefit to the employee is defined as some percentage (often between 1% and 2% for each year of service) of the employee's average salary during his last five years of employment. For example, a 2% formula for an employee with 30 years of service would define a benefit of 60% of the average of salary earned between years 26 through 30.

Contribution deadlines

For qualified plans, corporate contributions must be made by the date the corporate tax return is filed.

Profit-sharing plans and ESOPs

Profit-sharing plans are considered "defined contribution" and are subject to the rules outlined above ensuring equal treatment of employees. Note that the employer need not contribute when there is no profit and can vary the amount contributed.

Employer contributions to Employee Stock Ownership Plans (ESOPs) are made in the form of shares in the company. This means employees build a position of ownership; it also means their pension funds are subject to the fluctuations in market value of the stock. In most cases, employers who use ESOPs as pension plans can deduct their contributions from firm income without any cash expenditure.

RETIREMENT PLANS FOR SMALL EMPLOYERS AND SELF-EMPLOYED

Aside from employer pension plans, there is a wide range of individual plans that offer some tax advantages. These include Individual Retirement Accounts (IRAs), Keogh (H.R.10) Plans, Simplified Employee Pension Plans (SEPs), and Section 401(k) Plans.

Keogh plans (H.R.10) for the self-employed

Keogh (pronounced "Key-oh") plans offer tax advantages on retirement-oriented investments for self-employed individuals and their employees. These funds can be invested in any investment approved by the IRS. These include annuities, mutual funds, trust or savings accounts, most securities, nonterm life insurance, and mortgages.

One feature of Keogh plans is that all eligible employees must be covered at the same rate. Physicians who set up Keogh plans and contribute the maximum 25% of net compensation must contribute that proportion of their nurses' salaries as well.

Contribution deadlines   A Keogh must be established by the end of the tax year. However, additional contributions—up to the limits allowed—can be made up to the time the tax return is due—April 15 of the following year.

Self-employed individuals include those who are employed by others but have separate earned income from consulting, royalties, or from work as independent contractors.

Contribution Limits   Contributions are limited to 25% of net compensation with a maximum of $30,000 for a defined contribution plan. Eligibilities, vesting, and fairness requirements for all employees of self-employed individuals are the same as those for employer pension plans.

Simplified Employee Pension plans (SEPs)

A Simplified Employee Pension plan allows a small employer to set up a pension plan with individual retirement accounts for each covered employee. It greatly reduces the paperwork and is in other ways simpler than an employer benefit plan.

Under an SEP, the employer may, but is not compelled to, make contributions to the individual accounts each year. The maximum elective contribution is indexed for inflation. The total contribution, including amounts from the employer and those elected by the employee, is limited to 15% of compensation but no more than $30,000.

Vesting in an SEP is immediate. Eligibility requirements are like those for employer pension plans.

401(k) plans

A final pension option is the tax-deferred retirement plan known as 401(k). 401(k) plans resemble employer pension plans, but are less restrictive. Contributions to such plans are treated like additions to a defined contribution plan. Elective employee contributions to such a plan are similar to those in the SEPs and employer contributions are allowed up to 15% of compensation with a $30,000 maximum.

Note: the total contribution by an employee to all SEP and 401(k) plans is limited to 25% of net compensation with a maximum of $10,000.

To qualify as a tax-deferred plan, a 401(k) may not discriminate in favor of highly compensated employees. That is, the actual deferral percentage for highly compensated employees cannot exceed that of lower-paid employees by too large an amount. Vesting in the employee contribution is immediate; vesting in the employer portion is subject to the same rules as those for employer pension plans.

Individual Retirement Accounts (IRAs)

Any individual may open and maintain an Individual Retirement Account (IRA). Since IRAs were first established in 1981, limits on these accounts have changed several times, and they may well change again. With passage of the 1997 "Taxpayer Relief Act," the following limits apply (but note this act also creates new forms of IRA, described below):

Contribution limits   Individuals who are not active participants in an employer-sponsored retirement plan may contribute up to 100% of income or $2,000, whichever is less, into an IRA and deduct that sum from income before figuring taxes. For a married couple filing jointly, up to $2,000 can be contributed to each spouse's IRA —even if one spouse has little or no earnings— or up to $4,000 for the year. When compensation is unequal, however, the IRA of the spouse with less income cannot exceed the couple's total income after deducting the higher-earning spouse's IRA contribution.

If either spouse is covered by an employer retirement plan, IRA deductions may be further limited. However, individuals with adjusted gross income below $50,000 (for a married couple $60,000) covered by a retirement plan at work are allowed a full IRA deduction. For those earning more, an IRA contribution is no longer tax-deductible; however, any interest earnings or other gains in the account are tax-deferred until withdrawals begin.

Distributions   Once established, IRAs are treated much like the plans described above: taxes are deferred on any gain to the account. Funds distributed before age $59\frac{1}{2}$ are subject to income tax and to a 10% penalty unless they are used for buying a first home (up to $10,000), funding a college education for the holder or for his or her spouse, children, and grandchildren, or where medical expenses exceed $7\frac{1}{2}\%$ of adjusted gross income.

Distribution of funds must begin by age $70\frac{1}{2}$ and meet minimum distribution requirements or a penalty must be paid for "insufficient distribution."

An individual who receives a lump-sum distribution from a qualified employer plan, for example on leaving a job, may "roll it over" into an IRA. The $2,000 limit does not apply, but the money must be rolled over within 60 days. All or part of the sum can be so handled. If only part is rolled over, the balance is taxed as normal income.

At payout, IRA distributions are taxed as regular income.

"Roth IRA"

A new type of Individual Retirement Account, called a Roth IRA, was introduced in the 1998 tax year. This is a nondeductible account—unlike eligible contributions to an ordinary IRA, the taxpayer cannot claim a deduction for contributing to a Roth IRA, but if certain requirements are met all earnings in the account are tax free, and neither the original contributions nor any amount they have earned are taxable when they are withdrawn.

Withdrawals are taxed and subject to a penalty if the account is less than five years old, with the exceptions noted above (for home-buying, education, and medical care) for regular IRAs.

Roth IRAs are available whether or not the taxpayer participates in a retirement plan at work. Income limits are $95,000 for individuals, $150,000 for couples. Unlike conventional IRAs, there is no age-linked requirement for withdrawal: Roth IRAs can be held (and added to) after age $70\frac{1}{2}$.

Nonqualified retirement plans

Not all plans meet the ERISA standards. These "nonqualified plans" are most often termed "deferred compensation" plans, and are effectively contracts between employer and employee in which the employee agrees that some portion of his or her compensation will not be paid until termination, retirement, disability or death. The tax savings anticipated are based on the likelihood that the individual will be in a lower tax bracket at that time.

IRS approval is not required, nor is there any fairness requirement: such plans can be offered only to selected employees.

The agreement may include provisions for forfeiture if the employee engages in activity unacceptable to the employer. Note that such plans give the employee no recourse if the business should fail, and, as noted above, that contributions to the plan are not tax deductible; tax is only deferred until the time when payment is received.

TERMS

Tax shelters   Specialized investment plans allow investors to defer taxes or to incur paper losses. Under the Tax Reform Act of 1986, such losses cannot be used to shelter income except from tax shelters; certain types of real estate still offer tax advantages.

Direct Participation Programs (DPP)   Allow investors to participate directly in gain or loss and tax consequences

Limited Partnership (LP)   Most important type of DPP

Qualifications for LP   Must differ fundamentally from corporation; *e.g.*, have limited life, restrict transferability

General partner   Unlimited liability; usually active in management

Limited partner(s)   Provide most of capital; share profits or losses; not active in management; limited liability

Sponsor (syndicator)   Organizes and registers partnership with authorities

Formation   Certificate must be filed in state of origin; gives details of partnership, partners

Agreement   Describes rights and responsibilities of limited and general partners

Evaluating limited partnership   Assess economic soundness; examine sponsor's earlier offerings, especially potential conflicts of interest and real basis of investment; gauge potential risks (lack of liquidity, etc.)

Recourse loans due the partnership   Limited partner personally liable to partnership

Managed offerings   Like mutual funds

Non-managed offerings   Sold directly through a wholesaler or RR

Subscription agreement   Between investors and general partner or sponsor; investors attest they can satisfy all requirements

- RR must assure that participants understand the program

- No sales until general partner accepts subscribers as limited partners

Real estate programs

Investors usually completely passive

Basic incentives   Income, capital appreciation, diversification, and tax relief

Non-recourse loans   No claim on limited partner's assets

Tax relief   Expenses, mortgage interest, and depreciation allow income losses and cash flow

Types of programs   New construction, government-aided housing, existing properties, land, condominium securities, REITS

Oil and gas programs

Chance to deduct intangible drilling costs and depletion allowance

Overriding royalty interest   Sponsor shares revenues but not costs

Reversionary (subordinate) working interest   Sponsor does not share cost, shares revenues only when investment recovered

Functional allocation   Investors contribute all deductible costs; sponsor all non-deductible costs

Drilling programs   Exploratory (in unproved area) or development (drilling in or near proven fields)

Income programs   Acquiring producing properties

Combination programs

Equipment Leasing Programs   Purchase and subsequent lease of major capital cost equipment

Annuities

Annuity   Contract between insurance company and investor ("annuitant"); company agrees to pay stipulated amount for specified period for one or several payments; benefits may be immediate or deferred

Fixed annuity   Company guarantees to pay fixed dollar amount at specified intervals; assumes mortality risk and investment risk, annuitants assume inflation risk

Variable annuity   No guarantee of payout amount or interest rate, annuitant assumes investment risk

Contracts   Must be registered as open-end investment companies

Taxation   Earnings tax deferred

Separate account   Moneys paid for variable annuities must be segregated

Investment advisor   Manages funds under board of managers

Guaranteeing against loss   Prohibited

Accumulation units   Expresses value of variable annuity while annuitant pays in; measure of proportionate interest in separate account

Value of contract   Value = accumulation unit × number of units

Annuity unit   Measure of how much annuitant will receive based on value of accumulation unit when payout begins and "Assumed Interest Rate" of separate account; actual payout based on actual performance of portfolio

Purchase/payout combinations   Single Payment Immediate Annuity; Single Payment Deferred Annuity, Periodic (Installment) Payment Deferred Annuity

Possible forms of payout   Life Annuity; Life Annuity, Joint and Survivor; Life Annuity, Period Certain; Life Annuity, Unit Refund; Installment for Designated Period (Limited Installment, Fixed Period); Installment for Designated Amount; Investment Income

Charges and fees   Usually fixed percentage of payment; can be reduced at breakpoints or with rights of accumulation; front-end load like mutual funds

Tax treatment   Contributions accumulate income tax free; treatment of payouts depends on whether contributions made after-tax or before-tax

Retirement plans

Employer-sponsored plans   To be tax-qualified must meet standards of vesting, eligibility, fairness

Individual plans include:

Keogh plans   Up to 25% of all net earned income from self-employment

Simplified Employee Pension (SEP) plans

401(k) plans

IRA   Individual Retirement Accounts, principally for individuals who are not active participants in an employer-sponsored plan

Non-qualified plans   Basically contracts between employer and employee; principal effect is to defer taxation

REVIEW QUESTIONS

1. If a Direct Participation Program does not have a legitimate economic purpose it is called:

   (A) a tax shelter
   (B) a direct shelter
   (C) a deduction shelter
   (D) an abusive shelter

2. Due diligence must be exercised on a real estate limited partnership by the:

   (A) registered representative
   (B) managing underwriter
   (C) investor
   (D) SEC

3. The Ozark Oil Drilling Partnership requires the limited partners to pay labor costs and the general partner to pay for producing well equipment. This type of arrangement is called:

   (A) functional allocation
   (B) overriding royalty interest
   (C) reversionary working interest
   (D) disproportionate sharing

4. All of the following are risks of a direct participation program EXCEPT:

   (A) there is no guaranteed return
   (B) the program may not get favor-
      able tax treatment
   (C) the investment may be illiquid
   (D) potential loss could be larger than contracted for

5. A limited partnership is most likely to differ from a corporation in which of the following ways?

   I. limited liability
   II. centralized management
   III. difficulty of transferring ownership
   IV. continuous life

   (A) I and II
   (B) II and III
   (C) III and IV
   (D) I and IV

6. An investor in a buy-leaseback arrangement would expect all of the following EXCEPT:

   (A) risk of default
   (B) freeing up of capital
   (C) depreciation deductions
   (D) regular cash distributions

7. The Keogh Act would allow each of the following to set up a self-retirement fund EXCEPT:

   (A) a lawyer in private practice
   (B) a municipal employee with an income from selling paintings
   (C) a broker with the funds from a Christmas bonus
   (D) a salaried plumber from free-lance plumbing income

8. One may rollover the proceeds from an IRA (for the benefit of the same person) tax-free as long as the transfer occurs within:

   (A) 30 days
   (B) 60 days
   (C) 90 days
   (D) 6 months

9. Eligibility for an employee in a Keogh Plan takes place:

   (A) at once
   (B) after one year
   (C) after three years
   (D) after five years

10. An individual can receive distributions from an IRA without penalty at the age of:

    (A) 59
    (B) $59\frac{1}{2}$
    (C) 60
    (D) $60\frac{1}{2}$

11. An individual must begin distributions from an IRA by age:

    (A) 62
    (B) 65
    (C) 70
    (D) $70\frac{1}{2}$

12. All of the following are permissible investments for an IRA EXCEPT:

    (A) options
    (B) variable annuities
    (C) corporate bonds
    (D) CDs

13. The maximum allowable annual contribution to a Keogh Plan is:

    (A) $2,000
    (B) $10,000
    (C) $15,000
    (D) $30,000

14. The value of an accumulation unit in a variable annuity is directly dependent on:

    (A) the prime rate
    (B) the Dow Jones Industrials Average
    (C) the NAV in the separate account
    (D) a broad-based securities index

15. If an investor purchases insurance completion with a variable annuity, who receives the benefit if the investor dies?

    (A) the fund's custodian
    (B) the estate's executor
    (C) the fund's trustee
    (D) the estate of the deceased

16. The potential advantages of a tax shelter investment are:

    I. long-term capital gains
    II. generation of current losses which can offset income
    III. generation of current income

    (A) I and II
    (B) I and III

    (C) II and III
    (D) I, II, and III

17. All of the following are true of variable annuities EXCEPT:

    (A) there is a guaranteed minimum return
    (B) the portfolio may include convertible bonds
    (C) the portfolio may include mutual funds
    (D) the payout may begin 10 years after contributions end

18. To qualify, a Keogh Plan must cover the following employees EXCEPT:

    (A) there are no exceptions
    (B) full time employees of at least one year
    (C) employees who work more than 1,000 hours for one year
    (D) employees who work less than 1,000 hours for two years

19. A basic feature of oil and gas drilling programs is:

    (A) depletion allowance
    (B) current income
    (C) investment tax credit
    (D) safety of investment

20. All of the following are true about REITs EXCEPT:

    (A) they invest in long-term mortgages
    (B) they pass 95% of net earning to investors
    (C) they make short-term loans
    (D) there are at least 100 beneficial owners

21. In a direct participation program, "phantom income" occurs when:

    (A) cash flow exceeds depreciation
    (B) cash flow exceeds income
    (C) income is diminished by depreciation
    (D) income exceeds cash flow

22. In a DPP the general partner's liability is limited to:

    (A) there is no limit
    (B) the total contribution of all partners
    (C) his original investment plus all non-recourse loans
    (D) his original contribution plus all recourse loans

23. The basis for an investor's share of a DPP is $25,000. During the year, he receives a $10,000 distribution, and at the end of the year, his share of losses is $20,000. How much of the loss can he realize that year against ordinary income?

    (A) $3,000
    (B) $5,000
    (C) $10,000
    (D) $0

24. If a drilling program has granted a 20% royalty interest to holders of the surface rights, the limited partners realize:

    (A) 80% of the return
    (B) less than 80% of the return and most of the risk
    (C) 80% of the return for 80% of the risk
    (D) 20% of the return for 80% of the risk

25. All of the following are characteristics of profit sharing plans EXCEPT:

    (A) contributions are only made in years where there is a profit
    (B) it is a defined benefit plan
    (C) all eligible employees must be included
    (D) vesting must obey ERISA guidelines

The following information is for questions 26 and 27.

The income statement for a rental property includes:

revenues	$450,000
expenses	$150,000
depreciation	$200,000
interest	$150,000

26. The cash flow for this year is:

    (A) ($50,000)
    (B) $0
    (C) $50,000
    (D) $150,000

27. The income for this year is:

    (A) ($50,000)
    (B) $0
    (C) $50,000
    (D) $150,000

28. The underwriting fees for a DPP are limited to:

    (A) NASD's fair and reasonable 5%
    (B) $8\frac{1}{2}$ %
    (C) 10%
    (D) 0%

29. An equipment leasing program can take advantage of all of the following EXCEPT:

    (A) accelerated depreciation
    (B) interest deductions for purchase of the equipment
    (C) reduced cash outflow because of leasing
    (D) limited liability

30. The number of annuity units at payout is based on:

    (A) the original form of payments
    (B) T-bill rates
    (C) the life expectancy of the annuitant
    (D) the performance of the stock market during accumulation

ANSWERS TO REVIEW QUESTIONS

1. **(D)** In order to qualify for the favorable tax treatment, it must have a legitimate economic purpose.

2. **(B)** The underwriting firm is responsible for due diligence.

3. **(A)** The sponsor contributes for the development of productive wells.

4. **(D)** The point of such a program is that liability is limited.

5. **(C)** These are the two ways in which limited partnerships differ from corporations.

6. **(B)** The seller-lessee would have capital freed up, not the buyer-lessor.

7. **(C)** All of the other sources of income are from self-employment. This one is from income at his regular job.

8. **(B)** This rollover can only occur once in any year. It is not limited to $2,000 but rather can be all of any existing IRA.

9. **(B)** Vesting occurs after five years of eligibility or in increments of 20% from year 3 to year 7.

10. **(B)** Death or disability also allow penalty-free distributions.

11. **(D)** At that time the moneys are subject to income tax.

12. **(A)** While options are generally not a permissible investment, a mutual fund that wrote covered options to enhance return would be permissible

13. **(D)** The maximum is the smaller of $30,000 and 25% of income.

14. **(C)** A variable annuity must have a separate account. This is different from a fixed annuity whose assets may be commingled with those of the insurer.

15. **(A)** The custodian is responsible for seeing that the premiums in the plan are paid.

16. **(D)** All of these are potential advantages of such a program.

17. **(A)** A variable annuity does not guarantee any fixed return but does offer the possibility that the return will be sufficient to offset the effects of inflation.

18. **(D)** All those employed for at least one year, except those who work less than 1,000 hours per year, must be covered.

19. **(A)** None of the others are basic features of a drilling program.

20. **(C)** They are required to invest in real property or government securities.

21. **(D)** It is called phantom income because the investor gets less money than the income credited to his or her account.

22. **(A)** The general partner has unlimited liability.

23. **(D)** The loss can be applied only to passive income. In this case, the $10,000 distribution reduces his basis to $15,000. This is the amount he can apply to other passive income.

24. **(B)** Since the general partner will also get some of the return, less than 80% will be available for the limited partners even though they put up most of the money.

25. **(B)** A defined benefit plan will specify how much the employee receives, so it cannot depend on the company's profits.

26. **(D)** The cash flow will be the revenue less the cash actually expended. Depreciation is not expended cash.

27. **(A)** The income from this investment is revenue less all expenses and depreciation.

28. **(C)** This limit applies to the total of all expenses related to the underwriting.

29. **(C)** The lessor is the one who benefits from reduced cash outlay because he avoids having to purchase the equipment.

30. **(C)** The annuity units are determined by actuarial methods using an assumed interest rate (AIR) and the expected remaining life of the annuitant.

CHAPTER SIX

new issues

When a corporation wants to raise money for long-term needs, it usually issues securities. (Bank borrowing is generally reserved for short-term use and relatively small amounts.) This chapter describes the mechanisms and rules involved in issuing new securities.

THE INVESTMENT BANKER

Corporations can sell their own securities to investors, but they customarily work with an investment banker. This relationship is a long-term one, since the services provided require that the investment banker have an intimate knowledge of the corporation.

These investment banking firms act as middlemen between corporations seeking capital and individuals or institutions seeking to invest. Working with responsible corporate officers, the investment banker decides on the amount of money to be raised, the type of securities to offer, and how and when to offer them.

Most often, the investment banker underwrites the issue, that is, buys securities from the issuer and resells them to the public. These transactions require considerable capital, and margins (the difference between the cost of buying securities and the price at which they are resold) are relatively low, so investment banking is considered a risky and highly technical business. Especially because of the risk, regulations prevent commercial banks from entering into the investment banking business (see Chapter 15).

TYPES OF OFFERINGS

Offerings of securities can be divided into two basic types:

Primary offerings

Here the investment banker distributes previously unissued securities. (The first time a firm offers shares publicly is called the "initial public offering.") *Proceeds from primary offerings go directly to the issuer, and they cannot be bought on margin.*

Secondary offerings

Here the investment banker distributes securities held by individual owners (for example, a large block of stock belonging to a corporate official). Treasury stock (see page 12) can fall into this category. *Proceeds from these transactions go directly to the seller. Margin purchases are sometimes permitted.*

At times, an issue of stock will include both a primary and secondary offering. This is called a "split offering" or "combined distribution."

PRIVATE PLACEMENTS

A completely separate category of new issue is one that can go directly to one or several major individual or institutional investors. This is called a "private placement." Under this procedure, the security is never made available to the general public. (See page 381.)

The advantage of a private placement is that it is not regulated as stringently as a public offering and is therefore much less costly for the corporation. On the assumption that the private investors are sophisticated and do not need the protection that the general public does, it does not have to be registered with the SEC. Investors supply an investment letter attesting to this.

In addition, it affords the issuing company a great deal more privacy about its finances than would a public offering. Most private placements are for bonds, and the purchaser of a privately-placed issue is drawn by the fact that these pay a slightly higher rate than do comparable public offerings.

NEGOTIATED OFFERING

Most new issues of corporate securities involve a "negotiated offering." (Some involve competitive bidding, but since this is more common with municipal issues, it is discussed later in this chapter). In the process of negotiation, the investment banker will investigate the issuer's financial condition, relations with employees, plans for future growth, etc., and the general condition of the industry in which it is engaged, as well as examining the salability of the securities to be offered.

Once both sides are satisfied, the issuer and the investment banker enter into a contract under which the investment banker agrees to buy the issue at a specified price. (The securities are subsequently sold to the public at a higher price; see below.)

THE UNDERWRITING AGREEMENT

This contract is called the underwriting agreement. It must be filed with the SEC as part of the registration statement (see Chapter 15) and is usually not finally signed until just before the new issue goes on sale to the public.

The agreement includes the following elements:

- name and amount of securities being offered

- the issuer's pledge that the issue will meet SEC requirements

- the issuer's agreement to sell a stated amount of securities

- the investment banker's agreement to buy a stated amount of securities

- *the price at which securities will be offered to the investment banker*

- *the price at which securities will be offered to the public (the public offering price or POP)*

- *dealer concession*

- provisions concerning payment—how, where, and when the issuer will be paid for the securities

- conditions required for the underwriter to meet its commitment (for example, independent review of the issue's legality and of the issuer's financial statements)

- responsibility for meeting both federal and state registration requirements and for preparing and distributing the prospectus and registration

- *indemnifying each side from liability for anything not its fault*

- *terminating with "market out" clause (see below)*

- provisions dealing with the possibility of default by the underwriter

- postponement in case of some catastrophic event

TYPES OF UNDERWRITER COMMITMENTS

As principal

Usually, the investment banker buys outright the full amount of the new offering and guarantees the proceeds to the issuer—that is, the underwriter assumes financial liability for any unsold shares and acts as a principal in the transaction. This is called "firm commitment" underwriting.

"Standby"   The issuer tries to sell its securities directly to investors (for example, to existing shareholders as part of a rights offering), and the investment banker "stands by" to assist in selling any remaining shares.

"Mini-max"   The investment banker makes a "firm commitment" to sell a certain portion of the issue and agrees to make a "best effort" with the balance. The agreement is not canceled if the minimum is met, even though the maximum is not sold.

Example

In a "1 million, 1.5 million mini-max" agreement, the underwriter commits to purchasing 1 million shares and to make a "best effort" to sell the remaining .5 million shares without actually buying these shares.

As agent

The investment banker or underwriter can also act as an agent in one of several ways:

"Best efforts"   The underwriter agrees to make its "best effort" to sell as much of the issue as it can, but assumes no actual financial liability. This entails less risk and is most common with relatively small issues or where the issuer does not feel particularly pressed for funds.

"All or none" (AON)   The investment banker again makes a best effort, but must work within a time limit (usually some days or weeks). If the entire issue is not sold in that time, the agreement (and the offering itself) is canceled. With such an approach, no sales to investors are final until and unless all shares are sold.

Market-out clause

All types of underwriter commitments may, and usually do, include a "market-out clause." This allows the agreement to be canceled in case of a dramatically unfavorable turn of events, for example, a strong downturn in the market, a sudden change in the issuer's financial position, some adverse government ruling, or some drastic change in the economy as a whole.

FORMATION OF UNDERWRITERS' SYNDICATE

If the new issue is too large for one investment banker to handle, the underwriter will usually turn to other investment bankers and form a syndicate to sell the issue. Typically, the issuer would select a senior manager and perhaps several junior managers. This management group would then choose other investment bankers to join them in an underwriting syndicate. Members of the syndicate sign an "agreement among underwriters" that details arrangements between the several members and between members and the managing underwriter. It generally includes provisions on:

- terms of the offering
- proportion of each underwriter's participation
- the length of the association (30 days is usual)
- appointment of the managing underwriter to represent the syndicate and a listing of its responsibilities
- the fee for management
- members' obligations for expenses
- the method of handling the liability for unsold issues
- the time and method of delivering the securities and paying for them

An important feature of most such agreements (sometimes called purchase group agreements) is a clause penalizing members who sell shares to customers interested in a speedy profit. The "penalty syndicate clause" says that if a member's customer sells to the managing underwriter in the after-market at the stabilizing price (see page 152), then that syndicate member earns no commission on the transaction and is subject to other penalties.

TYPES OF UNDERWRITERS' AGREEMENTS

These agreements can be:

Divided account (or limited liability or Western account)

This arrangement is the one usually employed with corporate issues. Syndicate members are "severally, but not jointly" liable, *i.e.*, each member is liable only for his agreed-upon participation. For example, a firm with 5% participation in a $20 million issue is responsible for only $1 million of the shares and bears no responsibility for other unsold shares, nor would it share in any profit from those other shares.

Undivided account (Eastern account)

Here each member is "severally and jointly liable"—responsible both for its own and for other members' participation. This approach is normally used only with municipal issues. If a member takes 5% participation in a $20 million issue, it is liable to sell $1 million, but even if that commitment is met—even exceeded—each member is still responsible if other members fail to sell their allotted shares. Thus, if $2 million remained unsold, the member would be responsible for 5% of that $2 million.

In all cases, the syndicate dissolves when the transaction is complete.

The managing underwriter has several duties, including forming the syndicate, that are discussed in the following sections. For their part, members of the underwriting syndicate agree to offer the securities at the established price. They can be released from this pledge if the issue proves particularly difficult to sell, but only with the authorization of the managing underwriter.

THE SELLING GROUP

If the managing underwriter decides that the underwriting syndicate will not be able to sell the entire new issue without assistance, it will put together a "selling group" composed of NASD member firms for help in marketing the issue. Securities held by the syndicate and sold directly, not through the selling group, are called "retained shares" or the "retention."

Members of the selling group do not actually buy the securities, that is, they take no financial responsibility, are not underwriters. But each one commits to sell a certain amount, either as allotted by the syndicate or as subscribed to. This is often called a "firm subscription." Members of the group sign an agreement with the syndicate manager that generally echoes the underwriters' own agreement. These firms receive a "selling concession," which is part of the underwriter's spread (see page 154).

PREPARATION OF NEW ISSUES

Registration

All new issues of securities must be registered with the SEC. The investment banker usually assists in preparing the registration statement which is supposed to provide "full disclosure" about the issue to potential investors.

Exempt securities

Some securities are exempt from the registration requirements. These include securities issued or guaranteed by the U.S. government or its agencies and obligations issued by any state or other political subdivision; thus, municipals are exempt.

Other exempt securities include commercial paper (corporate debt) and banker's acceptances maturing in less than 270 days; instruments issued by railroads, trucking companies, airlines and others regulated by the Interstate

Commerce Act; banks or trust companies; savings and loan associations; building and loan societies' co-op banks; and nonprofit groups.

Securities issued intrastate are also exempt, as are issues of $1.5 million or less, fixed annuity contracts and insurance policies, and "private placements" where the issuer makes no public offering.

Cooling-off period

Once this statement is filed, a "20-day cooling-off period" begins to allow the SEC to review the statement. In actual practice this period can be—and most often is—extended in 20-day increments, but 20 days is the minimum time that must elapse before the "effective date," *i.e.*, the date on which securities may be sold to investors.

During this period, both issuer and underwriter take a number of steps, including:

"Preliminary prospectus"   May be issued. This is designed to provide potential investors with information sufficient for them to judge the worth of the offering. Though they cannot yet purchase securities, they can make "indications of interest."

This preliminary prospectus is also called a "red herring" because it includes these words, stamped or printed in red: "this is not an offer to sell and any solicitation of sale is unlawful." It contains much of the information in the SEC registration statement and in the final prospectus, with some important omissions: *it does not show the public offering price, the underwriter's spread, the date securities will be available, or the total amount of the sale.* In most cases, the underwriter distributes the preliminary prospectus. It may indicate an expected price range, *e.g.*, "$20–$25 per share."

"Blue-skying"   During the cooling-off period, the managing underwriter registers the issue in each state where securities are to be offered for sale, under the laws of that state. This is called "blue-skying" the issue. Additionally, registered representatives who sell in any state must register in that state.

"Due diligence meeting"

At or near the end of the cooling-off period, the managing underwriter calls a "due diligence meeting." This involves not only the underwriters, but also responsible officers of the issuing corporation and, usually, accountants and attorneys acting on behalf of both parties.

At the meeting, participants review the registration statement and the final prospectus to make sure that all is in correct order before the public sale begins.

An underwriter wishing to withdraw can do so at this meeting without incurring any liability. Formal terms of the contract between issuer and underwriter are usually negotiated. The underwriter establishes the final public offering price, the spread, and the sales concession. By that time, responses to the preliminary prospectus should have provided a good idea of how the public will receive the offering.

SALE OF NEW ISSUES

Although actual sales to the public can start at any time beginning with the effective date on the registration statement, they usually begin on the day following.

Once sales open, syndicate and selling group members contact those who have given indications of interest and ask for firm orders.

All purchasers must receive a final prospectus. The final prospectus must remain available for 40 days following offering date of a primary or secondary distribution and for 90 days following an initial public offering.

"Tombstone announcements"

When sales to the public begin, the underwriter may place a "tombstone" announcement in the press. This is specifically an announcement, not an advertisement designed to sell the issue. It includes the name of the issuing company, the type of securities being offered, the amount of the issue, and the price of each unit. Names of underwriter(s) are included, with the managing underwriter(s)'s displayed above that of the other underwriters.

Opening and closing the books

When sales begin ("opening of the books"), the managing underwriter receives subscriptions from members of the selling group and from outside dealers. If enough subscriptions are received, the managing underwriter may "close the books."

"Closing the books" is at the discretion of the managing underwriter and can take place almost immediately. Such quick closings are often accompanied by an announcement that the issue is "oversubscribed." This does not necessarily mean that all the securities have been sold, but only that dealers—who may still have to sell the securities—have subscribed for the entire issue.

In general, a certain amount of oversubscription is anticipated. Along with providing for clerical errors, the underwriter must anticipate some last-minute cancellations.

"Stabilizing the issue"

If public interest in the issue proves lower than expected, the underwriter may be required to engage in "stabilizing the issue." This requirement, if it exists, is usually described in the prospectus.

Stabilizing is an effort to keep the issue from losing value too quickly. For a time after the sale date until the price stabilizes on its own, the underwriter may need to stand ready to buy the securities back at or below the public offering price.

Obviously, stabilizing never requires purchases when the price is at a premium to the offering price. Stabilizing is the only type of price manipulation allowed by the SEC. This readiness to buy provides a partial floor for the market value at or close to the offering price.

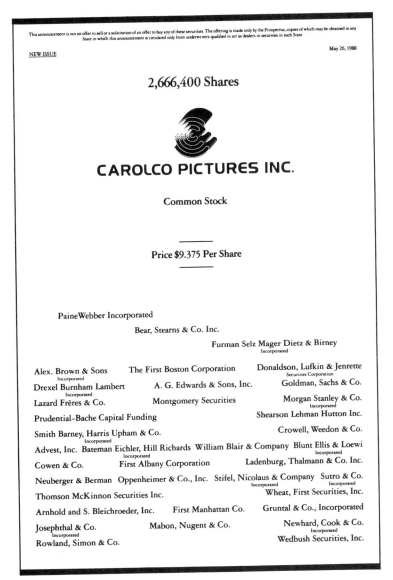

This announcement is not an offer to sell or a solicitation of an offer to buy any of these securities. The offering is made only by the Prospectus, copies of which may be obtained in any State in which this announcement is circulated only from underwriters qualified to act as dealers in securities in such State.

NEW ISSUE   May 26, 1988

2,666,400 Shares

CAROLCO PICTURES INC.

Common Stock

Price $9.375 Per Share

PaineWebber Incorporated

Bear, Stearns & Co. Inc.

Furman Selz Mager Dietz & Birney
Incorporated

Alex. Brown & Sons   The First Boston Corporation   Donaldson, Lufkin & Jenrette
Incorporated   Securities Corporation
Drexel Burnham Lambert   A. G. Edwards & Sons, Inc.   Goldman, Sachs & Co.
Incorporated
Lazard Frères & Co.   Montgomery Securities   Morgan Stanley & Co.
                                                             Incorporated
Prudential–Bache Capital Funding   Shearson Lehman Hutton Inc.

Smith Barney, Harris Upham & Co.   Crowell, Weedon & Co.
Incorporated
Advest, Inc. Bateman Eichler, Hill Richards William Blair & Company Blunt Ellis & Loewi
                         Incorporated   Incorporated
Cowen & Co.   First Albany Corporation   Ladenburg, Thalmann & Co. Inc.

Neuberger & Berman Oppenheimer & Co., Inc. Stifel, Nicolaus & Company Sutro & Co.
                                                  Incorporated   Incorporated
Thomson McKinnon Securities Inc.   Wheat, First Securities, Inc.

Arnhold and S. Bleichroeder, Inc.   First Manhattan Co.   Gruntal & Co., Incorporated

Josephthal & Co.   Mabon, Nugent & Co.   Newhard, Cook & Co.
Incorporated   Incorporated
Rowland, Simon & Co.   Wedbush Securities, Inc.

Figure 6.1 Tombstone

An agreement among underwriters may state that subscribers can sell securities back to the managing underwriter if the price falls, but at a penalty.

"Hot issues"

Some issues of stock are labeled "hot issues" because there is a larger public demand for them than the existing supply. Such an issue is likely to sell at a premium immediately in the secondary or after-market. (Trading in the new issue after the effective date by broker-dealers is called trading in the "after-market.")

Typically, some purchasers of these shares are eager to take a profit and therefore offer to resell immediately. For this reason, the underwriter will often "overallot" or "oversell" the issue, that is, allot or sell more securities than actually exist (usually up to 10%) and buy up the shares offered for resale to make up for this oversold condition.

Any losses incurred because such purchases were made at a premium are prorated among syndicate members in the manner specified in the agreement among underwriters.

In many cases, the issuer grants the underwriter the option to buy additional securities at the public offering price less the spread, and these can be used to cover the oversold position. Any new stock issued for this purpose must be registered with the SEC in an amendment to the registration statement.

Profits, if any, from distributing these additional shares are prorated among syndicate members.

NASD rules governing the handling of hot issues (see page 398) are designed to ensure that broker-dealers make a genuine effort to distribute a new issue at the public offering price and forbid members from withholding a portion of the allotted securities for their own use. In general, these rules say that all potential customers must be treated equally and that no individual or group gets favored treatment.

COMPENSATION

Usually, the issuer pays all expenses connected with getting securities to the underwriter—preparing and distributing the registration and both preliminary and final prospectus and blue-skying the issue. The underwriter is responsible for its own legal expenses, for any advertising costs, and for the costs of stabilizing the issue and distributing securities to syndicate members.

The spread

The difference between the public offering price ("POP") and the actual amount paid to the issuer is called the underwriter's "spread" or gross spread. This discount for the managing underwriter will vary according to the type of securities. Spreads are generally higher on common stocks than on preferred, higher on preferred than on bonds, and usually increase with smaller issues, more speculative issues, or issues that are expected to be difficult to sell.

Management fee

In exchange for his or her extra responsibilities, the manager of the syndicate usually receives some part of the spread on every share sold. This is called the management fee.

Underwriter's concession ("takedown")

Shares distributed by the rest of the syndicate earn the spread minus the management fee. The difference between this price and the POP is called the "underwriter's concession" or the underwriter's takedown.

Selling concession

Members of the selling group then can earn the "selling concession," a portion of the underwriter's concession.

Reallowance

Finally, for shares ultimately disposed of by non-members of the selling group, including syndicate members who require more shares than they are allotted by the syndicate managers, there is a reallowance that is typically less than half of the selling concession.

Example

If the public offering price for a stock was $20. and the spread was $.75, then the managing underwriter would earn $.75 on each share that he sold. If the management fee was $.05, the syndicate members would earn an underwriter's concession or takedown of $.70 on shares that they distributed (and the manager would earn $.05). Members of the selling group would earn the selling concession, say $.40, leaving $.35 for the syndicate member which, of course, includes the $.05 management fee. Finally, a reallowance of $.20 might be earned by a non-member of the selling group who distributed shares. The selling group member then earns $.20 on these shares and the syndicate member the remaining $.30, never forgetting the additional $.05 management fee.

Discount to:	Manager	Takedown	Selling Concession	Reallowance
	$.75	$.70	$.40	$.20

Price to:	Manager	Underwriter	Selling Group Member	Non-member
	$19.25	$19.30	$19.60	$19.80

NEW ISSUES OF MUNICIPALS

Though there are many similarities, the process of offering new municipal securities usually differs from new corporate offerings in important ways. Perhaps most significant is the fact that competitive bidding by underwriters—rarely required with corporate issues—occurs regularly. Negotiated offerings take place for revenue bonds. The issuer selects an underwriter. The issuer usually gives the underwriter an Official Statement which describes the issuer, the type of security, the details of its size and terms, and its purposes and uses. Indeed, competitive bidding for general obligation municipal bonds is required by law in most states.

Where there is competitive bidding, prior contact with underwriters is strictly forbidden. Competition occurs in the sense that syndicates bid for this issue and for the right to resell it to the public. To begin with, the issuer publishes an official Notice of Sale which describes details of the proposed new offering. The underwriters submit sealed bids, and the bid that provides the lowest net interest cost (NIC) to the issuer wins the competition. Sometimes bids are stated in terms of True Interest Cost (TIC), which also takes into account the time-value of money. However, it is the NIC that determines the winning bid.

Some firms act as financial advisors to municipalities. If such firms wish to participate in an underwriting, they must alert the issuer in writing of their intention, providing details on the amount of remuneration they expect to receive from the underwriting. This is particularly applicable in smaller municipalities where government officials may be part-time and may also practice law or work in financial businesses.

There are several sources of information on these matters. The most commonly used are:

The *Blue List*

This publication covers only the secondary market, showing yields to maturity on dealer-held inventories of municipal bonds. It provides a listing of the current supply of such bonds being offered by dealers. It contains no background information, not even bond ratings. An additional service of the *Blue List* is called *Munifacts*. This is a wire service that provides constantly updated information about prices and new issues.

Daily Bond Buyer

This publication indicates new issue market conditions, as it shows the "placement ratio," that is, what proportion of new issues placed on sale have actually been sold. It also includes the *Bond Buyer Index* which lists 20 bonds of 20-year terms and shows the average yield to maturity each month, thereby indicating current interest rates in the market.

Additional indices are a G.O. index of eleven 20-year AA-rated bonds and a revenue bond index that consists of 25 three-year revenue bonds of different types—transportation, housing, etc. Lastly, it has the *Visible Bond Supply*, a listing of municipals scheduled to be sold in the coming 30 days. This is significant because if too many issues are entering the market, this will tend to lower the price of a new issue, and vice versa.

MUNICIPALS: BIDDING AND SELLING PROCEDURES

If a municipality or agency decides to issue securities in a situation requiring a competitive bid, it must publish an Official notice of Sale in the financial press (usually the *Daily Bond Buyer*). This notice must contain complete information about the proposed issue itself and about bidding procedures. It includes:

- the date, time, and place of sale

- a description of the issue (the purpose, type, and amount of securities; maturities and amounts maturing in each period)

- manner of bidding (oral or sealed written bid)

- class of bond (general obligation or revenue issue)

- agency or official authorizing the sale

- limits on interest rates (if there is a statutory ceiling)

- dates on which interest will be paid

- denomination of securities and form (book-entry, registered, etc.)

- minimum acceptable bid

- "good faith deposit" required with a sealed bid

- name of the bond attorney

- place and method of settlement

- right to reject any and all bids

- person authorizing the sale

Naturally, the Official Notice of Sale does not specify the underwriter nor the rating of the proposed issue. One difference between municipal underwriting and corporate underwriting is that municipal syndicates can take indications of interest from prospective investors even before they are awarded the issue. Investors can enter pre-sale orders knowing that the order will not be filled if the syndicate does not win the bidding.

Once the underwriting agreement has been signed (for both negotiated and competitive offerings), the manager issues a letter called the agreement among underwriters or syndicate account letter. Among other things, this letter specifies the priority of orders described below.

The syndicate tries to sell the issue out as quickly as possible. Sometimes, the issue is completely sold out in pre-sale orders; if not, there is an "order period" during which the issue is sold. If an issue is oversubscribed, MSRB specifies a strict order for allocations of these bonds. This is:

1. Pre-sale orders.

2. Group net orders. These have the highest priority during the order period. An investor wishing highest priority stipulates as much. These orders are credited to the entire syndicate no matter which member brings them in.

3. Net designated orders. These are orders brought in by syndicate members in which an investor specifies who is to receive credit for the sale. For example, an order of 1,000 bonds might specify that 500 be credited to member A, 300 to member B, and 200 to member C.

4. Member at takedown (or member takedown orders). These are orders for bonds entered by a member and credited to that member only.

Compensation ("spread")

The underwriting syndicate for municipal issues sells securities to the public at a price higher than that bid (or negotiated); as with corporate issues, the difference is called the underwriting spread.

A portion of the spread goes to the syndicate itself as a fee for management and to pay for expenses; the balance is called the "takedown," and this is the compensation for syndicate members. The takedown may, in turn, be further divided to allow a non-syndicate member to purchase the securities at a price lower than the public offering price: this last division is called a "concession" or "selling concession"; that portion of the takedown that remains with the member is sometimes called "additional takedown."

Before the underwriter will buy the issue, he customarily ensures that the legal opinion (see Chapter 2) is on the face of the bond or attached to it. If this is missing, the bond is not in "good delivery form." Such bonds can be traded (as "ex legal"), though usually only at a discount.

Since municipals always trade "with interest," newly-issued securities always include the "dated date," *i.e.*, the day on which interest begins to accrue. New issues are usually traded "when issued."

Disclosure

Although the governmental entities and agencies that issue municipal bonds are not subject to federal regulation, those who underwrite these issues and/or sell them to the public are subject to rules governing securities trading, in particular those against fraud. On this basis, the SEC has found that an underwriter must have a "reasonable basis" to recommend the purchase of a municipal bond.

Thus, a municipal offering is not subject to the SEC review that faces new issues of corporate securities, but the underwriter is expected to review the accuracy, truthfulness, and completeness of the official statement that accompanies these offerings. This investigation can involve any of a number of sources, including the underwriter's own personnel and others in the municipal securities industry.

Directly governing this requirement is SEC Rule 15c2-12, which pertains to most initial offerings of municipals valued at $1 million or more, excepting small issues of short-term high-denomination instruments. Under this rule, an underwriter must obtain and review an official statement before entering a bid for the securities. Pre-sale customers in negotiated underwritings must be sent the most recent copy of the preliminary official statement within one day of making a request; the same rule holds for the final official statement for at least 25 days from the end of the underwriting period. For this reason, the underwriter must contract with the issuer to receive sufficient quantities of the final official statement to comply with the rules.

TERMS

Investment bankers   Middlemen between corporation seeking capital and investors; cannot be commercial bank

Underwriter   Buys securities from issuer and resells to public

Primary offerings   Previously unissued securities, proceeds directly to issuer; cannot be bought on margin

Secondary offerings   Securities held by individual owners, proceeds directly to seller; margin purchases permitted

Split offering or combined distribution   Both primary and secondary offering in one issue

Private placement   Securities not available to public, SEC registration not required

Underwriting agreement   Contract between issuer and investment banker; must be filed with the SEC

Firm commitment   Underwriter/investment banker buys full offering and guarantees proceeds to issuer; *i.e.*, acts as a principal

Best efforts   Underwriter assumes no financial liability; acts as agent

All or none   Best effort within a time limit; canceled if entire issue not sold in that time

Standby   Issuer tries to sell directly to investors; investment banker stands by to assist in selling any remaining shares

Mini-max   Firm commitment to sell portion of issue; best effort with the balance

Market-out clause   Agreement can be canceled in case of a dramatically unfavorable turn of events

Managing underwriter(s)   Underwriter(s) who form a syndicate

Agreement among underwriters   Details arrangements between members

Divided (Western) account   Each member liable only for agreed-upon participation

Undivided (Eastern) account   Each member responsible both for its own and other members' participation

Selling group   Put together by managing underwriter to help market issue; takes no financial responsibility

Retained shares ("retention")   Securities held by syndicate and sold directly, not through the selling group

Firm subscription   Selling group members commitment to sell a certain amount

Selling concession   Amount received by selling group

Registration   New issues generally must be registered with SEC; statement provides full disclosure

Cooling-off period   20-day period after statement filed to allow SEC review; can be extended

Effective date   Date when securities may be sold to investors

Preliminary prospectus   May be issued during cooling-off period

Blue-skying   Registering issue in each state where securities are to be sold

Due diligence meeting   Underwriters and corporate officers review registration statement and final prospectus and establish final public offering price, spread, and sales concession

Final prospectus   Must go to all purchasers

Tombstone announcement   May be placed when sales begin; provides basic information, not an advertisement

Opening the books   Sales begin

Closing the books   At discretion of managing underwriter

Stabilizing the issue   Underwriter may buy securities back at or below public offering price to keep the issue from losing value too quickly

Hot issues   Where public demand exceeds existing supply

Overallotment   In hot issue, underwriter can allot or sell more securities than actually exist and buy up shares offered for resale; any profits or losses incurred are prorated among syndicate members

Spread   Difference between public offering price and amount paid issuer

Management fee   Portion of spread given syndicate manager

Underwriter's concession or takedown   Spread minus the management fee

Selling concession   Selling group member's portion of underwriter's concession

Reallowance   Amount allotted for shares sold by non-members of selling group or by syndicate members who require more shares than allotted

Municipal securities underwriting   Usually by competitive bidding; issuing agency must examine market

Blue List   Covers secondary market, showing yields to maturity; lists dealer-held inventories; publishes *Munifacts* wire service

Daily Bond Buyer   Shows proportion of new issues actually sold

Bond Buyer Index   Shows average yield to maturity on selected bonds

Visible Bond Supply   List of municipals to be sold in next 30 days

Official Notice of Sale   Must contain complete information about proposed issue and bidding procedures

Precedence for filling muni orders

- pre-sale orders

- group net orders

- net designated orders

- members at takedown

Good delivery form   Bond with legal opinion; otherwise bonds can only be traded "ex legal"

Dated date   Day on which interest begins to accrue

Blue Sky laws   State laws dealing with registration of representatives and securities

REVIEW QUESTIONS

1. The preliminary prospectus would contain all of the following EXCEPT:

   (A) a description of the uses to which the funds will be put
   (B) the names of the officers of the company
   (C) the offering price
   (D) a disclaimer of SEC approval

2. In an underwriting syndicate, arrange the following in order from largest to smallest:

   I. underwriting spread
   II. reallowance
   III. selling concession

   (A) II, III, and I
   (B) III, II, and I
   (C) I, II, and III
   (D) I, III, and II

3. If the manager says that the retention is 80% for an underwriter who has 100,000 shares, the shares available to that underwriter for his own customers is:

   (A) 20,000
   (B) 80,000
   (C) 100,000
   (D) 100,000 plus 80% of the remainder

4. Which of the following occurs during the cooling-off period?

   (A) stabilization
   (B) reallowance
   (C) due diligence meetings
   (D) setting of the final price

5. The selling price of a new issue is affected by all of the following EXCEPT:

   (A) anticipated earnings
   (B) the underwriter's feel for the market
   (C) the selling group
   (D) anticipated dividends for the first year

6. An underwriter in an Eastern account has a 15% participation. The underwriting is for $10 million and he has sold $1.5 million. If $1 million remains unsold, what is his liability?

   (A) nothing
   (B) $100,000
   (C) $150,000
   (D) $1 million

7. A broker who is a member of the selling group would get which of the following discounts?

   (A) spread
   (B) concession
   (C) takedown
   (D) reallowance

8. Which of the following is not allowed to the manager of an underwriting?

   (A) Increasing the number of shares offered
   (B) Increasing the offering price
   (C) Stabilizing after distribution begins
   (D) Setting aside some percentage of each member's share, for institutional buying

9. If an investment banker may return to the issuer all securities not sold, we have a:

   (A) best effort offering
   (B) contingency offering
   (C) firm commitment
   (D) limited offering

10. Another name for a tombstone is:

    (A) preliminary prospectus
    (B) final prospectus
    (C) request for bids
    (D) announcement of a new offering

11. An investment banker is likely to participate in which of the following?

    I. Arranging a 6-month loan
    II. Arranging a 15-year bond issue
    III. Participating in a third market distribution
    IV. Arranging a new issue of securities

    (A) I and III
    (B) II and IV
    (C) II, III, and IV
    (D) All of the above

Questions 12–15 are based on the following information: A Western syndicate agrees to purchase 10 million shares from a corporation for a total of $89 million. These are to be offered to the public at $10 per share.

12. If the manager is to receive $.10 per share, then the underwriter's concession is:

    (A) $1.00 per share
    (B) $1.10 per share
    (C) $1.20 per share
    (D) subject to further negotiation

13. If an underwriter with a 10% share has sold 900,000 shares and if the entire syndicate has sold 8 million shares, this underwriter is responsible for an additional:

    (A) 100,000 shares
    (B) 200,000 shares
    (C) 1,000,000 shares
    (D) 2,000,000 shares

14. If the selling group concession is $.40, then a member of the selling group would receive:

    (A) $.40 per share
    (B) $.60 per share
    (C) $.70 per share
    (D) none of the above

15. Which of the following would be an example of stabilizing?

    (A) A pre-sale bid of $11
    (B) A pre-sale bid of $9
    (C) A post-distribution bid of $11
    (D) A post-distribution bid of $9

16. If an underwriter agreed to an All or None offering, he would:

    (A) take all of the unsold issue for his account
    (B) take none of the unsold issue for his account
    (C) sell all of the issue to an institution
    (D) sell all of the issue or return it all to the issuer

17. Which of the following new issue debt instruments is most likely to be purchased through competitive bidding?

    (A) corporate debentures
    (B) corporate adjustment bonds
    (C) municipal general obligation bonds
    (D) municipal water and sewer bonds

18. A "best effort" underwriting can be characterized as one in which the underwriter is a(n)

    (A) broker
    (B) dealer
    (C) principal
    (D) owner

19. A firm is to make its first public offering. The firm is located in New York and does some business in New Jersey and Connecticut, and therefore the broker will offer the shares in those two states as well. Which of the following hold?

    I. registration takes place in New York only
    II. blue-sky laws of all three states must be satisfied
    III. tombstones must be published in all three states
    IV. registered reps must be licensed in any state in which they sell the issue

    (A) I and III
    (B) II and III
    (C) II and IV
    (D) II, III, and IV

20. The solicitation of an investment letter from a prospective purchaser is normally associated with:

    (A) secondary distributions
    (B) private placements
    (C) no-load funds
    (D) Rule 144 distributions

21. A new stock offering suggests that between 2 million and 2.5 million shares will be sold depending on the market. This is called a:

    (A) conditional underwriting
    (B) best effort
    (C) all-or-none underwriting
    (D) mini-max offering

22. A "due diligence" meeting is called for a new issue in order to:

    (A) establish the reallowance and the selling concession
    (B) set the final price of the offering
    (C) allow the underwriter to meet with the issuing firm
    (D) all of the above

Questions 23–25 are based on the following information: An initial offering of Consolidated Amalgamated Incorporated is to be underwritten by a syndicate. Of the 10 million shares being offered, 2.5 million are allocated to the selling group. The public offering price is $18 per share, of which CAI is to get $17. Assume the management fee is set at $.15 and the selling concession is $.60.

23. How large is the spread?

    (A) $.40
    (B) $.60
    (C) $.85
    (D) $1.00

24. What does the managing underwriter get for his services?

    (A) $400,000
    (B) $850,000
    (C) $1,000,000
    (D) $1,500,000

25. How much will a syndicate member realize on each share that he sells to a member of the selling group?

    (A) $.25
    (B) $.40
    (C) $.60
    (D) $.85

26. Which of the following securities are exempt from the registration requirements of the Securities Act of 1933?

(A) municipal bonds
(B) U.S. government securities
(C) state chartered banks
(D) all are exempt

27. In an underwriting, the selling group may do all of the following EXCEPT:

    (A) have financial liability
    (B) assist in the marketing of the issue
    (C) get some of the underwriting spread
    (D) be an advisor on the issue

28. The announcement of a common stock offering includes the following information: Offering price $16 per share; takedown, $1.20; concession $.90; additional take-down $.30; and management fee $.40. If the offering is sold out, what are the proceeds per share to the issuer?

(A) $13.20
(B) $14.10
(C) $14.40
(D) $14.80

29. A new issue comes to market at $22. If the inside quote on this issue is $21\frac{1}{2}-22\frac{1}{2}$ the issue may be stabilized at all of the following prices EXCEPT:

    (A) $21
    (B) $21.25
    (C) $21.50
    (D) $22

30. In a municipal syndicate account which is Eastern, an account member's liability is determined from the number of bonds:

    (A) he has sold
    (B) required to make up his percentage share
    (C) left unsold in the offering
    (D) unsold divided by the number of syndicate members

ANSWERS TO REVIEW QUESTIONS

1. (**C**) The price is not set until just before distribution begins.

2. (**D**) The underwriting spread is the largest. From this the selling concession would be offered to the selling group who might in turn offer a reallowance to others.

3. (**A**) The retention is those shares that are retained by the syndicate for group sales.

4. (**C**) All of the others occur later.

5. (**C**) The selling group does not take part in the price setting.

6. (**C**) In an Eastern account, each underwriter is jointly and severally responsible. Therefore, this underwriter is responsible for 15% of the unsold shares.

7. (**B**) The concession goes to members of the selling group.

8. (**B**) The price may never be changed after the offer price has been made; however, a lower bid may be made to help stabilize the issue.

9. (**A**) The underwriter makes his "best effort," and the issuer accepts whatever he gets.

10. **(D)** The tombstone is merely an announcement.

11. **(B)** (I) would be done by a bank and (III) involves listed stocks, not new issues.

12. **(A)** The total spread is the difference between the offering price, $10, and what the issuer receives, $8.90, less the $.10 manager's fee, leaving $1.00.

13. **(A)** In a Western syndicate, each underwriter is responsible for his share; in this case, 10% of 10 million is 1 million shares.

14. **(A)** This is the definition of the selling concession. This concession is the discount available to a non-member of the syndicate.

15. **(D)** Stabilizing takes place only after distribution and at a price no higher than the offering price.

16. **(D)** The definition of "All or None."

17. **(C)** In most cases, this is a legal requirement.

18. **(A)** The underwriter does not actually buy the issue, but rather takes a commission for any shares sold.

19. **(C)** The issue must be registered in any state in which it is offered. The tombstone is not required anywhere.

20. **(B)** The letter asserts that the investor is sophisticated and aware of the risks.

21. **(D)** The lower bound is a firm commitment; the rest is on a best efforts basis.

22. **(D)** The meeting allows a review of the registration statement and the final prospectus.

23. **(D)** The difference between the price and what the issuer gets.

24. **(D)** $.15 × 10 million shares.

25. **(A)** After the $.15 management fee and the $.60 selling concession, there is $.25 left.

26. **(D)** All of these are exempt from the registration requirements.

27. **(A)** Members of the selling group have no direct financial liability. Only the underwriters assume liability.

28. **(A)** The takedown equals the concession plus the additional takedown. Net proceeds are $16 less the takedown, $1.20, and less the management fee, $.40.

29. **(D)** Stabilization can take place at any price not above the offering price, but also not above the highest bid by independent market makers.

30. **(C)** An Eastern account means undivided liability. Thus, each member of the syndicate is responsible for his proportion of any unsold bonds even if he has already sold the amount equal to his percentage of the undertaking.

over-the-counter market (OTC)

THE FOUR MARKETS

Traders distinguish four types of transactions:

- trading of listed securities on an exchange

- trading of unlisted securities over the counter (These are called the "secondary market" or "after market" to distinguish them from new issue transactions, which are known as the "primary market.")

- "third market" refers to trading of listed securities in OTC markets. This occurs, for example, with some listed securities that can be traded only by members of the listing exchange but can be sold over the counter to a nonmember broker/dealer. Third market transactions are also popular with institutional traders who do not want to place a large block of stock on an exchange at one time as such an action might depress the price of the security.

- "fourth market"—direct trades between institutions, for example, mutual funds or insurance companies, without using any middleman or broker. Some of these transactions take place through "Instinet."

OVER-THE-COUNTER TRADING

The term "over the counter" or OTC is used to describe securities trading that does not take place on an exchange. There is no single centralized marketplace for this trading. Rather, individual firms are willing to make a market (have an inventory from which they are willing to buy and sell to others) in some securities. Different firms make a market in different securities, although a single firm may make a market in several securities.

The types of securities that are traded over the counter include all securities not listed on an exchange, of course, but any security can be traded over the counter. There are significant differences between trading on an exchange (discussed in Chapter 8) and OTC trading.

Differences between OTC and exchange markets

The exchanges are auction markets, with transactions made on the exchange floors, subject to the rules of the exchanges and with prices determined by bidding. In the OTC market, price is reached through negotiation: someone who wishes to buy will make a bid; someone who wishes to sell will ask or offer a certain price. The difference between bid and asked price is called "the spread."

OTC transactions are governed by NASD rules. On the exchanges, there are "listing requirements" which a security must meet in order to be eligible for exchange trading. In contrast, in the OTC market there are no such requirements. These exchange requirements set certain minimums for capitalization, number of shares outstanding, and breadth of ownership. Thus, most unlisted securities tend to be smaller and newer than—though not necessarily inferior to—those traded on an exchange.

Types of issues traded OTC

In addition to unlisted securities, traders generally prefer the OTC market for closely-held issues, for high-value shares, and for instruments that tend to be traded in large blocks.

The following securities—listed and unlisted—are commonly traded over the counter: shares of bank and trust companies and insurance companies, U.S. government securities, municipal bonds, open-end investment company (mutual fund) shares, new issues, corporate bonds, foreign securities, and

ADRs. Overall, more issues of all types are traded over the counter than on the exchanges, although overall trading volume is greater on the exchanges.

THE MARKET MAKER

Some over-the-counter dealers "make a market" in certain securities. In some respects, the market maker is like a stock specialist (see page 189), but he acts as a dealer, not a broker.

In general, the market maker owns (has a position in) a particular security and sells to or buys from customers—individual investors, or other broker/dealers. Earnings come from a markup or markdown rather than from a commission. The market maker regularly publishes bid and offer quotes and stands ready to buy or sell securities at the quoted price.

BROKER OR DEALER

It is important to distinguish between an agent acting as broker and one acting as dealer:

A dealer sells securities to (or buys securities from) a customer from (or for) his own inventory. This is acting as a principal. The dealer earns money on the difference between the price he is willing to pay and the price he will sell at. This is called the *markup*.

A broker acts as an agent, bringing a buyer and seller together, or buying for a customer from a market maker and charging a fee, or commission, for this service. In OTC transactions, the price the customer pays, including the markup, is called the "net price."

One may not act as broker and dealer in one transaction—i.e., one cannot earn both a markup and a commission.

However, "dual agency" is possible. The broker can act as agent for both buyer and seller *and can earn commissions on both transactions.* This must, however, be disclosed when confirming the transaction.

CONFIRMATION

When a trade is completed, the broker/dealer must send the customer a written notice of confirmation. For trades between dealers, this confirmation must be sent by the end of the first business day after the trade date. For trades involving retail customers, confirmation must be sent by the date on which the transaction is completed (the settlement date).

The notice of confirmation must say whether the broker/dealer acted as a broker or a dealer. If as a broker, the confirmation must include the name of the other party to the transaction (or an offer to provide the name) and the amount of commission earned. If the firm acted as dealer, selling from its inventory, it need not disclose the amount of markup; however, if it buys the securities for immediate resale to the customer in what is known as a "riskless" trade, it must disclose the amount of markup.

TYPES OF QUOTES

In the OTC market, quotes can be "subject" or "firm."

"Subject quotes"

The quoted price is subject to confirmation. The quoting broker/dealer may or may not buy or sell at this price. Here are samples of subject quotes:

"It is quoted $15–15\frac{1}{2}$" (where 15 is bid, $15\frac{1}{2}$ offered).

"It is $15–15\frac{1}{2}$ subject."

A variation is the "workout" quote. This indicates a possible buying or selling price if the broker/dealer is given time to execute the order. Such a quote might occur when a broker/dealer has so many buy and sell orders for a particular security that he must "work out" his position before filling an order. The quote "15–17 workout" means that any trade will be executed in that range.

"Firm quote"

This is the actual buying or selling price for a security (sometimes called "actual quote"). Examples would be:

"It is $15–15\frac{1}{2}$."

"The market is $15–15\frac{1}{2}$."

A dealer giving a firm quote must be ready and able to buy or sell at the quoted price in a quantity equal to at least one usual trading unit—usually 100 shares of stock or five bonds.

"Bid or offer wanted"

When a broker/dealer wants to trade in a security, but is receiving no orders, he may make a "bid wanted" ("BW") quote. This shows no price, but requests bids from potential buyers. Conversely, an "offer wanted" ("OW") comes from a broker/dealer seeking possible sellers of a particular security. These are usually found in the "sheets" described on pages 172–173.

TYPES OF ORDERS

Because the OTC is a negotiated market, there are basically two types of orders allowed, market orders and limit orders.

The various kinds of stop orders are not allowed.

In a market order, the customer asserts that he is willing to pay (or receive) the best currently available price. In a limit order, he says that he will pay no more than (accept no less than) some specified amount, his limit. Either order may be for one day only or may remain open until it is filled or canceled.

Example

A client puts in an order to buy 100 ACI "at the market." If your firm makes a market in ACI and it is currently 20–21, you would sell them to the client at 21. If you did not make a market in that stock, you would call a market maker and buy from him. If you bought at 21, you would sell it to the client at 21 and would charge a commission of perhaps $.80 per share bringing the cost to $2,100 plus $80 in commission.

WHOLESALE AND RETAIL TRADING

A trade between brokers is a wholesale transaction. A trade between a firm and a client is called a retail transaction. A market maker or a broker/dealer who trades only with other dealers or with large institutions is called a wholesale trader. Dealers who sell to the public (often after buying from wholesalers) are said to operate in the retail market. In general, the spread between the bid and offer price is greater in the retail market.

THE NASDAQ SYSTEM

The channel for negotiating many over-the-counter prices is the NASD Automated Quotation Service, or NASDAQ. This electronic system links broker/dealers, market makers, and others through a network of computer terminals. It gives quotes by registered market makers on authorized securities, as well as some indications of trading volume. Note that NASDAQ is not an up-to-the-minute record of trades. It shows the volume of trading for each security at day's end, not trades or volume as they occur.

There are three levels of NASDAQ quotes. Level 1 is essentially for retail trade. It provides the highest bid and lowest offer (the inside price) currently available. Level 2 shows all market makers and their current bids and offers. Finally, Level 3 is used by market makers. It allows them to enter changes in their current quotations. Thus, an order room would see the quotes and the firms making them on its Level 2, but only a Level 3 system would enable one to make changes in a current quote. *All of these quotes are firm quotes.*

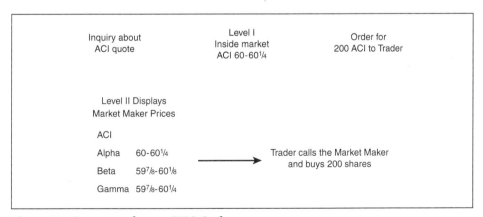

Figure 7.1 Sequence for an OTC Order

Requirements for NASDAQ listing

To be included in the NASDAQ system, securities must be registered under the Securities Act of 1934 or the Investment Company Act of 1940, have at least 100,000 publicly-held shares and at least 300 shareholders. In addition, to be listed:

- they must have a minimum bid price of $5

- the issuer must have capital and surplus of at least $1 million and assets of at least $2 million

- there must be at least two market makers for domestic issues, three for foreign issues

To qualify for participation in NASDAQ, a market maker:

- must remain open for business from 8:30A.M. to 4:30P.M. Eastern time

- must maintain a net capital position of at least $2,500 for each security in which he makes a market ($500 for securities priced at $5 or less)

- must execute a trade for at least the normal trading unit (100 shares of stock or 5 bonds) at the price shown on the screen when the order is received; in other words, the NASDAQ quote is a "firm quote"

- must report a trade within 90 seconds of execution

- must provide bid and ask quotations

- must report volume for his securities daily and monthly

OTHER SOURCES OF OTC INFORMATION

The National Market System, NMS
Introduced in 1982, the National Market System marked a significant improvement in providing information about the market. NMS provides up-to-the-minute reports of actual transactions and total volume, as well as the quote information available on NASDAQ. Over $\frac{3}{4}$ of the securities in NASDAQ are eligible for the NMS. The SEC encourages the inclusion of eligible issues, and the Federal Reserve allows stocks in the NMS to be bought on margin.

Small Order Execution System
A further improvement instituted in 1984, the Small Order Execution System (SOES) allows trades in NMS and NASDAQ stocks to be executed automatically at the inside price. Up to 1,000 shares for NMS stocks and up to 500 shares of NASDAQ stocks can be traded without contacting other brokers. Market and limit orders can be filled this way.

Computer-Aided Execution System
The Computer-Aided Execution System (CAES) allows automatic execution of both listed securities and NMS

stocks. There is some overlap with SOES, but CAES accepts listed (but not all NASDAQ) stocks and does not limit the size of the trade, while SOES accepts NASDAQ (but not listed) stocks and limits the size of the trade.

Consolidated Quote Service (CQS)   Provides quotes on common and preferred stocks, warrants, and rights traded on the exchanges and over the counter and for some stocks listed only on regional exchanges—"third market" trades. NASD members, identified as CQS market makers, can enter size and bid and asked quotes into CQS.

The National OTC-NASDAQ list or "national list"   Published daily in the *Wall Street Journal* and other financial pages, it includes issues with the highest trading volume (in dollar terms). Figures shown in these listings are the last dealer-to-dealer quotes for that day, not the public price (*i.e.,* they do not include commissions, markups or markdowns). These are "subject" quotes.

Additional list   950 additional issues that don't qualify for the national list.

Local lists   Several separate lists are published in specific areas and include items of interest in those localities. These can include both NASDAQ and non-NASDAQ securities.

Pink sheets   Published every business day, these sheets show the names and telephone numbers of market makers and the subject quote of each market maker. If there is no quote from a market maker, it will show a blank and will have OW (BW) if the market maker is looking for offers (bids). These are inter-dealer "subject" quotes and do not include commissions or markups. NASDAQ stocks have their symbols listed, and marginable stocks have an M preceding their listing.

Yellow sheets   These sheets cover OTC trading in unlisted corporate bonds and their market makers.

NASD MARKUP POLICY

NASD Rules of Fair Practice make reference to "fair" and "reasonable" prices and commissions. This has led to the "5% markup policy" for markups and markdowns in OTC trading. The basis for this markup is always the current offer to other dealers. Specifically, it is *not* the price that this dealer actually paid for the shares originally. That price is irrelevant. This is a guideline, not a firm rule; a greater (or lesser) percentage may be reasonable under certain conditions. Under the Rules, the following factors may be considered in deciding on the fairness of a markup (or commission):

Type of security   For example, the markup percentage is usually higher on common stock than on a bond and higher on a more speculative than on a less speculative issue.

Market activity Markups should be lower on an actively traded security. Unusual effort required to obtain an inactive security may justify a higher markup.

Price In general, the percentage markup goes down as the price of the security goes up, as handling costs involved in trading low-priced issues are proportionately higher.

Dollar value of transaction Handling expenses may be greater, in percentage terms, with a small transaction.

Disclosure Telling a customer that the markup is high (and explaining why) does not itself justify unfair charges, though such a practice would be considered if a dealer were to be accused of imposing an excessive markup.

Patterns While each transaction must be fair, the pattern of a broker's markups overall will be considered.

Services offered Some broker/dealers provide more, or more elaborate, services for their clients, and such costs may be considered, to some degree, in deciding on the fairness of the markup. Note that "excessive expenses" cannot be used to justify unreasonable markups.

The 5% guidelines apply on the following types of OTC transactions:

"Riskless" or "simultaneous" transactions These occur when a dealer has an order for a security and buys the same security to fill that order.

Sales from dealer's inventory The markup is calculated on the basis of the current market price. Profit (or loss) experienced because the dealer's inventory has appreciated (or depreciated) is not considered.

The same rules apply when making purchases of securities from customers—the markdown (amount deducted from the price dealers bid in interdealer transactions) must be reasonable. Also, when acting as an agent in a transaction, the broker/dealer must charge a fair commission.

"Designated securities" Low-priced stocks (so-called "penny stocks") are subject to special rules regarding solicited orders from new customers. The account must be approved for these trades after suitability has been carefully established. In addition, the first three such trades must also include a written agreement from the customer which describes the name and quantity of security to be purchased.

"Proceeds transactions" If a client sells securities to a dealer, and uses the proceeds of that sale to purchase other securities from the same dealer, this must be viewed as one transaction—*i.e.*, any profit or commission on the first part of the transaction must be considered in deciding on the fairness of the markup charged on the second part.

Note

The 5% is a guideline, and some of the factors mentioned above may justify some modification. Also note that in calculating markup or markdown, one begins with the current offering (or bid) price of the security among dealers, not the dealer's original cost.

This guideline does not apply to exempt securities. These include issues sold with a prospectus or at a specific public offering price, in other words, to new issues (or registered secondary issues) or to open-end investment company shares.

OTC MUNICIPAL BOND TRADING

As all municipal bonds are traded OTC, it will be helpful to review some of the material covered in Chapter 2.

The primary source for information on municipal bond trading is the *Blue List*, the daily publication that lists the securities each dealer has available for sale. It describes the bonds, the quantity available, and the price (usually expressed in terms of yield to maturity). In addition, the *Blue List* offers a computer service showing current yield, which is displayed on a terminal.

The *Daily Bond Buyer*, a newspaper for the bond market, includes articles and statistics about bonds. It also provides indices of average yields for different categories of bonds and has a wire service with up-to-the-minute information about bonds, syndicates, and winning bids.

Transactions between dealers are done on a concession basis. That is, they are sold at some given yield less a discount to the purchasing broker. For example, in a sale of 20 bonds at "$8\frac{1}{4}$ less $\frac{3}{8}$," the bonds are priced to yield $8\frac{1}{4}$%, and the buyer receives a concession of \$75 ($20 \times \$3.75$).

TERMS

Types of transactions:

Trading of listed securities on an exchange

Trading of unlisted securities over the counter (OTC) "secondary market"

Third market   Trading of listed securities OTC

Fourth market   Direct trades between institutions

OTC trading   Can involve any security; price reached through negotiation; transactions governed by NASD

Spread   Difference between bid and asked price

Market maker   Like exchange specialist but acts as dealer; must maintain certain holdings, honor NASDAQ quotes, etc.

Dealer   Acts as principal; sells or buys securities; earns a markup or markdown

Broker   Acts as agent; earns commission. One party may not act as broker and dealer in one transaction

Subject quotes   Price subject to confirmation

Workout quote   Possible price given time

Firm quote   Actual price to buy or sell at least one usual trading unit

Bid or offer wanted   Request for bids or offers from potential buyers or sellers

Market order   Customer will pay (or receive) best available price

Limit order   Customer will pay no more than (accept no less than) specified amount

Stop orders   Not allowed OTC

Time limits   Orders may be for one day only or good until filled or canceled

NASDAQ   NASD Automated Quotation Service; electronic link; gives firm quotes; volume only at day's end

National Market System, NMS   Gives last-sale prices and current volumes for some NASDAQ securities

Small Order Execution System (SOES)   For trades in NMS and NASDAQ stocks

Computer Aided Execution System (CAES)   For executing orders for both listed securities and NMS stocks

The National OTC-NASDAQ List ("National List")   Published daily in financial pages

Pink sheets   Show market makers and subject quotes from each

Yellow sheets   Cover OTC trading in unlisted corporate bonds

Markup policy   NASD Rules of Fair Practice call for "fair" and "reasonable" prices and commissions

5% markup policy   Maximum for markups and markdowns; guideline, not a rule; does not apply to new issues or mutual fund shares; based on current offer

REVIEW QUESTIONS

1. In an agency transaction, an over-the-counter dealer would consider all of the following in determining the commission EXCEPT:

   (A) dollar value of the transaction
   (B) actual costs of execution
   (C) liquidity of the market for that security
   (D) original price to the dealer for the security

2. Which of the following are traded over the counter?

   I. municipal bonds
   II. treasury bonds
   III. corporate bonds
   IV. common stocks

   (A) I and II
   (B) I and III
   (C) I, II, and III
   (D) I, II, III, and IV

3. Firm A acting for Firm B makes securities transactions not for Firm A's account. Firm A is said to be acting as a:

   (A) principal
   (B) broker
   (C) dealer
   (D) middleman

4. In an over-the-counter transaction, the "spread" refers to the:

   (A) markup from cost
   (B) difference between the current bid and asked
   (C) difference between purchase and sale prices
   (D) allowable charge on the transaction

5. All of the following are true of the over-the-counter market EXCEPT:

   (A) it is a negotiated market
   (B) it is a secondary market
   (C) it is an auction market
   (D) it handles large secondary distributions

6. On the NASDAQ System, all of the following would be shown EXCEPT:

   (A) market makers' change of quotes
   (B) transactions as they occur
   (C) report on daily volume
   (D) quoting requirements

7. An investor sells $50,000 of ACI and uses all of the proceeds to buy stock in CAI. A single firm acts as a dealer in both transactions. Which of the following is true?

   I. each markup is determined separately
   II. a "fair" markup must take both transactions together
   III. this is illegal
   IV. this is a "proceeds transaction"

   (A) I only
   (B) I and IV
   (C) II and IV
   (D) III only

8. On the NASDAQ, Level III provides which of the following?

   (A) firm quotes
   (B) level quotes
   (C) subject quotes
   (D) negotiated quotes

9. A purchaser of stock from a market maker in that stock can expect to pay:

   (A) no markup
   (B) a markup and a commission
   (C) a markup
   (D) a commission

10. Exchange-listed securities which are bought and sold over the counter are traded in the:

    (A) primary market
    (B) second market
    (C) third market
    (D) fourth market

11. If a dealer were said to have a position in a security he would:

    (A) own the security
    (B) have issued a position paper on this security
    (C) be recommending it
    (D) be in a position to acquire a large block of it

12. A market maker has purchased stock for his account at prices ranging from \$3 to \$10, with an average of \$8. If the stock is currently selling at 4 bid, $4\frac{1}{4}$ asked, NASD Rules of Fair Practice require him to base his offer on:

    (A) \$3
    (B) \$8
    (C) \$10
    (D) the current market price

13. For over-the-counter securities, the inside market is:

    (A) the highest bid available coupled with the lowest offer
    (B) the bid and offer of any market maker
    (C) the lowest bid available coupled with the highest offer
    (D) the narrowest bid and offer from some market maker

14. Which of the following would be considered a firm quote?

    I. "We can do ACI at $20-20\frac{3}{8}$"
    II. "ACI is $20-20\frac{3}{8}$"
    III. "The market in ACI is $20-20\frac{3}{8}$"

    IV. "ACI is quoted around $20-20\frac{3}{8}$"

    (A) I only
    (B) I and II only
    (C) III and IV
    (D) I, II, and III

15. In the over-the-counter market, stock prices are determined by:

    (A) negotiation between buyers and sellers
    (B) bidding among buyers
    (C) bidding among sellers
    (D) the 5% markup rule

16. A quote of "8.0 for one hour and five" means:

    (A) a firm offer of 8.50
    (B) a firm offer good for one hour and five minutes
    (C) a firm offer good for one hour
    (D) a firm offer of \$8.05

17. The SOES:

    I. handles only National Market System shares
    II. is an automated trading system
    III. handles trades of no more than 1,500 shares
    IV. is part of the Computer-Assisted Execution System (CAES)

    (A) I and II
    (B) II and IV
    (C) I, II, and III
    (D) II and III

18. Which of the following is governed by the NASD 5% policy?

    (A) exchange distributions
    (B) underwriting spreads on new issues
    (C) simultaneous or riskless transactions
    (D) secondary distributions

19. Level I of the NASDAQ has:

    (A) the most recent transaction for every security
    (B) the highest bid and the lowest offer for every security
    (C) the average bid and offers for each security
    (D) none of the above

20. A pension fund buys 10,000 shares of ACI from some other fund. We would call this a trade on the:

    (A) second market
    (B) third market
    (C) fourth market
    (D) over-the-counter market

ANSWERS TO REVIEW QUESTIONS

1. (**D**) As an agent, he charges a commission. The first three are relevant to this commission.

2. (**D**) All four are traded OTC, although some stocks and bonds are also traded on exchanges.

3. (**B**) Choices A and C are incorrect and D is not common usage.

4. (**B**) This spread is the quote that a customer would get.

5. (**C**) The exchanges are auction markets.

6. (**B**) There are no transactions reported on NASDAQ.

7. (**C**) It is not "fair" to charge for two transactions.

8. (**A**) These are always firm quotes, however, they can be changed at will.

9. (**C**) A commission would be charged by a broker, and it is illegal to charge both.

10. (**C**) This is the definition of the third market.

11. (**A**) None of the other choices describes having a position.

12. (**D**) The 5% rule applies to the current price.

13. (**A**) The quote which has the "inside track."

14. (**D**) Only IV is not a firm quote.

15. (**A**) It is a negotiated market.

16. (**C**) An offer good for one hour with a five minute warning that someone else wants to accept.

17. (**D**) It is an automated system that handles up to 1,000 shares of NMS and 500 shares of NASDAQ securities.

18. (**C**) None of the others comes under the 5% rule.

19. (**B**) This is called the inside price.

20. (**C**) The fourth market represents trades between investors.

exchange markets

An exchange market is a place where buyers and sellers come together to trade securities. The best-known and largest exchange is the NYSE, which handles well over half of all transactions. The AMEX, the Boston Stock Exchange, the Pacific Stock Exchange, the Midwest Stock Exchange, the Philadelphia Stock Exchange, and other exchanges have rules and procedures not unlike those of the NYSE. Therefore, our description of the NYSE will serve as a model for the others.

The NYSE is a large room dotted with booths known as "trading posts" staffed by "specialists" each of whom handles certain securities. All transactions in listed securities take place on the floor of that room.

The exchange is not itself involved in the market, though it acts to enforce certain rules to ensure fairness. A board of directors (the NYSE is a corporation) sets policy, decides which stocks are eligible for listing and who will be a member of the exchange, and approves specialists.

MEMBERSHIP

Membership is limited to 1,366 "seats" and is *open only to individuals.* Corporations or partnerships may not hold seats. Seats are sold by bid to any qualified person. The price varies according to demand and has ranged from under $50,000 to over $1,000,000. Brokerage firms can operate on the floor if a member of the firm (usually a partner or director) holds a seat; these are called member firms. Only a member of the exchange, or a person who has leased a seat from a member, can transact business on the floor. The board of directors (10 from the public, 10 exchange members and a full-time chairman who can vote only to break a tie) is chosen by a nominating committee of exchange members not on the board.

Categories of membership

Commission house brokers   Act for themselves or for non-members; execute customers' orders for their firms and charge a commission for their services.

Floor brokers or "two-dollar brokers"   Execute orders for other brokers when the latter are too busy to execute orders themselves. They usually charge a fee for each transaction (once $2, hence the name).

Registered trader or competitive trader   Usually execute orders for their own account; if they do agree to act for others, they must give those orders strict priority.

Specialist or market maker   This role is discussed in detail below. The specialist is always at his or her post, the booth where the security he or she specializes in is traded. A broker will come to that booth to trade that security. The specialist will not handle every transaction in the stocks in which he or she specializes (most trades are handled directly between members) but is responsible for all odd-lot trading (see page 192).

Bond members   Deal exclusively in bonds.

Allied members   Are allowed on the exchange floor, but not to trade. They include general partners, directors, and executives of member firms.

NYSE listing requirements

Only certain securities are traded on the NYSE, namely those listed there.

To be eligible for listing on the NYSE, stocks must meet minimum requirements as to market value, number of shares outstanding, number of shareholders, and corporate earnings. These requirements are periodically changed. Directors also consider whether there is national interest in the firm (a corporation with strength concentrated in one region might be held to higher standards) and the general condition and future prospects of the corporation. The listing agreement requires that the firm solicit proxies and provide timely disclosure of information important to investors.

Delisting

The NYSE generally disapproves of delisting a corporation which remains eligible. However, a firm that wishes to be delisted can do so if:

- holders of $\frac{2}{3}$ of the outstanding common stock vote to delist *and*

- holders of no more than 10% of outstanding shares object *and*

- a majority of the corporation's directors agree

A corporation can be involuntarily delisted if it fails to issue proxies or issues non-voting common stock.

OPERATION OF THE EXCHANGE

Trading on the exchange involves a "double auction." In the usual auction, one seller hears bids from many potential buyers. This, however, is a two-way affair: buyers shout bids while sellers shout offers. In all cases, the highest bid and lowest offer prevail. Although prices are quoted per share, the basic trading unit is 100 shares (a round lot).

Thus, a broker who bids "$29\frac{1}{2}$" is willing to buy 100 shares at $29.50 each. One who offers "$29\frac{3}{4}$" is willing to sell 100 shares at $29.75. A quote includes the current highest bid and lowest offer (*e.g.*, "$29\frac{1}{2}$ bid, $29\frac{3}{4}$ offered" or just "$29\frac{1}{2}$, $29\frac{3}{4}$"). The difference between bid and offer is called the spread.

A quote may also include the quantity being bid or offered ("quote and size"). For example, "$29\frac{1}{2}$, $29\frac{3}{4}$, 200 either way" would mean 200 shares are bid at $29\frac{1}{2}$, 200 offered at $29\frac{3}{4}$. The same price quote followed by "100 by 300" or "1 by 3" would mean 100 bid, 300 offered. When no size is mentioned, all trades are for one round lot.

Auction rules

The minimum bid from a buyer must be $\frac{1}{8}$ point higher than the last bid, from a seller $\frac{1}{8}$ point lower. A bidder cannot enter a lower bid in an attempt to confuse other bidders. All bids must be audible; no secret deals are allowed.

Once all offers or bids are removed by a trade or trades, a new auction begins. Since so many transactions in a particular security take place at one trading post, exchange rules determine the order in which bids (and offers) must be considered.

Priority   Since the highest price or best offer succeeds, the first to make a bid or offer at a given price is given priority. Only one individual can have priority, even if he is no longer at the trading post.

Precedence   If more than one broker makes the high bid at the same time, the largest order prevails. For example, Broker A enters the highest bid of 25 for 400 shares of PDS. Simultaneously, Broker B also bids 25, but for 700 shares. Broker C, who is offering 700 shares, must sell to B, as he can fill the order.

Parity   If two or more members offer the same price at the same time for the same quantity (*i.e.*, no one has priority or precedence) they must match (usually by tossing a coin) to see who gets the order. In other words, once the priority order is filled, others who have offered the best price are equal. If one can fill all orders, he wins the bid; if more than one can fill all orders, the first to bid wins. If no one is first, they match.

TYPES OF ORDERS

Investors can enter different kinds of orders which limit transactions in terms of price, time, or broker's discretion.

Market order

An order to move at the "best available price," *i.e.*, to buy or sell at the lowest offer or highest bid when the order is received. The customer knows the order will be executed, but not at what price.

Limit order

An order to buy or sell only at a specified price "or better," *i.e.*, a minimum selling price or a maximum buying price. If the limit is not reached, the order is not executed.

As a limit order is always entered above the current selling price (or below the current buying price), the broker will seldom be able to fill the order on the floor. So he usually leaves the order with a specialist to execute if and when the limit is reached.

The specialist enters such orders in his book (see page 190) in the order received. The most recent will not be executed until all those entered earlier are filled. A limit order can be partially filled; *e.g.*, on an order to sell 500 shares of ABC at $30; only 200 shares might be sold.

For a customer, the advantage of a limit order is that he knows what price he will receive (or pay) for a security. The disadvantage is that there is no assurance a transaction will take place: the limit may not be reached. Even if it is reached, other orders may have priority.

Stop order

This also sets a specified price, but automatically becomes a market order when that price is reached. Thus, if the stop price is reached, execution is guaranteed—but not the price, as the transaction is executed at the next available price.

For example, consider an order to buy 200 XYZ at 80 on a stop. If successive transactions were 79, $79\frac{1}{2}$, 80, the order would become a market order, and the specialist would take the next offer whether it was at 80 or above (or below).

Both buy and sell stop orders can be entered. They are usually executed by a specialist since the stop price is not (usually) at the market price, and a broker would be reluctant to wait at the booth until the order could be filled. Stop orders are used in two ways: to protect profits or limit losses and (by technical traders) to trigger orders at support levels (see Chapter 12).

Example

An investor is willing to risk $500 on the 100 shares of XYZ which he purchased at $55. By placing a sell stop order in at $50 he is assured that even if he is not following the stock carefully his loss will be limited to about $500 because if the price falls to $50, his sell stop becomes a market order and is automatically executed.

This same order could be used to protect a profit. If the customer in the previous example had actually bought XYZ at $25 and it was now trading at $55, he might still put in a sell stop at $50 guaranteeing himself most of his current profit. In a similar fashion, an investor could use a buy stop if he currently were short (see Chapter 11).

Stop-limit orders

A stop order that automatically becomes a limit order (not a market order) once the stop limit is reached. For example, "Sell 100 ABC at 50 stop $49\frac{1}{2}$ limit." Though this avoids the risk of a stop order (not being filled at 50), there is the possibility that the market may move in the wrong direction once the stop price is reached, and the order might not be executed.

Time qualifications on orders

Day Order   Good only until the close of trade that day and canceled if not executed by then. Orders are assumed to be day orders unless otherwise marked.

Good-Till-Canceled (GTC) or open order   Valid until it is executed (or canceled). Such orders are automatically canceled twice a year: at the end of April and the end of October, to clear the specialist's book. They can then be immediately renewed and retain their priority order position.

Shorter term orders, good for a week or good for a month, are handled by the broker, who places a GTC order with the specialist, then cancels it. *It is the broker's responsibility to cancel such an order, and a customer would not be liable for an order executed after his cancellation date.*

Not held order or market not held

This is a market order with the additional proviso that the floor broker is given some leeway in filling it. If he feels that it should not be filled immediately, he may wait to get a better price. The broker is, however, "not held" responsible if the order is not filled within a particular time or at a particular price. This type of order is often used with a large order where the broker may prefer to sell a little at a time.

Time qualifications on orders

At the opening   An order to buy or sell at the opening price. If it is not executed then, it is to be canceled.

At the close   To be executed at the close of trading with no guarantee that it will be done at the closing price.

Other qualifications on orders

Fill or kill   This must be completed entirely immediately in one trade or the order is canceled.

Immediate or cancel   Like Fill or Kill, but can be partially filled; the remainder is then canceled.

All or none   An order (for bonds only) that must be filled in its entirety or not at all. Unlike Fill or Kill it does not require immediate execution. The order can be either a market or a limit order.

Do Not Reduce (DNR) and Do Not Increase (DNI)   The price named should not be adjusted for ex-dates or for stock splits.

Automated order execution systems

Each exchange has an automated system to help speed the execution of relatively small orders. The NYSE has DOT (Designated Order Turnaround System) and Super DOT. Others, modeled on DOT, include PACE (Philadelphia Exchange Automated Communication and Execution System); MAX (Midwest Automated Exchange); SCOREX (Securities Communications Order Routing and Execution System, Pacific Stock Exchange); OSS (Order Support System) and RAES (Retail Automatic Execution System), both on CBOE; and AUTO PER and AUTO AMOS for equity and options transactions on the AMEX.

With DOT, an order form completed by a registered representative is sent from the firm's wire room directly to the DOT system. The system looks for an order to sell that matches the order to buy; if the system does not already contain such an order, the buy order is directed to a specialist, bypassing the floor broker.

Orders can be both market and limit orders. The volume on the automated systems continues to grow.

BLOCK TRADES

Because a large buy or sell order for a particular security can distort the market, the NYSE has developed special procedures for dealing with what are called block trades. With respect to these procedures, there is no fixed definition of a "block." The amount varies according to the typical volume of trading in a security, which can change from time to time.

The NYSE does record the number of trades involving 10,000 or more shares and calls them block trades, but these are not the only trades for which the special procedures can be invoked. If a broker decides the market cannot absorb a particular large trade in some security, he can get exchange permission to use one of the special methods described below.

Block trade procedures may require notification of the SEC and sometimes registration of the stock. In particular, notification is required if:

- the stock is not registered

- the stock was acquired through stock options

- the owner is an officer (or insider) of the firm

- the owner has more than 10% of the shares outstanding

The four basic methods are: special offer or bid, exchange distribution or acquisition, specialist block purchase or sale, and secondary distribution.

Special offer, special bid

This involves the sale (or purchase) of a large block. Special offer is an announcement on the tape offering a block with no commission to the buyer. Trading is executed on the floor and reported on the tape. Price shown is net to buyer plus a commission which is offered as an inducement to brokers. If the offering is oversold, each bidder receives a proportionate share (*e.g.*, if 90,000 are offered and bids for 100,000 shares are received, each bidder gets 90% of his bid).

Conversely, in a special bid, a firm will announce on the tape its intention to buy a large block at a price (and the commission it will pay). Unless otherwise announced, the offer (or bid) must remain open for at least 15 minutes.

Example

XYZ Pension Fund wants to sell 100,000 shares of Amalgamated Consolidated (ACI), currently at 23. After negotiations, your firm agrees to purchase the block at $21\frac{1}{2}$ in a private transaction. With exchange permission, you then print notice of a special offer on the tape:

Myfirm Special Offer ACI 100,000s.23 less 1.

This means your firm is willing to pay $1 for every share ordered. As orders are received, they are crossed ("crossing" occurs when a member holds buy and sell orders within the current market for an equal number of shares of the same stock) on the floor and appear on the tape in the usual manner until the order is complete.

While this procedure is supposed to protect the seller from having his block drive the price down, news of the offer will sometimes affect the market. In such cases, the special offer can be withdrawn.

Special bid procedures are just the opposite of those outlined above. In either case, the tape announces "deal is done" once the offer or bid is completed.

Exchange distribution (exchange acquisition)

The broker representing a client with a large sell (buy) order finds buyers (sellers) privately. When he has assembled enough orders to complete the transaction, and with the approval of the exchange, he crosses the block on the floor of the exchange.

Notice of the sale appears on the tape once the transaction is completed, but not before, with the symbol DIST. All brokerage costs are paid by the seller (buyer), allowing the broker to attract buyers (sellers) with a lower (higher) net price.

Example

Your client wants to sell 45,000 shares of ACI, now on the market at 25. After negotiation, your firm buys the stock for $24\frac{1}{2}$ in a private transaction. Your sales people then offer these shares at 25 net, *i.e.,* the customer pays no commission. When they have sold 45,000 shares, those orders are accumulated into one block and brought onto the exchange floor with the sell order from your firm's account, and the two blocks are crossed. The transaction must take place during market hours and involve only member firms.

Specialist block purchase or sale

This is basically a private sale, where the broker feels that activity in a particular security is so thin that selling (buying) a block would cause a sharp drop (rise), yet the quantity involved does not justify a special bid or offer, or exchange distribution or acquisition.

A specialist block transaction may also be necessary when speedy execution is important. In a purchase, a broker will ask the specialist if he is interested in the block. As the specialist can expect to have to hold the securities in inventory for a time, he usually offers a price below the market.

The transaction, which must be approved by a floor governor of the exchange, is completed privately off the floor and never appears on the tape. *It also does not appear on the specialist's book.* A specialist block sale involves the same procedure on the sell side.

Secondary distribution

For an extremely large block of shares, the methods outlined above may not be practicable, and the seller will turn to a secondary distribution. Some of these must be treated as new issues and require SEC registration, a cooling-off period, a prospectus, etc. (see Chapter 6). Others also resemble a new offering in that an underwriting syndicate is formed to buy the shares and sell them to the public, but with special permission, the shares are handled on the exchange.

A secondary distribution is announced on the tape, usually near the market close. The message will show the name of the head of the syndicate, the code for the stock, number of shares available, the price, and the commission offered.

The stock is offered at a net price, *i.e.*, with no commission. After the announcement, trading in these securities takes place off the floor. *Although the other types of special block sales can involve only exchange members, non-members can participate in a secondary distribution because the number of securities involved is usually very large.*

THE SPECIALIST

To work properly, an exchange market must continually offer the opportun-ity to buy and sell in an orderly fashion. Much of a specialist's work is directed to ensuring that such a market exists: he is ready to trade when no one else will, and he acts to stabilize the market in the issues in which he is a specialist. Often several specialists will combine in partnerships or joint accounts. Specialists are selected by the exchange board of directors.

Exchange rules say that the specialist is required to meet at least once a year with the officers of the corporation(s) in whose securities he specializes. However, neither the specialist nor his associates (including clerks) may serve as officers or directors of those corporation(s). They are also not permitted to participate in proxy contests in firms in whose stock they are specialists.

On the floor of the exchange, about 25% of the members are specialists. They act as both agents and dealers. As an agent, a specialist is in effect a broker's broker, filling orders for floor brokers. For this, he earns commissions from the floor broker's firm. As a dealer, the specialist buys or sells for his own account. When trading for his own account, he *must* buy only on a downtick and sell only on an uptick. In short, he trades against the market to help stabilize it.

He plays a further stabilizing role by stepping in to buy or sell when no one else will. Specialists typically form specialist units as partnerships or joint accounts. They are required to meet minimum capital requirements, as well as minimum requirements on maintaining positions in stocks for which they are specialists.

Trading rules for specialists

A specialist's trading practices are subject to specific restrictions. The specialist cannot accept orders from:

- officers, directors, or principal shareholders of a corporation in whose shares he is a specialist
- profit-sharing funds or pension funds
- a bank, trust company, insurance company, or investment company

In addition, the specialist:

- may not make a transaction for his own account that causes a stop order to be executed. Thus, if the last transaction is at $47\frac{1}{2}$ and he has a buy stop at 48, he may not offer stock at 48 himself. *In general, the specialist stops stock when he is acting as an agent. As a dealer he may not stop stock. Thus, he may never stop stock for his own account.*

- may not buy or sell for his own account while holding a market order not yet executed. (Though he may buy while holding a sell order and vice versa.)

- may not buy (or sell) at a limit order before a customer recorded in his book

- may not, acting for his own account, trigger a limit order on his book

- may not act as both broker and dealer in the same transaction

One final, and important, restriction on a specialist is that he may not "cross" orders without first offering the stock higher than his bid (*e.g.*, if a specialist has an order to buy 300 shares at 32 from one broker and an order to sell the same quantity at the same price from another broker, he must ask $32\frac{1}{8}$ or more (or bid $31\frac{7}{8}$ or less) in an attempt to get a better price before making a cross).

The specialist's book

To keep his transactions as an agent firmly separated from his transactions as a dealer, the specialist enters other broker's orders in his book. These are kept according to price and, within each price, in the sequence in which they were received. This book is closed to all but exchange or SEC officials.

The specialist accepts only limit and stop orders (no market or not held orders) on either a day or GTC basis. A day order reentered as a GTC order is treated as a newly entered order and is placed last in line.

Each page is headed by the symbol for the stock and usually covers only one point beginning with the point and ending at $\frac{7}{8}$. See Figure 8.1.

A specialist will always quote the highest bid and lowest offer currently in his book, *i.e.*, the price at which a market order to buy or sell can be immediately executed. Thus, with ACI, as shown in Figure 8.1, the quote would be "$20\frac{1}{4}$–$20\frac{1}{2}$," meaning he will execute a buy order at $20\frac{1}{4}$ or a sell order at $20\frac{1}{2}$.

The specialist may quote prices more favorable than those in his book. For example, floor brokers or other specialists trading in one of "his" stocks may make a higher bid (say $20\frac{3}{8}$ in our example), so the current quote becomes "$20\frac{3}{8}$–$20\frac{1}{2}$."

While he may not show his book, the specialist will, on request, announce the number of shares at the current quotation level *but not above or below these levels*. Thus, "300 by 400" or "3 by 4" indicates the 300 buy and 400 sell orders in ACI.

SPECIALIST'S BOOK

BUY	ACI	SELL
	20	
2 ML / 1 DW / 3 BACHE	$\frac{1}{8}$	
1 DW (STOP) / 2 SCHWAB	$\frac{1}{4}$	
	$\frac{3}{8}$	
	$\frac{1}{2}$	3 ML / 1 SCHWAB
	$\frac{5}{8}$	2 DW / I DREX / 2 ML
	$\frac{3}{4}$	
	$\frac{7}{8}$	

Figure 8.1 Page from Specialist's Book

It is not always possible for the specialist to execute limit orders, even though the limit price is reached. He may be holding earlier orders ("stock ahead"). In the illustration, the 300 to buy for Bache would not be filled even if 300 were sold, since Merrill would get 200 and DW 100 before that order could be filled; or he may lose a match.

Stopping stock

If—and only if—a broker asks, the specialist can agree to "stop" an order. This means he guarantees to execute a market order at the current price, while allowing the broker a (usually short) time to shop for a better price. The specialist must honor his guarantee, that is, must buy or sell at the stop price, even if he has failed to act on time. Under NYSE rules, a specialist:

- cannot stop stock for his own account, for another specialist in the same stock, or for another exchange member. *Stopping is for public orders only.*

- cannot stop stock unless the currently quoted spread is greater than the minimum (in other words, $\frac{1}{4}$ point or more)

- cannot reduce the size of an offer on his book once a stop is granted

- cannot guarantee the stop once another trade has been executed at the stop price (except to correct an error)

Again using Figure 8.1, the specialist could buy for his own account at $20\frac{3}{8}$ since any lower purchase would trigger the stop. In the same way, he could sell from his own account at $20\frac{3}{8}$.

"Arranging the opening"

Before trading begins for the day, the specialist reviews orders received since the previous close (often from foreign clients) and attempts to match them so the day's trading will begin in an orderly fashion.

If the volume of buy orders considerably exceeds the volume of sell orders (or vice versa), the price may move swiftly up (or down) at the opening. To prevent this, the specialist often supplies (buys) stock from (for) his own account. If this is not possible, and the security will open significantly up or down ($2 on stocks at $20 or more, $1 on stocks less than $20) from its previous closing price, he must get exchange approval to open at the new price, and the symbol OPD (opening delayed) appears on the tape.

If supply and demand are grossly unequal, the specialist may not begin trading until late in the day or not at all. In the most extreme situation, the specialist may ask the exchange governors to halt trading in the security.

Ex-sales and the specialist

Once a stock goes ex-dividend or ex-rights, it often drops in price. Thus, the specialist reduces the price in his book on certain orders entered below the current market. These are:

Open Buy Limit Orders   Open Sell Stop Orders

(Remember the initials OBLOSS.) These are orders in which the buyer (or seller) is interested in the "value" of the security.

Orders entered above the current market are not changed:

Open Sell Limit   Open Buy Stop

DNR (Do Not Reduce) orders are also not changed. Since dividends may not exactly equal a trading unit, the specialist rounds to the next lowest $\frac{1}{8}$, *e.g.*, a dividend of 55 cents would mean a reduction down $\frac{5}{8}$.

Example

If Consolidated Amalgamated Inc. (CAI) selling at $30\frac{1}{4}$ goes ex-dividend of $.70, the specialist (rounding up to $\frac{3}{4}$) would reduce a limit order to buy at 29 to the new price of $28\frac{1}{4}$ and a sell stop order at $29\frac{5}{8}$ would be lowered to $28\frac{7}{8}$. A buy stop at 34 and a limit sale at 32 would be unaffected. Similarly, any order marked DNR would be unchanged.

ODD-LOT TRADING

Orders to buy or sell less than a round lot (usually 100 shares) are also handled by the specialist. In these transactions, he acts as a principal. Only round-lot transactions appear on the tape. A specialist may buy several odd lots adding up to a round lot. If he then trades those shares, the transaction will appear on the tape.

Share price in an odd-lot purchase is based on the round-lot price, so an odd-lot order cannot be executed until a round-lot sale of that security has been recorded. This is called the "effective sale price." Most specialists charge a "differential fee" for handling odd-lots, usually $\frac{1}{8}$ point (12.5 cents) per share, buy or sell.

"Part round lot" is the term for an odd-lot order entered as part of a round lot, for example, 150 shares. The odd-lot portion is executed at the round-lot price.

"Bunched orders" If several customers (or one broker acting for several accounts) enter odd-lot buy or sell orders, they can be bunched into a round lot with customer approval. Dividing round lots into odd lots is not allowed.

Types of odd-lot orders

Odd-lot orders can be market, limit, or stop orders. A market order is executed at the next round-lot buy or sell price, plus the differential. Short sales in odd lots are subject to the plus tick and zero plus tick rules based on the next round-lot sale.

Example

A market order to buy 70 shares of CAI would be executed after the next round-lot transaction. If this occurred at $25\frac{1}{2}$ (the effective price), the order would be filled at $25\frac{5}{8}$ (the execution price). At the same time, a market order to sell 30 shares would be executed at $25\frac{3}{8}$.

Limit orders Are handled similarly to those for round-lots, but must consider the differential. A buy limit order, for instance, is based on the first round-lot sale below the odd-lot limit by at least $\frac{1}{8}$ point. Thus, a buy limit order for 70 shares at 28 would not be executed until the stock reached $27\frac{7}{8}$. Similarly, a sell limit of 50 shares at 28 would not be executed until the price reached $28\frac{1}{8}$. In both cases, the customer would then be assured of getting at least the price that he set.

Stop orders Odd-lot stop orders are also handled as with round lots and are allowed on both the NYSE and the American Exchange. Thus, an odd-lot stop is triggered by the first round-lot sale at or above the stop price on a buy order (at or below on a sell order) and is executed on the next round-lot sale, whatever the price. The differential is not considered.

Example

With the market at 31 for ACI, an order to buy 40 shares at $31\frac{1}{2}$ on a stop is received. Subsequent round-lot trades occur at $31\frac{3}{8}$, $31\frac{1}{2}$ and $31\frac{3}{4}$. The client's order would be triggered by the $31\frac{1}{2}$ and become a market order. The *next* sale at $31\frac{3}{4}$ would be the effective price, and the customer would pay $31\frac{7}{8}$.

A sell stop would work in the opposite direction.

BOND TRADING

Most corporations that list their stocks on the exchange also list their bonds. However, trading on the exchange is relatively light as most bonds are traded in over-the-counter markets. Bond brokers typically act as broker's brokers for a "give-up commission" since the volume of trading does not warrant individual firms' maintaining their own operations. The exchange bond room includes the "free" or "active" crowd and the "cabinet" crowd.

Types of trading

Active trading
Involves verbal bids and offers on an "all or none" basis for lots of at least 50 bonds (the usual trading block). A typical transaction would be "Bid 104 for 50 ACI; Offer 50 ACI at $104\frac{1}{2}$. Take them." Notice the bid begins with price, then volume, and finally name, whereas the offer has volume, then name, then price. This is the standard procedure for trades in the active crowd. Only GTC and day orders are handled; market, limit, and stop orders may be used.

"Cabinet" trading
Literally involves filing bids and offers in a cabinet. Orders can be day orders or good for a week or month or GTC. Stop orders are not accepted.

A broker who wishes to buy and who finds a filed offer card at an acceptable price takes it to the ring and makes a verbal bid at that price. If no better offer is available, the filed offer consummates the trade. An offer on file can be canceled only by physically removing the offer card.

Pricing

Bond trading has the same auction rules as do stocks. New bids must be better than existing bids (by at least $\frac{1}{8}$) to get priority, and lower bids are not allowed. Similarly, offers must be lower to get priority.

The "nine bond rule"

To encourage trading on the exchange, especially by small traders, the NYSE has promulgated a "nine bond rule." This holds that any order for nine bonds or less must be shown on the floor before being traded over the counter. If there is no sale in a reasonable time (one hour), the broker may go outside the exchange. This rule does not apply to:

- federal, state, or municipal securities
- bonds with a call or redemption date within 12 months

- bonds for which the customer orders no trading on the floor

- lots of 10 or more

Bond quotations

In bond quotes, the letter "M" is used to indicate $1,000. Thus, an order for 4M is an order for four bonds with a face value of $1,000 each.

READING THE TAPE

News of stock transactions is carried on the "consolidated tape," which shows information about volume and price seconds after a transaction occurs. The selling broker sends this information. The tape has two channels or "networks."

Network "A" covers trades in all stocks, warrants, rights, etc. listed on the NYSE, whether executed on the NYSE or on regional exchanges and in the third and fourth markets. The "B" Network shows AMEX trades and transactions on regional exchanges for stocks that meet the listing requirements of the NYSE or AMEX. Additionally, the Consolidated Quotation Service provides quotes on exchange-listed securities that are traded OTC. Quotes can be entered on the consolidated tape only by NASD members. Those members identified as designated reporting members *must* report trades to the service within 90 seconds.

Tape symbols

The "ticker symbol" (abbreviation) for a particular stock appears on the top line; the number of shares sold and the price are shown immediately below. If the trade involves 100 shares, only the price appears.

Trades in multiples of 100 are shown with a single digit followed by an "s." Thus 3s is 300 shares, 7s is 700 and so on. The "s" is always placed between the volume and the price: "6s33" means 600 shares at $33. If the transaction being reported involves more than 10,000 shares, the entire amount appears on the tape: 11,000s35 means 11,000 shares traded at $35.

If more than one transaction is being reported, a period is used to separate them. Thus $24.7s23\frac{1}{2}$ means 100 shares at 24, 700 shares at $23\frac{1}{2}$. A series of trades at the same price is reported in a string: 3s 5s 2s25 indicates separate trades, in sequence, of 300, 500, and 200 shares at 25.

Reporting of errors

When they occur, errors are corrected on the tape. (Note that a quote to a customer based on a tape error does not hold; the customer must pay the correct price.)

Late reports   Although all trades are supposed to appear on the tape as soon as possible, a trade will sometimes appear out of order. These late trades carry the symbol "SLD." Thus: SLD T/ 2s.90 means that 200 shares of Telephone were traded at $90 sometime earlier. It is not possible to tell how much earlier.

Abbreviated quotes

When volume is particularly heavy, the quotation may be "abbreviated" by removing the first digit of the price. Thus for a stock where the last trade was 33, the tape might show $4s3\frac{1}{2}$, indicating 400 shares at $33\frac{1}{2}$, etc. The full figure would reappear if the shares went up or down through the next ten-point level, *i.e.*, to 40 or 20.

Inactive or rarely traded stocks

If listed on the NYSE, normally trade in round lots of 10 shares. There is no trading booth for inactive stocks, rather orders are filed in a cabinet as with inactive bonds. When these are traded, the number of shares sold appears on the tape with the symbol [ss]. Thus, 4 [ss]35 means 40 shares traded at 35. This is not an odd-lot trade.

Preferred stocks

The symbol Pr identifies preferred stocks. Thus, T Pr/75 indicates 100 shares of Telephone preferred traded at $75 per share.

When-issued shares

If new shares of an already-traded stock are being issued because of a stock split, these are shown on the tape as W/I, for "when issued." For example, if PDS stock is trading at 70 and the corporation offers a two-for-one stock split, the when-issued stock will trade at 35. A sale of 700 new shares after the split would show on the tape as PDS 7s35 W/I.

Rights

Trades in rights are signified with the symbol RTS. These values (rights customarily trade for less than $1) are expressed in fractions: those below 50 cents trade in 32nds; those at 50 cents to $1 trade in 16ths.

Thus, XYZ.RTS /900s 12/16 means 900 shares of XYZ rights traded at 12/16.

Bankruptcy

Companies in bankruptcy that continue to trade are identified with the letter Q. So PDS Q/ 5s.3 means the bankrupt PDS company traded 500 shares at $3.

Other tape messages

From time to time, the tape will carry messages not strictly related to a particular transaction, for example, to report "TRADING HALTED" or "OPENING DELAYED" (or the code OPD) for a particular security.

Finally, as noted above, certain block trades (special offers and special bids, exchange distributions and exchange acquisitions) appear on the tape with the codes SP OFF, SP BID, DIST and ACQ.

TERMS

NYSE membership 1,366 seats

Types of members

Commission house brokers Act for themselves or for non-members

Floor brokers Execute orders for other brokers, usually for a fee

Registered trader Usually acts for own account; if acting for others, must give their orders priority

Specialist or market maker

Bond members

Allied members

Exchange Practices

Listing requirements   To be listed, stock must meet certain financial and other tests

Trading on exchange   Double auction—highest bid and lowest offer prevail

Basic trading unit   100 shares (a round lot)

Spread   Difference between bid and offer

Quote and size   Includes quantity being bid or offered

Auction rules   Minimum bid difference $\frac{1}{8}$ point

Order in which bids (and offers) must be considered

Priority   First to make a bid or offer at given price

Precedence   If more than one broker enters high bid at same time, largest order prevails

Parity   If no one has priority or precedence, they must match for the order

Types of orders

Market order   Order to move at "best available price"

Limit order   Order to act only at a specified price "or better"

Stop order   Sets a specified price, automatically becomes a market order when that price is reached

Stop-limit order   Stop order that automatically becomes limit order once stop limit is reached

Day order   Good only until close of trade that day

Good-Till-Canceled (GTC) or open order   Valid until executed (or canceled)

Shorter term order   Broker places GTC order, takes responsibility for canceling

Not held order (or market not held)   Market order that broker can wait to execute

Fill or kill   Completed entirely in one trade or canceled

Immediate or cancel   Like Fill or Kill, but can be partially filled

All or none   Order for bonds that must be filled entirely or not at all

At the opening (or at the close)   To be executed as near as possible to opening (or closing) price

Do Not Reduce (DNR) and Do Not Increase (DNI)   Named price not adjusted for ex-dates or splits

Automated order execution systems   DOT (NYSE), PACE (Philadelphia), MAX (Midwest), AUTO PER, AUTO AMOS (AMEX)

Block trades special procedures

Special offer, special bid   Announced on tape; trade on floor reported on tape

Exchange distribution (exchange acquisition)   Broker finds buyers (sellers) privately; stock crossed on floor; notice of sale appears on tape

Specialist block purchase or sale   Private sale off floor; never appears on tape

Secondary distribution   For extremely large blocks, announced on tape, trade off floor

Specialist

Works to ensure an orderly market; acts as both agent and dealer; as dealer must trade against the market in accord with strict trading rules. For other broker's orders; only limit and stop orders, day, or GTC; always quotes highest bid and lowest offer in book

Stopping stock   Specialist can agree to stop an order, guaranteeing execution at current price, while broker seeks better price; stopping for public orders only

Arranging the opening   Specialist attempts to match orders received since the previous close so day's trading will begin in orderly fashion; must get exchange approval to open at price significantly up or down; in extreme situation, may ask to halt trading in the security

Ex-sales   When a stock goes ex-dividend or ex-rights, specialist must reduce price in book on Open Buy Limit orders, Open Sell Stop orders (OBLOSS)

Odd-lot share price   Based on recorded round-lot price

Part round lot   Odd-lot order entered as part of a round lot

Bunched orders   Several customers' odd-lot orders can be bunched into a round lot with customer approval

Odd-lot order   Can be market, limit, or stop orders based on applicable round-lot sale

Bonds

Active trading   Verbal bids and offers, "all or none" basis, minimum lot 50 bonds; only GTC and day orders; market, limit, and stop orders allowed

Cabinet trading   Bids and offers filed; day, week, month, GTC orders allowed; no stop orders

Nine-bond rule   Generally, any order for nine bonds or less must be shown on the floor before being traded over-the-counter

Pricing   Bond auction rules like stocks

Bond quotations   "M" indicates $1,000 value

REVIEW QUESTIONS

1. An investor enters an order valid for six weeks. Who bears responsibility for canceling the order at the end of the six-week period?

   (A) the investor
   (B) the registered representative
   (C) the specialist
   (D) the member firm

2. An investor enters an order to buy 100 ACI at 55, GTC. ACI is currently selling at 60 and goes ex-dividend $1 before the order is filled. The specialist's book will contain an open order to:

   (A) buy 100 at 60
   (B) buy 100 at 59
   (C) buy 100 at $58\frac{7}{8}$
   (D) buy 100 at 54

3. The quote "40 to $40\frac{1}{2}$ 300 either way" on the NYSE signifies:

   (A) the broker will sell 300 shares at 40 or better
   (B) quote and size
   (C) the broker will buy 300 shares at $40\frac{1}{2}$ or better
   (D) all of the above

4. All of the following are acceptable on the AMEX EXCEPT:

   (A) stop-limit orders
   (B) round-lot limit orders

   (C) odd-lot orders
   (D) all are acceptable

5. A group of brokerage firms organizes to sell a large block of stock off the floor. This is called a(n):

   (A) secondary distribution
   (B) special offer
   (C) exchange distribution
   (D) special bid

6. An order to be filled immediately is most likely to be:

   (A) a market order
   (B) a stop order
   (C) a fill or kill order
   (D) a limit order

7. All of the following are reported on the Consolidated Tape EXCEPT:

   (A) options trades
   (B) preferred stock trades
   (C) exchange distributions
   (D) third market trades

8. All of the following would be accepted by a specialist EXCEPT:

   (A) GTC orders
   (B) day orders
   (C) not held orders
   (D) limit orders

9. What does the symbol OPD on the NYSE tape mean?

   (A) the daily opening
   (B) opening delayed
   (C) delete the trade in OP
   (D) none of the above

10. The number of members of the NYSE is:

    (A) 500
    (B) 1,066
    (C) 1,366
    (D) 2,001

11. A buy order which converts to a market order after a transaction at or above a specified price is called a:

    (A) market order
    (B) buy stop
    (C) buy limit
    (D) buy stop-limit

12. None of the following can take place on the NYSE floor without prior announcement EXCEPT:

    (A) special bid
    (B) exchange distribution
    (C) secondary distribution
    (D) special offer

13. The following symbols appeared on the tape: ACI 25s 45. One would read this as saying:

    (A) 2,500 shares of ACI were sold at 45
    (B) 250 shares of ACI were sold at 45
    (C) 2,500 shares of ACI were sold short at 45
    (D) 25 shares of ACI were sold at 45

14. A specialist can stop stock for himself if:
    (A) he gets approval from an exchange officer

    (B) he gets approval from an exchange governor
    (C) he chooses to
    (D) under no circumstances

15. A stock closes today at $45\frac{1}{2}$. The stock will trade ex-dividend tomorrow morning. The most recent dividend was $1.40. If the stock were to open unchanged, it would open at:

    (A) 44
    (B) $44\frac{1}{8}$
    (C) $44\frac{1}{4}$
    (D) 45

16. An order for corporate bonds is marked "3M92." What is the dollar amount which the customer proposed for these bonds?

    (A) $276
    (B) $2,760
    (C) $3,000
    (D) $30,000

17. The "nine-bond" rule on the NYSE requires that orders for listed bonds be presented for execution on the floor of the exchange EXCEPT when:

    (A) the order is for less than ten bonds
    (B) the bonds are revenue bonds
    (C) the bonds are debentures
    (D) the bonds have been called

18. A sell stop could be used in any of the following situations EXCEPT:

    (A) to safeguard a profit on a long position
    (B) to limit a loss on a long position
    (C) to limit a loss on a short position
    (D) to establish a new position

19. An investor sells 100 shares of CAI at 45. That afternoon his broker informs him that the sale was at $44\frac{3}{4}$. The investor:

    (A) can demand a sale at 45
    (B) must accept the sale at $44\frac{3}{4}$
    (C) can cancel the order
    (D) has grounds for a grievance

20. A broker receives an order to buy 1,000 ACI at 40 "fill or kill." The following trades appear on the tape: ACI 5s40 3s41 6s40. How many shares will the customer get?

    (A) 500 shares
    (B) 600 shares
    (C) 1,000 shares
    (D) no shares

21. Which of the following can own a seat on the NYSE?

    I. Mr. Smith
    II. Smith & Jones Partners
    III. Smith & Jones Inc.
    IV. Jones and Jones Brokers

    (A) I only
    (B) I and II only
    (C) I, II, and III
    (D) I, II, III, and IV

22. The DOT system:

    (A) is an automated order system
    (B) is an AMEX system
    (C) is used by floor brokers
    (D) never goes through the specialist

23. If ACI is currently selling at 45 and an investor enters an order to buy 200 shares at 48 stop and will not pay more than 49, what kind of order has he entered?

    (A) a buy stop order
    (B) a market "not held" order
    (C) a buy limit order
    (D) a buy stop-limit order

24. Two of the functions of this individual are to maintain an orderly market and to act as a broker for other brokers. He is a(n):

    (A) principal
    (B) floor trader
    (C) specialist
    (D) odd-lot broker

25. To be listed on the NYSE, a firm is required to have all of the following EXCEPT:

    (A) pre-tax earnings of $2.5 million in the previous year
    (B) at least 2,000 round-lot owners
    (C) one million shares outstanding
    (D) net worth of $5 million

26. An investor buys 300 shares of CAI at $90. After a 3 for 1 split and no other changes, he will own:

    (A) 300 shares at $30
    (B) 900 shares at $30
    (C) 300 shares at $90
    (D) 900 shares at $90

Questions 27–28 are based on the following stretch of ticker:
CAI. SLD 45 ACI Pr 45s 102 ACI 2s 55

27. The CAI trade shows

    (A) 100 shares of CAI were sold
    (B) 100 shares of CAI were sold short
    (C) 100 shares of CAI were sold and reported out of sequence
    (D) 100 shares of CAI were part of a secondary distribution

28. The trade in ACI preferred shows:

    (A) 45 shares of ACI preferred sold at 102
    (B) 450 shares of ACI preferred sold at 102
    (C) 4,500 shares of ACI preferred sold at 102
    (D) 450 shares of ACI preferred sold short at 102

Questions 29–30 are based on the following excerpt from a specialist's book:

AMALGAMATED CONSOLIDATED INCORPORATED

BUY		SELL
200 Bache	55	
100 Reynolds	$\frac{1}{8}$	
100 Shearson	$\frac{1}{4}$	
	$\frac{3}{8}$	
	$\frac{1}{2}$	200 Merrill
	$\frac{5}{8}$	100 Kidder
	$\frac{3}{4}$	300 Schwab
	$\frac{7}{8}$	

29. What is the size of the quote?

    (A) 400 by 600
    (B) 200 by 100
    (C) 200 by 300
    (D) 100 by 200

30. For his own account, the specialist may bid as low as:

    (A) 55
    (B) $55\frac{1}{4}$
    (C) $55\frac{3}{8}$
    (D) $55\frac{1}{2}$

ANSWERS TO REVIEW QUESTIONS

1. (**B**) The registered rep would cancel any order longer than a day order.

2. (**D**) Remember open buy limit and open sell stop (OBLOSS) orders are reduced.

3. (**B**) This quote gives both the "bid and asked" and the size on each side.

4. (**D**) Only stop limit orders for odd lots are not permitted on the AMEX.

5. (**A**) All of the others take place on the floor of the exchange.

6. (**A**) Choices B and D are not immediate, and C may not be filled.

7. (**A**) The others are all carried for listed stocks.

8. (**C**) These can be accepted by a broker who would use his discretion as to when it is filled.

9. (**B**) By definition.

10. (**C**) This number is fixed and membership is limited to individuals.

11. (**B**) If there is also a maximum price which may be paid, it is a buy stop limit.

12. (**B**) Choices A and D require prior announcement, and C is done off the floor.

13. (**A**) The symbol "s" following a number means that number of round lots.

14. (**D**) He may only stop stock for public orders.

15. (**B**) The adjusted price of 44.10 would be rounded to the next highest eighth.

16. (**B**) This means three $1,000 bonds selling at $920 each.

17. (**D**) The rule does not apply to bonds callable within one year.

18. (**C**) A short position has already sold and hence could not use a sell stop.

19. (**B**) He must accept it unless his was a limit order.

20. (**D**) Since he couldn't fill the order in one transaction, it is killed.

21. (**A**) Seats may only be purchased by individuals.

22. (**A**) The DOT system is an automated system that bypasses floor brokers. If it cannot match orders, it sends them through the specialists.

23. (**D**) There is a triggering stop and a limit on the price.

24. (**C**) These are the main functions of the specialist who must also keep a book on orders to be filled.

25. (**D**) This is not required, but it is necessary that the market value of outstanding shares be at least 16 million dollars.

26. (**B**) With no other changes, the value must remain the same, and hence, if the number of shares tripled, the value of each share must be cut into a third of its original value.

27. (**C**) The symbol SLD means trade reported out of sequence.

28. (**C**) The Pr means preferred and the s is the number of round lots.

29. (**D**) The size is the amount of the highest bid and the lowest offer.

30. (**C**) For his account, he must bid higher than any of the bids of his customers

CHAPTER NINE
options

An option is the right to buy something at a specified price and within a given time; the buyer pays for this *right*. For example, a film producer takes an option on a book, or a real estate agent takes an option on a house. These payments don't provide title to the book or the house, but rather give the holder the option to acquire title. With securities, options involve the right to buy (call) or sell (put) securities (usually 100 shares of a stock) at a set price and until a specified future date.

The holder, or buyer, of the contract pays the writer (or seller) a fee, called a "premium." The holder need not exercise the right to buy or sell, but has the "option" to do so. If the holder does "call," the writer must sell the called securities at the specified price. If the holder "puts," the writer must buy the securities at the specified price.

Trading in options

Options contracts are negotiable. They are traded both over the counter and through exchanges; the latter are called "listed options." OTC trading in options, as with other securities, takes place in a negotiated, rather than an auction, market. But trading is not continuous, as there is no active secondary market. This is particularly crucial since options have a limited life.

In the OTC market, one can have an option in any security for which someone is willing to write an option. These differ from listed options in important ways: there is no need to meet any regulatory requirement, no mechanism for getting continuous price information, and no limit on the number or amount of options an individual may hold; in addition, settlements are on the same day, expirations are not uniform, and exercise prices are not standardized. For all of these reasons, the OTC market is very small, and the remainder of this chapter concerns only listed options.

The Options Clearing Corporation

In 1973, the need for a really liquid market, standardized terms, and a centralized marketplace led to the establishment of the Options Clearing Corporation. Working with several national exchanges, the OCC sets option terms, provides forms for traders, ensures a continuous market for securities (just as the NYSE provides for common stocks listed there), and supplies daily quotations to the financial press. The OCC acts as principal in every options transaction for listed options contracts. It is owned by the five exchanges where options are currently traded. These are the American, Pacific, Philadelphia and New York Stock Exchanges and the Chicago Board Options Exchange.

As principal, it issues all listed options, guarantees the contracts, and is the legal entity on the other side of every transaction. In effect, the OCC makes it possible for buyers and sellers to act independently.

FORMS OF OPTIONS

Options contracts are traded in two forms: the contract to buy is classified as a "call option"; the contract to sell as a "put option."

Call options

The holder of the call has the right to buy *at a specified price* (to call) securities from the person who writes the contract. The writer in turn has the obligation to sell if the holder calls. The right and obligation have a finite lifetime, after which they simultaneously expire.

Thus, the call holder has the *right* to call from the writer; the call writer has the *obligation* to sell if the option is called (or exercised.) The call buyer pays a fee (the premium) for this right.

Put options

With a put, the holder has a right to sell (to put) securities to the writer at a specified price. The writer is obliged to buy if the holder exercises his option.

The put holder has the *right* to sell to the writer; the writer has the *obligation* to buy if the option is exercised. As with the call option, the right and obligation have a finite lifetime.

Note

The holder or buyer of the contract is said to be "long" the option. The terms "long a call" or "long a put" are sometimes used to describe this position. Conversely, the writer or seller is "short" the option. Here, the terms "short a call" or "short a put" are used.

TERMINOLOGY

The following terms are used in describing options trading.

Exercise price or strike price

This is the price fixed in the options contract at which the option can be exercised; *i.e.*, the price at which the call holder can buy or the put holder can sell. With listed options, choices for this price are set by the OCC, usually at $2.50 intervals for stocks trading at less than $25 a share; $5 intervals for issues between $25–$200; and $10 intervals for those over $200. On the over-the-counter market, the exercise price is usually set at the current market value per share of the underlying stock.

Expiration date

The month in which the contract expires is the expiration date. These are set by the OCC for all listed options. In that month, all listed options expire on the Saturday following the third Friday of the month at 11:59 P.M. Eastern Time.

OTC options usually are for terms of 90 days or 6 months plus 10 days, but can be for as little as 35 days.

Type

The two basic types of options are calls and puts.

Class

All options of one type for a given stock are a "class" of option. For example, all IBM calls or all IBM puts are termed a class, whatever the price or expiration date.

Series

Series are options that are identical in class, expiration date, and execution price; *e.g.* all IBM Aug 60 Puts.

Premium

A premium is the fee charged by the writer whether or not the option is exercised. It varies with the price of the underlying stock and other factors. (See page 210.)

Example

With these definitions in mind, we can read the following quote: "3 PSM Nov 60 C at 2"

3—the number of contracts for 100 shares of the underlying stock,

PSM—abbreviated name of the underlying security,

Nov—expiration month,

60—execution price or strike price,

C—type of option (call or put),

2—premium (these trade in fractions as small as $\frac{1}{16}$, though most examples here use whole numbers).

Thus, 3 PSM Nov 60 C at 2 describes an option giving the buyer the right to buy 300 shares (3 × 100) of PSM for $60 per share until some time in November for a premium of $600 ($2 per share × 3 × 100 shares). Note that the standard contract is for 100 shares of stock.

BASIC OPTIONS POSSIBILITIES

Every options contract involves one of two present actions (buying or writing) *and* one of two potential actions (calling or putting). Let us look first at the four basic possibilities (for simplicity, we will generally ignore premiums in this section).

Call holder (or buyer)

The call holder has the option to buy at a particular price. He hopes the market price of the underlying stock will rise. If it does, he will exercise his option to buy the stock at the strike price and then profit by reselling it at the higher market price.

Example

Mrs. A buys a PSM Nov 70 Call at 6 when the market price of the underlying stock is 70. PSM rises on the market to 80. She calls 100 shares at 70, sells them in the market at 80, and makes a profit of $400, $1,000 less the $600 she paid as a premium. If the stock falls below 70, Mrs. A simply lets the option expire, since to exercise would mean buying at 70 a stock that she can buy in the market for less than 70.

Call writer (or seller)

The call writer sells the option to buy. He hopes the price of the underlying stock will not go up. If it doesn't, the call holder will let the option expire, and the writer will profit by the amount of the premium collected at the time the option was written. If the security's market price rises, however, the option will be exercised, and the call writer must provide the stock at the agreed price taking whatever loss this involves.

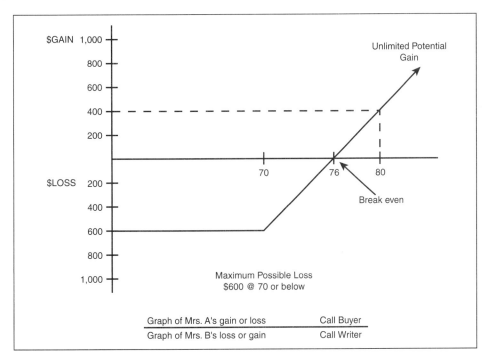

Figure 9.1 Buying a Call

Example

Assume Mr. B. wrote the PSM Nov 70 Call option that Mrs. A (in the example above) bought. When the stock rose to 80, Mrs. A exercised at 70 so Mr. B. must buy at 80 (or provide from his portfolio) and sell at 70. Mr. B will lose $1,000, again minus the $600 premium which he collected originally.

Put holder

The put holder purchases the right to sell at a specified price. He hopes the market price of the underlying stock will fall. He will then exercise his option to sell to the writer at the (now higher) strike price, buy in the market at a lower price, and realize a profit on the difference.

Example

Mrs. A. buys PSM Nov 70 Put at 4 when the market price of PSM is $70. The price drops to $63. She can exercise the option, sell at $70 a share securities which she can buy at $63, and realize a gain of $7 a share or $700 for the contract (less the $400 premium). If the market value of the stock rises, she will let the option expire, since exercising it would create a loss.

Put writer

The put writer has sold the right to sell; *i.e.*, he has assumed the obligation to buy from the put holder at the exercise price. Thus, the put writer hopes the market value of the underlying stock will not fall. Then the put holder will not exercise the option, and the writer will profit by the amount of the premium.

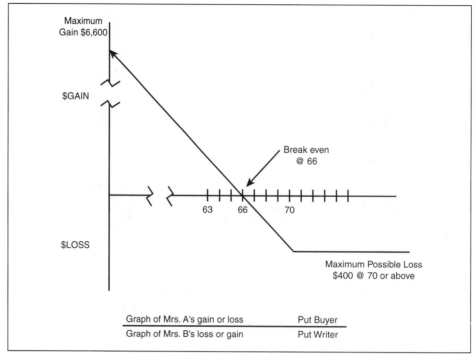

Figure 9.2 Buying a Put

Example

Mr. B writes PSM Nov 70 Put when the market price of PSM is $70. The stock drops to 63. He must now buy from Mrs. A at $70 per share PSM which has a value of only $63 in the market, a loss of $7 per share, or $700 minus the $400 previously collected premium.

Note

In general, if an option is exercised, the holder's gain from exercising is offset by the writer's loss. If the writer already owns the stock or, in the case of a Put, is short the stock, the loss is an opportunity loss, *i.e.*, loss of the opportunity to sell at the (better) market price since the writer must sell (or buy back the short) at the exercise price.

In summary, the put holder has the right to sell at a specified price and hopes the market price falls; the put writer must buy if the option is exercised so hopes the price doesn't fall.

PREMIUMS

While bidding determines the actual price of an option, it is customary to distinguish two components of the value of an option.

Intrinsic value

This is the value reflected in a call option with an exercise price below the current price of the underlying stock or a put option with an exercise above the current value of its underlying stock. It is the amount of money the owner of the option can make by exercising the option at the moment and immediately reversing that transaction in the stock market. For this reason, such an option is called "in the money."

For example, a call option with a strike price of $40 on a stock selling at $50 has an intrinsic value of $10, since one could exercise the option getting the stock for $40 and then selling it at once for $50. Call options with a strike price above market price are called "out of the money," and those whose strike prices exactly equal market prices are called "at the money."

For put options, in and out of the money are reversed. A put with a strike price of $40 on a stock selling at $50 is out of the money, and one with a strike price above market price (*e.g.*, market price at $30) is "in the money." *However, even out of the money options are worth something.*

Time value

In general, we ascribe all value not explicitly intrinsic to time value. For in the money options, this value is the difference between premium price and intrinsic value. For out of the money options, all value is time value. The actual length of time until expiration of the option plays a role, and the premium tends to go up if the time to expiration is longer, *i.e.*, there is greater time value to the option.

Here are several examples, all of which involve buying PSM Nov 40 Calls.

- If the premium is $4, but PSM itself is trading at $38 a share, or $2 out of the money, the buyer is not paying for any intrinsic value, but rather hopes for PSM stock to rise over time.

- If the premium is $6 when PSM is selling for $44, it reflects a time value of $2 above the intrinsic value.

With a put, obviously, the situation is reversed. For example, a PSM Nov 70 Put is in the money by $4 if PSM sells at $66. In this case, $4 of the premium would represent the intrinsic value.

Volatility

To understand premium pricing, one additional element must be included, namely the volatility of the underlying stock price. If this is high, if the stock price fluctuates greatly, then the value of an option is increased since the likelihood that the option will have substantial intrinsic value is increased. Conversely, if the stock price tends to be stable, the option will have less time value.

Note that while the time value increases with volatility, only the intrinsic value can be cashed in by exercising the option. Of course, since options are traded as instruments in their own right, one can buy an option and resell it later at a higher price.

COVERED VS. UNCOVERED OPTIONS

Writing options can be extremely risky. If a call option is exercised, the call writer must pay the difference between the market price and the strike price; the greater this difference, the greater the loss. In principle, there is no limit to the writer's risk since there is no limit to the price the underlying security might reach before the option expires. The put writer must pay the difference between the market price and the strike price. This limits the risk to the price of the underlying security, since that could go to $0.

Limiting risks on call writing

These risks can be moderated. If a call writer owns the underlying security which has been called, then he merely needs to deliver it. His risk has now been converted to an opportunity loss (since he no longer owns this security and cannot himself benefit from its rise). Of course, by owning the security, he also assumes the risk that this underlying security might fall in price.

A writer who owns the underlying security is referred to as a "covered writer." Those with no such protection are termed "uncovered" or "naked" option writers. Variations of covering include owning a security convertible to the underlying stock, or owning an escrow or depository receipt, *i.e.*, legal evidence that the writer has the stock on deposit. (This is often used by large institutions.)

A call writer can also limit risk by holding an unexpired long call on the same stock at the same or some other strike price. If the call he wrote is exercised, he can, where necessary, exercise his own long call to obtain the stock needed to fill his obligation.

Example

A writer of a 50 ACI Call who owns a 60 ACI Call has his risk limited to the $10 between 50 and 60. If the price rises above $60, he exercises his call and delivers the shares to the 50 call holder. The writer's loss is limited to $10 per share (minus the premium he collected, but plus the premium he paid for the 60 call).

Limiting risks on put writing

A put writer can limit risk by selling the underlying security short or by owning a put on the same security. If he is short the security, he of course assumes the risk that the security will rise in price.

Example

A writer of a 50 ACI Put who owns a 35 ACI Put risks a maximum of $15 since he can sell ACI at 35 and must buy at 50. Of course, if he owns a higher put, say an ACI 60, then he has no risk; if exercising the 50 put makes sense, then so does exercising the 60 put, and he will make $10 per share.

Note

In this case, the premium he paid for his 60 put is probably higher than that which he received for writing his 50 put.

BREAK-EVEN POINTS

The break-even point is that point at which an investor who trades in options literally "breaks even" in regard to some transaction or combination thereof. We will analyze such points *before the imposition of transaction costs*.

Buyers

For buyers of options, the break-even point is readily determined. The buyer of a call will break even when the underlying security is priced at the strike price plus the premium. The buyer of a 40 call with a premium of 5 breaks even when the stock goes to 45. By exercising there, he would buy at 40 and sell at 45, thereby recapturing the premium of 5 which he paid originally.

Conversely, the buyer of a put will break even when the stock price equals the strike price minus the premium. The buyer of a 40 put at a premium of 5 needs to have the stock price at 35 in order to break even.

Writers

For writers, the issue is somewhat more complex. For a covered call writer, the break-even point is the original cost to the writer of the underlying security *minus* the premium. For example, if ACI was originally purchased at 35 and a call was written at 35 with a premium of 7, the writer is said to break even when the stock reaches 28. The loss of 7 per share on the stock is exactly made up by the 7 premium collected when the option was written.

It is worth noting that if a stock goes up in price, there is no break-even point—the writer is always ahead. This is true because the break-even is now based on two combined transactions.

Similarly, for a put writer who is short the stock, the break-even is the short sale price *plus* the premium. If ACI was shorted at 35, and subsequently a 35 put is written for a premium of 4, the writer breaks even at 39. Here again two transactions are combined.

For an uncovered call writer, the break-even is the strike price *plus* the premium. If one writes an uncovered call on ACI with a 35 strike price and collects a $4\frac{1}{2}$ premium, the break-even occurs when ACI reaches $39\frac{1}{2}$.

Conversely, an uncovered put writer breaks even at the strike price *minus* the premium. A 35 put with a premium of 6 causes the writer to break even at 29.

STRATEGIES: HEDGES, STRADDLES, COMBINATIONS, SPREADS

Aside from the basic strategies of buying and writing puts and calls, there are other more complex strategies. In this section, the more common of these investments will be outlined.

Hedges

Hedges are strategies similar to insurance policies. Just as with insurance, one pays a premium and is then protected against catastrophic loss. There are two basic hedges: long call/short stock and long put/long stock.

Long call/short stock
Buying a call on a stock and selling the same stock short. This procedure, "hedging a short sale," provides insurance to a short seller who otherwise faces unlimited risk. It guarantees the right to buy at a price that puts a ceiling over any loss from the short sale.

Example

Sell 100 shares PSM short at 50 and buy 1 PSM Nov 50 Call at 5. If PSM went to 100, the short seller would lose $5,000. With the call, however, the loss is only the premium, or $500, since the investor has the right to buy the stock at 50 for the term of the option. If the stock falls, the short seller will not realize a profit unless and until the drop exceeds the amount of the premium, which in the above example, is below 45.

The maximum loss for the call buyer would be the $500, and his theoretical maximum gain—if the stock went to $0—would be $5,000 – $500 = $4,500. A naked writer of the call would have no limit on his potential maximum loss and would have a maximum possible gain of $500 if the call was not exercised.

Long put/long stock
This means buying a put and buying shares of the same stock. It limits risk if the market price of the stock falls.

Example

Buy 100 PSM at 50 and buy 1 PSM 50 put at 5. The put guarantees being able to sell the stock at 50. Thus, the loss cannot exceed $500, *i.e.*, the premium or cost of placing the put. Again, no profit will be realized until the stock rises enough to cover the premium; which means the break-even point is the cost of the stock plus the premium, or 55 in the above example.

Again, the maximum loss for the put buyer is the $500 premium, but his theoretical maximum gain is now unlimited.

Note

Writing covered options is a partial hedge. It insures against some limited amount of loss. For instance, writing a covered call on ACI at 70 for a premium of 6 provides the writer with protection against a fall in the price of ACI up to 64. The writer is thus partially protected, but should ACI fall below 64 he again assumes the risk.

Straddles

A straddle is the simultaneous buying (or writing) of a put and a call on the same stock with the same expiration date and strike price.

Long straddle (buy a straddle)
This means buying a put and a call of the same expiration date and execution price for one security. The buyer expects movement in the stock, but is unsure whether it will rise or fall.

Example

Buy 1 PSM Nov 70 Call at 7 and buy 1 PSM Nov 70 Put at 5. Assume the underlying stock goes to 74, the call is exercised, and the put expires. The holder of the straddle has paid $1,200 in premiums ($700 for the call, $500 for the put), and earned $400 from the exercised call (buy at 70, sell at 74)—a net loss of $800. Here, the break-even point is reached when the underlying stock rises or falls in the market enough to cover both premiums—in this example, up to 82 or down to 58.

The maximum loss for the purchaser is now $1,200, equaling the maximum possible gain for the writer. This occurs only if both options expire unexercised.

Note

In the above example, if the call were exercised at 74 before the put expired, and subsequently the stock fell to 62, that would also represent a break-even.

Short straddle (write or sell a straddle)   Writing a put and a call on the same security, with the same expiration date and execution price. Here, the writer hopes for relatively little movement in the market price of the underlying security. He gets two premiums. This, like call writing or put writing, is often used to improve the return on capital.

Example

Sell 1 PSM Nov 70 Call at 5; sell 1 PSM Nov 70 Put at 3. If by expiration date, PSM goes to 73, the call is exercised, and the put is allowed to expire. The writer has received $800 in premiums, and this gain is offset by a loss of $300. The writer's break-even points would be 78 or 62, *i.e.*, he would make money if the stock remained within that range and would lose outside of it.

Combinations

Combinations are variations on a straddle. They involve the purchase (or sale) of a put and a call on the same security with different expirations, different strike prices, or both. Two examples follow.

- buy 1 ACI May 60 Call and buy 1 ACI Aug 60 Put

- sell 1 ACI May 60 Call and sell 1 ACI May 50 Put

Like the long straddle, the first example would be employed when considerable movement was expected, especially if one thought it might first go up and then down. The second combination might be used if the writer believed the price would fluctuate between 50 and 60. In that case, neither option would ever be in the money.

Spreads

Buying and selling a call or buying and selling a put on the same security, *i.e.*, on options of the same type and class, with either different expiration dates or different strike prices or both, is called "putting on a spread" or "spreading." Such a procedure involving self-canceling positions—any gain on one side would be offset, dollar for dollar, by a loss on the other—may seem odd. However these positions are not exactly opposite. Here, the term "spread" refers to the difference between the premium paid and the premium received on the two positions (*e.g.*, long call/short call) and determines the gain or loss.

If the only difference is the strike price, this is called a "vertical spread" or "price spread." If they differ in expiration date only, it is called a "horizontal spread" or "time spread." Spreads which differ in both time and price are called "diagonal spreads." (These terms reflect the way options are listed in the newspaper: successive strike prices are shown one above the other, successive expirations along one line.)

Let us examine the two situations:

Debit spread (also called a bull price spread or "buying the spread")

If the premium paid for the long call is greater than the premium received for the short call, the transaction is called a "debit spread." The position is more profitable if the market price of the underlying stock goes up and widens the spread.

Example

With PSM at 76, buy 1 PSM Nov 70 C at 7 and sell 1 PSM Nov 80 C at 1; net debit, $600. With this spread, the maximum loss would come if the market price drops below 70—both calls expire "out" and the $600 net premium cost is lost.

Alternately, maximum gain occurs if the price rises above 80. The written call would be exercised, and the spreader would have to deliver at 80. He, in turn, exercises the held call at 70, for a gain of $1,000 less premium of $600, or a total of $400.

Note

The difference between the long and short call—10 points here—is the maximum possible gain, whatever the market price. Of course, some lesser gain is possible if the underlying stock reaches a point between 70 and 80. The break-even here is obviously at 76.

Credit spread (also bear price spread or "selling the spread")   If the premium paid on the long call is less than the premium received on the short call, a "credit spread" occurs. There is greater profit if the market price falls and the spread narrows.

Example

Buy 1 PSM 80 C at 1, sell 1 PSM 70 C at 7; net credit $600, assuming market price is 76. This situation is the reverse of the bull spread. Maximum gain is realized if the price falls below $70, leaving both calls "out of the money" so that both options expire, and the spread earns $600 net (premiums). Maximum loss occurs if the underlying stock climbs above 80. Both calls are then in the money, will be exercised, and the holder of the spread must deliver shares purchased at 80 for 70. The loss is $1,000 less the $600 gain on premiums, or a net loss of $400. Here again, the break-even is at 76.

OBJECTIVES OF OPTIONS TRADERS

It is possible to identify four separate but related objectives for options purchasers:

1. To speculate in a security while limiting risk. For example, a $10 ACI 100 call would return a profit of $2,000 on a $1,000 investment if ACI goes to 130, or 200%. Purchasing ACI outright would require a $10,000 investment and bring a return of 30%.

2. To diversify a portfolio. An investor with $5,000 who believed the market was due to rise could buy calls on *five different stocks* (assuming a $10 premium on each) but could only buy 100 shares of *one* $50 stock.

3. To hedge a position. An investor owning 100 shares of ACI could protect that investment against catastrophic loss by buying a put on ACI. If ACI drops sharply, the investor's loss is limited to the premium on the put option, and he can still profit from any rise in ACI (minus the cost of the put).

4. To delay a decision. A relatively small investment in a call allows an investor to take advantage of a rise in the price of the security while not committing a large amount of capital. This is an important advantage in cases where the capital might not be available until some later date. By buying a call, the investor defers the decision without giving up all the potential gain.

MARGINS

Though margins are covered in detail in Chapter 11, some margin requirements pertain specifically to options. Only writers of uncovered options must meet margin requirements.[*] Buyers, under OCC rules, must settle on the next business day. The buyer of a put or call must pay the full amount of the premium, even if that individual has an active margin account for stocks, *i.e.*, long options have no loan value, and the broker cannot lend against them even if they appreciate.

Applied to a margin purchase, "covered" means the brokerage firm is not at risk, while covered writer, on the other hand, refers to protecting the investor.

On calls

A call writer is considered covered for margin purchases if he:

- holds a long position in the underlying stock, or

- holds a security convertible to the same stock, or

- has an escrow or depository receipt showing the stock is held in a bank and will be delivered if the call option is exercised, or

- holds a long call option on the same stock with the same or later expiration date and the same or lower strike price

In any such case, there is no margin requirement on the writer of a call.

[*]The margin requirements are changed from time to time by the various exchanges.

On puts

A put writer is covered if he:

- is short the underlying stock, or

- holds a long put option with same expiration date or longer, or

- holds a long put option with same strike price or greater. Technically being short stock and writing a put is not a covered put position, but for margin purposes, it is covered since there is no additional margin requirement.

Deposits

Uncovered writers are required to have a minimum on deposit, in most cases $2,000, before any transactions are undertaken. After that, the requirements are governed by maintenance margin, and further deposits are not required except to meet those margins. For options traded through OCC, the minimum margin on one transaction is $250 per contract.

Margin for writers of naked equity options

The current requirement is that 20% of the value of the underlying stock plus the premium collected from the buyer be on deposit as margin. This total is decreased by the "out of the moneyness" of the option, and there is a minimum requirement of the premium plus 10% of the value of the underlying stock.

For uncovered puts, the requirement is similar, namely 20% of the market price plus the premium and minus any out of the moneyness, again with a minimum of 10% of market value. Further, this requirement is "marked to market" at the end of each day. That is, every day at the close, the new premiums and market prices are used to determine the necessary amount.

Example 1

If ACI is selling at 52, and the investor writes 3 ACI Nov 50 calls at 3, the required deposit would be:

$$3(20\% \times \$5,200 + \$300) = 3(\$1,040 + \$300) = \$4,020$$

Example 2

If ACI is selling at $58, and the investor writes 5 ACI Nov 60 calls at 1, the required deposit is:

$$5(20\% \times \$5,800 + \$100 - \$200 \text{ [out of money]}) = \$5,300$$

Example 3

If CAI is selling at 24, and the investor writes a CAI Nov 30 call at 1/2, the required deposit would be:

$$20\% \times \$2,400 + \$50 - \$600 = -\$70$$

Since this is less than the 10% minimum, the required deposit becomes:

$$\$50 + 10\% \times \$2,400 = \$290$$

Spread margins

Covered spread   Although there is no margin requirement for covered spreads, the difference between the premium collected on the written option and that required for the purchased option would have to be deposited.

Call spread   A call spread is covered when the long option has a strike not higher than, and an expiration not earlier than, the short option. For example:

- buy 1 ACI Jun 55 Call at 7
- sell 1 ACI Jun 60 Call at 3

If the 60 Call is exercised, then the 55 can be as well. There is no margin requirement, but the $400 difference in premiums must be deposited.

Put spread   If the long option has a strike price no lower, and an expiration not earlier than the short option, then the put spread is covered. For example:

- buy 1 ACI Sep 60 Put at 6
- sell 1 ACI Jun 60 Put at 3

Here, a later date is chosen for the long put rather than a higher price. In any case, if the short put is exercised, the long put can be as well. Again, there is no margin requirement, and the $300 between premiums must be deposited.

OPTION TRANSACTION PROCEDURES

Issuing a contract

The option contract is issued by the OCC as a "new offering" of a security. Therefore, under the Securities Act of 1933, all potential purchasers must receive a prospectus and any solicitation of a customer to buy (or write) an option must be accompanied by a prospectus. Whenever a prospectus is updated, existing customers must get a copy of the new prospectus with or before the confirmation of their next trade. In options, the prospectus is often called the "Option Disclosure Document" or "Option Disclosure Statement."

Ordering options

In ordering listed options, the following steps occur. After the customer enters an order for a buy or sell option contract through a brokerage firm, the order is executed on the floor of a member exchange. After the trade is completed, it is then submitted to the OCC, which "clears" the transaction and issues the option contract to the buyer or seller.

OPTION ORDER TICKET

ERRORS COST YOU MONEY

Primary Market: □ VS   Phone Orders: □ IO

Secondary Market Exchange Codes: CBOE □ AMOE □ PBOE □ PCOE □ OTCO □   Other Exch. Codes

Action Combinations If Required: □ CXL □ CFM □ Foned □ Spread* □ Straddle* □ Combo* *Use Lines 2 & 3

Buy/SL: **Buy** (CFO)

Option: □ Put ☒ Call □ Put □ Call

Contracts: **5**

Description — Symbol: **IBM** Month: **May** Strike Price: **110**

Price: **6 ½**   Qualifier: **Limit**   Spd. Std. □ Net □ DBT □ CDT □ Even Qual.

Dur.: □ Open ☒ Day □ Open □ Day

Branch: **0 1 3** Account Number: **9 8 0 2 4 6** Type FA

Position Information: □ Cover ☒ Open ☒ Cust □ Uncover □ Close □ Firm

Write In Area — Account Name: **John Doe**

Additional Order Handling Info (Qualifies Manner In Which It Is Handled By Trader): $ ___

Trailer Info (For Commision Or Figuration Purposes): □ Via □ For   □ No Credit □ Sol □ Full Credit □ Unsol

Position Information for Spread, Straddle, Combo's and (MULTI ACCOUNT NUMBERS):
□ Buy □ Sell □ Cover □ Uncover □ Open □ Close □ Cust □ Firm
□ Buy □ Sell □ Cover □ Uncover □ Open □ Close □ Cust □ Firm
□ Buy □ Sell □ Cover □ Uncover □ Open □ Close □ Cust □ Firm

Option Trade Level

Manager Approval

Form 8044 REV 3/97   Read Back This Order To Client   WIRE OPERATOR INPUT COPY

Figure 9.3 Option Order Ticket

Exercising an option

When a customer exercises an option, he notifies his broker; the brokerage firm notifies the OCC directly; and then the OCC assigns the contract to one of the firms representing writers on a random basis. That firm in turn must assign the contract among its clients equitably. This can also involve random selection, or "first in first out," but must be fair—for example, not to the customer who has the largest position. In short, the OCC holds the option contract obligation and acts as intermediary between buyer and seller.

Required forms

Because option trading is risky and specialized, the OCC will not issue a contract until certain documentation is completed. No customer can participate in options transactions unless and until all four of these forms are completed.

Option information form This form concerns the customer's financial standing, background, and interests. It must be signed by both the customer and the registered representative who is recommending the customer for this type of trading and must be approved by the firm's branch manager (who must be a Registered Option Principal if the branch has four or more registered representatives involved in options transactions). This approval must be confirmed in writing within 15 days by a Compliance Registered Options Principal (CROP). In addition, the CROP must also approve any promotional or educational material. Said materials must also be submitted to the Options Exchanges at least 10 days before they are used.

Branch | Account No.

Check One ☐ For initial option transaction(s). ☐ To up-date level changes, background and financial information to an already existing option account.

1 Client's Name / Address

Attention Client
Please read the reverse side of this Option Client Information Form and Agreement prior to signing at the bottom of this page.

2 (Area Code) Home Phone Number | ☐ Rent ☐ Own Residence | Does anyone have power of attorney? If "Yes", attach a new account form for the agent ☐ Yes A/C# or Name ☐ No | **Is power of attorney FA?** ☐ No ☐ Yes

3 Is client retired? ☐ Yes ☐ No | Is client a student? ☐ Yes ☐ No | Employer's name or check if self-employed: ☐ | Type of Business | Job Function

4 Marital Status (Please Check) ☐ Single ☐ Married ☐ Divorced ☐ Widow(er) ☐ Separated | No. of Dependents | Date of Birth Mo. Day Year / / | Client's Stated Annual Income $ .00 | Client's Stated Net Worth Exclusive of Family Residence $ .00 | Estimated Liquid Net Worth $ .00

INVESTMENT EXPERIENCE	NO. OF YEARS
OPTIONS	
EQUITIES	
BONDS	
COMMODITIES	
OTHER	

Client's Stated Option Investment Objective(s) (Please Check) ☐ Income ☐ Investment Hedge ☐ Speculation

Client's Options Investment Experience

5 Types of trades in past year have been ☐ Cash ☐ Both ☐ Margin ☐ Neither | The activity has been ☐ Writing Covered ☐ Buying ☐ Uncovered (Sales) ☐ Various Strategies ☐ No Activity | Past Trading History ☐ Actively ☐ Moderately ☐ Infrequently ☐ No Trading

6 Type of option transactions **anticipated:** ☐ Writing Covered Calls ☐ Buying Options ☐ Writing Puts ☐ Spreading ☐ Writing Uncovered Calls ☐ Writing Straddles & Combinations ☐ All Types

7 FA Name Typed or Printed | FA Signature | Date | Manager's Signature | Date

8 Types of transactions for which account is **approved:**

☐ Level 1 Writing covered call options
☐ Level 2A Level 1 plus buying options including listed index and foreign currency warrants.
☐ Level 2B Level 1 and 2A, plus spreading listed options, buying straddles and combinations, writing puts on equities.
☐ Level 3 Level 1 and levels 2A and 2B plus all other types of transactions, selling of uncovered index puts, selling of uncovered call options, including variable (ratio) hedging, straddles, combinations and the short sale of listed index and foreign currency warrants.

* Foreign Currency Option Trading requires the additional completion of Form 4811 (Foreign Currency Option Supplement).

9 **In my capacity as R.O.P., I have reviewed the client's financial conditions, investment objective(s) and investment experience, and on that basis feel the above level of trading is suitable for this client.** | **Signature of R.O.P.** | **R.O.P. LOG ON I.D.** | **DATE**

10 **By signing this agreement, the customer acknowledges that he/she has received, read, and understood a copy of this agreement. This agreement contains a pre-dispute arbitration clause on reverse at paragraph 10.**

11 Client's Signature **X** | Date | Joint Party Signature **X** | Date

NEW ACCOUNT COPY
(SEE REVERSE SIDE FOR INSTRUCTIONS)

Figure 9.4 Option Account Agreement and Information Form

Standard option agreement This explains the firm's procedures for dealing with the account, any transactions, notices of execution, delinquencies, etc. It must be signed by the customer within 15 days after the account is opened.

Prospectus (options disclosure document) At or before the time that options trading begins, the client must be provided with the risk disclosure statement "Characteristics and Risks of Standardized Options," published by the OCC.

A new account form (See Chapter 10)

Options clearing agreement Finally, within 15 days after the account is approved, the customer must sign an agreement with the OCC itself. This "options clearing agreement" specifies OCC regulations pertaining to the customer.

Trading in listed options is carried out without certificates. Rather, confirmations of transactions and regular statements are sent by the broker.

"Opening" and "closing" transactions

Options orders must show if the customer is "opening" or "closing" a position and if that position is long (buyer or holder) or short (seller or writer). There are only the following four possibilities:

Opening buy—Long, *i.e.*, establishing a long call or put position as holder

Closing sell—Long, *i.e.*, liquidating a long call or put position

Opening sell—Short, *i.e.*, establishing a short call or put position as writer

Closing buy—Short, *i.e.*, liquidating a short call or put position

These designations allow options trading exchanges to provide a daily accounting of "open interest," which is an important indicator of liquidity in particular options contracts. This figure, published in the financial press, shows the number of contracts still open in a given series.

OPTIONS PRICING

When a listed option of a particular series expires, the options exchange will introduce a new series based on the current market price of the underlying stock. The offered puts and calls usually "bracket" this price. For example, if PSM is selling at $68 when the January contracts expire, the exchanges will offer October PSM 65 and October PSM 70.

In general, strike (exercise) prices are offered at $2.50 intervals for equities below $25/share, at $5 intervals for stocks up to $200, and at $10 intervals for those above $200.

OCC RULES AND REGULATIONS

Expirations

All options contracts expire at 10:59 P.M. Central Time (since much options trading takes place in Chicago, times are often given in both Central and Eastern zones), 11:59 P.M. Eastern Time, on the Saturday following the third Friday of the expiration month.

Although options contracts expire on a Saturday, trading in a particular option must cease at 3:02 P.M. Central (4:02 P.M., Eastern) time the business day preceding the expiration date. In addition, even though trading in the option has been halted, an option can be exercised until 5:30 P.M. Eastern Time on the business day preceding the expiration date. An option can be exercised, but not sold, even if trading in the option and the underlying stock have been suspended.

Each listed option has a cycle of four expiration months, *e.g.*, Jan, Apr, Jul, and Oct; or Mar, Jun, Sep, and Dec. At any given time, only the next three of these expirations are available. For instance, if Feb, May, and Aug are available, then Nov does not become available until Feb expires.

Adjustments in contracts

Cash dividends   With exchange-traded options, there is no adjustment in price when a cash dividend is issued for the underlying stock. With over-the-counter options, the option price is reduced by the amount of the dividend. The dividend belongs to the stockholder, hence the ex-dividend date represents the dividing line for options contracts. Thus, the holder of a call must exercise before that date to get the dividend, and the holder of a put may not exercise until the ex-dividend date in order to keep the dividend.

Stock dividends   For a stock dividend, the number of shares is increased and the exercise price is decreased to reflect the dividend, beginning on the ex-dividend date. These changes are made to the nearest whole share and the nearest $\frac{1}{8}$ of a point. This keeps the dollar amount needed to exercise close to the amount before the dividend.

Example

If ACI declares a 5% stock dividend, then a May ACI 50 Call would become a May ACI 47 $\frac{5}{8}$ of 105 shares ($5,000 ÷ 105 = $47.6190). The premium is now multiplied by 105 after the split.

Stock splits   For whole number splits (*e.g.*, 2 for 1), the number of contracts is increased, and the price reduced.

Example

1 PSM Nov 90 Put after a 3 for 1 stock split becomes 3 PSM Nov 30 Puts.
In a fractional split (*e.g.*, 5 for 4), the number of shares per contract is increased, and the price is reduced.

Example

1 PSM Nov 90 Put becomes one PSM Nov 60 Put for 150 shares after a 3 for 2 stock split.

Exercise notice

The option agreement sets forth the customer's responsibility to deliver stock if exercised on a call or to deliver money (to buy stock) if exercised on a put. An American-style option can be exercised as soon as ownership is confirmed. There are a few European-style options that permit exercise only in the time just before expiration. Once exercised, the stock must be delivered, and settlement made, in five business days. For the writer, this will be four business days after assignment.

POSITION LIMITS

Because a large investor could conceivably use leverage to control the market, the OCC limits the number of contracts an individual investor can hold at any one time. "Individual" includes investors acting in joint accounts or partnerships, investment advisors, and those representing many accounts.

An individual investor cannot exceed the position limit on the "same side" of the market, *i.e.*, such that they would benefit from moves in the same direction. The easy way to think of this is in terms of "bullish" and "bearish" holdings. In other words, a long call and a short put are both bullish; short calls and long puts are bearish.

Position limits are currently set on three levels by the OCC.[*]

1. 8,000 contracts on a side for options where the underlying stock meets one of the two following criteria:

    *   120,000,000 shares outstanding and a trading volume of at least 30,000,000 shares during the most recent six-month trading period

    *   trading volume of at least 40,000,000 shares during the most recent six-month trading period, independent of shares outstanding

2. 5,500 contracts on a side for options where the underlying stock meets one of the two following criteria:

    *   40,000,000 shares outstanding and a trading volume of at least 15,000,000 shares during the most recent six-month trading period

    *   trading volume of at least 20,000,000 shares during the most recent six-month trading period, independent of shares outstanding

3. 3,000 contracts on a side for all other listed options

Exercise limits

*   These same limits apply to the number of contracts that an investor may exercise in any consecutive five-business-day period.

EXCHANGES

The OCC is owned by five exchanges on which options are traded. They are:

New York Stock Exchange—NYSE

Chicago Board Option Exchange—CBOE

American Stock Exchange—ASE

Philadelphia Stock Exchange—PBX

Pacific Stock Exchange—PSE

[*]Position limits may also change from time to time.

Options are bought and sold on these exchanges in an auction market similar to the stock markets. Commission charges, set by brokers and the exchange, are based on premiums. Limit and market orders are permitted.

All exchanges but the CBOE use a specialist system similar to that described in Chapter 8, with firms acting as both brokers and dealers on the floor. On the CBOE, there are no specialists; rather their functions are divided into:

- Order Book Official (OBO) who maintains an orderly market. The OBO, an employee of the CBOE, accepts only customer market orders and limit orders from brokers; he cannot trade for his own account.

- market maker who performs a dealer function, trading for his own account

The OCC guarantees puts and calls listed on its exchanges, and supervises the listing of options. An option to be listed must meet the following rigorous requirements as to value, volume traded, and financial health of the issuing firm.

1. The underlying stock must have a value of at least $10 per share.

2. At least 8 million shares of the underlying stock must be publicly held, with at least 10,000 different shareholders.

3. At least 1.2 million shares must have traded each year in the two preceding years.

4. The firm issuing the underlying stock must have had a net after-tax income of at least $1 million in three of the last four fiscal years, including the most recent fiscal year.

5. The issuing firm must be current in its dividend and sinking fund obligations to preferred shareholders and in its debt payments.

TAX ON OPTIONS

A chapter of this book is devoted to taxes. This section will describe some options trading tax consequences. An investor who closes out an option position always realizes a capital gain or loss. For tax purposes, gain or loss is defined by the way the option position is ended, *i.e.*, expired, exercised, traded or sold.

Expired options

When an option expires, it is treated as worthless for tax purposes. It is therefore a capital loss to the owner. The writer of such an expired option always has a short-term capital gain.

Traded options

The liquidation of an options position by sale generates a capital gain, or loss, of net proceeds less acquisition cost. Thus, an investor who bought a contract with a premium of $300 and resold it at $600 has realized a $300 capital gain. The gain is found in similar fashion with the repurchase of a written option.

Exercising

Taxes are calculated only when the security is sold, and call premiums are included in the basis or cost of acquisition.

Buy a call   A customer buys PSM Nov 60 Call at 3 on June 4, and exercises the option August 12. The cost of acquiring the stock is $63 per share. If the stock is sold for $64 per share, the gain is $100. The holding period begins on the day the option is exercised, in this case August 12. Note that for tax purposes, the cost basis for the stock acquired by exercising now includes the cost of the option.

Write a call   A customer writes PSM Nov 60 Call at 3 on June 4 and is exercised on August 12. Net proceeds would be $6,300. Acquisition cost must be the price actually paid for the stocks. If this is an uncovered option, then the current market price is used. For the writer, the holding period ends when the call is exercised.

Write a put   A customer writes a PSM Nov 60 Put at 3 on Sep 4 which is exercised. He must buy at $60, but acquisition cost is $57.

Buy a put   An investor buys a PSM Nov 60 Put at 4 on Aug 6 and exercises Sep 7. His proceeds are $5,600. If he had owned stock long term, the put does not affect its status; however, for stock owned short term, the holding period is eliminated and cannot begin again until the put is disposed of.

Spreads

For spread transactions each option is taxed separately.

SUITABILITY

Options are inherently risky. A registered representative must exercise special care in determining the suitability of this type of investment for each client. This includes recognizing that a situation in which covered options are suitable is not automatically a situation in which the riskier uncovered options are suitable and that, in general, no more than 15% or 20% of a client's assets should be involved with options. In addition, a client must be advised of the generally higher fees and commissions charged in options trading. The RR (Registered Representative) should also alert clients to the possible tax consequences of options trading on existing stock positions.

STOCK INDEX OPTIONS

Stock indexes are weighted averages of groups of stocks. Options based on these indexes have also been introduced. Although trading in these options resembles other options trading, there are some significant differences.

Trading in index options is a way to diversify over a range of equities without having large amounts of capital and without the problems and paperwork of trading many separate stocks. In this way, stock indexes resemble mutual funds. They differ in that there are no management fees associated with index trading and no professional management of the portfolio; one simply chooses an index, *e.g.*, S&P 100, and trades it.

Some indexes are quite broad, like the S&P 500, the Major Market Index, or the Japan Index; others are much narrower or more specific, such as indexes comprised exclusively of stocks in a single field, *e.g.*, computer technology or precious metals.

Indexes are computed in several ways. The most straightforward method is to sum the prices of all included stocks and divide that total by the number of different equities, without considering the size of each component. Another method is to multiply each stock by the number of shares outstanding before finding a total and then averaging. Finally, some indexes are computed by averaging the percentage change over a stated period in each component stock.

In all cases, the value at some given date is considered a base value of the index. This base may be modified periodically to reflect changes in the capitalization of a component stock or even by adding or dropping a stock. Finally, the value of an index changes each day with changes in the prices of the component stocks.

Reasons for buying index options

Recall that investment risk is often separated into several components, including "company risk," which is the risk that a particular company will not perform as expected. Diversification can overcome this risk. Similarly, the indexes provide opportunities for moderating "industry risk" (the risk associated with a particular industry) and "market risk" (the risk that the entire equities market will not perform as expected).

Investors use index futures and index options just as they do stock options. An investor who feels that computer stocks are going to appreciate, but is unsure which stock will do best, might buy a call on an index of computer stocks.

Options also provide a method for hedging stock portfolios. For example, an investor who holds stocks with large capitalizations could augment the return on such a portfolio by writing options on MMI (Major Market Index), an index of blue chip stocks. The premiums collected would augment the return on this portfolio.

Characteristics of index options

Contract size   The value of an options contract is, with some exceptions, $100 times the value of the index. Thus, if the S&P 100 is at 275.40, the value of one options contract for that index is $27,540. In this way, the 100 multiplier is like the 100 shares of stock in a stock option.

Settlement   The major difference between index and stock options is that all settlements in index options are cash transactions. They take place the next business day. There is no opportunity to call an index in the sense of actually buying the securities. Rather, when an index option is exercised, the short (writer) pays the long (holder) the difference between the strike price and the index value times the multiplier (usually 100) at the time of exercise. This difference affects margins in that there are no covered options. The basis for payment is the closing price on the day of the transaction rather than the price at the time of the transaction.

Note that exercisers must be careful: since settlement is based on the close of day price, it is possible to exercise an option while it is in the money, only to find that it was out of the money by day's end.

Example

An S&P 100 June 1,000 call is exercised when the index is at 1006. If the index closed that day at 997, the exerciser would not only not get the $500 expected when he exercised, but would have to pay the writer $300, because settlement is based on the closing price.

Exercise and expiration
Exercise prices for these options are in dollars. They are set at five-point intervals, or as necessary. Expiration and exercise times are exactly like those for stock options: all contracts expire at 10:59 PM CT (11:59 PM ET) on the Saturday following the third Friday of the expiration month. Trading ends at 3:02 PM CT (4:02 PM ET) on the business day preceding the expiration date, but an option can be exercised until 4:30 PM CT (5:30 PM ET) on that day.

Margin requirements*

For long positions, 100% of the premium must be deposited. As mentioned earlier, there are no covered short positions. In calculating margins, "narrow-based" are distinguished from "broad-based" index options. The former are indexes of a specific industry and entail greater risk.

The margin requirement for a broad-based index is 15% of the value of the index plus the premium and minus the out of the moneyness.

The minimum requirement is 10% of the value of the index plus the premium. In either case—exactly as with stock options—the premium that has been collected would be subtracted from the margin requirement to determine the cash requirement, and a minimum $2,000 initial deposit would be required.

Example 1

With the S&P 100 at 272.50, a 275 Call with a premium of 7 would have a margin requirement of:

$$\$700 + (15\% \times \$27,250) - \$250 = \$4,537.50$$

Example 2

With the MMI at 440, a 400 Put with a premium of $\frac{1}{16}$ would require:

$$\$6.25 + (15\% \times \$43,000) - \$4,000 = \$2,456.25$$

---

*These too are subject to change.

which is obviously below the minimum, so the requirement becomes:

$$\$6.25 + (10\% \times \$43,000) = \$4,306.25$$

For narrow-based indexes, the requirement is 20% of the value plus the premium and minus the out of the moneyness, with a minimum of 10% of value plus the premium.

Example 3

With the Gold and Silver Index at 95.00, a 100 Put with a premium of 6.50 means that the requirement is:

$$\$650 + (20\% \times \$9,500) = \$2,550$$

Position limits

As with stock options, concern about an individual's ability to influence the market has caused the SEC to establish position and exercise limits of 25,000 on the same side of the market for index options.

Capped and long-term options (Caps and LEAPS)

Recently, two new types of options have been introduced. One, the "capped" option, puts a predetermined limit or cap on the gain an investor can realize. The other is a long-term option, with expirations of one or more years. Interest in these options has varied over time; they are described on page 237.

INTEREST RATE OPTIONS

At times, options on interest rates—including a long-term interest rate index, T-note, and T-bond options—have been offered through the OCC and traded on major exchanges. The primary use of these options is to speculate on the direction of interest rates or to hedge portfolios of fixed income securities.

For instance, if rates are expected to rise (and hence prices to fall), puts might be bought. If these expectations are realized, one could exercise and reap the reward; if not, one's loss would be limited to the cost of the puts. On the other hand, the manager of a portfolio of fixed-income securities could write call options, increasing the yield on the portfolio and protecting against some modest rate rise as well. Of course, he has the risk that if the rates fall, his portfolio would be called away.

While these options are not currently available, they may be offered again in the future. A brief discussion of the three most popular interest rate options follows. Note that the details of trade practice are offered here only to give a sense of the strategies involved; actual rules regarding contract size, expiration, and pricing may vary.

T-bill options

The contract size is $1,000,000 of 13-week T-bills. The expiration cycle is Mar., Jun., Sep. and Dec., with the three nearest active at all times, *e.g.*, when March expires December begins trading. The exercise of a T-bill option is settled by delivery of $1,000,000 of 13-week T-bills on Thursday (the usual day of issue) of the following week.

Exercise and strike prices are based on the discount yield for 1-year bills. Thus, if the current discount is 6.20, the current price is given as $100 - 6.20 = 93.80$. As noted earlier, each .01 is called a basis point; 1.00 is 100 basis points. The 6.20 annualized discount is adjusted to a 91-day maturity to compute the actual discount and the resulting principal or exercise price as follows:

$$6.20 \times \frac{91}{360} = .015672$$

$$.015672 \times \$1,000,000 = \$15,672$$

the actual discount which results in a principal of:

$$\$1,000,000 - \$15,672 = \$984,328$$

Notice that the inverse relationship between rates and prices still obtains. This method of converting discount yield to a price does the inversion automatically. Thus, if yield goes from 6.20 to 6.40, the price declines from 93.80 to 93.60. Strike prices usually are set at 20 basis point intervals bracketing current market price; occasionally they are set at 50 basis point intervals.

While each point represents $\frac{1}{100}$ of 1% or $100 on a $1,000,000 1-year bill, these are 13-week bills (or $\frac{1}{4}$ of a year), so each basis point is worth $25 (or $\frac{1}{4}$ of $100). Thus, a 20 point move from 93.80 to 94.00 is an increase of $500.

Premiums are quoted in terms of 100 basis points to the unit. Thus, a premium of 1.24 would cost $3,100 ($25 × 124).

T-note options

Contract size is $100,000 face value of the appropriate notes. Prices are quoted as a percentage of par and $\frac{1}{32}$ of a percent. Quotation style is similar to notes: 102.08 means 102 and $\frac{8}{32}$% of par. Since 1% of par is $1,000, each $\frac{1}{32}$ is worth $31.25, so that 102.08 equals $102,250.

Strike prices are set at two-point intervals bracketing current market price. Premiums are quoted like prices: a premium of 2.10 would mean $2,312.50. Settlement of an exercise notice is in two business days.

T-bonds

The size of this contract is also $100,000 worth of the listed bond. Quotations and premiums are the same as for notes. Strike prices are at two-point intervals. Thus, if the bonds were trading at 98.12 when the option came into existence, its cost would be $98,375, and strike prices would be set at 98 and 100.

Margin requirements

Margin requirements for all debt instrument options have the following qualities in common:[*]

1. All longs are required to deposit the entire premium.

2. Shorts can be covered or uncovered. They are considered covered if:

    - for calls, the appropriate underlying security is on deposit in the account, or an escrow receipt for the same

    - for puts, a bank guarantee letter

    - for calls (puts) being long, a similar option with a not higher (lower) and a not earlier expiration date

For uncovered options, the basic margin required is the current premium, less the amount out of the money, plus a percentage of the amount of the option (0.35% for T-bills; 3.5% for T-bonds, and 3.0% for T-notes). Minimum margin requirements are premium plus .05% for bills, plus .50% for bonds and notes.

Objectives of interest rate options traders

As noted above, investors in these options have two general objectives: to speculate on the direction of future interest rates and to hedge existing portfolios. The former is not unlike the situation with any options trader: longs want increased leverage and limited risk; shorts hope to collect the premium. Hedging strategies are more complex, however. Here are some typical potential uses of interest rate options:

Example 1

A portfolio manager has some T-bonds at 90. He believes that rates will rise soon, but is unwilling (for tax or other reasons) to sell his bonds. He buys "at the money" puts, and if bond prices decline (*i.e.*, if rates rise), the decline in the value of his portfolio is offset by the rise in the value of the options. If bond prices rise, then the cost of the options is at least partly offset by the increase in the value of the portfolio. The maximum loss of this strategy is limited to the cost of the options.

Example 2

A portfolio manager wishes to increase the yield on her T-notes. She can do this by writing call options and adding the premium to the interest collected on the notes. Of course, if rates decline, and her notes are called away, she may no longer be able to provide that yield.

Example 3

A corporate treasurer must commit funds for a project some time before corporate bonds are issued to actually finance the project. Fearing a rise in rates, he buys puts on treasury securities of similar maturity to his bonds. These are

[*]Again, these are subject to change.

not identical instruments, but can act as a partial interest rate hedge since corporate and treasury rates are likely to go in the same direction, and he will be able to offset some of the additional cost of his bonds by selling his puts at a higher price.

FOREIGN CURRENCY OPTIONS

Trading in foreign currencies occurs on an enormous scale. Such trading consists of exchanging one currency for another at a specified exchange rate.

Most transactions occur in the following currencies:

- Australian dollars (AD)
- European Currency units (ECU)
- U.S. dollars (US$)
- Canadian dollars (CD)
- Deutsche marks (DM)
- Swiss francs (SF)
- French francs (FF)
- British pounds (BP)
- Japanese yen (JY)

There are now three basic marketplaces for these transactions; only one is directly involved with options sales.

Interbank

The Interbank market, as its name implies, involves currency trading among commercial banks. It operates 24 hours, conducts business by telephone and Telex, has no central marketplace, is self-regulated, and is dominated by banks and multinational corporations.

Because trading is continuous, there is no "last trade" information, but rates are extremely uniform due to ease of arbitrage. Quotations are available world wide via Reuters and other quote systems in one of two formats:

European terms   Units of a foreign currency per U.S. dollar (*e.g.,* 2DM = $1)
or

U.S. terms   Units of U.S. dollars in that currency (*e.g.,* $0.5 = 1 DM).

As our interest is confined to trades between U.S. dollars and all other currencies, we do not consider trades involving only non-U.S. currencies.

The outcome of a currency transaction is to credit an account with some number of units of one currency and debit it the appropriate number of units of the other currency. Two types of transactions can occur on the Interbank market, "spot" and "forward" transactions. Spot transactions settle in two business days, except in Canada where they settle in one day. Forward transactions settle in more than two days, with the usual transactions for one month, three months, six months, and one year.

The International Monetary Market (IMM)

The International Monetary Market in Chicago began trading currency futures contracts in 1972. Unlike Interbank transactions, these contracts are for a fixed size and for fixed delivery (on the third Wednesday in Mar., Jun., Sep., and Dec. only). Unlike the Interbank, it is an exchange market in which trades are between individual institutions.

A futures contract is an agreement to buy (or sell) a specified number of units of currency at a future date stipulated in the contract. An initial margin (technically "good faith money") is required; the account is marked to market every day; and deficiencies from a maintenance margin must be made good immediately. The IMM is monitored by the Commodity Futures Trading Commission, CFTC.

Currency options markets

In 1982, a third market for trading currencies was opened when the Philadelphia Stock Exchange (PHLX) began trading currency options in the foreign currencies listed above. Trades are all in terms of U.S. dollars and are quoted in U.S. terms.

Expirations There are six expirations: Mar., Jun., Sep., Dec., and two others chosen so that there are always one-, two-, and three-month options available. Currently, only the three nearby expirations are traded.

Trading rules As with all other listed options, the OCC issues options contracts and the same trading rules prevail: trading stops at 2:30 PM ET. Options must be exercised by 5:30 PM on the Friday preceding the third Wednesday in the expiration month and expire at 11:59 PM on the day after trading ends.

Exercise and settlement Settlement of a foreign currency option requires that the buyer deliver U.S. dollars and the writer deliver the foreign currency. Exercise may be European style (with settlement three business days after exercise) or American style (settlement four business days after exercise).

Specifications Figure 9.5 gives specifications on options contracts for the Philadelphia exchange.

The options contract expresses in U.S. terms the exercise price per unit of the foreign currency. As the table shows, the BP, SF, CD, AD, and DM are quoted in cents ($.01), the FF in $\frac{1}{10}$ cents ($.001), and the JY in $\frac{1}{100}$ cents ($.0001). Strike prices were originally at 5-cent intervals for the BP; 1-cent for the SF, DM, and CD; $\frac{1}{2}$ cent for the FF; and $\frac{1}{100}$ cent for the JY. These are modified as necessary.

CURRENCY OPTIONS SPECIFICATIONS
PHILADELPHIA STOCK EXCHANGE

Currency	Number $ of Units	Usual Strike Price Intervals	Minimum Price Change	Value of a $.01 Price Change
Australian Dollars	50,000	$.01	1/100 of a cent	$500
British Pounds	31,250	$.025	1/100 of a cent	$312.50
Canadian Dollars	50,000	$.005	1/100 of a cent	$500
Deutsche Marks	62,500	$.01	1/100 of a cent	$625
European Currency Unit	62,500	$.01	1/100 of a cent	$625
French Francs	250,000	$.005	1/1,000 of a cent	$250
Japanese Yen	6,250,000	$.01	1/10,000 of a cent	$625

Figure 9.5 Options specifications for the Philadelphia Exchange

Example 1

The contract size for the DM is 62,500. Therefore, buying:

$$\text{1 DM Jun 48 Call at } \frac{3}{4}$$

would be the right to buy 62,500 Deutsche marks at $.48 per mark any time between now and expiration. For this right the premium is $\frac{3}{4}$ cent per mark or $.0075 × 62,500 = $468.75. The total value of the contract is 62,500 × $.48 = $30,000.

Example 2

The contract size for the JY on the PHLX is 6,250,000. Therefore, buying:

$$\text{1 JY Sep Put 65 at 1}$$

would be the right to sell 6,250,000 Japanese yen at $.0065 per yen. The total value is 6,250,000 × $.0065 = $40,625. The premium would be found by moving the decimal four places, 6,250,000 × .0001 = $625.

Example 3

The PHLX BP contract is for 12,500. A premium of 6 for a BP option would represent a total premium of 12,500 × $.06 = $750.

Premium quotes

Since the units of the currencies involved have very different values in U.S. dollars, premium quotes are also in different units. They conform to the quotes of the currencies as listed above.

Minimum changes are also listed in the table, along with the dollar value of these changes. Thus, the minimum premium change in the FF is .05, and since the FF is in units of $\frac{1}{10}$ cent ($\frac{1}{1000}$ of a dollar), the decimal is moved 3 places to the left, and we have:

$$125{,}000 \times \$.00005 = \$6.25$$

as the minimum change in the total price of an FF option.

Margin requirements

As with all other options, there is no margin requirement for long option positions. Rather, the total purchase price must be deposited.

Covered   For writers of options, again we distinguish covered and uncovered positions. Here, it is useful to bear in mind that the underlying security is money in the form of some currency. Thus, a call writer must have the foreign currency, and a put writer must have U.S. dollars.

There are two basic forms. The first is an option guarantee letter from an approved bank. The letter states that the bank has on deposit, and will deliver from the investor's account, the appropriate number of units of the named currency (or the requisite number of units from the reciprocal currency). Thus, a call writer must have foreign currency to be delivered against dollars, and a put writer must have dollars for delivery against the foreign currency.

The second is an irrevocable letter of credit from the bank to the broker. This letter states that it will deliver on demand the requisite number of units of the currency.

Uncovered   For uncovered positions (short), the structure of the margin requirement is similar to that for equity options. It is the premium, plus 4% of the current value of the contract, minus the out of the moneyness. There is a minimum margin of the premium plus $\frac{3}{4}$ of 1% of the contract value.

Example 1

If the spot (current) price of the DM is .48 then:

1 DM Sep 49 Call at .24

on the Philadelphia Exchange has a margin requirement of $150 (premium) + .04 × $30,000 − $625 (out of the money) = $725. (The minimum would have been $375.)

Example 2

With the same spot price:

1 DM Sep 49 Put at 1.2

on the PHLX would have a margin requirement of $750 (premium) + .04 × $30,000 (spot value) = $1,950.

Spread margins   Here again, the logic of margins duplicates that of stock options. Call (put) spreads are covered when the long strike price is not higher (not lower) than the short strike price. Covered spreads have no margin requirement, but the difference in premiums must be deposited.

For uncovered spreads, the margin is the lesser of:

1. the margin on the short position

2. the dollar value of the difference in the strike prices

Example

With the JY spot at 65.40
Sell 1 Dec JY 65 Call at 1.00
Buy 1 Dec JY 66 Call at .60
(1) \$625 (premium) + .04 × 6,250,000 × .006540 = \$2,260
(2) 6,250,000 × (\$.0066 − \$.0065) = \$625

The lesser of these is \$625 from (2).

Straddle margins

Long straddles require that the premiums be on deposit. Short straddles require the larger of the two short margins.

Example

On the PHLX with the CD spot at .7450
Sell 1 Sep CD 75 Call at 0.5
Sell 1 Sep CD 75 Put at 1.0
Call Margin: \$250 (premium) + .04 × 50,000 × \$.7450 − \$250 (out of money) = \$1,490.
Put Margin: \$500 (premium) + .04 × 50,000 × \$.7450 = \$1,990.

In general, the (more) in the money option will have the higher margin. In this case, it is the put margin of \$1,990.

Position and exercise limits

With the usual definition of being on the same side, *i.e.,* long call and short put or long put and short call, the position limit is 100,000 contracts on the PHLX. Furthermore, these limits also govern the number of contracts that may be exercised over any five-consecutive-business-day period.

Option strategies

Individuals, or firms, engaged in foreign trade must continually consider the risks associated with the shifting relationships between the U.S. dollar and other currencies. For example, a firm doing business in Germany does so in DM and must make any purchases in that currency; similarly, any profits from such business would be in marks and must be converted to dollars before being reverted to the U.S.

Options allow one to hedge the risk in such a future conversion. For instance, if one felt the dollar was going to appreciate relative to the DM, one might buy DM puts, insuring (at the cost of the put premium) that one could later sell those DM at the strike price rather than at the "anticipated" lower price.

For speculators, the situation is analogous to that in stock options. By thinking of the foreign currency as a security with a current price and an anticipated future price, all of the same strategies apply. For example, if one felt exchange rates were going to remain stable, one might sell (write) puts or calls or straddles. On the other hand, if the opposite were true, one would buy such instruments.

Caps and LEAPS

Capped options are currently available on two stock indexes, the S&P 500 (SPX) and S&P 100 (OEX). Both are traded on the CBOE as "European-style" options, *i.e.*, they can only be exercised at expiration. Caps are set at 30 points above (for calls) and 30 points below (for puts) the strike price. For example, an SPX call with a strike price of 550 would have a cap of 580.

Note

These options are *automatically exercised* if the closing price is at or above the cap for calls (at or below the cap for puts). This is true even though the option has not expired, on the understanding that there is no point in holding the option any longer.

Example

An investor buys an SPX call with a strike price of 550. The S&P 500 closes at 580; the option is automatically exercised, and the investor realizes $30 \times \$500$ or $15,000, less the premium paid.

Although these options are normally exercised only at expiration, an investor can realize a profit earlier by selling the option.

Long Term Equity Anticipation Securities (LEAPS) are stock and index options with expirations of up to three years in the future. This longer term means they have higher premiums than traditional options; it also means that investors can focus on long-term considerations and avoid the risk of having their judgment invalidated by a short-term fluctuation—in other words, it reduces the role played by timing alone.

With respect to trading units, hours, settlement, exercise, and expiration, rules governing LEAPS stock options trading are the same as those for regular stock options. For premiums below $3, the minimum variation is $6.25 ($\frac{1}{16}$); above $3, the minimum is $12.50 ($\frac{1}{8}$).

LEAPS index options are available on the S&P 500 (SPX), a European-style option, and the S&P 100(OEX), an American-style option. Both are valued at 10% of the underlying contract. For example, with the S&P 100 at 525, strike prices for OEX leaps would typically be 50, $52\frac{1}{2}$, 55, etc., with the $52\frac{1}{2}$ option "at the money." If the index moved to 580, the holder of an option at $52\frac{1}{2}$ could exercise it and realize a gain of $5\frac{1}{2} \times \$100 = \$550$, less the premium.

TERMS

Option   Right to buy at specified price within given time; buyer pays for this right

Call option   Right to buy (call)

Put option   Right to sell

Holder   Buyer of contract

Writer   Seller of contract. If holder calls, writer must sell at specified price; if holder puts, writer must buy at specified price

Premium   Fee holder pays writer

Securities option   Usually 100 shares of stock

Options trading   OTC and through exchanges; no active secondary market

Options Clearing Corporation   Sets terms, provides forms, makes continuous market, supplies daily quotations; acts as principal in every transaction for listed options

Exchanges trading options   American, Pacific, Philadelphia, and New York Stock Exchanges, and the Chicago Board Options Exchange

Call options

Call holder   Has right to call (buy) from writer

Call writer   Has obligation to sell if option is called

Put options

Put holder   Has right to sell securities to writer

Put writer   Has obligation to buy if holder exercises his option

Terminology

Long an option   Holder of contract

Short an option   Writer of contract

Exercise or strike price   Price fixed in contract at which option can be exercised

Expiration month, listed options   Set by OCC in three quarterly cycles; expire Saturday following third Friday, 11:59 P.M. ET

Expiration OTC options   Varying terms

Types   Calls and puts

Class   All options of one type for a given stock

Series   Options identical in class, expiration date, and execution price

Premium   Fee charged by writer

Call holder (buyer)   Has right to buy at particular price; profits if market price of underlying stock rises

Call writer (seller)   Sells option to buy; takes loss if market price of underlying stock rises

Note   Call writer's loss generally equals call holder's gain and vice-versa

Put holder   Purchases right to sell at specified price; profits if market price of underlying stock falls

Put writer   Sells right to sell; must buy if option is exercised; takes a loss if market value of underlying stock falls

Intrinsic value   Value reflected if call (put) option exercise price is below (above) the current price of the underlying stock

In the money call   Option with strike price below market price

Out of the money call   Option with strike price above market price

At the money option   Strike price exactly equals market price

Out of the money put   Option with strike price below market price

In the money put   Strike price above the market price

Time value   All value not explicitly intrinsic; increases with volatility

Covered options

Covered call writer   Owns underlying security or holds unexpired long call on same stock

Covered put writer   Sells underlying security short or holds unexpired put on the security

Break-even points

Call buyer's break-even   When underlying security price = strike price + premium

Put buyer's break-even   When underlying security price = strike price – premium

Covered call writer   Break-even = original cost of underlying security – premium

Put writer short the underlying stock   Break-even = strike price + premium

Uncovered call writer   Break-even = strike price + premium

Uncovered put writer   Break-even = strike price – premium

Hedges

Long call/short stock   Buy call and sell short same security

Long put/long stock   Buying a put and buying shares of same stock

Straddles

Long straddle (buy a straddle)   Buy a put and a call of same expiration date and execution price for one security

Short straddle (write or sell a straddle)   Write a put and a call of same security, expiration date, and execution price

Combinations

Purchase (or sale) of a put and a call on the same security but with different expirations or different strike prices or both

Spreads

Buying and selling a call or a put on one security with either different expiration dates or different strike prices or both; spread = difference between premium paid and premium received on the two positions

Debit spread (buying the spread)   If premium paid is greater than premium received

Credit spread (selling the spread)   If premium paid is lower than premium received

Margin requirements

Apply only to writers of uncovered options

Covered call writer   No margin requirement if long underlying stock; holds long call on same stock with same or later expiration date and same or lower strike price

Covered put writer   Short underlying stock or holds long put option with same or later expiration date, same or greater strike price

Deposit requirements   Uncovered writers must have minimum deposit before any transactions

Margin for naked equity options   20% of value of underlying stock plus premium minus the out of the moneyness; minimum: premium plus 10% of the value of the underlying stock

Marked to market   Day's premiums and market prices are used to determine the necessary amount

Covered spreads   No margin requirement; customer must deposit difference between premium collected and the premium required

Call spread   Covered when long option has not higher strike and not earlier expiration than the short option

Put spread   Covered if long option has strike price no lower and expiration not earlier than short option

Transaction procedures

Issuing a contract   OCC contract is new offering under Securities Act of 1933; must provide prospectus (Option Disclosure Document)

Ordering procedure   Customer orders through brokerage firm; order executed on exchange floor; OCC clears transaction and issues the option contract

Exercise procedure   Customer exercises option; brokerage firm notifies OCC; OCC assigns contract to firm representing writers; firm assigns contract equitably

OCC   holds option contract obligation and acts as intermediary between buyer and seller

Required forms

Option information form   Signed by both customer and RR and approved by branch manager

Standard option agreement

Prospectus (options disclosure document)

New account form

Options clearing agreement   Between customer and OCC

Opening and closing transactions

Opening buy—long   Establishing long call or put position

Closing sell—long   Liquidating long call or put position

Opening sell—short   Establishing short call or put position

Closing buy—short   Liquidating short call or put position

Open interest   Number of shares still open long and short in a given series

Price   Strike (exercise) prices usually bracket current market price of underlying stock when introduced; then at $2.50 intervals for equities below $25/share, $5 intervals for those up to $200, and $10 above $200

Trading   Must cease at 3 P.M. CT on business day preceding expiration date; can be exercised until 5:30 P.M. ET that day

Expirations   Each listed option has four expiration months; at any given time, only the next three are available

Adjustments in contracts

Cash dividends   Exchange-traded options, no adjustment in price when dividend issued; over-the-counter options, option price reduced by amount of dividend

Stock dividends   Number of shares increased and exercise price decreased to reflect dividend on ex-dividend date

Stock splits   Number of shares or contracts and price adjusted

Position limits   (imposed on same side of option = long call and short put; short call and long put)

Tax

Expired options   Capital loss to holder, short-term capital gain to writer

Traded options   Sale of options position generates capital gain (or loss) of net proceeds less acquisition cost

Exercising   Taxes calculated only when security is sold; call premiums included in cost of acquisition

Spreads   Each option taxed separately

Stock index options

Contract size   Usually $100 times the value of the index

Settlement   Cash transactions, writer pays holder difference between strike price and the index value

Covered options   Do not exist

Expiration and exercise times   Exactly like stock options

American-style options   Can be exercised any time before expiration date

European-style options   May only be exercised during some specific period; no intrinsic value except during this period

Interest rate options   Including long-term index, T-note, and T-bond options, sometimes offered

REVIEW QUESTIONS

1. What percentage of the premium on a listed option must be deposited?

   (A) 25%
   (B) 50%
   (C) 60%
   (D) 100%

2. What would the owner of 1 ACI 45 Call have after a 3-for-2 stock split?

   (A) 1 ACI 45 Call
   (B) 1 ACI 45 Call for 150 shares
   (C) 1 ACI 30 Call
   (D) I ACI 30 Call for 150 shares

3. A writer of a CAI Dec 50 Call would be considered covered by OCC rules if he owned (was long):

(A) 1 CAI Dec 60 Call
(B) 1 CAI Sep 50 Call
(C) 1 CAI Mar 40 Call
(D) 1 CAI Dec 50 Put

Questions 4–5 are based on the following information: An investor buys 2 ACI Mar 45 Calls for a premium of 4 each. The current market price of ACI is 47. Answer all questions without regard to commissions.

4. What is the most that an investor could lose on this trade?

(A) $200
(B) $400
(C) $600
(D) $800

5. What is the break-even point?

(A) $45
(B) $47
(C) $49
(D) $51

6. All listed options are issued and guaranteed by the:

(A) SEC
(B) option writer
(C) exchange on which they are traded
(D) Options Clearing Corporation

7. All listed options expire at:

(A) 2:30 Central Time on the third Friday of expiration month
(B) 3:30 Central Time on the third Friday of expiration month
(C) 4:30 Central Time on the third Friday of expiration month
(D) 10:59 Central Time on the Saturday after the third Friday

8. Being long a straddle means:

(A) short a call and long a put
(B) short a call and short a put
(C) long a call and long a put
(D) long a call and short a put

9. Which of the following is true for listed options?

(A) cash dividends raise the strike price
(B) cash dividends reduce the strike price
(C) stock dividends raise the number of shares controlled by an option
(D) stock dividends raise the strike price

10. When a brokerage firm is notified that an investor wishes to exercise an option, it notifies the:

(A) writer
(B) OCC
(C) AMEX or CBOE
(D) exerciser

11. An uncovered put writer will suffer a loss if:

(A) the option expires unexercised
(B) the price of the stock rises
(C) the price of the stock drops by less than the premium
(D) the price of the stock drops by more than the premium

12. An investor buys 200 shares of ACI at $50. At the same time, he writes 1 ACI Dec 55 Call at 2. If the option expires without being exercised, what profit (or loss) will the investor realize on the stock?

(A) –$400
(B) $200
(C) $600
(D) cannot be determined

13. An investor bought 100 shares of CAI at 38 and, at the same time, wrote 1 CAI Feb 35 Call at 5. At what price will he break even?

    (A) $30
    (B) $33
    (C) $35
    (D) $38

Questions 14–15 are based on the following information: An investor buys 1 ACI Dec 45 Call at $1\frac{1}{2}$ and simultaneously sells 1 ACI Dec 40 Call at $5\frac{1}{2}$. Assume ACI is selling at 43 at that time.

14. These option transactions would be called:

    (A) a long straddle
    (B) a short straddle
    (C) a bull spread
    (D) a bear spread

15. If the options are held to expiration, the investor will have a maximum profit if ACI:

    (A) closes above 45
    (B) closes at or below 45
    (C) closes above 40
    (D) closes at or below 40

16. Which of the following pairs are on the same side?

    I. long calls, long puts
    II. long calls, short puts
    III. short calls, long puts
    IV. short calls, short puts

    (A) I and III
    (B) I and IV
    (C) II and III
    (D) II and IV

17. The largest limit on the number of listed stock options of the same class held by any individual or group acting in concert is:

    (A) 2,000
    (B) 4,000
    (C) 6,000
    (D) 8,000

18. Which of the following would be considered the same class of options?

    (A) 1 ACI Dec 50 Call and 1 ACI Dec 50 Put
    (B) 1 ACI Dec 45 Call and 1 CAI Sep 40 Call
    (C) 1 CAI Sep 40 Call and 1 CAI Mar 60 Call
    (D) 1 CAI Sep 45 Call and 1 CAI Mar 45 Put

19. The price an investor pays for buying an option is called:

    (A) strike price
    (B) exercise price
    (C) premium
    (D) listed cost

Questions 20–22 are based on the following information: In May of 1987, an investor bought 100 shares of Amalgamated Consolidated Incorporated (ACI) at $53 per share. In July, 1987, he then bought 1 ACI Dec 50 Put at $\frac{1}{2}$.

20. If the put expires without being exercised, what are the tax consequences for the investor regarding the premium?

    (A) a $50 capital loss
    (B) a $50 income loss
    (C) an addition of $50 to his cost of the ACI stock
    (D) cannot be determined until the stock is sold

21. If the investor sells the stock for $50 in August, what are the tax consequences of that transaction?

    (A) he realizes a $300 capital loss
    (B) he realizes a $350 capital loss
    (C) he realizes a $300 capital gain
    (D) there are no consequences until the option expires

22. If the option is exercised and no other transactions take place, what is the investor's net stock position?

    (A) long 0 shares
    (B) long 100 shares of ACI
    (C) long 200 shares of ACI
    (D) short 100 shares of ACI

23. The most speculative of the following options transactions is probably:

    (A) sell a call and buy the stock
    (B) sell a call and short the stock
    (C) buy a call and short the stock
    (D) buy a call

    Questions 24 and 25 assume that the margin requirement includes 20% of the value of the underlying stock.

24. What is the margin requirement for writing an uncovered CAI Sep 30 Put at 4 if CAI is selling at 28?

    (A) $400
    (B) $560
    (C) $960
    (D) $2,000

25. What is the margin requirement for writing an uncovered CAI Jun 40 Call at 2 if CAI is selling at 37?

    (A) $200
    (B) $300
    (C) $640
    (D) $940

26. The premium on an option not in the money is said to be:

    (A) the strike price
    (B) its intrinsic value
    (C) its time value
    (D) its out of the moneyness

27. An investor owns 1 ACI Aug 45 Call. A cash dividend is declared with an ex-dividend date of July 10. The investor is entitled to that dividend:

    (A) never
    (B) always
    (C) if he exercises before July 10
    (D) if he exercises after July 10

28. A premium of 1.20 on a T-bill option would require payment of:

    (A) $1,200
    (B) $3,000
    (C) $12,000
    (D) $30,000

    Questions 29 and 30 assume an investor buys 2 at the money ACI Dec 70 Calls and 2 ACI Dec 70 Puts for a total premium of $2,000.

29. The investor can do no better than break even if:

    I. ACI goes to 80
    II. ACI goes to 76 and subsequently falls to 66
    III. ACI goes to 50
    IV. ACI goes to 60 and then rises to 70

    (A) I only
    (B) I and III only
    (C) I, II, and III
    (D) I, II, and IV

30. The maximum possible results from this position are:

    (A) $1,000 loss and $7,000 gain
    (B) $2,000 loss and $14,000 gain
    (C) $2,000 loss and unlimited gain
    (D) cannot be determined

ANSWERS TO REVIEW QUESTIONS

1. **(D)** The full premium price must be deposited when purchasing options.

2. **(D)** The number of shares is increased, and the strike is decreased equivalently. The same is true when stock dividends are declared.

3. **(C)** The covering call option must have a not higher strike and a not earlier expiration.

4. **(D)** If they expire unexercised, the investor loses the premium $2 \times \$400$.

5. **(C)** To break even, the investor must recapture the premium. He does this by exercising at 49.

6. **(D)** The OCC takes the other side on all listed options contracts.

7. **(D)** Since most options trade in the midwest, expiration time is often quoted in Central Time.

8. **(C)** A straddle is a put and a call of the same strike and expiration. Being long means owning both options.

9. **(C)** There is no adjustment for cash dividends. Stock dividends increase the number of shares and decrease the strike.

10. **(B)** When an investor wishes to exercise, he notifies his broker who in turn notifies the OCC (or does so through a clearing member of the exchange).

11. **(D)** The writer collects a premium. If the exercise price is lower than the strike minus the premium, the writer loses.

12. **(D)** All we know is that he collected the premium and the price of the stock is not above $55.

13. **(B)** By collecting a $500 premium, the investor is protected until the price drops below $33, the break-even point.

14. **(D)** A bear spread is profitable if the price of the stock drops.

15. **(D)** The maximum profit occurs if neither option is exercised. This occurs at or below 40.

16. **(C)** Holding II, you would like the stock price to rise; with III you would like it to fall.

17. **(D)** This limit holds for stock with 120 million shares outstanding and 30 million in trading volume over six months.

18. **(C)** A class is all options of a type (call or put) in the same stock.

19. **(C)** Choices (A) and (B), the strike or exercise price, are prices at which the investor can buy the stock, not the option.

20. **(A)** The asset became worthless.

21. **(A)** The option has no tax consequence unless sold or exercised or it expires.

22. **(A)** When the investor exercises a put he sells the 100 shares which had been bought.

23. **(B)** Choice D risks the premium, A is a covered option, and C loses if the stock goes up. B loses more since he is short a call.

24. **(C)** The margin is 20% of $2,800 + $400 premium or $960.

25. **(C)** 20% × $3,700 + $200 − $300 out of the money or $640.

26. **(C)** The intrinsic value is the amount it is in money.

27. **(C)** If he exercises before July 10, he then owns the stock and is the owner of record when the dividend is declared.

28. **(B)** The premium is quoted on the basis of $25 for a basis point. Hence, 1.20 or 120 points × $25 = $3,000.

29. **(D)** If ACI goes to 50, he can do better than break even by exercising the put and collecting $4,000. In all other cases, he can break even.

30. **(C)** The maximum possible loss is the $2,000 of premium. The maximum gain is unlimited since the stock price can rise without limit.

CHAPTER TEN
client accounts

This chapter outlines procedures and rules for opening and maintaining customer brokerage accounts. All customer accounts with a brokerage firm are either cash accounts or margin accounts.

The cash account customer who purchases securities pays the full amount required. A margin account customer pays for his purchases by borrowing some portion of its cost from the firm and putting up the difference himself. Margin accounts are discussed fully in Chapter 11, though they are mentioned here when applicable.

OPENING A NEW ACCOUNT

The registered representative is responsible for knowing the relevant facts about the customer. This responsibility is spelled out in NYSE Rule 405, the "Know Your Customer" rule, which is one of the most crucial of the exchange's regulations.

249

Under this rule, member brokerage firms, their partners, officers, managers, and registered representatives are charged to "use due diligence to learn the essential facts relative to every customer, every order, every cash or margin account accepted or carried" by the firm.

The new account form

To satisfy NYSE Rule 405, every firm requires that a new account form be filed for each prospective customer and be approved by the firm's management. Essentially, this is written proof that an individual is legally authorized to open an account. The form varies from firm to firm, but all contain at least the following information:

- name(s)—family name and at least one full name; an initial is not sufficient

- address and telephone number—usually for both residence and business

- social security number (or tax identification number)—required by the IRS to identify dividend recipients and often also required by transfer agents

- age

- marital status

- occupation and employer and type of business; certain employees connected with financial institutions (see below) cannot open an account without special approval

- bank reference

- brokerage reference—from any other brokerage accounts

- citizenship—non-citizens may be subject to certain taxes on dividends

- cash or margin account

- relationship—to the registered representative, if any

- investment objectives

Information about the customer's income and assets may also be sought. If more than one person is authorized to trade in the account, names and occupations of all others should also be included. This is particularly important when a husband and wife have independent accounts.

Such a form is required for *every* new account. It must be reviewed and approved by an executive officer or general partner of the firm. In some cases, a branch manager can provide interim approval while the form is forwarded to the responsible official.

…

NEW ACCOUNT FORM

Check if updating existing account:	Acct. Type	Citizenship (if not U.S.) ↓	Household Search Name: _____ A/C No.: _____		Branch	Account No.	FA	Doc. ID **40**

PSI Retirement Documents? ↑

1. Client Information

Legal Name/Title and Address:
__ Mr. __ Mrs.
__ Ms. __ Dr. _____
__ Mr. __ Mrs.
__ Ms. __ Dr. _____
__ Mr. __ Mrs.
__ Ms. __ Dr. _____

☐ SSN ☐ EIN   Date of Birth   TIC%

City, State, ZIP _____

Mailing (NAD 1) Title/Address (if different)

Foreign Zone Code: _____ Country Code: ___ ___ City, State, ZIP _____

1. Home Tel. No.: ( )	2. Business Tel. No.: ( )	3. Cellular Tel. No.: ( )	4. Fax. Tel. No.: ( )

2. Client Profile

Assets ☐ All parties ☐ 1st party Currency: (Int'l only) _____

Stated Annual Income: ___ ___

Is Client on a Fixed Income ☐ Yes ☐ No

Stated Net Worth (excl. res.): ___ ___

Stated Liquid Net Worth: ___ ___

Federal Tax Bracket: ___ ___

Personal

Gender: ☐ Male ☐ Female

☐ Single ☐ Married ☐ Widow ☐ Divorced

Number of Dependents: ___ ___

Residence: ☐ Owns ☐ Rents Yrs. There: ___

Mother's Maiden Name: _____

Formal Education: ___ ___

Employment Status: ___ ___

Occupation: ___ ___

Is Client employed, or Associated Person, in the securities brokerage industry? ☐ Yes ☐ No

If no, Industry: ___ ___

Employer: _____ Yrs. ___

Is Client or any other member of Client's immediate family (spouse, parents, children and their spouses, brother or sister, or any in-laws) employed by or otherwise affiliated with a broker/dealer, bank, insurance company, savings and loan institution or other financial institution?
☐ Yes ☐ No

Client's corporate relationship, if any:

☐ 10% Stockholder ☐ Officer ☐ Director

If publicly traded, Symbol/CUSIP _____

FA has known Client ☐ less than one year, or _____ years.

Introduction source: ___ ___

Client's Investment Experience

Number of years in: Equities: _____ Bonds: _____

Options: _____ Futures: _____ Mutual Fds. _____

Spousal Information
(For 1st Person Named in the Title)

Name: _____

Employment Status: ___ ___

Occupation: ___ ___

Is **spouse** employed, or Associated Person, in the securities brokerage industry? ☐ Yes ☐ No

If no, Industry: ___ ___

Employer: _____ Yrs. ___

Client's Other Brokerage Account

Firm: _____

A/C No. (PSI Employees): _____

Type: ___ ___

3. Account Classification

Stated Investment Objective

You must choose at least one. You may rank up to 2 objectives (1=primary, 2=secondary).

Preservation of Capital: _____ Speculation: _____

Income: _____ Growth: _____

Short Term Gain: _____ Hedge: _____

Client's Risk Tolerance ___ ___

Initial Transaction ☐ Account Transfer

☐ Rec'd Securities ☐ Rec'd Check/Funds

☐ Purch. of: _____ ☐ Sale of: _____

Kind of Account

☐ Securities ☐ Speculative Futures

☐ T-Bill ☐ Hedge Futures

Pledge Account: ☐ Flex Res. ☐ Prime Res.

☐ Margin ☐ Cash

☐ COMMAND ☐ Custom COMMAND

☐ BusinessEdge

☐ CMMD Essentials ☐ Cust. Essentials

Money Fund Instructions ___ ___

Dividend Options

☐ Auto. Div. Payment - Monthly Check

  ☐ Excl. principal ☐ NYC Bonds

Div. Reinvestment Program ☐ Yes ☐ No

COMMAND Dividend Instructions

Monthly Dividend Payment Date(s): _____

Monthly **Fixed** Payment:

Amount: _____ Date: _____

COMMAND Fee Payment Election:

☐ Annual ☐ Monthly

☐ Broker Book

Does Client object to PSI disclosing name, address and securities positions to corporate issuers under an SEC rule designed to permit users to communicate directly with non-objecting owners?

☐ Objects/OBO ☐ Doesn't Obj./NOBO

Retirement Accounts (check all that apply)

Is this a rollover account? ☐ Yes ☐ No

Custodian? ☐ PSI ☐ Other:

Whose Account? ☐ Employee ☐ Employer

Related Retirement A/C: _____

Additional Classifications

DVP: ___ ___ REPO: ___ ___

Managed Program/Outside Inv. Mgr.: _____

MCSI #: ___ ___ ___ - ___ ___

Fee Arrangement: ☐ Wrap ☐ Fee + Comm ☐ VIP

Power of Attorney*: ☐ No If yes, _____
*(FA Full Power needs Compliance approval)

Employee Account

Employee at? ☐ PSI Branch ☐ Other: _____

Employee Related Account

  Financially dependent? ☐ Branch ☐ HO/Reg.

  Financially independent ☐

Related Employee Name: _____

Related Employee SS #: ___ - ___ - ___

POA's, Agent or other XTOP: _____

City, State, ZIP _____

XTOP receives: ☐ Statements ☐ Confirms
For: ☐ Securities ☐ Futures

4. Review / Signature

The information contained herein has been obtained from the Client
FA(Print): _____ Signature: _____ Date: _____

Manager has verified that FA is properly state registered.
Manager(Print): _____ Signature: _____ Date: _____

Figure 10.1 New Account Form

Other customer forms

Other forms may be required, often as part of a customer's agreement. Depending on the type of account, these include:

Hypothecation agreement   An agreement that must be signed for a margin account; it gives the broker the right to pledge the customer's securities as collateral to secure a bank loan (see Chapter 11).

Credit agreement   An agreement required for margin accounts to spell out the method of calculating and charging interest on balances.

Loan consent agreement   An agreement for margin accounts allowing the broker to lend customer securities to other brokerage firms, *e.g.,* for short sales.

Options agreement   As outlined in Chapter 9, this agreement is required if options will be traded in either cash or margin accounts.

Power of attorney   If someone other than the customer has authority to act in the account, such a power must be obtained for either cash or margin accounts.

TYPES OF CUSTOMER ACCOUNTS

Individual account

This is a cash or margin account in one name, owned by one person.

Joint account

A cash or margin account in the names of two or more individuals either as:

- "Tenants in common account" (or agreement)—In which interest is divided; should one of the tenants die, that person's portion of the interest becomes the property of his or her estate; or

- "Joint tenants with rights of survivorship"—In which each party's interest is undivided; should one tenant die, the deceased's portion goes to the surviving party(ies) and not to the estate. This agreement is most common between married couples.

In opening a joint account, the registered representative must obtain a joint account agreement in addition to the new account and other forms mentioned above.

Corporate account

This is held in the name of a corporation. The registered representative and the brokerage firm must be sure they are dealing with a person or persons specifically authorized to conduct securities transactions. For this reason, a copy of the corporate resolution authorizing specific persons to trade, passed by the board of directors and signed by the corporation secretary, is required.

This resolution must state that the corporation is legally incorporated and that its charter and by-laws permit stock trading. Requirements for a corporate margin account are similar. These forms are required in addition to all pertinent documents mentioned above.

Partnership account

Held in the name of a partnership, these require not only new account and other pertinent forms, but a copy of the partnership agreement, which makes the action of each individual partner binding on the other partner(s).

Unincorporated associations

Accounts held in the name of investment clubs, nonprofit organizations (charities, schools, churches, hospitals, etc.) and hedge funds. These require a copy of the group's constitution or other document authorizing securities transactions and a copy of a resolution naming specific persons to act for the organization, in addition to any other needed forms.

Fiduciary accounts

"Fiduciary" is the term for a person or institution legally authorized to act on behalf of an individual, such as a trustee or guardian, the administrator or executor of an estate, or a receiver in bankruptcy. A fiduciary can open only a cash account; margin accounts are usually not allowed.

With these accounts, in addition to the new accounts form, the brokerage firm must obtain a legal document certifying the individual's authority to transact business. For example:

- Trustees—must present a copy of the trust whether it has been established in a will or is a "living trust," *i.e.,* one set up by a living person.

- Guardians—must present a court certificate showing their appointment as guardian, *i.e.,* as the person designated to handle the affairs of a minor or of someone deemed incompetent.

- Executors and administrators of estates ("executor" is the person designated in a will, an "administrator" is usually appointed by a court when an individual dies without a will)—must present copies of the death certificate and will, a court order recognizing the executor, waivers on inheritance tax, and proof of domicile.

- Receivers in bankruptcy—must present the court order showing they have been appointed receivers.

- Conservator for an incompetent—must present the court order appointing him or her as conservator of someone judged incapable of handling his or her own affairs.

Unless they are specifically granted legal permission to do otherwise, fiduciary accounts must be handled according to the rules on securities investment in their state. These laws are of two types:

"Legal list"   Some states provide a list of approved securities, and the fiduciary is allowed to buy only items on that list.

"Prudent man rule"   Some state statutes do not restrict the fiduciary's investment, except to say that purchases and sales must be "reasonably prudent," *i.e.*, to bring a reasonable income and preservation of capital.

Investment advisors' accounts

Some individuals may be registered with the SEC as investment advisors under the Investment Company Act of 1940. A registered advisor may open an "omnibus account," which shows the advisor as the person who introduced the customer but lists each account separately.

The advisor must present a power of attorney, a new account form, and a trading authorization for each customer, as well as written instructions indicating where to send duplicate confirmations. (The original goes to the advisor.)

CUSTODIAN ACCOUNTS FOR MINORS

Minors are not legally entitled to own securities, as they cannot execute a contract, *e.g.*, endorse a stock certificate. Thus, a registered representative can prudently maintain an account for a minor only through an adult custodian. Such accounts are regulated in all states by the Uniform Gifts to Minors Act (UGMA), which includes the following rules for custodian accounts:

1. All gifts to minors must be irrevocable. This means the donor gives up all rights and may not withdraw the gift, nor can the minor return it. Gifts must be "new"; property already owned by the minor cannot be part of a gift.

2. The donor can give cash or securities of any type; there is no limitation on the amount. In most (but not all) states, gifts under the UGMA cannot be established through a will.

3. The donor appoints the custodian who may be the donor or another party. However, when the gift is bearer securities, the custodian must be someone else.

    Specifically with regard to brokerage accounts, the law holds:

4. Custodian accounts cannot purchase securities on margin (be margin accounts) or pledge securities for a loan. Securities donated as a gift cannot be purchased on margin.

5. There can only be *one* custodian and *one* minor for each account. Neither joint custodians nor joint tenants are permitted.

6. Securities bought for or sold from the account must be in registered form, in the customer's name, showing the minor as legal owner. For example, "John Doe as custodian for Sally Doe under the Uniform Gifts to Minors Act of the State of Ohio."

   Bearer instruments and stocks held in a "street name" cannot be held in the account. This also excludes options, since there is no evidence of ownership. (Bearer securities can be given to a minor if accompanied by a Deed of Gift, but the donor may not designate himself or herself as the custodian of such securities.)

7. Any payment from the account must be in the name of the custodian acting on behalf of the minor and never in the custodian's name alone.

8. The account must show the minor's tax identification number; the minor bears tax liability for the account.

9. The account is completely controlled by the custodian who may buy or sell securities and exercise (or not exercise) rights, warrants, or options solely as he or she sees fit. This also means that the custodian cannot enter into an agreement allowing a third party to trade in the account.

10. If the custodian dies or resigns, a new custodian must be appointed by a court (unless the custodian designates a successor).

11. If the minor dies, the account is terminated, and the gift becomes part of the minor's estate.

12. Money may be taken from the account for the minor's benefit; for example, for his or her support or education.

13. Proceeds from sales or dividends may be held in the account for a reasonable amount of time; if they are not then reinvested, they must be put in a bank.

14. The custodian must maintain proper records. He or she is entitled to a reasonable sum for services in operating the account and to reimbursement for expenses if he or she is not the donor.

15. Once the minor reaches the age of majority, all securities and cash in the account must be transferred into his or her name.

Note

A guardian has no control over a custodial account (unless of course the guardian is the custodian).

The term "beneficial owner" is often used in discussing custodial accounts. This is the person for whom property is being held, in this case, the minor. No special documents, beyond the New Account Form, are required to open a custodial account under the UGMA.

RESTRICTIONS ON NEW ACCOUNTS

Restricted persons

Under NYSE Rule 407, a registered representative cannot open an account for certain persons without special written approval. These include:

NYSE employees   These employees must have written permission from their employers to open a cash or margin account. This applies to employees and members of AMEX and other exchanges and to spouses of employees of the above.

Registered representatives and other employees, including partners, of brokerage firms and their spouses   Must have written permission from their employer (or another partner if a partner is involved) to open a cash or margin account. After each trade, duplicate copies of each confirmation must be sent to a designated person (partner or officer) in the employing firm.

Individuals employed by a bank, insurance company, trust company or other financial organization   Must have written permission from their employers to open a margin account (but not for a cash account). This does not include officers of such companies, who are not considered employees.

Aliens   There are some restrictions on persons who are not citizens of the United States.

"Control persons" and those holding restricted securities   They are subject to certain conditions on transactions according to the Securities Act of 1933 and SEC rules (see Chapter 15.)

Other restrictions on accounts

Discretionary accounts   The holder of an account can give another party (including a registered representative) the right to make decisions about, and transactions in, that account. In such cases, the account holder must provide written authorization. All orders for such accounts:

*   must be marked discretionary

*   must be suitable for the account

*   must be approved on the day they are entered by a partner or officer of the brokerage firm or by some person in the firm specifically named to provide such approval

Discretionary accounts allow the broker to decide not only when to buy and sell, and at what price, but to choose the securities to be traded. Lacking a discretionary account, the customer must specify the security.

Both NYSE and NASD rules require that these accounts be reviewed frequently by a member of the firm other than the person exercising discretion. A particular concern is to avoid "churning," or excessive trading in an account simply to generate more commissions without regard to the benefit of the client.

Power of attorney   If a customer wants another party to have the authority to trade in the account, a written power must be obtained. In such accounts, the original confirmation of a transaction is sent to the holder of the power of attorney, and a duplicate is sent to the customer.

"Refusal to receive duplicate confirmation"   This refusal can be entered by a customer with an account under power of attorney.

Numbered account   A customer who wishes to keep his or her identity a secret may have transactions conducted so that only a number appears. Holders of such accounts must provide the brokerage firm with a letter stating the actual ownership of the account.

Second accounts   A customer who opens more than one account with a firm should sign a "Two or More Accounts Form."

REQUIREMENTS IN DEALING WITH DECEASED PERSONS' ACCOUNTS

When an account-holder dies, all unexecuted orders must be canceled, and all records of the account should be marked to show date of death. Any assets in the account should be considered frozen until the necessary documents are presented by a legally authorized person to transfer ownership to the proper beneficiary. The actual documents needed vary according to the type of account. Similar rules apply for accounts held by a person declared incompetent or bankrupt.

Individual account

- copy of will; if there is no will, a Surrogate Court Certificate
- copy of death certificate
- appointment of executor as stated in the will; if there is no will, court appointment of administrator
- tax waivers (this document attests to the payment of inheritance taxes; it may be necessary to have one from both the state of domicile and the state of incorporation)
- certificate of domicile (showing state in which the deceased resided)

Joint tenants with rights of survivorship

- copy of death certificate
- tax waivers

Tenants in common

All documents listed for an individual account and written instructions on transferring the securities from the executor (or administrator) are required.

Partnership account

If one partner dies, the partnership no longer exists. Surviving partner(s) must then file a new partnership account form and give written instructions on how to dispose of the deceased's share.

Account with power of attorney

If the signer of the power of attorney dies, the power of attorney is terminated.

ORDER PROCEDURES FOR CLIENT ACCOUNTS

The order ticket

Orders from a customer must be presented, in writing, to the firm's wire room or order room. A standardized form (or order ticket) is used. These vary slightly but must include:

- client's name and account number
- registered representative's identification number
- description of securities involved—name (or symbol) and number of shares or bonds (*e.g.*, 100 shares Xerox, or 5M PG&E 7% of 2015)
- market on which the security is traded (*e.g.*, NYSE or OTC)
- price limitations—if it is a limit, stop, or market order
- time limitations—if it is a day or GTC order
- nature of the order, *i.e.*, buy, sell (long, short); if an option order: buy, write (covered or uncovered), open, close
- type of account (cash, margin, etc.)
- special instructions—*e.g.*, on settlement or payment

The customer's name must appear on the ticket; blank tickets are not allowed. If the name is incorrect, or if the wrong customer's name appears, it can be changed only with the permission of an officer of the firm. All errors on order tickets must be reported to an officer immediately.

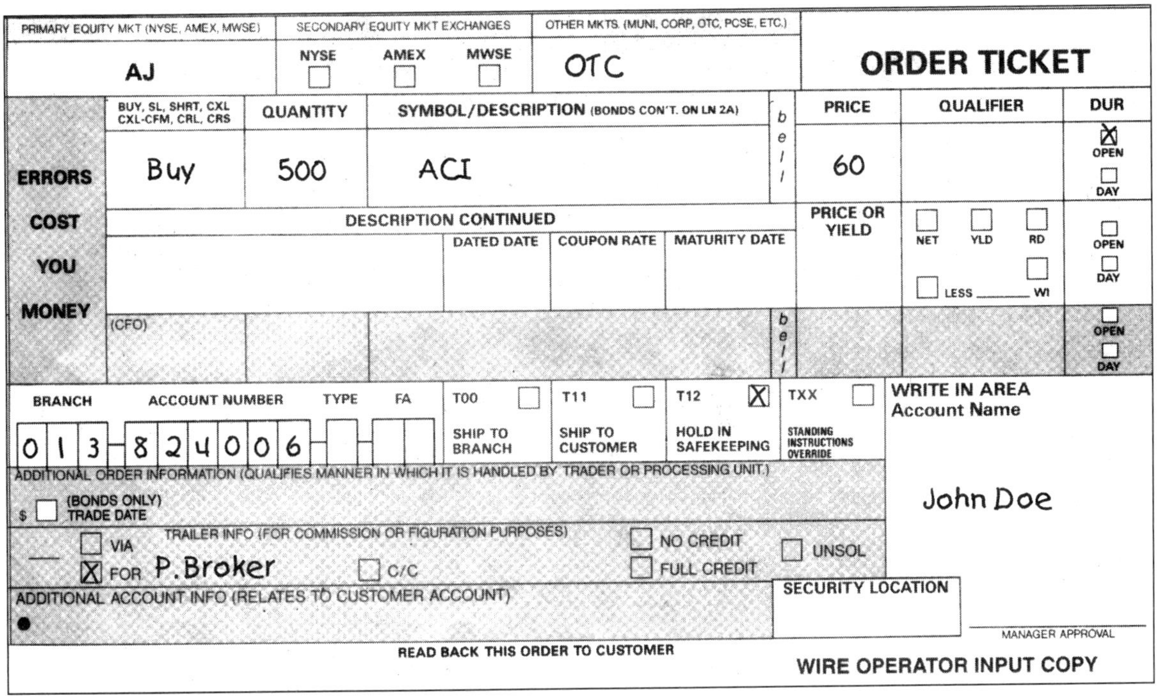
PRIMARY EQUITY MKT (NYSE, AMEX, MWSE) | SECONDARY EQUITY MKT EXCHANGES | OTHER MKTS. (MUNI, CORP, OTC, PCSE, ETC.)
AJ | NYSE AMEX MWSE | OTC
ORDER TICKET
ERRORS COST YOU MONEY
BUY, SL, SHRT, CXL CXL-CFM, CRL, CRS: Buy
QUANTITY: 500
SYMBOL/DESCRIPTION (BONDS CON'T. ON LN 2A): ACI
b e l l
PRICE: 60
QUALIFIER
DUR: [X] OPEN / DAY
DESCRIPTION CONTINUED
DATED DATE | COUPON RATE | MATURITY DATE
PRICE OR YIELD
NET YLD RD
LESS ____ WI
OPEN DAY
(CFO)
BRANCH: 013 | ACCOUNT NUMBER: 824006 | TYPE | FA
T00 SHIP TO BRANCH | T11 SHIP TO CUSTOMER | T12 [X] HOLD IN SAFEKEEPING | TXX STANDING INSTRUCTIONS OVERRIDE
WRITE IN AREA Account Name: John Doe
ADDITIONAL ORDER INFORMATION (QUALIFIES MANNER IN WHICH IT IS HANDLED BY TRADER OR PROCESSING UNIT.)
$ (BONDS ONLY) TRADE DATE
TRAILER INFO (FOR COMMISSION OR FIGURATION PURPOSES)
VIA
[X] FOR P.Broker
C/C
NO CREDIT
FULL CREDIT
UNSOL
ADDITIONAL ACCOUNT INFO (RELATES TO CUSTOMER ACCOUNT)
SECURITY LOCATION
MANAGER APPROVAL
READ BACK THIS ORDER TO CUSTOMER
WIRE OPERATOR INPUT COPY

Figure 10.2 Order Ticket

Client confirmations

With every transaction, a client must receive a written confirmation. This document must include:

- Client's name and account number
- Broker's name
- Trade and settlement dates
- Price bought [or] sold
- Market on which traded
- Commission
- Interest, taxes, registration fees, and/or postage
- Net amount

In addition, for municipal bond trades, confirmation must disclose whether it is a dealer or broker transaction and the bond's dated date.

Reviewing the report of execution

Once a transaction has been executed, a report is sent to the broker who initiated it. This report must be compared to the order ticket; if there is a discrepancy, it must be reported to an officer of the firm at once before any other action is taken. Customers are not bound by errors arising from this discrepancy.

However, an error *in reporting* is not binding on the broker. That is, if the confirmation is inaccurate but the order was filled correctly, the actual trade is binding on the customer. For example, a registered representative receives a confirmation that a particular "at the market" buy order was executed at $35\frac{1}{2}$. Later, he learns the actual price was 36. The customer must accept the price of 36.

Records of customer's transactions

A broker must keep a cross-indexed record of a client's holdings, *i.e.*:

- a "customer book" which gives details of each client's security positions
- a stock record which breaks down customer's holdings by security

"Back office" order processing

The clerical duties in a brokerage firm are handled in several departments, usually referred to as "the back office." Following the trail of a transaction, they are:

Order department (or wire room or order room) The order ticket goes first to this department which transmits it to the proper market for execution. When that market confirms the transaction verbally, this confirmation is noted on the ticket. One copy of the order ticket is retained in the Order Department; the others go to:

Purchase and sales (P&S) department This department prepares a confirmation for the customer, computes all of the consequences of the transaction, records them in customer accounts, and handles billings.

Margin department This section is responsible for collecting monies due from both cash and margin accounts. It learns of a trade from the order ticket but does not act until it receives figures from the P&S department. It then handles all activities involving credit, computing when and how much money customers must deposit in cash or margin accounts.

Bookkeeping department Copies of the order ticket also go to this department, which maintains an updated record of all client accounts for the previous six years.

Registered representative Finally, the order ticket is sent back to the registered representative who gives it a last check for errors.

Other back office functions

Cashiering department This department is responsible for receiving and delivering securities and money. All transactions are recorded daily on a "blotter" kept by the cashier. This department also keeps a record, called a "box," of all securities currently in the firm's possession. Upon receipt of instructions from the margin department (called "transfer and ship"), the cashier will remove the named securities from the box, send them to the transfer agent, and then deliver them to the customer once his or her name has been registered. Similarly, the cashier will issue payment on instructions from the margin department.

Securities held by a brokerage firm are usually held in a street name, *i.e.*, the firm's name, until transferred.

Dividend department   Ensures that dividends and interest payments on securities held by the firm for customers are properly credited to customer accounts.

Proxy department   Ensures that proxy statements and information, such as financial reports, go to customers whose securities the firm is holding.

Reorganization department   Advises customers of reorganizations involving securities that the firm is holding for them. This department also oversees calls when issued by a corporation, handles conversions at the customer's request, assists in subscriptions for new shares in a rights offering, etc.

Stock record department   This department maintains a record of all securities held by the firm by name of security and customer and number of shares.

Controller's department (or controller)   The controller oversees the cashier's department and is responsible for the firm's internal accounts (payroll, etc.), for record-keeping, and for filing reports required by regulatory bodies.

TERMS

Cash account   Purchaser pays full amount required

Margin account   Purchaser borrows portion of cost from firm

NYSE Rule 405 "Know Your Customer"   RR is responsible for knowing all pertinent facts about any customer

Required forms

New account form   For each prospective customer, reviewed and approved by executive officer or general partner

Margin account   Hypothecation agreement, credit agreement, loan consent agreement

Others   Options agreement, power of attorney, joint account agreement

Types of accounts

Individual account   Cash or margin account owned by one person

Joint account   Cash or margin account in the names of two or more individuals, as tenants in common or joint tenants with rights of survivorship

Corporate account   Held in name of corporation; requires copy of corporate resolution authorizing trade

Partnership account   Held in name of partnership; requires copy of partnership agreement

Unincorporated associations   Require copy of document authorizing securities transactions and resolution naming specific person(s) to act

Fiduciary accounts   Held by person or institution legally authorized to act on behalf of an individual; margin accounts usually not allowed; require legal document authorizing fiduciary to transact business

Legal list   State-approved list of securities for fiduciaries

Prudent man rule   Statute holding purchases and sales by fiduciaries must be "reasonably prudent"

Investment advisor's accounts   Individuals registered with SEC as investment advisors may open omnibus account; must present power of attorney and trading authorization for each customer

Minors' accounts   RR can maintain only through adult custodian under Uniform Gifts to Minors Act (UGMA):

Numbered account   Customer must provide firm with letter stating actual ownership

Two or more accounts form   From customer who opens more than one account with a firm

Death of account-holder   All unexecuted orders canceled; assets frozen until documents presented to transfer ownership to beneficiary

Order procedure

Order ticket   In writing to wire room or order room

Order department   Transmits order to proper market; when market confirms, sends copies of order ticket to purchase and sales

Purchase and sales (P&S)   Prepares confirmation for customer, records transaction in customer accounts, handles billings

Margin department   Collects monies due from both cash and margin accounts and computes amount due from customers

Bookkeeping department   Maintains updated records of all client accounts

Cashiering department   Receives and delivers securities and money

Dividend, proxy, reorganization departments   Ensure that securities held for customers are properly credited with dividends, etc.

Stock record department   Maintains a record of all securities held by firm

Controller   Oversees cashier; handles internal accounts; files reports required by regulatory bodies

REVIEW QUESTIONS

1. On opening a new account, the registered representative has a responsibility to determine which of the following?

   I. the customer's investment objectives
   II. the customer's prior trading record
   III. the customer's financial means

   (A) I only
   (B) I and II
   (C) I and III
   (D) I, II, and III

2. A customer enters a GTC order and then goes on vacation. If the customer wants the stock but will not return in time to pay for it by the settlement day, the account executive should:

   (A) pay for it himself and be reimbursed
   (B) request an extension
   (C) cancel the order
   (D) transfer the order to a house account

3. The term limited trading authority allows its possessor to:

   (A) enter orders without further authorization
   (B) withdraw cash from the account
   (C) withdraw securities from the account
   (D) none of the above

4. When a client dies, the registered representative must:

   I. close the account
   II. cancel all open orders
   III. await the instructions of the executor
   IV. fill or kill all open orders

   (A) I and II
   (B) II and III
   (C) II and IV
   (D) I, II, and III

5. All of the following customer records must be kept by the registered representative EXCEPT:

   (A) each customer's current position
   (B) each customer's purchase and sale for the past three years
   (C) each customer's dividend income for the past three years
   (D) a cross-indexed file of his entire customer holdings

6. Under the Uniform Gift to Minors Act, which of the following is true with respect to the custodian and the donee?

   (A) The relationship is automatically terminated at majority
   (B) The custodian is responsible for all taxes
   (C) Payments from the account can be in the custodian's name alone
   (D) The relationship is terminated after majority when the donee instructs the firm to terminate

7. For a discretionary account which of the following is true?

    I. It must be accepted by a principal of the firm
    II. It must have written authorization on file before any trading takes place
    III. The account must be reviewed periodically by an authorized employee of the firm
    IV. All orders must be marked discretionary

(A) I and II
(B) I and III
(C) I, II, and III
(D) I, II, III, and IV

8. Stock registered in "street" name has as beneficial owner the:

(A) brokerage firm
(B) client
(C) registrar
(D) transfer agent

9. "Street" name stock has as owner of record the:

(A) brokerage firm
(B) client
(C) registrar
(D) transfer agent

10. A confirmation will include all of the following EXCEPT:

(A) trade date
(B) broker's ID
(C) limit or stop order
(D) settlement date

11. Which of the following would require that all confirmations and statements be sent to the investor's employer?

(A) an account for an employee of the NYSE
(B) a margin account for an employee of another broker
(C) a margin account for an employee of a bank
(D) none of the above

12. On the death of one tenant of an account with joint tenancy with rights of survivorship, the:

(A) account passes to the other tenant
(B) account passes to the estate of the deceased
(C) account is automatically closed
(D) brokerage firm becomes the custodian of the account

13. Under NYSE rules, which of the following requires prior permission from the investor's employer?

    I. a margin account for an employee of a bank
    II. an account for an employee of the exchange
    III. a cash account for an employee of another broker

(A) I and II
(B) II and III
(C) I and III
(D) I, II, and III

14. All of the following are allowed under the Uniform Gifts to Minors Act EXCEPT:

(A) gifts of mutual fund shares
(B) purchases in margin accounts
(C) gifts of letter stock
(D) gifts of real estate

15. In processing an order, the information will go through which sequence?

(A) Order room, P&S, cashier, margin
(B) Order room, P&S, margin, cashier
(C) Order room, cashier, margin, P&S
(D) Order room, margin, cashier, P&S

16. A custodian account may include:

    (A) a custodian and one minor
    (B) a custodian and two minors
    (C) two custodians and one minor
    (D) two custodians and two minors

17. If a registered rep has been told to use his judgment but has no written authorization, he may make choices about:

    (A) which stock to buy or sell
    (B) what price to execute at
    (C) which bond to buy or sell
    (D) how much of a security to buy or sell

    The following information is to be used for questions 18–20: An investor wishes to provide his young ward with a gift of cash and securities. Under the Uniform Gifts to Minors Act:

18. If some of the securities are in "bearer" form, they:

    (A) may not be accepted in the account
    (B) may be accepted in the account if accompanied by a Deed of Gift
    (C) must be converted to "street name" to be accepted
    (D) may have the donor as custodian

19. The custodian account must have the Social Security (or Tax I.D.) number of the:

    (A) guardian
    (B) custodian
    (C) minor
    (D) minor and the custodian

20. If the custodian dies, the:

    (A) account is frozen until the minor chooses a new custodian
    (B) court appoints a new custodian
    (C) account is liquidated
    (D) account reverts to the donor

ANSWERS TO REVIEW QUESTIONS

1. **(C)** The client's prior trading record is not required, but detailed information on his background is.

2. **(B)** He may request an extension as long as the privilege is not abused.

3. **(A)** The authority is limited to trading. No cash or other assets may be transferred from the account.

4. **(B)** The account is not closed, but it is frozen.

5. **(C)** The dividend record is not required. In particular, if the client received dividends directly, the rep would not know about them.

6. **(A)** The other choices are incorrect since taxes are the owner's responsibility, and the securities must be marked with the minor as legal owner.

7. **(D)** All are required. Oversight is especially required out of particular concern that the account not be churned to generate commissions.

8. **(B)** The beneficial owner is the one who benefits from ownership. This is obviously the client.

9. **(A)** By definition.

10. **(C)** The trade price is given.

11. **(B)** All of them would require prior approval to open an account.

12. **(A)** The most common form for married couples. It allows the survivor to manage the account immediately.

13. **(D)** As noted above. For choices II and III, this applies to both cash and margin accounts. For I, only to margin accounts.

14. **(B)** Margin accounts are not allowed.

15. **(B)**

16. **(A)** Every such account is set up with one custodian and one minor.

17. **(B)** This is not trading authority. The broker has been given discretion over price and/or time.

18. **(B)** The securities must show the beneficial owner; hence, if in bearer form they require a Deed of Gift to identify the owner.

19. **(C)** The tax liability is the minor's. Therefore, his Tax I.D. is required.

20. **(B)** A custodian is court-appointed or is designated by the previous custodian.

CHAPTER ELEVEN
margins and
short sales

PART ONE
Margins

Margin accounts are accounts in which the customer puts up only a certain percentage of the amount required to purchase securities and a broker/dealer extends credit for the balance. In effect, the broker/dealer becomes a creditor (lends money), and the customer becomes a debtor.

For investors, the principal advantage of such an account is "leverage," *i.e.*, the opportunity to buy a given quantity of securities with fewer dollars than required in a cash purchase.

All securities bought on margin are registered in the firm's name (the "street name") because the customer is a debtor. The brokerage firm is then the "nominee," the customer the "beneficial owner."

Terminology

Terms used in margin transactions include:

Margin   The margin is the percentage of that the sales price the customer must deposit. Under federal regulation, the current margin requirement is 50%. This means that for every dollar of securities purchased on margin, the customer puts up 50¢, and the broker/dealer lends 50¢. This Regulation T requirement varies. It has been as low as 40% and as high as 100%.

Hypothecation   Hypothecation is the practice of pledging securities as collateral for loans, *e.g.*, when customers leave securities on deposit with a broker as a pledge for purchases.

Rehypothecation   Rehypothecation occurs when a broker pledges a customer's pledged securities with a bank (or other source of funds).

Loan value   The percentage of the security's market value that the brokerage firm lends the customer is called the loan value. If the margin requirement is 50%, the loan value is 50%; if the requirement is raised to 65%, the loan value is reduced to 35%.

REGULATION OF MARGIN ACCOUNTS

Under the Securities Exchange Act of 1934, the Federal Reserve Board is given the power to set margin requirements and to regulate credit practices in the securities industry. In addition, the NYSE, NASD, and individual brokerage firms set their own margin requirements, which tend to be more stringent than those of the FRB.

The three pertinent FRB regulations are:

Regulation U—limits the amount banks can lend to brokers who use any securities as collateral

Regulation G—limits the amount non-bank lenders can lend to brokers who use customer securities as collateral

Regulation T—limits the amount brokers can lend to customers on securities of various types. Reg T does this in part by specifying the proportion and method of payment required for different types of accounts as follows:

Cash account

Customers holding such accounts may buy any type of security but must pay in full promptly. "Promptly" is defined as no more than five business days after the trade date. Reg T covers these purchases as a way of limiting the free credit a broker grants a customer. In fact, firms usually require payment in three business days (to conform with "regular way" settlement).

Long account

The customer may buy stocks by putting up the FRB required margin. As above, payment is due in five days, but most firms demand payment in three to meet "regular way" dates.

Frozen accounts

Under Reg T, if a customer does not pay in seven days, the brokerage firm must cancel or liquidate the transaction and "freeze" the account for 90 days. When an account is frozen, no trades can be made in the account unless they are paid in cash in advance.

There are, however, a few exceptions. Margin requirements of $500 or less need not meet the time requirements; purchases of "when-issued" securities are subject to other requirements; and extensions can be allowed "for exceptional circumstances," including illness, postal problems, etc. The broker may request a time extension for payment from a registered stock exchange or from an NASD district office. To ensure that this privilege is not abused, no more than five (5) such extensions may be granted in any one-year period.

Note

An account must be frozen if the broker does not receive payment on time or if a customer sells a security before making payment. For example, Mrs. Y enters a buy order for 100 shares of PSM at $50; the stock goes up to $55 two days later, and she sells out, taking a profit without sending a check for the buy. Her account is frozen. A customer must actually send money to the broker/dealer. If the payment is made within five (5) days, the account is automatically unfrozen.

CHARACTERISTICS OF MARGIN ACCOUNTS

Since they involve extending credit, margin accounts are subject to some special requirements imposed by regulators and brokerage firms.

Opening a margin account

Registered representatives who open margin accounts must have their customers sign a margin agreement form in addition to the usual new accounts form. The margin agreement form states that all transactions are subject to the pertinent laws and rules of all regulatory authorities, exchanges, etc. In addition, by signing, the customer further agrees, among other provisions, that:

- all securities may be pledged or repledged in the broker's general loans,

- interest will be charged on debt balances in the account,

- if equity is inadequate, the brokerage firm may sell the customer's securities with or without notifying the client.

A margin agreement form is usually combined with a consent to lend agreement, authorizing the firm to borrow the customer's securities for its own use or to lend to other brokers. (This usually involves short sales; see Part Two of this chapter.)

Individuals requiring special approval

In general, customers who must receive prior approval for a cash account also require similar approval for a margin account. Such customers include officers or employees (or their spouses) of other exchange members and employees of the NYSE, NASD, and any of their subsidiaries. All such potential customers must have written permission from their employers before a margin account can be opened. In addition, under NYSE rules, any employee of any organization dealing in any form of securities—such as banks, trusts, and insurance companies—must have such permission to trade in a margin account. This does not include, however, corporate officers or independent insurance agents.

Approval

The registered representative may not open a margin account without a branch manager's approval. Many firms also require a credit check and/or a cash deposit.

Ineligible accounts

Margin purchases may not be made for accounts held under the Uniform Gifts to Minors Act (UGMA). Fiduciary accounts are also barred, unless there is specific authorization to engage in such trading.

Eligible securities

Under Reg T, only certain securities may be purchased on margin. They are known as "marginable securities" and are defined as follows:

- any "listed" securities, *i.e.,* those traded on a national securities exchange,
- securities traded over the counter must be on the OTC margin list, which means they meet certain requirements. This list is updated regularly.

Exempt securities

Certain securities are specifically exempted from Reg T margin requirements, including debt securities issued by the federal government or its agencies, by state or municipal governments, or by other taxing entities. Brokerage firms can assign higher loan values to these instruments because they are exempt.

Governments   Initial and maintenance margin requirements on U.S. government securities are related to maturity and range from 1% to a maximum of 6% for issues that will not mature for 20 years or more.

Municipals   Initial and maintenance margin requirement on municipal bonds is the greater of 7% of the principal amount or 15% of market value.

Other margin requirements

When-issued stock is treated like issued stock, *i.e.*, subject to standard FRB requirements. Under NYSE/NASD rules, a buyer must deposit 25% to purchase when-issued stock in a cash account.

REG T INITIAL MARGIN REQUIREMENT

Under Reg T, a customer who makes a margin purchase must provide an initial amount equal to stated requirements. If Reg T margin is 50%, and the customer wants to buy $20,000 worth of securities, he or she must put up 50% of the total worth, or $10,000; the brokerage firm lends the rest. The amount the customer must put up is termed the "call" or "initial call."

CALCULATIONS INVOLVING MARGIN ACCOUNTS

Long market value

This is the customer's gross cost, including any charges or commissions (charges and commissions are ignored in the examples below for the sake of simplicity), on the trade date; it is used for purposes of calculating the initial margin requirement. After this, securities in the account are valued at their current market price.

Debit balance

Debit balance is the amount lent to the customer by the brokerage firm (the complement of the margin requirement) and for which it charges interest. With an initial purchase of $20,000 and a 50% margin, the debit balance is $10,000. It is useful to bear in mind that the debit balance (often called the debit record) does not change as market value changes.

Equity

The margin customer's net worth in the account is the equity. To calculate equity, the following formula is used.

$$\text{Market Value} - \text{Debit Balance} = \text{Equity}$$

In our example:

Market Value	$20,000
Debit Balance	$10,000
Equity	$10,000

In other words, the customer buys $20,000 in securities by meeting the initial $10,000 margin requirement (the equity), and the brokerage firm puts up $10,000 (the debit balance).

This ability to purchase $20,000 worth of securities with only $10,000 in cash indicates the leverage offered in a margin transaction. This is often called "buying power"; a formula for calculating it would be:

$$\text{Buying Power} = \text{Cash Available} \div \text{Margin } \%$$

In this case, $10,000 \div 50\% = $20,000; a $10,000 investment in a margin account has the buying power of $20,000. If the Reg T requirement is 60%, then the buying power of $10,000 is $10,000 \div 60\% = $16,666.67.

Loan value

As noted above, the loan value, or the complement of the margin requirement, is the amount the broker can lend to the customer. If the Reg T requirement is at 60%, the loan value of $20,000 would be:

$$\$20,000 \times (100\% - 60\%) = \$8,000$$

FRB Reg U limits the amount of customer securities a broker can pledge to a bank for a margin loan. Under this regulation, a broker cannot pledge securities worth more than 140% of the customer's debit balance. Continuing with the above example, this means 140% of $10,000; or $14,000 of the $20,000 in securities purchased. The bank, in turn, will lend up to 70% of the value of the securities pledged as collateral, or $14,000 \times 70\% = $9,800. This sum is very close to the amount that the broker lends the customer.

With Reg T at 60%, the broker could pledge 140% \times $8,000, or $11,200 worth of securities. Note that 140% is the most that may be pledged, and if a bank requires less than that in collateral, then the lesser amount is pledged. In any case, securities not pledged must be segregated and marked as belonging to the customer.

The rate that banks charge the brokerage firm on such a loan is called the broker loan rate. The call rate, the rate that the firm then charges its customer, is typically 1% higher than this.

Buying power of deposited securities

A customer may purchase on margin by depositing fully paid securities with the broker. The broker then rehypothecates them to a bank for a loan. In other words, the customer purchases securities with the loan. Just how great a quantity of securities must be deposited depends on the margin requirement. The formula is:

fully paid securities deposit = amount of purchase × margin % ÷ (100% − margin %)

Thus, a customer who wishes to purchase $5,000 in securities by depositing fully paid securities with a 50% margin requirement must deposit:

$5,000 × 50% ÷ 50% = $5,000 (in fully paid securities)

Or:

Market Value	$10,000
Debit Balance	$5,000 (loan with securities as collateral)
Equity	$5,000 (fully paid securities on deposit)

This meets the 50% initial margin requirement. Note that the loan equals the purchase, and the loan itself is collateralized by the deposit of securities.

Again, with a 60% requirement, a customer purchasing $5,000 of securities would deposit:

$5,000 × 60% ÷ 40% = $7,500

and the account would read:

Market Value	$12,500
Debit Balance	$5,000
Equity	$7,500

Margin requirements on transactions including options

Recall that option premiums are not marginable; *i.e.*, they must be paid in full. This affects the margin requirements on certain hedge transactions. For instance, suppose an investor buys 100 ACI at 60 on margin and writes 1 ACI Dec 60 Call at 5. The margin requirement at 50% is $3,000, but the $500 premium received can be used to meet this call, and the customer would need to deposit only an additional $2,500 to meet this call. On the other hand, if a customer wished to hedge the purchase of that 100 ACI by buying 1 ACI Dec 60 Put at 4, the total purchase is $6,000 for the stock and $400 for the put, or $6,400. But recalling that the option is not marginable, the amount required for deposit by the customer in this margin account is $3,000 + $400, or $3,400.

Excess equity

If the market value of the securities in a margin account increases, the equity in the account increases correspondingly. Look again at the example that we have used after the initial purchase.

Market Value	$20,000
Debit Balance	$10,000
Equity	$10,000

or a margin of 50% ($10,000/20,000).

Now assume the securities go up in value on the market to $30,000.

Market Value	$30,000
Debit Balance	$10,000
Equity	$20,000

The equity goes up exactly as much as the market value. If the customer were to sell out at this point, he or she would realize $30,000 which, after paying off the $10,000 loan, would leave $20,000 (the equity).

This increase in value, then, creates "excess equity."

To find the excess equity, simply subtract equity required for the new, higher market value from actual equity. In the example above, current equity is $20,000, required equity at 50% is $15,000; therefore, excess equity is $5,000. The customer can choose to withdraw the excess equity in cash, apply it to a new margin purchase, or leave it in the account.

Withdrawing cash   If a customer withdraws the excess equity in cash, *i.e.*, reduces the account by $5,000 to its allowable position, the debit balance increases, because market value − equity = debit balance. In other words, the loan value increases and interest will be charged on the higher amount.

Purchasing stock   Assume the customer uses excess equity to purchase additional securities in the same account. The excess now has buying power, and the $5,000 can purchase $10,000 in securities. The account looks like:

	Current Position	New Position
Market Value	$30,000	$40,000
Debit Balance	$10,000	$20,000
Equity	$20,000	$20,000
		(50% margin)

The customer can simply let the account stand as is.

RESTRICTED ACCOUNTS

Consider a situation in which the market value of securities in an account declines. If a customer has purchased $10,000 of PSM stock when the margin requirement is 50%, the account looks like this:

Market Value	$10,000
Debit Balance	$5,000
Equity	$5,000

Just as equity rises along with an increase in value, so it falls with a decrease. If the value of the PSM securities a customer has purchased should fall to $7,500, the account would be:

Market Value	$7,500
Debit Balance	$5,000
Equity	$2,500

Note the margin also declines along with market value: here, from 50% to 33%.

Under Reg T, there is no legal limit on how far the account can decline. Even if the stock loses all value, the FRB would neither take nor demand action. (The NYSE, NASD, and individual firms do set limits, however; these are discussed below.) But such accounts do have a different status: whenever the equity in a margin account falls below the initial margin requirement, it becomes a restricted account, and as such, it is subject to certain rules governing any sales. (An account can also become restricted because commissions or other charges have been added to the debit balance.) This is called the retention requirement.

To recap, the Federal Reserve imposes both an initial margin requirement (which dictates how much the customer must put up with a purchase) and a retention requirement (which dictates how much a customer must retain if anything is withdrawn from the account). Federal rules on restricted accounts do not require payment from the customer or bar new trading or withdrawals from the account.

Additional purchases in a restricted account

If a customer with a restricted account wants to purchase additional securities, he or she need only comply with the initial margin requirement for those new shares. Look again at the above example and assume the customer buys an additional $5,000 in securities and the margin requirement is 50%. The account looks like this:

Market Value	$7,500 + $5,000 = $12,500
Debit Balance	$5,000 + $2,500 = $ 7,500
Equity	$2,500 + $2,500 = $ 5,000

The account is still restricted because it is still below the 50% margin requirement.

Selling securities from a restricted account

When selling securities from a restricted account, on the other hand, the retention requirement states that only a portion of the proceeds may go to the customer. The balance stays in the account, reducing the credit balance (raising the margin). This could, conceivably, remove the account from restricted status.

Assume $5,000 worth of securities is sold from the following account:

Market Value	$20,000
Debit Balance	$12,500
Equity	$7,500

If the proceeds of the sale were left in the account, then:

Market Value	$20,000 – $5,000 sold = $15,000
Debit Balance	$12,500 – $5,000 = $ 7,500
Equity	$ 7,500 = $ 7,500

returning the margin to 50%. However, if the customer took the allowable portion of the proceeds of the sale in cash, thereby reducing equity by $2,500 (to $5,000) and increasing the debit balance an equivalent $2,500 (to $10,000), the margin actually drops to 33%.

Withdrawing cash from a restricted account

Cash may be withdrawn from restricted accounts without selling securities. To do so requires deposit of additional margin securities, while the customer receives only the current loan value of those securities. Should a client wish to take $5,000 cash from an account, with the Reg T requirement at 50%, he must deposit $10,000 in marginable securities.

Withdrawing securities from a restricted account

Customers may withdraw stock from a restricted account, but must replace it with cash or with other securities. In either case, the amount must meet the retention requirement. For example, if Mrs. Y is holding:

Market Value	$15,000 – $5,000 = $10,000
Debit Balance	$10,000 – $2,500 = $7,500
Equity	$5,000 – $2,500 = $2,500

With equity at only 33%, this is a restricted account. If she wishes to take out $5,000 worth of stock and put cash in the account, she would have to deposit $2,500 because 50% of the value of the withdrawn stock must be retained in the account.

If she wanted to withdraw $5,000 worth of PSM and replace it with another stock she is holding, she must deposit securities with a loan value equal to the retention requirement. In the above example, she must deposit the equivalent of $2,500 to take out $5,000 worth of stock due to the retention requirement. However, this $2,500 is calculated in terms of loan value: if Reg T is 50%, she will have to bring in $5,000 worth of the securities for deposit in the account.

Note

There are two steps to this calculation: figuring the retention requirement and then finding the loan value.

Liquidation of securities to meet Reg T calls

It is possible to meet a Reg T call for a new purchase by liquidating securities in a restricted account, although this is prohibited as a regular practice. It is necessary, then, to remember the retention requirement, *i.e.*, 50% of the value of the sold stock must remain in the account. Therefore, to meet an initial call of $2,000, for example, the customer must liquidate $4,000 in securities.

Simultaneous purchase

There is an exception to requirements generally facing restricted accounts, namely, same-day substitution of equal dollar amounts. A customer who buys, say, $7,000 of one stock and sells $7,000 of another on the same day need not put up additional margin.

Simultaneous transactions of unequal value

When same-day transactions are not exactly even, then Reg T requirements do come into play. If the buy side is greater than the sell side, the customer must meet the margin requirement on the difference, *e.g.*, buy $7,000 and sell $5,000; he or she must put up $1,000, or 50%, of $2,000. If the sell side is greater, only 50% of the difference can be withdrawn; *e.g.*, in buying $5,000 and selling $7,000, only $1,000 can be received.

INDUSTRY REQUIREMENTS

NYSE and NASD initial requirements

As noted above, the securities industry's self-regulatory agencies impose requirements on margin accounts which are stricter than those under Reg T.

For new accounts, these rules require the customer to put up an equity of $2,000, or 100% of the cost of the securities if the total purchase is less than $2,000. For example, if a customer wished to open an account by purchasing 100 PSM at 70, and the margin requirement is 50%, the call follows the Reg T pattern.

Market Value	$7,000
Debit Balance	$3,500
Equity	$3,500

This satisfies both the initial margin requirement and the $2,000 minimum. But if PSM is at 35, then

Market Value	$3,500
Debit Balance	$1,750
Equity	$1,750

satisfies Reg T, but not the $2,000 minimum. The customer must be called, and the account looks like:

Market Value	$3,500
Debit Balance	$1,500
Equity	$2,000

In effect, a margin of about 58% has been put up.

However, a customer need never put up more than the full purchase amount. If PSM were selling at $17, with the margin requirement at 50%, the account would be:

Market Value	$1,700
Debit Balance	$0
Equity	$1,700

When-issued securities are subject to the same minimum rules. In a cash account, NASD regulations require a 25% deposit for purchases of when-issued stock.

Industry maintenance requirements

As we have seen, Reg T does not set any limit on how far the market value of securities held in a margin account may fall. However, NYSE and NASD rules do impose a minimum maintenance requirement. In a long account, a customer must maintain equity of 25%, or $2,000, whichever is greater. As with the initial requirement, the account is not required to hold more than the full cost of the securities.

Thus, neither the customer nor the broker/dealer can act in any way that brings the account below $2,000. However, if the market value of the securities in the account drops below $2,000, no call is issued as long as the 25% minimum is satisfied.

These are industry-wide minimums. Many brokerage firms demand even higher minimums, which are often called a "house requirement."

Differences between Reg T and maintenance calls

If the market value of shares in a long account falls below the 25% minimum, the firm sends the customer a maintenance call. This must be met immediately (most firms allow 48 hours). If it is not, the broker may sell shares from the customer's account.

The customer may meet the call by depositing cash or additional securities in the account or by liquidating some of the securities held, as described in the calculations below.

Important differences between a maintenance call and a Reg T call include:

- The maintenance call, once met, brings equity in the account up to the 25% level, not the 50% of the initial call.

- A Reg T call must be met in five business days; a maintenance call is due on demand.

- A Reg T call must be met by the customer. As indicated above, an initial purchase requires an initial margin payment, even if the shares are sold or increase dramatically in value. A maintenance requirement, however, may be met by market action. If the market price of the securities in the account increases sufficiently to put the account above the maintenance requirement, then the call is met.

Calculations: maintenance calls

Consider the case below where stocks decline in value.

	Opening $	1st Decline	2nd Decline
Market Value	$10,000	$7,500	$7,000
Debit Balance	$5,000	$5,000	$5,000
Equity	$5,000	$2,500	$2,000

The margin here has dropped from 50% to 33% (2,500 ÷ 7,500) after the first decline and to about 28% after the second. This is still above the NYSE and NASD minimum, although it may be below the house requirement.

However, if the securities drop in value below $6,666, a maintenance call would be issued:

Market Value	$6,666
Debit Balance	$5,000
Equity	$1,666

or a margin of 25% (1,666 ÷ 6,666).

The formula for determining the market value at which a NYSE or NASD maintenance call must be issued is

$$\frac{4}{3} \times \text{Debit Balance} = \text{Minimum Maintenance Level Market Value}$$

In the example above, $\frac{4}{3} \times \$5,000 = \$6,666$ is the balance triggering a maintenance call.

Example

In an account with a market value of $24,000 and equity of $14,400, the maintenance level is found by determining the debit balance and then multiplying the debit balance by $\frac{4}{3}$.

If:

$$\$24,000 \div \$14,400 = \$9600 \times \tfrac{4}{3} = \$12,800$$

then:

Market Value	$12,800
Debit Balance	$9,600
Equity	$3,200

where equity is 25% of market value.

Note

This calculation is based on the debit balance, which remains constant. Another way to express minimum maintenance requirement is:

Equity $= \frac{1}{3}$ of Debit Balance

Since market value = debit balance + equity, $\frac{1}{3}$ of the debit balance requirement yields:

Market Value $= \frac{4}{3}$ of Debit Balance

which agrees with the first version above.

Meeting maintenance calls

Assume the stock values continue to drop to:

Market Value	$6,000
Debit Balance	$5,000
Equity	$1,000

The market value has now fallen below the minimum maintenance requirement (25% of $6,000 = $1,500), and a maintenance call for $500 would be issued.

Depositing cash to meet maintenance call

There are several ways to meet a maintenance call. The simplest is to deposit cash. Thus, the equity increases, and the credit balance decreases. In our example, a deposit of $500 would create:

Market Value	$6,000
Debit Balance	$4,500
Equity	$1,500

Depositing securities to meet maintenance call

A customer may meet a maintenance call by depositing fully paid securities. The necessary amount is determined by the formula:

$\frac{4}{3}$ Maintenance Call = Securities Required

In this example, $\frac{4}{3} \times \$500 = \$667$. The account now reads:

Market Value	$6,667
Debit Balance	$5,000
Equity	$1,667

and the equity is $\frac{1}{4}$ of the market value as required. The point is that since $\frac{1}{4}$ of the amount deposited must be used as maintenance for the increase in market value, $\frac{3}{4}$ of it is available for meeting the maintenance call. Since $\frac{3}{4} \times \frac{4}{3} \times$ maintenance call = maintenance call, the requirement is met.

Liquidating securities to meet maintenance call

Finally, a customer could meet the call by liquidating securities in the account. Although this is not proper as a regular practice for meeting a Reg T call, it is acceptable for a maintenance call. The formula here is:

$4 \times$ Maintenance Call = Value of Securities to be Liquidated

In the example above,

Market Value	$6,000
Debit Balance	$5,000
Equity	$1,000

If $2,000 is liquidated ($4 \times \$500$ call), the account reads:

Market Value	$4,000
Debit Balance	$3,000
Equity	$1,000

SPECIAL MEMORANDUM ACCOUNT (SMA)

The Special Memorandum Account (SMA) is so called because amounts are kept on the basis of a "memorandum" entry. Funds are not actually moved into the account; an SMA is more like a line of credit than a bank account. A customer who uses the money in an SMA increases the debit balance in the margin account and, therefore, pays interest on the amount withdrawn.

An SMA *balance* is created in a margin account when there is excess equity. This means that the client can either purchase new securities or remove cash from the account without violating any of the margin requirements. The account serves to protect the buying power of that excess equity because the amount in an SMA is not affected by a drop in the value of the securities in the account.

The SMA balance can be created by a rise in the value of the securities in a margin account.

Effect of excess equity on SMA balance

Look again at a margin account holding securities that have risen in value:

Market Value	$30,000
Debit Balance	$10,000
Equity	$20,000

The $5,000 excess equity is credited to an SMA. SMA, like excess equity, can be withdrawn in cash (in which case, the debit balance is increased), used to buy additional securities under the buying power formula, or simply allowed to stand.

Note what happens in the above example if the securities decline in value:

	Original	Decline
Market Value	$30,000/SMA $5,000	$24,000/SMA $5,000
Debit Balance	$10,000	$10,000
Equity	$20,000	$ 14,000

The result is that equity is reduced (because the debit balance is unchanged, but market value has dropped); but the SMA balance remains unaffected and its buying power is preserved.

Adding to SMA

The SMA balance can be generated in a number of ways in addition to a rise in the market value of stock beyond Reg T requirements:

Cash   A customer may deposit cash in a margin account, which is credited to the SMA if it is not needed to meet a margin call.

Marginable securities   When a customer deposits marginable securities into an account, the securities' loan value is transferred into the SMA.

Cash dividends and earned interest   If stocks held in the account pay dividends, those dividends may be credited in full to an SMA. A customer is entitled to withdraw all dividends and interest from the SMA even if the account is restricted.

Liquidating securities   When a customer sells securities in a margin account, 50% of the proceeds are automatically released to an SMA. This reflects the retention requirement.

Reducing SMA

Cash withdrawals   Cash withdrawals from an SMA mean the customer must pay interest on a larger credit balance. These withdrawals are allowed even if the account is restricted. There is, however, one important proviso: SMA withdrawals cannot leave the equity in the account below the maintenance level.

Equity is involved because the debit value is increased, thereby decreasing equity. Assuming an SMA of $14,000, consider the following example:

Market Value	$24,000
Debit	$14,000
Equity	$10,000

Margin is now at 42% (10,000 ÷ 24,000), making the account restricted; the SMA is the result of earlier activity. How much may this customer withdraw before the account reaches the maintenance level? If there is no change in market value, the maximum withdrawal is $4,000.

Market Value	$24,000
Debit	$14,000 + $4,000 = $18,000
Equity	$10,000 − $4,000 = $6,000

Withdrawing securities   With no SMA, as noted above, the margin account customer must make a cash deposit of 50% of the value of the withdrawn securities. Similarly, with an SMA, the SMA is debited by 50% of the value of the withdrawn securities.

This requirement is imposed because the broker has made outstanding loans using the securities as collateral. By making the customer replace securities with cash, the broker's position is unchanged. The formula here is:

SMA ÷ 50%

Thus, a customer with $4,000 in an SMA could withdraw $8,000 in securities, leaving nothing in the SMA.

Other possibilities include combining an SMA and cash. For a customer with $2,000 in an SMA who then wishes to withdraw $7,000 worth of securities, a total of $3,500 is needed.

$7,000 × 50% = $3,500 Total Needed

From this amount, subtract the amount of the SMA:

$3,500 − $2,000 SMA = $1,500 cash must be deposited

A customer with an SMA could also withdraw securities from the account by replacing them with other marginable securities (see below). In this case, one would determine the deposit required, then divide that by the loan value to calculate the amount of securities needed.

For example, a customer wishes to withdraw securities worth $6,000 and replace them with fully paid securities. He has $2,000 in an SMA.

Initial requirement = $3,000 ($6,000 × 50%)

Less SMA	$2,000
Net required	$1,000

Therefore, the client will have to deposit $2,000 ($1,000 ÷ 50% loan value) in fully paid securities.

Summary of SMA calculations

Consider the following margin account (with Regulation T at 50%):

Market Value	$60,000 SMA $10,000
Debit Balance	$20,000
Equity	$40,000

At this point the customer can choose one of the following three options:

Withdrawing cash
By withdrawing cash from the account, the client, in effect, borrows some (or all) of the cash available in the SMA, thereby increasing the debit balance. If the customer took $5,000, the account would now read:

Market Value	$60,000/SMA $5,000
Debit Balance	$25,000
Equity	$35,000

Buying additional securities
The customer could buy up to $20,000 of additional securities without putting up any money. If Reg T were at 60%, then his buying power in the account would be:

Buying power = SMA ÷ 60% = $10,000 ÷ .6 = $16,667

Inactive account
If the account were left alone and the market value dropped precipitously so that the account showed:

Market Value	$35,000/SMA $10,000
Debit Balance	$20,000
Equity	$15,000

The margin would now be 42.86% ($15,000 ÷ $35,000), and the account would be restricted, *i.e.*, between the 25% maintenance and 50% Reg T. At this point, either buying or selling could be considered.

- Buying securities—The customer could still buy up to $20,000 in marginable securities using the SMA.

Market Value	$55,000/SMA $0
Debit Balance	$40,000
Equity	$15,000

Notice that the margin has now dropped to 27.27% ($15,000 ÷ $55,000), which is very close to the 25% maintenance requirement.

- Selling securities—If the customer sold securities, the situation would be reversed. Assume, instead of buying $20,000 in securities, the customer sold $10,000. The client can either take the proceeds, in which case the account would read:

Market Value	$25,000/SMA $10,000
Debit Balance	$15,000
Equity	$10,000

Or leave them in the account, in which case the account would read:

Market Value	$25,000/SMA $15,000
Debit Balance	$10,000
Equity	$15,000

With market value at $25,000, the equity in the account cannot go below $6,250, which is 25% of the market value.

PART TWO
Short Sales

A short sale is any sale of security which the seller either does not own, or owns but chooses not to deliver. Thus, a short sale is any sale which is consummated by the delivery of a borrowed security by, or for the account of, the seller. To make delivery in such a transaction, the broker borrows the subject stock. Because the customer does not own the stock, he must buy the stock at some future date to meet his sales commitment ("cover the short position") or deliver some stock he owns.

At this time, the Reg T requirement on short sales is 50%. Thus, a customer selling short 100 shares of ACI at 50 would be required to deposit $2,500 into his account. Notice that by selling short the customer is effectively creating additional shares of ACI. The required deposit mitigates the effect of this new wealth in the economy. Additionally, this deposit acts as security for the broker, since the customer does not actually have the stock that has been sold.

Customers who sell short expect the value of a security to decline. If the stock appreciates in value, the short-seller loses the difference between the amount he must pay when he eventually buys the shares and the amount he received when he sold them originally. Alternately, if the security declines in value, the strategy is profitable as the customer can buy back for less than the selling price.

Example

An investor sells short 100 shares of ACI at 50. Subsequently, the price of ACI falls to 40. The investor buys back the ACI at 40 realizing a profit of $1,000 less transaction costs. Of course, if ACI had risen to 75 instead, and the investor, afraid of even further rises, bought it back at that point, he would realize a loss of $2,500 plus commissions.

Note

Short sales may be transacted only in margin accounts. Legally, any security can be sold short; in practice, however, only "marginable" securities are usually so traded. The reason is that, in a short sale, the broker must be able to borrow the actual securities. This is difficult or impossible with nonmarginable securities, since they generally are not available for borrowing purposes. Customers sign loan agreements allowing the broker to borrow securities in a margin account, but these would not include nonmarginable securities. Indeed, most firms limit short sales to listed securities and avoid over-the-counter issues.

Note further that while short sales take place in margin accounts, they do not involve borrowing money from the broker, creating debit balances; rather credit balances are created by the sum of the market value of the securities sold and the required margin deposit.

In the above example, we have:

Credit Balance $5,000 (100 ACI at 50) + $2,500 (margin) = $7,500

The equity in the account is the credit balance less the market value of the securities. Here, it is simply the $2,500 deposited by the client.

PURPOSE OF SHORT SALES

Speculation

Many of those who sell short are simply speculating. This means the client expects a stock to drop in price and hopes to make a profit on that drop. Such transactions often include stop and limit orders (see Chapter 8).

Hedging

Another use of short sales is as part of a hedging strategy, *e.g.*, taking a short position in a firm's common stock while holding a long position in a convertible debt instrument issued by the same firm. These strategies are covered in some detail in Chapter 9.

Tax purposes, or sales against the box

Sometimes a customer will sell short securities he owns, or will soon own, "against the box." In these transactions, the seller makes delivery by borrowing stock, not using his own holdings. Later, he may use his stock to repay the lender or buy in the open market to close out the transaction. The usual reason for such sales is to lock in a profit on a security without actually realizing the profit in that tax year.

Example

A customer owns 100 shares of CAI which he bought at 40 and is now selling at 75. If he were to sell, the customer would realize a capital gain of $3,500 and incur the accompanying tax liability. If, instead, he were to sell CAI short against the box at 75, a profit of $35 per share is guaranteed without actually realizing the profit at that time. This is often called "locking in" the profit. At some later date, in another taxable year, he can unwind the transaction by covering his short and selling the security he owned.

Short sales against the box are also used to hedge a long position.

Future delivery

A customer can sell short simply to delay delivery. For example, someone who is traveling and cannot actually endorse the certificates might sell short until he can deliver the requisite instrument.

Market arbitrage

This sophisticated trading technique involves trading the same stocks in different markets. For example, if PSM were trading at a slightly higher price on the Pacific Exchange than in New York, the trader might buy in San Francisco and sell in New York—but sell short because regular-way delivery is not physically possible. The margin requirement for arbitrage transactions is 10% of the long position.

Arbitrage between equivalent securities

It is sometimes profitable to buy a convertible bond and simultaneously sell short the equivalent stock. This usually involves a newly issued convertible instrument in which the arbitrageur would hold the new issue as a hedge against a short position in the common stock.

RIGHTS OF LENDERS

As defined above, a short sale can be effected only when a broker can borrow stock to deliver to the buyer. The short-seller's broker can supply the securities from its own stock (in other words, lend them to the customer). Or, the broker can borrow from another firm, in which case, the borrowing firm must deposit the total market value of the securities in cash with the lender. The lender of the stock can lend the deposited funds and earn interest. For this reason, such loans of stock are usually without charge ("flat"), though a premium can be charged. Sometimes, when interest rates are high, the lender actually pays interest on the money received for the loaned stock, effectively splitting the amount earned on the money.

CLOSING OUT A SHORT SALE

Normally, a short position is closed out when the short-seller "covers" by buying the requisite securities and delivering those shares to the lender who returns the deposited funds.

The following special rules can apply to these transactions.

Mark to the market

If the market value of the borrowed securities rises, the lending broker may demand that the borrower deposit enough additional cash so that the total equals the new, current market value of the borrowed stock. This is called "mark to the market." As a stock loan for a short sale must be 100% secured by cash, the borrower must meet the demand for additional funds immediately. If the market value declines, the lender returns surplus cash.

Dividends from loaned stock

If a dividend is declared on this borrowed stock, there are two claimants for it: the investor and the lender. The investor who bought the stock and has the securities will get the dividend from the corporation; however, the lender of the stock also owns shares. Therefore, the short-seller must pay the lender an amount equal to any dividends paid on loaned shares. This amount is usually charged to the short-seller's account. The short-seller must also pay in a timely fashion, *i.e.*, when the dividends are normally paid. The lender does lose the privilege of voting the shares which he has lent.

Return of stock

Under NYSE rules, a loan of securities can be canceled by either side at any time. The lending firm may return the money and demand the securities, or vice versa. This is usually done through a clearing corporation, but it can simply involve the two firms.

MARGIN REQUIREMENTS FOR SHORT SALES

As noted above, in a short sale, the customer's account is credited with proceeds from the sale of the securities. In the following example (which we will carry forward for further transactions), suppose a client sells short 100 PSM at 100 with Reg T at 50%. The account looks like this:

Credit Balance	$15,000
Market Value	$10,000
Equity	$ 5,000

In this case it is the credit balance which remains constant as the sum of the market value and the equity.

NYSE rules

In addition, NYSE rules require a $2,000 initial deposit on any margin account. However, the alternative ("or 100% of purchase") is not applicable in short accounts; even if the initial transaction is for less than $2,000, a $2,000 deposit is required.

Minimum maintenance (NYSE/NASD)

In short accounts, minimum maintenance is set by the NYSE and NASD at $2,000 or 30% of market value, whichever is greater. For stocks valued at less than $5.00 per share, a margin of $2.50 per share, or 100%, whichever is greater, must be maintained. For stocks valued at $5 or more, the minimum is $5 a share or 30% of the market value, whichever is greater.

REGULATION OF SHORT SALES

The Securities Exchange Act of 1934 gives the Federal Reserve Board power to fix margin requirements on short sales. It also prohibits a firm's directors, officers, and principal shareholders from selling stock short in their own companies. It also sets legal penalties for those who sell short on a national security exchange in violation of SEC rules. Perhaps the most important of these is the "plus tick rule" adopted in 1937.

The plus tick rule

This rule is designed to prevent investors from driving down the price of a stock by continuing to sell it short. The rule holds that individuals, whether acting as principal or agent, may not make a short sale on any national security exchange except at a price higher than the last change in price.

The plus tick terminology is straightforward, and includes:

Plus tick   A plus tick is a movement upward by a minimum price change. It is usually $\frac{1}{8}$ point above the previous transaction. For example, in the following series of trades:

(a) 34   (b) $34\frac{1}{8}$ (c) $34\frac{1}{8}$

(d) $34\frac{1}{4}$ (e) $34\frac{1}{8}$

the trades labeled (b) and (d) would be plus tick.

Zero plus tick   A zero plus tick is a price showing no change from a previous plus tick transaction. The trade labeled (c) above is a zero plus tick.

Minus tick (or down tick)   The minus tick is a downward movement. In the example above, (e) is the down tick.

Note

Under SEC rules, a short sale can be made only on a plus tick or a zero plus tick.

Exceptions to the rule

The plus tick rule does not apply to U.S. government and municipal securities or to over-the-counter short sales. Some odd lot orders are also exempt.

Identification of sell orders as short

SEC rules also require that all orders to sell securities be clearly identified as either long or short. Thus, any order for a short transaction must be so labeled.

CALCULATIONS IN SHORT SALES ACCOUNTS

Decrease in market value

When selling short, a decline in market value means a gain for the customer. Assume PSM, in the previous example, falls to $80 per share on the market. The account now looks like:

Credit Balance	$15,000
Market Value	$8,000
Equity	$7,000

The credit balance stays the same, similar to the debit balance in a long account, and the margin goes up. It is now 87.5% ($7,000 ÷ $8,000). In a short account, too, the difference between actual equity and required equity is excess equity, and this can be part of an SMA. In the above example:

	Actual	Required (at 50%)
Credit Balance	$15,000	$12,000
Market Value	$8,000	$8,000
Equity	$7,000	$4,000

So excess equity is $3,000.

As with any margin account, the excess equity may be allowed to stand, or be taken in cash. If the customer takes cash, then the credit balance and equity are reduced accordingly. In the example, if the client takes the SMA in cash, the account would look like:

Credit Balance	$12,000
Market Value	$8,000
Equity	$4,000

Buying power of SMA balance

If the customer with excess equity wishes to sell additional securities short or to buy securities, it is possible to calculate buying power. As in a long margin account, buying power is determined by:

Buying Power = SMA ÷ Margin Requirement

In the above example, $3,000 ÷ 50% = $6,000; thus, the buying power is $6,000. If a client chooses such a course, the account would look like:

Credit Balance	$12,000 + $9,000 = $21,000
Market Value	$8,000 + $6,000 = $14,000
Equity	$4,000 + $3,000 = $ 7,000 (50% margin)

Effect on SMA of increase or decrease in short market value

Increase in short market value   Should the market price of shares sold short increase in value, the customer loses. Although the credit balance is unchanged, equity in the account decreases. Recall the original account:

Credit Balance	$15,000
Market Value	$10,000
Equity	$5,000

and assume market value increases to $11,000:

Credit Balance	$15,000
Market Value	$11,000
Equity	$4,000

thus producing a margin of about 36% ($4,000 ÷ $11,000). The maintenance margin is 30%, and the level at which maintenance will be reached can be found as a function of the credit balance as follows:

Credit Balance ÷ 130% = Market Value

In the example above:

$15,000 ÷ 130% = $11,538

an equity of $3,462 remains. Since the credit balance remains unchanged, the maintenance level is reached when the credit balance is 130% of market value. This then implies that the equity is 30% of the market value, since equity + market value = credit balance.

As with long accounts, should the margin in a short account fall below the 50% requirement but remain above the maintenance level, the account is restricted. The computations for restricted short accounts are similar to those for long accounts. The obvious difference is that purchasing stock (covering short positions) frees cash, while selling stock short encumbers cash.

For example, assume that the account now looks like:

Credit Balance	$60,000/SMA $5,000
Market Value	$42,000
Equity	$18,000

The client could sell short $10,000 in stock,

Credit Balance	$70,000/SMA $0
Market Value	$52,000
Equity	$18,000

and the margin would be reduced from 42.86% ($18,000 ÷ $42,000) to 34.62%. Of course, the client could also deposit the additional $5,000 in margin leaving the SMA at $5,000. In which case:

Credit Balance	$75,000/SMA $5,000
Market Value	$52,000
Equity	$23,000

and the margin would be 44.23% ($23,000 ÷ $52,000).

Or the client could take the $5,000 from the account:

Credit Balance	$55,000/SMA $0
Market Value	$42,000
Equity	$13,000

and the margin would now be 30.95% ($13,000 ÷ $42,000).

Or the client could repurchase $10,000 of securities.

Credit Balance	$50,000/SMA $10,000
Market Value	$32,000
Equity	$18,000

The important requirements are the 30% maintenance level and the $2,000 minimum balance. These restrictions apply in all cases, except for low-priced stocks where the requirement is more stringent.

Combination long and short accounts

An account will often contain both long and short positions. The requirements on such accounts treat these positions separately. That is, each position must separately conform to the appropriate requirements.

For example, if an account is long 200 ACI at $50 and short 100 CAI at $80, the initial margin requirements (assuming 50% Reg T) would look like:

	Long	**Short**
Market Value	$10,000	$ 8,000
Debit (Credit)	$5,000	$12,000
Equity	$5,000	$4,000

In fact, the $4,000 in equity in the short account would be applied to the debit balance, thereby reducing the outstanding loan to $1,000. Maintenance margin would be computed separately as 25% of the long market value and 30% of the short market value. Here, it would be:

$$25\% \times \$10,000 + 30\% \times \$8,000 = \$4,900$$

If the equity fell below this amount, there would be a margin call.

TERMS

Margins

Margin accounts   Customer puts up only a percentage of the amount required to purchase securities; broker/dealer extends credit for balance. Securities bought on margin are registered in firm's name (street name); firm is nominee; customer is beneficial owner

Margin   Percentage of sales price customer must deposit

Margin requirements   Set by Federal Reserve Board under law; currently 50%, can be changed; NYSE, NASD, and brokerage firms can set their own requirements

Hypothecation   Pledging securities as collateral for loans

Rehypothecation   When broker pledges customer's pledged securities for loan

Loan value   Reciprocal of margin requirement; *i.e.*, percentage of market value lent by broker to customer (if margin requirement is 50%, loan value is 50%)

Applicable FRB regulations

Reg U   Limits amount banks can lend brokers who pledge securities

Reg G   Limits amount nonbank lenders can lend brokers who pledge customer securities

Reg T   Limits amount brokers can lend customers on securities; specifies different types of accounts

Special requirements on margin accounts

Opening account   Customer must sign margin agreement in addition to new accounts form

Approval   RR may not open margin account without branch manager's approval

Ineligible   Accounts held under Uniform Gifts to Minors Act (UGMA); fiduciary accounts absent specific authorization

Eligible securities   Any listed securities, securities traded OTC must be on OTC margin list

Ineligible securities   All OTC stocks not on the list

Reg T initial margin requirement   Customer who buys on margin must provide initial amount equal to stated requirements, termed the call or initial call

Terms used in calculations

Long market value   Customer's gross cost on trade date for purposes of calculating initial margin requirement; after this, current market price

Debit balance   Amount lent customer by brokerage firm (reciprocal of margin requirement)

Equity   Margin customer's net worth in account

Market value   Debit balance + Equity

Buying power   Leverage offered in margin transaction

Buying power = cash available/margin %

Loan value   Amount broker can lend to customer (reciprocal of margin requirement)

Buying power of deposited securities   Customer may purchase on margin by depositing fully paid securities with broker

Fully paid securities deposit = amount of purchase × margin % ÷ (100% − margin %)

Excess equity   If market value of securities in margin account increases, equity in the account increases correspondingly: "excess equity"

Customer with excess equity can:

- Withdraw cash, increases debit balance, *i.e.*, loan value increases, interest is charged on higher amount

- Purchase stock

- Let account stand

Restricted accounts

- If market value of securities in an account declines, margin declines correspondingly making it a restricted account; certain rules dictate how much customer must retain if anything is withdrawn (retention requirement)

Industry requirements

NYSE/NASD initial requirements   For new accounts: customer must put up $2,000 equity, 100% of cost of securities if total purchase below $2,000 or full purchase price, whichever is less (when-issued securities subject to same rules)

Industry maintenance requirements   In a long account, customer must maintain equity of 25% or $2,000, whichever is greater, although no more than full cost of securities

- Many brokerage firms demand even higher minimums (house requirement)

- If market value of shares in long account falls below 25% minimum, firm sends maintenance call, which must be met immediately (usually 48 hours); if not, broker may sell shares from account

- Customer may meet call by depositing cash or additional securities or by liquidating some securities

Differences between maintenance call and a Reg T call

- Meeting maintenance call brings equity up to 25% level, not 50%

- Reg T call must be met in seven business days; maintenance call on demand

- Reg T call must be met by customer payment; maintenance call may be met by market action

Calculating maintenance calls

To determine market value at which NYSE and NASD maintenance call must be issued:

$\frac{4}{3} \times$ Debit balance = minimum maintenance level market value

or:

Equity = $\frac{1}{3}$ of debit balance

Meeting maintenance calls

- Deposit cash, *i.e.,* increase equity, decrease credit balance
- Deposit fully paid securities under the formula:

  $\frac{4}{3}$ Maintenance call = securities required

- Liquidate securities under the formula:

  $4 \times$ Maintenance call = value of securities to be liquidated

Special Memorandum Account (SMA)

- Amounts kept on basis of "memorandum" entry
- Customer who uses money in SMA increases debit balance in margin account, pays interest on amount withdrawn
- Created in margin account when there is excess equity; customer can purchase new securities or withdraw cash without violating margin requirements
- Not affected by drop in value of securities in account
- Can be created by rise in value of securities in a margin account
- Deposit of cash
- Marginable securities (loan value goes into SMA), etc., add to SMA, and withdrawing securities reduces SMA
- Customers may also combine SMA and cash or withdraw securities by replacing them with other marginable securities

Short sales

Short sale Any sale of a security that the seller does not own, or owns but chooses not to deliver; thus, any sale consummated by delivery of a borrowed security by, or for the account of, the seller

- To make delivery, broker borrows subject stock; customer does not own the stock, but must buy or deliver it at some future date
- Reg T requirement on short sales currently 50%
- Short-sellers expect security to decline in value
- Short sales may be transacted only in margin accounts

Short sales do not involve creating debit balances, but creating credit balances (market value of securities sold + required margin deposit):

Equity = credit balance − market value of securities

Purpose of short sales:

- Speculation

- As one part of a hedging strategy

- For tax purposes (sales against the box)

- To delay delivery

- In market arbitrage (trading the same stocks in different markets)

- In arbitrage between equivalent securities (*e.g.*, buying convertible bond and simultaneously selling short the equivalent stock)

Rights of lenders

- Broker must have stock to deliver to buyer; can supply from its own stock

- If broker borrows from another firm, must deposit total market value of securities in cash with lender

- Lender can lend and earn interest on those funds

Closing out short sales

- Normally, short-seller covers by buying requisite securities and delivering shares to lender; special rules apply to these transactions

Margin requirements for short sales

- In a short sale, customer's account is credited with proceeds from sale of the securities

  Credit balance = market value + equity

- NYSE rules $2,000 initial deposit even if initial transaction is for less than $2,000

- Minimum maintenance (NYSE and NASD) $2,000 or 30% of market value, whichever is greater

Regulations

- Firm's directors, officers, and principal shareholders may not sell stock short in that firm

- Plus tick rule: no individual may make a short sale on any national security exchange except at a price higher than the last change in price

- Identification: all orders to sell securities must be clearly identified as either long or short

Calculations

- Decrease in market value means a gain for the customer

    Credit balance – market value = equity

- Excess equity: difference between actual equity and required equity; can be part of SMA; can be let stand or taken in cash

- Buying power of SMA balance in short account (to sell additional securities short or buy securities)

$$\text{Buying power} = \frac{\text{SMA}}{\text{margin requirement}}$$

REVIEW QUESTIONS

1. Which of the following are exempt securities?

    (A) convertible bonds
    (B) municipal bonds
    (C) listed stocks
    (D) OTC stocks

2. After placing an order to buy 200 shares of ACI, an investor informs the registered rep that he cannot pay for the stock. The registered rep should:

    (A) liquidate the position and freeze the account for 90 days
    (B) notify the NASD to freeze all other accounts
    (C) liquidate all other positions of this customer
    (D) bar any future trading by this customer

3. If an account is frozen, which of the following is true?

    I. all purchases must be paid in advance
    II. all sales require previous delivery of the securities
    III. no activity is allowed without NASD approval

    (A) I only
    (B) I and II

    (C) III only
    (D) I and III

The following information is to be used in connection with Questions 4–7: With margin set at 50% by Reg T, an investor's margin account has the following positions:

Security	Market Price
200 ACI	40
300 CAI	20
100 ATT	60
Market Value	$20,000
Debit	$8,000
Customer's Equity	$12,000

4. What is the customer's excess equity?

    (A) $2,000
    (B) $4,000
    (C) $6,000
    (D) $8,000

5. How much buying power does the account have?

    (A) $2,000
    (B) $4,000
    (C) $6,000
    (D) $8,000

6. If the customer wished to add 200 shares of ACI at its current price to his holdings, how much cash would he need to deposit?

   (A) $0
   (B) $2,000
   (C) $4,000
   (D) $8,000

7. If he wished to deposit fully marginable securities to meet the requirement, how much would he need to deposit?

   (A) $2,000
   (B) $4,000
   (C) $6,000
   (D) $8,000

8. Which of the following are true of a maintenance call?

   I. it is due within 7 days
   II. it is set by the FRB
   III. it can be met by market action
   IV. it is at least 25% of market value

   (A) I and III only
   (B) II and IV only
   (C) II and III only
   (D) III and IV only

9. An investor sells 100 shares of CAI at 30. If he does not already own these shares, we say his position is:

   (A) hedged
   (B) short
   (C) short against the box
   (D) arbitraged

10. If this sale were in a new account, his margin call would be for:

   (A) $1,000
   (B) $1,500
   (C) $2,000
   (D) $3,000

11. All of the following have set regulations regarding margin requirements EXCEPT the:

   (A) Federal Reserve
   (B) NYSE
   (C) SEC
   (D) broker/dealer

12. Maintenance requirements on margin accounts are set by the:

   (A) Federal Reserve
   (B) NYSE
   (C) SEC
   (D) broker

13. The pledging of a customer's securities as collateral for a debit balance is called:

   (A) hypothecation
   (B) rehypothecation
   (C) intermediation
   (D) disintermediation

14. The only account in which a short sale can take place is a:

   (A) cash account
   (B) margin account
   (C) special account
   (D) short account

15. If an investor is short against the box and wishes to liquidate the long side of the position only, what notations should appear on the order ticket?

   (A) none since it is liquidating a long position
   (B) short sale, with the normal up or zero plus tick
   (C) short sale with no tick requirement
   (D) none, but with the up or zero plus tick requirement

16. All of the following could open a margin account EXCEPT:

   (A) two brothers in a joint tenant account
   (B) a corporation
   (C) the custodian under the Uniform Gifts to Minors Act
   (D) a married couple in a common tenancy account

17. With Regulation T at 75%, an investor sells 100 ACI short at 30. How much would she need to deposit to meet the margin requirement?

    (A) $1,500
    (B) $2,000
    (C) $2,250
    (D) $3,000

18. All of the following may grant an extension under the Reg T requirement EXCEPT the:

    (A) NASD
    (B) American Stock Exchange
    (C) SEC
    (D) NYSE

19. What is the maximum amount that can be waived under the Reg T requirement?

    (A) $0
    (B) $250
    (C) $500
    (D) $1,000

20. An investor buys $20,000 of ACI which is marginable and sells $15,000 of CAI on the same day. If he had a $1,000 SMA, how much additional margin would he have to deposit?

    (A) $1,500
    (B) $2,000
    (C) $2,500
    (D) $3,000

21. If in the previous question the SMA had been $2,200, what would the margin call have been?

    (A) $0
    (B) $300
    (C) $500
    (D) $1,400

22. An investor sells short 200 shares of ACI at 40. If he makes the appropriate Reg T deposit of 50%, his credit balance will read:

    (A) $4,000
    (B) $8,000
    (C) $12,000
    (D) $16,000

23. If subsequently ACI rises to 50, his credit balance will now read:

    (A) $0
    (B) $4,000
    (C) $8,000
    (D) $12,000

24. If an investor decided to withdraw $20,000 of marginable securities from his account, how much cash would have to be deposited to maintain the same buying power?

    (A) $10,000
    (B) $20,000
    (C) $40,000
    (D) it depends on his SMA account

25. All of the following are true about selling short against the box EXCEPT:

    (A) it results in locking in a profit
    (B) it can result in deferring a tax liability
    (C) it must be done on an up or zero plus tick
    (D) it converts ordinary income to a capital gain

26. If an investor has a restricted account, his margin is:

    (A) below 25%
    (B) below 50%
    (C) at 50%
    (D) above 50% but with no cash in the account

27. All of the following can be transacted in a special cash account EXCEPT:

    (A) sell convertible bonds
    (B) sell stock short
    (C) buy common stock
    (D) buy covered calls

28. The buying power in a margin account can be described as:

    (A) cash available
    (B) the cash available times the Reg T requirement
    (C) the cash available divided by the Reg T requirement
    (D) the equity in the account

29. The amount of an investor's securities that a broker may pledge to a bank for a margin loan is:

    (A) 50% of the market value of the account
    (B) 140% of the debit balance
    (C) 140% of the SMA
    (D) 240% of the debit

30. An investor has an account with a market value of $40,000 and a debit of $25,000. If $10,000 of securities are sold from the account, the investor may withdraw from the account up to:

    (A) $0
    (B) $2,500
    (C) $5,000
    (D) $10,000

ANSWERS TO REVIEW QUESTIONS

1. (**B**) All of the others are subject to Reg T except that some OTC are not marginable at all.

2. (**A**) See question 3.

3. (**B**) When an account is frozen, all transactions must be done on a cash-and-carry basis.

4. (**A**) The excess equity is the amount in the account not needed for margin requirements. Here, $20,000 of market value requires $10,000 of margin.

5. (**B**) The excess equity can be used for margin at 50%.

6. (**B**) 200 shares would cost $8,000 or $4,000 in margin of which $2,000 are already in the account. Alternatively, $8,000 would bring the market value to $28,000, requiring $14,000 in margin of which $12,000 are in the account.

7. (**B**) To purchase with marginable securities the $4,000 of securities not yet covered, he needs $4,000 × 50% ÷ (100% − 50%) or $4,000.

8. (**D**) I and II are not true; a maintenance call is due as soon as possible, and it is set by NASD, NYSE, and individual firms.

9. (**B**) By definition.

10. (**C**) The minimum deposit in a new account even though it exceeds the Reg T requirement.

11. (**C**) The Fed sets initial margin requirements, the NYSE establishes maintenance requirements, and brokers set house rules which are often more stringent than those of the NYSE.

12. **(B)** See question 11.

13. **(A)** Rehypothecation is the pledging of the customer's securities to the bank for margin loans.

14. **(B)** A short sale always involves margin.

15. **(A)** This is not a short sale.

16. **(C)** These are not allowed under UGMA.

17. **(C)** $\$3,000 \times 75\% = \$2,250$.

18. **(C)** The SEC has nothing to do with this requirement.

19. **(C)** This is at the discretion of the brokerage house.

20. **(A)** In same day transactions, only the difference need be margined. Here, the $5,000 of new securities requires $2,500 of margin, of which $1,000 were in the account.

21. **(A)** The $300 required, however, would not have to be met.

22. **(C)** The credit balance is the sum of the market value $8,000 and the margin $4,000 (equity).

23. **(D)** The credit balance would not change, the market value would rise, and the equity would fall.

24. **(A)** With Reg T at 50%, cash has twice the buying power of fully paid securities.

25. **(D)** The transactions all result in capital gains (or losses).

26. **(B)** An account is restricted if it falls below initial requirements.

27. **(B)** Short sales take place in a margin account.

28. **(C)** By definition.

29. **(B)** Since the bank will lend up to 70% of the value, we have 1.40×70 ($= 98\%$) of the required margin.

30. **(C)** Although this account is restricted, the client may withdraw up to 50% of the proceeds of the sale.

CHAPTER TWELVE
analyses

PART ONE
Economic Analysis

The end purpose of all investment analysis is to find the value of a particular security or category of securities. That value, in turn, depends on the state of the economy as a whole. For this reason, the registered representative must have some ongoing knowledge of the broader economic picture and, in particular, of how general trends and government actions are conventionally thought to affect securities markets.

NATIONAL INCOME AND GNP

The broadest measure of the overall economy is the "Gross National Product," or GNP. This figure is the total value (Gross) of all goods and services produced

(Product) in the nation (National) in a year. GNP measures final use. For example, the leather sold to a shoe factory is not counted; its price is included in the price of the shoes sold to consumers. Therefore, adding the leather into GNP would mean counting it twice.

In short, GNP is the sum of all individual consumer spending, all government spending (except for interest payments and "transfer payments" like pensions), and all private sector capital-forming investment (*i.e.*, facilities needed to create jobs and products).

GNP can be expressed in current dollars, *i.e.*, the actual amounts paid for all its constituents, or in terms of some base year's dollars, such as 1982 dollars. The latter eliminates the effects of inflation since the same yardstick is used to compare two years. The Commerce Department publishes its estimate of GNP once every quarter.

Components of GNP

Analysts break the GNP figure into several components.

Net National Product (NNP)
The NNP is the GNP less depreciation, the amount used to replace plants and equipment worn out over the year.

National Income (NI)
The NI is wages, rents, interest, and profits paid to all those who produce goods and services; it is calculated by subtracting business taxes paid from the NNP.

Personal Income (PI)
The PI is the consumer's pre-tax income; it is derived by subtracting business profits from the NI.

Disposable Income (DPI)
The DPI is reported quarterly and reflects what people have after taxes, including transfer payments; it is calculated by NNP less taxes and retained corporate earnings, but plus transfer payments.

Generally speaking, the GNP is viewed as the most complete measure of economic activity and is watched closely.

BUSINESS CYCLES

In general, GNP has gone up over time, but the growth is uneven, and there have been periods of decline. The economy has experienced cycles of growth and decline of varying length and varying levels of height and depth.

There is a general growth period called expansion which, at some point, reaches a peak and is then followed by decline. This decline reaches bottom at the trough, or low point, after which expansion begins again.

In recent years, the United States has been experiencing a prolonged period of expansion, yet—contrary to conventional wisdom—unemployment has continued to drop and inflation has remained essentially dormant. Nevertheless, it is generally agreed that the idea of a business cycle is still valid, and we can expect a period of contraction. A lasting decline or contraction is called a recession.

Recession

A recession is commonly defined as two successive quarters of decline in GNP. In terms of investment strategies, a recession is conventionally thought to hurt first and foremost firms that produce durable goods (items like automobiles, major appliances, and goods involved in home-building). This is because recession is almost certainly accompanied by increasing unemployment, which in turn means fewer people are able to buy nonessential items.

As durable goods last for a long time, potential purchasers can decide to put off purchasing them until economic conditions improve. A similar logic holds for any items considered nonessential; however, this analysis should be used with caution as the sales of some non-essential goods do not obey this logic.

Affected industries are often called cyclical industries and are contrasted with those that produce staple items, like foods and drugs, which are essential at all times. These producers of essentials are sometimes called noncyclical industries precisely because they are usually less affected by the business cycle.

Business cycle indicators

No one can precisely predict when the economy will begin to contract nor, more generally, when upturns or downturns will occur. However, economists have identified some indicators that they believe give clues to likely turning points in the economy. Based on this work, the Conference Board (assuming a task formerly performed by the U.S. Department of Commerce) has constructed three composite indices of indicators: the index of leading indicators (10); the index of coincident indicators (4); and the index of lagging indicators. These have been somewhat useful, although, as one economist joked, "The index of leading economic indicators has predicted eleven of the last six turns in the economy."

As their name implies, leading indicators are supposed to change direction before the GNP does, so they draw the most attention from those interested in predicting what the economy will do. The most recent version of the list includes:

1. Average weekly hours for workers in manufacturing

2. Average weekly initial claims for unemployment insurance (inverted: *i.e.*, a drop in this figure is a positive sign)

3. New orders to manufacturers for consumer goods and materials

4. Vendor performance; index of companies receiving slow deliveries

5. New orders to manufacturers for nondefense capital goods

6. Building permits, new private housing units

7. Stock prices, 500 common stocks

8. Money supply (M-2)

9. Interest-rate spread, 10-year T-bonds vs. Fed Funds (in terms of percent of change)

10. Index of consumer expectations

Inflation

Inflation occurs when the dollar price of a fixed "basket of goods" rises over an extended period of time. This is not to be confused with a onetime rise in prices caused, perhaps, by a natural disaster or the exercise of monopoly power by an economic entity.

Inflation is measured in several ways. The most familiar is the "consumer price index" (CPI), published monthly by the U.S. Department of Labor. This gauges the price of a market basket of goods deemed necessary for a hypothetical average family in the United States.

Explaining inflation

There are several theories that purport to explain inflation. Primarily an indication of their proposers' economic biases, these theories merely start at different points in the cycle of spiraling prices and then say the same thing.

Demand-pull theory
One popular theory is called "demand-pull." If the amount of money available to buy goods and services increases faster than the amount of goods and services produced (real GNP), then prices will move up as more money chases fewer goods in the marketplace. That is, since demand outstrips supply, prices rise.

A classic example of demand exceeding supply is wartime. The productive capacity is used to produce goods that are available for purchase only by the government. Since everyone is working, more money is available to purchase what few consumer goods are around. However, if taxes are raised, this extra cash is not available, *i.e.*, because the government is paying for its purchases.

Cost-push theory
Another popular theory is called "cost-push." When prices begin to rise (for example, because of demand-pull) the cost of producing goods also rises. In particular, workers will want higher wages to continue buying the same amount of goods. To maintain required profit levels, producers add these new costs into their prices. This leads into a spiral: the new higher prices bring demands for higher pay, which brings higher prices, and so on. In short, increased demand increases inflation.

Other pressures
Expectations about continuing inflation, or the fear of future inflation, can also contribute inflationary pressures. Consumers then tend to buy more, fearing that if they wait, they will be forced to pay higher prices. This increasing demand can also contribute to inflation.

Effects of inflation

There is a sort of brake built into the spiral: as demand for goods increases, so does demand for money. If the money supply does not grow, interest rates will rise. Rising rates make it harder to profit from economic activity, thus slowing the entire economy. Workers are laid off, and those still employed tend to reduce purchases and forego wage increases, which, in theory, breaks the cycle. However, real economic activity rarely follows any neat rules for any length of time: for example, recessions have historically been times of low inflation, but in the late 1960s and for much of the 1970s, there were periods of persistent inflation despite a stagnant economy—a condition dubbed "stagflation."

More recently, as mentioned above, the U.S. economy has been behaving contrary to conventional wisdom, with sustained moderate to strong economic growth without any appreciable inflation.

Changing interest rates have an immediate effect on certain securities. Recall that as rates rise, the price of existing bonds falls and vice versa. Equities in companies with a great deal of debt (utility companies are typically so financed) are also affected.

While some inflation is necessary—some even say healthy—rapid inflation has harmful effects, especially on those economic entities with relatively fixed incomes, such as pensioners or businesses unable to raise their prices as other prices rise around them.

CONTROLLING THE CYCLES—THE MONETARY APPROACH

Just as there are different theories about inflation, there are different theories about controlling the cycle. The best known of these are called "monetarist" and "Keynesian."

Monetarist theory says that if the supply of money is allowed to grow at the same rate as the economy is growing, inflation will be kept in check because the amount of money available will match the goods and services available. Keynesian theory says that the government should act as a balance wheel to the economy, spending more and generating economic activity when the rest of the economy is not growing, and doing the opposite when the economy is growing rapidly.

In addition, there is the theory that the economy is best left alone, with government interfering as little as possible. This is variously called "laissez faire," or "supply side," and dates back to Adam Smith's idea of an "invisible hand," which almost magically provides the impetus for economic well-being. This school of thought emphasizes lower taxes and less government interference in economic activity.

Each of these theories has some adherents, and so, not surprisingly, government policy in the United States (and the rest of the developed world) is a mixture of these theories.

The Federal Reserve System

In the United States, the flow of money and credit is the concern of the Federal Reserve System (the "Fed") and particularly of its board of governors, seven members appointed by the President and confirmed by the Senate. This board directly controls 12 government-owned Federal Reserve Banks around the country. In addition, most commercial banks are Fed members and must abide by its rules.

In general, the Fed tries to keep the money supply growing at the same rate as real GNP is growing.

Measuring the money supply

The supply of money is measured in several ways. The most closely watched, although not necessarily the most important, is called "M-1."

M-1   This includes currency in circulation, plus travelers checks, plus the balances in all demand deposits, *i.e.,* accounts from which funds can be drawn by writing a check, including NOW accounts, automatic transfer accounts, and credit union shares. A second important figure is "M-2."

M-2   This includes all funds in M-1, plus deposits in regular savings accounts, all time-deposits under $100,000 (where the depositor has agreed to leave money in an account for a period of time), money-market mutual funds other than those restricted to institutional investors, and IRAs. M-2 also includes overnight repos and Eurodollars.

M-3   This is M-2 plus large time deposits, term (not overnight) repos at banks and savings and loans, and institutional money-market mutual funds.

These figures are followed closely by those concerned with securities, on the understanding that the Fed's mechanisms for changing growth rates (if that is deemed necessary) may lead to changes in interest rates which in turn affect investors' decisions on the relative attractiveness of stocks and bonds.

Changing the money supply

When the Fed wishes to change the growth rate of the money supply, it does so by acting in one (or more) of several ways. The most immediate method of affecting the money supply, and the easiest to reverse, involves "open market operations."

Open market operations   Every month, the Fed's "Open Market Committee" (FOMC) meets to look at the most recent money supply figures in light of the Fed's own guidelines. The committee works to exert short-term control by buying or selling government securities in the open market. If the FOMC feels the money supply is growing too fast, it will sell U.S. government obligations (such as T-bills) in the market. This will draw funds out of commercial banks, thereby reducing the amount of money banks have available for loans.

Conversely, if the Fed thinks money supply growth is too slow, it buys government securities on the open market, and these funds soon end up in commercial banks. This generally increases the amount of funds banks have available, and in effect, puts more money into the system.

Other methods open to the Fed involve discount rates, reserve requirements, and margin requirements.

In addition, the Fed can and does buy or sell "repos" (see Chapter 3) to affect the money supply.

Discount rate   Banks that are temporarily unable to meet their reserve requirements have the "privilege" of borrowing at the "discount window" of their regional Federal Reserve Bank. The rate at which they may borrow is called the "discount rate" and is set by the Fed. The discount window should be considered as a fall-back resource; continuous use of this window is thought inappropriate.

If the Fed raises this rate, banks tend to borrow less (or be less inclined to let their reserves fall to the point where they need to borrow). If the discount rate is cut, they tend to borrow more. Thus, a higher discount rate tends to constrict the money supply and vice versa.

Reserve requirements   Banks in the Federal Reserve system are required to retain a certain stated reserve, that is, to hold aside a certain percentage of their deposits of all types (though the requirement is higher for demand deposits). This money cannot be lent out to customers.

The reserve requirement is of particular importance because banks, in effect, create money. If a bank lends a client $10,000, it credits the client's checking account with $10,000, "creating" money for the client to spend. The client's checks are in turn deposited and lent again. This is called the "multiplier effect," and it explains why the Fed's reserve requirement is particularly powerful.

For example, assume the requirement is 20%, and Bank A has deposits of $1,000. With a 20% reserve requirement, the bank must keep $200 but can lend $800. These funds are eventually deposited in Bank B. Bank B must then keep $160 but can lend $640 and so forth until there is nothing left to lend.

Mathematically, the multiplier effect is derived from the reserve requirement by the formula:

$$\text{Multiplier} = 1 \div (\text{Reserve Requirement})$$

In this example, the multiplier is $1 \div .2 = 5$. Thus, the actual supply available to banks for loans is five times the amount deposited. A relatively minor change in reserve requirements can change the money supply considerably. For example, if there is a 25% requirement, then the multiplier effect is only 4. For this reason, the Fed makes such a change infrequently.

Margin requirements   Since the Fed sets margin requirements under Reg T (see page 269), it can also affect the supply of money by adjusting this figure. Again, a tighter policy—higher requirements—drives the money supply down; a looser policy brings the money supply up. This can curb speculation, but it is the least powerful of the Fed's tools as it affects only the securities market.

Moral suasion   Finally, the Fed can use "moral suasion," asking member banks, often through statements in the media, to pursue a more or less tight policy. Since the banks are dependent on the Federal Reserve Bank, they are not likely to ignore this "jawboning."

Effects of Fed's actions on securities markets

The Fed's monetary actions can strongly affect stock markets. For example, if the Fed perceives a threat of inflation, it uses one or more of the tools described to reduce the amount of money available for loans. Thus, interest rates are pushed up. Consequently, companies reduce the amount they invest (as their cost of acquiring money goes up); as investment drops, output and employment go down, which tends to slow the entire economy. In general, corporate securities will offer lower returns and investors will tend to turn away from stocks toward bonds or other instruments which offer a better return.

Other money supply rates and measures

Here are other regularly published monetary figures analysts watch.

Prime rate   The prime rate is a nominal rate that commercial banks charge their best customers, although they often lend these customers money at lower rates.

Federal funds rate   A commercial bank with deposits in excess of its reserve requirements may lend to other banks that are temporarily unable to meet the requirements. These are called "federal funds," and are negotiable money market instruments (see Chapter 3). This rate is set by the supply and demand for funds, and it is highly volatile. Many other short-term rates are keyed to it.

Call loan rate   The rate banks charge brokers for margin loans also may change daily.

Interest rates and inflation

Interest rates represent the cost of money. A lender gives up the current use of his money in the expectation of getting more money some time in the future. The lender must take into account the value of the money he will receive later. Inflation can reduce this value, so a lender usually demands an interest rate that compensates for this erosion of value.

It is possible to think of the stated interest rate (or nominal interest rate) as made up of two components: the expected rate of inflation and the real rate. Under this model, interest (R) is $R = R(I) + R(R)$ where $R(I)$ is the rate of inflation and $R(R)$ the real rate of interest. For example, if the current rate for T-bills is 5% and inflation is estimated at 2%, the real rate of return on T-bills is 3%. It is possible to estimate the real rate of return for any investment in the same fashion. This explains why inflation is an important issue for investors: with high inflation, interest rates go up, and this in turn tends to dampen economic activity because investors find fewer opportunities that provide returns commensurate with risk.

CONTROLLING THE CYCLES—FISCAL POLICIES

Economic policies other than monetary are usually called "fiscal policies." Until recently, these policies have been based on the Full Employment Act of 1946, which charges the government with:

- minimizing the impact of business cycles

- working to promote a growing, high employment economy

- keeping prices as stable as possible

To meet these goals, the government uses its basic powers to tax and spend. In very simplified terms, the government increases taxes and reduces spending in an inflationary period; it lowers taxes and increases spending in a downturn.

Automatic responses

Some government responses to excessive swings in the business cycle are in effect built in or "automatic," and work opposite the direction of the cycle. For instance, some transfer payments (government funds which go directly to individuals, like unemployment insurance) are automatic under certain conditions. They work to mute the effects of a downturn by helping limit the decline in consumption. Conversely, when the economy is expanding, more people are working and contributing to these programs and, thus, have that much less disposable income.

Saving is another automatic response. When the economy dwindles, people are forced to rely more on their savings. This provides additional demand beyond that generated by income, and so consumption does not fall as sharply. Conversely, when the economy booms, people save more of their income, and consumption does not grow as rapidly.

Discretionary policies

In addition to automatic stabilizers, the federal government can take deliberate actions to boost employment and/or modify the business cycle.

Perhaps the most familiar of these discretionary tools is simply spending. When the economy is moving downward, the government tends to spend more (on defense, public works, etc.); when the economy seems to be expanding too quickly, the government tends to spend less.

Another familiar discretionary tool is changing tax rates and structures. In general, it is thought that lowering personal income taxes should increase the amount of disposable income and consumption, while raising them should have the opposite effect. Thus, tax reforms enacted in 1986, 1993, and 1997 have been more or less neutral with respect to total amounts of taxation; they have changed tax policy in ways that are intended to help the economy.

INTERNATIONAL FACTORS

Just as securities markets operate within the economy as a whole, so the U.S. economy must operate within the context of a world economy. Trade among nations currently accounts for 25% of the world economy, and this proportion continues to rise. There is no handy global equivalent to GNP, but investors need to have some sense of the global economy in making their decisions.

A key factor in world trade is the relative value of the currencies of the countries involved. Basically, if country A's currency moves up (appreciates) with respect to that of country B, then A's exported goods and services become more expensive for buyers of imports in B; conversely, if A's currency moves down (depreciates) relative to the currency of country B, then A's exports will be cheaper in B.

The relative value of currencies reflects a complex combination of strengths and weaknesses beyond the scope of this book, but one important underlying element is supply and demand. This is measured by the "balance of payments."

Balance of payments

"Balance of payments" is the term used to denote the net flow of money in or out of a country. If inflow exceeds outflow, there is a surplus; if outflow exceeds inflow there is a deficit.

Balance of payments figures are calculated in two ways.

Current account   This is the up-to-date figure for exports and imports of merchandise, tourist expenditures, shipping, military spending, investments by U.S. firms, and bank loans.

Capital account   This is U.S. money invested abroad on the debit side; foreign investments within the U.S. on the credit side.

Factors affecting the balance of payments

The direction of these flows is affected by many things such as:

- if interest rates are higher in one country, then investors will tend to buy debt in that country

- if inflation is higher in one country, holders of that country's currency will try to exchange it for currency of another

- if there is a persistent trade imbalance, then the country with the surplus trade will have the stronger currency. For example, if more German goods are bought in the U.S. than U.S. goods in Germany, more Deutsche marks will be needed by dollar holders than vice versa

- finally, if the climate for investment in securities, or industry, or real estate is attractive in a country, then a demand for the currency of that country increases

While the trade component of the balance of payments often draws a great deal of attention, it is clear that interest rates, investment opportunities, and perceptions about prospects for the future play a major role in determining the value of a currency.

In any case, these factors affect the economy as a whole, not only individual industries and individual firms within those industries. To this extent at least, an analyst—and, in fact, the registered representative—should keep these various factors in mind when trying to determine a course of investment action.

PART TWO
Technical and Fundamental Analysis

Attempts to analyze the behavior of securities markets are generally called either "technical" or "fundamental" although, in practice, most analysts use elements of both.

Technical analysts look at price movements in the market for clues as to when to buy or sell. They pay particular attention to indexes and averages, such as the Dow Jones or S&P, and to "charting" price movements of individual stocks.

Fundamental analysts are more concerned with basic economic factors and with measuring the soundness of particular industries and companies.

In other words, technical analysts think they can learn all they need to know about a security's future price movements by examining data on past price movements and the movement of relevant indicators. These analysts claim they do not need information such as a company's earnings or a particular industry's strength or weakness. Fundamental analysts disagree. They say that only basic economic data can provide the information necessary for buy and sell decisions.

TECHNICAL ANALYSIS

Averages and indexes

Technical analysts pay much attention to stock averages and indexes. An "average" can be just that—the sum of market prices of all stocks in a group divided by the number of stocks in that group. A securities "index" tends to be broader and more sophisticated; it is weighted to account for the fact that the outstanding shares of some firms have considerably greater dollar value than outstanding shares of others. Depending on the elements considered, different indexes can show different results, especially in chart form. Yet over the long term, most popular market indexes show remarkable similarity.

Dow Jones Average   By far the most widely quoted (and the oldest) stock average is the Dow Jones, or simply "The Dow." In fact, it is four averages:

- 30 industrial stocks, principally manufacturers (the "industrial average" or DJIA)

- 20 transportation stocks including airlines, trucking, railroads (the transportation average)

- 15 utilities (the utilities average)

- 65 stocks, total of all those above (the composite average)

The specific stocks included in the averages have been chosen because they are large, actively traded issues and account for nearly 30% of the value of all listed stocks.

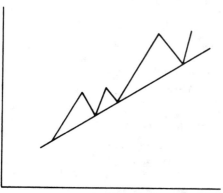

Figure 12.1-a Rising support line　　　　*Figure 12.1-b Declining resistance line*

Piercing the resistance line at A will often lead to the line becoming a support line B.

Thus, a Dow quote does not represent dollars and cents, although it is sometimes described in terms such as "the Dow gained $5 today," or "it lost $12.50 today." Also, dramatic numeric moves can represent very small percentages. If the Dow is reported "up 81 points" when it is at 9,000, a rise of only 0.9% has occurred.

Standard & Poor's 500

This is a composite index of 500 stocks: 400 industrials, 20 transportation, 40 financial, and 40 public utilities. It includes a larger and broader selection than the Dow, representing 75% to 80% of the value of all issues listed on the NYSE. S&P's 500 is also more refined: each stock is weighted to reflect the value of its outstanding shares. For example, a company with $100,000,000 in shares outstanding will have 10 times the weight of a firm with $10,000,000 outstanding.

NYSE Index

This figure represents the average price per share of all common stocks traded on the NYSE. It is weighted, like the S&P 500, by the total value of outstanding shares. Sub-indexes cover industrials, transportation, utilities, and finance. Preferred stocks are not included.

Wilshire 5000 Stock Index

The broadest popular stock index, the "Wilshire 5000" includes 5,000 stocks from the New York and American Exchanges and the OTC market. It, too, is dollar-weighted.

NASDAQ-OTC price indexes

These indexes include a composite index for the 2,000-plus stocks listed on NASDAQ and sub-indexes for industrial, transportation, utilities, banks, insurance, and "other finance." It is prepared by the NASD. Mutual funds, though traded OTC, are not included.

Market theories

Technical analysts consider averages and indexes in judging overall market strength or weakness and in discerning a "bullish" or "bearish" market. When technical factors show a strong market, they recommend that investors buy; when the market looks weak, they recommend selling or selling short.

In making these determinations, technicians use one or more of several theories. Keep in mind that these theories are supposed to show general trends in the market, not the worth or attractiveness of an individual security.

Dow theory   This oldest of the technical theories is supposed to indicate when a major, long-term trend in the market is about to change either up or down. Dow theory distinguishes these "primary trends" (lasting a year or more) from "secondary reactions" (lasting a few weeks to a few months) and "fluctuations" (which last some hours or days).

These distinctions are important because stocks rarely move in a straight line; there are almost always corrections in the other direction. Dow theorists say these smaller moves can point to a primary trend: a rising market when the chart shows each secondary low is higher than the preceding low (and each high is higher) or a falling market if the lows (and highs) show a descending pattern (see Figures 12.1a & b).

Indeed, such changes at the secondary level—lows starting to fall below previous levels in a rising market and vice-versa—may signal a new trend.

Both the industrial and transportation indexes must be rising to show an upward trend; a rise in only one is considered a false signal, especially if the other is falling. The reasoning here is that an increase in industrial production cannot be sustained unless the means to distribute (transportation) grows accordingly. Conversely, if both industrials and transportations are down, a downtrend is indicated. (Note that this is more of an economic argument and, hence, more in keeping with fundamental analysis than with technical analysis.)

Once the Dow theorist determines that a primary trend exists, investors are urged to go with the trend, *i.e.,* to buy in a bull market and sell short in a bear market.

There have been many challenges to the Dow's validity as a measure of the market, but, perhaps because of its age, the Dow's popularity continues. Like the Dow index itself, Dow theory has been criticized as imprecise, slow to show changes, and often (some studies say half the time) simply wrong; but like the Dow, it is still widely used.

Advance-decline ("breadth of market") theory   This theory counts the number of traded issues moving up in price (advanced), less the number moving down (declined), to arrive at a net figure. For example, if 2,200 different securities trade, with 1,200 up, 800 down, and 200 unchanged, the advance-decline figure would be plus 400. If, over time, the figure is positive (advances exceed declines), the situation is bullish; a negative number signals a bearish market.

The time period measured can vary; the important indicator is a net change in either direction. This figure can be negative even when a stock index is rising, since the net change measures numbers of different shares only, while indexes are weighted averages. In fact, many advance-decline theorists look for such a disparity and think a noticeable rise or fall in the advance-decline line presages a movement up or down in the market as a whole.

As the advance-decline theory considers all traded issues, this approach provides a broader measure of securities prices than Dow theory. It is usually employed in conjunction with other theories.

Volume of trading

Here the number of shares traded (the volume) is compared with changes in market price. High volume in a rising market is generally considered a bullish sign, low volume a bearish one; the idea here is that low volume means an absence of buyers, as sellers are always present.

Specifically, this theory holds that volume tends to fall before a major turn in price averages; in other words, declining volume indicates the end of a bull market and is a "sell" signal. By the same token, a surge of volume after an extended decline suggests stocks have "bottomed out" and a reversal is due; this is a "buy" signal.

Those who follow this indicator hold that volume and price must move together. They consider a price rise with low volume, or high volume with no increase in price, as signs of a technically weak market.

Odd-lot theory

This theory suggests that small investors always move in the wrong direction, that they act on poor or late information, so they buy or sell incorrectly or too late.

To gauge small investor sentiment, this theory examines the number of transactions for odd lots (less than 100-share units, which small investors prefer). This is usually translated into an index, showing odd-lot sales as a percentage of all sales. If the number is high (*i.e.*, if more odd lots are being bought, this is considered a sell signal; if the number falls, it is a buy signal).

Short interest theory

"Short interest" refers to the number of outstanding shares sold short. Technicians usually calculate short interest in proportion to average daily volume or some other volume figure; this is the "short interest ratio."

Here, the underlying premise is that short-sellers, since they must eventually enter the market and buy to cover their positions, will tend to act as a brake in a declining market. Thus, a high short interest ratio (more short-sellers) is considered bullish; a low ratio is bearish.

Confidence index

This index attempts to measure how confident investors are that markets will go up or down. It looks to the bond market, since bond holdings often reflect the judgment of those who manage portfolios for large institutions. If they are pessimistic, the theory holds, they will tend to move strongly toward the highest-rated bonds; if optimistic, toward lower-rated but higher-yielding bonds.

To measure the relative attraction of the two, the technician might use a ratio derived by comparing the yield on Barron's high grade 10-bond average with the yield on the Dow Jones 40-bond average, which includes some lower-rated bonds. If lower-grade bond yields are improving, this is a bullish signal.

Charting—the technical analysis of individual securities

In deciding whether to buy a particular security, a technical analyst usually turns to "charting." (In fact, technicians are often also called "chartists.") Charting means plotting the stock's price movement over time on a graph.

The "levels"   Here, dozens of different methods are in use, but almost all recognize "support" and "resistance" levels, "head and shoulders" formations, and "trendlines." If, in the time period covered by the chart (see Figure 12.2), the security being tracked has moved up and down in price, but has remained within a band bounded by the line LL below and the line HH above, then LL is called a "support level" and HH a "resistance level."

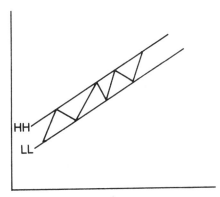

Figure 12.2 Rising channel

Chartists think that once a stock "breaks through" such a level, *e.g.*, falls below LL, then it is likely to decline considerably further. Similarly, if the price were to penetrate above HH, it would be an indication that the price will continue to rise.

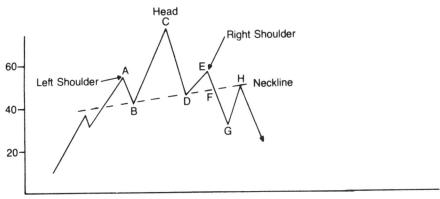

Figure 12.3 After breaking the neckline at F, the neckline becomes a resistance line.

One strategy is to buy securities near LL and to sell them near HH; another is to wait until such a level has been penetrated and then to "ride that trend." It should be noted that, since there are many chartists, any time a clearly defined band exists, the theory will tend to be self-fulfilling, since the chartists will all act as if it were true.

Reading such a chart (or any of the others that are in use) to discover the correct pattern is something of an art and, hence, provides many opportunities for chartists to disagree.

The patterns   There are many chart patterns that are believed to be significant. Without attempting to be exhaustive, we note the popular chart formation called a "head and shoulders" pattern (see Figure 12.3).

Some chartists think such a formation indicates that a stock has peaked (top form) and will start to fall; an inversion of this pattern would indicate that a stock has bottomed out and is ready to rise.

Note

With the arrival of substantial computational and graphic tools, analysts have been using more and more sophisticated mathematical forms to model the price movements of securities. These include moving averages, exponential smoothings, and other more complex techniques. The goal of all of these tools is the same: to predict the future price of a security based upon information about past prices and volumes. This distinguishes them from fundamental analyses.

FUNDAMENTAL ANALYSIS

While technical analysts look at price movements in the market, the fundamental analyst looks at underlying economic factors: basic conditions in the economy itself, in a particular industry, and in particular companies within that industry. An "industry" can be more or less broadly defined, *e.g.*, electronics or microchips, rubber or tires.

Industry categories

Analysts often group industries into three broad categories.

Noncyclical industries   These are relatively resistant to business cycle ups and downs and can be considered "defensive investments." Examples are the food and drug producers and utilities. In general, investments in these firms tend to be less risky, but, therefore, often bring relatively low returns.

Cyclical industries   The opposite of the above, cyclical industries are most affected by downturns and recoveries. Examples are producers of "durable goods," such as automobiles, heavy equipment, housing materials, etc. When the economy slows, or inflation is rising rapidly, individual consumers and businesses both tend to delay purchases of such goods.

Growth industries   This grouping is less influenced by business cycles than by investors' expectations that these producers will grow faster than the economy as a whole. Such firms often concentrate heavily on research (recent examples include lasers and biotechnology).

Industry life cycles

Of course, no industry can grow forever. Recognizing this, the fundamental analyst may also look at an industry in terms of its "life cycle" and speak of phases like:

Pioneering   This is a period of strong and rapid expansion because the industry is relatively new (exploiting a technological innovation, perhaps). This is also often a period of keen competition as many firms rush to enter the market. Those that succeed reward their investors handsomely, but, of course, most firms will not succeed, with unhappy consequences for the investors. Genetic engineering is an industry in the pioneering stage. At this writing, it is not clear which of the many firms in the industry will ultimately be its leaders.

Growth   In this phase, the industry expands rapidly. This tends to be a period of only modest consolidation; many firms sell their products to this growing market. Minicomputers have been an example of a growth industry.

Maturity   A time of slower growth, stagnation, or even actual decline, with a few surviving firms accounting for nearly all the industry's output. The automobile industry in this country is certainly mature. As companies move through this cycle, the potential for further growth, and hence rapid price appreciation, goes down; investors look for higher dividends to compensate for this lower capital appreciation.

Other factors considered by fundamental analysts

In addition to examining broad measures, the fundamental analyst will explore a number of specific quantitative factors concerning an industry, relying on both government sources (such as the Federal Reserve Banks and the Department of Commerce) and commercial, trade, and financial publications. Items of concern include statistics on sales (both raw figures and changes over time as compared to GNP); production and inventory levels; industry wage rates, price levels, and profit margins; information about the financial health of an industry; and chances for industry growth.

The fundamental analyst tends to specialize in an industry or even a single company. This analyst looks at quantitative and qualitative indicators of a company's position within its industry, as well as its current financial position, stability, and expected growth.

PART THREE
Securities Analysis

A registered representative is often called on to analyze an individual firm, either to select a promising investment or to evaluate continuing performance. Financial statement analysis is the "window" into a company's operations.

This analysis requires a great deal of skill and experience, and the registered representative will usually rely on the research of professionals who have acquired this experience. However, the rep needs training to put this research into practice and should be able to read financial statements.

This part explains how to read financial statements and outlines measures used to gauge a firm's overall performance, its profitability, and the soundness of its financial position. The closing sections deal with investment risks as they relate to assembling an investment portfolio.

The two fundamental financial statements are the balance sheet and the income statement.

THE BALANCE SHEET

This is perhaps the most familiar form of financial statement. It provides a snapshot, usually taken at the end of the fiscal year, which shows the company's monetary position at that moment in time.

The two elements that must balance are usually displayed side by side: on one side, assets; on the other, liabilities and shareholder equity (sometimes called net worth). The idea is that the assets of the firm minus its liabilities belong to the owners or shareholders. The equation of balance is written:

Total Assets = Total Liabilities + Shareholders' Equity

Each side will be examined in turn.

AMALGAMATED CONSOLIDATED INC.
BALANCE SHEET
DECEMBER 31, 1994

Assets

• Current Assets
Cash	$ 400,000
Marketable Securities	100,000
Accounts Receivable	300,000
Inventory	200,000
Total Current Assets	$1,000,000

• Fixed Assets
Plant & Equipment	$2,500,000
Less: Accumulated Depreciation	(600,000)
Net Plant & Equipment	$1,900,000

• Intangibles
Patents	$90,000
Goodwill	$10,000

Total Assets	$3,000,000

Liabilities

• Current Liabilities
Accounts Payable	$ 250,000
Notes Payable	100,000
Income Taxes Payable	100,000
Dividends Payable	50,000
Total Current Liabilities	$500,000

• Long-Term Liabilities
10% Bonds Payable (due in 2003)	$1,000,000
Total Liabilities	$1,500,000

Shareholder's Equity
Preferred Stock 5% (100 par value)	$200,000
Common Stock ($2 par)	400,000
Additional Paid-in Capital	600,000
Retained Earnings	300,000
Total Shareholders' Equity	$1,500,000
Total Liabilities and Shareholders' Equity	$3,000,000

Figure 12.4

Assets

Anything the corporation owns is considered an asset. These are listed on the left side of the balance sheet in decreasing order of liquidity, *i.e.,* beginning with those that are most easily converted into cash. Further, they are separated into:

Current assets   These are assets that normally would be convertible into cash within the accounting cycle, usually one year. They are:

- **Cash**   The actual total, not an estimate

- **Marketable securities**   These are short-term investments in marketable instruments

- **Accounts receivable**   Items for which payment is due within a year

- **Inventories**   All goods on hand that will be converted into cash within 12 months

- **Prepaid expenses**   Expenditures for goods and services not yet received

Fixed assets (or long-term assets)   This category, sometimes called plant and equipment, includes:

- **land,**

- **plant** (buildings, machinery, other equipment), *less*

- **accumulated depreciation** or the allowance made for amortization of costs over the assumed useful life of the asset. This deduction applies to most fixed assets other than land.

Intangible assets   These are nonphysical items, such as trademarks, patents and copyrights, good will, and so on.

Liabilities

Anything the corporation owes is considered a liability. Liabilities are also divided into two categories: current and long-term.

Current liabilities   These include obligations payable in cash within one year, such as:

- accounts payable, or bills not yet paid

- notes payable, or money owed for loans

- taxes payable, or federal or other taxes due

- dividends payable or dividends declared but not yet paid

- interest on debt

Long-term liabilities   Debt not due within the next 12 months: bonds, mortgages, and long term loans.

Total Liabilities = Current Liabilities + Long-Term Liabilities

Shareholders' equity or net worth

This is the third element of the balance sheet; in fact, the balance equation is often written as:

Shareholders' Equity = Total Assets − Total Liabilities

It includes shareholders' original contribution plus any earnings retained over the years. It represents the shareholders' residual claims against the assets of the firm. For both accounting and legal purposes, it is divided as follows:

Capital stock   This includes both preferred and common stock valued at par. Recall that preferred stock takes precedence over common stock both in the payment of dividends and in the return of original investment on the dissolution of the corporation. Preferred stock usually has a par value of $100 per share.

Paid-in surplus or paid-in capital   This is the difference between the actual issued price and par. It is the surplus amount that shareholders have paid for issued common stock.

Retained earnings or earned surplus   Retained earnings are net earnings still held. Thus:

Retained earnings = Total profits − Total paid out dividends

Footnotes to the balance sheet

Reading the fine print, in this case the footnotes, can be critical. On a balance sheet, these often describe such important matters as the accounting methods used.

THE INCOME STATEMENT

The income statement provides a summary of all revenues and expenditures for a given period, usually the company's fiscal year. Unlike the "freeze frame" of the balance sheet, the income statement shows activity over the most recent period. It summarizes the profit (or loss) over that period from the sale of goods and services, minus the expenses incurred. For this reason, the income statement is often a better indicator of future performance. Figure 12.5 is the hypothetical income statement for Amalgamated Consolidated Inc.

The items in the income statement can be interpreted as follows:

Gross sales   Total sales of products to customers, less:

Returns   Returns from customers equal:

Net sales   Gross sales minus returns.

Cost of goods sold   Includes raw materials, manufacturing costs, utilities, etc.

General operating expenses   Not directly connected with manufacture, *e.g.*, for sales, staff, administration, advertising, research, and development.

Depreciation   Amortization of plant and equipment used to produce revenues over the productive lifetime of this plant and equipment.

Operating income   *I.e.*, net sales less cost of goods, general operating expense, and depreciation.

Nonoperating income (income from other sources)   Royalties, earnings from subsidiaries, rents, interest, or income from investments.

Total income   The sum of operating and nonoperating income, often called earnings before interest and taxes (EBIT).

AMALGAMATED CONSOLIDATED INCORPORATED
INCOME STATEMENT
FOR THE YEAR ENDED DECEMBER 31, 1994

Gross Sales	$1,100,000
Less: Returns	100,000
Net Sales	1,000,000
Less: Cost of Goods Sold	400,000
Gross Profit on Sales	600,000
Less: Operating Expenses	200,000
Less: Depreciation	100,000
Operating Income	300,000
Other Income	50,000
Operating Income (Earnings Before Interest & Taxes)	350,000
Interest Expenses	100,000
Taxable Income	250,000
Taxes (40%)	100,000
Net Income	150,000
Preferred Dividends	10,000
Net Income Available for Common	140,000
(Earnings per Share of Common $140,000 ÷ 200,000 = $.70	
Dividends for Common Stock ($.30 per share)	60,000
Additions (Losses) to Retained Earnings	$ 80,000

Figure 12.5 An income statement

Interest and other nonoperating expenses Most often, this is interest on long-term debt.

Taxable income (Earnings Before Taxes, EBIT) less:

Taxes leaves:

Net income before preferred dividends.

Preferred dividends Paid to holders of preferred stock leave:

Net income The famous "bottom line"; the difference between revenue and expenditure for the period. Any dividends for common must be based on this figure.

Earnings per share of common Net income divided by the number of shares of common outstanding.

Dividends for common The amount of earnings actually paid out in dividends to common stock holders.

Additions to retained earnings As defined, the residual funds that are retained and can now be added to previously retained earnings.

Footnotes As with balance sheets, footnotes on the income statement can include crucial information, *e.g.,* one-time events such as the sale of a subsidiary or a plant. SEC regulations require registered firms to report such items separately.

STATEMENT OF CHANGES IN FINANCIAL CONDITION

A third financial statement is called the Statement of Changes in Financial Condition or Funds Statement. While the balance sheet shows net working capital (defined as current assets less current liabilities) at a given moment, this form shows changes over the fiscal year and, more importantly, how these changes have arisen, namely, the sources and uses of working capital.

The Statement of Changes is derived from the two balance sheets that bracket the income statement. In our illustrations, then, we would need to compare the balance sheet for Dec. 31, 1989, with the one shown. The 1990 Statement of Changes might look like the example on the next page. As the illustration shows, this statement is usually divided into two parts, showing funds coming in and funds going out.

1990 Statement of Changes for Amalgamated Consolidated Inc. (Sources and Uses of Funds Statement)

Sources		Uses	
Net Income	$150,000	Dividends for Preferred	$ 10,000
Depreciation	100,000	Dividends for Common	60,000
Increase in Acc. Pay.	40,000	Increase in Inventory	50,000
Decrease in Market. Sec.	20,000	Increase in Acc. Rec.	60,000
	$310,000	Increase in Plant & Eqp.	50,000
		Increase in Ret. Earn.	80,000
			$310,000

Figure 12.6 A sources and uses of funds statement

Items that are sources

- net income (from operations) or profits

- depreciation (a noncash expense); it has the effect of increasing working capital since it is deducted when figuring net income, thus reducing taxes paid

- sale of securities, or of noncurrent assets; this increases capital although it does not affect total assets

Items that are uses

- net operating losses (cash outflow)

- purchase of noncurrent assets, *e.g.*, land, plant, patents; decreases capital, although it does not affect total assets

- cash dividends; even the declaration of a dividend creates a current liability and so reduces working capital

- repayment of debt

Within the Funds Statement, those items that increase current assets or decrease current liabilities lead to working capital increases and vice versa.

VALUATION PRACTICES

Different accounting methods can produce different values for the same assets or liabilities, so it is important to know which approach is being used.

Inventories

Most assets are valued at original cost. In a period of consistent inflation, such a figure could be very different for two identical items of inventory, especially if one were long-held. The cost of goods sold then depends on which item from inventory has been liquidated. There are two accounting methods in general use for valuing inventories.

FIFO (First In, First Out)
This assumes the first items bought (*i.e.*, the items held the longest) are the first items sold. In practice, this is usually the case; but in an inflationary period, this method will cause the cost of goods to be low, thus raising earnings and hence taxes. It also causes the inventory to be highly valued since only the new, more expensive inventory remains, thus raising the value of current assets.

LIFO (Last In, First Out)
This assumes the last items bought (*i.e.*, the newest items) are the first sold. This has the opposite effect, lowering taxable earnings and current assets.

Depreciation

Fixed assets are depreciated using one of two accounting methods, "straight-line" or "accelerated."

Straight line
This method simply divides the cost of the asset by its expected useful life. Thus, a $100,000 stamping press with a usable life of 10 years is depreciated at $10,000 per year. The formula is:

Original Cost − Salvage Value ÷ Years of Life = Annual Depreciation

Accelerated
This method permits the firm to depreciate an asset more quickly and to use large depreciation allowances in the early years of an asset's life and relatively smaller ones in later years. Accelerated methods will tend to lower a firm's earnings, and hence its taxes, in early years.

EFFECTS OF CORPORATE CHANGES

Some actions by a corporation's board of directors, in particular those changing the number of outstanding shares, have a significant effect on financial statements.

New issue of stocks or bonds

The issue of new securities increases both assets (working capital) and shareholders' equity (if stocks) or long-term liabilities (if bonds).

Example

If Amalgamated Consolidated Inc. were to issue 50,000 new shares at $10, then working capital and shareholder's equity (SE) would be increased by $500,000. Note that the original 200,000 shares would now be increased to 250,000 with the accompanying dilutions of voting rights, dividends, etc.

If the firm had sold the same amount of bonds, long-term liabilities would have increased instead of SE, and there would not be any dilution. However, in this case, the debt to asset ratio (see page 329) would be increased.

Exercise of rights and warrants

This also raises capital. When rights- or warrant-holders exercise their privileges, the issuing firm must sell them shares at the specified price. This is, in effect, like issuing new shares, and, as above, increases equity and capital surplus while diluting ownership.

Conversion of convertible securities

When the holder of a convertible bond or convertible preferred stock exercises the right to convert, there is an increase in the entries for common stock at par and a decrease in bond amount or preferred stock outstanding.

Example

If in the above example there had been no new issue but rather the conversion of $500,000 of bonds to 50,000 shares of common stock, then there would be no change in working capital. The dilution would still occur and the debt to asset ratio would be decreased.

Stock splits

A decision to split stock is usually taken to lower the market price and, thereby, attract more investors. Such an action reduces par value and increases the number of shares proportionately (*e.g.*, a 2-for-1 split doubles the number of shares but cuts par value in half), but has no effect on total stockholders' equity. A reverse split (*e.g.*, 1-for-2), has the opposite effects on par and number of shares but, again, no effect on stockholders' equity.

Dividends

Cash dividends, when declared, are taken from retained earnings to become current liabilities; when they are paid, cash and dividends payable are both reduced. With stock dividends, though, there is a resemblance to a split; the value of the dividend is taken from retained earnings and is added to stockholders' equity on the balance sheet, divided between common stock and capital surplus.

Example

A company with SE (Stockholders' Equity) of $20 (stock at 1, capital surplus 9, retained earnings 10) declares 10% stock dividend. It still has $20 SE, but now 1.1 stock, 9.9 surplus, 9 retained.

Other actions

Other actions can affect the balance sheet. For example, if cash is used to buy new equipment, current assets are decreased and fixed assets are increased although total assets remain unchanged. On the other hand, if a current liability is paid from cash, then both current assets and current liabilities are decreased. In either case, however, the balance in the balance sheet is preserved.

PART FOUR
Financial Ratios and Investment Policies

Using information revealed by financial statements as raw material, more sophisticated analyses concerning a firm's liquidity, operating efficiency, profitability, and the value of its shares can be performed. This analysis is based on a series of measures usually expressed as the ratio of two amounts.

As mentioned above, accurate analysis requires skill and experience. Bearing this in mind, one can use the ratios discussed below to track a company's performance over time (*e.g.*, are profit margins increasing?), or to compare one firm with another. Much data on the average values for these measures for different industries, as well as individual companies, has been published.

In what follows, these ratios will be described and illustrated with the financial statements of Amalgamated Consolidated Inc. (see Figure 12.4). The first group of measures describes the firm's liquidity. These are primarily of interest to short-term lenders since they describe the firm's ability to meet short-term obligations.

LIQUIDITY RATIOS

The difference between current assets and current liabilities is:

Net Working Capital = Current Assets − Current Liabilities

This describes the resources available over the coming year—literally, capital to work with. At ACI, the net working capital is $1,000,000 − $500,000 = $500,000. This figure is an absolute number, and, as such, it is hard to judge its significance.

The next measure uses the same two numbers to form a ratio which can be used to compare firms of different sizes.

Current Ratio = Current Assets ÷ Current Liabilities

The higher the ratio, the greater the liquidity. At ACI:

Current Ratio = $1,000,000 ÷ $500,000 = 2

A more rigorous measure of liquidity, the acid test ratio, does not include inventories because at times inventories become obsolete or are otherwise not quickly converted to cash.

Acid Test Ratio (Quick Ratio) = (Current Assets − Inventories) ÷ Current Liabilities

At ACI, then:

$$\text{Acid Test Ratio} = \frac{(\$1,000,000 - \$200,000)}{\$500,000} = 1.6$$

The most rigorous of all liquidity ratios recognizes that even accounts receivable may not be liquid. This is called a cash assets ratio:

$$\text{Cash Assets Ratio} = \frac{(\text{Cash} + \text{Marketable Securities})}{\text{Current Liabilities}}$$

At ACI:

$$\text{Cash Assets Ratio} = \frac{(\$400,000 + \$100,000)}{\$500,000} = 1$$

DEBT RATIOS

The second group of ratios is of interest to long-term debt holders.

Debt to Asset Ratio = Long-term Debt ÷ Total Assets

The ratio of long-term debt to total capitalization. At ACI:

Debt to Asset Ratio = $\$1,000,000 \div \$3,000,000 = \frac{1}{3}$

As the firm must pay interest on this debt (or face bankruptcy), too high a ratio can signal a potentially unsound situation. Accordingly, the firm's ability to cover its interest expense should also be considered.

Times Interest Earned = Income Before Interest and Taxes ÷ Interest

At ACI:

Times Interest Earned = $\$350,000 \div \$100,000$ (10% of $\$1,000,000$) = 3.5

Similarly this coverage can be considered for preferred stockholders. The significant difference is that since preferred stock dividends are paid after taxes, the numerator of this ratio is after tax income; the denominator is dividends for preferred stockholders.

Preferred Dividend Coverage = After Tax Income ÷ Preferred Dividends

At ACI:

Preferred Dividend Coverage = $\$150,000 \div \$10,000 = 15$

CAPITALIZATION RATIOS

This group of ratios describes the manner in which a firm has capitalized itself. It compares the components of long-term capitalization—long term liabilities, preferred stock, common stock—to the total of this capitalization (TC):

Bond Ratio = long-term liabilities ÷ TC

Preferred Stock Ratio = Par Value Preferred Stock ÷ TC

Common Stock Ratio = Total Value of Common Stock ÷ TC

For ACI these are:

$$\text{Bond Ratio} = \frac{\$1,000,000}{\$2,500,000} = 0.4$$

$$\text{Preferred Stock Ratio} = \frac{\$200,000}{\$2,500,000} = 0.08$$

$$\text{Common Stock Ratio} = \frac{(\$400,000 + \$600,000 + \$300,000)}{\$2,500,000} = 0.52$$

ASSET UTILIZATION RATIOS

The next set of ratios is often called asset utilization ratios. They describe some aspects of how well a firm is using its assets. The first equation measures the ability to convert inventory to sales. A high ratio is better as rapid turnover cuts the cost of storage and the risk of obsolescence.

Inventory Turnover Ratio = Net Sales ÷ Inventory

At ACI:

Inventory Turnover = $1,000,000 ÷ $200,000 = 5

Another measure of asset use is:

Receivables Turnover = Net Sales ÷ Accounts Receivable

This ratio describes the firm's ability to convert its receivables into cash. It is useful in assessing a firm's use of credit to enhance sales and its general control over its operations. Here again, a high value is good since it says that receivable collections are achieved in a timely fashion. At ACI:

Receivables Turnover = $1,000,000 ÷ $300,000 = 3.3

PROFITABILITY RATIOS

The first profitability ratio is net profit margin; it usually would consider only operating income. Its interpretation is obvious.

Net Profit Margin (before taxes) = Net Operating Profit ÷ Net Sales

At ACI:

Net Profit Margin = $300,000 ÷ $1,000,000 = 30%

Two other profitability ratios are:

Return on Assets = Net (after tax) Profit ÷ Total Assets

and:

Return on Common Equity = Earnings for Common ÷ Common Equity

At ACI:

Return on Assets = $150,000 ÷ $3,000,000 = 5%

and:

Return on Common = $140,000 ÷ ($1,500,000 − $200,000) = 10.77%

CASH FLOW

Another important measure is a company's cash flow. It describes the actual amount of cash generated by the firm. As such, cash flow is in many ways more important than net income; it differs from net income primarily in that cash flow includes depreciation.

Thus, the use of accelerated depreciation has a twofold effect. On the one hand, income for the year is decreased because taxes are lowered; on the other hand, cash flow is increased since depreciation is added back in. This is illustrated below using ACI:

Cash Flow = Net Income + Current Depreciation

At ACI:

Cash Flow = $150,000 + $100,000 = $250,000

If for example an accelerated method for depreciation yields a current depreciation of $150,000, the income statement would reflect this larger depreciation by showing:

Taxable Income = $250,000 − $50,000 (additional depreciation)

= $200,000

Taxes (at 40%) = $ 80,000

Net Income = $120,000

and

Cash Flow = $120,000 + $150,000 = $270,000

Thus, while income has decreased, cash flow has increased. It follows that firms that need to show earnings currently are less likely to avail themselves of the benefits of accelerated depreciation. Conversely, for firms that desire additional cash flow, net income may appear to be unduly depressed.

VALUATION RATIOS

Valuation ratios describe ways to value a company. By comparing these values to the market value, the price for which one can actually buy the company (more realistically, the shares of the company), one can judge the desirability of such an investment. The most common valuation ratio is book value.

Book value per common share

This shows the "theoretical" liquid value—"theoretical" because it is unlikely assets could actually be liquidated at their listed value—of each common stock share. A stock with a market price below book value is often said to be undervalued.

$$\text{Book Value of Common} = \frac{(\text{Common Equity} - \text{Intangible Assets})}{\text{Common Shares Outstanding}}$$

Thus, for ACI:

$$\text{Book Value per Share} = \frac{(\$2,900,000 - \$1,500,000 - \$200,000)}{200,000 \text{ shares}}$$

$$= \$6.00 \text{ per share}$$

This ratio is sometimes called "tangible asset" value per share because only tangible assets are included in the valuation. Also, common equity means that both liabilities and preferred equity have been subtracted from the book value.

Since this ratio's denominator is shares of common stock, one must be alert to the possibility that this number could change. This is especially true for firms with convertible securities outstanding. If they are converted, the value is diluted. However, to the extent that bonds (debt) are converted, liabilities are decreased and common equity is increased. A similar analysis applies to the conversion of preferred stock.

EARNINGS RATIOS

Finally, ratios that compare earnings, dividends, and stock prices are examined. The first is:

(1) Earnings Per Share = Earnings for Common ÷ Common Shares Outstanding

If, for instance, ACI's \$1,000,000 long-term debt were a convertible bond (at \$50) the bond could be converted into 20,000 shares so that the fully diluted earnings per share would be:

Earnings Per Share = \$140,000 ÷ 220,000 shares = \$.636 per share.

Here again, this figure does not provide an accurate picture when a firm has any convertible securities, rights, options, or warrants outstanding. If these are converted into, or used to buy, common shares, the number of outstanding shares will increase and earnings per share will decline.

In such a situation, it is necessary to report "earnings after dilution" or "fully diluted earnings." To arrive at this figure, one increases the number of shares outstanding by the number of shares that would be issued if options, warrants, and rights were exercised. The calculation also requires that earnings be changed to reflect reduced interest (or preferred dividend) on those issues.

Another ratio of interest is:

(2) Dividend Payout Ratio = Dividends per Share ÷ Earnings per Share

At ACI:

Dividend Payout Ratio = \$.30 ÷ \$.70 = 42.86%

As noted in Chapter 1, this figure tends to be lower for growth (usually newer) firms which keep earnings to aid in expansion and higher for firms (usually more mature) where investors expect less growth but higher returns.

Finally, two widely used ratios are:

(3) Current Yield = Dividends per Share ÷ Share Price

and

(4) Price Earnings (P/E) Ratio = Share Price ÷ Earnings per Share

The first measures the current return on a share of stock. It specifically does not consider the possibility of appreciation in share price. The second expresses a stock's price as a multiple of earnings. Other considerations being equal, a higher P/E ratio reflects expectations of higher future growth.

PART FIVE
Investment Risks

All investment in securities involves some risk. On the simplest level, the investor risks losing some or all of the amount invested. Investors expect rewards to be commensurate with risks; that is, the greater the risk, the greater the return. This concept is at the heart of all investment decisions.

Risks are conventionally divided into several categories.

Financial risk, or business risk

Investors are concerned about the safety of their principal and of their return (dividends or interest payments).

Market risk

The market price of a company's securities can change even if there has been no material change in the company's condition or prospects. This happens, for example, when the stock market as a whole moves strongly in response to news.

Purchasing-power risk

This is simply the risk that the invested dollar will not grow at the same pace as overall inflation, *i.e.*, that returns will actually buy less (have less real purchasing power).

Interest-rate risk

If interest rates rise, the value of an investment, particularly a long-term investment, may fall.

Marketability or liquidity risk

A security should be readily tradeable. If it is not, the investor may not be able to sell or buy it at the most advantageous time. Marketability risk occurs principally when the securities are thinly traded, either because the total number of outstanding shares is quite small or because the shares are closely held, *i.e.*, most outstanding shares are held by a few individuals. Thus, low volume can indicate that a security carries this risk. Another indicator is a large spread between bid and asked prices.

Call risk

Holders of bonds or preferred issues with a call provision face the risk that the issue will be called. As noted earlier, most issues pay a premium when calling and provide time limits on calling, both of which provide additional return in exchange for the risk.

PORTFOLIO POLICIES

No two individual investors have precisely the same resources or goals. It is the task of the registered representative to design a program tailored to each client, *i.e.*, to build a portfolio meeting that client's needs with the lowest possible risk.

Investment objectives

The first step involves determining the client's goals and resources. In other words, what does the client expect? How much money is or will be involved? An important task here is to project retirement needs. The careful representative will try to offer all available services suitable to the client's total situation, even though the plan may contain elements (insurance, estate planning) that will require advice from other professionals.

Financial position

The current and expected future financial status should be taken into account to help choose appropriate investment objectives. This should involve some of the steps used in examining a corporation: drawing up a personal balance sheet, perhaps even an income statement. This will help determine the present or future assets available for investment.

Constraints on investment

Once the registered representative has some idea of a client's goals and resources, it is important to know preferences that might limit investment options. For example:

- Is the client able and willing to risk loss of principal?

- Is the client able and willing to risk loss of income?

- Can the client assume purchasing-power risk?

- Can the client hold investments for a long period?

- What is the client's tax status?

Building the portfolio

Portfolios should suit the investor's needs, resources, and willingness to assume risk. Portfolio strategies are usually divided into three categories: aggressive, defensive, and mixed.

Aggressive   For those (often younger) investors who seek high returns and are willing to take the higher risks associated with such returns. Such a portfolio tends to include speculative securities and margin and options purchases since leverage is an important ingredient of an aggressive strategy. It might also have relatively little diversification.

Trading strategy for such a portfolio might call for moving between stocks and bonds and "timing" transactions, *i.e.*, buying and selling to take advantage of expected fluctuations in the market.

Defensive   For those (often older) investors most concerned with the safety of their principal and income and less inclined to take risks. Such portfolios are characterized by:

- high-rated bonds, blue chips, and/or other quality common stocks

- broad diversification, thereby spreading the risk among different types of issues

- both long- and short-term bonds, the former for steady, predictable income, even though changing interest rates lead to fluctuations in the principal value; the latter to protect the principal, although changing interest rates mean different rates of return when funds are reinvested

- an investment plan that controls amounts invested over time, for example, dollar cost averaging or constant dollar plans (see page 96)

- holding securities for relatively long periods

Mixed   These combine aggressive and defensive strategies to meet the needs (and temperament) of the individual client

PART SIX
Portfolio Theory

There are a number of ideas about the operation of markets that employ sophisticated mathematical techniques. They begin with a basic premise: investors behave rationally. Rational investor behavior requires that riskier investments have larger expected returns. It follows then that given a choice between two investments with identical risks but differing returns, investors would prefer the one with higher return. And, that given a choice between investments with identical expected returns and differing risks, investors would choose the less risky one. No judgment is made about investments with differing risks and returns except the one stated above, *i.e.*, that higher risk requires higher return.

Defining return

By expected return, we mean the average return one should expect over time from this investment. This formulation recognizes that the return for any investment is not constant, but rather that it fluctuates. One can, however, find an average (historical) return for any investment, and that is the expected return. This theory includes an implicit assumption that the *future* expected return is equal to the *past* average return.

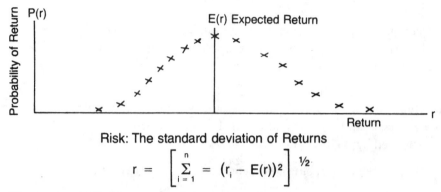

$$r = \left[\sum_{i=1}^{n} = (r_i - E(r))^2 \right]^{1/2}$$

Figure 12.7 Risk: The standard deviation of returns

Defining risk

Risk is defined as deviation (technically, the "standard deviation") from the expected return. Figure 12.7 shows a chart plotting return against the probability of that return.

Characteristic line

Using a complex set of assumptions and rationales, detailed explanations of which are beyond the scope of this book, one arrives at the idea of a *characteristic line* for each security.

In Figure 12.8, this line is fitted to data that plots the return on ACI against the return on the market over some time period. (In practice, the S&P 500 is usually used as a surrogate for the market as a whole.) The slope of this line is called *beta*. It describes the return for a security in terms of the return for the market.

Example

Investment A has a beta = 2, B has beta = 1, C has beta = .5, and D has beta = −1. If the market has a return of 10% for some period, A would be expected to return 2 × 10% or 20%, B to return 1 × 10% (the same as the market on the whole), C to return .5 × 10% or 5%, and D to return −1 × 10% or −10%.

The point on the characteristic line where it crosses the Y-axis is called *alpha*, which represents the expected return for this security when the expected return for the market as a whole is 0.

Using the characteristic line

One uses this set of ideas in two ways.
1. For an individual security—The beta of an individual security describes the volatility of its return relative to the market as a whole. An investor who is *confident* the market will rise might seek a security with a high

positive beta to get a high return; at another time, he might choose a less volatile performer. In fact, if he felt the market was likely to fall, he would seek a security with a negative beta. This can be thought of as the quantification of the ideas of cyclical and counter-cyclical securities.

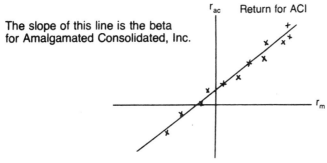

Figure 12.8 The Characteristic Line for Amalgamated Consolidated, Inc.

2. For a portfolio—The second way in which these concepts are employed is in constructing a portfolio of securities. For instance, by combining investments with the same expected return and with betas of opposite sign, one can construct a portfolio with an equivalent return but with lower risk.

In light of an earlier observation about investor behavior, this implies the combination of these two investments is preferable to either one alone. Extensions of this reasoning are used to construct portfolios of investments that lower risk for a given expected return.

Efficient Market Hypothesis or EMH

The term "efficient market" means one where new information is quickly and broadly disseminated and is immediately reflected in the market price. Conceptually, then, this hypothesis implies that no information, whether technical, fundamental, or even "insider," is useful in predicting future price movements.

In fact, the three generally accepted versions of this hypothesis—the "weak form," the "semi-strong form," and the "strong form"—respectively deny the usefulness of technical, fundamental, and insider information for predicting future price movements.

Random walk hypothesis

One version of the EMH is the random walk hypothesis. This hypothesis asserts that price fluctuations occur randomly in the short run. The implications of this hypothesis are that there is no correlation between the return in one period and the return in the next period, and that for any time period, the chances of any particular return—say a gain of 10% or a loss of 30%—are the same as they are for any other time period.

Not surprisingly, the efficient market hypothesis, which was developed by theoreticians at universities, is not too well accepted by market practitioners. It is true that larger portfolios, especially some mutual funds, strive to mirror the performance of the market at the lowest possible transaction cost, effectively admitting that they cannot "beat the market." Nevertheless, most professionals believe that some form of analysis—technical or fundamental, or both combined—is worthwhile and that professionals can help a client achieve investment objectives with such an approach.

TERMS

Economic analysis

Gross National Product (GNP)   Total value of all goods and services produced in the nation in a year; can be in current or fixed dollars

GNP components

Net National Product (NNP)   GNP less depreciation

National Income (NI)   NNP less business taxes

Personal Income (PI)   NI less business profits

Disposable Income (DPI)   NNP less taxes; retained corporate earnings less transfer payments

Business cycles

Expansion   Time of general growth

Recession   Usually defined as two consecutive quarters of decline in GNP

Cyclical industries   Those most likely to be adversely affected by recession (*e.g.,* durable goods)

Noncyclical industries   Usually less affected by the business cycle (*e.g.,* staples)

Leading indicators   Point to changes in the business cycle

Inflation   Continuous rise in dollar price of fixed basket of goods over extended time

Consumer Price Index (CPI)   Monthly price of basket of goods deemed necessary for average family

Demand-pull theory of inflation   If amount of money available increases faster than amount of goods and services, producer prices will move up

Cost-push theory   When prices begin to rise, cost of producing goods also rises, leading into a spiral

Stagflation   Persistent inflation when economy is stagnant or actually declining

Monetary policies

Attempts to smooth business cycle by smoothing growth of money supply

M-1   Currency in circulation plus balances in all demand deposits

M-2   M-1 plus deposits in regular savings accounts, time deposits under $100,000, some money market funds, IRAs, and repos

M-3   M-2 plus large time deposits, term repos, and institutional money funds

Federal Reserve System   Tries to keep the money supply growing at same rate as real GNP

Open market operations   Fed's Open Market Committee (FOMC) exerts short-term control by buying or selling government securities in the open market

Reserve requirements   Banks in Fed System must retain a certain percentage of their deposits; changing this requirement has a multiplier effect

> Multiplier = 1 ÷ Reserve Requirement

Discount rate   To meet reserve requirements banks borrow from Fed; Fed can raise or lower interest on these loans (discount rate)

Margin requirements   Set by Fed

Moral suasion   Asking member banks to pursue a policy that is more or less tight

Effects on securities markets   If Fed tightens, interest rates rise, investors tend to turn away from stocks

Prime rate   Rate commercial banks nominally charge their best customers

Federal funds rate   Rate charged by commercial banks for loans needed by other banks to meet their reserve requirements

Call loan rate   Rate banks charge brokers for margin loans

Fiscal policies

Government   Increases taxes and reduces spending in inflationary period; lowers taxes and increases spending during downturn

Automatic responses   Built-in correctives to cyclical changes

International factors

Balance of payments   Net flow of money in and out of the country

Current account   Exports and imports of merchandise, tourist expenditures, shipping, military spending, investments by U.S. firms, bank loans

Capital account   Money spent by U.S. corporations abroad, U.S. purchases of foreign bonds and securities on debit side; foreign investments in the U.S. on credit side

Technical and fundamental analysis

Technical analysts   Look at historical data about price movements, particularly indexes and averages

Fundamental analysts   Look at basic economic factors and soundness of industries or companies

Averages   Can be simple arithmetic average

Indexes   Usually weighted to consider relative value of constituents

Dow Jones Averages   (weighted total market price of the stocks is divided by a constant)

Standard & Poor's 500   Weighted to reflect value of shares

NYSE Index   Average price per share of all common stocks traded on the NYSE, weighted like the S&P 500

Wilshire 5000 Stock Index   Broadest popular index; includes 5,000 stocks; is dollar-weighted

NASDAQ-OTC Price Indexes   Composite index and subindexes; mutual funds not included

Market theories

Dow theory   Indicates when a major trend is about to change either up or down

Advance-decline (breadth of market) theory   Counts number of issues increasing in price less those that decreased

Volume of trading   Compares number of shares traded with changes in market price

Odd-lot theory   Examines number of odd-lot transactions, usually as a percentage of all sales

Confidence index   Measures yield on high grade vs. lower grade bonds; bullish if index is up, bearish if down

Charting   Graphing stock's price movement over time

Fundamental analysis

Noncyclical industries   Relatively resistant to ups and downs of business cycle

Cyclical industries   Most affected by ups and downs

Growth industries   Often concentrate on research and development

Securities analysis

Balance sheet   Snapshot picture of company's monetary position

Total Assets = Total Liabilities + Shareholders' Equity

Income statement   Summary of all revenues and expenditures for a given period

Statement of Changes in Financial Condition   Shows changes over the fiscal year and sources and uses of working capital

Portfolio theory

Investors behave rationally; riskier investments must have larger expected returns

Return   Average return expected over time; historical return

Risk   Deviation from expected return

Diversifiable risk   Represents risk which can be eliminated by diversifying a portfolio

Market risk   Measures how much of a stock's price change reflects moves in overall market

Characteristic line   Relates return available from the security to the return available from market as a whole

Beta   Slope of characteristic line

Alpha   Represents expected return for the security when expected return for market as a whole is 0

Efficient Market Hypothesis (EMH)   Says new information is reflected in market price immediately; implies that information is not useful for predicting price movements

Random walk   Holds that there is no correlation between present and future returns; and the probability of any particular return is the same in each period

REVIEW QUESTIONS

1. Which of the following are part of the index of leading indicators?

   I. housing starts
   II. new unemployment insurance claims
   III. orders for plant and equipment
   IV. prices of the S&P 500

   (A) I and II only
   (B) I and IV only
   (C) II and III only
   (D) I, II, III, and IV

2. The "Odd-Lot Theory" suggests that:

   (A) sophisticated investors spread their purchases
   (B) mutual funds allow one to take advantage of pooled buying
   (C) investors who trade in odd lots are usually right
   (D) investors who trade in odd lots are usually wrong

3. On a balance sheet, retained earnings are part of:

   (A) shareholders' equity
   (B) assets
   (C) liabilities
   (D) income

4. A fundamental analyst would be likely to use which of the following information?

   I. the advance-decline ratio
   II. projected earnings
   III. trading volume
   IV. industrial production

   (A) I and II
   (B) II and IV
   (C) I and III
   (D) II and III

5. All of the following are likely EXCEPT:

   (A) a growth company would pay high cash dividends
   (B) investors might buy stocks as a source of income
   (C) a high P/E ratio suggests high expectations about future growth
   (D) a blue chip stock pays dividends regularly

6. A stable P/E ratio of 14 and a projected price of $35 for the next year suggest that next year's earnings will be:

   (A) $2.00
   (B) $2.50
   (C) $5.00
   (D) impossible to estimate

7. If a corporation has total assets of $1,000,000 and short-term liabilities of $600,000 and no long-term debt, then the shareholders' equity is:

   (A) $ 400,000
   (B) $ 600,000
   (C) $1,000,000
   (D) impossible to determine

8. A breakout from a "Head and Shoulders" pattern would indicate to a technical analyst that the price was:

   (A) likely to move downward
   (B) likely to drift sideways
   (C) likely to move up
   (D) pointing to a resistance line

9. "Disintermediation" is the name for which of the following?

   (A) the withdrawal of time deposits from banks
   (B) the analysis of future moves by the FOMC
   (C) the depositing of a customer's stock in a bank

(D) the effect of raising margin requirements

10. The "Dow Industrials" comprises:

    (A) all NYSE stocks
    (B) 65 industrial stocks
    (C) 30 industrial stocks
    (D) all NYSE industrial stocks

11. A highly leveraged company has only a small portion of its assets in the form of:

    (A) bonds
    (B) convertible debentures
    (C) common stock
    (D) liabilities

12. A technical analyst would be likely to enter a sell stop at which of the following points?

    (A) above a resistance line
    (B) at new highs for the security
    (C) when a support line was penetrated
    (D) when potential profit can be maximized

13. The totality of goods and services produced by the U.S. is called:

    (A) total savings
    (B) Gross National Product
    (C) total income
    (D) accumulated wealth

14. The conversion of convertible bonds to common stock would result in a(n):

    I. increase in debt
    II. decrease in leverage
    III. increase in stockholder's equity
    IV. increase in total assets

    (A) I and II
    (B) II and III
    (C) II and IV
    (D) I, II, and III

15. The tangible assets of a corporation would correspond most closely with:

    (A) par value
    (B) market value
    (C) book value
    (D) working capital

16. If the Fed acted to increase the money supply by buying securities, the rate that would reflect this first is the:

    (A) prime rate
    (B) discount rate
    (C) Fed funds rate
    (D) commercial paper rate

17. The rate which commercial banks usually charge their best customers is called the:

    (A) bank rate
    (B) Fed funds rate
    (C) discount rate
    (D) prime rate

18. Money can be drained by the Fed if it:

    (A) increases the discount rate
    (B) decreases the discount rate
    (C) sells government securities
    (D) does less "jawboning"

19. Typically the most highly leveraged companies are:

    (A) utility companies
    (B) growth companies
    (C) automobile companies
    (D) computer companies

20. An index which includes 500 securities is known as the:

    (A) Value Line index
    (B) Dow Industrials
    (C) S&P index
    (D) Dow composite

21. The CAI corporation earned $2.50 per share last year. If CAI paid $1.50 in dividends, the dividend payout ratio was:

    (A) 40%
    (B) 50%
    (C) 60%
    (D) impossible to determine

22. A recession is:

    (A) one quarter of decline in the GNP
    (B) two consecutive quarters of decline in the GNP
    (C) one year of decline in the GNP
    (D) whatever the Council of Economic Advisors decides

23. The acid test ratio is:

    (A) current assets ÷ current liabilities
    (B) total assets ÷ total liabilities
    (C) (current assets – inventory) ÷ current liabilities
    (D) current assets – current liabilities

24. If the Federal Reserve Board lowers reserve requirements, all of the following would occur EXCEPT:

    (A) the multiplier would increase
    (B) the multiplier would decrease
    (C) money would become easier
    (D) banks would have more money to lend

25. The rationale for the treatment of depreciation in financial statements is to:

    (A) amortize the cost of equipment over its useful life
    (B) increase taxes
    (C) increase the firm's income
    (D) lower cash flow

26. The declaration of a cash dividend results in:

    (A) increase in long-term liabilities
    (B) increase in current liabilities
    (C) decrease in current liabilities
    (D) decrease in total assets

27. If prices remain constant and costs are decreasing, which method of inventory valuation will show the best earnings picture for the period?

    (A) FIFO
    (B) LIFO
    (C) replace as needed
    (D) don't replace inventory

28. All of the following would be defensive stocks EXCEPT:

    (A) utility stocks
    (B) supermarket stocks
    (C) computer stocks
    (D) generic drug stocks

29. The book value of a corporation could be affected by which of the following?

    I. a decrease in the market price of the stock
    II. an increase in the market price of the stock
    III. the sale of an asset at a loss
    IV. an increase in retained earnings

    (A) I and II
    (B) II and III
    (C) III and IV
    (D) I and IV

Questions 30–32 are based on the following information: Amalgamated Consolidated Incorporated, ACI, was capitalized at $50 million. This consisted of $30 million in common stock with 1 million shares issued and $20 million in 9% long-term bonds. ACI earned $5 million before interest and taxes (at 25%) and paid a dividend of $.60 per share.

30. What were the earnings per share?

    (A) $1.80
    (B) $2.40
    (C) $3.00
    (D) $5.00

31. What is the return on investment (ROI)?

    (A) 8%
    (B) 24%
    (C) 48%
    (D) 56%

32. What was the dividend payout ratio?

    (A) 20%
    (B) 25%
    (C) 50%
    (D) 60%

33. A stock with a beta of −1 would perform best during a period when the market:

    (A) went down by 10%
    (B) went down by 5%
    (C) was unchanged
    (D) went up by 10%

34. One form of the efficient market hypothesis implies that:

    (A) prices increase at a random rate over time
    (B) technical analysis is better than fundamental analysis
    (C) fundamental analysis is randomly applied
    (D) current prices reflect all useful information

35. The FOMC is:

    (A) Federal Reserve Open Market Committee
    (B) Federal Oversight Management Committee
    (C) Fair, Open Markets Committee
    (D) Federal [regulation] On Making Commitments

ANSWERS TO REVIEW QUESTIONS

1. (**D**) All of these are leading indicators.

2. (**D**) The little investor is least likely to be right.

3. (**A**) The retained earnings are what is left after all required payments like bond interest and dividends; thus, they belong to the stockholders.

4. (**B**) A fundamental analyst would be interested in the economic condition of the firm.

5. (**A**) A growth firm would want to keep its earnings for investment in expansion.

6. (**B**) If the price to earnings ratio is 14, then $\dfrac{\$35}{\text{earnings}} = 14$ or earnings = $2.50.

7. (**A**) Total Assets = Liabilities + Shareholders' Equity.

8. (**A**) With a "Head and Shoulders," a breakout would be downward. An inverted one would have an upward breakout.

9. (**A**) A bank intermediates by aggregating deposits and lending them. When funds are withdrawn, this is disintermediation.

10. (**C**) The 65 Dow stocks are 30 industrials, 20 transports, and 15 utilities.

11. **(C)** The firm is leveraged because its assets are a large multiple of its equity.

12. **(C)** A sell stop would be used to protect a profit or limit a loss. A technician would use a support line as a signal point and enter a sell stop below it.

13. **(B)** By definition.

14. **(B)** Converting debt to equity would reduce debt and increase equity. The ratio of debt to equity (leverage) would thus be reduced.

15. **(C)** The market value is what the outstanding stock is worth, the par value is relatively meaningless now, and working capital refers only to current assets and liabilities.

16. **(C)** This is the most volatile of the rates.

17. **(D)** Of the others, discount rate is charged by the Fed to member banks, and the Fed funds rate is the rate between banks for overnight loans of excess reserves.

18. **(C)** By selling securities, it collects money, thereby draining money.

19. **(A)** The cash flow of utilities is very stable since customers pay these bills regularly. This makes utilities less vulnerable to business risk and allows a highly leveraged structure.

20. **(C)** The Value Line Index has about 1,700 stocks; the Dow has 65.

21. **(C)** The ratio of dividends to earnings.

22. **(B)** By definition.

23. **(C)** The acid test is more stringent than the current ratio because it recognizes that inventory is not always liquid.

24. **(B)** By lowering reserve requirements, a smaller percentage of each dollar is set aside. In addition, the number of times each dollar is loaned increases. Thus, the multiplier also increases.

25. **(A)** The equipment is used to produce revenues over its useful life, hence its cost should be spread over that life.

26. **(B)** When a dividend is declared, it must be paid and, thus, becomes a current liability.

27. **(B)** By charging the most recent inventory (last in, first out), when costs are declining, the profit margin increases.

28. **(C)** The others have stable sales and therefore earnings do not fluctuate as much.

29. **(C)** I and II do not affect the intrinsic value of the firm.

30. **(B)** Earnings are after interest and taxes. The former is $1.8 million, leaving $3.2 million. After taxes, this is $2.4 million, and with 1 million shares outstanding, this gives $2.40 per share.

31. **(A)** With an investment of $30 million, the return of $2.4 million represents 8%.

32. **(B)** $.60 is 25% of $2.40 earnings per share.

33. **(A)** A beta of −1 means that it does exactly the opposite of the market and will do best when the market does its worst.

34. **(D)** If "useful" includes insider information, then this is the strong form of the hypothesis.

35. **(A)** By definition.

CHAPTER THIRTEEN
taxation

Recent federal legislation—especially the Tax Reform Act of 1986 and the Omnibus Budget Reconciliation Act of 1993—has radically affected the tax treatment of investment income. Actual writing, implementation, and interpretation of specific rules designed to meet the requirements of these laws will occupy the Internal Revenue Service and the investment industry for many years to come. For that reason, this chapter is concerned principally with broad tax considerations as they affect investment decisions. (Note, too, that taxation is discussed in many particular instances throughout this book.)

GENERAL INFORMATION

Progressive and regressive taxes

Taxation schemes are conventionally divided into two categories: "progressive" and "regressive." A progressive tax takes a larger proportion of individual income as earnings increase; for example, in 1986 U.S. taxpayers were taxed at 15 different rates, ranging from 11% to 50%, depending on their income. A regressive tax, on the other hand, does not consider income. Examples include sales or excise taxes.

The Tax Reform Act of 1986 considerably reduced the progressive nature of income tax, with most taxpayers paying either 15% or 28% of their incomes (a few paid 31%). In 1993, however, new brackets were added for those in upper-income categories: a 36% rate for individuals with a taxable income over $115,000 (over $140,000 for couples) and a 39.6% rate for those with taxable incomes above $250,000. Taxes on Social Security recipients with high income also were raised.

An Alternative Minimum Tax, first introduced in 1979, provides (as its name implies) both an alternative method of figuring one's tax liability and a minimum amount of tax that must be paid: this is 26% on the first $175,000 of defined AMT income and 28% with AMT income above $175,000. This is directed particularly at those who take large deductions known as "preference items." Those affected must calculate both minimum and regular taxes and pay the higher amount.

Many of these preference items were eliminated by the 1986 law (especially those for long-term gains), but new ones appeared: examples include untaxed appreciation of real property, charitable donations, and most municipal bond income.

Types of income

The Internal Revenue Code separates "ordinary income," which includes all types of earnings, interest and dividends, from "capital gains income," i.e., any gains (or losses) realized from the sale of an asset (including securities). Capital gains income in turn is further subdivided into "short-term" and "long-term" gain, the former basically for assets held less than one year, the latter for those held one year or more.

Under the Tax Reform Act of 1986, these distinctions were basically eliminated, although the category "capital gains" was still used as an accounting category, and it was thought that the practice of taxing such income at a different level would reappear. So it did in the 1993 tax law, which made the maximum rate for long-term capital gains 28% even for those who pay up to 39% on ordinary income. The 1997 tax bill introduces more complexity with a variety of rates starting as low as 10% (depending on the taxpayer's overall tax level and the amount of time the asset has been held), with new categories for certain assets held more than six months, and even lower for some even longer-term gains. It seems likely that new variations will again appear.

Favorable tax treatment of certain kinds of gains is supposed to encourage certain kinds of investment. For individual investors, and for registered representatives, laws and rulings on capital gains lead to a number of investment strategies, some of them quite complex, to ensure that income is of the right kind for the specific investor's circumstances.

An important distinction in the tax law concerns net capital losses. A maximum of $3,000 of such losses may be charged against ordinary income in any tax year. Any additional net capital losses may be carried forward to future years and again first charged against any capital gains for that year and then again can be charged against ordinary income for that year with the same $3,000 limit. This process can be continued until such losses have been exhausted.

Example

Mrs. Y sells some assets and experiences a loss of $10,000 in 1992. She may deduct $3,000 of that from her 1992 income; the remaining $7,000 is carried forward. If, in 1993, she realizes a capital gain of $2,000, she may deduct the $7,000, thus showing a net loss of $5,000. Again, $3,000 of this may be charged against income; the remaining $2,000 can be carried forward.

Note that this is different from ordinary losses or expenses, which can be used to offset income with no annual dollar limitation, though they cannot exceed the amount of income.

TREATMENT OF INCOME FROM SECURITIES

Dividend income

In general, all dividends on investments, including cash distributions that are automatically reinvested, are treated as ordinary income. There are two exceptions to this rule: stock dividends where the investor is not offered the option of accepting cash payment and dividends treated as "return of capital." In these cases, the dividend is considered to reduce the "cost basis" of the asset.

Corporate dividend income

For a corporation owning up to 20% of the stock of another corporation, 70% of the dividend income is excluded. This exclusion rises to 80% if the corporation owns between 20% and 80% of the corporation issuing the dividend; above 80%, the issuer is considered wholly owned and all dividends are excluded. This does not apply to interest payments: a corporation receiving "dividends" from a mutual fund distributing income from debt securities would not be eligible for this exclusion.

Interest income

Interest income is taxable with the distinctions noted in the chapter on bonds. For instance, interest income on municipal securities is generally exempt from federal taxes and in some cases from state and local taxes as well. However, under the 1986 Tax Reform Act, certain industrial development bonds issued by municipalities that are deemed to be for "nonessential purposes" are no longer tax exempt.

Interest expense

In general, a taxpayer can deduct interest expenses incurred in making an investment from income, but the amount deducted cannot exceed net investment income. Any interest expense in excess of that amount can be carried forward and charged against net investment income in subsequent years. There is one notable exception: interest paid on loans obtained to purchase tax-exempt instruments is not deductible.

Capital gains and losses—determining "cost basis"

A capital gain (or loss) is simply the profit (or loss) realized when an asset held for investment purposes is sold or exchanged. In recent years, these have been taxed like ordinary income except for those in the highest earnings brackets, but with the 1997 tax bill, differential treatment—taxing long-term gains at a rate lower than conventional income—has returned. In addition, under the 1997 law, gains on securities held for a period in excess of 18 months are taxed at a rate lower than those held between 12 and 18 months. The 1997 law has, in effect, created two classes of long-term gains.

In the simplest case, of course, the gain (or loss) realized from the sale of an asset is simply the difference between the selling price and the purchase price. But with securities held over time, a number of things can change the per-share cost, such as the issuing of dividends or rights. Thus, there are a number of rules that apply to the problem of determining the "cost basis" of an investor's holdings.

Stock dividends and rights
When a stock dividend is issued, a new cost basis is determined. This is the out-of-pocket cost (the total of the purchase price plus any commissions and taxes) divided by the new total number of shares. Stock rights are not immediately taxable, and if used to purchase stock, help determine the cost basis. However, if the rights are sold, the net proceeds are treated as ordinary income.

Example

A client buys 100 shares of PSM at $42, then receives a stock dividend of 5 shares. Ignoring commissions, the out-of-pocket cost was $4,200; the new cost basis per share is:

$4,200 ÷ 105 shares = $40 per share

Gifts of securities
The recipient of a gift of securities assumes the donor's cost basis if the current value or the eventual sale price exceeds the donor's cost. If the value drops between the time of gift and the time of sale, the cost basis is the market value at the time of gift.

Inheritance
The cost basis of inherited stock is the value of the stock on the date of the testator's death.

Selling part of a position

A client wishing to sell part of a portfolio that contains securities which have different cost bases can choose to sell certain items and thereby enjoy some tax advantage. The IRS assumes a FIFO method (first in, first out), but the investor may choose LIFO (last in, first out).

Additionally, an investor can sell "identified shares" by (a) delivering those certificates or (b) by instructing the broker to deliver those shares if they are held in a street name.

Wash sales

An exception to these general rules concerns a "wash sale." A wash sale involves the sale and purchase of a security so as to create a loss. Such a loss will generally not be recognized by the IRS if the repurchase takes place within thirty days of the sale that creates the loss. Specifically, the investor cannot deduct the loss if he or she buys or has an option to buy the sold stock at any time between 30 days before and 30 days after the sale that creates the loss.

For example, if a client sells 100 shares of ACI at a loss on Dec. 15, 1992, and buys the same shares after Nov. 15 or before Jan. 14, 1993, then the loss may not be deducted for 1992.

TREATMENT OF DEBT INSTRUMENTS

Cost basis

The cost basis for a debt instrument varies depending on whether it was purchased at issue or in the secondary market and whether it was issued at par or as an Original Issue Discount (OID) or an Original Issue Premium (OIP).

At par

A bond issued at par, or purchased in the market at par, has par as its cost basis. If purchased later at a premium (or a discount), then the basis is the purchase price. This is assumed to return to par on a straight line basis as the bond ages to maturity. For example, a purchase at $920 with ten years to maturity would have its basis increase by $8 per year so that at maturity the basis would again be at par. Similarly, a purchase at $1,150 with six years to maturity would have its basis decrease by $150/6 = $25 each year. If such a bond were sold after two years, the basis at the time of sale would be $1,100 and any gain or loss would be computed from that basis. The decrease (increase in the previous example) in basis would be considered a change in ordinary income.

OID or OIP

When an OID (or OIP) is purchased at issue, then the basis for this bond changes on an "economic accrual" basis. This is the compound interest rate necessary to bring the basis to par at maturity. That is the compound rate at which the issue price would have to grow (or decline) to reach par at maturity. Normally, the schedule of these accruals (or amortizations) is included with the bond to ease the burden of determining the basis.

Example

A client buys a 10-year bond at issue for $800. Two years later the schedule says that the bond has accrued $35.60. If he now sells the bond for $900, the capital gain is $900–$835.60 = $64.40. Note that the $35.60 of accrual is considered as interest income and is taxable except for the case of a municipal bond, where the interest is tax free. A similar calculation would apply to an OIP.

Accrued interest

As noted in Chapter 2, a bond transaction that takes place between the dates when interest is paid involves the buyer paying and the seller receiving interest accrued until the trade date. This accrued interest is not part of the cost basis of the bond.

MUTUAL FUNDS

Dividends and capital gains distributions are treated as described above. It is important to remember that reinvesting these distributions does not alter the tax liabilities.

OPTIONS

Tax consequences of options transactions and positions are covered in Chapter 9. A key point to remember is that the cost basis for stocks bought in conjunction with the purchase of an option includes the price of the option. For example, an investor who bought 100 shares of ACI at 50 and also bought 1 ACI Nov 50 Put at 3 would be considered to have a cost basis of 53 for the stock.

GIFTS AND ESTATES

Assets acquired as gifts are subject to the gift tax in lieu of income tax. There is a $10,000 per person per annum income exemption from this tax. For example, a couple could give a total of $20,000 to each of their children each year without any gift tax being levied. This allows one to begin transferring an estate without incurring estate taxes. (There is no gift tax on a spousal gift.)

For gift tax purposes, the amount of a gift is its fair market value at the time of the gift. This is different from the basis for determining a capital gain (or loss).

Gifts to minors

Gifts made under the Uniform Gifts to Minors Act (UGMA) are irrevocable; hence, the income and resulting tax liability (if any) are always the responsibility of the minor.

TAX-ADVANTAGED INVESTMENTS

These are described in Chapter 5. Since these instruments are designed in terms of their tax consequences, some key points are summarized here, and some additional points are included.

- Income and loss flow through to limited partners of direct participation programs and for REITs.

- Losses for passive investors can be used only to offset income from passive investments. Additional losses may be carried forward to offset passive income in future years. However, if a partner sells his interest in the passive investment, then any of the losses carried forward can be deducted first against passive income and then against any other income.

- For qualified deferred income plans, 401(k) contributions by employers are deductible when made. Eligibility requirements cannot be more strict than one year's employment for all employees who work over 1,000 hours per annum.

- Individuals may set up Individual Retirement Accounts (IRAs). The maximum contribution is $2,000 per annum; a married couple filing jointly can deduct up to $4,000 if this does not exceed their income. Individuals who do not qualify for the deduction may still contribute up to $2,000 to an IRA. In all cases, IRA income accrues on a tax-deferred basis.

- Self-employed individuals may contribute no more than 25% of their income to Keogh Plans, up to a maximum of $30,000. Note that individuals who are employed by others but have income from self-employment may make contributions from that income.

- Certain uniform distribution rules apply to all tax-favored retirement plans. Distribution may begin at age $59\frac{1}{2}$ and must begin by age $70\frac{1}{2}$. Premature distributions are subject to a 10% excise tax, except in the case of death or disability, for deductible medical expenses, or for certain persons aged 55 who have met early retirement provisions.

- Taxpayers who receive lump sum distributions from a plan can, after age $59\frac{1}{2}$, use five-year-income averaging once.

TERMS

Progressive tax   Takes a larger proportion of income as earnings increase

Regressive tax   Does not consider income

Recent tax legislation   Most taxpayers pay either 15% or 28% of their income; three higher brackets (31%, 36%, 39.6%) affect high-income taxpayers

Types of income   Ordinary income (all earnings, dividends); capital gains (realized from sale of an asset)

Capital gains   Taxed as ordinary income but at no more than the 28% rate

Net capital losses Up to $3,000 may be charged against income in tax year; any over $3,000 may carry forward and charge against capital gain

Ordinary losses Expenses can be offset up to 100% of income; no dollar limitation

Dividends to individuals Taxed as ordinary income, except dividends paid exclusively in stock or as return of capital reduce "cost basis"

Dividends to corporations On domestic stocks from 70% to 100% excluded, depending on extent of holdings.

Interest income Generally taxable

Calculating capital gain (loss) Difference between selling price and purchase price or cost of an asset

Wash sales Sale and purchase of a security to create a loss generally not recognized by IRS if stock repurchased within 30 days of sale

Year of loss (gain) Can report loss only at time of trade; gain at trade or settlement date

Gift and estate taxes $10,000 per person per annum exempt; spousal gift exempt; gift value = fair market value at time of gift

Gifts to minors Tax liability to minor

Tax-advantaged investments See Chapter 5

REVIEW QUESTIONS

1. An investor with a self-directed IRA would be least likely to choose which of the following?

   (A) common stocks
   (B) corporate bonds
   (C) municipal bonds
   (D) growth fund

2. An investor in the 28% bracket has a 13-month capital gain of $10,000. The tax liability for this will be:

   (A) $1,120
   (B) $1,400
   (C) $2,000
   (D) $2,800

3. A tax shelter specifically designed for self-employed individuals is a(n):

   (A) IRA
   (B) limited partnership
   (C) Keogh plan
   (D) qualified pension plan

4. To escape tax liability, the moving of an IRA from one investment to another must be accomplished within:

   (A) 15 days
   (B) 30 days
   (C) 60 days
   (D) 90 days

5. For estate tax purposes, real property may be valued at the time of death or at:

   (A) six months prior to death
   (B) six months after death
   (C) one year prior to death
   (D) one year after death

6. An investor buys a 10% coupon $10,000 face value municipal bond in the secondary market for $8,800. If it is held to maturity, the federal tax liability will be based on:

(A) $0 income
(B) $1,200 interest income
(C) $1,200 capital gains
(D) $1,200 capital gains + annual coupon interest

7. For an investor in the 28% bracket, a municipal bond with a 10% coupon is equivalent to a corporate bond with a coupon of:

(A) 7.2%
(B) 10%
(C) 12.8%
(D) 13.9%

8. The taxable portion of ACI's $100,000 of dividend income from other U.S. corporations is:

(A) $0
(B) $15,000
(C) $30,000
(D) $80,000

9. An investor buys a $100,000 T-bond with six years to maturity at 106. If he sells it four years later for 102, his capital gain (or loss) is:

(A) $0
(B) $2,000 gain
(C) $2,000 loss
(D) $4,000 loss

10. An investor buys an original issue municipal with a 20-year maturity at a discount price of $8,000. He sells it after 10 years for $9,500. His taxable gain is approximately:

(A) $0
(B) $500
(C) $1,500
(D) $9,500

11. A divorced couple wish to give their child a cash gift. The maximum this child can receive from them in one year without incurring gift tax is:

(A) $5,000
(B) $10,000
(C) $20,000
(D) $40,000

12. An investor reinvests the capital gains distribution from a mutual fund. The tax consequences are:

(A) taxed as income when sold
(B) taxed as capital gain when sold
(C) taxed as income when received
(D) taxed as capital gain when received

13. An investor is given the choice of a 5% stock dividend or its cash equivalent. If he chooses the stock, he is taxed:

(A) as capital gain when received
(B) as income when received
(C) as capital gain when stock is sold
(D) as income when stock is sold

14. A lump sum distribution from a qualified pension plan for a person born after 1936 is eligible for forward averaging of:

(A) only one year
(B) three years
(C) five years
(D) ten years

15. The following describes the tax consequences for transactions in the last five business days of the year:

(A) gain or loss on trade date
(B) gain or loss on settlement date
(C) gain on trade date, loss on settlement or trade date
(D) gain on settlement or trade date, loss on trade date

16. An investor has a $14,000 capital loss for 1991. With no other capital transactions, the investor will have deductions until:

    (A) 1991
    (B) 1992
    (C) 1994
    (D) 1995

17. Which of the following are exempt from all taxes for residents of New York State?

    I. New York State bonds
    II. New Jersey bonds
    III. U.S. bonds
    IV. Puerto Rico bonds

    (A) I and III
    (B) II and IV
    (C) I and IV
    (D) I, II, and IV

18. An investor buys a 10-year $1,000 corporate bond at an original issue discount of $100. If he holds it to maturity, the total taxable income is:

    (A) interest each year + $100 interest income at maturity
    (B) interest each year + $100 capital gain at maturity
    (C) interest + accrual interest each year
    (D) interest + accrual capital gain each year

19. An investor sold a municipal bond for $18,000 + $300 of accrued interest. For U.S. tax purposes, he experienced:

    (A) sale price of $18,000 + $300 interest income
    (B) sale price of $17,700
    (C) sale price of $18,000
    (D) sale price of $18,300

20. An investor bought 1 ACI Dec 70 Call at 4. If ACI went to 80 and he exercised the call and sold the stock, he would have a capital gain (ignoring transaction costs) of:

    (A) $0
    (B) $400
    (C) $600
    (D) $1,000

21. The income from a custodian account under the Uniform Gifts to Minors Act is the responsibility of the:

    (A) minor
    (B) donor
    (C) custodian
    (D) depends on whether the gift is more than $10,000 or not

22. An employee of an advertising agency with a qualified pension plan has a freelance business as well. His contribution to a Keogh is limited to:

    (A) $0
    (B) $7,000 less the contribution to the pension plan
    (C) $30,000 less the contribution to the pension plan
    (D) $30,000

23. A T-bill bought in 1991 is held to maturity in 1992. For tax purposes there is:

    (A) capital gain pro rated between 1991–1992
    (B) interest income pro rated between 1991–1992
    (C) capital gain in 1992
    (D) interest income in 1992

24. An investor bought 100 shares of CAI at $100. Subsequently, a 25% stock dividend was declared. If he eventually sold his shares for $90, he would realize a:

(A) $15-per-share loss
(B) $10-per-share loss
(C) $10-per-share gain
(D) $25-per-share gain

25. For gift tax purposes, fair market value is determined:

(A) when gift is given
(B) when gift is sold
(C) at donor's cost
(D) average of donor's cost and sale price

ANSWERS TO REVIEW QUESTIONS

1. **(C)** The IRA income is already tax deferred. One is less likely to choose the lower return of a municipal.

2. **(D)** The new act does away with the distinction between capital gain and income, so the investor's tax bracket is irrelevant. The tax rate on the long-term gain for a security held less than 18 months is 28%.

3. **(C)** By definition. Keoghs (H.R.10) were specifically set up for self-employed individuals.

4. **(C)** This rollover applies to any amount of money, not just the $2,000 of a particular year.

5. **(B)** The more beneficial of these values may then be chosen.

6. **(C)** Municipal bonds bought in the secondary market are treated as an asset. This asset appreciated by $1,200.

7. **(D)** The equivalent yield is computed from the formula:

    EQ. Y. = coupon ÷ (1 − tax rate)
    = 10% ÷ (1 − .28)

8. **(C)** The corporate dividend exclusion for holdings of up to 20% is 70%.

9. **(A)** The T-bond purchased at a premium has that premium amortized over its remaining life to find that adjusted cost.

10. **(B)** An original issue municipal purchased at a discount has the discount accrued (on an economic basis) over time. The accrual on a straight line basis would yield $9,000 after 10 of the 20 years to maturity. Thus, at $9,500, the investor realized a $500 gain. The accrual on an economic basis would be slightly different, but $500 would still be the closest answer.

11. **(C)** The law allows up to $10,000 per person per year. Their marital status is irrelevant.

12. **(D)** A dividend would be taxed as income when it is received.

13. **(B)** The stock dividend is treated as income when received because the investor had a choice. If there had been no choice and a 5% stock dividend had been received, it would have resulted in changing the cost basis for the stock.

14. **(C)** This is a change from the ten years previously available to all.

15. **(D)** The investor has a choice for the gain, but no choice for the loss.

16. **(D)** The investor can take up to $3,000 each year beginning in 1991. The $14,000 would be exhausted in 1995.

17. **(C)** Generally residents of a state are exempt from taxes on that state's municipals. Bonds from Puerto Rico are exempt from all federal, state, and local income taxes.

18. **(C)** The bond purchased at a discount is assumed to accrue additional interest on an annual basis.

19. **(C)** The municipal does not generate interest income.

20. **(C)** The $400 cost of the call is added to his $7,000 cost basis, leaving a gain of $600.

21. **(A)** The gift is irrevocable and the assets, income, and tax liability belong to the minor.

22. **(D)** The Keogh is independent of any pension plan as long as it comes from self-employment monies. The maximum allowable contribution is 25% of net income (effectively 20% of gross income) up to $30,000.

23. **(D)** T-bills although sold at a discount are treated as interest income payable when the bill matures or is sold.

24. **(C)** The 25% stock dividend gives him 125 shares for which he paid $10,000, for a reduced cost basis of $80 per share.

25. **(A)** This is different from the basis for income tax purposes.

reading the financial news

Every day, the registered representative must read the financial press. Although stock market quotations and other reports always cover past events, they contain information essential to this day's investment decisions.

This chapter is a guide to the major items on the financial pages: reports of trading in securities on the exchanges and over the counter, corporate reports and announcements, government and municipal bond listings, etc.

NEW YORK STOCK EXCHANGE ISSUES

The table below is called consolidated or composite because it includes all trading in listed stocks on all exchanges and over the counter.

Reading from left to right:

CONSOLIDATED TRADING

365-Day High	Low	Stock	Div	Yld %	P/E	Sales 100s	High	Low	Last	Chg
		A								
14 5/8	10 3/4	AAR	48	3.5	...	1236	14 1/4	13 1/2	13 7/8	
29 3/8	13 3/4	AL Lab	.18	1.2	30	4742	16 1/8	15	15	− 7/8
33	22 5/8	AbbtLab	68	2.4	17	62059	29 1/4	27 5/8	27 7/8	− 1/2
5 7/8	2 7/8	Abex n	...	...	...	1628	3 3/4	3 3/8	3 1/2	− 1/4
12 5/8	8 1/4	Abtibi	...	...	...	100	10 5/8	10	10 1/4	+ 1/8
15 5/8	8 1/4	Acpls s	...	...	15	591	14 3/4	14	14 1/8	− 3/8
5 3/4	2 1/4	Acpls wt	...	...	5	331	5	4 3/8	4 3/8	− 1/4
36	25 1/2	AceLtd n	40	1.3	8	5811	32 3/4	29 1/4	30 1/8	−2 3/8
12	10 3/4	ACMIn	1.10e	9.4	q	7762	11 3/8	11 1/2	11 3/4	+ 1/4
10 1/8	9	^ACMOp	.79	8.0	q	1240	10 1/4	9 7/8	9 7/8	− 1/8
11 5/8	9 7/8	ACMSc	1.10	9.6	q	10180	11 5/8	11 3/8	11 1/2	...
10	8 5/8	ACMSp	.79e	8.0	q	6637	10	9 3/4	9 7/8	...
15 1/8	15	ACM MD n	...	...	q	2972	15 1/8	15	15	...
11 3/4	9 5/8	ACM M n	...	...	q	1090	11 3/4	11 5/8	11 3/4	...
9 7/8	8 5/8	ACMMM	.72e	7.9	q	831	9 1/4	9 1/8	9 1/4	...
15 1/8	13 1/4	ACMMSI n	.90	6.4	...	917	14 3/8	14	14	− 1/4
12 3/8	7 1/8	AcmeC	44	4.6	13	366	10 1/2	9 3/8	9 5/8	− 3/4
57 1/8	37 1/8	^AmPresd	.60	1.0	13	1873	57 1/2	55 1/4	57 1/2	+2
41 3/4	27	▾AmRe n	...	...	23	6703	30 1/8	26	28	− 7/8
9 3/8	6 1/8	AmREst	.50	5.7	7	461	8 3/4	8 5/8	8 3/4	+ 1/8
15 5/8	5 5/8	AmRtys	...	...	...	79	12 5/8	12	12	− 5/8
15 1/8	14 1/2	AmrSelct n	...	...	...	335	14 3/4	14 1/2	14 1/2	− 1/8
2 5/8	9/16	▾AmShip	...	...	...	70	1/2	1/2	1/2	− 3/16
49 1/4	36 1/4	AmStr	.80	2.0	12	7037	41 1/4	39 3/4	40 1/8	− 3/8
16 7/8	15 1/8	ASIP n	1.35	8.2	q	248	16 5/8	16 3/8	16 1/2	− 1/4
16 1/8	14 3/4	ASIPII n	1.35e	8.6	q	693	16	15 5/8	15 3/4	− 1/4
15 5/8	14 3/4	ASIPIII n	1.27	8.3	q	888	15 3/8	15	15 1/4	...
65	42 3/8	AT&T	1.32	2.4	18	96258	58 3/8	55	56 1/8	−1 3/8
3 3/4	1 3/4	AmWste	...	...	13	7228	2 3/8	1 7/8	2	...
32 1/4	24 1/8	AmWtr	1.00	3.4	14	1341	31 1/8	29	29 1/2	−1 1/2
22 1/2	18 3/8	^AmWtr pfA	x1.25	5.9	...	18	23	21 1/4	21 1/4	−1 1/4
2 1/2	1 7/8	AmHotl	...	...	...	120	2 3/8	2 3/8	2 3/8	− 1/8
8	2 3/4	AmriCr	...	...	...	6008	8	6 7/8	7 1/4	+ 1/4
91 1/8	63 3/4	Amrtch	3.68	4.4	15	11966	85 3/8	82 3/8	82 7/8	−1 7/8
38 7/8	30 7/8	Amron	1.28	3.5	15	109	36 5/8	36	36 1/4	− 5/8
17 1/2	12 3/8	Ametek	68	5.1	23	2820	13 3/4	13 1/8	13 1/4	− 1/2
59 1/4	46 3/4	Amoco	2.20	4.0	15	31311	55 7/8	53 7/8	54 7/8	−1

Figure 14.1

365-Day High-Low   This is the range of prices over the preceding year, not including the current day, given in dollars and fractions of a dollar. Arrows indicate a high greater than, or a low less than, the high (or low) level for the preceding year; a two-headed arrow indicates both a new high and a new low.

Stock   Name of the company issuing the stock (usually an abbreviation or initials); "pf" indicates preferred; "s" a stock split within the past year; "n" a new issue. Other letter codes (over a dozen are used) include "x" for the first day a stock trades ex-dividend and "wt" for warrants.

Div.   Gives the annual rate of dividend payment on the basis of the most recent declared dividend.

Yld %   This is current yield, *i.e.*, annual dividend divided by the closing market price for that day.

P/E   Price/Earnings ratio: the ratio of price to earnings over the last year, *i.e.*, current market price divided by reported earnings per share.

Sales 100s   Round lots traded during the day.

High   Highest price trade during the day.

Low   Lowest price trade during the day.

Last   Last trade of the day (this may be from the Pacific Exchange, which closes three hours after New York).

Change   Difference between this day's closing price and the close at the end of the previous day.

Bold type   Stocks that rose or fell 4% or more (if the change was at least 75¢).

Underlining Stock traded more than 1% of its total shares outstanding; on NASDAQ, more than 2% of outstanding shares.

Other symbols and abbreviations scattered throughout the table are explained in accompanying text.

NYSE BOND TRADING

Bonds are quoted in terms of a percentage of the par, or face value, with 100 equaling par. Current yield is the annual percentage return at the current price. As with stocks, fluctuations are expressed in fractions. The High, Low, Last, and Net Change figures are also derived as with the NYSE stock table.

This table does not cover most bond trading, which is conducted over the counter, nor does it include any municipal bonds.

NEW YORK STOCK EXCHANGE BOND TRADING

Bonds	Current Yield	Sales in $1000	Last	Chge.
A	B	C	D	
AForP 5s30	7.3	3	68⅛	− 1¼
AMR 9s16	8.4	3	107	+ 1½
AMR 8.10s98	7.7	10	105¼	− ¼
Aclava 9½98	9.5	22	100¼	− ¼
Advst 9s08	cv	20	101	+ ¾
AirbF 6¾01	cv	113	112½	− 1
AlskAr 6⅞14	cv	1	87½	− ¼
AlskAr zr06	...	82	40	− ¼
Albnylnt 5s02	cv	11	97	...
AlldC zr98	...	25	76½	...
AlldC zr2000	...	4	66⅝	− ⅝
AlldC zr01	...	5	60¾	− ¾
AlldC zr03	...	10	52⅞	− ⅛
AllgWt 4s98	4.3	11	92⅞	− ⅛
AlgLud 02	cv	10	116	− 1
Allwst 7¼14	cv	9	91	...
AmBrnd 9⅛16	8.4	5	109⅛	− ¾
ATT 4¾98	4.9	35	97⅞	+ ⅜
ATT 4⅜96	4.4	35	99½	+ ⅜
ATT 4⅜99	4.6	5	94⅝	− ¼
ATT 6s00	6.0	49	100¾	+ ⅛
ATT 5⅛01	5.3	41	96	+ ¼
ATT 7⅛02	6.7	200	105⅜	− ¼

Bonds	Current Yield	Sales in $1000	Last	Chge.
Clmt zrD96	...	12	76⅛	− 1⅞
Clmt zrD97	...	13	69⅛	− ½
Clmt zrD98	...	26	61½	...
Clmt zrD01	...	20	43⅞	− ⅛
Clmt zrD04	...	11	32	− ¼
Clmt zrD05	...	37	29¼	+ ⅜
Clmt zrD07	...	5	25¼	+ 1¼
ClevEl 8¾05	8.6	135	102	+ ⅛
ClevEl 9¼09	8.9	10	103½	− ⅛
ClevEl 8⅜11	8.4	14	99½	− ⅛
ClevEl 8⅜12	8.4	11	99½	+ ⅜
ColeWld zr13	...	66	27¼	− ¼
viColG 9s94f	...	20	115 9/32	+ 1
viColuG 8¾s95f	...	15	116⅝	+ ⅛
viColuG 9⅛s95f	...	6	116¾	+ ¼
viColuG 8⅞s96f	...	10	115	+ 1½
viColuG 8¼s96f	...	10	115	− 1½
viColuG 9⅞99f	...	6	120	...
viColuG 10½12f	...	5	124⅝	+ ⅝
CmwE 7⅝03F	7.5	10	101½	...
CompUSA 9½00	9.4	43	100¾	− ¼
ConrPer 6¾01	cv	166	90⅝	+ ⅜
ConrPer 6½02	cv	80	94	+ ⅛
CnNG 5⅞98	5.8	2	100¾	...

	U.S. Gov't. Bonds	Other Dom. Bonds	Foreign Bonds	Total All Bonds
Today's Sales	$	$ 29,850,000	$ 80,000	$ 29,930,000
Friday	$	$ 19,880,000	$ 175,000	$ 20,055,000
Yr. to Date	$ 470,000	$ 952,040,000	$ 20,615,000	$ .972,655,000
1994 Yr. to Date	$ 150,000	$ 1,408,377,000	$ 4,063,000	$ 1,412,440,000

a—Includes International Bank Bonds

BOND ISSUES TRADED

	Issues	Advance	Declines	New High	New Lows
Feb.14	380	155	145	18	9
Feb.11	264	95	92	6	2
Feb.10	359	130	149	13	9

Bonds	Current Yield	Sales in $1000	Last	Chge.
HostM 10⅞01	10.6	182	103	...
HostM 11¼05	10.8	244	103¾	− ⅛
HostM 10½06	10.2	225	102⅞	− ½
HostM 11s07	10.7	215	103⅛	+ ⅜
HostM 10⅜11	10.1	88	102½	+ ¼

Bonds	Current Yield	Sales in $1000	Last	Chge.
PhilEl 7⅜01	7.1	20	103¼	+ ⅞
PhilEl 7¾23	7.6	18	101⅜	...
PhilEl 7¼24	7.4	25	97⅜	+ ¼
PacTT 7¼08	7.1	10	102⅜	...
PacTT 7⅜09	7.4	4	102½	− ⅛

Figure 14.2

OVER-THE-COUNTER QUOTATIONS (NASDAQ NATIONAL MARKET)

Over the counter trading is recorded in two different tables. The NASDAQ National Market, or National List, includes those issues that meet certain SEC requirements (for trading volume, market value, etc.) and others that have asked to be included.

Entries in this table are like those in the NYSE stock table but do not include Yield % or P/E Ratio.

Other over the counter quotes are shown in the NASDAQ Supplemental List. This includes only the name of the stock and dividend; the Bid (*i.e.*, the price dealers are willing to pay); and Ask (or Offer, the price at which a dealer is willing to sell). Net Change shows any movement from the previous day's last reported bid price.

These quotations do not necessarily represent actual trades.

NASDAQ NATIONAL MARKET

365-Day High	Low	Stock	Div	Yld %	P/E	Sales 100s	High	Low	Last	Chg
		A								
83/4	43/4	ATS Med	...	...	...	85	51/2	53/8	51/2	...
131/8	7	Aames s	.30	3.3	9	159	10	9	9	– 1/2
103/4	21/2	Aaon s	...	...	24	191	101/8	93/4	93/4	– 3/8
15	101/4	AarnR A	.06	0.4	17	69	143/4	141/4	141/2	...
151/4	91/2	AarnR B	.08	0.6	17	130	141/2	141/4	141/2	– 1/4
81/2	4	Abaxis	...	...	...	632	63/4	6	6	– 3/4
291/2	163/4	AbyHlth	...	...	17	933	291/4	285/8	29	...
183/4	12	ABC Rail	...	...	24	91	171/8	163/4	171/8	...
121/2	81/2	AbingSv	...	...	8	132	11	101/4	103/4 +	1/4
12	7	Abiomd	...	...	...	23	81/8	71/2	8	...
121/2	63/4	Abraxas	...	...	...	66	111/2	101/2	111/2 +	1/4
141/2	65/8 ^ABS s	.20	1.3	23	240	153/8	133/4	153/8 +11/8		
161/2	31/8	AbsEnt	...	...	36	66	43/8	41/8	43/8 +	1/4
30	15	ABT Bld	...	...	19	129	281/2	273/4	281/4 –	1/4
221/2	101/2	ACC Cp s	.12	0.6	57	677	191/4	173/4	187/8	...
51/4	27/8 ^Accel	...	...	...	101	51/2	5	5 +	1/8	
133/8	61/4	AcesHlt	...	...	66	223	123/4	117/8	117/8 –1	
313/4	102/2	Aclaim s	...	...	29	13686	225/8	213/8	213/4 +	3/8
157/8	63/4	AceCsh	...	...	23	69	111/2	103/4	103/4 –	1/8
143/4	123/4	Aceto s	.26b	2.0	10	32	137/8	131/2	133/4 +	1/4
10	73/4	Acmt	...	...	17	202	81/4	81/4	81/4 –1	
251/2	13	AcmeMt	...	...	22	1081	251/4	233/4	243/4 +	3/4
111/2	37/8	ArtistG	.10	1.7	21	439	6	55/8	6	...
14	91/4	AsanteTch	...	...	30	1082	123/4	121/4	123/4 +	1/2
141/2	5	Aseco	...	...	13	34	73/4	63/4	71/4 –	1/2
281/8	81/8	ASKgp	...	...	...	2032	85/8	81/4	81/2 –	1/8
46	141/4	AspctTl	...	...	31	2204	351/4	331/2	333/4 –11/4	
20	101/2	AspenBk	.20	1.1	15	44	19	181/2	19	...
40	313/8	AssdBnc	1.00	2.9	12	17	36	347/8	347/8 +	1/8
341/4	171/4	AssdCm A	...	...	...	97	271/4	26	26 –	3/4
331/4	16	AssdCm B	...	...	...	4	271/4	271/4	271/4 +1	
323/4	123/4 ^AST	...	...	...	8631	33	31	313/8 –	7/8	
165/8	97/8	Astec s	...	...	14	421	151/2	143/4	151/8	...
311/4	273/4	AstorFn	...	...	32.	277	303/8	293/4	297/8 –	1/2
151/4	91/2	AstrM	.12	1.0	19	5	12	111/2	12 +	1/8
31/4	2	Astron	.04	1.5	9	19	25/8	25/8	25/8 –	1/4
43/4	37/8	Astrosy	...	...	21	30	41/4	4	41/8 +	1/8
163/4	93/4	AsyetTch	...	...	27	118	161/4	141/2	141/2 –	3/4
191/4	121/4	AtchCast	...	...	45	195	181/2	177/8	18 –	1/4
13	61/4	Athena	...	...	...	439	10	93/4	93/4 –	1/4
73/4	53/4	Athey	...	...	...	138	73/4	61/4	73/4 +13/4	
201/2	113/4	Atlfd s	36b	2.3	15	20	153/4	15	153/4 –	1/2
23/4	15/8	AtlAm	...	...	12	48	21/2	21/4	21/4	...
7	53/4	AtlBevr	...	...	...	31	63/4	61/2	63/4 +	1/4
17	71/2	AtlCstAr	...	...	...	95	8	73/4	8	...
111/4	43/4	AtlGulf	...	...	...	69	11	101/8	103/4 +	1/4
39	221/2	AttS Ar s	.32	0.9	29	1371	363/4	353/4	361/4 –	1/2

Figure 14.3

TREASURY BILLS, BONDS, AND NOTES

T-bills are issued regularly and are purchased at a discount with the difference between discount and face determining the yield. (The higher the purchase price, the lower the yield.)

In Figure 14.4, the date shown is the maturity date. Bid and ask prices are quoted in terms of yield to maturity. Change is quoted in basis points. Yield is annual return at the current price, also quoted in basis points, as T-bills have a $10,000 face value.

Bonds and notes are treated somewhat differently. Again, maturity date is shown first, followed by an "n" for a note (those with no symbol are bonds). Here, the next column shows the coupon rate. Bid, ask, and change, however, are quoted in 32nds, and yield is yield to maturity.

TREASURY BILLS, BONDS AND NOTES

Prices in 32d of a point, bill yields in basis points.

TREASURY BILLS Date	Bid	Ask	Chg.	Yield	BONDS & NOTES Date	Rate	Bid	Ask	Chg.	Yield	BONDS & NOTES Date	Rate	Bid	Ask	Chg.	Yield
-1994-					Jul 95 p	41/4	100-03	100-07+	01	4.09	May 99 p	91/8	116-28	117-00—	02	5.36
Feb 17	2.97	2.94	+0.10	2.98	Aug 95 p	41/8	100-19	100-23+	01	4.13	Jul 99 p	63/8	104-09	104-13—	03	5.42
Feb 24	2.54	2.50	–0.28	2.54	Aug 95 p	81/2	106-05	106-09—	01	4.14	Aug 99 p	8	112-03	112-07—	01	5.40
Mar 3	2.97	2.94	+0.02	2.98	Aug 95 p	101/2	109-02	109-06—	03	4.12	Oct 99 p	102-14	102-18—	04	5.47	
Mar 10	3.06	3.03	+0.02	3.08	Aug 95 p	37/8	99-14	99-18—	01	4.17	Nov 99 p	77/8	111-20	111-24—	03	5.46
Mar 17	3.02	2.97	–0.05	3.02	Sep 95 p	37/8	99-11	99-15—	01	4.22	Jan 00 p	63/8	104-09	104-13—	02	5.49
Mar 24	2.97	2.94	–0.13	2.99	Oct 95 p	83/4	106-28	107-00		4.21	Feb 95-00	77/8	103-22	103-26—	02	3.95
Mar 31	3.05	3.00	–0.08	3.05	Oct 95 p	37/8	99-08	99-12—	01	4.26	Feb 00 p	81/2	115-03	115-07—	03	5.49
Apr 7	3.13	3.09	–0.06	3.15	Nov 95 p	51/2	101-09	101-13		4.28	Apr 00 p	81/2	100-01	100-04—	03	5.47
Apr 14	3.13	3.09	–0.06	3.15	Nov 95 p	81/2	106-30	107-02		4.25	May 00 p	87/8	117-16	117-20—	01	5.50
Apr 21	3.21	3.16	–0.03	3.22	Nov 95 p	91/2	108-22	108-26+	01	4.20	Aug 95-00	83/8	105-26	105-30+	01	4.25
Apr 28	3.24	3.19	–0.02	3.25	Nov 95	111/2	112-01	112-05		4.20	Aug 00 p	83/4	116-31	117-03—	06	5.58
May 5	3.27	3.22		3.29	Nov 95 p	41/4	99-25	99-29		4.30	Aug 00 p	81/2	115-25	115-29—	06	5.63
May 12	3.28	3.25		3.32	Dec 95 p	41/4	99-23	99-27		4.34	Feb 01 p	73/4	111-28	112-00		5.65
May 19	3.30	3.25	+0.02	3.32	Jan 96 p	71/2	108-23	108-27		4.38	Feb 01	113/4	135-00	135-04—	08	5.61
May 26	3.30	3.25		3.33	Jan 96 p	4	99-07	99-10+	01	4.37	May 01 p	8	113-12	113-16—	05	5.70
Jun 2	3.34	3.31	+0.01	3.39	Jan 96 p	71/2	105-21	105-25—	01	4.39	May 01	131/8	143-28	144-00—	11	5.64
Jun 9	3.33	3.28	–0.01	3.36							Aug 01 p	77/8	112-25	112-29—	07	5.73
Jun 16	3.35	3.31	+0.01	3.40	Feb 96 p	43/4	100-09	100-13		4.41	Aug 96-01	8	107-25	107-29		4.62
Jun 23	3.37	3.34	+0.02	3.43	Feb 96 p	77/8	106-14	106-18		4.41	Aug 01	133/8	146-17	146-21—	05	5.66
Jun 30	3.36	3.31		3.40	Feb 96 p	87/8	108-11	108-15		4.40						
Jul 7	3.37	3.34	–0.02	3.44	Feb 96 p	71/2	105-25	105-29		4.43						
Jul 14	3.39	3.34		3.44	Mar 96 p	73/4	106-14	106-18		4.47	Nov 01 p	71/2	110-18	110-22—	05	5.77

Figure 14.4

GOVERNMENT AGENCY BONDS

These are bonds issued by government agencies but not guaranteed by the federal government. They are listed like government bonds: maturity date, coupon rate, bid, ask, and change in 32nds, and yield to maturity.

GOVERNMENT AGENCY BONDS

Prices in 32d of a point.

FEDERAL NATIONAL MTGS											
Date		Rate	Bid	Ask	Chg.	Yield	Date		Rate	Bid Ask	Chg. Yield
Apr	94	7.65	100-20	100-23		3.23	Jul	01	8⅞	108-17 108-23+	05 4.99
Apr	94	9.60	100-30	101-01		3.27	Aug	01	8.40	106-27 107-01—	05 5.39
May	94	9.30	101-11	101-14		3.36	Nov	01	7.99	107-01 107-19—	03 4.97
Jun	94	8.60	101-18	101-21		3.48	Dec	01	7.56	105-27 106-13—	04 5.12
Jul	94	7.45	101-16	101-19—	01	3.55	Feb	02	7½	109-02 109-06—	07 6.04
Aug	94	8.90	102-16	102-19—	01	3.59	Mar	02	7.89	102-27 103-01—	04 6.78
Oct	94	10.10	104-02	104-06—	01	3.67	Apr	02	7.90	106-12 106-30—	12 5.48
Nov	94	9¼	103-27	104-01—	01	3.72	Apr	02	7.55	109-10 109-16—	09 6.06
Dec	94	5½	101-10	101-14—	01	3.77	Jun	02	7.80	106-13 106-17—	10 5.62
Jan	95	9	104-14	104-18		3.86	Jul	02	7.30	104-01 104-11—	16 5.87
Jan	95	11.95	107-02	107-06—	01	3.86	Aug	02	7	103-07 103-17—	01 5.87
Feb	95	11½	107-06	107-10		3.95	Nov	02		105-26 106-04	6.13
Mar	95	8.85	104-30	105-02		4.01	Jan	03	6.80	104-13 104-19—	10 6.12
May	95	11.70	108-31	109-03—	03	4.13	Mar	03	6.40	99-13 99-23—	06 6.44
Jun	95	11.15	108-27	109-01—	01	4.12	Aug	03	6¼	98-12 98-18—	10 6.45
Sep	95	10½	109-07	109-13		4.29	Oct	03	5.45	95-04 95-08—	07 6.11
Nov	95	8.80	107-08	107-14—	03	4.33	Nov	03	6.20	97-18 97-22—	04 6.52
Nov	95	10.60	110-07	110-11—	03	4.38	Dec	03	5.80	97-11 97-15—	10 6.15
Jan	96	9.20	108-15	108-19—	02	4.44	Jan 04		6.40	98-29 99-01—	05 6.53
Feb	96	7	104-18	104-24—	02	4.49	Mar	14	12.65	100-17 100-27	2.05
Feb	96	7.70	99-27	99-31+	06	7.72	Jul	14		22-19 22-31—	04 7.34
Feb	96	9.35	109-02	109-06—	03	4.50	Dec	15	10.35	138-02 138-12—	18 6.92
Apr	96	8	100-19	100-23		3.50	Mar	16	8.20	114-10 114-20—	10 6.90
							Feb	18	8.95	123-03 123-21—	09 6.92
							Aug	19	8.10	113-14 114-09—	10 6.92

Figure 14.5

STOCK OPTIONS

Listed options are shown in Figure 14.6 (terms are explained in Chapter 9). For each option (on a line of bold type):

Stock Name of the company.

Exchange A one-letter abbreviation of the exchange (or exchanges) on which the option is traded.

Close Closing price of the stock on that day. On subsequent lines for each entry, the table offers:

Date Expiration date.

Strike Exercise price.

Call Price of a call option.

Put Price of a put option.

MUTUAL FUNDS

These tables are usually quite abbreviated. More elaborate tables are offered in some cases at week's end, and some publications provide additional information on sales charges or returns in a column that changes each day. Terms are discussed in Chapter 4.

TRADING IN STOCK OPTIONS

Stock Date	Exch Strike	Close Call	Put	Stock Date	Exch Strike	Close Call	Put
AbbtLab	X	28 1/2		Feb. 94	20	11/16	1
Feb. 94	30	1/8	1 1/2	Feb. 94	22 1/2	1/4	r
May 94	30	1	2 1/8	March 94	20	1 1/4	1 3/4
Adapt	A	18 3/8		March 94	22 1/2	1/2	r
Feb. 94	20	1/8	1 3/4	April 94	20	1 3/4	2 1/16
Adobe S	P	29 1/4		April 94	30	3/16	r
Feb. 94	25	5 1/4	1/8	July 94	20	2 3/4	3 1/8
March 94	30	1 7/8	2 9/16	**ColgP**	C	60 7/8	
AdvMD	P	21 3/4		Feb. 94	55	6 1/2	r
Feb. 94	20	1 3/4	1/8	**ColHither**	A	40 1/2	
March 94	20	3 1/4	1 1/2	Feb. 94	35	5	1/16
March 94	22 1/2	2	2 7/8	**Comcst**	X	28	
April 94	20	3 3/4	2 1/4	July 94	20	2 9/16	r
July 94	22 1/2	3 3/8	4 3/8	**Compaq**	P	89 1/2	
AsInLf	A	62 1/4		Feb. 94	75	14 1/2	1/16
April 94	55	r	1/4	Feb. 94	80	9 1/2	1/16
Agnico	P	12 1/4		Feb. 94	85	4 7/8	1/4

Figure 14.6

Fund family
The name in bold type is that of the fund or the sponsor of a group of funds.

Fund name
Name of specific funds within a fund family.

NAV
The Net Asset Value per share, or the amount at which the fund may be bought (plus sales charges) or redeemed (less redemption charges).

Daily % ret
Increase or decrease NAV from the previous close, adjusted for dividends.

MUTUAL FUNDS

Sales Charge	Fund Family / Fund Name	NAV	Daily % Ret
	First Omaha		
NL	Equity b	10.72	+0.3
NL	FixIn b	10.41	...
	First Prairie		
4.50	DivrAst m	13.01	-0.1
4.50	MuniBdInt m	12.30	-0.1
	First Priority		
NL	EquityTr	10.58	...
NL	FixIn Tr	10.40	...
NA	LtdMetGov	9.96	-0.1
	First Union		
4.00	Bal BInv m	12.25	+0.1
4.00	Bal CInv m	12.25	+0.1
NL	Bal Tr	12.26	+0.1
NL	FixIn Tr	10.40	...
4.00	InsTaxFB m	11.12	-0.1
4.00	InsTaxFC m	11.12	-0.1
NL	MgdBd Tr	10.45	...
4.00	NCMuBd C m	10.59	-0.1
4.00	USGovBInv m	10.01	-0.1
4.00	USGovCIv m	10.01	-0.1
4.00	Val BIv m	17.77	+0.1
4.00	Val CIv m	17.76	+0.1
NL	Value Tr	17.77	+0.1
.100	FixInLtd m	10.13	...
	General Electric		
NL	ElfDivr	14.22	+0.1
NL	ElfGlob	17.18	...
NL	ElfInc	11.64	+0.1
NL	ElfTrusts	34.02	+0.1
NL	ElfTxEInc	12.22	...
4.25	FixIn A m	12.08	...
NL	S&SLgTm	11.60	+0.1
NL	S&SProg	37.26	...
NL	USEq D	16.37	...
	Gintel		
NL	Erisa b	29.58	...
NL	Gintel	15.69	+0.7
	Glenmede		
NL	Equity	13.28	+0.4
NL	IntGovt	10.64	...
NL	Intl	13.63	+0.7
NL	MuniInt	10.56	+0.1
NL	SmCapEq	14.43	+0.7
	GoldOakIA	10.09	...
	Goldman Sachs		
5.50	CapGrow m	15.82	+0.6
4.50	GlobInc m	14.93	-0.1
5.50	GrowInc m	15.65	+0.6
5.50	IntlEq m	17.78	+0.1
	John Hancock		
5.00	Discov B m	9.40	+0.3
5.00	Growth A m	17.11	+0.2
NL	IndDivCor b	13.15	+0.1
3.00	LtdTmGvA m	8.74	...
5.00	MgdTxE B m	11.97	...
3.00	ShTmStrB m	8.89	...
5.00	SpecEq A m	15.88	+0.9
5.00	SpecEq B m	15.80	+0.9
5.00	SpecOppA m	8.65	+0.1
5.00	SpecOppB m	8.63	+0.1
4.50	StrInc A m	7.74	-0.1
5.00	StrInc B m	7.74	-0.1
4.50	TaxECA m	12.12	...
4.50	TaxEInc m	11.17	-0.1
4.50	TaxEMA m	12.31	...
4.50	TaxENY m	12.50	...
	John Hancock Freedom		
5.00	Glob A m	13.75	-0.1
5.00	GlobIncB m	9.45	...
5.00	GlobTech f	18.82	+0.7
5.00	NatAviat f	11.48	+0.6
5.00	PacBasin m	15.68	-0.8
5.00	RegBankA m	20.57	+0.2
5.00	RegBankB m	20.50	+0.2
5.00	OppGrow f	10.54	+0.5
	MAS		
NL	Balanced	11.80	...
NL	EmgGrow	17.77	+0.6
NL	Equity	21.40	+0.2
NL	FixInc	11.90	-0.1
NL	FixIncll	11.39	-0.2
NL	GloFixIn	10.64	+0.6
NL	HiYldSec	9.70	-0.1
NL	IntlEq	15.44	-0.7
NL	LtdDurFI	10.53	...
NL	MtgBack	10.50	-0.1
NL	MuFixIn	11.04	+0.1
NL	SelEq	18.00	+0.1
NL	SelFixIn	10.67	-0.1
NL	SmCapVal	17.46	+0.3
NL	SpecPurp	12.47	-0.1
NL	Value	12.51	+0.2
	MFS		
4.75	ALMuBd A m	10.89	+0.1
4.75	ARMuBd A m	10.37	+0.1
4.75	Bond A m	13.71	...
4.75	CAMuBd A m	5.87	...
5.00	CapGro B m	13.89	...
5.75	EmgGro A m	19.25	+0.8
4.00	EmgGro B m	19.21	+0.8
	Merrill Lynch		
4.00	AZMuni B m	11.04	-0.1
3.00	AdjRt A m	9.73	...
3.00	AdjRt B m	9.74	...
3.00	AmerIncB m	10.63	-0.5
6.50	BalInv A f	12.52	-0.2
4.00	BalInv B m	12.62	-0.2
6.50	BasicValA f	23.79	...
4.00	BasicValB m	23.57	...
4.00	CAInsMuB m	10.19	-0.1
4.00	CAMuni A f	12.05	-0.1
4.00	CAMuni B m	12.06	...
6.50	CapitalA f	28.53	-0.1
4.00	CapitalB m	28.13	-0.1
NL	ConsIntl b	12.76	+0.9
4.00	CorHIncA f	8.48	...
4.00	CorHIncB m	8.48	...
2.00	CorIntTA f	11.88	...
2.00	CorIntTB m	11.88	...
4.00	CorIvGrA f	11.92	-0.1
4.00	CorIvGrB m	11.92	...
6.50	DevCapMk f	17.78	-0.7
4.00	Dragon A m	17.19	-2.1
4.00	Dragon B m	17.14	-2.1
6.50	EuroFd A f	15.12	-0.2
4.00	EuroFd B m	14.59	-0.2
	Morgan Stanley		
4.75	AsianGrA m	16.95	-1.7
1.00	AsianGrB m	16.89	-1.7
	Morgan Stanley Inst		
NL	ActivCoun	12.06	-0.7
NL	AsianEq	23.09	-1.8
NL	EmgGrow	16.17	+0.7
NL	EqGrowth	12.11	+0.2
NL	FixInc	10.64	-0.2
NL	GloFixIn	11.34	+0.2
NL	HiYield	11.10	+0.1
NL	IntlEq	14.65	+0.5
NL	IntlSmCo	16.50	+0.7
NA	RealYld	10.20	+0.1
NL	ValueEq	12.06	+0.1
5.00	MuniBdR m	10.82	+0.3
4.75	MutualBen f	18.27	+0.2
	Mutual Series		
NL	Beacon	31.89	...
NL	Discover	13.65	+0.3
NL	Qualified	27.19	...
NL	Shares	81.13	...
	NCC		
NL	EquityIs	13.85	+0.1

Figure 14.7

Note

Only open-end funds are included; closed-end funds are listed in stock tables.

CORPORATE SALES AND EARNINGS REPORTS

These are very brief summaries, often footnoted.

They usually (though not always) cover a quarterly period and often offer figures for a six-month period or for a year, permitting a reader to derive several important ratios. Customarily, these show sales or revenues, net income, earnings per share, and average number of shares outstanding.

COMPANY EARNINGS

For periods shown. (N) indicates stock is listed on the New York Stock Exchange, (A) the American Stock Exchange and (O) Over-the-Counter.

American Brands Inc.(N)

Qtr to June 30	1991	1990
Revenue $	2,937,000,000	2,952,400,000
Net inc	181,600,000	158,400,000
Share earns	.88	.81
Shares outst	202,000,000	191,800,000
6mo rev	6,794,200,000	6,156,100,000
Net inc	398,300,000	353,800,000
Share earns	1.94	1.81
Shares outst	201,600,000	191,700,000

The company said all share earnings and shares outstanding reflected a 2-for-1 stock split in the form of a 100 percent dividend, which became effective in October 1990.

American Cyanamid Co. (N)

Qtr to June 30	1991	1990
Sales $	1,420,400,000	1,228,300,000
Net inc	131,800,000	b111,400,000
Share earns	1.41	1.16
6mo sales	2,733,200,000	2,380,800,000
Net inc	236,600,000	b202,300,000
Share earns	2.53	2.11

b-Included income of $3,000,000, or 3 cents a share, in the quarter and a loss of $3,000,000 in the 6 months, both from discontinued operations.

The company said the discontinued operations were related to the Shulton Group, the company's divested consumer products business.

Arco Chemical (N)

Qtr to June 30	1991	1990
Revenue $	703,000,000	705,000,000
Net inc	33,000,000	102,000,000
Share earns	.34	1.06
6mo rev	1,385,000,000	1,390,000,000
Net inc	85,000,000	b227,000,000
Share earns	.89	2.37

b-Included gain of $43 million from cumulative effect of change in accounting principle.

The company said second-quarter results include a $12 million pre-tax favorable adjustment for property and casualty liability costs recorded in 1990 related to the plant incident and shutdown in Channelview, Texas.

Black & Decker (N)

Qtr to June 30	1991	1990
Revenue $	1,106,500,000	1,224,600,000
Net inc	7,300,000	16,100,000
Share earns	.11	.26
6mo rev	2,194,100,000	2,228,000,000
Net inc	11,400,000	26,100,000
Share earns	.18	.43

Burlington Northern Inc.(N)

Qtr to June 30	1991	1990
Revenue $	1,080,000,000	1,172,000,000
Net loss	b420,000,000	c71,000,000
Share earns	—	.92
Shares outst	76,396,000	76,794,000
6mo rev	2,212,000,000	2,355,000,000
Net loss	b428,000,000	c134,000,000
Share earns	—	1.74
Shares outst	76,315,000	76,664,000

Central & South West Corp.(N)

Qtr to June 30	1991	1990
Revenue $	717,000,000	649,000,000
Net inc	94,000,000	59,000,000
Share earns	.93	.54
6mo rev	1,365,000,000	1,208,000,000
Net inc	157,000,000	191,000,000
Share earns	3.44	1.87

Colgate Palmolive (N)

Qtr to June 30	1991	1990
Revenue $	1,516,400,000	1,452,900,000
Net inc	93,300,000	81,900,000
Share earns	.66	.58
Shares outst	133,533,000	131,966,000
6mo rev	2,978,200,000	2,754,100,000
Net inc	184,600,000	163,100,000
Share earns	1.31	1.16
Shares outst	133,441,000	131,958,000

Dana Corp.(N)

Qtr to June 30	1991	1990
Sales $	1,134,300,000	1,323,700,000
Net inc	4,600,000	31,600,000
Share earns	.11	.78
6mo sales	2,185,500,000	2,590,600,000
Net inc	6,700,000	54,700,000
Share earns	.16	1.34

The company said 1991 second quarter net income included a gain of $5.9 million from the sale of a subsidiary. First quarter 1991 net income includes a $6 million gain on sales of subsidiaries net of additional reserves.

Figure 14.8

DIVIDENDS DECLARED

IRREGULAR

	Period rate	Stk of record	Payable
FutureGermany Fd	.02	9-5	9-13
Germany Fund	.10	9-5	9-13
Merrimac Ind	x .075	9-5	9-19

x-commences quarterly

	Period rate	Stk of record	Payable
New Germany Fd	.07	9-5	9-13

INCREASED

	Period rate	Stk of record	Payable
Am Filtrona	Q .235	8-9	8-25
Consol Rail	Q .45	8-30	9-16
Golden Corral	Q .27	7-31	8-14
Metro Bnchsrs	Q .15	7-29	8-13
Omni Capital	Q .11	7-29	8-12
Schwab,Charles	Q .05	8-1	8-15
Unifi Inc	Q .15	8-19	8-26

OMITTED

Baltek Corp
CalFed Inc

SPECIAL

	Period rate	Stk of record	Payable
FstFdlSv Charlotte	.20	7-31	8-9

REGULAR

	Period rate	Stk of record	Payable
AmericusTr Xerox	x .6475	8-2	8-16

x-payable on prime & units.

	Period rate	Stk of record	Payable
Ashland Oil	q .25	8-22	9-15
Athlone Ind	q .25	8-2	8-16
Barnett Bks	Q .33	9-9	10-1
Burlington Nth	Q .30	9-9	10-1

REGULAR

	Period rate	Stk of record	Payable
CA Water Svc	Q .45	8-1	8-15
CIM Hi YldSecur	M .07	7-26	8-5
Charter Pwr	Q .0275	8-6	8-14
Cinn G&E,	Q .30	8-1	8-15
Cinn G&E,	Q .62	7-29	8-15
Coca Cola Co	Q .24	9-15	10-1
CommerceBncp NJ	.1125	-31	8-15
Constar Intl	Q .16	8-13	9-3
Core Ind	Q .12	-30	9-23
Crompton Knowles	Q .13	8-2	8-23
DF Stheastern	Q .05	7-31	8-9
Dreyfus Corp	Q .13	8-5	8-14
FstFed FinclSvc	.14	8-2	8-22
FstFedS&L Lenawee	Q .22	7-30	8-15
FstFdlSv Charlotte	Q .15	7-31	8-9
FstFidel Bncptn	Q .30	7-29	8-6
Firstar Corp	Q .36	7-29	8-15
Ft Wayne Ntl	Q .27	9-13	10-1
Fuller HB,	Q .155	8-1	9-5
Fulton Fincl	Q .20	9-20	10-15
Gorman Rupp	Q .155	8-1	8-15
Hawaiian El	Q .25	8-9	9-10
Heritage Fin	Q .55	8-12	9-10
Hewlett Packard	Q .14	7-29	8-9
Horizon Ind	Q .125	9-25	10-16
Iowa NtlBkshrs	Q .02	8-1	8-15
	Q .38	7-31	8-7

REGULAR

	Period rate	Stk of record	Payable
Kansas P&L,	Q .465	9-4	10-1
Massbank Corp	Q .11	7-31	8-16
NY Times	Q .14	9-6	9-25
Newhall Land	Q .20	8-2	9-9
Nthwst NaturGas	Q .42	7-31	8-15
ONEOK Inc	Q .21	7-31	8-15
Occidntl Petrol	Q .25	9-10	10-15
Oppenheimr MulGv	M .076	7-26	8-9
PPG Indust	Q .42	8-12	9-12
Pacific G&E,	Q .41	-16	10-15
Provident Bkshrs	Q .05	7-29	8-9
RMI Titanium	Q .025	8-1	9-1
Safecard Svcs	S .075	7-31	9-16
Skyline Corp	Q .12	9-12	10-1
Sonoco Prod	Q .23	8-16	9-10
Sthwstn Ntl	Q .24	8-10	9-10
Summit Bncp	Q .20	9-1	9-15
Summit Bncp adjpf	Q .3781	9-1	9-15
Time Warner	Q .25	8-23	9-10
Tultex Corp	Q .09	9-6	10-1
United Mobile	Q .05	8-15	9-16
Valero Energy	Q .09	7-30	9-6
ValliCorp Hold	Q .05	8-1	8-15
Village Fincl	Q .05	7-29	8-12
WPL Holdings	Q .45	7-31	8-15
West One Bncp	Q .24	9-30	10-17

g-Payable in Canadian Funds.

Figure 14.9

This announcement is not an offer to sell or a solicitation of an offer to buy any of these securities. The offering is made only by the Prospectus, copies of which may be obtained in any State in which this announcement is circulated only from underwriters qualified to act as dealers in securities in such State.

NEW ISSUE   May 26, 1988

2,666,400 Shares

CAROLCO PICTURES INC.

Common Stock

———

Price $9.375 Per Share

———

PaineWebber Incorporated

Bear, Stearns & Co. Inc.

Furman Selz Mager Dietz & Birney
Incorporated

Alex. Brown & Sons Incorporated	The First Boston Corporation	Donaldson, Lufkin & Jenrette Securities Corporation
Drexel Burnham Lambert Incorporated	A. G. Edwards & Sons, Inc.	Goldman, Sachs & Co.
Lazard Frères & Co.	Montgomery Securities	Morgan Stanley & Co. Incorporated
Prudential–Bache Capital Funding		Shearson Lehman Hutton Inc.
Smith Barney, Harris Upham & Co. Incorporated		Crowell, Weedon & Co.

Advest, Inc. Bateman Eichler, Hill Richards William Blair & Company Blunt Ellis & Loewi
Incorporated   Incorporated

Cowen & Co.   First Albany Corporation   Ladenburg, Thalmann & Co. Inc.

Neuberger & Berman Oppenheimer & Co., Inc. Stifel, Nicolaus & Company Sutro & Co.
Incorporated   Incorporated

Thomson McKinnon Securities Inc.   Wheat, First Securities, Inc.

Arnhold and S. Bleichroeder, Inc.   First Manhattan Co.   Gruntal & Co., Incorporated

Josephthal & Co.   Mabon, Nugent & Co.   Newhard, Cook & Co.
Incorporated   Incorporated
Rowland, Simon & Co.   Wedbush Securities, Inc.

Figure 14.10 Tombstone

CORPORATE DIVIDEND REPORTS

These brief announcements of regular dividends show the company's name, payment frequency (*e.g.*, quarterly), dollar amount per share, date the dividend will be paid, and record date (date on which a shareholder must own the share to receive the dividend).

Irregular dividends are similarly reported when announced (usually at the end of a fiscal year), as are stock dividends (showing percentage rather than a dollar amount). Notices will show when a dividend has increased or has been omitted.

TOMBSTONE ANNOUNCEMENTS

It is important to note that these are announcements, not advertisements, as, under SEC regulations, sales cannot be made from the announcement.

A firm is not legally required to publish this announcement; if it does, it can include only:

- the name of the security (A date can be included showing when a primary offering is issued or simply the date on which the announcement appears.)

- number of shares being offered (or number of bonds)

- offering price

- managing underwriter (the seller)

- members of the underwriting syndicate. Usually arranged in order of the size of their commitment and alphabetically within each group. Members of the selling group are not shown.

Note

The disclaimers must be included because the SEC holds that an investor cannot buy shares without a copy of the prospectus.

BLUE LIST (SECONDARY MARKET FOR MUNICIPALS)

The *Blue List* contains secondary market municipal bond listings. Included are:

- name of issuing agency

- coupon rate

- maturity date

- bid price, expressed as a percentage of par (considered to be $1,000)

- asked price, as a percentage of par

- change in price from previous day

- yield to maturity

Note

The "f" indicates the bond is trading flat, *i.e.*, without accrued interest.

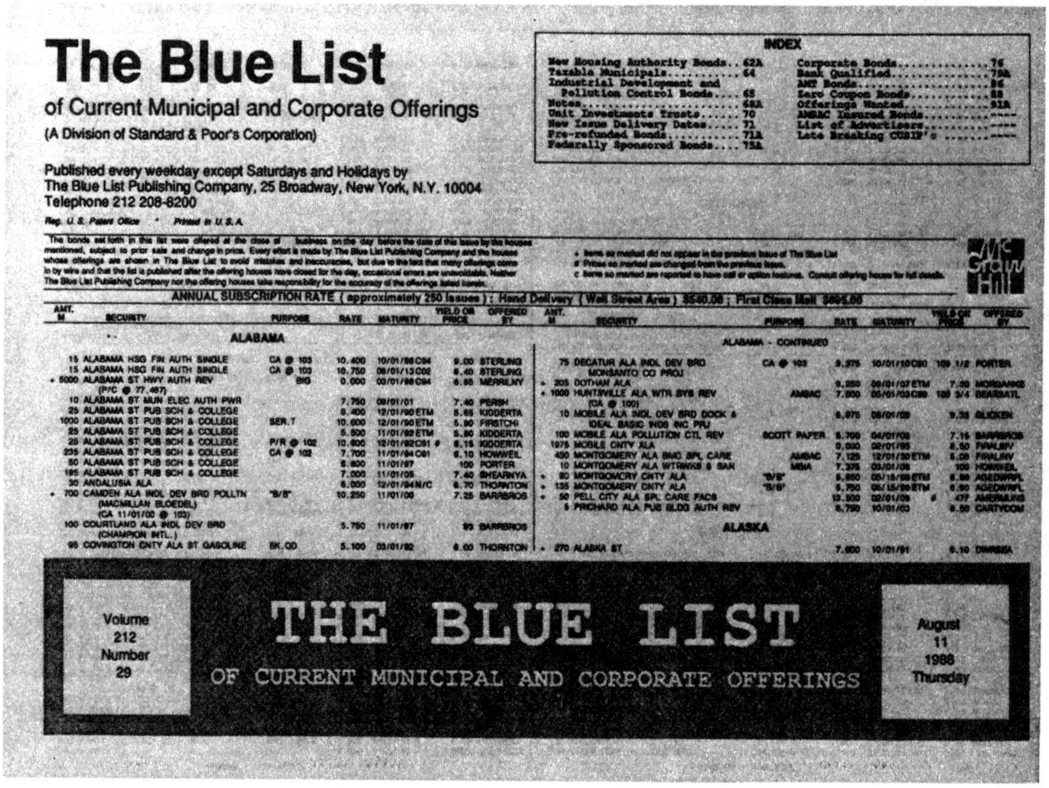

The Blue List

of Current Municipal and Corporate Offerings

(A Division of Standard & Poor's Corporation)

Published every weekday except Saturdays and Holidays by
The Blue List Publishing Company, 25 Broadway, New York, N.Y. 10004
Telephone 212 208-8200

Reg. U.S. Patent Office • Printed in U.S.A.

INDEX

New Housing Authority Bonds	62A	Corporate Bonds	76
Taxable Municipals	64	Bank Qualified	79A
Industrial Development and Pollution Control Bonds	65	AMT Bonds	86
Notes	68A	Zero Coupon Bonds	88
Unit Investments Trusts	70	Offerings Wanted	91A
New Issue Delivery Dates	71	AMBAC Insured Bonds	----
Pre-refunded Bonds	71A	List of Advertisers	----
Federally Sponsored Bonds	75A	Late Breaking CUSIP's	----

The bonds set forth in this list were offered at the close of business on the day before the date of this issue by the houses mentioned, subject to prior sale and change in price. Every effort is made by The Blue List Publishing Company and the houses whose offerings are shown in The Blue List to avoid mistakes and inaccuracies, but due to the fact that many offerings come in by wire and that the list is published after the offering houses have closed for the day, occasional errors are unavoidable. Neither The Blue List Publishing Company nor the offering houses take responsibility for the accuracy of the offerings listed herein.

+ Items so marked did not appear in the previous issue of The Blue List
# Prices so marked are changed from the previous issue.
c Items so marked are reported to have call or option features. Consult offering house for full details.

ANNUAL SUBSCRIPTION RATE (approximately 250 issues): Hand Delivery (Wall Street Area) $540.00; First Class Mail $695.00

AMT. M	SECURITY	PURPOSE	RATE	MATURITY	YIELD OR PRICE	OFFERED BY
	ALABAMA					
15	ALABAMA HSG FIN AUTH SINGLE	CA @ 103	10.400	10/01/98C94	9.00	STERLING
15	ALABAMA HSG FIN AUTH SINGLE	CA @ 103	10.750	08/01/13C02	8.40	STERLING
+ 5000	ALABAMA ST HWY AUTH REV (P/C @ 77.467)	BIG	0.000	03/01/98C94	6.95	MERRILNY
10	ALABAMA ST MUN ELEC AUTH PWR		7.750	09/01/01	7.40	PERSH
25	ALABAMA ST PUB SCH & COLLEGE		8.400	12/01/90ETM	5.65	KIDDERTA
1000	ALABAMA ST PUB SCH & COLLEGE	SER.T	10.600	12/01/90ETM	5.90	FIRSTCHI
25	ALABAMA ST PUB SCH & COLLEGE		5.500	11/01/92ETM	5.80	KIDDERTA
25	ALABAMA ST PUB SCH & COLLEGE	P/R @ 102	10.600	12/01/92C01 #	6.15	KIDDERTA
235	ALABAMA ST PUB SCH & COLLEGE	CA @ 102	7.700	11/01/94C01	6.10	HOWWEIL
50	ALABAMA ST PUB SCH & COLLEGE		6.800	11/01/97	100	PORTER
195	ALABAMA ST PUB SCH & COLLEGE		7.000	11/01/05	7.40	SHEARNYA
30	ANDALUSIA ALA		6.000	12/01/94N/C	6.70	THORNTON
+ 700	CAMDEN ALA INDL DEV BRD POLLTN (MACMILLAN BLOEDEL) (CA 11/01/00 @ 103)	"B/B"	10.250	11/01/00	7.25	BARRBROS
100	COURTLAND ALA INDL DEV BRD (CHAMPION INTL.)		5.750	11/01/97	93	BARRBROS
95	COVINGTON CNTY ALA ST GASOLINE	BK.QO	5.100	03/01/92	6.00	THORNTON
	ALABAMA - CONTINUED					
75	DECATUR ALA INDL DEV BRD MONSANTO CO PROJ	CA @ 103	9.375	10/01/10C90	109 1/2	PORTER
+ 205	DOTHAN ALA		9.250	09/01/07ETM	7.30	MORGANKE
+ 1000	HUNTSVILLE ALA WTR SYS REV (CA @ 100)	AMBAC	7.800	05/01/03C99	100 3/4	BEARSATL
10	MOBILE ALA INDL DEV BRD DOCK & IDEAL BASIC INDS INC PRJ		6.875	09/01/09	9.35	GLICKEN
100	MOBILE ALA POLLUTION CTL REV	SCOTT PAPER	5.700	04/01/09	7.15	BARRBROS
1975	MOBILE CNTY ALA		0.000	02/01/95	6.50	FIRALINV
490	MONTGOMERY ALA BMC SPL CARE	AMBAC	7.125	12/01/30ETM	5.00	FIRALINV
10	MONTGOMERY ALA WTRWKS & SAN	MBIA	7.375	03/01/08	100	HOWWEIL
+ 90	MONTGOMERY CNTY ALA	"B/B"	6.850	05/15/98ETM	6.80	AGEDWRPL
+ 135	MONTGOMERY CNTY ALA	"B/B"	6.750	05/15/99ETM	6.90	AGEDWRPL
+ 50	PELL CITY ALA SPL CARE FACS		13.500	02/01/09 #	477	AMERMUNS
5	PRICHARD ALA PUB BLDG AUTH REV		6.750	10/01/03	8.50	CARTYCOM
	ALASKA					
+ 270	ALASKA ST		7.800	10/01/91	6.10	DWRSEA

Volume 212 Number 29

THE BLUE LIST

OF CURRENT MUNICIPAL AND CORPORATE OFFERINGS

August 11 1988 Thursday

Figure 14.11 Blue List

Reprinted with permission of Standard & Poor's Corporation.

MUNICIPAL BOND OFFICIAL NOTICE OF SALE

These include the following:

- name of issuing agency
- total amount of issue
- date, time, and place of sale
- maturity(ies) of bonds
- call features
- type of bond (G.O. or revenue, etc.)
- denomination(s)
- dates on which interest will be paid
- bidding instructions (minimum bid, amount of good-faith deposit required, bidding procedure, bid form)
- name of bond counsel
- method and place of settlement
- person authorizing sale

This announcement is not an offer to sell or a solicitation of an offer to buy any of these securities.
The offering is made only by the Prospectus.

NEW ISSUE

September 30, 1986

2,148,315 Shares

M. A. Hanna Company

$2.125 Convertible Exchangeable Preferred Stock

The shares of $2.125 Convertible Exchangeable Preferred Stock, with a liquidation preference of $25 per share, of the Company are convertible at the option of the holder at any time, unless previously redeemed, into shares of the Common Stock of the Company at a conversion price of $24.875 per share, subject to adjustment under certain conditions.

The Preferred Stock also is exchangeable in whole at the option of the Company on any dividend payment date beginning December 30, 1989, for the 8.50% Convertible Subordinated Debentures Due December 30, 2016 of the Company at the rate of $25 principal amount of Debentures for each share of Preferred Stock. The Debentures, if issued, will be convertible at the option of the holder at any time, unless previously redeemed, into shares of Common Stock at a price equivalent to the conversion price applicable to the Preferred Stock for which the Debentures were exchanged.

Price $25 Per Share
plus accrued dividends, if any, from date of issuance.

Copies of the Prospectus may be obtained in any State in which
this announcement is circulated only from such of the Underwriters as are qualified to act as dealers in securities in such State.

PaineWebber Incorporated	The First Boston Corporation

Bear, Stearns & Co. Inc.	Alex. Brown & Sons Incorporated	Dillon, Read & Co. Inc.
Donaldson, Lufkin & Jenrette Securities Corporation	Drexel Burnham Lambert Incorporated	A. G. Edwards & Sons, Inc.
Goldman, Sachs & Co.	Hambrecht & Quist Incorporated	E. F. Hutton & Company Inc.
Kidder, Peabody & Co. Incorporated	Lazard Frères & Co.	Merrill Lynch Capital Markets
Montgomery Securities	Morgan Stanley & Co. Incorporated	Prudential-Bache Securities
L. F. Rothschild, Unterberg, Towbin, Inc.	Salomon Brothers Inc	Shearson Lehman Brothers Inc.
Smith Barney, Harris Upham & Co. Incorporated	Wertheim & Co., Inc.	Dean Witter Reynolds Inc.

Figure 14.12 Tombstone

MUNICIPAL BOND BUYER INDEX

This is an index of investment grade long-term tax-exempt bonds. It shows the average yield for such bonds by category within the revenue bonds and general obligation bonds.

BOND BUYER INDEXES

AVERAGE MUNICIPAL BOND YIELDS—COMPILED WEEKLY

	20 G.O. BONDS (1)	11 G.O. BONDS (1)	25 REV. BONDS (2)	TREASURY BONDS (3)
May 21	8.31	8.17	8.68	9.00
May 14	7.82	7.70	8.20	8.72
May 7	7.86	7.74	8.20	8.64
Apr. 30	7.85	7.72	8.13	8.44
Apr. 23	7.82	7.69	8.16	8.53
Apr. 15	7.90	7.77	8.28	8.27
Apr. 9	7.27	7.14	7.54	8.07
Apr. 2	6.93	6.80	7.26	7.91
Mar. 26	6.79	6.67	7.11	7.55
Mar. 19	6.68	6.55	7.08	7.50
Mar. 12	6.61	6.48	7.02	7.51
Mar. 5	6.54	6.40	6.92	7.44
Feb. 26	6.59	6.45	7.01	7.49
Feb. 19	6.62	6.49	7.05	7.53
Feb. 12	6.67	6.53	7.09	7.58
Feb. 5	6.57	6.43	6.98	7.46
Jan. 29	6.56	6.43	6.98	7.44
Jan. 22	6.54	6.40	6.92	7.36
Jan. 15	6.65	6.51	7.04	7.37
Jan. 8	6.70	6.57	7.01	7.31

Figure 14.13

20 GO Bond Index: The average yield of 20 general obligation bonds with 20-year maturities. The average rating for the 20 bonds is "A."

11 GO Bond Index: The average yield on 11 of the 20 bonds in the 20 Bond Index. The average rating for the 11 bonds is "Aa."

Revenue Bond Index: The average yield on 25 revenue bonds with 30-year maturities.

VISIBLE SUPPLY OF MUNIS

SAMPLE OF DATA FROM THE VISIBLE SUPPLY

The 30-day visible supply is compiled daily from the Bond Buyers Guide. It shows the total dollar volume expected to come to the market during the next 30 days. Along with the total there is also a breakdown into competitive and negotiated offerings.

1987	Competitive	Negotiated	Total
10/30	1,113,865,950	1,305,275,000	2,419,140,950
10/23	1,104,170,000	750,410,000	1,809,580,000
10/16	1,362,092,000	360,715,000	1,722,807,000

Figure 14.14

MUNICIPAL BOND INDEX
MERRILL LYNCH 500

Week ended Wednesday, July 23, 1986

The following index is based on yields that about 500 major issuers, mainly of investment grade, would pay on new ? long term tax-exempt securities. The securities are presumed to be issued at par; general obligation bonds have a 20-year maturity and revenue bonds a 30-year maturity. The index is prepared by Merrill Lynch, Pierce, Fenner & Smith Inc., based on data supplied by Kenny Information Systems, a unit of J.J. Kenny & Co.

–OVERALL INDEX–

7.83 –0.63

–REVENUE BONDS–

Sub-index 7.97 –0.85

	2-23-88	Change in Week
AAA-Guaranteed	7.77	–0.00
Airport	7.00	–0.00
Electric-Retail	7.00	–0.00
Electric-Wholesale	8.10	–0.00
Hospital	7.00	–0.00
Housing	8.00	–0.00
Miscellaneous	7.81	–0.00
Pollution Control/		
Ind. Dev.	8.15	–0.00
Transportation	7.90	–0.00
Utility	7.92	–0.00

–GENERAL OBLIGATIONS–
Sub-index 7:40 –0.00

Cities	7.51	–0.00
Counties	7.11	–0.00
States	7.27	–0.00
Other Districts	7.68	–0.00

The transportation category airport utility includes electrics. The transportation category each airport utility includes electrics.

Figure 14.15

MUNICIPAL BONDS TOMBSTONE

Information in this announcement includes:

- name of bond counsel

- description of the denomination and type(s) of bonds. All municipal bonds must be registered, but both serial and term bonds can be combined in one issue

- for serial bonds, a listing of the amount, due date, interest rate, and price. This is called the "scale"; those which mature over a longer term pay a higher rate of interest. The price quoted is a percent of par

- the date on which interest begins to accrue (the "dated date")

- class of bond (revenue or G.O., etc.)

- dates on which interest will be paid

- names of managing underwriter(s) and of firms in the underwriting syndicate, arranged as with a corporate tombstone

STANDARD & POOR'S STOCK GUIDE

A much more complete view of securities activity is provided by *Standard & Poor's Stock Guide,* which gives up-to-date information on some 4,000 stocks. Reading from left to right, it includes:

- ticker symbol and name of the issue

- market(s) where stock is traded

- Standard & Poor's rating of the issue

- par value

- institutional holdings

- brief description of the firm's business

- high and low prices for the issue for several past periods

- average number of shares sold and high, low, and last prices for most recent month

- current dividend yield and P/E ratio

- past dividend payment record and current dividend

- financial position and capitalization from most recent balance sheet

- earnings per share for the preceding five years, the current year, and interim earnings, if any

Standard & Poor's Stock Guide also includes the Mutual Fund Data Sheet.

Agency Rent-A-Car

3033

NASDAQ Symbol AGNC (Incl. in Nat'l Market; marginable)

Price	Range	P-E Ratio	Dividend	Yield	S&P Ranking	Beta
Mar. 28'88 19	1988 21-17	19	[2]---	[2]---	B+	NA

Summary

Agency believes it is the nation's largest company specializing in the insurance replacement automobile rental market. With a fleet of about 32,500 vehicles, Agency conducts its business through more than 500 offices in the U.S. and Canada. Growth in the rental fleet, increased fleet utilization and higher rental rates aided earnings in recent periods. Nearly 60% of the shares are closely held.

Business Summary

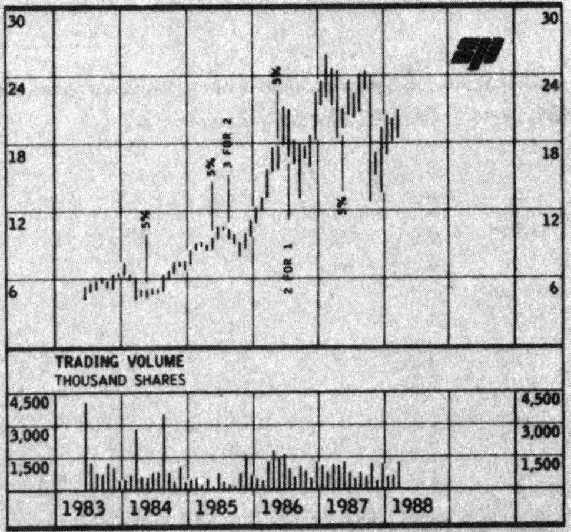

Agency Rent-A-Car, Inc., rents automobiles on a short-term basis, primarily to customers whose insurance coverage entitles them to a replacement vehicle in the event that their own car is damaged, stolen or requires major repairs. Based on its fleet of about 32,500 vehicles, Agency believes that it is the largest firm in its specialized segment of the U.S. car rental market. Wholly owned TransAutomotive Insurance Co. is a multiline insurance company chartered in Texas. The unit had been writing long-haul motor carrier excess liability, physical damage, and general liability and cargo reinsurance coverage, but it ceased underwriting operations in 1982 pending improvement in the commercial casualty insurance business.

As of 1987-8 year-end, Agency was operating 510 car rental offices in the U.S. and Canada. Generally, an insured requiring a replacement vehicle is referred to the company by the insurance adjuster or agent handling his claim. Insurance replacement rental rates range from $15 to $18.50 and business and vacation rentals are approximately $24 a day. Approximately 8% of revenues were derived from car rentals to business or vacation travelers. The company acquires its fleet through two wholly owned automobile agencies.

The rates charged for insurance replacement rentals are usually substantially lower than those charged by the large business and vacation automobile rental companies because business and vacation travelers demand a wide selection of automobiles and often rent for high mileage travel resulting in considerable wear and tear on the automobile. Insurance replacement rentals are usually used as a family car replacement for routine, low mileage, local use. The business and vacation rental companies also have to locate in expensive space in airport locations to be competitive, while the insurance replacement rental company operates in suburban locations so it can deliver the customer's car directly to their home or business.

Important Developments

Mar. '88—The company reported that at 1987-8 year-end it was operating 510 offices in 41 states and 2 Canadian provinces and expected to add 75 offices in 1988-9. Since becoming a public company in 1983, Agency has opened 320 new offices.

Next earnings report due in June.

Per Share Data ($)

Yr. End Jan. 31	1988	1987	1986	1985	1984	1983	1982	1981	1980	1979
Book Value	NA	3.38	2.65	2.01	1.47	1.06	0.82	0.55	0.35	0.25
Earnings	1.01	0.82	0.64	0.54	0.41	0.24	0.28	0.21	0.10	0.08
Dividends[1]	Nil	Nil	Nil	Nil	Nil	$0.00\frac{1}{4}$	$0.00\frac{1}{8}$	$0.00\frac{1}{4}$	Nil	Nil
Payout Ratio	Nil	Nil	Nil	Nil	Nil	1%	1%	1%	Nil	Nil
Calendar Years	1987	1986	1985	1984	1983	1982	1981	1980	1979	1978
Prices—High	26	$22\frac{5}{8}$	$11\frac{1}{4}$	$7\frac{5}{8}$	$6\frac{5}{8}$	NA	NA	NA	NA	NA
Low	$12\frac{7}{8}$	$10\frac{7}{8}$	$7\frac{3}{8}$	$4\frac{1}{4}$	$4\frac{3}{8}$	NA	NA	NA	NA	NA
P/E Ratio—	26-13	28-13	18-12	14-8	16-11	NA	NA	NA	NA	NA

Data as orig. reptd. Adj. for stk. divs. of 5% May 1987, 100% Jul. 1986, 5% May 1986, 50% Aug. 1985, 5% May 1985, and 5% May 1984. 1. Paid prior to public offering. 2. Pays stk. (see Dividend Data). NA-Not Available.

Standard OTC Stock Reports
Vol. 54/No. 39/Sec. 2

April 6, 1988

Standard & Poor's Corp.
25 Broadway, NY, NY 10004

Figure 14.16 Standard & Poor's Stock Guide

Reprinted with permission of Standard & Poor's Corporation

CHAPTER FIFTEEN
federal and state regulations

This chapter covers federal and state laws and regulations concerning the issuance of, and trading in, securities. Much of this information has already been presented in earlier chapters; however, it is discussed here in depth because a registered representative must be familiar with the legislation itself.

Note that this text refers to certain rules by number (usually assigned by the SEC or NSDA) for convenience, but test questions concern only the content of rules and not their numbers.

PART ONE
The Securities Act of 1933

The Securities Act of 1933 was the first federal legislation designed to regulate interstate activities in securities. It affects only new issues (primary or secondary distributions); it is basically designed to ensure that investors receive complete, accurate information. The act is administered and enforced by the Securities and Exchange Commission (SEC).

Although the act contains many provisions and definitions, its aim is to require full and fair public disclosure of important elements of new issues and to prevent fraud.

REGISTRATION REQUIREMENTS

Under the act, all newly issued securities sold through interstate commerce must be registered with the SEC. Registration is accomplished by filing an "S-1" statement, which gives detailed information about both the issuing entity and the issue. The S-1 statement must be accompanied by a prospectus. The prospectus is an abbreviated version of the registration: it contains the same information but omits supporting documentation.

The S-1 statement

The S-1 statement includes:

- nature of issuer's business

- information about corporate officers and directors (name and address, business history, etc.)

- specific description of how proceeds of the new issue will be used

- financial statements, including balance sheet and income accounts, showing capitalization and funded debt for preceding three years

- amount of corporate securities held by officers, directors, and beneficial owners holding 10% or more of these securities

- statement describing any legal action pending against the company

- cost of promoting the new issue

- legal opinion

- articles of incorporation

- underwriter's spread

Penalties for misleading statements

If the S-1 statement proves to be misleading, either because it contains false statements or omits important information, all those who have signed it can be prosecuted for fraud. Maximum criminal penalties, if convicted of this crime, are three years in prison or a $5,000 fine for each count. Civil remedies are also available. Within three years of the offering, or within one year of the time the fraud is discovered, a purchaser has the "right of recovery" from all those who are named in, or have signed, the registration statement. This includes not only corporate partners and directors but underwriters, attorneys, accountants, and appraisers—anyone, in fact, who signs a report supporting facts in the statement.

SEC review process

As discussed in Chapter 6, the SEC must review the registration before the new issue can be sold to the public. Once registration is filed (the "filing date"), the law calls for a 20-day "cooling-off" period. This period allows the SEC time to review and dampens the effect news of a new issue may have on the market. When the review is complete, sales can begin; this is called the "effective date."

Deficiency letters   In practice, the cooling-off period is often longer than 20 days. The SEC may need more information; if this is the case, it will issue one or more "deficiency letters" asking for certain specific amendments. Once these are received, 20 days can again pass before the effective date.

Note

The SEC has the power to lengthen or shorten the cooling-off period.

Stop orders   If the SEC thinks the registration statement contains misstatements or omits important facts, it can suspend the entire registration process with a "stop order." The issuer is then entitled to a hearing before such an order is promulgated.

Note

The SEC cannot be said to "approve" a new issue. It makes no judgment on the accuracy of the registration statement or on the quality of the issue itself, but simply reviews for completeness. The prospectus must include wording explaining this "nonapproval."

The preliminary prospectus

While SEC review is in progress, no sales of the new issue are allowed, but the issuer can produce and circulate a preliminary prospectus to get indications of interest from prospective purchasers. This is similar to the final prospectus, but lacks the final price, the date certificates will be ready for delivery, or the underwriters' spread.

On its face, the preliminary prospectus must say that:

- registration has been filed but is not yet effective
- the information is subject to change
- this is not an offer to sell or a solicitation to buy

This material must be printed in red, which is why the preliminary prospectus is often called a "red herring."

In addition, during the waiting period, the underwriter cannot make any predictions about the issuer's performance, though it is proper to answer unsolicited inquiries about the new issue.

As noted in Chapter 6, the offering price and underwriters' spread are the last amendments to be filed with the SEC.

Selling the new issue

As soon as the registration is effective, but not before, the new issue may be sold, subject to the following regulations:

Primary distribution   Anyone who purchases the new issue within 90 days of the effective date must receive the prospectus.

Secondary distribution   When the issuer already has shares outstanding, anyone who purchases the new issue within 40 days of the effective date must receive the prospectus.

Note

In all cases, the prospectus must be delivered to the buyer before, or no later than, confirmation of the sale.

Advertising   Dealers cannot advertise the new issue for 90 days after the effective date, except by delivering the prospectus. Tombstone ads (see Figure 14.12) are allowed.

Mutual funds   If the prospectus is used more than nine months after the effective date (as with mutual funds), the information it contains must be no more than 16 months old.

EXEMPT SECURITIES

Under the Act, certain securities are exempt from the registration requirements (though not from the fraud provisions). These include:

1. Securities issued or guaranteed by the U.S. government or by U.S. government agencies

2. Obligations issued by any state or other political subdivision (thus municipals are exempt)

3. Commercial paper (corporate debt) or bankers' acceptances with maturities of less than 270 days

4. Instruments issued by common carriers (railroads, trucking companies, airlines) which are regulated by the Interstate Commerce Act

5. Domestic banks or trust companies, savings and loans associations, building and loan societies, and co-op banks are all exempt

6. Nonprofit groups (churches, schools, etc.)

7. Private placements (see below)

8. Intrastate issues

9. "Regulation A" filings, *i.e.*, issues of $1.5 million or less (see page 384)

10. Fixed annuity contracts and insurance policies

EXEMPT TRANSACTIONS

Even with those securities that are not exempt, some transactions are not subject to the requirements of the Act. These include:

1. Transactions between "private individuals" (*i.e.*, not the issuer, underwriter, or a dealer)

2. Private placements (*i.e.*, where the issuer makes no public offering, see below)

3. Unsolicited broker transactions

PRIVATE PLACEMENT (REGULATION D)

Securities placed with selected investors, and never offered to the public, are exempt from registration and prospectus requirements. However, they are still subject to the anti-fraud provisions of the Act and must meet some standards: they may not be advertised; there must be disclosure in some cases; and the securities' price must be negotiated.

Further, the issuer may not sell to an underwriter and cannot sell to more than 35 people in any 12-month period. Securities sold in this fashion may be resold only in accordance with Rule 144 (see below) or if they are registered with the SEC.

Regulation D governs private placements. The conditions for a private placement include:

- issuer must have reason to think the buyer is a sophisticated investor and that the buyer will not resell the securities quickly. The buyer usually furnishes an "investment letter"

- buyer must be provided with an "offering memorandum," which gives the same financial information as a prospectus

Rule 501

This regulation defines "accredited investors." Such investors are not included in the limit of 35 purchasers of private placements. Accredited investors include:

- any financial institution (banks, insurance companies, and employee benefit plans)

- any individual with net worth of over $1,000,000 (including joint net worth with spouse)

- any individual with an income of over $200,000 in each of the preceding two years and a "reasonable expectation" of continuing to earn such an income

- directors, executives, and general partners of the issuer

Additionally, the regulation spells out the conditions under which a security would be exempt from SEC regulations.

Other rules

Other rules under Regulation D require:

- an issuer claiming exemption must file a "notice of sale" with the SEC

- purchasers, for the most part, must have access to the same information as in a registration statement

- any company not required to report to the SEC or any investment company can issue up to $500,000 of securities without registering them. There is no limit on the number of investors, but general solicitation is prohibited

- any noninvestment company (including partnerships) be exempt from registration requirements on issues of $5,000,000 or less to no more than 35 unaccredited investors (there is no limit on the number of accredited investors)

- any issue to 35 or fewer "sophisticated" investors (again, accredited investors don't count toward this total). This rule does allow others to participate if they act through a "purchaser's representative" who is "sophisticated"

SALE OF RESTRICTED AND CONTROL SECURITIES (RULE 144)

Securities acquired through a Reg D transaction (private placement) or through an employee stock option plan are "restricted" or unregistered. Securities held by a person in control (a corporate officer or director or a major shareholder) are called "control securities."

Restricted or unregistered securities

These provisions apply to the sale of securities that have never been registered (*e.g.*, acquired through a private placement or a merger).

Ownership   The seller must have owned (fully paid for) the securities for at least two years. This period excludes any time in which the seller has a short position or owned puts in this stock. If ownership of the new securities is transferred, a new two-year period begins, unless they are a gift.

Broker's role   The securities can be sold by the broker only on an agency basis. That is, the broker can execute a sell order but cannot solicit an order to buy.

SEC notification   The seller of restricted securities must file a notice of intention to sell (Form 144) with the SEC and act within 90 days of filing (or file a new form). This requirement does not apply if the transaction involves 500 or fewer shares and does not exceed $10,000.

Limits on quantity   A seller may sell only 1% of the total number of shares currently outstanding or an amount equal to the weekly average number of shares sold during the four weeks prior to the SEC filing—whichever is greater. Such a sale may be made only once in a three-month period.

Control securities

A number of rules cover securities transactions involving corporate officers, directors, or those who own at least 10% of any class of outstanding securities. In addition:

Public information   Control securities can be sold only if certain information is available to the buyer, either the annual or quarterly reports filed with the SEC (which include income statements and balance sheets) or equivalent information from firms which do not file ("nonreporting companies").

Holding period   Same as for restricted securities, including the exemption on a smaller issue. However, if the control securities are registered, the two-year wait does not apply.

Limits on quantity   These limits are the same as for restricted securities; the Rule includes all members of the control person's immediate family.

"Nonaffiliated persons"

A person who is not in a position of control but holds restricted securities is called "nonaffiliated." He may sell all his holdings after three years and is exempt from the filing and information requirements of Rule 144.

INTRASTATE TRANSACTIONS (RULE 147)

Under Rule 147, securities sold only to residents of the state in which the issuer is also a resident and operator of a business are exempt from registration requirements. The rule stipulates:

Residence   The issuer must reside in and do business within the state at the time of the offering.

Doing business "Doing business" means: the issuer's main office is located in that state, has at least 80% of its assets within that state, and derives 80% of gross revenues from operations within that state.

Use of proceeds Issuer will be using at least 80% of the proceeds from the Rule 147 transaction for operations within that state.

Resale For nine months after the issuer's last sale, these securities can be resold only to residents of that state.

Purchaser's residence All purchasers must live within the state (an individual's main residence or a corporation's main office must be within the state) and provide written proof of that to the issuer.

Certificate The issuer must place, on each certificate, a legend stating that the security is not registered under the Act and describing the resale restrictions.

Transfer The issuer must give its transfer agent "stop transfer" instructions to prevent illegal transactions in the after-market.

REGULATION A OFFERINGS

Certain small-scale and limited offerings are exempt from the Act's registration and prospectus requirements. Regulation A sets qualifying conditions for these exemptions.

Size Reg A offerings cannot exceed $5,000,000 in total value in a 12-month period.

Filing The issuer must file a notification form at a regional SEC office within 10 days before the initial offering. Filing alone is not sufficient; the SEC must review the information and decide whether the issue qualifies.

Time limits The offering must take place within 90 days of the filing date or the SEC will consider that the issuer has "abandoned" the matter.

"Offering circular" Reg A issues of more than $100,000 must be accompanied by an offering statement describing the issue. A copy of this statement must be filed with the SEC within 10 business days prior to its public distribution; purchasers must receive a copy at least 48 hours before the confirmation of sale is mailed.

The only advertising permitted is a tombstone containing basic information (name of issuer and name, amount, and price of the offered securities).

ADVERTISING

Regulations govern the amount and kind of information that may be released to the public during the "cooling-off" period, *i.e.,* after the registration statement is filed but before the issue is registered. It provides a guide for the underwriters of a proposed distribution.

Advertisements *must* include:

- wording to the effect that the registration statement has been filed with the SEC but has not yet become effective

- a statement as to whether the security is offered in connection with a distribution by the issuer or by a security holder, or both; and whether this represents new financing or refunding, or both

- name and address of a person who can provide a written prospectus

- notice that securities may not yet be sold

- a statement that the communication is not an offer to sell nor a solicitation of an offer to buy

Advertisements or other communications during the "cooling-off" period *may* include:

- identification of the issuer

- title and amount of securities to be offered

- some indication of the issuer's general type of business (if an investment company, its classification)

- the price of the security or method of determining its probable price range

- names of underwriters

- whether, in the opinion of counsel, the security is a legal investment

PART TWO
The Securities Exchange Act of 1934

The purpose of this act is to bar unfair practices once securities have been issued. It regulates exchanges, over-the-counter markets, brokers and dealers and is, in general, designed to ensure that the market is fair and orderly.

Note

The Securities Act of 1933 concerns new issues; the Securities Exchange Act of 1934 regulates trading of issued securities in the secondary market.

Perhaps the most significant feature of the 1934 Act is the creation of the Securities and Exchange Commission (SEC) as an enforcing authority for the securities industry. Its five commissioners are appointed by the president, are approved by the Senate for five-year terms and are barred from any business or stock activity when they are serving.

The SEC is specifically charged with establishing rules regulating credit, brokers' treatment of customers' securities, etc., all detailed below. The Act also defines terms like "broker" and "dealer" and includes provisions for regulating exchanges.

RULES GOVERNING REGISTRATION

The 1934 Act calls on exchanges to regulate themselves; but all national securities exchanges must register with the SEC, agree to abide by the law, and supply up-to-date information about the organization's rules and membership, including its provisions for dealing with members who conduct business in ways that violate the principles of the Act.

Others who must register with, and are regulated by, the SEC are individuals or firms engaged in securities transactions in interstate commerce. These include exchange members who deal with the public, such as specialists, brokers, or dealers who engage in over-the-counter transactions, and members of national securities associations. Also, securities themselves must be registered with the SEC.

Exempted from registration requirements are small local exchanges, brokers/dealers who do not do business with the public or who work only intrastate (though anyone who uses the mail is subject to the Act), and issues that are exempt (government, intrastate, and some smaller issues).

CREDIT REGULATIONS

Under the 1934 Act, the Federal Reserve Board is given authority to control the amount of credit "initially extended and subsequently maintained" on securities (see page 268). The board does this by restricting the borrowing of members, brokers, and dealers under its Regulation T, which is enforced by the SEC.

It is unlawful for any member of a national securities exchange, or any broker/dealer who transacts business through such a member, to borrow on any listed security except through an FRB member bank or to have a total indebtedness in excess of 15 times its net capital. These requirements do not apply to exempt securities (direct federal government obligations, or government-guaranteed obligations).

HYPOTHECATION AND COMMINGLING OF CUSTOMERS' SECURITIES

No member of a national exchange or broker or dealer may:

- pledge a customer's securities (hypothecate) to a bank as security for a loan without the customer's written consent

- commingle a customer's securities with those of other customers or of the firm without written permission

When the firm does have permission to commingle and hypothecate customer's securities, it may not pledge them for an amount in excess of the debit balance in the customer's account.

MANIPULATION AND DECEPTION

SEC regulations prohibit fraud and/or the manipulation of securities' prices.

Manipulative devices

It is unlawful to act so as to give a false appearance of active trading in a security; any device(s) used to manipulate markets is prohibited. These include:

"Wash sales" One person buys and sells to create the misleading appearance of active trading.

"Matching orders" Two or more individuals act together and enter identical (or almost identical) orders simultaneously, so the transaction appears on the tape although there has been no true change of ownership.

False information For example, urging a transaction in a particular security by saying some person is going to move in a way that will affect its price.

Short sales

Another way in which the Act guards against manipulation is with rules concerning short-selling. The specific intent here is to prevent an investor from cornering the market by continually selling short and driving a security's price down, then buying the securities back cheaply.

Thus, the basic rule is the "plus tick" rule: no short sales are permitted at a price lower than the last reported regular-way sale. In other words, selling short is allowed only at a price higher than the last reported sale (a plus tick) or at a price which is the same as the last reported sale but higher than the last reported sale at a different price. (See Chapter 11.)

With odd lots, the plus tick rule is applied in terms of the last reported round lot sale price.

Someone who holds a short position in a security may not tender that security in response to a tender offer.

Other prohibited activities

Solicitation Because it is possible to manipulate prices by soliciting purchases on an exchange, the law prohibits distributors of securities (underwriters) to solicit trade in those securities. There are some exceptions, including:

- unsolicited customer orders

- bids offered for the purpose of stabilizing the issue by managing underwriters

- "market making" transactions that take place 10 business days before distribution

Tenders
To prevent those who make a tender offer from purchasing in the market, the rules prohibit anyone who makes a tender (or exchange) offer for a particular security from purchasing that security except under the terms of that offer.

Credit disclosure
To guard against deception, credit terms must be disclosed in margin transactions. This means a customer must receive a written statement of rates and charges at the time a margin account is opened. No credit can be extended on the purchase of new issues.

Note
All these rules are issued pursuant to the anti-fraud provisions of the 1934 Act. While some particular transactions are exempted from requirements of the Act, as noted, none are exempt from anti-fraud provisions.

STABILIZATION

As noted in Chapter 6, the 1934 Act permits stabilization of a new issue, provided it:

- takes place prior to the effective date of the issue

- is disclosed in the prospectus

- is not used to raise the price of the offered security (stabilization can only be used to prevent a drop in the market price during distribution)

- is not performed by anyone other than the managing underwriter

- does not involve a bid higher than the current offering price

INSIDER RULES

The Act restricts the activities of "insiders." An insider is defined as:

- an officer or director of a corporation

- anyone holding 10% or more of the shares (of any class of equity security) issued by the corporation and immediate family members

- anyone who has information about the corporation not available to the public

Basically, insiders are not allowed to profit from their information by trading in a stock before that information is public. For that reason, those who become insiders must file a personal statement with the SEC.

If an insider makes a profit on the corporation's stock in a period of less than six months, the corporation can legally recover that profit. Insiders must report all personal transactions in securities of their corporations no later than 10 days after the end of the calendar month in which they occur. Generally, insiders are barred from any short selling.

PROXIES

Solicitation of proxies is also regulated by the SEC under the Act. A shareholder can give someone power to vote in his or her behalf through a proxy. The regulations state that companies that solicit proxies must provide shareholders with accurate, detailed information about any proposals up for vote; this information must also be submitted to the SEC for review.

In a situation where control of a company is at stake, usually called a "proxy contest" (*e.g.*, where another firm is trying to acquire a company), those involved in soliciting proxies must register with the SEC as "participants." This does not include anyone (such as a broker) who is asked for advice; the key concept is "unsolicited advice." Those who fail to register can face criminal penalties.

RECORD-KEEPING AND REPORT-FILING REQUIREMENTS

Every broker or dealer and every national securities exchange must keep detailed records; copies must be filed with the SEC as that agency deems necessary to protect investors. A representative of the SEC or the NASD may examine such records at any time without warning.

All registered brokers or dealers must annually file an income statement and balance sheet, certified by an independent accountant, with the SEC. Copies of these reports must go to the firm's customers.

All individuals involved—partners, officers, directors, or employees—in a listed exchange, brokerage, or dealership must submit their fingerprints to the U.S. Attorney General.

OTC REGULATIONS

Under Section 15A of the 1934 Act (The Maloney Amendment), the National Association of Securities Dealers (NASD) was established to regulate the over-the-counter market. The NASD itself must be registered with the SEC; any nonmember broker/dealer whose business involves any interstate commerce or transactions involving national securities exchanges is directly regulated by the SEC.

Recommendations   In recommending any security to a customer, registered brokers and dealers must be sure it is reasonable and suitable for the particular customer. (NASD bylaws are set forth on pages 396–406.)

Supervision   The Act requires close supervision of all "associated persons" (employees) of a broker or dealer. Thus, all member firms must have on file written procedures for such supervision. Duties of a designated supervisor include:

- reviewing and approving (in writing) each new customer account and conducting frequent examinations of established accounts

- reviewing and approving (in writing) all security transactions and correspondence by associated persons

- reviewing customer complaints

Customer accounts   Member firms are required to:

- establish a particular form for new accounts

- maintain current records on each customer

- keep detailed records on discretionary accounts to show that transactions in the account are not excessive

- maintain current information about the companies, especially with respect to dividends, splits, rights subscriptions, etc.

- keep all customer complaints on file

CAPITAL REQUIREMENTS

Net capital requirements: SEC Rule I5c3-1

To ensure that brokers or dealers remain solvent, the law limits the total indebtedness of member firms to a specific percentage of net capital. The rule sets the requirements for various categories of brokers and stipulates the elements that must be considered as debt or capital.

Use of customer free credit balance: SEC Rule I5c3-2

"Free credit balance" effectively refers to cash in the customer's account; *i.e.*, any liability payable to the customer on demand. The rule holds that the broker/dealer can use these amounts for its business operations if the customer is advised in writing every three months of:

- the amount of the free credit balance

- funds that are not segregated and may be used by the broker/dealer for its own business

- the funds that are payable to the customer on demand

Customer protection: Rule I5c3-3

Essentially, this rule holds that the broker must keep physical control over all customers' fully paid securities (*i.e.*, not including those pledged for a bank loan).

This rule also requires those who are selling stock on behalf of a customer to buy the stock in the market for delivery to the buyer if the customer fails to deliver the stock within 10 business days of the settlement date.

In addition, every broker or dealer must maintain a "special reserve bank account for the exclusive benefit of customers" separate from any other bank account, containing an amount worked out according to a formula provided (basically, the amount by which the firm's obligation to customers exceeds customer obligations to the firms).

PART THREE
Other Regulations

INVESTMENT COMPANY ACT OF 1940 (ICA 1940)

Most of the provisions of the Investment Company Act of 1940 are presented in Chapter 4, Mutual Funds, so this will be only a very brief review.

This Act defines the three principal types of investment companies: face amount certificate companies; unit investment trusts; and management companies including diversified, nondiversified, open-end, and closed-end companies. Like the 1933 and 1934 Acts, this legislation is enforced by the SEC and extends the requirements of those acts to investment companies, especially portions of those acts ensuring a fair and equitable issuance of securities. A related law, the Investment Advisers Act of 1940, requires all investment advisers to register with the SEC.

Various provisions of the Act require registration of investment companies, restrict the choice of directors, prohibit certain types of transactions, outline shareholders' rights, and so on. All are covered in Chapter 4.

Two amendments to the Securities Exchange Act of 1934 are the Maloney Act of 1938 and the Securities Acts Amendments of 1975. The first gave OTC markets the power of self-regulation and led to the creation of the NASD. The second extended self-regulation to municipal securities and led to the creation of the MSRB.

FEDERAL RESERVE BOARD REGULATIONS

As noted above, the SEC authorized the Federal Reserve Board to regulate credit involved in securities purchases. Two regulations govern such matters.

Regulation U

Banks are limited in the amount of credit they may extend for the purchase of listed stocks or bonds. Customers who borrow under the Regulation must file a statement indicating the purpose of the loan, and banks must keep this statement for three years after the loan is repaid. Loans made for other purposes are called "nonpurpose loans."

Regulation T

Reg T sets rules on extending credit in securities transactions; these apply to all securities broker/dealers and members of national securities exchanges.

Basically, the Regulation limits the amount of credit a broker/dealer may extend to clients who are purchasing securities on margin (not including municipal or U.S. government or commodity transactions).

SECURITIES INVESTOR PROTECTION CORPORATION (SIPC)

In 1970, Congress created the Securities Investor Protection Corporation (SIPC) to provide limited protection to customers of securities firms that are forced to liquidate and to promote confidence in the securities industry. In effect, it protects an investor's cash and securities (but not commodity accounts) up to $500,000.

SIPC membership

SIPC is not an agency of the government, but a nonprofit membership corporation composed of members: all broker/dealers registered under the 1934 Act, all members of national securities exchanges, and most NASD members. It is financed by an assessment on members' securities-related business and can receive emergency funding from the Treasury with SEC approval.

Liquidation procedures

When it is determined that a member must liquidate, the SIPC may ask a federal court to appoint a trustee to supervise the liquidation. The trustee must:

1. Notify customers of the liquidation.

2. See that customers receive securities registered in their name or those in the process of being registered (*i.e.*, any securities that can be identified as belonging to a specific client). There is no limit on the value of the returned property.

3. See that customers receive all other "customer property" (cash and securities) held by the firm, divided on a pro rata basis. Again, there is no limit on the value of the returned property.

4. See that remaining claims are satisfied by the SIPC, subject to certain limitations.

Limits on customer claims

The SIPC covers claims of up to $500,000 per separate customer, of which not more than $100,000 may be in cash. This is not coverage "per account." Under the SIPC Act, when a single customer holds accounts in different forms, each account is considered separate. For example, consider an investor who has an individual account, a joint account with his or her spouse, and acts as trustee in yet a third account, all with the same broker/dealer. In liquidation, these would be considered three "separate customers."

However, a person who has one or more individual accounts (say, a cash account and a margin account) with one firm is considered a single customer and will be covered for only $500,000 in liquidation.

Clients must file claims directly with the SIPC trustee. Claims are valued as of the date the trustee begins liquidation. Reimbursement is "in kind," *i.e.*, claims for securities are satisfied by delivery of those securities. Customers are not protected if securities rise or fall in value between the time of filing and date of delivery.

TRUST INDENTURE ACT OF 1939

Requirements of this act are covered in Chapter 2. Basically, it concerns all corporate bonds issued to the public interstate and requires that a trustee be appointed to safeguard the rights of bondholders; it also mandates full disclosure of information in the written agreement between the corporation and its creditors (the trust indenture), etc.

STATE REGULATIONS

Although the securities industry is also regulated at the state level, it is not possible to discuss each state's particular regulations in detail. However, some general similarities do exist. For example, the Uniform Securities Act is actually a model followed by many states in formulating their own laws.

State "blue sky laws," discussed in Chapter 6, provide protection in securities transactions similar to that provided by federal legislation. Most states also require the regulation and registration of securities, broker/dealers, and individual agents; many impose capital requirements for those active in the securities industry. In addition, many states have antifraud regulations.

Uniform gifts to minors

This, too, is a model act; it has been adopted by most states. It is discussed in some detail in Chapter 10.

Prudent man rule

In many states, some version of this rule applies to the investment-related activities of fiduciaries or trustees. In essence, it holds that people acting on behalf of another can invest only in those securities that a reasonably prudent man who is seeking reasonable income and preservation of capital would choose.

Legal lists

These are published by the banking departments of some states. They list securities that institutions (*e.g.*, banks, insurance companies) may purchase. Its purpose, like that of the prudent man rule, is to prevent speculative activity with funds belonging to others. In some states that lack the prudent man rule, the list also governs the behavior of trustees and fiduciaries.

Law of agency

This stipulates that a registered representative acts on behalf of his or her employer as an agent, and may not:

- act on behalf of a third party whose interests conflict with those of the employer
- acquire private interests that conflict with the employer's interests
- work for another firm in the same business, except with the employer's permission

Questions on federal and state regulations follow Chapter 16.

CHAPTER SIXTEEN
industry regulations

PART ONE
NASD Regulations

The National Association of Securities Dealers, Inc. (NASD) is a self-regulating body that sets standards for the over-the-counter securities market. It was established as a "national securities association" under the Maloney Act, which became law in 1938. That law is now Section 15A of the Securities Exchange Act of 1934.

A set of bylaws, printed in the NASD Manual, sets forth requirements for qualifying and registering as a member. Other important units are the:

- Rules of Fair Practice, which concern member firms' dealings with the public

- Uniform Practice Code, which covers dealings between brokerage firms

- Code of Procedure, which deals with violations of NASD rules

- Code of Arbitration, which deals with settling disputes between members and between members and the public

PURPOSES

In its Certificate of Incorporation, the NASD declares its purposes. These include:

1. To promote the investment banking and securities business, standardize its principles and practices, promote high standards of commercial honor, and encourage observance of applicable laws.

2. To provide a medium which enables members to work with government and other agencies on problems affecting investors, the public, and those engaged in the investment banking and securities business.

3. To adopt and enforce rules of fair practice and rules preventing fraud and manipulation; to promote just and equitable principles of trade for the protection of investors.

4. To promote self-discipline among members and to deal with grievances between members and between members and the public.

BYLAWS: MEMBERSHIP

Eligibility

NASD bylaws say that any broker or dealer or securities underwriter legally authorized (under federal or state law) to transact business in the investment banking or securities field, who actually transacts such business in the United States, and who pledges to abide by NASD rules, is eligible for membership.

Commercial banks are specifically excluded. Under certain conditions, individuals can be disqualified from membership or from seeking membership. These include:

1. Anyone suspended or expelled from a self-regulatory organization (such as the NASD or any national securities exchange).

2. Anyone who has been subject to an SEC order suspending or revoking broker or dealer registration.

3. Anyone who has been convicted of a felony or misdemeanor involving securities trading, perjury, bribery, embezzlement, and so on, in the preceding 10 years.

Registration of members

Under the bylaws, members must register as principals or representatives. Principals are those actively engaged in the investment banking or securities activities of a member firm, including officers, directors, partners, and supervising managers. Representatives are those who engage in such activities as employees of a member.

Branch offices Every member firm is required to register its branch offices and inform the board of governors of any branch opening or closing.

Exemptions No registration is required for:

- those who deal exclusively in exempt securities, commodities, or listed securities (those traded on a national exchange)

- clerical or administrative personnel

- persons who provide capital but are not directly engaged in the member firm's activities

Conditions Both principals and representatives must pass a qualifying exam. For registered representatives, registration is nontransferable. If they change employers, they must reregister in the new position. If more than two years elapse, the former members may have to requalify.

Those who wish to terminate their registration must submit a written resignation to the NASD.

Advantages Although NASD membership is voluntary, it does carry certain benefits. Member firms receive preference when they underwrite and trade in the over-the-counter market; members may deal with nonmembers only on the same basis as with the general public, and members cannot join in an underwriting with nonmembers.

Operations

Under the bylaws, a 27-member Board of Governors, the governing body of the NASD, is responsible for administering its affairs. This board divides the country into 13 geographical districts. In each, a District Committee functions to provide administration on the local level. At times, this becomes the District Business Conduct Committee and acts as a disciplinary body (see page 407).

Assessments

The Board of Governors draws up a budget annually and imposes assessments on members to meet financial needs. Charges include: a basic membership fee plus a percentage of gross income; a fee for each registered representative, principal, and branch office; and fees for registration and membership applications and exams.

RULES OF FAIR PRACTICE

As noted, these rules principally concern relations between members and their customers. They are intended to ensure just and equitable charges and customs in retail transactions and to prevent fraud and manipulation.

Perhaps the most general (and most important) rule is entitled Business Conduct of Members. It simply states that members "shall observe high standards of commercial honor and just and equitable principles of trade."

Executing retail transactions in the OTC market

When buying or selling for a customer, a member must find the best inter-dealer market for the securities; *i.e.*, must get the best price possible in the current market.

A member may not turn to a third party, *i.e.*, channel the transaction through another broker/dealer, unless it will demonstrably reduce the cost to the customer.

Prompt receipt and delivery of securities

Purchases   No member may accept a purchase order for securities from a customer unless he is certain the customer agrees to pay for them promptly (in seven business days) and to receive securities against payment, even for executions that represent only part of a larger order.

Sales   A member cannot execute a customer's sell order unless:

1.   The member has possession of the security; or

2.   The customer is long in that security in his account with the member; or

3.   The member has reasonable assurance (a) the customer will deliver the security within five business days of the execution of the order; or (b) the security is on deposit with a qualified institution that has been instructed to deliver the securities against payment.

Forwarding of proxy and other materials

Members must forward proxy materials, annual reports, and other legally required information to each beneficial owner of shares held by the member (in a street name). This material is furnished by the issuer, which also pays the cost of distributing it.

"Free riding and withholding"

Members must make a bona fide public distribution at the public offering price for securities that trade at a premium in the secondary market ("hot issues"). Failure to do so is termed "free riding and withholding"; this rule is designed to prevent a broker/dealer from artificially raising prices by holding securities off the market in the face of considerable demand. It applies no matter how the member acquired the securities: as underwriter, as selling group member, or from an underwriter or selling group member.

More specifically, the rules say a member:

1. Cannot hold any such securities in the member firm's account.

2. Cannot sell such securities to any officer, director, employee, agent, or associate of the member (or of another broker/dealer) or to members of any such person's immediate family. (This includes parents, children, brother or sister, spouse, and father-, mother-, brother-, and sister-in-law, as well as any other person materially supported by the member.)

3. Cannot sell such securities to a finder or anyone acting in fiduciary capacity to the managing underwriter or to members of his or her immediate family.

4. Cannot sell such securities to senior officers of institutions (*e.g.*, banks, savings and loans, insurance companies), or to employees of such institutions whose work involves securities transactions, or to members of their immediate families.

Exceptions

A member may sell securities to those described in items 3 and 4 above, to family members of those described in item 2 above, or to any account in which thatthose persons have a beneficial interest provided that:

1. The member can demonstrate the securities were sold in accordance with those persons' normal investment practices; *i.e.*, that it reflects a customary—in terms of frequency and amount—purchase from the member; a consistent policy of purchasing only hot issues would not be likely to qualify as "normal" *and*

2. That the total amount of securities sold is insubstantial and not disproportionate to total public sales. (Insubstantial is not defined in any fixed way but applies to both aggregate sales and sales to any one individual. As for disproportionate, this obviously depends on the size and price of the issue; the Manual suggests, as a guideline only, 10% of the member's total participation in the issue.)

A member cannot sell these securities at or above the public offering price to another broker/dealer; however, he may sell all or part of these securities to another member broker/dealer if that member provides written assurance that the purchase is for public customers.

Special regulations adopted by the SEC concern sale practices connected with so-called "penny stocks." These are basically stocks valued at less than $5 a share and traded over the counter (*i.e.*, not listed on an exchange or NASDAQ).

These regulations call on broker/dealers to furnish a Risk Disclosure Document detailing the particular risks involved with these stocks before completing any transaction. Further, customers must be notified of the current quoted price for the stock and the amount of compensation for both the registered representative and the broker/dealer. This information must be provided for each and every transaction.

The rule is aimed at firms in which these stocks provide a significant portion of income: if a broker/dealer's earnings from penny stocks (commissions and markups) amount to less than 5% of total earnings, the rule does not apply. The rule is also designed to protect unsophisticated investors, exempting those involved with the issuing firm, private placements, institutional investors, and customers who have a continuing relationship with the broker/dealer.

Recommendations to customers ("fair dealing")

In recommending a security transaction to a customer, a registered representative must have reasonable grounds to believe that it is suitable in terms of the customer's other holdings, resources, and needs. More specifically, this means members:

1. Cannot recommend speculative, low-priced securities without attempting to get information about the customer's financial situation.

2. Cannot engage in excessive trading or "churning."

3. Cannot trade in mutual fund shares, as these are not considered suitable for short term trades.

   Also, members cannot engage in fraudulent conduct, specifically:

4. Establish fictitious accounts to execute prohibited transactions (*e.g.,* purchase of hot issues) or to disguise actions contrary to a firm's policy.

5. Conduct transactions in discretionary accounts without the customer's written permission.

6. Execute transactions without customer authorization or to send confirmations to customers, thereby making them accept transactions not agreed to.

7. Borrowing customer's funds or securities without written authorization.

8. Engage in any illegal fraudulent activity such as forgery, misstatement, or manipulation.

Members are also advised that recommending purchase of securities beyond a customer's financial ability is an unfair practice.

Charges for services performed

A member is allowed to charge for such services as collection of dividends and interest due, transfer of securities, appraisals, safekeeping, etc. Such charges must be reasonable and fair (not discriminatory between customers).

Fair prices and commissions

In all over-the-counter securities transactions, a member must buy or sell at a price that is fair and reasonable, considering all relevant factors; if the member is acting as an agent, any commission or service charge must be similarly fair and reasonable. The guiding interpretation here is the "5% markup policy." It is important to note that this is a guide, not a rule: greater (or smaller) markups may be considered fair under certain circumstances including:

- the type of security (common stocks tend to have a higher markup than bonds, for example)

- market conditions for the security (if market activity is slow, the markup may be higher than in a more active market)

- price of the security (lower-price securities might warrant a higher percentage markup)

- size of transaction (handling expenses may be less in percentage terms on a larger transaction)

- expenses involved in obtaining the security

- services rendered in completing the transaction

However, excessive expenses (such as high salaries or high rent) are not considered to justify a higher markup. Markups must be based on current market value. This guideline applies to transactions in which a member:

- buys a security to fill an order received from a customer for that security ("riskless" or "simultaneous" transactions)

- sells a security to a customer from inventory (markup should be based on current market price, not the broker/dealers' cost)

- buys a security from a client (here the rule applies to markdown, not a markup)

- acts as agent

- participates in a "proceeds transaction" (In these trades, a customer sells securities to or through a broker/dealer, and the proceeds are used to pay for other securities purchased from or through that broker/dealer at or about the same time. This is considered a single transaction.)

Note

NASD markup policy is not applicable to securities where a prospectus is required and securities are sold at a public offering price. This effectively excludes new issues and mutual fund shares.

Publication of transactions and quotations

Members cannot publish any communication (advertisement, circular, etc.) that reports a security transaction unless the member believes it represents a bona fide sale or purchase. Similarly, members cannot report a bid or asked price unless they believe it represents a bona fide bid or offer (a firm quote). Nominal (approximate) quotes can be used, but they must be clearly identified.

This rule also explicitly prohibits publishing a figure as a firm quote unless a bona fide transaction took place at that price. Using false or misleading quotations to induce a customer to purchase securities is considered manipulation and fraud.

Offers at stated prices

Members cannot offer to buy or sell securities at a stated price unless they are prepared to trade at that price. In short, quotations should be firm; the action of refusing to honor an offered quotation is called "backing away." Although the rules acknowledge that "subject" quotes are sometimes necessary, a member making a "firm trading market" in a security is expected to buy or sell a normal unit at the quoted price.

Disclosure of price in selling agreements

Selling-group agreements must state the public price of the securities involved. They must also stipulate who gets concessions (if any) and under what circumstances.

Securities taken in trade

The term "taken in trade" refers to a transaction in which a member purchases (as agent or principal) a security from a customer as part of an agreement that the customer will purchase securities that are part of a fixed price offering from the member. The rule holds that such securities must be purchased at a fair market price, *i.e.*, what a dealer in that security would normally pay. If the member is acting as agent, a normal commission must be charged.

Use of information obtained in fiduciary capacity

A member acting as paying agent, transfer agent, trustee, or the like may not use any information received in that capacity to solicit trades, unless asked to do so by the issuer.

Influencing or rewarding employees of others

No member or associated person shall give anything of value worth more than $100 in any year to any person (or any agent or employee of any person) if the gift is in relation to that person's (or employer's) business (*e.g.*, bribing another firm's order clerk to channel orders to a member). This does not, however, prohibit business-related expenses such as meals or theater tickets.

Payment designed to influence market prices

Members cannot give anything of value to induce anyone to publish information that could affect the market price of a security (*e.g.*, paying a market-letter publisher or journalist for favorable comment). This rule explicitly excepts clearly defined paid advertising.

Disclosure on confirmation

At or before the time a transaction with a customer is completed, members must provide written confirmation showing whether the member acted as broker or dealer; if the member acted as a broker, the member must report, or offer to report, the identity of the other party and other details of the trade.

Note

Commission amounts must be disclosed (but not markups except on riskless transactions) and a broker or dealer member cannot act as both principal and agent in the same transaction.

Disclosure of control

A member controlled by or controlling the issuer of a security or in a "control position" must so inform customers prior to entering into a contract for purchase or sale of such security. This disclosure must be delivered in writing at or before the completion of any transaction.

This would include, for example, a situation in which officers of the issuing company are also officers of the member firm or when the shares offered are in a company that owns interest in the member firm.

Disclosure of participation or interest in primary or secondary distribution

This echoes the preceding rule: a member who participates in distribution of a security as broker or as dealer must inform customers in writing of that involvement at or before the completion of any transaction involving that security.

Discretionary accounts

This reinforces the "fair dealing" rule mentioned above and forbids a member or registered representative from exercising any authority over a customer's account without written authorization. All such activity must be approved in writing by the member, especially with regard to avoiding excessive transactions (churning).

Offerings "at the market"

A member who is in any way financially involved in the primary or secondary distribution of a security not traded on a national exchange may not tell a customer that it is being offered "at the market" unless the member has reason to believe there is another market other than the one made or controlled by the member.

Solicitation of purchases on an exchange to facilitate a distribution of securities

It is prohibited for a member who has a financial interest in the distribution of a security to pay someone to buy any security of that same issuer on an exchange or to pay someone to solicit another person to buy such a security unless the purchase is for that member's own account. This rule is intended to avoid creating false trading activity.

Use of fraudulent devices

This catchall rule simply prohibits members from using manipulation, deception, or fraud to effect any transaction.

Customers' securities or funds

In holding that a member may not make "improper use" of funds or securities belonging to a customer, this rule specifically incorporates the provisions of Rule 15c3-3 (see page 391). In addition, members or associated persons are forbidden to:

1. Lend securities carried for any customer's account without that customer's written authorization (a "loan consent agreement").

2. Lend securities carried for any customer's account which are fully paid for or are excess margin securities (*i.e.*, which exceed the customer's indebtedness) without written authorization. Such securities must be segregated and clearly identified.

3. Guarantee a customer against loss.

4. Share directly or indirectly in the profits or losses of any customer's account without prior written authorization. Any such sharing must be in direct proportion to the financial contributions made to the account by each person. (Note that this provision on proportion does not apply to the accounts of the immediate family of the member or associated person.)

Installment or partial payment sales

Basically, a member cannot transact business for or with a customer on an installment plan.

Books and records

Members are required to keep all records and books in compliance with applicable laws and NASD regulations. In particular, complete customer account forms must be on file. Written complaints from customers, and actions taken in response, must be recorded in a separate file.

Disclosure of financial condition

Members must provide a copy of the firm's most recent balance sheet to any bona fide customer who requests it.

Net prices to persons not in investment banking or securities business

Members may not offer any concession, discount, or other allowance in a securities transaction to any person outside the securities industry. Trades with the general public must be at the net price.

Selling concessions

A member may pay or receive selling concessions only for services rendered; these can be paid only to brokers or dealers actually involved in the investment banking or securities business. Members are prohibited from granting concessions to nonmembers who are not involved in a distribution or to the general public.

Dealing with nonmembers

This rule repeats the strictures on dealing with nonmembers in an underwriting and also forbids transactions with nonmembers on any terms or for any charges other than those offered the general public. An exception is made for nonmember broker/dealers trading in a foreign country and ineligible for membership in a registered securities association. If the transaction involves some allowance, however, the foreign firm must agree to abide by this rule.

Investment companies

Much of the contents of this rule is covered in Chapter 4. It defines terms associated with investment company offerings and includes the following provisions:

Underwriters   Members who are underwriters of an investment company may not sell its shares to any broker/dealer except at the public offering price unless a sales agreement between the parties is in effect.

Sales charge   Members are barred from offering or selling shares in an open-end investment company, or "single payment" plans of a registered unit investment trust, if the public offering price is excessive. Basically, this means any sales charges in excess of 8.5% of the offering price; lower rates are stipulated if dividend reinvestment is not available or if "rights of accumulation" or quantity discounts are not offered.

Other provisions   Members are prohibited from "selling dividends" or with-holding orders so as to make a profit. Members may not purchase these securities from an underwriter (or as an underwriter from the issuer) except to cover purchase orders already received or for their own investment.

Favoring   In selling or distributing shares, members may not favor or disfavor any particular company on the basis of sales commissions or sales incentives.

Supervision

Each member must establish and enforce written procedures that allow proper supervision of each registered representative and associated person to ensure they comply with all applicable laws and rules.

Members are responsible for proper supervision and must designate a partner, officer, or manager in each office of supervisory jurisdiction, including the main office, to carry out the written procedures. An office of supervisory jurisdiction is one designated as responsible for the review of activities of registered representatives in that office or any other office of the member.

In addition, members must periodically review securities transactions and correspondence, customer accounts, etc.

Transactions for personnel of another member

A member who knowingly executes a securities transaction for the employee of another member should try to determine that the transaction will not have an adverse effect on that member's employer. In these cases, the member who executes the order must notify the employer in writing and provide duplicate confirmation to that firm if requested. Notification is not required with investment companies' securities.

A person employed by a member who transacts securities business with another member should notify the employing member of that fact.

Variable contracts of an insurance company

This rule defines variable contracts, sets limits on sales charges, and lists procedures for handling (see page 126).

Margin accounts

Members are prohibited from effecting margin transactions in any manner that does not meet NASD requirements (see page 277). Particulars are set forth in Appendix A to the Rules.

THE UNIFORM PRACTICE CODE

These are rules governing delivery of securities and other practices connected with securities transactions described in Chapter 10.

CODE OF PROCEDURE

This code applies to all proceedings relating to disciplining members, eligibility requirements, and limiting or denying services. As noted above, each of the 13 NASD district committees becomes a District Business Conduct Committee for these purposes.

The District Business Conduct Committee   This committee may issue a complaint itself (for example, if a routine inspection reveals some violation of laws or rules) or can act when it receives a complaint. In either case, the complaint must be detailed in writing; a copy must be sent to the party or parties named in the complaint.

The party(ies) named in the complaint must answer in writing; when the answer is filed, any of those involved (complainant, respondent, or the committee) may request a hearing. The entire committee may sit as a hearing panel or may appoint a hearing panel. At a hearing, both complainant and respondent are entitled to testify and be represented by counsel; documentary evidence, if any, must be submitted before the hearing.

Decisions may be appealed to the NASD Board of Governors, which may uphold the decision and/or reduce or increase any penalty or sanction. Further appeals can be made to the SEC, which can uphold or reverse penalties or sanctions. The SEC may lower, but cannot increase, penalties or sanctions.

CODE OF ARBITRATION

This covers disputes among members and between members and associated persons, public customers, and registered clearing agencies. The NASD board of governors appoints a national arbitration committee, including representatives from the public, which sets rules for arbitration and establishes a pool of arbitrators. A director of arbitration appoints panels from this pool.

Under the code, disputes are arbitrated at the instance of a member against another member, a member against an associated person (or vice versa), an associated person against another associated person, and with any dispute involving a registered clearing agency.

PART TWO
NYSE Regulations

The rules and regulations of the New York Stock Exchange, set out in its Constitution, serve as a model for other, smaller, national exchanges. Details about operation of the exchange are covered in Chapter 8; some of these reflect exchange rules and will be recapitulated here.

THE REGISTERED REPRESENTATIVE

A registered representative is an employee of a NYSE- or NASD-member firm who is licensed to operate as a broker/dealer and who has passed the qualifying ("Series 7") exam. Acting on behalf of that employer, the registered representative is an agent who solicits business (including orders for securities trades) and provides information on investments. The representative must deal fairly with clients.

Note

The term "registered representative" does not apply to those who act only as securities traders or arbitrageurs or who solicit only commodities contracts. A person who sells only government or municipal issues (exempt securities) for a NASD member firm would not be required to take the exam. This exception does not apply to those employed by a NYSE member firm.

Qualifications

Passing the Series 7 Exam is only one step in the registration process. Registered representatives must also be registered with and approved by the exchange itself (employers are responsible for verifying an employee's work record). Candidates must have reached legal majority in the state in which they are working and usually are required to register with that state's securities department.

The registered representative's agreement

All registered representative candidates are required to sign a statement agreeing to abide by the constitution and rules of the NYSE. They must agree to notify their firm in the case of arrest, personal bankruptcy, or involvement in any investigation or litigation involving the securities industry. The firm, in turn, notifies the NYSE. A person confined in a mental institution must also notify his employer, although, in this case, the employer does not necessarily have to inform the exchange.

In addition, prospective registered representatives agree:

- not to agree to pay or actually pay a customer's debit balance without the written consent of the NYSE

- not to guarantee a customer against loss or guarantee a profit

- not to share in the profits or losses of a customer's account

- not to rebate any part of commissions or any other compensation to a customer

- not to keep a personal account except with a member firm or a bank, and that with employer's consent

- not to accept any sort of compensation for a transaction except from the employer without written permission from the NYSE

Fixed duties of registered representative

Full time   The registered representative must devote full time to the job (unless explicitly hired as a part-time employee).

Other work   A representative may accept an after-hours position in another business only with the permission of the employer and the NYSE.

Leave   A registered representative may take leave for up to one year, with the employer's permission (NYSE permission is not required), provided he or she accepts no other employment during that time; the rep may not enter the employer's premises while on leave.

Teaching   A registered representative may teach evening classes on a financial subject for a reasonable fee with an employer's permission.

Termination   Whenever a registered representative or officer leaves a firm, or is transferred to another office, the NYSE Department of Member Firms must be notified of that fact and of the reasons for termination. Registration is not transferable: the representative who joins a new firm must reregister with that firm.

PUBLIC COMMUNICATIONS (ADVERTISING AND SPEAKING)

Published material   All advertising, for use in any medium, and all other communications (research reports, brochures, market letters, etc.) must meet standards of truthfulness and good taste. Members are expected to avoid exaggerated claims or statements; recommendations must be reasonably based and supported by factual information—including the current market price.

Other rules reflect NASD regulations. For example, if a firm recommends a security in which it has some interest, that interest must be disclosed. If testimonials are used, it must be clear that they may not indicate future performance or be said to reflect all customers' experience; any projections must be explicitly identified as estimates.

All literature must be approved by the member firm (usually by an authorized person in the firm); research reports must be approved by a supervisory analyst.

Speaking   The registered representative must get permission from the employer for each speech or lecture course he or she offers. The firm assumes responsibility for the content of any speech or lecture and must keep a record for three years showing:

- sponsoring group's name and the name and address of the person who chaired the program

- topic(s) discussed

- approximate number of people in attendance

- speaker's name

CONDUCT OF ACCOUNTS

A number of rules deal specifically with the handling of customer accounts.

"Know your customer" rule

Every member firm must know the essential facts about every one of its customers, every new or continuing cash or margin account, and every order.

Accordingly, one person in the firm (a general partner, principal executive, or other designated supervisor) is responsible for seeing that essential facts about each customer are recorded and for diligently supervising all the registered representatives' accounts. When a new account is opened, it must be specifically approved before or just after the first transaction is executed. This may be done by a branch manager who determines that all essential facts pertaining to the customer are on record. But the account must still be approved by the firm's designated principal.

Corporate accounts
Special rules apply to dealings with corporations. Member firms cannot open a corporate margin account without determining that the corporation's charter and bylaws permit such transactions. With either a cash or margin account, the member firm must ensure that the individual conducting business in that account is authorized to do so by the corporation.

Other rules
When an account is opened for someone acting as an agent, members must have on file the name of the principal and written proof of the agent's authority. The registered representative is responsible for obtaining certain information about new accounts (see pages 249–250).

It is never permissible to open an account for a third party (though customers can grant power of attorney or open accounts in trust for minors).

Designation of accounts

Accounts carried on a member firm's books must be in the customer's own full name. Customers who wish to transact business through a numbered account may do so, but the firm must have on file a written statement, signed by the customer, attesting to ownership of the account.

"Street name" accounts

When customer-owned securities are held in the name of the broker/dealer, this is called "in street name." The firm is then the "owner of record"; the actual owner is "the beneficial owner."

Voting rights stay with the beneficial owner, who must tell the owner of record how to vote. However, if there is nothing of importance to be voted on, and the firm has mailed proxies 15 days prior to the meeting and received no answer within five days, "in street name" stock may be voted by the firm. This rule was established to make it easier for a corporation to reach a legal quorum at stockholders' meetings.

Accounts of members and allied members in other member firms

Member firms cannot have the account of a member or allied member of another member firm without prior written consent from that firm. This must be signed by a general partner or principal executive, and all transactions must be reported to the person who granted approval.

Accounts of employees of other member firms

Cash accounts   Individuals employed by the NYSE, or by a corporation in which the NYSE has majority holdings, or by any member organization cannot open a cash account at another member firm without written permission from their employers.

Margin accounts   NYSE and member firm employees, as well as employees of banks, trust companies, insurance companies, or of any firm that deals in securities, cannot open a margin account at a member firm without written permission from their employers.

Discretionary accounts

Some accounts (see page 256) give the registered representative power to act on the customer's behalf in choosing securities and in deciding when and how much to buy or sell. All such accounts activity is valid only if there is prior written authorization from the customer giving discretionary power to a third party. (This is not required when the customer simply asks the registered representative to decide when to enter an order or to get, *e.g.*, the "best price.")

Member firms must review such accounts frequently to be sure there is no churning, or excessive trading.

Statements of account

Member firms must send their customers' statements showing securities and cash positions at least quarterly. If the customer so instructs the firm in writing, originals of these statements, as well as confirmations of particular transactions, may be sent to a person holding power of attorney with a duplicate going to the customer.

Designation on orders

No order can be executed on the exchange floor unless the customer's name (or some information designating an account) is on the order. Any change in this designation must be authorized and approved in writing on the order itself.

Records

Member firms are required to keep records of all orders sent to the floor for at least three years.

Errors

The actual price at which an order is executed is binding, even if the price is erroneously reported to the customer verbally or in writing on the confirmation.

Audit

Member firms must be audited by an independent public accountant annually.

ARBITRATION

Disputes

All disputes involving members—for example, between a registered representative and a firm, between two firms, etc.—are handled by the arbitration board of the NYSE. Findings in the arbitration are compulsory and binding; there is no appeal.

Disputes involving nonmembers, such as customers, may also be handled through arbitration if the nonmember agrees to this process. Customers are usually asked to sign an agreement to arbitrate when opening a new account. Arbitrators are chosen from a panel of experienced and knowledgeable individuals. Panels consist of three or four except in disputes involving large sums of money, when there are five arbitrators.

Discipline

Accusations against a NYSE member's employee must be detailed in writing and signed. The accused has 15 days in which to answer in writing. He is entitled to counsel and to cross-examine any witnesses before the panel convened to consider the charge(s). That panel's findings may be appealed to the exchange board of directors, but no further. Unlike NASD rules, NYSE rules do not permit appeals to the SEC or to the courts. The exchange must keep a record of the proceedings and the findings.

LISTING

Chapter 8 gives details of current standards for listing on the NYSE. To recapitulate, a corporation must have at least:

- 2,000 owners of 100 shares or more
- 1.1 million shares publically held
- monthly trading volume of 100,000 shares

- market value of $18,000,000, or net tangible assets of $18,000,000

- earnings of $2.5 million for the last fiscal year and $2 million for the two previous fiscal years to be eligible for listing

These standards are altered occasionally.

PART THREE
MSRB Regulations

Because the courts have ruled that the Constitution bars direct federal regulation of other governmental entities (states, cities, municipal agencies, etc.), municipal securities are not subject to the Securities Act of 1933, mandating registration of new issues, nor do the issuers of such securities have to meet the reporting requirements of the Securities Exchange Act of 1934.

For these reasons, trading in municipals was generally unregulated until 1975, when the Municipal Securities Rulemaking Board (MSRB) was created as part of the Securities Acts Amendments. The 15-member board has five representatives each from banks, brokerage firms, and the public.

While the 1975 legislation could not extend SEC jurisdiction to municipals or their issuers, it could and did effectively extend the provisions of the 1934 Act to those who work professionally in the municipals market—securities firms and banks. The federal anti-fraud provisions and some further rules now apply to transactions involving municipals; in particular, the underwriting of municipal bonds is now subject to federal regulation.

Thus, the MSRB, though it owes its existence to an act of Congress, is not a government agency. It is a self-regulatory organization, the principal rule-maker for the municipal securities industry, financed solely by private firms and banks operating in that industry.

Although MSRB rules have the force of law, *i.e.*, they are issued in compliance with SEC regulations, the board itself does not have the authority to enforce those laws or to inspect industry activities.

Instead, under the 1975 Amendments, authority in the municipal securities industry is delegated to the SEC, NASD, and federal bank regulatory agencies. The 1975 Act assigns these functions as follows:

- MSRB has rulemaking authority only

- SEC has primary enforcement, inspection, and rulemaking authority

- NASD has inspection and enforcement authority for those NASD members who are subject to MSRB rules

Three bank regulatory agencies have the authority to enforce MSRB rules for bank dealers: Comptroller of the Currency (enforces rules governing national banks), Federal Reserve Board (enforces rules governing nonnational banks that are members of the Federal Reserve System), and Federal Deposit Insurance Corporation (FDIC) for all other banks.

Note

NASD member firms that are not members of a national exchange must maintain a fidelity bond. Non-NASD member firms face the same requirement—but these rules do not apply to bank dealers. Hence, the three bank regulatory agencies enforce the appropriate rules for such dealers.

RULES

MSRB Rules are often referred to by number (G1 to G35). It is not possible to discuss each one in detail.

Standards of professional qualification, G2, G3

Only registered representatives may effect transactions. A prospective representative must serve a 90-day apprenticeship during which time he or she would be expected to pass the general securities exam or the municipal securities representative exam. As apprentices, they may not receive commissions (as opposed to straight salary). An apprenticeship can be extended 90 days.

In addition, each firm must have at least two principals who have passed the municipal securities principal's qualifying exam responsible for management and supervision of any activities involving the public. (Firms with 10 or fewer employees need have only one.) An individual whose sole responsibility is supervision of sales may qualify as a municipal securities sales principal by passing this exam. A person who oversees the preparation of financial reports to be filed with the SEC must qualify as a financial and operations principal.

Brokers, G4–7

- Anyone expelled or suspended from any exchange or securities association is disqualified from working as a municipal securities broker.

- A fidelity bond is required for every municipal securities broker.

- A prospective municipal securities broker must furnish an employment record of at least 10 years, including any disciplinary action taken against him.

Keeping of records, G8–10

Municipal securities brokers must keep current books and records. Some records must be kept for six years:

- blotter entries (records of original entries)

- customer accounts

- all positions held in each security

- syndicate transactions
- customer complaints

In addition, other records must be kept for at least three years:

- transactions in progress (transfers, validations, etc.)
- confirmations
- customer information

Municipal underwriting, G11

Sets out requirements for underwriting agreements (see page 147).

Settlement and delivery, G12

Good delivery of bearer bonds requires that the coupons be attached, the legal opinion be imprinted or attached, and that the bonds be uncalled and in denominations of $1,000 and $5,000. Registered bonds must have a proper assignment; these may be in denominations of $1,000 to $100,000.

Quotations, G13

Published quotations must be bona fide bids or offers; nominal quotations (quotes for information) are allowed only if they are so identified.

Reports of purchase and sale, G14

Any reported transaction must represent an actual trade—fictitious or deceptive reports are not permitted.

Customer confirmations, G15

A municipal securities broker or dealer must send a customer written confirmation at or before the completion of a transaction. This must describe the transaction in detail. It must also indicate (among other things):

- a description of the securities
- whether or not the firm acted as principal or agent
- if the securities are callable

Periodic examinations, G16

Every municipal securities firm must be examined by the NASD at least every two years.

Customer treatment, G17, G18

A municipal securities broker/dealer must deal with customers in a fair and honest way. He must try to get the best possible price when executing trades for a customer.

Know your customer, G19

As in the NASD Rules of Fair Practice, municipal securities broker/dealers must believe their recommendations are suitable for the customer; excessive trading (churning) is prohibited.

Gifts, G20

No municipal securities broker/dealer or sales representative may receive (or give) business-related gratuities or gifts valued at more than $100 to or from one person in any one year. This does not include business expenses allowable under the IRS rules, *e.g.,* business dinners or entertainment.

Advertising, G21

False and misleading communications are prohibited. All advertising (including new issue tombstones) and other literature must have prior written approval from a principal of the firm.

Control relationships, G22

Any control relationship between the issuer and the municipal securities professional must be disclosed. Examples would include situations where the professional works for the municipality or where the broker/dealer has financial interest in a firm affected by industrial revenue bonds.

Financial advisors, G23

When a municipal securities firm acts as financial advisor to an issuer, the terms of the relationship (including compensation) must be set out in writing. If the firm sells shares of the issue to its customer, the relationship must be disclosed. If the firm wishes to participate in an underwriting it:

- may be required to terminate its relationship
- must get written permission from the issuer
- must disclose the details of the previous arrangement

Ownership information obtained in fiduciary capacity, G24

This prohibits anyone in the municipal securities industry from using "inside" information in trading except with the issuer's consent.

Improper use of assets, G25

A municipal securities broker/dealer may not misuse municipal securities or funds held on another person's behalf, may not guarantee a customer against loss, and may not share in a customer's profits or losses.

Administration of discretionary accounts, G26

As with other rules governing discretionary accounts (see page 256), customer approval is required. In addition, each transaction must be reviewed and approved in writing by a municipal securities principal of the firm.

Supervision, G27

Sales must be supervised: each firm is required to designate a municipal securities principal and a financial and operations principal; further, each firm must establish and maintain written supervisory procedures in conformance with MSRB rules, including procedures for opening new accounts, for all transactions and related correspondence, for handling customer complaints, and for periodic examination of accounts.

Transactions with employees of other firms, G28

Again, as with NASD rules, no account may be opened for an employee of another municipal securities broker/dealer without prior written notice to the employer; that firm must also receive a duplicate of every confirmation of a trade in the account.

Availability of board rules, G29

All municipal securities broker/dealers must keep a copy of MSRB Rules and make them available to any customer who requests them.

Prices and commissions, G30

When a broker/dealer acts as a principal, he must buy or sell at a price that is fair and reasonable, including the markup or markdown; when acting as an agent, commissions charged must also be fair and reasonable. While this echoes the NASD Rule, there is no 5% guideline policy.

Reciprocal dealings with municipal securities investment companies, G31

A broker who sells for an investment company may not accept any compensation from that company except the normal sales charge nor make any other special deals.

New issue disclosure, G32, G33

Customers who purchase a new municipal issue must receive a final copy of the official statement (or offering circular) either with or prior to final confirmation of the transaction.

In addition, if the new issue involves a negotiated underwriting (see page 147), the customer must also be advised of:

- the amount of the underwriting spread
- the amount of the commission received by the firm
- the offering price for each maturity in the issue

Rule G33 sets out the computations for accrued interest—a 360-day year comprising twelve 30-day months.

An underwriter may not publish an announcement offering new issues unless they are available at the end of the presale period, although such an announcement may indicate certain maturities are available.

CUSIP numbers, G34

A municipal broker or dealer who is the managing underwriter of a new municipal securities issue must apply for a CUSIP (Committee Uniform Securities Identification Procedure) number for the issue and ensure that the number appears on all certificates. This rule took effect July 8, 1983, for all municipal securities that have:

- a par value of at least $500,000, or
- a par value of $250,000 or more where the issuer's outstanding debt exceeds $250,000, or
- where the issuer's outstanding debt exceeds $500,000 (In these cases, an issue of any amount must have a CUSIP number)

Local assessment bonds or notes with maturities of one year or less are exempt from this requirement.

Dispute and arbitration, G35

Disputes within the municipal securities industry are handled with the MRSB code of arbitration. It provides a board of arbitration that is similar to the one used at NASD. There is a six-year statute of limitations of issues brought to the board.

TERMS

Securities Act of 1933

Purpose of act   To ensure that investors receive complete, accurate information on new issues

Registration   All newly issued securities sold interstate must be registered by filing S-1 statement; includes detailed information about issuer and issue

Review process   SEC must review registration before new issue can be sold to public

Cooling-off period   Renewable 20-day interval set aside for review

Effective date   When review has been completed and sales can begin

Deficiency letters   Sent by SEC asking for more information

Stop orders   Issued if SEC thinks registration statement contains misstatements or omissions

Note   SEC does not approve issue, simply reviews for completeness

Preliminary prospectus   Can be issued during review; omits final price, delivery date, and underwriters' spread; must state that this is not an offer to sell or a solicitation to buy

Selling the new issue

Prospectus   Registration data without documentation; must be delivered to purchasers

Advertising   Dealers cannot advertise new issue for 90 days after effective date, except by prospectus or tombstone ads

Mutual funds   If prospectus used more than nine months after effective date, information must be no more than 16 months old

Exempt securities (not subject to registration requirements; subject to anti-fraud provisions)   Government securities; municipals; commercial paper or bankers' acceptances with maturities less than 270 days; instruments issued by common carriers, domestic banks, trust companies, savings and loans, building and loan societies, co-op banks, and nonprofit groups; private placements; intrastate issues; Regulation A filings; fixed annuity contracts and insurance policies

Exempt transactions   Between private individuals; unsolicited broker transactions; private placement, subject to Reg D

Restricted or unregistered securities   Acquired through Reg D transaction or through an employee stock-option plan; governed by Rule 144

Control securities   Those held by a person in control (corporate officers, directors or owners of at least 10% of any class of outstanding securities); also governed by special rules

Intrastate transactions (Rule 147)   Securities sold only intrastate (strictly defined) may be exempt from registration requirements

Reg A offerings

- cannot exceed $1,500,000 in total value in a 12-month period

- issuer must file a notification; offering must take place within 90 days

- if for more than $100,000, must be accompanied by an offering statement

- only advertising permitted is a tombstone

Advertising   Regulates any communication after statement is filed but before issue is registered

Securities and Exchange Act of 1934

Purpose   To bar unfair practices once securities have been issued; regulates exchanges, over-the-counter markets, brokers, dealers; creates SEC as enforcing authority

Registration   All national securities exchanges and any individual or firm engaged in interstate securities transactions must register with (and be regulated by) the SEC

Exemptions   Small local exchanges; brokers who do no business with the public

Prohibited activities

Hypothecation and commingling   Forbidden without written permission

Manipulation and deception   Prohibited, specifically including wash sales, matching orders, false information

Short sales (plus tick rule)   No short sales at a price lower than last reported regular-way sale

Solicitation   Firms may not trade in securities they are underwriting except to stabilize or as market-making transactions 10 business days before distribution

Tender offer   Anyone who makes tender (or exchange) offer may not purchase that security except under terms of that offer

Credit disclosure   Credit terms must be disclosed in writing in margin transactions

Note   No transactions are exempt from Act's anti-fraud provisions

Records

Every broker or dealer, every national securities exchange must keep detailed records

Registered brokers or dealers   Must file income statement and balance sheet annually

Over-the-counter transactions

NASD   Established by Section 15A of 1934 Act to regulate OTC market

Recommendation   Recommendations must be reasonable and suitable for customer

Supervision   Employees of a broker or dealer must be closely supervised

Designated supervisor   Must approve each new account, all security transactions, correspondence, and review customer complaints

Capital requirements

Set by SEC Rules

Investment Company Act of 1940   Defines principal types of investment companies; extends requirements of 1933 and 1934 Acts to them

Investment Advisers Act of 1940   All investment advisers must register with SEC; Amendments (1970 and 1975) govern sales charges

Federal Reserve Board Regulations

Reg U   Limits credit that banks may extend for purchase of listed stocks or bonds

Reg T   Covers extending credit in securities transactions

Securities Investor Protection Corporation (SIPC)

Claim limits   Up to $500,000 per separate customer, not per account, of which not more than $100,000 in cash

Trust Indenture Act of 1939

Concerns corporate bonds; requires appointment of trustee, trust indenture

State regulations

Uniform Securities Act   Model followed by many states

Blue Sky laws   Provide protection similar to federal legislation

Uniform Gifts to Minors Act   Model adopted by most states

Prudent Man rule   State rule governing fiduciaries' actions

Legal lists List of securities institutions may purchase

NASD regulations

Rules of fair practice Concerns member firms' dealings with the public

Uniform practice code Covers dealings between brokerage firms

Code of procedure Deals with violations of rules

NASD code of arbitration For disputes

Eligibility for membership Any broker, dealer, or securities underwriter

Ineligible Commercial banks; anyone suspended or expelled from a self-regulatory organization or by SEC or convicted of certain crimes in preceding 10 years

Registration Member must register as principal or representative

Exemptions Those who deal exclusively in exempt securities, commodities, or listed securities; clerical or administrative personnel; persons who only provide capital

Conditions Principals and representatives must pass qualifying exam; RR's registration is nontransferable

Investment companies

Investment company underwriters may not sell its shares to any broker except at public offering price, unless sales agreement is in effect; sales charge cannot be in excess of 8.5% of the offering price

Members may not

- sell dividends or withhold orders to make a profit
- purchase these securities from underwriter (or from issuer) except to cover purchase orders or for own investment
- favor or disfavor any particular company on the basis of sales commissions or sales incentives

Supervision Members must establish and enforce written procedures of supervising of each RR and associated persons

Transactions for personnel of another member In executing transaction for employee of another member, should determine that transaction will not adversely affect that member's employer; must notify employer in writing

NYSE regs

Registered Representative (RR) Employee of NYSE- or NASD-member firm licensed to operate as a broker

Qualifications   Must pass Series 7 Exam, be registered with and approved by exchange, agree to abide by NYSE Rules; generally must devote full time to job; after-hours work, leave of absence, etc., restricted

Termination   If RR or officer leaves firm or is transferred, NYSE must be notified

Public communications   All published communications must be truthful, in good taste, approved by member firm

Speeches or lectures   RR must get employer permission; firm assumes responsibility for content

Arbitration   Disputes involving members handled by NYSE arbitration committee; findings compulsory and binding; no appeal

MSRB Regs

Municipal securities rulemaking board   Extends provisions of 1934 Act to professionals in municipals market; rulemaking authority only

Professional qualification   Any broker or dealer who conducts transactions in municipal securities must be qualified

Records   Municipal securities broker must keep current books and records

Rules on published quotations, confirmations, execution, recommendations, etc.   Like NASD Rules of Fair Practice

Gifts   No business-related gratuities or gifts worth more than $100 to or from one person in any year

Advertising   Like rules covering other securities

Control relationships   Between issuer and municipal securities professional must be disclosed

Information obtained as fiduciary; use of assets, discretionary accounts, supervision, transactions with employees of other firms   All as with NASD rules

Prices and commissions   Must be fair and reasonable; no 5% guideline policy; special deals not allowed

New issue   Purchasers of new municipal issue receive copy of Official Statement

CUSIP numbers   Managing underwriter of new municipals issue must apply for CUSIP numbers and ensure that number appears on all certificates

REVIEW QUESTIONS

1. All of the following are subject to MSRB regulation EXCEPT:

   (A) the municipal bond department of a NYSE member firm
   (B) the issuing municipalities
   (C) underwriters of municipal bonds
   (D) municipal bond sales personnel

2. The financial statement of a broker/dealer would contain all of the following EXCEPT:

   (A) the firm's balance sheet
   (B) any loans outstanding
   (C) the firm's trading record
   (D) the firm's income statement

3. If a new issue is considered "hot," the rules of fair practice forbid "free riding." Which of the following would fall into that category?

   I. allocating stock to a member of the underwriting firm
   II. allocating stock to partners of other brokerage firms
   III. allocating stock to partners of the underwriting firm

   (A) III only
   (B) I and III only
   (C) II and III only
   (D) I, II, and III

4. Form 144 remains in effect for:

   (A) 30 days
   (B) 45 days
   (C) 60 days
   (D) 90 days

5. The length of time covered by a single registration under Rule 145 is:

   (A) 1 year
   (B) 2 years

   (C) 5 years
   (D) 7 years

6. Which of the following requires full disclosure for public offerings?

   (A) Securities and Exchange Act of 1934
   (B) The Trust Indenture Act of 1939
   (C) The Securities Act of 1933
   (D) The Holding Company Act of 1935

7. The Trust Indenture Act of 1939 applies to all of the following EXCEPT:

   (A) convertible bonds
   (B) revenue bonds
   (C) corporate debentures
   (D) T-bonds

8. All of the following are prohibited under SEC Rule 144 EXCEPT:

   (A) adding a special commission to
       the seller's cost
   (B) selling before notification to the SEC
   (C) selling on an exchange without announcing that it is 144 stock
   (D) soliciting orders from the broker's customers

9. The maximum size of a Reg A offering is:

   (A) $1 million
   (B) $1.5 million
   (C) $2 million
   (D) $5 million

10. On distributing a "hot issue" one may allocate stock to which of the following, provided it is part of one's normal pattern of investment and it is not a substantial part of the total offering?

I. a registered rep of the member firm

II. the father of an employee of the member firm

III. the member firm for its account

IV. an officer of an insurance company

(A) I and II
(B) II and III
(C) II, III, and IV
(D) II and IV

11. The rules on withholding and "free riding" apply to which of the following?

(A) a new issue selling at a discount
(B) a new issue selling at a premium
(C) any listed security
(D) any security

12. Which of the following new issue debt instruments is most likely to be purchased through competitive bidding?

(A) corporate debentures
(B) corporate adjustment bonds
(C) municipal general obligation bonds
(D) municipal water and sewer bonds

13. The bidding procedure on a new municipal bond issue coming out under competitive bidding would be described in the:

(A) Official Notice of Sale
(B) Preliminary Prospectus
(C) *Blue List*
(D) Official Statement

14. Under NASD rules, a mutual fund underwriter may give an account executive which of the following?

(A) A $40 ticket to a Broadway show
(B) a $125 gift certificate
(C) a discount from the price listed in the prospectus
(D) a commission added to the one listed in the prospectus

15. How long after the effective date for a new issue is it before a firm can accept orders for a margin account?

(A) 30 days
(B) 45 days
(C) 60 days
(D) 90 days

16. The decision to allow an over-the-counter stock to be bought on margin is made by the:

(A) NASD
(B) Federal Reserve Board
(C) SEC
(D) market makers

Questions 17 and 18 are based on the following information: An investor enters an order to sell short 100 ACI at $45\frac{1}{2}$ on a stop limit. The last recorded round lot sale was at $45\frac{7}{8}$. Subsequently there are round lot sales at $45\frac{3}{8}$, $45\frac{3}{8}$, $45\frac{5}{8}$ and $45\frac{1}{2}$.

17. The sale that triggers this order is at:
(A) $45\frac{3}{8}$
(B) $45\frac{1}{2}$
(C) $45\frac{5}{8}$
(D) $45\frac{7}{8}$

18. The sale that causes this order to be executed is at:
(A) $45\frac{3}{8}$
(B) $45\frac{1}{2}$
(C) $45\frac{5}{8}$
(D) $45\frac{7}{8}$

19. If a registered representative and a firm agree to an arbitration proceedings in some dispute, NYSE rules say that the decision:

   (A) may never be appealed
   (B) may be appealed to the NYSE
   (C) may be appealed to the NASD
   (D) may be appealed to the SEC

20. What is the margin account value of listed long call options?

   (A) the same as the premium
   (B) the premium minus the out of the moneyness
   (C) the in the moneyness minus the premium
   (D) they have no value for margin account uses

21. Trading volume in ACI over the past six weeks was:

   last week   20,000 shares
   two weeks ago   25,000 shares
   three weeks ago 20,000 shares
   four weeks ago   24,000 shares
   five weeks ago   20,000 shares
   six weeks ago   15,000 shares

   If there are 2 million shares outstanding and an investor owns 100,000 shares of restricted stock, what is the maximum number he could sell under Rule 144?

   (A) 20,000
   (B) 25,000
   (C) 22,250
   (D) 24,250

22. Which legislation empowered the Federal Reserve to set margin requirements?

   (A) The Securities Act of 1933
   (B) The Securities and Exchange Act of 1934
   (C) The Banking Act of 1937
   (D) The Trust Indenture Act of 1940

23. The amount banks may lend on rehypothecated securities is regulated by:

   (A) Reg T
   (B) Reg U
   (C) SEC rules
   (D) what the bank feels is prudent

24. The Securities Act Amendments of 1975 set enforcement responsibility of MSRB rules with all of the following EXCEPT:

   (A) NASD
   (B) NYSE
   (C) SEC
   (D) Comptroller of the Currency

25. All of the following are represented on the MSRB EXCEPT:

   (A) banks
   (B) bond attorneys
   (C) brokerage firms
   (D) the general public

ANSWERS TO REVIEW QUESTIONS

1. **(B)** MSRB rules do not regulate the issuer.

2. **(C)** The trading record of the broker is not part of the firm's financial statement.

3. **(D)** All of these are forbidden.

4. **(D)** After this period, a new notification to the SEC is required.

5. **(B)** Rules for disposing of the stock mirror those of Rule 144. The difference is in how the stock was acquired.

6. **(C)** This was the first major legislation regulating securities. It was designed to prevent fraud in the issuance of new securities.

7. **(D)** U.S. government securities are specifically exempt from the provisions of the act.

8. **(A)** Such a fee may be allowed. It takes into account the potentially more difficult task of selling such stock.

9. **(D)** By definition.

10. **(D)** The others are forbidden to receive stock under any circumstances.

11. **(B)** The rules apply to hot issues. Only choice B fits that description.

12. **(C)** Municipal general obligation bonds usually must be sold through competitive bidding.

13. **(A)** This is usually published in the daily *Bond Buyer's Guide.*

14. **(A)** Gifts are limited to $100. The other two choices are not allowed.

15. **(D)** The Fed decides which securities are marginable.

16. **(B)** In general, listed stocks are marginable, and some OTC stocks are after designation by the Fed.

17. **(A)** A sell stop is a stop below the market. Hence $45\frac{3}{8}$ triggers the stop.

18. **(C)** This is an up tick and satisfies the $45\frac{1}{2}$ limit.

19. **(A)** There is no appeal from NYSE arbitration.

20. **(D)** Long options have no margin value since they expire after some time. If an option is exercised, the stock received may have margin value.

21. **(C)** The average for the past four weeks is 22,250 and 1% of 2 million shares is 20,000. Under Rule 144 the larger of these two amounts may be sold.

22. **(B)** This act empowers the Fed to set margin requirements and to regulate exchanges and brokers.

23. **(B)** The amount of stock the broker may use as collateral is restricted to 140% of the debit balance.

24. **(B)** Other bank regulatory agencies (FDIC, FRB) also have enforcement responsibility.

25. **(B)** The fifteen members of the board are chosen five each from the other three groups.

THREE PRACTICE EXAMINATIONS

practice
examination
one

PRACTICE EXAMINATION ONE
Answer Sheet

PART ONE

1 Ⓐ Ⓑ Ⓒ Ⓓ	37 Ⓐ Ⓑ Ⓒ Ⓓ	73 Ⓐ Ⓑ Ⓒ Ⓓ	109 Ⓐ Ⓑ Ⓒ Ⓓ
2 Ⓐ Ⓑ Ⓒ Ⓓ	38 Ⓐ Ⓑ Ⓒ Ⓓ	74 Ⓐ Ⓑ Ⓒ Ⓓ	110 Ⓐ Ⓑ Ⓒ Ⓓ
3 Ⓐ Ⓑ Ⓒ Ⓓ	39 Ⓐ Ⓑ Ⓒ Ⓓ	75 Ⓐ Ⓑ Ⓒ Ⓓ	111 Ⓐ Ⓑ Ⓒ Ⓓ
4 Ⓐ Ⓑ Ⓒ Ⓓ	40 Ⓐ Ⓑ Ⓒ Ⓓ	76 Ⓐ Ⓑ Ⓒ Ⓓ	112 Ⓐ Ⓑ Ⓒ Ⓓ
5 Ⓐ Ⓑ Ⓒ Ⓓ	41 Ⓐ Ⓑ Ⓒ Ⓓ	77 Ⓐ Ⓑ Ⓒ Ⓓ	113 Ⓐ Ⓑ Ⓒ Ⓓ
6 Ⓐ Ⓑ Ⓒ Ⓓ	42 Ⓐ Ⓑ Ⓒ Ⓓ	78 Ⓐ Ⓑ Ⓒ Ⓓ	114 Ⓐ Ⓑ Ⓒ Ⓓ
7 Ⓐ Ⓑ Ⓒ Ⓓ	43 Ⓐ Ⓑ Ⓒ Ⓓ	79 Ⓐ Ⓑ Ⓒ Ⓓ	115 Ⓐ Ⓑ Ⓒ Ⓓ
8 Ⓐ Ⓑ Ⓒ Ⓓ	44 Ⓐ Ⓑ Ⓒ Ⓓ	80 Ⓐ Ⓑ Ⓒ Ⓓ	116 Ⓐ Ⓑ Ⓒ Ⓓ
9 Ⓐ Ⓑ Ⓒ Ⓓ	45 Ⓐ Ⓑ Ⓒ Ⓓ	81 Ⓐ Ⓑ Ⓒ Ⓓ	117 Ⓐ Ⓑ Ⓒ Ⓓ
10 Ⓐ Ⓑ Ⓒ Ⓓ	46 Ⓐ Ⓑ Ⓒ Ⓓ	82 Ⓐ Ⓑ Ⓒ Ⓓ	118 Ⓐ Ⓑ Ⓒ Ⓓ
11 Ⓐ Ⓑ Ⓒ Ⓓ	47 Ⓐ Ⓑ Ⓒ Ⓓ	83 Ⓐ Ⓑ Ⓒ Ⓓ	119 Ⓐ Ⓑ Ⓒ Ⓓ
12 Ⓐ Ⓑ Ⓒ Ⓓ	48 Ⓐ Ⓑ Ⓒ Ⓓ	84 Ⓐ Ⓑ Ⓒ Ⓓ	120 Ⓐ Ⓑ Ⓒ Ⓓ
13 Ⓐ Ⓑ Ⓒ Ⓓ	49 Ⓐ Ⓑ Ⓒ Ⓓ	85 Ⓐ Ⓑ Ⓒ Ⓓ	121 Ⓐ Ⓑ Ⓒ Ⓓ
14 Ⓐ Ⓑ Ⓒ Ⓓ	50 Ⓐ Ⓑ Ⓒ Ⓓ	86 Ⓐ Ⓑ Ⓒ Ⓓ	122 Ⓐ Ⓑ Ⓒ Ⓓ
15 Ⓐ Ⓑ Ⓒ Ⓓ	51 Ⓐ Ⓑ Ⓒ Ⓓ	87 Ⓐ Ⓑ Ⓒ Ⓓ	123 Ⓐ Ⓑ Ⓒ Ⓓ
16 Ⓐ Ⓑ Ⓒ Ⓓ	52 Ⓐ Ⓑ Ⓒ Ⓓ	88 Ⓐ Ⓑ Ⓒ Ⓓ	124 Ⓐ Ⓑ Ⓒ Ⓓ
17 Ⓐ Ⓑ Ⓒ Ⓓ	53 Ⓐ Ⓑ Ⓒ Ⓓ	89 Ⓐ Ⓑ Ⓒ Ⓓ	125 Ⓐ Ⓑ Ⓒ Ⓓ
18 Ⓐ Ⓑ Ⓒ Ⓓ	54 Ⓐ Ⓑ Ⓒ Ⓓ	90 Ⓐ Ⓑ Ⓒ Ⓓ	
19 Ⓐ Ⓑ Ⓒ Ⓓ	55 Ⓐ Ⓑ Ⓒ Ⓓ	91 Ⓐ Ⓑ Ⓒ Ⓓ	
20 Ⓐ Ⓑ Ⓒ Ⓓ	56 Ⓐ Ⓑ Ⓒ Ⓓ	92 Ⓐ Ⓑ Ⓒ Ⓓ	
21 Ⓐ Ⓑ Ⓒ Ⓓ	57 Ⓐ Ⓑ Ⓒ Ⓓ	93 Ⓐ Ⓑ Ⓒ Ⓓ	
22 Ⓐ Ⓑ Ⓒ Ⓓ	58 Ⓐ Ⓑ Ⓒ Ⓓ	94 Ⓐ Ⓑ Ⓒ Ⓓ	
23 Ⓐ Ⓑ Ⓒ Ⓓ	59 Ⓐ Ⓑ Ⓒ Ⓓ	95 Ⓐ Ⓑ Ⓒ Ⓓ	
24 Ⓐ Ⓑ Ⓒ Ⓓ	60 Ⓐ Ⓑ Ⓒ Ⓓ	96 Ⓐ Ⓑ Ⓒ Ⓓ	
25 Ⓐ Ⓑ Ⓒ Ⓓ	61 Ⓐ Ⓑ Ⓒ Ⓓ	97 Ⓐ Ⓑ Ⓒ Ⓓ	
26 Ⓐ Ⓑ Ⓒ Ⓓ	62 Ⓐ Ⓑ Ⓒ Ⓓ	98 Ⓐ Ⓑ Ⓒ Ⓓ	
27 Ⓐ Ⓑ Ⓒ Ⓓ	63 Ⓐ Ⓑ Ⓒ Ⓓ	99 Ⓐ Ⓑ Ⓒ Ⓓ	
28 Ⓐ Ⓑ Ⓒ Ⓓ	64 Ⓐ Ⓑ Ⓒ Ⓓ	100 Ⓐ Ⓑ Ⓒ Ⓓ	
29 Ⓐ Ⓑ Ⓒ Ⓓ	65 Ⓐ Ⓑ Ⓒ Ⓓ	101 Ⓐ Ⓑ Ⓒ Ⓓ	
30 Ⓐ Ⓑ Ⓒ Ⓓ	66 Ⓐ Ⓑ Ⓒ Ⓓ	102 Ⓐ Ⓑ Ⓒ Ⓓ	
31 Ⓐ Ⓑ Ⓒ Ⓓ	67 Ⓐ Ⓑ Ⓒ Ⓓ	103 Ⓐ Ⓑ Ⓒ Ⓓ	
32 Ⓐ Ⓑ Ⓒ Ⓓ	68 Ⓐ Ⓑ Ⓒ Ⓓ	104 Ⓐ Ⓑ Ⓒ Ⓓ	
33 Ⓐ Ⓑ Ⓒ Ⓓ	69 Ⓐ Ⓑ Ⓒ Ⓓ	105 Ⓐ Ⓑ Ⓒ Ⓓ	
34 Ⓐ Ⓑ Ⓒ Ⓓ	70 Ⓐ Ⓑ Ⓒ Ⓓ	106 Ⓐ Ⓑ Ⓒ Ⓓ	
35 Ⓐ Ⓑ Ⓒ Ⓓ	71 Ⓐ Ⓑ Ⓒ Ⓓ	107 Ⓐ Ⓑ Ⓒ Ⓓ	
36 Ⓐ Ⓑ Ⓒ Ⓓ	72 Ⓐ Ⓑ Ⓒ Ⓓ	108 Ⓐ Ⓑ Ⓒ Ⓓ	

PRACTICE EXAMINATION ONE
Answer Sheet

PART TWO

126 Ⓐ Ⓑ Ⓒ Ⓓ 162 Ⓐ Ⓑ Ⓒ Ⓓ 198 Ⓐ Ⓑ Ⓒ Ⓓ 234 Ⓐ Ⓑ Ⓒ Ⓓ
127 Ⓐ Ⓑ Ⓒ Ⓓ 163 Ⓐ Ⓑ Ⓒ Ⓓ 199 Ⓐ Ⓑ Ⓒ Ⓓ 235 Ⓐ Ⓑ Ⓒ Ⓓ
128 Ⓐ Ⓑ Ⓒ Ⓓ 164 Ⓐ Ⓑ Ⓒ Ⓓ 200 Ⓐ Ⓑ Ⓒ Ⓓ 236 Ⓐ Ⓑ Ⓒ Ⓓ
129 Ⓐ Ⓑ Ⓒ Ⓓ 165 Ⓐ Ⓑ Ⓒ Ⓓ 201 Ⓐ Ⓑ Ⓒ Ⓓ 237 Ⓐ Ⓑ Ⓒ Ⓓ
130 Ⓐ Ⓑ Ⓒ Ⓓ 166 Ⓐ Ⓑ Ⓒ Ⓓ 202 Ⓐ Ⓑ Ⓒ Ⓓ 238 Ⓐ Ⓑ Ⓒ Ⓓ
131 Ⓐ Ⓑ Ⓒ Ⓓ 167 Ⓐ Ⓑ Ⓒ Ⓓ 203 Ⓐ Ⓑ Ⓒ Ⓓ 239 Ⓐ Ⓑ Ⓒ Ⓓ
132 Ⓐ Ⓑ Ⓒ Ⓓ 168 Ⓐ Ⓑ Ⓒ Ⓓ 204 Ⓐ Ⓑ Ⓒ Ⓓ 240 Ⓐ Ⓑ Ⓒ Ⓓ
133 Ⓐ Ⓑ Ⓒ Ⓓ 169 Ⓐ Ⓑ Ⓒ Ⓓ 205 Ⓐ Ⓑ Ⓒ Ⓓ 241 Ⓐ Ⓑ Ⓒ Ⓓ
134 Ⓐ Ⓑ Ⓒ Ⓓ 170 Ⓐ Ⓑ Ⓒ Ⓓ 206 Ⓐ Ⓑ Ⓒ Ⓓ 242 Ⓐ Ⓑ Ⓒ Ⓓ
135 Ⓐ Ⓑ Ⓒ Ⓓ 171 Ⓐ Ⓑ Ⓒ Ⓓ 207 Ⓐ Ⓑ Ⓒ Ⓓ 243 Ⓐ Ⓑ Ⓒ Ⓓ
136 Ⓐ Ⓑ Ⓒ Ⓓ 172 Ⓐ Ⓑ Ⓒ Ⓓ 208 Ⓐ Ⓑ Ⓒ Ⓓ 244 Ⓐ Ⓑ Ⓒ Ⓓ
137 Ⓐ Ⓑ Ⓒ Ⓓ 173 Ⓐ Ⓑ Ⓒ Ⓓ 209 Ⓐ Ⓑ Ⓒ Ⓓ 245 Ⓐ Ⓑ Ⓒ Ⓓ
138 Ⓐ Ⓑ Ⓒ Ⓓ 174 Ⓐ Ⓑ Ⓒ Ⓓ 210 Ⓐ Ⓑ Ⓒ Ⓓ 246 Ⓐ Ⓑ Ⓒ Ⓓ
139 Ⓐ Ⓑ Ⓒ Ⓓ 175 Ⓐ Ⓑ Ⓒ Ⓓ 211 Ⓐ Ⓑ Ⓒ Ⓓ 247 Ⓐ Ⓑ Ⓒ Ⓓ
140 Ⓐ Ⓑ Ⓒ Ⓓ 176 Ⓐ Ⓑ Ⓒ Ⓓ 212 Ⓐ Ⓑ Ⓒ Ⓓ 248 Ⓐ Ⓑ Ⓒ Ⓓ
141 Ⓐ Ⓑ Ⓒ Ⓓ 177 Ⓐ Ⓑ Ⓒ Ⓓ 213 Ⓐ Ⓑ Ⓒ Ⓓ 249 Ⓐ Ⓑ Ⓒ Ⓓ
142 Ⓐ Ⓑ Ⓒ Ⓓ 178 Ⓐ Ⓑ Ⓒ Ⓓ 214 Ⓐ Ⓑ Ⓒ Ⓓ 250 Ⓐ Ⓑ Ⓒ Ⓓ
143 Ⓐ Ⓑ Ⓒ Ⓓ 179 Ⓐ Ⓑ Ⓒ Ⓓ 215 Ⓐ Ⓑ Ⓒ Ⓓ
144 Ⓐ Ⓑ Ⓒ Ⓓ 180 Ⓐ Ⓑ Ⓒ Ⓓ 216 Ⓐ Ⓑ Ⓒ Ⓓ
145 Ⓐ Ⓑ Ⓒ Ⓓ 181 Ⓐ Ⓑ Ⓒ Ⓓ 217 Ⓐ Ⓑ Ⓒ Ⓓ
146 Ⓐ Ⓑ Ⓒ Ⓓ 182 Ⓐ Ⓑ Ⓒ Ⓓ 218 Ⓐ Ⓑ Ⓒ Ⓓ
147 Ⓐ Ⓑ Ⓒ Ⓓ 183 Ⓐ Ⓑ Ⓒ Ⓓ 219 Ⓐ Ⓑ Ⓒ Ⓓ
148 Ⓐ Ⓑ Ⓒ Ⓓ 184 Ⓐ Ⓑ Ⓒ Ⓓ 220 Ⓐ Ⓑ Ⓒ Ⓓ
149 Ⓐ Ⓑ Ⓒ Ⓓ 185 Ⓐ Ⓑ Ⓒ Ⓓ 221 Ⓐ Ⓑ Ⓒ Ⓓ
150 Ⓐ Ⓑ Ⓒ Ⓓ 186 Ⓐ Ⓑ Ⓒ Ⓓ 222 Ⓐ Ⓑ Ⓒ Ⓓ
151 Ⓐ Ⓑ Ⓒ Ⓓ 187 Ⓐ Ⓑ Ⓒ Ⓓ 223 Ⓐ Ⓑ Ⓒ Ⓓ
152 Ⓐ Ⓑ Ⓒ Ⓓ 188 Ⓐ Ⓑ Ⓒ Ⓓ 224 Ⓐ Ⓑ Ⓒ Ⓓ
153 Ⓐ Ⓑ Ⓒ Ⓓ 189 Ⓐ Ⓑ Ⓒ Ⓓ 225 Ⓐ Ⓑ Ⓒ Ⓓ
154 Ⓐ Ⓑ Ⓒ Ⓓ 190 Ⓐ Ⓑ Ⓒ Ⓓ 226 Ⓐ Ⓑ Ⓒ Ⓓ
155 Ⓐ Ⓑ Ⓒ Ⓓ 191 Ⓐ Ⓑ Ⓒ Ⓓ 227 Ⓐ Ⓑ Ⓒ Ⓓ
156 Ⓐ Ⓑ Ⓒ Ⓓ 192 Ⓐ Ⓑ Ⓒ Ⓓ 228 Ⓐ Ⓑ Ⓒ Ⓓ
157 Ⓐ Ⓑ Ⓒ Ⓓ 193 Ⓐ Ⓑ Ⓒ Ⓓ 229 Ⓐ Ⓑ Ⓒ Ⓓ
158 Ⓐ Ⓑ Ⓒ Ⓓ 194 Ⓐ Ⓑ Ⓒ Ⓓ 230 Ⓐ Ⓑ Ⓒ Ⓓ
159 Ⓐ Ⓑ Ⓒ Ⓓ 195 Ⓐ Ⓑ Ⓒ Ⓓ 231 Ⓐ Ⓑ Ⓒ Ⓓ
160 Ⓐ Ⓑ Ⓒ Ⓓ 196 Ⓐ Ⓑ Ⓒ Ⓓ 232 Ⓐ Ⓑ Ⓒ Ⓓ
161 Ⓐ Ⓑ Ⓒ Ⓓ 197 Ⓐ Ⓑ Ⓒ Ⓓ 233 Ⓐ Ⓑ Ⓒ Ⓓ

PART ONE

Time   3 Hours

Questions   1–125

DIRECTIONS

Each of the questions or incomplete statements below is followed by four suggested answer options. Choose the best answer and then blacken the corresponding space on the answer sheet.

1. All of the following transactions must be executed in a cash account EXCEPT:

    (A) buying a call
    (B) buying a put
    (C) buying a marginable security
    (D) buying a spread

2. Options expire at:

    (A) 3:00 P.M. Central Time on the third Friday of the expiration month.
    (B) 4:30 P.M. Central Time on the third Friday of the expiration month.
    (C) 4:30 P.M. Central Time on the third Saturday of the expiration month.
    (D) 10:59 P.M. Central Time on the third Saturday of the expiration month.

3. An out-of-the-money option has a premium of $400. This premium reflects:

    (A) $400 of intrinsic value
    (B) $400 of time value
    (C) $200 of intrinsic and $200 of time value
    (D) some indeterminable mix of intrinsic and time value

4. Under which of the following circumstances may a registered representative purchase a hot issue from his own firm?

    (A) Never
    (B) If it is part of his regular trading pattern
    (C) For family members, if it is in their regular pattern
    (D) If the purchase represents a small part of the total issue

5. A mutual fund bid at $9.30 has a 7% load. What is the offer price?

    (A) $8.65
    (B) $9.30
    (C) $10.00
    (D) $10.70

6. Registering an offering with the SEC ensures that the:

    (A) SEC has changed the facts in the registration statement
    (B) SEC has approved this investment
    (C) statement includes the relevant facts about the issue
    (D) issue is suitable for investment by the public

7. Under NASD rules, a guilty finding by the District Business Conduct Committee may be appealed first to:

(A) NASD Board of Arbitration
(B) NASD Board of Governors
(C) SEC
(D) courts in the state where the alleged infraction takes place

Use the following information to answer Questions 8 and 9.

A firm has $100,000,000 in convertible securities outstanding. These pay 5% and have a conversion price of $40. The firm induces investors to trade $60,000,000 of these convertibles into nonconvertibles by paying a $5,000,000 premium.

8. If the firm has 10,000,000 shares outstanding and all of the remaining convertible securities are converted, the firm will experience dilution of:

(A) 5%
(B) 10%
(C) 15%
(D) 20%

9. The effect of trading $60,000,000 for nonconvertible securities will be:

(A) to increase the debt and decrease the cash position of the firm
(B) to increase the potential dilution effect and decrease the cash position
(C) to decrease the potential dilution effect and to decrease the cash position
(D) to decrease the potential dilution effect and to increase the debt position

10. Which of the following trades would appear on the consolidated tape?

I. Exchange market
II. Primary market
III. Options market
IV. Third market

(A) I and II
(B) II and IV
(C) I and III
(D) I and IV

11. Which investment would provide Amalgamated Consolidated Inc., with the best return? Assume a 25% tax rate.

(A) 4% municipal bond
(B) 6% corporate bond
(C) Common stock yielding 5%
(D) Preferred stock yielding 6%

12. All of the following change the terms of a listed option EXCEPT:

(A) a 2% stock dividend
(B) a 1 for 3 reverse split
(C) a $.10 cash dividend
(D) a rights distribution

13. A fund with NAV of $10 sells at $9.50. It is:

(A) a closed-end fund
(B) an open-end fund
(C) a front-end load fund
(D) a no-load fund

14. A depreciation deduction would be available on each of the following EXCEPT:

(A) subsidized housing
(B) a shopping center
(C) developable acreage
(D) single-family homes

15. The NYSE margin requirements for $50,000 of municipals which sold for $30,000 would be:

(A) $3,000
(B) $3,500
(C) $4,500
(D) $30,000

16. Eurodollar bonds are:

    I. denominated in a European currency
    II. denominated in U.S. dollars
    III. issued in the U.S.
    IV. traded in the U.S.

    (A) I and III
    (B) II and III
    (C) I and IV
    (D) II and IV

17. If a municipal bond issue is pre-refunded, all of the following are true EXCEPT:

    (A) the interest, principal, and call premium are covered
    (B) covering funds are on deposit in an escrow account
    (C) covering funds are invested in U.S. Treasury securities
    (D) this usually occurs when rates rise

18. A quote of 101.08 for a $100,000 T-bond would mean a dollar amount of:

    (A) $100,108
    (B) $100,250
    (C) $101,080
    (D) $101,250

19. Stocks with a high negative beta could be characterized as being:

    (A) defensive
    (B) aggressive
    (C) low volatility
    (D) blue chip

20. The purchaser of an index option call would be hoping for:

    (A) a decline in the stock market
    (B) a rise in the stock market
    (C) a rise in the bond index
    (D) a decline in the bond index

21. After-tax income is maximized for someone in the 28% tax bracket by purchasing a:

    (A) 7% T-bill
    (B) 8% corporate bond
    (C) 6% tax-exempt municipal bond
    (D) $7\frac{1}{2}$% T-bond

22. A broker might be disqualified by the MSRB for all of the following reasons EXCEPT:

    (A) conviction on an attempt to defraud a customer
    (B) expulsion from the NASD
    (C) conviction of a failure to make full disclosure of a conflict of interest on a transaction
    (D) conviction on a moving traffic violation

23. Dollar cost averaging results in:

    (A) buying the same number of shares each time
    (B) buying more shares when the price is high
    (C) buying more shares when the price is low
    (D) buying an average number of shares each year

Questions 24 and 25 refer to the following:

Write 2 ACI Mar 40 Calls at 6

Buy 2 ACI Mar 50 Calls at $1\frac{1}{2}$

24. The maximum possible profit on these trades is:

    (A) $900
    (B) $1,200
    (C) $1,400
    (D) $2,300

25. The maximum loss would occur if, at expiration, ACI is:

    (A) 40
    (B) $41\frac{1}{2}$
    (C) 46
    (D) 50

26. An investor buys a $10,000 par value municipal bond in the market for $8,800. Assume he is in the 28% tax bracket. If he holds it to maturity, his taxable income is:

    (A) none
    (B) $1,200 of ordinary income
    (C) $1,200 of capital gain
    (D) $600 of ordinary income and $600 of capital gain

27. If ACI has a high dividend payout ratio, we can expect:

    (A) stockholders' equity will grow slowly
    (B) earnings per share will rise rapidly
    (C) stockholders' equity will shrink
    (D) earnings per share will shrink

28. The margin requirement specified by the NYSE for investors wishing to purchase when-issued stock is:

    (A) 15%
    (B) 25%
    (C) 30%
    (D) 50%

29. Which of the following is most likely to generate large current deductions and possible future cash flow?

    (A) Oil and gas development programs
    (B) Buying triple-net leasebacks
    (C) Undeveloped land
    (D) Oil and gas exploratory programs

30. All of the following are quoted in 32nds EXCEPT:

    (A) T-bonds
    (B) T-bills
    (C) GNMAs
    (D) T-notes

31. To get the most complete financial information about a new issue of municipal securities, one should consult the:

    (A) prospectus
    (B) official statement
    (C) registration statement
    (D) tombstone

32. The yield on a common stock is determined from:

    (A) earnings and P/E (price/earnings) ratio
    (B) dividends and P/E
    (C) dividends and price
    (D) earnings and assets

33. Regulations for municipal securities are issued by all of the following EXCEPT:

    (A) SIPC
    (B) MSRB
    (C) NASD
    (D) SEC

34. When investors redeem CDs and buy common stocks, they are causing:

    (A) inflation
    (B) diversification
    (C) refinancing
    (D) disintermediation

35. All of the following are likely to be in a syndication letter EXCEPT:

    (A) the amount of the bid
    (B) the duration of the account
    (C) the type of account
    (D) the member participation level

36. What are Fannie Mae securities?

    (A) Packages of commercial mortgages
    (B) Short-term discount notes and debentures
    (C) Packages of FHA and VA mortgages
    (D) Industrial development bonds

The following information is to be used in connection with Questions 37–39.

Shares	Purchase Price	Market Price	Market Value
200 ACI	$40	$35	$7,000
100 CAI	$50	$40	$4,000
100 XYZ	$70	$30	$3,000
Debit Balance			$10,000

37. For the account to become unrestricted again, how much cash would the investor have to deposit?

(A) $250
(B) $2,000
(C) $3,000
(D) $3,500

38. What is the minimum maintenance requirement on this account?

(A) $2,000
(B) $3,500
(C) $5,000
(D) $6,500

39. At which of the following market values would a maintenance margin call be sent?

(A) $12,500
(B) $13,500
(C) $14,500
(D) A call would already have been sent.

40. The coverage on revenue bonds refers to the ratio of:

(A) gross revenue to operating expenses
(B) gross revenue to interest expenses
(C) net revenue to debt service
(D) net revenue to annual interest expense

Questions 41–43 refer to the information below:

An investor's margin account has the following information:

Long Market Value	Debit Record	SMA
$40,000	$23,000	$1,500

41. What is the buying power in the account?

(A) $0
(B) $750
(C) $1,500
(D) $3,000

42. How much equity does the investor have?

(A) $1,500
(B) $17,000
(C) $23,000
(D) $40,000

43. If the investor sold $5,000 from this account, what is the total amount the investor could remove?

(A) $0
(B) $1,500
(C) $2,500
(D) $4,000

44. According to MSRB rules, all of the following would be an acceptable gift from one registered representative to another EXCEPT:

(A) two $40 tickets to the theater
(B) video tapes worth $75
(C) a $200 business dinner
(D) a gift certificate for $50

45. With Regulation T at 50%, a customer sells short 200 shares of ACI at 50 and deposits the appropriate margin. If the price of ACI drops to 40, how much

excess cash can the customer remove from the account?

(A) $1,000
(B) $2,000
(C) $3,000
(D) $5,000

The following information should be used to answer Questions 46 and 47:

An investor writes an ACI Nov 60 straddle at 4. The put is exercised at expiration when the market price is 50. The investor resells 100 shares of ACI for $5,000.

46. His net for these transactions is:

(A) $400 profit
(B) $600 profit
(C) $600 loss
(D) $1,000 loss

47. If prior to being exercised, the investor had bought the same straddle at 9, he would realize:

(A) $900 capital loss
(B) $900 ordinary loss
(C) $500 capital loss
(D) $500 ordinary loss

Questions 48–50 refer to the following choices:

(A) balanced fund
(B) income fund
(C) growth fund
(D) load fund

Choose the type of fund that best describes the funds listed in the questions below:

48. AAA Fund invests primarily in money market instruments.

49. BBB Fund is loaded up with equities of firms that reinvest most earnings.

50. CCC Fund has a portfolio of stocks, bonds, and preferred stocks.

51. An investor would like to find a large inventory of New York City general obligation bonds. He should consult the:

(A) pink sheets
(B) yellow sheets
(C) *Blue List*
(D) *Bond Buyer Index*

52. A put option is out of the money if the strike price is:

(A) below the market price
(B) at the market price
(C) above the market price
(D) below the exercise price

53. One of two partners in a partnership account dies. The registered representative should:

(A) close the account
(B) freeze the account
(C) liquidate all short positions
(D) accept only cash orders

Questions 54–56 are based on the following combination of trades:

Mr. Smith buys 1 ACI Nov 50 Call at 7 and 1 ACI Nov 50 Put at 3.

54. What is the maximum possible loss on these trades?
(A) Unlimited
(B) $300
(C) $700
(D) $1,000

55. What is the maximum possible gain on these trades?

(A) Unlimited
(B) $300
(C) $700
(D) $1,000

56. If ACI goes to 30 at expiration and the investor has not exercised beforehand, his profit (or loss) would be:

(A) $1,000
(B) $1,300
(C) $1,700
(D) $2,000

57. The effective return on a municipal bond with a coupon of 8% for an investor in the 28% bracket is:

(A) 8%
(B) 10.8%
(C) 11.1%
(D) 12.8%

Questions 58–61 make use of the following information:

An investor buys $100,000 of a real estate program. For 1991, his portion generates revenues of $200,000 and expenses of $150,000. Additionally, there are $50,000 of interest payments and $25,000 of depreciation.

58. What net gain (loss) is passed through to this investor for 1991?

(A) $25,000 gain
(B) $0
(C) $25,000 loss
(D) $50,000 loss

59. How much operating income is generated?

(A) $25,000 loss
(B) $0
(C) $25,000 gain
(D) $50,000 gain

60. What is the cash flow for his portion of the program?

(A) $0
(B) $15,000
(C) $25,000
(D) $40,000

61. If the investor is in the 31% tax bracket and has $40,000 of other passive income, this program will result in a:

(A) net tax saving of $12,300
(B) net tax saving of $7,750
(C) total tax bill for passive income of $12,300
(D) total tax bill for passive income of $7,750

62. Which of the following is true of T-bonds?

(A) They have little inflation risk.
(B) They have little interest rate risk.
(C) They have little credit risk.
(D) They are not widely available.

63. Which of the following pairs are on the same side of the market?

 I. Long calls and long puts
 II. Long calls and short puts
 III. Short calls and long puts
 IV. Short calls and short puts

(A) I and II
(B) I and IV
(C) II and III
(D) III and IV

Questions 64 and 65 can be answered with the following information:

ACI sells at $40 per share. Last year, it had earnings of $4 per share and a dividend payout ratio of 60%.

64. ACI's P/E is:

(A) 1/10
(B) 4
(C) 6
(D) 10

65. ACI's dividend for last year (was):

(A) $1.60
(B) $2.40
(C) $4.00
(D) cannot be determined

66. An option is purchased and expires unexercised. For income tax purposes, the premium would be treated as:

    (A) a capital loss at the time of purchase
    (B) a capital loss at the time of expiration
    (C) an ordinary loss at the time of purchase
    (D) an ordinary loss at the time of expiration

67. A stockholder with 200 shares of ACI must vote to fill three positions on the board of directors. If voting rights are cumulative, he may use his votes in any of the following ways EXCEPT:

    (A) 200 votes for each of three candidates
    (B) 300 votes for each of two candidates
    (C) 600 votes for each of three candidates
    (D) 600 votes for one candidate

68. MSRB rules apply to all of the following EXCEPT:

    (A) municipal bond salesmen
    (B) municipal bond underwriters
    (C) municipal bond issuers
    (D) municipal bond dealers

Questions 69 and 70 refer to the following information:

ACI has a convertible bond with a conversion price of $50 per share.

69. The conversion ratio for these bonds is:

    (A) 2 to 1
    (B) 5 to 1
    (C) 20 to 1
    (D) 50 to 1

70. If the bond is currently selling at $1,100 and is at parity, the stock is selling at:

    (A) $22
    (B) $55
    (C) $220
    (D) $550

71. An investor buys 1 DM Sep 60 at 1.2. If the contract size is 125,000 German marks, his cost excluding commissions would be:

    (A) $125
    (B) $1,250
    (C) $1,500
    (D) $2,000

The following information is to be used in connection with Questions 72 and 73:

Consolidated Amalgamated has announced $25,000,000 of callable convertible debentures maturing in 2004. The conversion price is $12.50, and the bonds are issued at $1,000.

72. What is the conversion rate on these bonds?

    (A) 40
    (B) 80
    (C) 100
    (D) 125

73. If Consolidated Amalgamated were to call these bonds at 106 when the market price of the stock was $13 and at parity, an owner of these securities would do best to:

    (A) convert the bond and sell the shares
    (B) sell the bond
    (C) hold the bond and earn the interest
    (D) tender the bond

74. Which of the following is used by a technical trader?

    (A) Head and shoulders pattern
    (B) P/E
    (C) Quick ratio
    (D) Leverage

75. The "visible supply" refers to:

    (A) the supply of corporate bonds becoming available
    (B) the supply of T-bonds becoming available
    (C) the supply of new equities becoming available
    (D) the supply of municipal bonds becoming available

76. Which of the following positions requires maintenance margin?

    (A) A covered call
    (B) A covered put
    (C) An uncovered call
    (D) A long straddle

77. A customer buying an OTC stock from a firm that is a market maker in that stock, pays a price that:

    (A) includes a markup
    (B) does not include a markup
    (C) includes a commission
    (D) includes a commission and a mark up

78. If a municipal bond is purchased at a discount and is sold before maturity, the capital gain (loss) is measured from:

    I. cost basis for an original issue purchase
    II. cost basis for an aftermarket purchase
    III. accreted cost basis for an original issue purchase
    IV. accreted cost basis for an aftermarket purchase

    (A) I and III
    (B) I and IV
    (C) II and III
    (D) II and IV

79. The municipal issue most likely to require a sinking fund is a:

    (A) balloon issue
    (B) serial issue
    (C) term issue
    (D) revenue issue

80. What kind of investment company pays out 90% of its net investment income to its shareholders?

    (A) Registered
    (B) Diversified
    (C) Regulated
    (D) Balanced

81. An options contract for British pounds is for 25,000 BPs. If the strike price is 150, the value of the contract is:

    (A) $2,500
    (B) $3,750
    (C) $25,000
    (D) $37,500

82. If a client refuses to provide information about his financial status, needs, and investment objectives, a registered representative might recommend buying an option:

    (A) if it is approved by the firm's ROP
    (B) if the information is otherwise available
    (C) if he gets special permission
    (D) never

83. Amalgamated Consolidated, Inc. (ACI) had net income before taxes of $2,500,000. This included $500,000 of preferred dividends from XYZ corporation.

ACI owns 25% of XYZ, and ACI is in the 40% bracket. The total ACI tax bill would be:

(A) $800,000
(B) $840,000
(C) $860,000
(D) $1,000,000

84. A refunding is likely to occur for which of the following issues if all of them are selling at a current basis of 6.50?

(A) 5% coupon callable in 1991 at 102
(B) 6% coupon callable at par in 2001
(C) 6.5% coupon maturing in 1999
(D) 7% coupon maturing in 1994

85. An investor in a "plain vanilla" CMO who wished to achieve the highest possible return would choose:

(A) the first tranche
(B) the interest-only tranche
(C) the principal-only tranche
(D) the last tranche

86. If the board of directors declares a stock split, all of the following are true EXCEPT:

(A) liquidity increases
(B) it is easier for the public to buy the stock
(C) the stock price rises
(D) the stock price falls

87. An investor buys three New York State revenue bonds at 106. If the bonds mature in six years and she sells them after four years at 104, with respect to taxes she has a:

(A) $60 capital loss
(B) $60 capital gain
(C) $20 interest income gain
(D) none of the above

88. In an underwriting of a municipal bond issue, the additional takedown was $\frac{1}{2}$ and the concession was $\frac{1}{4}$.

If the manager's fee was $\frac{1}{16}$, then, for each bond sold, a member of the syndicate would receive:

(A) $\frac{1}{4}$
(B) $\frac{5}{16}$
(C) $\frac{9}{16}$
(D) $\frac{3}{4}$

89. If a municipality redeems outstanding bonds with the proceeds from a new bond issue, this is called:

(A) calling the bonds
(B) refunding the bonds
(C) sinking the bonds
(D) defending the bonds

90. In trying to sell shares in a mutual fund, the registered representative may:

(A) offer quantity discounts for large purchases arranged over an 18-month period
(B) compute yield based on all distributions made over the preceding five-year period
(C) consolidate income and capital gains distributions
(D) show net asset value at the beginning and end of the period discussed

91. An investor bought a 6.5% Ohio general obligation bond regular way on April 14. The last coupon date was February 15. How many days of interest must he add to the purchase price?

(A) 54
(B) 55
(C) 61
(D) 62

92. Having won a competitive bidding to underwrite a municipal bond, a syndicate now finds that rates have fallen as they are about to bring the issue to market. The syndicate would probably:

    (A) sell the bonds at a discount
    (B) sell the bonds at a premium
    (C) reduce the amount given to the municipality
    (D) not bring the issue to market.

Questions 93 and 94 refer to the following types of securities:

    (A) double-barreled bonds
    (B) special tax bonds
    (C) revenue bonds
    (D) special assessment bonds

Choose the type of security that best describes the bonds listed below.

93. A bond issued to build a new toll bridge with tolls paying off the bond.

94. A bond issued by a municipality backed by proceeds from assessments and further guaranteed by a state agency.

95. A trade made directly between an investment company and a bank is a:

    (A) first market trade
    (B) second market trade
    (C) third market trade
    (D) fourth market trade

96. In talking about a fidelity bond one is referring to:

    (A) insurance a broker/dealer must carry to protect against fraud judgments
    (B) good faith effort to sell a new issue
    (C) insurance provided by SIPC
    (D) protection of prerefunded bonds

Questions 97 and 98 are based on the following investments:

Long 1 ACI Feb 50 Call at 6

Short 1 ACI Feb 60 Call at 5

97. What is the maximum possible gain if the position is held to expiration?

    (A) $500
    (B) $900
    (C) $1,100
    (D) Unlimited

98. At what price would an investor break even?

    (A) 51
    (B) 56
    (C) 61
    (D) 65

99. Under what circumstances could an investor write an ACI June 40 call at 6 in a cash account?

    I. If the investor was short 100 ACI at 40
    II. If he was long 100 ACI in the account
    III. If he was long an escrow receipt for 100 ACI
    IV. If he was long warrants for 100 ACI

    (A) II and III
    (B) II and IV
    (C) I and III
    (D) I, II, and III

100. Defaulted bearer municipal bonds are traded:

    (A) flat and stripped of coupons
    (B) flat and with unpaid past-due coupons attached
    (C) with accrued interest to the date of delivery added to the price
    (D) with accrued interest to the date of delivery added to the price and with the unpaid coupons attached

101. If a corporation is conservatively capitalized, it will raise most of its capital by selling:

    (A) preferred stock
    (B) common stock
    (C) convertible bonds
    (D) bonds

102. All of the following are true of federal funds EXCEPT:

    (A) they represent funds in excess of reserve requirements
    (B) they are overnight loans
    (C) they are very sensitive indicators of rates
    (D) they are loans from the Fed to member banks

103. Under the UGMA, which of the following is true?

    (A) A donor may not be a custodian.
    (B) Twins may have a single account.
    (C) Trading in a margin account is not allowed.
    (D) Parents may be joint custodians.

104. A serial issue of municipals has maturities from 1993 to 2002 with the latter offering a 7% coupon to yield 7.50%. If the bonds are callable in 1994 at 103, in 1995 at 102, and at par thereafter, the bonds maturing in 2002 should be priced to the:

    (A) 1994 date
    (B) 1995 date
    (C) 1996 date
    (D) maturity date

105. The coupon rate on a municipal is:

    I. the nominal rate
    II. the current rate
    III. the yield to maturity
    IV. the rate stated on the bond

    (A) I and II
    (B) II and III
    (C) III and IV
    (D) I and IV

106. All of the following characterize variable annuities EXCEPT:

    (A) they often invest in mutual funds
    (B) they are professionally managed
    (C) they have a fixed minimum payout
    (D) their returns are based on market performance

107. An OTC dealer buys 100,000 shares of ACI at 20 and sells 1,000 immediately. Which of the following is closest to being fair and reasonable?

    (A) A markup of 7%
    (B) A sale at 22
    (C) A sale at 21 plus $.50 commission
    (D) The maximum suggested NASD markup

108. Compared to a bond without this feature, a bond with a call feature would:

    (A) be cheaper
    (B) be more expensive
    (C) be more attractive to investors
    (D) require lower coupon rates

109. All of the following should be determined about a new customer by a registered representative EXCEPT:

    (A) investment objectives
    (B) financial resources
    (C) financial requirements
    (D) prior investment results

110. To include a second dealer in a transaction unnecessarily is a violation of NASD Rules, and is known as:

(A) disintermediation
(B) churning
(C) twisting
(D) interpositioning

111. Which of the following would be considered a fair and reasonable reoffering price for 7% municipals purchased at a 7% basis?

I. 101
II. 107
III. 6.75
IV. 5.50

(A) I and IV
(B) II and III
(C) I and III
(D) II and IV

112. What is the dollar value of a $\frac{7}{8}$ change in an option's premium price?

(A) $7.80
(B) $8.75
(C) $78.00
(D) $87.50

The following information is to be used for Questions 113 and 114:

ACI has announced an offer of 1,000,000 units at $8. Each unit consists of one share of common, one share of preferred, and a warrant for $\frac{1}{4}$ share of common.

113. If the offering is successful and all warrants are exercised, how many new shares of common stock will be outstanding?

(A) 250,000
(B) 1,000,000
(C) 1,250,000
(D) 2,000,000

114. How much will ACI raise if the common is valued at $4 when issued?

(A) $1,000,000
(B) $4,000,000
(C) $5,000,000
(D) $8,000,000

115. A customer without a position writes 1 ACI Nov 60 Put and writes 1 ACI Nov 60 Call. The position established is a:

(A) long combination
(B) short combination
(C) short straddle
(D) long straddle

116. Before issuing revenue bonds, a municipal authority would probably do all of the following EXCEPT:

(A) have a ballot referendum
(B) do a feasibility study
(C) publish a notice of sale
(D) get a bond attorney

117. Tax-sheltered investments provide all of the following advantages to limited partners EXCEPT:

(A) opportunities to limit risk
(B) liquid investment
(C) opportunities to defer taxes
(D) opportunities to reduce taxes

118. An investor wishes to swap one municipal bond holding for another one. Which of the following would not enter into consideration of this transaction?

(A) Maturity
(B) Coupon
(C) Accrued interest
(D) Quality

119. With regard to NASD arbitration proceedings, which of the following is true?:

    (A) Nonmembers may not request their use in controversies involving members.
    (B) Members may not demand their use in controversies with other members.
    (C) The finding must be accepted by a member in controversy with a nonmember.
    (D) Members may demand their use in controversies with nonmembers.

120. Securities sold at "seller's option" can be delivered at the option of the seller if he gives written notice of:

    (A) one day
    (B) five weeks
    (C) seven days
    (D) ten days

121. A short straddle would be profitable if:

    (A) the market price differs from the strike price by more than the sum of the premiums
    (B) the market price differs from the strike price by less than the sum of the premiums
    (C) the premiums are large
    (D) the strike price is more than two times the larger premium

122. The takedown on a new municipal issue is $\frac{3}{8} + \frac{1}{8}$. For a member of the syndicate, the discount is:

    (A) $\frac{1}{8}$
    (B) $\frac{2}{8}$
    (C) $\frac{3}{8}$
    (D) $\frac{4}{8}$

123. Under SEC regulations, who among the following may be restricted in their use of nonpublic information about a public corporation?

    (A) Financial printers
    (B) Officers and directors
    (C) Underwriters
    (D) All of the above

124. A T-bill is characterized by all of the following EXCEPT:

    (A) it is issued at a discount
    (B) it has a $10,000 minimum denomination
    (C) it matures in no more than two years
    (D) it is in book-entry form

125. In executing an order for a public customer, a member asks the specialist in the stock to guarantee him a price while giving the customer an opportunity to obtain a better price. This is known as:

    (A) floor protection
    (B) a special deal
    (C) a stop order
    (D) stopping stock

PART TWO

Time   3 Hours

Questions   126–250

DIRECTIONS

Each of the questions or incomplete statements below is followed by four suggested answer options. Choose the best answer and then blacken the corresponding space on the answer sheet.

Questions 126 and 127 use the following information.

An investor bought $150,000 of a DPP and was also responsible for a $100,000 recourse loan.

126. The investor's basis in this program is:

   (A) $50,000
   (B) $100,000
   (C) $150,000
   (D) $250,000

127. Assume the investor had passive income of $300,000. What is the minimum possible passive income for this investor for the year?

   (A) $300,000
   (B) $200,000
   (C) $150,000
   (D) $50,000

128. A basis point on a corporate bond ($1,000 par) would be worth:

   (A) $.10
   (B) $1.00
   (C) $10.00
   (D) $100.00

Questions 129–131 refer to the following page from a specialist's book:

BUY	CAI	SELL
300 MERRILL	45	
1,000 BACHE	$\frac{1}{8}$	
200 DWR	$\frac{1}{4}$	
	$\frac{3}{8}$	
	$\frac{1}{2}$	500 STOP DREXEL
	$\frac{5}{8}$	400 MERRILL
		100 BACHE
	$\frac{3}{4}$	500 MERRILL
		200 DREXEL
	$\frac{7}{8}$	1,000 DWR
		500 BACHE

129. The current quote and size is:

   (A) $45-45\frac{7}{8}$ 1,500–2,800
   (B) $45\frac{1}{4}-45\frac{1}{2}$ 1,500–2,800
   (C) $45-45\frac{1}{2}$ 200–100
   (D) $45\frac{1}{4}-45\frac{5}{8}$ 200–500

130. For his own account, the specialist may bid no less than:

   (A) $45\frac{1}{4}$
   (B) $44\frac{3}{8}$
   (C) $45\frac{1}{2}$
   (D) he may not bid for the stock

131. If the last sale was at $45\frac{1}{2}$ on a minus tick, the lowest possible offer by a short seller would be:

    (A) $45\frac{1}{4}$

    (B) $45\frac{3}{8}$

    (C) $45\frac{1}{2}$

    (D) $45\frac{5}{8}$

Questions 132 and 133 are based on the following information:

An 8% municipal bond, of $10,000 par value maturing in ten years is trading at 90.

132. To the nearest .1%, what is the nominal yield?

    (A) 7.2%
    (B) 8.0%
    (C) 8.8%
    (D) 8.9%

133. To the nearest .1%, what is the current yield?

    (A) 7.2%
    (B) 8.0%
    (C) 8.8%
    (D) 8.9%

134. All of the following can be classified as money market instruments EXCEPT:

    (A) federal funds
    (B) American Depository Receipts
    (C) bankers' acceptances
    (D) commercial paper

135. The advance-decline line used by technical analysts is intended to gauge the:

    (A) direction of the market
    (B) volatility of the market
    (C) quality of the market
    (D) volume of activity in the market

136. When does Regulation T require payment for an option bought in a margin account?

    (A) On the seventh business day following the trade
    (B) On the trade date
    (C) On the next business day after the trade
    (D) On the fifth business day following the trade

137. When depositors withdraw money from savings institutions to invest in higher yielding instruments, this is called:

    (A) reverse repo
    (B) the multiplier effect
    (C) disintermediation
    (D) open market operations

138. When revenues exceed deductions in a DPP, we say that:

    (A) phantom income is generated
    (B) cash flow is positive
    (C) operating income is positive
    (D) the crossover point has been reached

139. Which of the following types of accounts are specifically prohibited by NYSE rules?

    I. Third-party accounts
    II. Accounts under an alias
    III. Code-number accounts
    IV. Limited discretion accounts

    (A) II and III only
    (B) I only
    (C) II and IV only
    (D) I and IV only

140. When interest rates on bonds rise, which of the following happens to old bonds outstanding?

    I. Dollar prices rise
    II. Yields rise
    III. Dollar prices decline
    IV. Yields decline

(A) I and II only
(B) I and IV only
(C) II and IV only
(D) II and III only

141. Offerings of new issues of municipal securities are exempted from all but the:

(A) 1933 Securities Act
(B) 1934 Securities Exchange Act
(C) 1935 Holding Company Act
(D) 1939 Trust Indenture Act

142. Under NYSE rules, opening an account for which of the following would require prior written consent and duplicate confirmations of all transactions sent to his employer?

(A) An employee in another member organization
(B) An employee of a registered investment company
(C) An officer of a trust company
(D) An independent insurance agent

143. In a municipal bond underwriting, which of the following is the correct order of allocation?

I. Pre-sale
II. Syndicate account less concession
III. Orders at the takedown prices
IV. Designated

(A) II, I, III, IV
(B) IV, III, II, I
(C) III, II, I, IV
(D) I, II, IV, III

144. A Direct Participation Program that does not have a legitimate business purpose is called a(n):

(A) tax shelter
(B) abusive shelter
(C) limited partnership
(D) passive shelter

145. A customer learns that he bought 100 ACI at $34\frac{1}{4}$. Today he discovers the correct price to be $34\frac{1}{2}$. As a result:

(A) the customer is permitted to cancel the trade
(B) the registered representative must pay the difference
(C) the customer is responsible for the price as executed
(D) the firm must take the transaction into its own error account

146. All of the following are true of most United States Government Agency bonds EXCEPT:

(A) they may have interest coupons attached
(B) they are freely traded
(C) they are considered relatively safe investments
(D) they are direct obligations of the United States Government

147. The document that stipulates the rights and obligations of the general and limited partners in a Direct Participation Program is called the:

(A) Agreement of Limited Partnership
(B) Certificate of Incorporation
(C) Partnership Papers
(D) Limited Liability Agreement

148. Option allocation assignments notices to customers may use which of the following methods?

I. Random selections
II. FIFO
III. LIFO
IV. Equitable allocation

(A) I, II, and IV only
(B) II, III, and IV only
(C) I and II only
(D) II and IV only

149. According to MSRB rules, each municipal securities dealer must keep a copy of those rules in:

(A) the main office of the firm
(B) any office of the firm where three or more representatives conduct municipal securities business
(C) each office of the firm
(D) any office of the firm that does not have a municipal securities principal in residence

150. During the "cooling-off" period in connection with an underwriting, all of the following usually take place EXCEPT:

(A) issuance of a red herring
(B) due diligence meetings
(C) blue sky filings
(D) stabilization

151. The owner of a call option is entitled to a dividend payable on the underlying stock:

(A) always
(B) never
(C) only if he exercises before the ex-dividend date
(D) only if he exercises after the ex-dividend date

152. What Act requires that municipalities file disclosures of pertinent information prior to a public offering?

(A) Securities Act of 1933
(B) Securities Exchange Act of 1934

(C) Trust Indenture Act of 1939
(D) No such law presently exists.

153. The accounting statement that presents a snapshot of a financial position of a business at a particular point in time (rather than over a period of time) is called the:

(A) balance sheet
(B) income statement
(C) sources and uses
(D) earnings statement

154. For listed options, the Options Clearing Corporation determines all but the:

(A) strike price
(B) premium amount
(C) contract size
(D) expiration

155. Municipal term bonds are usually quoted on a:

(A) discount basis
(B) current yield basis
(C) yield to maturity basis
(D) dollar price basis

The following choices apply to Questions 156–158:

(A) equity options
(B) interest rate options
(C) index options
(D) foreign currency options

Select the choice that best describes the options listed below.

156. Options that would be used to hedge a portfolio of three listed stocks.

157. Options for hedging FOMC moves.

158. Options affected by the interbank rate.

159. Settlement on an index option is made by:

    (A) cash
    (B) delivery of a futures contract
    (C) delivery of the underlying securities
    (D) any of the above

160. The balance sheet equation is:

    (A) assets = stockholder's equity
    (B) assets – liabilities = profits
    (C) total assets – total liabilities = profits
    (D) total assets – total liabilities = net worth

161. Options on foreign currencies are traded on the Philadelphia Stock Exchange. Which of the following currencies have listed options contracts?

    I. Japanese yen
    II. British pounds
    III. Canadian dollars
    IV. German marks

    (A) I, II, and IV only
    (B) II and III only
    (C) I and IV only
    (D) I, II, III, and IV

162. An investor purchases five ($1,000 par) 15-year municipal bonds at 107.50. Three years later, he sells them at 105. This results in a:

    (A) loss of $50
    (B) gain of $50
    (C) loss of $125
    (D) gain of $125

    Questions 163 and 164 refer to the choices listed below:

    (A) free riding
    (B) matched sales
    (C) wash sales
    (D) short against the box

    Select the choice that best describes the following activities:

163. Which activity describes buying and selling of equal totals of some security at the same price using a single broker and never actually changing the true owner of the securities?

164. Which activity describes buying and selling equal totals of some security to establish two separate positions?

165. A convertible bond selling at $1,110 has been called at 110. The bond is convertible at $50 to a stock that is currently selling at $54. Ignoring transaction costs, an investor should:

    (A) sell the bond
    (B) allow the bond to be called
    (C) convert and sell the stock
    (D) buy additional bonds and tender them

166. A trade to be settled "when as and if issued" will settle:

    (A) on the issue date
    (B) one day after issue
    (C) five days after issue
    (D) on a date to be assigned

167. All of the following are true of purchases of repos EXCEPT:

    (A) they are an investment in treasury instruments
    (B) they provide flexibility in the amount invested
    (C) they are a noncompetitive market
    (D) they offer money market rates

168. All of the following are part of the computation of cost depletion in a drilling program EXCEPT the:

    (A) extracted crude in storage
    (B) extracted crude sold
    (C) recoverable reserves
    (D) adjusted cost basis of the property

Questions 169 and 170 refer to the following information:

An investor buys 200 shares of CAI at 46 and sells 2 CAI Aug 50 Calls at 3.

169. With no previous exercise, her break-even point at expiration would be:

(A) 40
(B) 43
(C) 49
(D) 53

170. If the calls are exercised when CAI is at 56, she will realize a:

(A) $600 loss
(B) $200 gain
(C) $1,400 gain
(D) $2,600 gain

171. How often must an "open" order left with the specialist be reconfirmed?

(A) Daily
(B) Weekly
(C) Monthly
(D) Semiannually

172. The Trust Indenture Act of 1939 sets forth the following:

  I. the rules of the NASD
  II. the responsibilities of the trustee
  III. the rights of the stockbrokers
  IV. the obligations of the entity issuing the debt

(A) I and II only
(B) II and IV only
(C) I and III only
(D) I, II, III, and IV

173. Which of the following industries would be most likely to be hurt by interest rates increasing rapidly?

(A) Mining companies
(B) Chemical companies
(C) Railroad companies
(D) Utility companies

174. Who is the beneficial owner of stock registered in "street" name?

(A) The broker/dealer
(B) The transfer agent
(C) The registrar
(D) The customer

175. When do listed equity options cease to trade?

(A) 3:00 P.M. Eastern Time on the expiration date
(B) 10:59 A.M. Eastern Time on the business day prior to the expiration date
(C) 4:00 P.M. Eastern Time on the business day prior to the expiration date
(D) 10:59 P.M. Eastern Time on the business day prior to the expiration date

176. The writer of an option that has been exercised:

(A) may retender this obligation
(B) must make good on his obligation
(C) may buy an option to balance the position
(D) all of the above

177. A municipal bond is purchased at a premium. Order the yields from lowest to highest.

  I. Nominal yield
  II. Yield to maturity
  III. Current yield

(A) I, II, III
(B) III, II, I
(C) II, III, I
(D) III, I, II

178. All of the following are prohibited under SEC Rule 144 EXCEPT:

    (A) selling shares without notifying the SEC
    (B) sales on an exchange without advising purchasers they are acquiring 144 stock
    (C) solicitation of purchase orders from customers of the firm
    (D) charging the seller a special commission to compensate the firm for its extra distribution effort

179. The *New York Times* reported that Amalgamated Consolidated Incorporated announced a quarterly dividend of $1.20 with a record date of January 20. The dividend is payable February 28. An investor who purchased ACI on February 23 would:

    (A) receive the dividend
    (B) not receive the dividend
    (C) receive it if the trade had been for "cash"
    (D) receive $1 of dividend

180. The name for a written consent signed by all limited partners permitting the general partner to act outside the partnership agreement is a:

    (A) partnership democracy
    (B) flip-flop agreement
    (C) partnership agreement
    (D) certificate amendment

Questions 181–183 refer to the following customer margin account:

Long Market $60,000	Short Market $20,000
Debit Record $30,000	Credit Record $30,000

SMA -0-

181. What is the customer's equity?

    (A) $5,000
    (B) $40,000
    (C) $56,000
    (D) $80,000

182. If the market value of the short position falls to $10,000, what is the customer's equity?

    (A) $15,000
    (B) $40,000
    (C) $46,000
    (D) $50,000

183. What is the new SMA?

    (A) $5,000
    (B) $10,000
    (C) $15,000
    (D) $20,000

184. An investor purchases a 9% corporate bond in February at par. If she pays $30 in accrued interest and collects two semiannual interest payments on the bond, her tax liability is:

    (A) $0
    (B) $30
    (C) $60
    (D) $90

185. The length of time covered by a single SEC notification under Rule 144 is:

    (A) 60 days
    (B) 90 days
    (C) 180 days
    (D) 360 days

186. Free-riding and withholding are violations of the:

    (A) Securities Exchange Act of 1934
    (B) NYSE Constitution
    (C) NASD Rules of Fair Practice
    (D) Securities Act of 1933

187. All of the following oil and gas programs involve producing wells EXCEPT:

    (A) developmental
    (B) balanced
    (C) exploratory
    (D) income

188. A Regulation A offering cannot exceed:

    (A) $1,000,000
    (B) $1,500,000
    (C) $2,500,000
    (D) $5,000,000

189. To qualify as an "intrastate" offering under Rule 147, an offer must have:

    (A) 80% of the corporation's assets located in that state
    (B) 80% of the proceeds of the offering used in that state
    (C) 80% of the corporate revenues earned in that state
    (D) all of the above

190. An investor exercises an index option at noon on Tuesday. The exercise value used to determine his profit or loss is:

    (A) Monday's close
    (B) Tuesday's opening
    (C) Tuesday's noon value
    (D) Tuesday's close

191. Which of the following is true for qualified profit-sharing plans?

    (A) Contributions from the corporation are taxable.
    (B) Employee benefits are predetermined.
    (C) Contributions are mandatory whether the firm is profitable or not.
    (D) All income from the plan's assets are not taxed until received.

192. Which of the following options is "in the money"?

    (A) CAI Nov 40 Puts
        CAI stock at 45
    (B) ACI Nov 50 Calls
        ACI stock at 45
    (C) ACI Feb 55 Calls
        ACI stock at 55
    (D) CAI Feb 50 Puts
        CAI stock at 45

193. A T-bill was purchased at $9,500 in November 1992. If it matures at $10,000 in February 1993, the tax consequences are:

    (A) $500 capital gains 1993
    (B) $500 interest income 1993
    (C) $500 interest income divided proportionately between 1992 and 1993
    (D) $500 capital gains divided proportionately between 1992 and 1993

194. If a mutual fund had a portfolio consisting of a wide variety of biotechnology firms, it would best be characterized as a:

    (A) specialized fund
    (B) growth fund
    (C) closed-end fund
    (D) open-end fund

195. If federal funds rates decline over time, all of the following are likely EXCEPT:

    (A) the federal government is encouraging expansion
    (B) short rates are decreasing
    (C) the prime is decreasing
    (D) reserves are decreasing

196. An offering of $20,000,000 of 7% New York State highway bonds would pay semiannual interest totaling:

(A) $350,000
(B) $700,000
(C) $1,000,000
(D) $3,500,000

197. Customers with inactive accounts must receive statements at least:

(A) monthly
(B) every three months
(C) every six months
(D) annually

198. When a variable annuity contract is to begin payout, which of the following is true?

(A) The monthly dollars of payout is fixed.
(B) The number of units of payout is fixed.
(C) The value of each unit is fixed.
(D) The securities are liquidated.

199. For tax purposes, the first cash distributions from a depreciation in previous years must be added as taxable income. This is called:

(A) recapture
(B) return on equity
(C) limited partner costing
(D) reverse depreciation

Questions 200–202 refer to the following types of debt issues:

(A) T-bills
(B) federal funds
(C) commercial paper
(D) banker's acceptances

Which choice is best described in the following questions? (Remember that a choice might be used more than once.)

200. They are used to promote foreign trade.

201. They are quoted as an interest rate.

202. They are exempt from state and local taxes.

203. If a United States corporation owns common stock of another United States corporation, dividend payments received are:

(A) taxed as capital gains
(B) taxed as ordinary income
(C) effectively taxed at 30% of their normal rate
(D) taxed at 70% of the normal rate

204. Which method of payment yields the largest monthly payment from an annuity contract?

(A) Lump sum
(B) 15-year certain
(C) Life annuity
(D) Life annuity plus one survivor

205. ACI declares a 20% stock dividend. When ACI goes ex-dividend, an ACI Jun 60 Call would become:

(A) ACI Jun 60 Call for 120 shares
(B) ACI Jun 50 Call for 120 shares
(C) ACI Jun 60 Call for 100 shares
(D) ACI Jun 50 Call for 100 shares

206. If a margin account is restricted but has a positive SMA, how much may an investor withdraw from the account?

(A) No funds may be withdrawn from a restricted account.
(B) Fifty percent of the SMA may be withdrawn.
(C) All of the SMA may be withdrawn.
(D) All of the SMA up to an amount that leaves the account with 25% margin.

207. Which of the following transactions cannot be performed in a cash account?

    (A) Sell an ACI Call; buy ACI stock.
    (B) Buy an ACI Put; buy ACI stock.
    (C) Buy an ACI Call; buy ACI stock.
    (D) Sell an ACI Put; sell Short ACI stock.

208. The margin requirement for an investor who owned $100,000 of 6% T-notes that matured on 1/1/96 and who wrote a T-note call at 6 for notes maturing in January 1996 was:

    (A) 15% of market value plus the premium
    (B) 20% of market value minus the premium
    (C) 0
    (D) 20% of market value minus out of the moneyness

209. A certificate of limited partnership would need to be amended if any of the following occurred EXCEPT:

    (A) a new limited partner is added
    (B) a new general partner is added
    (C) a new financing arrangement is made
    (D) a new sharing arrangement is made

210. An end-of-year statement of a real-estate limited partnership contains the following information:

Rental income	$200,000
Expenses	$75,000
Depreciation	$50,000
Interest payments	$50,000
Principal payments	$50,000

The investor would report a gain (loss) on his tax return of:

    (A) $25,000 loss
    (B) $25,000 gain
    (C) $75,000 gain
    (D) $125,000 gain

211. Which of the following securities is not exempt from the registration requirements of the Securities Act of 1933?

    (A) Benevolent corporations
    (B) Municipal securities
    (C) Insurance companies
    (D) Bank issues

212. A customer purchases 1 CAI Dec 50 Call at 1. A few months later it is out of the money by 4. What is the customer's maximum possible loss?

    (A) $100
    (B) $200
    (C) $300
    (D) $400

213. The largest expense incurred in its first year by an open-ended investment company is usually the:

    (A) management fee
    (B) commission to salesmen
    (C) legal fees
    (D) accounting fees

214. A customer places an order to sell 100 ACI at $42\frac{5}{8}$ on a stop limit. Trades then take place as follows:

$42\frac{5}{8}$ $42\frac{1}{2}$ $42\frac{3}{8}$ $42\frac{1}{4}$

Execution takes place at:

    (A) $42\frac{1}{4}$
    (B) $42\frac{3}{8}$
    (C) $42\frac{1}{2}$
    (D) the order cannot be executed

215. Under the NASD Uniform Practice Code, which of the following is not a good delivery for a 700 share trade?

    (A) Twenty certificates of 35 shares each
    (B) Seven certificates of 40 shares each and seven of 60 shares each
    (C) One certificate for 200 shares and one certificate for 500 shares
    (D) One certificate for 700 shares

216. An investor has a $10,000 long-term loss in 1992 with no offsetting gains. What is the last year in which he has a carry forward loss?

    (A) 1992
    (B) 1993
    (C) 1994
    (D) 1995

217. Under Rule 144, every 90 days, one may sell:

    (A) an average of the past four weeks' trading volume
    (B) an average of the past six weeks' trading volume
    (C) one percent of the outstanding shares
    (D) whichever is greater of (A) or (C)

218. ACI closes at 45 on an uptick on the NYSE and goes ex-dividend $.60 the next day. The lowest possible price for a short sale on the opening the next day is:

    (A) $44\frac{3}{8}$
    (B) $44\frac{1}{2}$
    (C) $44\frac{5}{8}$
    (D) 45

219. For a mutual fund, net investment income is derived from:

    (A) dividend income
    (B) interest and dividend income
    (C) capital gains
    (D) interest and dividend income plus capital gains

220. If an OTC order is placed for 220 shares at the market on one ticket, and the market price is 40, then the order must be executed as:

    (A) 200 shares at 40 and 20 shares at $40\frac{1}{8}$
    (B) 220 shares at 40
    (C) 220 shares at $40\frac{1}{8}$
    (D) this cannot be placed as a single order

221. The "dated date" is the:

    (A) trade date
    (B) settlement date
    (C) date from which accrued interest starts
    (D) date from which all computations are made

222. An investor wants preservation of capital and a minimum amount of purchasing power risk. As a registered representative, you would suggest:

    (A) T-bonds
    (B) project notes
    (C) AA high-quality corporate bonds
    (D) revenue bonds

223. Which of the following ratios provides the most stringent test of liquidity?

    (A) (Current assets — inventory)/ current liabilities
    (B) Current assets/current liabilities
    (C) Assets/liabilities
    (D) Cash and marketable securities/liabilities

224. Municipalities would probably assess an *ad valorem* tax on:

    (A) population
    (B) property
    (C) sales of goods and services
    (D) income

225. List the following Moody's ratings in descending order:

    I. Aa
    II. Aaa
    III. A1
    IV. Baa

    (A) II, I, III, IV
    (B) III, II, I, IV
    (C) III, IV, I, II
    (D) II, III, I, IV

226. If total assets are $1,000,000 and short-term liabilities are $600,000 for a corporation that has no long-term debt, then the shareholder's equity is:

    (A) impossible to determine
    (B) $600,000
    (C) $400,000
    (D) $1,000,000

227. All of the following customer records must be kept by the registered representative EXCEPT:

    (A) each customer's current position
    (B) each customer's purchase and sale for the past three years
    (C) each customer's dividend income for the past three years
    (D) a cross-indexed file of his entire customer holdings

228. An investor pays a 7.5% sales commission on the purchase of 1,000 shares of a mutual fund offered at $15. If he sells it and must pay a .5% redemption fee,

and the fund has not changed in value, he will receive approximately:

    (A) $15,000
    (B) $14,925
    (C) $13,730
    (D) $13,800

229. The Keogh Act would allow each of the following to set up a self-retirement fund EXCEPT:

    (A) a lawyer in private practice
    (B) a municipal employee with an income from selling paintings
    (C) a broker with the funds from a Christmas bonus
    (D) a salaried plumber from freelance plumbing income

230. The Dow Industrials comprises:

    (A) all NYSE stocks
    (B) 65 blue-chip stocks
    (C) 30 blue-chip stocks
    (D) all NYSE industrial stocks

231. Under NYSE Rules, an investor can open a numbered account if:

    (A) he provides written evidence of responsibility for the account
    (B) he deposits $250,000 to cover the SIPC
    (C) he gets a bank letter of credit to cover the SIPC
    (D) it is not allowed

232. A mutual fund pays dividends and also has a capital gains distribution. An investor has owned shares in this fund for two years. The payouts would be treated as:

    (A) ordinary income
    (B) capital gains
    (C) ordinary income and capital gains
    (D) long-term capital gains

233. The maximum allowable contribution to a Keogh plan is:

    (A) $2,000
    (B) $7,500
    (C) $15,000
    (D) $30,000

234. Under NYSE rules, which of the following require prior permission from the investor's employer?

    I. A margin account for an employee of a bank
    II. An account for an employee of the exchange
    III. A cash account for an employee of another broker

    (A) I and II
    (B) II and III
    (C) I and III
    (D) I, II, and III

235. An investor writes 2 ACI Oct 40 Calls at 3 and at the same time writes 1 ACI Oct 40 Put at 5. If ACI goes to 44 and the calls are exercised and the put expires, the investor will realize:

    (A) a gain of $300
    (B) a gain of $600
    (C) a gain of $1,100
    (D) a loss of $800

236. If the manager says that the retention is 80%, an underwriter who has an allotment of 100,000 shares would have how many available for his customers?

    (A) 20,000
    (B) 80,000
    (C) 100,000
    (D) 100,000 plus 80% of the remainder

237. All of the following are true of the tax treatment of variable annuities EXCEPT:

    (A) early withdrawals are subject to a tax penalty
    (B) payments are considered part income and part return on investment
    (C) earnings are not taxed until withdrawal
    (D) all payments are taxed as received

238. Which of the following parties does an investor notify when he wishes to exercise an option?

    (A) The writer
    (B) The broker
    (C) The OCC
    (D) The AMEX or the CBOE

239. A registered representative who violates NYSE rules:

    I. is subject to expulsion
    II. is subject to fine
    III. is subject to censure
    IV. is subject to suspension

    (A) II and III
    (B) II and IV
    (C) II, III, and IV
    (D) I, II, III, and IV

240. The totality of final goods and services produced in the United States is called:

    (A) Total Savings
    (B) Gross National Product
    (C) Total Income
    (D) Accumulated Wealth

241. A general obligation bond has an official statement that says that property taxes may not rise above a certain level. This is an example of a:

    (A) moral obligation bond
    (B) fixed debt service bond
    (C) limited tax bond
    (D) limited obligation bond

242. The Revenue Bond Index is an average of:

    (A) 11 bonds
    (B) 20 bonds
    (C) 25 bonds
    (D) 30 bonds

243. The agreement between the issuer and the trustee of a municipal bond issue is written by the:

    (A) trustee's attorney
    (B) underwriter's attorney
    (C) bond counsel
    (D) syndicate manager

244. A premium of 1.20 on a T-bond option would require payment of:

    (A) $1,200
    (B) $3,000
    (C) $12,000
    (D) $30,000

245. All of the following recommendations from a registered representative would be acceptable EXCEPT:

    (A) ACI has been recommended by our research department.
    (B) CAI should go up by at least $10 next year.
    (C) CAI earnings are estimated to be $3 next year.
    (D) ACI looks good in the light of next year's projected GNP.

246. The conversion of convertible bonds to common stock would result in:

    I. an increase in debt.
    II. a decrease in leverage.
    III. an increase in stockholder's equity.
    IV. an increase in total assets.

    (A) I and II
    (B) II and III
    (C) II and IV
    (D) I, II, and III

247. All of the following are true of SIPC EXCEPT:

    (A) it is made up of broker/dealers
    (B) it is an arm of the federal government
    (C) it is a nonprofit corporation
    (D) membership is compulsory for broker/dealers who carry customer accounts

248. An underwriter in an Eastern account has a 15% participation. The underwriting is for $10 million, and he has sold $1.5 million. If $1 million now remains unsold, what is his liability?

    (A) Nothing
    (B) $100,000
    (C) $150,000
    (D) $1 million

249. If an account is frozen, which of the following is true?

    I. All purchases must be paid for in advance.
    II. All sales require previous delivery of the securities.
    III. No activity is allowed without NASD approval.
    IV. No activity is allowed without approval by a principal of the firm.

    (A) II and IV
    (B) I and II
    (C) III and IV
    (D) I and III

250. If a corporation changed its accounting from Accelerated Cost Recovery System to straight line, which of the following would occur?

    (A) Early years would show an increase in stated earnings.
    (B) Later years would show an increase in stated earnings.
    (C) Early years would show a decrease in stated earnings.
    (D) All years would show a decrease in stated earnings.

PRACTICE EXAMINATION ONE
Answer Key
PART ONE

1	C	37	C	73	D	109	D
2	D	38	B	74	A	110	D
3	B	39	A	75	D	111	C
4	A	40	C	76	C	112	D
5	C	41	D	77	A	113	C
6	C	42	B	78	C	114	D
7	B	43	D	79	C	115	C
8	B	44	C	80	C	116	A
9	C	45	C	81	D	117	B
10	D	46	C	82	B	118	C
11	D	47	C	83	B	119	C
12	C	48	B	84	D	120	A
13	A	49	C	85	D	121	B
14	C	50	A	86	C	122	D
15	C	51	C	87	B	123	D
16	D	52	A	88	D	124	C
17	D	53	B	89	B	125	D
18	D	54	D	90	D		
19	A	55	A	91	D		
20	B	56	A	92	B		
21	C	57	C	93	C		
22	D	58	C	94	A		
23	C	59	C	95	D		
24	A	60	A	96	A		
25	D	61	B	97	B		
26	C	62	C	98	A		
27	A	63	C	99	A		
28	B	64	D	100	B		
29	D	65	B	101	B		
30	B	66	B	102	D		
31	B	67	C	103	C		
32	C	68	C	104	D		
33	A	69	C	105	D		
34	D	70	B	106	C		
35	A	71	C	107	D		
36	B	72	B	108	A		

PRACTICE EXAMINATION ONE
Answer Key
PART TWO

126 D	162 A	198 B	234 D
127 D	163 C	199 A	235 A
128 A	164 D	200 D	236 A
129 D	165 A	201 B	237 D
130 B	166 D	202 A	238 B
131 D	167 C	203 C	239 D
132 B	168 A	204 C	240 B
133 D	169 B	205 B	241 C
134 B	170 C	206 D	242 D
135 A	171 D	207 D	243 C
136 D	172 B	208 C	244 B
137 C	173 D	209 C	245 B
138 D	174 D	210 B	246 B
139 B	175 C	211 C	247 B
140 D	176 B	212 A	248 C
141 D	177 B	213 B	249 B
142 A	178 B	214 D	250 A
143 D	179 B	215 A	
144 B	180 A	216 D	
145 C	181 B	217 D	
146 D	182 D	218 B	
147 A	183 C	219 B	
148 C	184 C	220 B	
149 C	185 B	221 C	
150 D	186 C	222 B	
151 C	187 C	223 A	
152 D	188 D	224 B	
153 A	189 D	225 A	
154 B	190 D	226 C	
155 D	191 D	227 C	
156 A	192 D	228 D	
157 B	193 B	229 C	
158 D	194 A	230 C	
159 A	195 D	231 A	
160 D	196 B	232 C	
161 D	197 B	233 D	

ANSWER EXPLANATIONS

PART ONE

1. All of the following transactions must be executed in a cash account EXCEPT:

   (A) buying a call
   (B) buying a put
   (C) buying a marginable security
   (D) buying a spread

   (C) None of the other choices can be bought in a margin account. Marginable securities, of course, can be.

2. Options expire at:

   (A) 3:00 P.M. Central Time on the third Friday of the expiration month.
   (B) 4:30 P.M. Central Time on the third Friday of the expiration month.
   (C) 4:30 P.M. Central Time on the third Saturday of the expiration month.
   (D) 10:59 P.M. Central Time on the third Saturday of the expiration month.

   (D) Note that trading is halted on the third Friday, and the options may be exercised until 4:30 P.M. Eastern Time of that day.

3. An out-of-the-money option has a premium of $400. This premium reflects:

   (A) $400 of intrinsic value
   (B) $400 of time value
   (C) $200 of intrinsic and $200 of time value
   (D) Some indeterminable mix of intrinsic and time value

   (B) An out-of-the-money option has no intrinsic value

4. Under which of the following circumstances may a registered representative purchase a hot issue from his own firm?

   (A) Never
   (B) If it is part of his regular trading pattern
   (C) For family members, if it is in their regular pattern
   (D) If the purchase represents a small part of the total issue

   (A) Never

5. A mutual fund bid at $9.30 has a 7% load. What is the offer price?

   (A) $8.65
   (B) $9.30
   (C) $10.00
   (D) $10.70

(**C**) The load is charged on the offer to yield the bid. Thus, $10 = \$9.30/93\%$.

6. Registering an offering with the SEC ensures that the:

    (A) SEC has changed the facts in the registration statement
    (B) SEC has approved this investment
    (C) statement includes the relevant facts about the issue
    (D) issue is suitable for investment by the public

(**C**) The SEC takes no responsibility beyond this.

7. Under NASD rules, a guilty finding by the District Business Conduct Committee may be appealed first to:

    (A) NASD Board of Arbitration
    (B) NASD Board of Governors
    (C) SEC
    (D) courts in the state where the alleged infraction takes place

(**B**) Subsequently, it could be appealed to the SEC, and finally, to federal court, not state courts.

Use the following information to answer Questions 8 and 9.

A firm has $100,000,000 in convertible securities outstanding. These pay 5% and have a conversion price of $40. The firm induces investors to trade $60,000,000 of these convertibles into nonconvertibles by paying a $5,000,000 premium.

8. If the firm has 10,000,000 shares outstanding and all of the remaining convertible securities are converted, the firm will experience dilution of:

    (A) 5%
    (B) 10%
    (C) 15%
    (D) 20%

(**B**) If the price of the common is $40, each $1,000 bond can be converted into 25 shares, and thus the remaining $40,000,000 of bonds can be converted into 1,000,000 shares or 10% of the 10,000,000 shares outstanding.

9. The effect of trading $60,000,000 for nonconvertible securities will be:

    (A) to increase the debt and decrease the cash position of the firm
    (B) to increase the potential dilution effect and decrease the cash position
    (C) to decrease the potential dilution effect and to decrease the cash position
    (D) to decrease the potential dilution effect and to increase the debt position

(**C**) The elimination of convertible decreases the potential dilution. Paying $5,000,000 reduces the cash position.

10. Which of the following trades would appear on the consolidated tape?

    I. Exchange market
    II. Primary market
    III. Options market
    IV. Third market

    (A) I and II
    (B) II and IV
    (C) I and III
    (D) I and IV

(D) No options transactions are reported, nor are new issues.

11. Which investment would provide Amalgamated Consolidated Inc., with the best return? Assume a 25% tax rate.

    (A) 4% municipal bond
    (B) 6% corporate bond
    (C) Common stock yielding 5%
    (D) Preferred stock yielding 6%

(D) The dividend income is subject to a 70% exclusion. The return is $(.7 \times 6\%) + [(.3 \times 6\%)(1 - .25)] = 5.5\%$. The tax free municipal would have a return of $4\% \div (1 - .25) = 5.33\%$. Answer B is incorrect because this represents interest income, which is subject to taxation.

12. All of the following change the terms of a listed option EXCEPT:

    (A) a 2% stock dividend
    (B) a 1 for 3 reverse split
    (C) a $.10 cash dividend
    (D) a rights distribution

(C) All of the others change the number of shares outstanding.

13. A fund with NAV of $10 sells at $9.50. It is:

    (A) a closed-end fund
    (B) an open-end fund
    (C) a front-end load fund
    (D) a no-load fund

(A) This fund is trading at a discount to NAV. No-loads trade at NAV and front-end loads trade at NAV plus sales charge. An open-end fund is sold by the fund and would not be offered for less than shares are worth.

14. A depreciation deduction would be available on each of the following EXCEPT:

    (A) subsidized housing
    (B) a shopping center

(C) developable acreage
(D) single-family homes

(**C**) Undeveloped land does not depreciate.

15. The NYSE margin requirements for $50,000 of municipals which sold for $30,000 would be:

(A) $3,000
(B) $3,500
(C) $4,500
(D) $30,000

(**C**) While there is no FRB margin requirement on municipal bonds, the NYSE requires the greater of 7% of face value or 15% of market value. In this case, 15% of $30,000 = $4,500 is larger than 7% of $50,000 = $3,500.

16. Eurodollar bonds are:

I.   denominated in a European currency
II. denominated in U.S. dollars
III. issued in the U.S.
IV. traded in the U.S.

(A) I and III
(B) II and III
(C) I and IV
(D) II and IV

(**D**) As their name suggests, they are denominated in dollars. They are issued in Europe but are traded in the United States as well.

17. If a municipal bond issue is prerefunded, all of the following are true EXCEPT:

(A) the interest, principal, and call premium are covered
(B) covering funds are on deposit in an escrow account
(C) covering funds are invested in U.S. Treasury securities
(D) this usually occurs when rates rise

(**D**) An issue would be prerefunded if the municipality could now borrow money more cheaply, *i.e.,* if rates have declined. All of the other choices are, in fact, requirements for the proceeds of the refunding.

18. A quote of 101.08 for a $100,000 T-Bond would mean a dollar amount of:

(A) $100,108
(B) $100,250
(C) $101,080
(D) $101,250

(**D**) The quote is for 101 and 8/32. Each point is $1,000.

19. Stocks with a high negative beta could be characterized as being:

    (A) defensive
    (B) aggressive
    (C) low volatility
    (D) blue chip

(A) Negative beta stocks would move in the opposite direction from the market. Incorporating them into a portfolio tends to smooth returns.

20. The purchaser of an index option call would be hoping for:

    (A) a decline in the stock market
    (B) a rise in the stock market
    (C) a rise in the bond index
    (D) a decline in the bond index

(B) An index option is an option on a stock index. The holder of a call would like to see stocks rise.

21. After-tax income is maximized for someone in the 28% tax bracket by purchasing a:

    (A) 7% T-bill
    (B) 8% corporate bond
    (C) 6% tax-exempt municipal bond
    (D) $7\frac{1}{2}$% T-bond

(C) All of the other securities are subject to a 28% tax. The largest of these is at $8\% \times (1 - .28) = 5.76\% < 6\%$.

22. A broker might be disqualified by the MSRB for all of the following reasons EXCEPT:

    (A) conviction on an attempt to defraud a customer
    (B) expulsion from the NASD
    (C) conviction of a failure to make full disclosure of a conflict of interest on a transaction
    (D) conviction on a moving traffic violation.

(D) All of the others are sufficient grounds for disqualification.

23. Dollar cost averaging results in:

    (A) buying the same number of shares each time
    (B) buying more shares when the price is high
    (C) buying more shares when the price is low
    (D) buying an average number of shares each year

(C) Dollar cost averaging requires investing the same amount each time. Thus, when the price is low, one buys more shares for the money.

Questions 24 and 25 refer to the following:

Write 2 ACI Mar 40 Calls at 6

Buy 2 ACI Mar 50 Calls at $1\frac{1}{2}$

24. The maximum possible profit on these trades is:

   (A) $900
   (B) $1,200
   (C) $1,400
   (D) $2,300

(**A**) Maximum profit will occur if the 40 calls are not exercised. The writer keeps the entire premium of $1,200. If this occurs, the 50 calls also expire worthless, and he loses $300 for a net of $900.

25. The maximum loss would occur if, at expiration, ACI is:

   (A) 40
   (B) $41\frac{1}{2}$
   (C) 46
   (D) 50

(**D**) At 50, his calls are worthless, and he loses $400 on each call that he wrote. Below 50, he loses less on the written calls.

26. An investor buys a $10,000 par value municipal bond in the market for $8,800. Assume he is in the 28% tax bracket. If he holds it to maturity, his taxable income is:

   (A) none
   (B) $1,200 of ordinary income
   (C) $1,200 of capital gain
   (D) $600 of ordinary income and $600 of capital gain

(**C**) For municipals purchased at a discount in the market, the increase is not interest income but capital gain

27. If ACI has a high dividend payout ratio, we can expect:

   (A) stockholders' equity will grow slowly
   (B) earnings per share will rise rapidly
   (C) stockholders' equity will shrink
   (D) earnings per share will shrink

(**A**) With a high dividend payout ratio, relatively less of the earnings are retained. Hence, stockholders' equity, which includes retained earnings, would grow slowly.

28. The margin requirement specified by the NYSE for investors wishing to purchase when-issued stock is:

(A) 15%
(B) 25%
(C) 30%
(D) 50%

(B) This is for purchase in a cash account. If an investor wished to buy these in a margin account the requirement would be 50%.

29. Which of the following is most likely to generate large current deductions and possible future cash flow?

    (A) Oil and gas development programs
    (B) Buying triple-net leasebacks
    (C) Undeveloped land
    (D) Oil and gas exploratory programs

(D) Choices A and B would both generate cash quickly, and choice C does not generate deductions. An exploratory program could not generate cash soon and would have deductions.

30. All of the following are quoted in 32nds EXCEPT:

    (A) T-bonds
    (B) T-bills
    (C) GNMAs
    (D) T-notes

(B) T-bills are quoted on a discount yield basis in .01s.

31. To get the most complete financial information about a new issue of municipal securities, one should consult the:

    (A) prospectus
    (B) official statement
    (C) registration statement
    (D) tombstone

(B) Since municipal securities do not have the SEC registration requirement, neither a prospectus nor a registration statement is required. The official statement provides the financial information usually provided in a prospectus.

32. The yield on a common stock is determined from:

    (A) earnings and P/E (price/earnings) ratio
    (B) dividends and P/E
    (C) dividends and price
    (D) earnings and assets

(C) The yield is the return on the investment in the stock. This is the dividend divided by the market price.

33. Regulations for municipal securities are issued by all of the following EXCEPT:

    (A) SIPC
    (B) MSRB
    (C) NASD
    (D) SEC

(A) The SIPC is a jointly owned investors' protective corporation.

34. When investors redeem CDs and buy common stocks, they are causing:

    (A) inflation
    (B) diversification
    (C) refinancing
    (D) disintermediation

(D) Disintermediation is the process of removing funds from financial intermediaries like banks. Redeeming CDs and buying common stock with the proceeds is an example of this process.

35. All of the following are likely to be in a syndication letter EXCEPT:

    (A) the amount of the bid
    (B) the duration of the account
    (C) the type of account
    (D) the member participation level

(A) The syndication letter goes to potential syndicate members. It includes the type of account, its duration, and the level of each member's participation. After the syndicate is formed, it submits a bid.

36. What are Fannie Mae securities?

    (A) Packages of commercial mortgages
    (B) Short-term discount notes and debentures
    (C) Packages of FHA and VA mortgages
    (D) Industrial development bonds

(B) These securities are issued as short-term discount notes and debentures. FNMA buys VA- and FHA-insured mortgages and packages them into bundles that provide the revenues to finance these securities.

The following information is to be used in connection with Questions 37–39.

Shares	Purchase Price	Market Price	Market Value
200 ACI	$40	$35	$2,000
100 CAI	$50	$40	$4,000
100 XYZ	$70	$30	$3,000
			Debit Balance $10,000

37. For the account to become unrestricted again, how much cash would the investor have to deposit?

    (A) $250
    (B) $2,000
    (C) $3,000
    (D) $3,500

    (C) With a market value of $14,000, the account would be unrestricted if the debit balance was 50%, or $7,000. The investor must deposit $3,000 to achieve this.

38. What is the minimum maintenance requirement on this account?

    (A) $2,000
    (B) $3,500
    (C) $5,000
    (D) $6,500

    (B) The NYSE maintenance requirement is 25% of market value, or $3,500.

39. At which of the following market values would a maintenance margin call be sent?

    (A) $12,500
    (B) $13,500
    (C) $14,500
    (D) A call would already have been sent.

    (A) The 25% of $12,500 is $3,125. With a debit balance of $10,000, the investor's equity is $2,500, and a maintenance call would be issued.

40. The coverage on revenue bonds refers to the ratio of:

    (A) gross revenue to operating expenses
    (B) gross revenue to interest expenses
    (C) net revenue to debt service
    (D) net revenue to annual interest expense

    (C) For a revenue bond, one compares the money available (net revenue) to the money required to pay for the bond (debt service). The ratio of one to the other is called the coverage.

    Questions 41–43 refer to the information below:

    An investor's margin account has the following information:

Long Market Value	Debit Record	SMA
$40,000	$23,000	$1,500

41. What is the buying power in the account?

    (A) $0
    (B) $750

(C) $1,500

(D) $3,000

(D) The buying power is twice the amount in the SMA.

42. How much equity does the investor have?

(A) $1,500

(B) $17,000

(C) $23,000

(D) $40,000

(B) The investor's equity is the difference between market value and the debit record.

43. If the investor sold $5,000 from this account, what is the total amount the investor could remove?

(A) $0

(B) $1,500

(C) $2,500

(D) $4,000

(D) The sale releases 50% of the proceeds to the SMA. The total of $1,500 plus $2,500 could be removed.

44. According to MSRB rules, all of the following would be an acceptable gift from one registered representative to another EXCEPT:

(A) two $40 tickets to the theater

(B) video tapes worth $75

(C) a $200 business dinner

(D) a gift certificate for $50

(C) MSRB rules permit gifts with value not exceeding $100.

45. With Regulation T at 50%, a customer sells short 200 shares of ACI at 50 and deposits the appropriate margin. If the price of ACI drops to 40, how much excess cash can the customer remove from the account?

(A) $1,000

(B) $2,000

(C) $3,000

(D) $5,000

(C) Initially, the account had $10,000 market value and $5,000 equity for a credit balance of $15,000. Now market value is $8,000, so the required margin is $4,000, leaving $3,000 of the credit balance which may be taken.

The following information should be used to answer Questions 46 and 47:

An investor writes an ACI Nov 60 straddle at 4. The put is exercised at expiration when the market price is 50. The investor resells 100 shares of ACI for $5,000.

46. His net for these transactions is:

(A) $400 profit
(B) $600 profit
(C) $600 loss
(D) $1,000 loss

(C) His loss is $1,000 minus the $400 of premium.

47. If prior to being exercised, the investor had bought the same straddle at 9, he would realize:

(A) $900 capital loss
(B) $900 ordinary loss
(C) $500 capital loss
(D) $500 ordinary loss

(C) He sold the straddle for $400 and bought it for $900 for a $500 capital loss.

Questions 48–50 refer to the following choices:

(A) balanced fund
(B) income fund
(C) growth fund
(D) load fund

Choose the type of fund that best describes the funds listed in the questions below:

48. AAA Fund invests primarily in money market instruments.

(B) Money market instruments have little opportunity for capital appreciation. They do generate income.

49. BBB Fund is loaded up with equities of firms that reinvest most earnings.

(C) Firms that reinvest earnings are giving up current income to achieve growth.

50. CCC Fund has a portfolio of stocks, bonds, and preferred stocks.

(A) A balanced fund has assets in both stocks and bonds generating income and (hopefully) capital appreciation.

51. An investor would like to find a large inventory of New York City general obligation bonds. He should consult the:

    (A) pink sheets
    (B) yellow sheets
    (C) *Blue List*
    (D) *Bond Buyer Index*

(C) The *Blue List* provides dealer offerings of outstanding municipal bonds. The Bond Buyer Index provides average yields for a group of 20 general obligation 20-year bonds. The other two do not refer to municipal bonds.

52. A put option is out of the money if the strike price is:

    (A) below the market price
    (B) at the market price
    (C) above the market price
    (D) below the exercise price

(A) One would have no incentive to exercise here because one could sell in the market at a higher price.

53. One of two partners in a partnership account dies. The registered representative should:

    (A) close the account
    (B) freeze the account
    (C) liquidate all short positions
    (D) accept only cash orders

(B) Each partner is a general partner, and when one dies the partnership is terminated. Hence, the account is frozen.

Questions 54–56 are based on the following combination of trades:

Mr. Smith buys 1 ACI Nov 50 Call at 7 and 1 ACI Nov 50 Put at 3.

54. What is the maximum possible loss on these trades?

    (A) Unlimited
    (B) $300
    (C) $700
    (D) $1,000

(D) If ACI expires at 50, he loses both premiums.

55. What is the maximum possible gain on these trades?

    (A) Unlimited
    (B) $300
    (C) $700
    (D) $1,000

(A) In principle, ACI can go up with no limit and hence his profit is (after subtracting $1,000 in premiums) unlimited.

56. If ACI goes to 30 at expiration and the investor has not exercised before-hand, his profit (or loss) would be:

   (A) $1,000
   (B) $1,300
   (C) $1,700
   (D) $2,000

(A) At 30, the investor realizes $2,000 minus $1,000 in premiums. The Call expires worthless.

57. The effective return on a municipal bond with a coupon of 8% for an investor in the 28% bracket is:

   (A) 8%
   (B) 10.8%
   (C) 11.1%
   (D) 12.8%

(C) The effective return $= \dfrac{\text{Coupon}}{1 - \text{Tax Rate}} = \dfrac{.08}{.72} = 11.1\%$

Questions 58–61 make use of the following information:

An investor buys $100,000 of a real estate program. For 1991, his portion generates revenues of $200,000 and expenses of $150,000. Additionally, there are $50,000 of interest payments and $25,000 of depreciation.

58. What net gain (loss) is passed through to this investor for 1991?

   (A) $25,000 gain
   (B) $0
   (C) $25,000 loss
   (D) $50,000 loss

(C) Both the interest and the depreciation are subtracted from the net of revenue minus expense to get net gain.

59. How much operating income is generated?

   (A) $25,000 loss
   (B) $0
   (C) $25,000 gain
   (D) $50,000 gain

(C) Operating income does not include interest payments.

60. What is the cash flow for his portion of the program?

   (A) $0
   (B) $15,000
   (C) $25,000
   (D) $40,000

(A) The cash flow adds depreciation back into net gain.

61. If the investor is in the 31% tax bracket and has $40,000 of other passive income, this program will result in a:

    (A) net tax saving of $12,300
    (B) net tax saving of $7,750
    (C) total tax bill for passive income of $12,300
    (D) total tax bill for passive income of $7,750

(B) The $25,000 loss is deducted from his passive income. At 31% this generates a saving of $7,750.

62. Which of the following is true of T-bonds?

    (A) They have little inflation risk.
    (B) They have little interest rate risk.
    (C) They have little credit risk.
    (D) They are not widely available.

(C) A and B are false because all coupon instruments rise and fall in price inversely with interest rates. There is little chance of default by the United States government, so C is true. Finally, there are many billions of dollars' worth of them available in the market.

63. Which of the following pairs are on the same side of the market?

    I. Long calls and long puts
    II. Long calls and short puts
    III. Short calls and long puts
    IV. Short calls and short puts

    (A) I and II
    (B) I and IV
    (C) II and III
    (D) III and IV

(C) If you are long calls, you want the market to go up. If you are short puts, you have written puts; hence, you also want the market to go up so that the put is not exercised. If you are short calls and long puts, you want the market to decline.

Questions 64 and 65 can be answered with the following information:

ACI sells at $40 per share. Last year, it had earnings of $4 per share and a dividend payout ratio of 60%.

64. ACI's P/E is:

    (A) 1/10
    (B) 4
    (C) 6
    (D) 10

(D) The P/E or price-earnings ratio is the market price ($40) divided by earnings per share ($4 = 10).

65. ACI's dividend for last year (was):

    (A) $1.60
    (B) $2.40
    (C) $4.00
    (D) cannot be determined

(B) The dividend payout ratio is the percentage of earnings paid as dividend. In this case, $4 × 60% = $2.40.

66. An option is purchased and expires unexercised. For income tax purposes, the premium would be treated as:

    (A) a capital loss at the time of purchase
    (B) a capital loss at the time of expiration
    (C) an ordinary loss at the time of purchase
    (D) an ordinary loss at the time of expiration

(B) An option is a capital asset that has tax consequences when it is disposed of. In this case, it expired worthless, and the loss is realized at expiration.

67. A stockholder with 200 shares of ACI must vote to fill three positions on the board of directors. If voting rights are cumulative, he may use his votes in any of the following ways EXCEPT:

    (A) 200 votes for each of three candidates
    (B) 300 votes for each of two candidates
    (C) 600 votes for each of three candidates
    (D) 600 votes for one candidate

(C) With cumulative voting rights, he can cast 600 in any way he chooses. Choice C, however, gives him 1,800 votes.

68. MSRB rules apply to all of the following EXCEPT:

    (A) municipal bond salesmen
    (B) municipal bond underwriters
    (C) municipal bond issuers
    (D) municipal bond dealers

(C) The MSRB rules apply to individuals and firms that trade in municipal bonds and not to issuers of these securities.

Questions 69 and 70 refer to the following information:

ACI has a convertible bond with a conversion price of $50 per share.

69. The conversion ratio for these bonds is:

    (A) 2 to 1
    (B) 5 to 1
    (C) 20 to 1
    (D) 50 to 1

(C) The conversion ratio is based on par. At $1,000 par, the $50 per share for common gives a ratio of 20 shares of common to 1 bond.

70. If the bond is currently selling at $1,100 and is at parity, the stock is selling at:

    (A) $22
    (B) $55
    (C) $220
    (D) $550

(B) With a 20 to 1 conversion and the bond selling at $1,100, each share would have to be worth $1,100/20 = $55 to have parity.

71. An investor buys 1 DM Sep 60 at 1.2. If the contract size is 125,000 German marks, his cost excluding commissions would be:

    (A) $125
    (B) $1,250
    (C) $1,500
    (D) $2,000

(C) The premium is quoted in cents per DM, so 1.2 × 125,000 DM amounts to $1,500.

The following information is to be used in connection with Questions 72 and 73:

Consolidated Amalgamated has announced $25,000,000 of callable convertible debentures maturing in 2004. The conversion price is $12.50, and the bonds are issued at $1,000.

72. What is the conversion rate on these bonds?

    (A) 40
    (B) 80
    (C) 100
    (D) 125

(B) A conversion price of $12.50 means that a $1,000 bond is convertible into 80 shares.

73. If Consolidated Amalgamated were to call these bonds at 106 when the market price of the stock was $13 and at parity, an owner of these securities would do best to:

    (A) convert the bond and sell the shares
    (B) sell the bond
    (C) hold the bond and earn the interest
    (D) tender the bond

(D) If the stock is at parity and is selling for $13, 80 shares of stock and the bond both are selling for $1,040, which is less than the call price of $1,060. Since the bond is called, holding the bond is not an option.

74. Which of the following is used by a technical trader?

    (A) Head and shoulders pattern
    (B) P/E
    (C) Quick ratio
    (D) Leverage

(A) This is a price chart pattern. The other choices are all part of fundamental analysis.

75. The "visible supply" refers to:

    (A) the supply of corporate bonds becoming available
    (B) the supply of T-bonds becoming available
    (C) the supply of new equities becoming available
    (D) the supply of municipal bonds becoming available

(D) This information for the next thirty days is compiled and published in the *Bond Buyer*.

76. Which of the following positions requires maintenance margin?

    (A) A covered call
    (B) A covered put
    (C) An uncovered call
    (D) A long straddle

(C) There is no maintenance margin on covered options (choices A and B). A long straddle would require both premiums immediately and nothing further.

77. A customer buying an OTC stock from a firm that is a market maker in that stock, pays a price that:

    (A) includes a markup
    (B) does not include a markup
    (C) includes a commission
    (D) includes a commission and a markup

(A) A market maker acts as principal; hence, the customer pays a mark-up and not a commission.

78. If a municipal bond is purchased at a discount and is sold before maturity, the capital gain (loss) is measured from:

    I.   cost basis for an original issue purchase
    II.   cost basis for an aftermarket purchase
    III. accreted cost basis for an original issue purchase
    IV.   accreted cost basis for an aftermarket purchase

    (A) I and III
    (B) I and IV
    (C) II and III
    (D) II and IV

(C) Original issue bonds have the discount treated as interest income so the basis is the accreted cost. This is not true for bonds bought in the after-market.

79. The municipal issue most likely to require a sinking fund is a:

    (A) balloon issue
    (B) serial issue
    (C) term issue
    (D) revenue issue

(C) Since all of the bonds of a term issue mature at one time, a sinking fund is usually required.

80. What kind of investment company pays out 90% of its net investment income to its shareholders?

    (A) Registered
    (B) Diversified
    (C) Regulated
    (D) Balanced

(C) Regulated investment companies are required to pay out a minimum of 90% of their net income annually to their shareholders.

81. An options contract for British pounds is for 25,000 BPs. If the strike price is 150, the value of the contract is:

    (A) $2,500
    (B) $3,750
    (C) $25,000
    (D) $37,500

(D) The strike price is given as 150 or $1.50. Hence, 25,000 BPs are worth $1.50 × 25,000 = $37,500.

82. If a client refuses to provide information about his financial status, needs, and investment objectives, a registered representative might recommend buying an option:

    (A) if it is approved by the firm's ROP
    (B) if the information is otherwise available
    (C) if he gets special permission
    (D) never

(B) Rule 405 (the "know your customer" rule) states that the representative must "use due diligence to *learn* the essential facts" but does not specify the source. If the broker knows that options are a suitable investment, he or she may recommend them.

83. Amalgamated Consolidated, Inc. (ACI), had net income before taxes of $2,500,000. This included $500,000 of preferred dividends from XYZ

corporation. ACI owns 25% of XYZ, and ACI is in the 40% bracket. The total ACI tax bill would be:

(A) $800,000
(B) $840,000
(C) $860,000
(D) $1,000,000

(B) If ACI owns more than 20% of XYZ, it receives an 80% dividend exclusion. Its taxable income is therefore $2,000,000 + 20% of $500,000 for a total of $2,100,000. At 40%, its tax bill is $840,000.

84. A refunding is likely to occur for which of the following issues if all of them are selling at a current basis of 6.50?

(A) 5% coupon callable in 1991 at 102
(B) 6% coupon callable at par in 2001
(C) 6.5% coupon maturing in 1999
(D) 7% coupon maturing in 1994

(D) This is the only issue with a higher coupon than current rates.

85. An investor in a "plain vanilla" CMO who wished to achieve the highest possible return would choose:

(A) the first tranche
(B) the interest-only tranche
(C) the principal-only tranche
(D) the last tranche

(D) In a "plain vanilla" collateralized mortgage obligation, the principal and interest would be paid to the tranches sequentially. The last tranche would have the highest risk of early repayment and therefore the highest return. A plain vanilla CMO would not have principal-only tranches.

86. If the board of directors declares a stock split, all of the following are true EXCEPT:

(A) liquidity increases
(B) it is easier for the public to buy the stock
(C) the stock price rises
(D) the stock price falls

(C) If the number of shares increases, the price of each share decreases.

87. An investor buys three New York State revenue bonds at 106. If the bonds mature in six years and she sells them after four years at 104, with respect to taxes she has a:

(A) $60 capital loss
(B) $60 capital gain
(C) $20 interest income gain
(D) none of the above

(B) Municipal bonds bought at a premium in the secondary market have their cost basis adjusted over the holding period. After four years, the basis for these bonds is 102, so a sale of three bonds at 104 represents a capital gain of $60.

88. In an underwriting of a municipal bond issue, the additional takedown was $\frac{1}{2}$ and the concession was $\frac{1}{4}$. If the manager's fee was $\frac{1}{16}$, then, for each bond sold, a member of the syndicate would receive:

    (A) $\frac{1}{4}$
    (B) $\frac{5}{16}$
    (C) $\frac{9}{16}$
    (D) $\frac{3}{4}$

(D) If the member sold the bonds, he would get the takedown, which is the additional takedown plus the concession.

89. If a municipality redeems outstanding bonds with the proceeds from a new bond issue, this is called:

    (A) calling the bonds
    (B) refunding the bonds
    (C) sinking the bonds
    (D) defending the bonds

(B) Calling bonds simply means redeeming them early. A fund is set aside for purposes of redemption.

90. In trying to sell shares in a mutual fund, the registered representative may:
    (A) offer quantity discounts for large purchases arranged over an 18-month period
    (B) compute yield based on all distributions made over the preceding five-year period
    (C) consolidate income and capital gains distributions
    (D) show net asset value at the beginning and end of the period discussed

(D) All other choices are incorrect. Choices B and C violate the Statement of Policy, and the maximum time span of a letter of intent is 13 months, not 18 months.

91. An investor bought a 6.5% Ohio general obligation bond regular way on April 14. The last coupon date was February 15. How many days of interest must he add to the purchase price?

    (A) 54
    (B) 55
    (C) 61
    (D) 62

(D) Interest is computed from coupon date February 15 up to, but not including, delivery date April 17, on a 30-day month basis. This yields (February) 16 plus 30 plus 16 (April) = 62.

92. Having won a competitive bidding to underwrite a municipal bond, a syndicate now finds that rates have fallen as they are about to bring the issue to market. The syndicate would probably:

    (A) sell the bonds at a discount
    (B) sell the bonds at a premium
    (C) reduce the amount given to the municipality
    (D) not bring the issue to market

(B) If rates have fallen, these bonds are now more attractive and can sell at a premium. This would increase the money going to the community.

Questions 93 and 94 refer to the following types of securities:

    (A) double-barreled bonds
    (B) special tax bonds
    (C) revenue bonds
    (D) special assessment bonds

Choose the type of security that best describes the bonds listed below.

93. A bond issued to build a new toll bridge with tolls paying off the bond.

(C) This is a revenue bond, since it is paid from revenues of the toll bridge.

94. A bond issued by a municipality backed by proceeds from assessments and further guaranteed by a state agency.

(A) There are two sources of payment, and that describes a double-barreled bond. Note that there is no special assessment, so choices C and D are incorrect.

95. A trade made directly between an investment company and a bank is a:

    (A) first market trade
    (B) second market trade
    (C) third market trade
    (D) fourth market trade

(D) Trading between institutions is termed "trading in the fourth market." The first market represents exchanges, the second market represents the OTC market, and the third represents OTC (NASD) trading of exchange-listed issues.

96. In talking about a fidelity bond, one is referring to:

    (A) insurance a broker/dealer must carry to protect against fraud judgments
    (B) good faith effort to sell a new issue

(C) insurance provided by SIPC

(D) protection of prerefunded bonds

(A) The fidelity bond is the insurance a broker/dealer must have to defend against fraud judgments.

Questions 97 and 98 are based on the following investments:

Long 1 ACI Feb 50 Call at 6

Short 1 ACI Feb 60 Call at 5

97. What is the maximum possible gain if the position is held to expiration?

(A) $500

(B) $900

(C) $1,100

(D) Unlimited

(B) At 60, the investor makes $400 on his long call at 50 and keeps the entire $500 on his short call.

98. At what price would an investor break even?

(A) 51

(B) 56

(C) 61

(D) 65

(A) At 51, the investor loses $500 on his long call ($100 profit – $600 premium) and earns the $500 premium on his short call.

99. Under what circumstances could an investor write an ACI June 40 call at 6 in a cash account?

    I. If the investor was short 100 ACI at 40

    II. If he was long 100 ACI in the account

    III. If he was long an escrow receipt for 100 ACI

    IV. If he was long warrants for 100 ACI

(A) II and III

(B) II and IV

(C) I and III

(D) I, II, and III

(A) A call can be written in a cash account if it is covered. Being long the shares or having an escrow receipt for the shares covers the call. Having the right to purchase the shares through a warrant is not considered covered.

100. Defaulted bearer municipal bonds are traded:

(A) flat and stripped of coupons

(B) flat and with unpaid past-due coupons attached

(C) with accrued interest to the date of delivery added to the price

(D) with accrued interest to the date of delivery added to the price and with the unpaid coupons attached

(B) Defaulted bonds trade "flat" (meaning without accrued interest) since interest on the bonds is not being paid by the issuer. To be a "good delivery," the defaulted bonds must have the unpaid past-due coupons attached.

101. If a corporation is conservatively capitalized, it will raise most of its capital by selling:

(A) preferred stock

(B) common stock

(C) convertible bonds

(D) bonds

(B) To be conservatively capitalized, the firm would avoid fixed payments, whether interest or dividends.

102. All of the following are true of federal funds EXCEPT:

(A) they represent funds in excess of reserve requirements

(B) they are overnight loans

(C) they are very sensitive indicators of rates

(D) they are loans from the Fed to member banks

(D) They are loans from banks with excess reserves to banks whose reserves are not adequate to meet federal requirements.

103. Under the UGMA, which of the following is true?

(A) A donor may not be a custodian.

(B) Twins may have a single account.

(C) Trading in a margin account is not allowed.

(D) Parents may be joint custodians.

(C) This is true; none of the other statements is true.

104. A serial issue of municipals has maturities from 1993 to 2002 with the latter offering a 7% coupon to yield 7.50%. If the bonds are callable in 1994 at 103, in 1995 at 102, and at par thereafter, the bonds maturing in 2002 should be priced to the:

(A) 1994 date

(B) 1995 date

(C) 1996 date

(D) maturity date

(D) Since the coupon is less than the yield to maturity, the bonds are at a discount. Therefore, they are priced to maturity.

488 Series 7: STOCKBROKER EXAM

105. The coupon rate on a municipal is:

    I.   the nominal rate
   II.   the current rate
  III.   the yield to maturity
  IV.   the rate stated on the bond

    (A) I and II
    (B) II and III
    (C) III and IV
    (D) I and IV

(D) These two terms are synonymous.

106. All of the following characterize variable annuities EXCEPT:

    (A) they often invest in mutual funds
    (B) they are professionally managed
    (C) they have a fixed minimum payout
    (D) their returns are based on market performance

(C) They do not have a fixed minimum payout precisely because their return is based on performance.

107. An OTC dealer buys 100,000 shares of ACI at 20 and sells 1,000 immediately. Which of the following is closest to being fair and reasonable?

    (A) A markup of 7%
    (B) A sale at 22
    (C) A sale at 21 plus $.50 commission
    (D) The maximum suggested NASD markup

(D) A greater-than-usual markup is permissible only on an extremely large or an extremely small transaction. This trade is neither. Since choice C has both markup and commission it is also not permitted.

108. Compared to a bond without this feature, a bond with a call feature would:

    (A) be cheaper
    (B) be more expensive
    (C) be more attractive to investors
    (D) require lower coupon rates

(A) This feature is not favorable to investors since they cannot be sure of getting the stated return until maturity; all of the other choices describe a bond that is better for investors.

109. All of the following should be determined about a new customer by a registered representative EXCEPT:

    (A) investment objectives
    (B) financial resources

(C) financial requirements

(D) prior investment results

(D) This is not required of the registered representative, although it might be helpful to him in "knowing his customer."

110. To include a second dealer in a transaction unnecessarily is a violation of NASD Rules, and is known as:

(A) disintermediation

(B) churning

(C) twisting

(D) interpositioning

(D) Interpositioning causes a customer to pay more or receive less on his order.

111. Which of the following would be considered a fair and reasonable reoffering price for 7% municipals purchased at a 7% basis?

   I. 101

  II. 107

 III. 6.75

  IV. 5.50

(A) I and IV

(B) II and III

(C) I and III

(D) II and IV

(C) A markup of one point or 25 basis points would be considered fair and reasonable.

112. What is the dollar value of a $\frac{7}{8}$ change in an option's premium price?

(A) $7.80

(B) $8.75

(C) $78.00

(D) $87.50

(D) The premium is multiplied by 100 because the option is for 100 shares.

The following information is to be used for Questions 113 and 114:

ACI has announced an offer of 1,000,000 units at $8. Each unit consists of one share of common, one share of preferred, and a warrant for $\frac{1}{4}$ share of common.

113. If the offering is successful and all warrants are exercised, how many new shares of common stock will be outstanding?

(A) 250,000

(B) 1,000,000

   (C) 1,250,000
   (D) 2,000,000

(C) If 1,000,000 units are sold, then 1,000,000 new shares are outstanding. If the 1,000,000 warrants are exercised, then 250,000 additional new shares will be outstanding for a total of 1,250,000 new shares outstanding.

114. How much will ACI raise if the common is valued at $4 when issued?

   (A) $1,000,000
   (B) $4,000,000
   (C) $5,000,000
   (D) $8,000,000

(D) If the units are sold at $8 each, then $8,000,000 will be raised.

115. A customer without a position writes 1 ACI Nov 60 Put and writes 1 ACI Nov 60 Call. The position established is a:

   (A) long combination
   (B) short combination
   (C) short straddle
   (D) long straddle

(C) A straddle is a put and a call on the same stock with the same strike price and the same expiration month. Since the customer wrote both a put and a call, this is a short straddle.

116. Before issuing revenue bonds, a municipal authority would probably do all of the following EXCEPT:

   (A) have a ballot referendum
   (B) do a feasibility study
   (C) publish a notice of sale
   (D) get a bond attorney

(A) A referendum is not likely since no additional taxes are involved. The other choices are likely.

117. Tax-sheltered investments provide all of the following advantages to limited partners EXCEPT:

   (A) opportunities to limit risk
   (B) liquid investment
   (C) opportunities to defer taxes
   (D) opportunities to reduce taxes

(B) Limited partnerships are usually highly illiquid. The other advantages do obtain.

118. An investor wishes to swap one municipal bond holding for another one. Which of the following would not enter into consideration of this transaction?

(A) Maturity
(B) Coupon
(C) Accrued interest
(D) Quality

(C) The accrued interest has no bearing on a swap transaction.

119. With regard to NASD arbitration proceedings, which of the following is true?

(A) Nonmembers may not request their use in controversies involving members.
(B) Members may not demand their use in controversies with other members.
(C) The finding must be accepted by a member in controversy with a nonmember.
(D) Members may demand their use in controversies with nonmembers.

(C) As part of the membership agreement, members are bound to accept such findings.

120. Securities sold at "seller's option" can be delivered at the option of the seller if he gives written notice of:

(A) one day
(B) five weeks
(C) seven days
(D) ten days

(A) With a seller's option, contract delivery can be effected if the buyer is given one day's written notice.

121. A short straddle would be profitable if:

(A) the market price differs from the strike price by more than the sum of the premiums
(B) the market price differs from the strike price by less than the sum of the premiums
(C) the premiums are large
(D) the strike price is more than two times the larger premium

(B) A short-straddle holder collects two premiums. He makes money if there is little movement in the market price. Choice B exactly describes the circumstances of his making money.

122. The takedown on a new municipal issue is $\frac{3}{8} + \frac{1}{8}$. For a member of the syndicate, the discount is:

    (A) $\frac{1}{8}$

    (B) $\frac{2}{8}$

    (C) $\frac{3}{8}$

    (D) $\frac{4}{8}$

    (D) The discount to a syndicate member is the total takedown. This consists of the concession ($\frac{3}{8}$) available to a nonsyndicate member and the additional takedown ($\frac{1}{8}$).

123. Under SEC regulations, who among the following may be restricted in their use of nonpublic information about a public corporation?

    (A) Financial printers
    (B) Officers and directors
    (C) Underwriters
    (D) All of the above

    (D) Anyone privy to material nonpublic information emanating from an "insider" is prohibited from making improper use of the information.

124. A T-bill is characterized by all of the following EXCEPT:

    (A) it is issued at a discount
    (B) it has a $10,000 minimum denomination
    (C) it matures in no more than two years
    (D) it is in book-entry form

    (C) Maximum maturity for T-bills is one year.

125. In executing an order for a public customer, a member asks the specialist in the stock to guarantee him a price while giving the customer an opportunity to obtain a better price. This is known as:

    (A) floor protection
    (B) a special deal
    (C) a stop order
    (D) stopping stock

    (D) This defines "stopping stock."

ANSWER EXPLANATIONS

PART TWO

Questions 126 and 127 use the following information.

An investor bought $150,000 of a DPP and was also responsible for a $100,000 recourse loan.

126. The investor's basis in this program is:

    (A) $50,000
    (B) $100,000
    (C) $150,000
    (D) $250,000

(D) The recourse loan is his risk and, hence, part of his basis.

127. Assume the investor had passive income of $300,000. What is the minimum possible passive income for this investor for the year?

    (A) $300,000
    (B) $200,000
    (C) $150,000
    (D) $50,000

(D) If his total investment, including the recourse loan, were lost, he would be left with $50,000.

128. A basis point on a corporate bond ($1,000 par) would be worth:

    (A) $.10
    (B) $1.00
    (C) $10.00
    (D) $100.00

(A) A basis point is .01 of a point. On a $1,000 bond, each point is worth $10. Hence, a basis point is $.10.

Questions 129–131 refer to the following page from a specialist's book:

BUY	CAI	SELL
300 MERRILL	45	
1,000 BACHE	$\frac{1}{8}$	
200 DWR	$\frac{1}{4}$	
	$\frac{3}{8}$	
	$\frac{1}{2}$	500 STOP DREXEL
	$\frac{5}{8}$	400 MERRILL
		100 BACHE

$\frac{3}{4}$ 500 MERRILL

200 DREXEL

$\frac{7}{8}$ 1,000 DWR

500 BACHE

129. The current quote and size is:

   (A) $45-45\frac{7}{8}$ 1,500–2,800

   (B) $45\frac{1}{4}-45\frac{1}{2}$ 1,500–2,800

   (C) $45-45\frac{1}{2}$ 200–100

   (D) $45\frac{1}{4}-4\frac{5}{8}$ 200–500

(D) The volume for the highest bid and the lowest offer. Stop orders are not considered in a quotation.

130. For his own account, the specialist may bid no less than:

   (A) $45\frac{1}{4}$

   (B) $44\frac{3}{8}$

   (C) $45\frac{1}{2}$

   (D) he may not bid for the stock

(B) A specialist must bid more than any existing bid in a trade for his own account.

131. If the last sale was at $45\frac{1}{2}$ on a minus tick, the lowest possible offer by a short seller would be:

   (A) $45\frac{1}{4}$

   (B) $45\frac{3}{8}$

   (C) $45\frac{1}{2}$

   (D) $45\frac{5}{8}$

(D) This is the only price that would represent the plus tick necessary in a short sale.

Questions 132 and 133 are based on the following information:

An 8% municipal bond of $10,000 par value maturing in ten years is trading at 90.

132. To the nearest .1%, what is the nominal yield?

   (A) 7.2%
   (B) 8.0%
   (C) 8.8%
   (D) 8.9%

(B) The nominal yield is the named yield (in this case, 8%).

133. To the nearest .1%, what is the current yield?

    (A) 7.2%
    (B) 8.0%
    (C) 8.8%
    (D) 8.9%

  (D) The current yield is the return available now. In this case, $800 ÷ $9,000
     = 8.888%.

134. All of the following can be classified as money market instruments
     EXCEPT:

    (A) federal funds
    (B) American Depository Receipts
    (C) bankers' acceptances
    (D) commercial paper

  (B) ADRs are depository receipts representing stock of foreign companies.
     The others are all money market instruments.

135. The advance-decline line used by technical analysts is intended to gauge
     the:

    (A) direction of the market
    (B) volatility of the market
    (C) quality of the market
    (D) volume of activity in the market

  (A) The advance decline ratio theory shows market direction and may indi-
     cate that a change in direction is near.

136. When does Regulation T require payment for an option bought in a
     margin account?

    (A) On the seventh business day following the trade
    (B) On the trade date
    (C) On the next business day after the trade
    (D) On the fifth business day following the trade

  (D) This is the Regulation T requirement. The OCC requires dealers to pay
     on the next business day. Most firms have house rules that require
     clients to do the same.

137. When depositors withdraw money from savings institutions to invest in
     higher yielding instruments, this is called:

    (A) reverse repo
    (B) the multiplier effect
    (C) disintermediation
    (D) open market operations

  (C) By definition.

138. When revenues exceed deductions in a DPP, we say that:

    (A) phantom income is generated
    (B) cash flow is positive
    (C) operating income is positive
    (D) the crossover point has been reached

  (D) This is the definition of the crossover point.

139. Which of the following types of accounts are specifically prohibited by NYSE rules?

     I.   Third-party accounts
     II. Accounts under an alias
     III. Code-number accounts
     IV. Limited discretion accounts

    (A) II and III only
    (B) I only
    (C) II and IV only
    (D) I and IV only

  (B) Third-party accounts are specifically prohibited. The other choices are permitted when properly documented.

140. When interest rates on bonds rise, which of the following happens to old bonds outstanding?

     I.   Dollar prices rise
     II. Yields rise
     III. Dollar prices decline
     IV. Yields decline

    (A) I and II only
    (B) I and IV only
    (C) II and IV only
    (D) II and III only

  (D) Rates up equals prices down. Prices down equals yield up.

141. Offerings of new issues of municipal securities are exempted from all but the:

    (A) 1933 Securities Act
    (B) 1934 Securities Exchange Act
    (C) 1935 Holding Company Act
    (D) 1939 Trust Indenture Act

  (D) This act about the trust indenture does apply to municipals.

142. Under NYSE rules, opening an account for which of the following would require prior written consent and duplicate confirmations of all transactions sent to his employer?

(A) An employee in another member organization
(B) An employee of a registered investment company
(C) An officer of a trust company
(D) An independent insurance agent

(A) Prior written permission is required to open any kind of account for an employee of another member organization; also, duplicate confirmations and statements must be sent to the employer.

143. In a municipal bond underwriting, which of the following is the correct order of allocation?

   I. Pre-sale
   II. Syndicate account less concession
   III. Orders at the takedown prices
   IV. Designated

   (A) II, I, III, IV
   (B) IV, III, II, I
   (C) III, II, I, IV
   (D) I, II, IV, III

(D) The normal account procedure.

144. A Direct Participation Program that does not have a legitimate business purpose is called a(n):

   (A) tax shelter
   (B) abusive shelter
   (C) limited partnership
   (D) passive shelter

(B) By definition, they are subject to legal attack by the Internal Revenue Service. Losses from them may not be accepted by the IRS.

145. A customer learns that he bought 100 ACI at $34\frac{1}{4}$. Today he discovers the correct price to be $34\frac{1}{2}$. As a result:

   (A) the customer is permitted to cancel the trade
   (B) the registered representative must pay the difference
   (C) the customer is responsible for the price as executed
   (D) the firm must take the transaction into its own error account

(C) Rule 411 of the NYSE requires that the report be corrected to the actual trade price.

146. All of the following are true of most United States Government Agency bonds EXCEPT:

   (A) they may have interest coupons attached
   (B) they are freely traded
   (C) they are considered relatively safe investments
   (D) they are direct obligations of the United States Government

(D) Most agency bonds are not directly guaranteed by the United States Government as to payment of principal or interest.

147. The document that stipulates the rights and obligations of the general and limited partners in a Direct Participation Program is called the:

(A) Agreement of Limited Partnership
(B) Certificate of Incorporation
(C) Partnership Papers
(D) Limited Liability Agreement

(A) The Agreement of Limited Partnership describes all of the rights, obligations, and limitations of the partners to the agreement.

148. Option allocation assignments notices to customers may use which of the following methods?

 I. Random selections
 II. FIFO
 III. LIFO
 IV. Equitable allocation

(A) I, II, and IV only
(B) II, III, and IV only
(C) I and II only
(D) II and IV only

(C) Only random selections or FIFO are allowed under OCC rules.

149. According to MSRB rules, each municipal securities dealer must keep a copy of those rules in:

(A) the main office of the firm
(B) any office of the firm where three or more representatives conduct municipal securities business
(C) each office of the firm
(D) any office of the firm that does not have a municipal securities principal in residence

(C) This is required under MSRB Rules (G-29).

150. During the "cooling-off" period in connection with an underwriting, all of the following usually take place EXCEPT:

(A) issuance of a red herring
(B) due diligence meetings
(C) blue sky filings
(D) stabilization

(D) Stabilization can occur only after the initial public offering.

151. The owner of a call option is entitled to a dividend payable on the underlying stock:

    (A) always
    (B) never
    (C) only if he exercises before the ex-dividend date
    (D) only if he exercises after the ex-dividend date

(C) When he exercises, the shares are his, and, hence, he is entitled to the dividend.

152. What Act requires that municipalities file disclosures of pertinent information prior to a public offering?

    (A) Securities Act of 1933
    (B) Securities Exchange Act of 1934
    (C) Trust Indenture Act of 1939
    (D) No such law presently exists.

(D) There are no requirements prior to a public offering.

153. The accounting statement that presents a snapshot of a financial position of a business at a particular point in time (rather than over a period of time) is called the:

    (A) balance sheet
    (B) income statement
    (C) sources and uses
    (D) earnings statement

(A) The balance sheet shows the condition of the corporation at a given point in time (usually the end of the year), while the income statement shows the result over a period of time (usually one year).

154. For listed options, the Options Clearing Corporation determines all but the:

    (A) strike price
    (B) premium amount
    (C) contract size
    (D) expiration

(B) The premium is determined in the market.

155. Municipal term bonds are usually quoted on a:

    (A) discount basis
    (B) current yield basis
    (C) yield to maturity basis
    (D) dollar price basis

(D) For this reason, term bonds are often called "dollar bonds."

The following choices apply to Questions 156–158:

(A) equity options
(B) interest rate options
(C) index options
(D) foreign currency options

Select the choice that best describes the options listed below.

156. Options that would be used to hedge a portfolio of three listed stocks.

(**A**) Options on each individual stock would be the best hedge.

157. Options for hedging FOMC moves.

(**B**) FOMC moves are moves by the Federal Reserve that affect the money supply and, hence, interest rates.

158. Options affected by the interbank rate.

(**D**) The interbank market is the market in foreign currencies.

159. Settlement on an index option is made by:

(A) cash
(B) delivery of a futures contract
(C) delivery of the underlying securities
(D) any of the above

(**A**) Exercise of index options is settled by payment of cash.

160. The balance sheet equation is:

(A) assets = stockholder's equity
(B) assets – liabilities = profits
(C) total assets – total liabilities = profits
(D) total assets – total liabilities = net worth

(**D**) By definition. It states that assets are made up of stockholders' equity plus liabilities.

161. Options on foreign currencies are traded on the Philadelphia Stock Exchange. Which of the following currencies have listed options contracts?

I. Japanese yen
II. British pounds
III. Canadian dollars
IV. German marks

(A) I, II, and IV only
(B) II and III only
(C) I and IV only
(D) I, II, III, and IV

(**D**) Options on all of these currencies exist.

162. An investor purchases five ($1,000 par) 15-year municipal bonds at 107.50. Three years later, he sells them at 105. This results in a:

    (A) loss of $50
    (B) gain of $50
    (C) loss of $125
    (D) gain of $125

 (A) The premium of $75 must be amortized over 15 years or $5 per year. After three years, the adjusted price is 106, so selling for 105 represents a $10 loss per bond.

 Questions 163 and 164 refer to the choices listed below:

    (A) free riding
    (B) matched sales
    (C) wash sales
    (D) short against the box

 Select the choice that best describes the following activities:

163. Which activity describes buying and selling of equal totals of some security at the same price using a single broker and never actually changing the true owner of the securities?

 (C) This is a description of a wash sale used to give the appearance of activity and trading interest in some security. Simultaneous buying and selling of some security at the same price is called *a matched purchase and sale* and accomplishes the same purpose.

164. Which activity describes buying and selling equal totals of some security to establish two separate positions?

 (D) One sells short (against the box) a security previously bought to lock in a profit on a long position without having the completed trade credited to the account at the time.

165. A convertible bond selling at $1,110 has been called at 110. The bond is convertible at $50 to a stock that is currently selling at $54. Ignoring transaction costs, an investor should:

    (A) sell the bond
    (B) allow the bond to be called
    (C) convert and sell the stock
    (D) buy additional bonds and tender them

 (A) This yields $1,110. The bond is called at $1,100 and, if converted, would give 20 shares selling at $54 each for a total of $1,080.

166. A trade to be settled "when as and if issued" will settle:

    (A) on the issue date
    (B) one day after issue

(C) five days after issue
(D) on a date to be assigned

(D) This is the correct answer although the date to be assigned could be one of the other choices.

167. All of the following are true of purchases of repos EXCEPT:

   (A) they are an investment in treasury instruments
   (B) they provide flexibility in the amount invested
   (C) they are a noncompetitive market
   (D) they offer money market rates

(C) They are, in fact, highly competitive markets.

168. All of the following are part of the computation of cost depletion in a drilling program EXCEPT the:

   (A) extracted crude in storage
   (B) extracted crude sold
   (C) recoverable reserves
   (D) adjusted cost basis of the property

(A) The cost depletion only considers the crude that has already been sold.

Questions 169 and 170 refer to the following information:

An investor buys 200 shares of CAI at 46 and sells 2 CAI Aug 50 Calls at 3.

169. With no previous exercise, her break-even point at expiration would be:

   (A) 40
   (B) 43
   (C) 49
   (D) 53

(B) She collects $600 in premiums but experiences a $600 loss on the stock purchased at $46 and currently at $43.

170. If the calls are exercised when CAI is at 56, she will realize a:

   (A) $600 loss
   (B) $200 gain
   (C) $1,400 gain
   (D) $2,600 gain

(C) Her profit is the $600 premium plus $800 on the 200 shares bought at $46 and delivered at $50.

171. How often must an "open" order left with the specialist be reconfirmed?

   (A) Daily
   (B) Weekly
   (C) Monthly
   (D) Semiannually

(D) Under NYSE Rules open order on the specialist's book must be renewed semiannually.

172. The Trust Indenture Act of 1939 sets forth the following:

    I. the rules of the NASD
    II. the responsibilities of the trustee
    III. the rights of the stockbrokers
    IV. the obligations of the entity issuing the debt

    (A) I and II only
    (B) II and IV only
    (C) I and III only
    (D) I, II, III, and IV

(B) The trust indenture does not define rights of stockholders and makes no mention of NASD regulations.

173. Which of the following industries would be most likely to be hurt by interest rates increasing rapidly?

    (A) Mining companies
    (B) Chemical companies
    (C) Railroad companies
    (D) Utility companies

(D) Public utilities are usually very sensitive to interest rate changes because most of their assets are funded with debt.

174. Who is the beneficial owner of stock registered in "street" name?

    (A) The broker/dealer
    (B) The transfer agent
    (C) The registrar
    (D) The customer

(D) The customer is the "beneficial" owner, and the broker/dealer is the owner of "record."

175. When do listed equity options cease to trade?

    (A) 3:00 P.M. Eastern Time on the expiration date
    (B) 10:59 A.M. Eastern Time on the business day prior to the expiration date
    (C) 4:00 P.M. Eastern Time on the business day prior to the expiration date
    (D) 10:59 P.M. Eastern Time on the business day prior to the expiration date

(C) This is the same as 3:00 P.M. Central Time.

176. The writer of an option that has been exercised:

    (A) may retender this obligation
    (B) must make good on his obligation

(C) may buy an option to balance the position

(D) all of the above

(B) The writer is obligated to deliver stock on a Call or buy it on a Put.

177. A municipal bond is purchased at a premium. Order the yields from lowest to highest.

I. Nominal yield
II. Yield to maturity
III. Current yield

(A) I, II, III
(B) II, III, I
(C) I, III, II
(D) III, I, II

(B) The bond is at a premium so the current yield is lower than the nominal yield. The yield to maturity is lower still since, at redemption, the investor does not recover the premium.

178. All of the following are prohibited under SEC Rule 144 EXCEPT:

(A) selling shares without notifying the SEC
(B) sales on an exchange without advising purchasers they are acquiring 144 stock
(C) solicitation of purchase orders from customers of the firm
(D) charging the seller a special commission to compensate the firm for its extra distribution effort

(B) Under Rule 144, this is permissible. None of the other items are permissible under the rule.

179. The *New York Times* reported that Amalgamated Consolidated Incorporated announced a quarterly dividend of $1.20 with a record date of January 20. The dividend is payable February 28. An investor who purchased ACI on February 23 would:

(A) receive the dividend
(B) not receive the dividend
(C) receive it if the trade had been for "cash"
(D) receive $1 of dividend

(B) The dividend is payable to those who own the stock on the record date.

180. The name for a written consent signed by all limited partners permitting the general partner to act outside the partnership agreement is a:

(A) partnership democracy
(B) flip-flop agreement
(C) partnership agreement
(D) certificate amendment

(A) This allows the general partner some latitude in his other activities.

Questions 181–183 refer to the following customer margin account:

Long Market $60,000   Short Market $20,000

Debit Record $30,000   Credit Record $30,000

SMA -0-

181. What is the customer's equity?

    (A) $5,000
    (B) $40,000
    (C) $56,000
    (D) $80,000

(B) The equity is $30,000 from the long account ($60,000 – $30,000) plus $10,000 from the short account ($30,000 – $20,000) = $40,000.

182. If the market value of the short position falls to $10,000, what is the customer's equity?

    (A) $15,000
    (B) $40,000
    (C) $46,000
    (D) $50,000

(D) At this point, the equity in the short account has increased to $20,000 ($30,000 – $10,000), so the total is now $50,000.

183. What is the new SMA?

    (A) $5,000
    (B) $10,000
    (C) $15,000
    (D) $20,000

(C) With a 50% Regulation T, the long account is fully margined. The short account now has a market value of $10,000, requiring $5,000 in margin. The additional $15,000 in customer's equity goes into the SMA.

184. An investor purchases a 9% corporate bond in February at par. If she pays $30 in accrued interest and collects two semiannual interest payments on the bond, her tax liability is:

    (A) $0
    (B) $30
    (C) $60
    (D) $90

(C) The $30 in accrued interest is subtracted from the $90 that she collects for the year, leaving tax due on $60 of interest income.

185. The length of time covered by a single SEC notification under Rule 144 is:

    (A) 60 days
    (B) 90 days
    (C) 180 days
    (D) 360 days

    (B) After 90 days, a new notification is needed.

186. Free-riding and withholding are violations of the:

    (A) Securities Exchange Act of 1934
    (B) NYSE Constitution
    (C) NASD Rules of Fair Practice
    (D) Securities Act of 1933

    (C) The prohibition against free-riding and withholding is found in the NASD Rules of Fair Practice.

187. All of the following oil and gas programs involve producing wells EXCEPT:

    (A) developmental
    (B) balanced
    (C) exploratory
    (D) income

    (C) An income program invests in producing properties. Developmental programs try to expand on existing fields where oil or gas has already been found. A balanced program is a combination of producing properties and drilling. Only exploratory programs don't involve producing wells.

188. A Regulation A offering cannot exceed:

    (A) $1,000,000
    (B) $1,500,000
    (C) $2,500,000
    (D) $5,000,000

    (D) The maximum value of an offering permitted under Regulation A is $1,500,000.

189. To qualify as an "intrastate" offering under Rule 147, an offer must have:

    (A) 80% of the corporation's assets located in that state
    (B) 80% of the proceeds of the offering used in that state
    (C) 80% of the corporate revenues earned in that state
    (D) all of the above

    (D) All of the choices are required for an offering to qualify as "intrastate."

190. An investor exercises an index option at noon on Tuesday. The exercise value used to determine his profit or loss is:

(A) Monday's close
(B) Tuesday's opening
(C) Tuesday's noon value
(D) Tuesday's close

(D) The exercise value is the quote for Tuesday's close.

191. Which of the following is true for qualified profit-sharing plans?

(A) Contributions from the corporation are taxable.
(B) Employee benefits are predetermined.
(C) Contributions are mandatory whether the firm is profitable or not.
(D) All income from the plan's assets are not taxed until received.

(D) Corporate contributions are deductible to the firm. The benefits depend on the firm's profitability and the profitability of the investments, and, as the name implies, if the firm has no profits, there is nothing to share (*i.e.,* the firm is not required to make contributions in years when it is not itself profitable).

192. Which of the following options is "in the money"?

(A) CAI Nov 40 Puts   CAI stock at 45
(B) ACI Nov 50 Calls   ACI stock at 45
(C) ACI Feb 55 Calls   ACI stock at 55
(D) CAI Feb 50 Puts   CAI stock at 45

(D) The put gives one the right to sell at 50 when the stock is at 45. This is obviously profitable.

193. A T-bill was purchased at $9,500 in November 1992. If it matures at $10,000 in February 1993, the tax consequences are:

(A) $500 capital gains 1993
(B) $500 interest income 1993
(C) $500 interest income divided proportionately between 1992 and 1993
(D) $500 capital gains divided proportionately between 1992 and 1993

(B) T-bills are sold at a discount. The appreciation is all interest income and is taxable in the year of maturity.

194. If a mutual fund had a portfolio consisting of a wide variety of biotechnology firms, it would best be characterized as a:

(A) specialized fund
(B) growth fund
(C) closed-end fund
(D) open-end fund

(A) The fund specializes in one type of stock. Note that most biotechnology firms might be considered growth stocks but are not necessarily so.

195. If federal funds rates decline over time, all of the following are likely EXCEPT:

    (A) the federal government is encouraging expansion
    (B) short rates are decreasing
    (C) the prime is decreasing
    (D) reserves are decreasing

  (D) If federal funds rates are declining, then the supply of reserves (the funds from which federal funds loans are made) is probably increasing, making more funds available and, hence, cheaper.

196. An offering of $20,000,000 of 7% New York State highway bonds would pay semiannual interest totaling:

    (A) $350,000
    (B) $700,000
    (C) $1,000,000
    (D) $3,500,000

  (B) The total payment is 7% of $20,000,000 or $1,400,000. The semiannual payment is half of that.

197. Customers with inactive accounts must receive statements at least:

    (A) monthly
    (B) every three months
    (C) every six months
    (D) annually

  (B) They may be and often are sent monthly, but the requirement is quarterly statements.

198. When a variable annuity contract is to begin payout, which of the following is true?

    (A) The monthly dollars of payout is fixed.
    (B) The number of units of payout is fixed.
    (C) The value of each unit is fixed.
    (D) The securities are liquidated.

  (B) The number of units is fixed, but the value of each unit and, hence, the dollar amount varies with market experience. Obviously, the securities are not liquidated (or the market experience would be irrelevant).

199. For tax purposes, the first cash distributions from a depreciation in previous years must be added as taxable income. This is called:

    (A) recapture
    (B) return on equity
    (C) limited partner costing
    (D) reverse depreciation

(A) This is the term used by the IRS to describe the process of reclaiming as ordinary income the amounts claimed against personal income in previous years.

Questions 200–202 refer to the following types of debt issues:

(A) T-bills
(B) federal funds
(C) commercial paper
(D) banker's acceptances

Which choice is best described in the following questions? (Remember that a choice might be used more than once.)

200. They are used to promote foreign trade.

 (D) These are used primarily with respect to foreign trade.

201. They are quoted as an interest rate.

 (B) All of the others are quoted on a discount basis.

202. They are exempt from state and local taxes.

 (A) This is true of United States Treasury securities in general. These are exempt from state and local taxes.

203. If a United States corporation owns common stock of another United States corporation, dividend payments received are:

(A) taxed as capital gains
(B) taxed as ordinary income
(C) effectively taxed at 30% of their normal rate
(D) taxed at 70% of the normal rate

 (C) They are 70% tax-exempt, so the effective rate is 30% of the normal rate. For example, if the normal rate is 35% and dividend payments are $10,000, then $7,000 is exempt and $3,000 is taxed at 35% to yield $1,050. This is effectively a rate of 10.5% on the total, which is 3/10 (30%) of the normal rates.

204. Which method of payment yields the largest monthly payment from an annuity contract?

(A) Lump sum
(B) 15-year certain
(C) Life annuity
(D) Life annuity plus one survivor

 (C) All of the others have some fixed minimum commitment from the insurer. This perforce lowers the amount available for monthly payments.

205. ACI declares a 20% stock dividend. When ACI goes ex-dividend, an ACI Jun 60 Call would become:

(A) ACI Jun 60 Call for 120 shares
(B) ACI Jun 50 Call for 120 shares
(C) ACI Jun 60 Call for 100 shares
(D) ACI Jun 50 Call for 100 shares

(B) The number of shares is raised to reflect the dividend, and, inversely, the strike price is lowered so that the total value is unchanged.

$$(100 \times \$60 = 120 \times \$50)$$

206. If a margin account is restricted but has a positive SMA, how much may an investor withdraw from the account?

(A) No funds may be withdrawn from a restricted account.
(B) Fifty percent of the SMA may be withdrawn.
(C) All of the SMA may be withdrawn.
(D) All of the SMA up to an amount that leaves the account with 25% margin.

(D) A restricted account is margined at between 25% (maintenance) and 50% (Regulation T requirement). The account may not go below maintenance, but, otherwise, SMA funds may be withdrawn.

207. Which of the following transactions cannot be performed in a cash account?

(A) Sell an ACI Call; buy ACI stock.
(B) Buy an ACI Put; buy ACI stock.
(C) Buy an ACI Call; buy ACI stock.
(D) Sell an ACI Put; sell Short ACI stock.

(D) The other choices can all be performed in a cash account. This one must be done in a margin account.

208. The margin requirement for an investor who owned $100,000 of 6% T-notes that matured on 1/1/96 and who wrote a T-note call at 6 for notes maturing in January 1996 was:

(A) 15% of market value plus the premium
(B) 20% of market value minus the premium
(C) 0
(D) 20% of market value minus out of the moneyness

(C) This is a covered option, and hence, there is no margin required.

209. A certificate of limited partnership would need to be amended if any of the following occurred EXCEPT:

(A) a new limited partner is added
(B) a new general partner is added
(C) a new financing arrangement is made
(D) a new sharing arrangement is made

(C) The certificate of partnership would not be affected by any change in how partnership investments are financed.

210. An end-of-year statement of a real estate limited partnership contains the following information:

Rental income	$200,000
Expenses	$75,000
Depreciation	$50,000
Interest payments	$50,000
Principal payments	$50,000

The investor would report a gain (loss) on his tax return of:

(A) $25,000 loss
(B) $25,000 gain
(C) $75,000 gain
(D) $125,000 gain

(B) Repayment of principal is not a loss, but the other items are deducted from income to arrive at net income.

211. Which of the following securities is not exempt from the registration requirements of the Securities Act of 1933?

(A) Benevolent corporations
(B) Municipal securities
(C) Insurance companies
(D) Bank issues

(C) Insurance companies' new issues are not excluded from registration under the Securities Act of 1933.

212. A customer purchases 1 CAI Dec 50 Call at 1. A few months later it is out of the money by 4. What is the customer's maximum possible loss?

(A) $100
(B) $200
(C) $300
(D) $400

(A) Buying an option, one can lose no more then the premium; in this case, $100.

213. The largest expense incurred in its first year by an open-ended investment company is usually the:

(A) management fee
(B) commission to salesmen
(C) legal fees
(D) accounting fees

(B) Sales commissions can be as high as $8\frac{1}{2}$%. Management fees are typically between $\frac{1}{2}$% and 1%.

214. A customer places an order to sell 100 ACI at $42\frac{5}{8}$ on a stop limit. Trades then take place as follows:

$42\frac{5}{8}$　　$42\frac{1}{2}$　　$42\frac{3}{8}$　　$42\frac{1}{4}$

Execution takes place at:

(A)　$42\frac{1}{4}$

(B)　$42\frac{3}{8}$

(C)　$42\frac{1}{2}$

(D)　the order cannot be executed

(D) A sell stop limit order is placed below the current market price and is used to liquidate a long position if the loss becomes too great. In this example, the first trade had gone to the "stop" price of $42\frac{5}{8}$, so the order is activated as a limit order at $42\frac{5}{8}$. Since the stock never trades as high as $42\frac{5}{8}$ again, the order to sell cannot be executed.

215. Under the NASD Uniform Practice Code, which of the following is not a good delivery for a 700 share trade?

(A)　Twenty certificates of 35 shares each
(B)　Seven certificates of 40 shares each and seven of 60 shares each
(C)　One certificate for 200 shares and one certificate for 500 shares
(D)　One certificate for 700 shares

(A) The rule is that shares must add up to 100 or be in round multiples of 100. Note: Since 40 + 60 = 100, choice B is good delivery. Only choice A fails the rule.

216. An investor has a $10,000 long-term loss in 1992 with no offsetting gains. What is the last year in which he has a carry forward loss?

(A)　1992
(B)　1993
(C)　1994
(D)　1995

(D) This allows deductions of $3,000 for 1992, 1993, and 1994, and $1,000 carried forward to 1995.

217. Under Rule 144, every 90 days, one may sell:

(A)　an average of the past four weeks' trading volume
(B)　an average of the past six weeks' trading volume
(C)　one percent of the outstanding shares
(D)　whichever is greater of (A) or (C)

(D) Rule 144 states that one can sell an average of the past four weeks' trading volume or 1% of the outstanding shares, whichever is greater.

218. ACI closes at 45 on an uptick on the NYSE and goes ex-dividend $.60 the next day. The lowest possible price for a short sale on the opening the next day is:

    (A) $44\frac{3}{8}$

    (B) $44\frac{1}{2}$

    (C) $44\frac{5}{8}$

    (D) 45

(B) A short sale can be made only on a plus tick or zero-plus tick. ACI closed at 45 on an uptick and the next day goes ex-dividend ($.60). When a stock goes ex-dividend, the price is reduced by the amount of the dividend or the next highest eighth if the dividend is not an amount divisible by $\frac{1}{8}$; here, the price is reduced by $\frac{1}{2}$, giving an adjusted plus tick price of $44\frac{1}{2}$.

219. For a mutual fund, net investment income is derived from:

    (A) dividend income
    (B) interest and dividend income
    (C) capital gains
    (D) interest and dividend income plus capital gains

(B) Net investment income is interest and dividends less expenses.

220. If an OTC order is placed for 220 shares at the market on one ticket, and the market price is 40, then the order must be executed as:

    (A) 200 shares at 40 and 20 shares at $40\frac{1}{8}$
    (B) 220 shares at 40
    (C) 220 shares at $40\frac{1}{8}$
    (D) This cannot be placed as a single order

(B) The OTC requirement is that an order of at least 100 shares must be made on each order ticket at the same price. Therefore, 220 shares at 40 is allowed.

221. The "dated date" is the:

    (A) trade date
    (B) settlement date
    (C) date from which accrued interest starts
    (D) date from which all computations are made

(C) By definition.

222. An investor wants preservation of capital and a minimum amount of purchasing power risk. As a registered representative, you would suggest:

    (A) T-bonds
    (B) project notes
    (C) AA high-quality corporate bonds
    (D) revenue bonds

    (B) Project notes are short-term debt backed by the full faith and credit of the United States Government. The short-term maturity reduces purchasing power risks.

223. Which of the following ratios provides the most stringent test of liquidity?

    (A) (Current assets — inventory)/current liabilities
    (B) Current assets/current liabilities
    (C) Assets/liabilities
    (D) Cash and marketable securities/liabilities

    (A) This is the quick ratio. It is more stringent than the current ratio, which includes inventory. The other choices have total liabilities in the denominator, and these do not reflect liquidity, since they are not necessarily payable soon.

224. Municipalities would probably assess an *ad valorem* tax on:

    (A) population
    (B) property
    (C) sales of goods and services
    (D) income

    (B) An *ad valorem* (to the value) tax is another name for a property tax.

225. List the following Moody's ratings in descending order:

    I. Aa
    II. Aaa
    III. A1
    IV. Baa

    (A) II, I, III, IV
    (B) III, II, I, IV
    (C) III, IV, I, II
    (D) II, III, I, IV

    (A) The Moody's rating system starts with a highest rating of Aaa. The A1 rating is higher than A but lower than Aa.

226. If total assets are $1,000,000 and short-term liabilities are $600,000 for a corporation that has no long-term debt, then the shareholder's equity is:

    (A) impossible to determine
    (B) $600,000

(C) $400,000
(D) $1,000,000

(C) Total assets = debt + shareholder's equity. In this case, all of the debt is short term.

227. All of the following customer records must be kept by the registered representative EXCEPT:

(A) each customer's current position
(B) each customer's purchase and sale for the past three years
(C) each customer's dividend income for the past three years
(D) a cross-indexed file of his entire customer holdings

(C) Records of dividends are not required.

228. An investor pays a 7.5% sales commission on the purchase of 1,000 shares of a mutual fund offered at $15. If he sells it and must pay a .5% redemption fee, and the fund has not changed in value, he will receive approximately:

(A) $15,000
(B) $14,925
(C) $13,730
(D) $13,800

(D) $15 × (1 − .075) = Bid = $13.875. If a 0.5% redemption fee is charged, the investor receives approximately $13.80, which, if multiplied by 1,000 shares, gives $13,800.

229. The Keogh Act would allow each of the following to set up a self-retirement fund EXCEPT:

(A) a lawyer in private practice
(B) a municipal employee with an income from selling paintings
(C) a broker with the funds from a Christmas bonus
(D) a salaried plumber from freelance plumbing income

(C) These bonus funds are not from self-employment and hence do not qualify for a Keogh.

230. The Dow Industrials comprises:

(A) all NYSE stocks
(B) 65 blue-chip stocks
(C) 30 blue-chip stocks
(D) all NYSE industrial stocks

(C) By definition.

231. Under NYSE Rules, an investor can open a numbered account if:

(A) he provides written evidence of responsibility for the account
(B) he deposits $250,000 to cover the SIPC

(C)   he gets a bank letter of credit to cover the SIPC

(D)   it is not allowed

(A) A numbered account is acceptable if the beneficial owner gives written proof of his ownership.

232. A mutual fund pays dividends and also has a capital gains distribution. An investor has owned shares in this fund for two years. The payouts would be treated as:

(A)   ordinary income

(B)   capital gains

(C)   ordinary income and capital gains

(D)   long-term capital gains

(C) The mutual fund acts as a conduit. The investors are responsible for all taxes.

233. The maximum allowable contribution to a Keogh plan is:

(A) $2,000

(B) $7,500

(C) $15,000

(D) $30,000

(D) The allowable deduction is 25% of net income up to a maximum of $30,000.

234. Under NYSE rules, which of the following require prior permission from the investor's employer?

  I.   A margin account for an employee of a bank

 II.   An account for an employee of the exchange

III.   A cash account for an employee of another broker

(A)   I and II

(B)   II and III

(C)   I and III

(D)   I, II, and III

(D) For I and II, this applies only to margin accounts. For III, it applies to cash and margin accounts.

235. An investor writes 2 ACI Oct 40 Calls at 3 and at the same time writes 1 ACI Oct 40 Put at 5. If ACI goes to 44 and the calls are exercised and the put expires, the investor will realize:

(A)   a gain of $300

(B)   a gain of $600

(C)   a gain of $1,100

(D)   a loss of $800

(A) He must purchase 200 shares at $44 and tender them at $40. This loss of $800 is subtracted from the $1,100 he collects in premiums.

236. If the manager says that the retention is 80%, an underwriter who has an allotment of 100,000 shares would have how many available for his customers?

    (A) 20,000
    (B) 80,000
    (C) 100,000
    (D) 100,000 plus 80% of the remainder

  (A) The retention is the amount retained by the syndicate for group sales. In this case, they retain 80% of the allotment, leaving 20% or 20,000 shares.

237. All of the following are true of the tax treatment of variable annuities EXCEPT:

    (A) early withdrawals are subject to a tax penalty
    (B) payments are considered part income and part return on investment
    (C) earnings are not taxed until withdrawal
    (D) all payments are taxed as received

  (D) Some of the payment is considered return of equity.

238. Which of the following parties does an investor notify when he wishes to exercise an option?

    (A) The writer
    (B) The broker
    (C) The OCC
    (D) The AMEX or the CBOE

  (B) When an investor wishes to exercise, he notifies his broker who in turn notifies the OCC.

239.   A registered representative who violates NYSE rules:

    I.   is subject to expulsion
    II. is subject to fine
    III. is subject to censure
    IV. is subject to suspension

    (A) II and III
    (B) II and IV
    (C) II, III, and IV
    (D) I, II, III, and IV

  (D) All of these are possible.

240. The totality of final goods and services produced in the United States is called:

    (A) Total Savings
    (B) Gross National Product

(C) Total Income
(D) Accumulated Wealth

(B) By definition.

241. A general obligation bond has an official statement that says that property taxes may not rise above a certain level. This is an example of a:

(A) moral obligation bond
(B) fixed debt service bond
(C) limited tax bond
(D) limited obligation bond

(C) A restriction on taxing power makes it a limited tax G.O. bond.

242. The Revenue Bond Index is an average of:

(A) 11 bonds
(B) 20 bonds
(C) 25 bonds
(D) 30 bonds

(D) There are also two G.O. indexes: a 20-bond index with average rating A and an 11-bond index with average rating Aa.

243. The agreement between the issuer and the trustee of a municipal bond issue is written by the:

(A) trustee's attorney
(B) underwriter's attorney
(C) bond counsel
(D) syndicate manager

(C) This is one of the bond counsel's responsibilities.

244. A premium of 1.20 on a T-bond option would require payment of:

(A) $1,200
(B) $3,000
(C) $12,000
(D) $30,000

(B) The premium is quoted on the basis of $25 for a basis point. Hence, 1.20 or 120 points × $25 = $3,000.

245. All of the following recommendations from a registered representative would be acceptable EXCEPT:

(A) ACI has been recommended by our research department
(B) CAI should go up by at least $10 next year
(C) CAI earnings are estimated to be $3 next year
(D) ACI looks good in the light of next year's projected GNP

(B) It is unacceptable to project future price increases.

246. The conversion of convertible bonds to common stock would result in:

    I.   an increase in debt
    II. a decrease in leverage
    III. an increase in stockholder's equity
    IV. an increase in total assets

    (A) I and II
    (B) II and III
    (C) II and IV
    (D) I, II, and III

(B) Converting debt to equity reduces leverage = (debt/equity) and obviously increases equity. Assets are unaffected.

247. All of the following are true of SIPC EXCEPT:

    (A) it is made up of broker/dealers
    (B) it is an arm of the federal government
    (C) it is a nonprofit corporation
    (D) membership is compulsory for broker/dealers who carry customer accounts

(B) It is not a part of the federal government but, rather, a corporation owned by broker/dealers.

248. An underwriter in an Eastern account has a 15% participation. The underwriting is for $10 million, and he has sold $1.5 million. If $1 million now remains unsold, what is his liability?

    (A) Nothing
    (B) $100,000
    (C) $150,000
    (D) $1 million

(C) In an Eastern account, each member has an undivided responsibility. In this case, if $1 million remains unsold and he has a 15% share, his responsibility is 15% of $1 million.

249. If an account is frozen, which of the following is true?

    I.   All purchases must be paid for in advance.
    II. All sales require previous delivery of the securities.
    III. No activity is allowed without NASD approval.
    IV. No activity is allowed without approval by a principal of the firm.

    (A) II and IV
    (B) I and II
    (C) III and IV
    (D) I and III

(B) A frozen account requires that all transactions be covered in advance.

250. If a corporation changed its accounting from Accelerated Cost Recovery System to straight line, which of the following would occur?

    (A) Early years would show an increase in stated earnings.
    (B) Later years would show an increase in stated earnings.
    (C) Early years would show a decrease in stated earnings.
    (D) All years would show a decrease in stated earnings.

(A) By changing to straight line, depreciation in early years is reduced. This increases earnings since depreciation is treated as a cost to be subtracted from revenues.

practice
examination
two

PRACTICE EXAMINATION TWO
Answer Sheet

PART ONE

1 Ⓐ Ⓑ Ⓒ Ⓓ	37 Ⓐ Ⓑ Ⓒ Ⓓ	73 Ⓐ Ⓑ Ⓒ Ⓓ	109 Ⓐ Ⓑ Ⓒ Ⓓ
2 Ⓐ Ⓑ Ⓒ Ⓓ	38 Ⓐ Ⓑ Ⓒ Ⓓ	74 Ⓐ Ⓑ Ⓒ Ⓓ	110 Ⓐ Ⓑ Ⓒ Ⓓ
3 Ⓐ Ⓑ Ⓒ Ⓓ	39 Ⓐ Ⓑ Ⓒ Ⓓ	75 Ⓐ Ⓑ Ⓒ Ⓓ	111 Ⓐ Ⓑ Ⓒ Ⓓ
4 Ⓐ Ⓑ Ⓒ Ⓓ	40 Ⓐ Ⓑ Ⓒ Ⓓ	76 Ⓐ Ⓑ Ⓒ Ⓓ	112 Ⓐ Ⓑ Ⓒ Ⓓ
5 Ⓐ Ⓑ Ⓒ Ⓓ	41 Ⓐ Ⓑ Ⓒ Ⓓ	77 Ⓐ Ⓑ Ⓒ Ⓓ	113 Ⓐ Ⓑ Ⓒ Ⓓ
6 Ⓐ Ⓑ Ⓒ Ⓓ	42 Ⓐ Ⓑ Ⓒ Ⓓ	78 Ⓐ Ⓑ Ⓒ Ⓓ	114 Ⓐ Ⓑ Ⓒ Ⓓ
7 Ⓐ Ⓑ Ⓒ Ⓓ	43 Ⓐ Ⓑ Ⓒ Ⓓ	79 Ⓐ Ⓑ Ⓒ Ⓓ	115 Ⓐ Ⓑ Ⓒ Ⓓ
8 Ⓐ Ⓑ Ⓒ Ⓓ	44 Ⓐ Ⓑ Ⓒ Ⓓ	80 Ⓐ Ⓑ Ⓒ Ⓓ	116 Ⓐ Ⓑ Ⓒ Ⓓ
9 Ⓐ Ⓑ Ⓒ Ⓓ	45 Ⓐ Ⓑ Ⓒ Ⓓ	81 Ⓐ Ⓑ Ⓒ Ⓓ	117 Ⓐ Ⓑ Ⓒ Ⓓ
10 Ⓐ Ⓑ Ⓒ Ⓓ	46 Ⓐ Ⓑ Ⓒ Ⓓ	82 Ⓐ Ⓑ Ⓒ Ⓓ	118 Ⓐ Ⓑ Ⓒ Ⓓ
11 Ⓐ Ⓑ Ⓒ Ⓓ	47 Ⓐ Ⓑ Ⓒ Ⓓ	83 Ⓐ Ⓑ Ⓒ Ⓓ	119 Ⓐ Ⓑ Ⓒ Ⓓ
12 Ⓐ Ⓑ Ⓒ Ⓓ	48 Ⓐ Ⓑ Ⓒ Ⓓ	84 Ⓐ Ⓑ Ⓒ Ⓓ	120 Ⓐ Ⓑ Ⓒ Ⓓ
13 Ⓐ Ⓑ Ⓒ Ⓓ	49 Ⓐ Ⓑ Ⓒ Ⓓ	85 Ⓐ Ⓑ Ⓒ Ⓓ	121 Ⓐ Ⓑ Ⓒ Ⓓ
14 Ⓐ Ⓑ Ⓒ Ⓓ	50 Ⓐ Ⓑ Ⓒ Ⓓ	86 Ⓐ Ⓑ Ⓒ Ⓓ	122 Ⓐ Ⓑ Ⓒ Ⓓ
15 Ⓐ Ⓑ Ⓒ Ⓓ	51 Ⓐ Ⓑ Ⓒ Ⓓ	87 Ⓐ Ⓑ Ⓒ Ⓓ	123 Ⓐ Ⓑ Ⓒ Ⓓ
16 Ⓐ Ⓑ Ⓒ Ⓓ	52 Ⓐ Ⓑ Ⓒ Ⓓ	88 Ⓐ Ⓑ Ⓒ Ⓓ	124 Ⓐ Ⓑ Ⓒ Ⓓ
17 Ⓐ Ⓑ Ⓒ Ⓓ	53 Ⓐ Ⓑ Ⓒ Ⓓ	89 Ⓐ Ⓑ Ⓒ Ⓓ	125 Ⓐ Ⓑ Ⓒ Ⓓ
18 Ⓐ Ⓑ Ⓒ Ⓓ	54 Ⓐ Ⓑ Ⓒ Ⓓ	90 Ⓐ Ⓑ Ⓒ Ⓓ	
19 Ⓐ Ⓑ Ⓒ Ⓓ	55 Ⓐ Ⓑ Ⓒ Ⓓ	91 Ⓐ Ⓑ Ⓒ Ⓓ	
20 Ⓐ Ⓑ Ⓒ Ⓓ	56 Ⓐ Ⓑ Ⓒ Ⓓ	92 Ⓐ Ⓑ Ⓒ Ⓓ	
21 Ⓐ Ⓑ Ⓒ Ⓓ	57 Ⓐ Ⓑ Ⓒ Ⓓ	93 Ⓐ Ⓑ Ⓒ Ⓓ	
22 Ⓐ Ⓑ Ⓒ Ⓓ	58 Ⓐ Ⓑ Ⓒ Ⓓ	94 Ⓐ Ⓑ Ⓒ Ⓓ	
23 Ⓐ Ⓑ Ⓒ Ⓓ	59 Ⓐ Ⓑ Ⓒ Ⓓ	95 Ⓐ Ⓑ Ⓒ Ⓓ	
24 Ⓐ Ⓑ Ⓒ Ⓓ	60 Ⓐ Ⓑ Ⓒ Ⓓ	96 Ⓐ Ⓑ Ⓒ Ⓓ	
25 Ⓐ Ⓑ Ⓒ Ⓓ	61 Ⓐ Ⓑ Ⓒ Ⓓ	97 Ⓐ Ⓑ Ⓒ Ⓓ	
26 Ⓐ Ⓑ Ⓒ Ⓓ	62 Ⓐ Ⓑ Ⓒ Ⓓ	98 Ⓐ Ⓑ Ⓒ Ⓓ	
27 Ⓐ Ⓑ Ⓒ Ⓓ	63 Ⓐ Ⓑ Ⓒ Ⓓ	99 Ⓐ Ⓑ Ⓒ Ⓓ	
28 Ⓐ Ⓑ Ⓒ Ⓓ	64 Ⓐ Ⓑ Ⓒ Ⓓ	100 Ⓐ Ⓑ Ⓒ Ⓓ	
29 Ⓐ Ⓑ Ⓒ Ⓓ	65 Ⓐ Ⓑ Ⓒ Ⓓ	101 Ⓐ Ⓑ Ⓒ Ⓓ	
30 Ⓐ Ⓑ Ⓒ Ⓓ	66 Ⓐ Ⓑ Ⓒ Ⓓ	102 Ⓐ Ⓑ Ⓒ Ⓓ	
31 Ⓐ Ⓑ Ⓒ Ⓓ	67 Ⓐ Ⓑ Ⓒ Ⓓ	103 Ⓐ Ⓑ Ⓒ Ⓓ	
32 Ⓐ Ⓑ Ⓒ Ⓓ	68 Ⓐ Ⓑ Ⓒ Ⓓ	104 Ⓐ Ⓑ Ⓒ Ⓓ	
33 Ⓐ Ⓑ Ⓒ Ⓓ	69 Ⓐ Ⓑ Ⓒ Ⓓ	105 Ⓐ Ⓑ Ⓒ Ⓓ	
34 Ⓐ Ⓑ Ⓒ Ⓓ	70 Ⓐ Ⓑ Ⓒ Ⓓ	106 Ⓐ Ⓑ Ⓒ Ⓓ	
35 Ⓐ Ⓑ Ⓒ Ⓓ	71 Ⓐ Ⓑ Ⓒ Ⓓ	107 Ⓐ Ⓑ Ⓒ Ⓓ	
36 Ⓐ Ⓑ Ⓒ Ⓓ	72 Ⓐ Ⓑ Ⓒ Ⓓ	108 Ⓐ Ⓑ Ⓒ Ⓓ	

PRACTICE EXAMINATION TWO
Answer Sheet

PART TWO

1 Ⓐ Ⓑ Ⓒ Ⓓ	37 Ⓐ Ⓑ Ⓒ Ⓓ	73 Ⓐ Ⓑ Ⓒ Ⓓ	109 Ⓐ Ⓑ Ⓒ Ⓓ
2 Ⓐ Ⓑ Ⓒ Ⓓ	38 Ⓐ Ⓑ Ⓒ Ⓓ	74 Ⓐ Ⓑ Ⓒ Ⓓ	110 Ⓐ Ⓑ Ⓒ Ⓓ
3 Ⓐ Ⓑ Ⓒ Ⓓ	39 Ⓐ Ⓑ Ⓒ Ⓓ	75 Ⓐ Ⓑ Ⓒ Ⓓ	111 Ⓐ Ⓑ Ⓒ Ⓓ
4 Ⓐ Ⓑ Ⓒ Ⓓ	40 Ⓐ Ⓑ Ⓒ Ⓓ	76 Ⓐ Ⓑ Ⓒ Ⓓ	112 Ⓐ Ⓑ Ⓒ Ⓓ
5 Ⓐ Ⓑ Ⓒ Ⓓ	41 Ⓐ Ⓑ Ⓒ Ⓓ	77 Ⓐ Ⓑ Ⓒ Ⓓ	113 Ⓐ Ⓑ Ⓒ Ⓓ
6 Ⓐ Ⓑ Ⓒ Ⓓ	42 Ⓐ Ⓑ Ⓒ Ⓓ	78 Ⓐ Ⓑ Ⓒ Ⓓ	114 Ⓐ Ⓑ Ⓒ Ⓓ
7 Ⓐ Ⓑ Ⓒ Ⓓ	43 Ⓐ Ⓑ Ⓒ Ⓓ	79 Ⓐ Ⓑ Ⓒ Ⓓ	115 Ⓐ Ⓑ Ⓒ Ⓓ
8 Ⓐ Ⓑ Ⓒ Ⓓ	44 Ⓐ Ⓑ Ⓒ Ⓓ	80 Ⓐ Ⓑ Ⓒ Ⓓ	116 Ⓐ Ⓑ Ⓒ Ⓓ
9 Ⓐ Ⓑ Ⓒ Ⓓ	45 Ⓐ Ⓑ Ⓒ Ⓓ	81 Ⓐ Ⓑ Ⓒ Ⓓ	117 Ⓐ Ⓑ Ⓒ Ⓓ
10 Ⓐ Ⓑ Ⓒ Ⓓ	46 Ⓐ Ⓑ Ⓒ Ⓓ	82 Ⓐ Ⓑ Ⓒ Ⓓ	118 Ⓐ Ⓑ Ⓒ Ⓓ
11 Ⓐ Ⓑ Ⓒ Ⓓ	47 Ⓐ Ⓑ Ⓒ Ⓓ	83 Ⓐ Ⓑ Ⓒ Ⓓ	119 Ⓐ Ⓑ Ⓒ Ⓓ
12 Ⓐ Ⓑ Ⓒ Ⓓ	48 Ⓐ Ⓑ Ⓒ Ⓓ	84 Ⓐ Ⓑ Ⓒ Ⓓ	120 Ⓐ Ⓑ Ⓒ Ⓓ
13 Ⓐ Ⓑ Ⓒ Ⓓ	49 Ⓐ Ⓑ Ⓒ Ⓓ	85 Ⓐ Ⓑ Ⓒ Ⓓ	121 Ⓐ Ⓑ Ⓒ Ⓓ
14 Ⓐ Ⓑ Ⓒ Ⓓ	50 Ⓐ Ⓑ Ⓒ Ⓓ	86 Ⓐ Ⓑ Ⓒ Ⓓ	122 Ⓐ Ⓑ Ⓒ Ⓓ
15 Ⓐ Ⓑ Ⓒ Ⓓ	51 Ⓐ Ⓑ Ⓒ Ⓓ	87 Ⓐ Ⓑ Ⓒ Ⓓ	123 Ⓐ Ⓑ Ⓒ Ⓓ
16 Ⓐ Ⓑ Ⓒ Ⓓ	52 Ⓐ Ⓑ Ⓒ Ⓓ	88 Ⓐ Ⓑ Ⓒ Ⓓ	124 Ⓐ Ⓑ Ⓒ Ⓓ
17 Ⓐ Ⓑ Ⓒ Ⓓ	53 Ⓐ Ⓑ Ⓒ Ⓓ	89 Ⓐ Ⓑ Ⓒ Ⓓ	125 Ⓐ Ⓑ Ⓒ Ⓓ
18 Ⓐ Ⓑ Ⓒ Ⓓ	54 Ⓐ Ⓑ Ⓒ Ⓓ	90 Ⓐ Ⓑ Ⓒ Ⓓ	
19 Ⓐ Ⓑ Ⓒ Ⓓ	55 Ⓐ Ⓑ Ⓒ Ⓓ	91 Ⓐ Ⓑ Ⓒ Ⓓ	
20 Ⓐ Ⓑ Ⓒ Ⓓ	56 Ⓐ Ⓑ Ⓒ Ⓓ	92 Ⓐ Ⓑ Ⓒ Ⓓ	
21 Ⓐ Ⓑ Ⓒ Ⓓ	57 Ⓐ Ⓑ Ⓒ Ⓓ	93 Ⓐ Ⓑ Ⓒ Ⓓ	
22 Ⓐ Ⓑ Ⓒ Ⓓ	58 Ⓐ Ⓑ Ⓒ Ⓓ	94 Ⓐ Ⓑ Ⓒ Ⓓ	
23 Ⓐ Ⓑ Ⓒ Ⓓ	59 Ⓐ Ⓑ Ⓒ Ⓓ	95 Ⓐ Ⓑ Ⓒ Ⓓ	
24 Ⓐ Ⓑ Ⓒ Ⓓ	60 Ⓐ Ⓑ Ⓒ Ⓓ	96 Ⓐ Ⓑ Ⓒ Ⓓ	
25 Ⓐ Ⓑ Ⓒ Ⓓ	61 Ⓐ Ⓑ Ⓒ Ⓓ	97 Ⓐ Ⓑ Ⓒ Ⓓ	
26 Ⓐ Ⓑ Ⓒ Ⓓ	62 Ⓐ Ⓑ Ⓒ Ⓓ	98 Ⓐ Ⓑ Ⓒ Ⓓ	
27 Ⓐ Ⓑ Ⓒ Ⓓ	63 Ⓐ Ⓑ Ⓒ Ⓓ	99 Ⓐ Ⓑ Ⓒ Ⓓ	
28 Ⓐ Ⓑ Ⓒ Ⓓ	64 Ⓐ Ⓑ Ⓒ Ⓓ	100 Ⓐ Ⓑ Ⓒ Ⓓ	
29 Ⓐ Ⓑ Ⓒ Ⓓ	65 Ⓐ Ⓑ Ⓒ Ⓓ	101 Ⓐ Ⓑ Ⓒ Ⓓ	
30 Ⓐ Ⓑ Ⓒ Ⓓ	66 Ⓐ Ⓑ Ⓒ Ⓓ	102 Ⓐ Ⓑ Ⓒ Ⓓ	
31 Ⓐ Ⓑ Ⓒ Ⓓ	67 Ⓐ Ⓑ Ⓒ Ⓓ	103 Ⓐ Ⓑ Ⓒ Ⓓ	
32 Ⓐ Ⓑ Ⓒ Ⓓ	68 Ⓐ Ⓑ Ⓒ Ⓓ	104 Ⓐ Ⓑ Ⓒ Ⓓ	
33 Ⓐ Ⓑ Ⓒ Ⓓ	69 Ⓐ Ⓑ Ⓒ Ⓓ	105 Ⓐ Ⓑ Ⓒ Ⓓ	
34 Ⓐ Ⓑ Ⓒ Ⓓ	70 Ⓐ Ⓑ Ⓒ Ⓓ	106 Ⓐ Ⓑ Ⓒ Ⓓ	
35 Ⓐ Ⓑ Ⓒ Ⓓ	71 Ⓐ Ⓑ Ⓒ Ⓓ	107 Ⓐ Ⓑ Ⓒ Ⓓ	
36 Ⓐ Ⓑ Ⓒ Ⓓ	72 Ⓐ Ⓑ Ⓒ Ⓓ	108 Ⓐ Ⓑ Ⓒ Ⓓ	

PART ONE

Time   3 Hours

Questions   1–125

DIRECTIONS

Each of the questions or incomplete statements below is followed by four suggested answer options. Choose the best answer and then blacken the corresponding space on the answer sheet.

1. ACI issued one million shares of convertible preferred (par $100). The shares are convertible at $45, and the common is currently selling at $36. If an investor paid $90 per share for 100 shares of preferred, which of the following is true?

    I. The conversion rate is 2.22.
    II. The conversion rate is 2.50.
    III. The preferred is selling below parity.
    IV. The preferred is selling above parity.

    (A) I and III
    (B) I and IV
    (C) II and III
    (D) II and IV

2. Which act empowered the Federal Reserve Board to regulate credit in securities transactions?

    (A) The Securities Act of 1933
    (B) The Securities Exchange Act of 1934
    (C) The Maloney Act of 1938
    (D) The Investment Company Act of 1940

3. CAI had earnings of $6 per share. If it paid quarterly dividends of $.60, its dividend payout ratio was:

    (A) 10%
    (B) 30%
    (C) 40%
    (D) 60%

4. Which of the following strategies has the greatest potential risk?

    (A) Writing naked puts
    (B) Buying naked puts
    (C) Writing naked calls
    (D) Buying naked calls

5. An investor owns 100 shares of ACI at $45.00. If she writes a straddle on ACI with a $45.00 strike, which subsequent event will create the greatest potential loss for her?

    (A) ACI remains unchanged.
    (B) ACI goes to 100.
    (C) ACI goes to 0.
    (D) Neither option is exercised.

6. All of the following are on the same side EXCEPT:

    (A) long call-short stock
    (B) long call-long stock
    (C) short call-short stock
    (D) short put-long stock

7. In 1987, an investor purchased a T-note with a May 12 settlement date. If the most recent interest payment had been January 15, how many days of accrued interest must he add to the purchase price?

(A) 116
(B) 118
(C) 120
(D) 121

8. An investor purchased a corporate bond with settlement on June 5. If the most recent payment had been on March 15, how many days of accrued interest must she add to the purchase price?

(A) 78
(B) 79
(C) 80
(D) 81

9. ACI is trading at 50. What is the loan value of an ACI Jun 30 Call trading at 22?

(A) $0
(B) $1,000
(C) $1,100
(D) $2,000

Questions 10–12 are based on the following information:

Regulation T is at 50%, house maintenance margin at 30% and NYSE maintenance at 25%.

Market Value	30,000
Debit Balance	17,000
SMA	5,000

10. How much in marginable securities would Mrs. P need to deposit to remove the account from restricted status?

(A) $0
(B) $1,000
(C) $2,000
(D) $4,000

11. At what market value will this account be at NYSE minimum maintenance?

(A) $20,000
(B) $22,667
(C) $24,287
(D) $25,000

12. How much cash can she currently withdraw from the account without any other transactions?

(A) $0
(B) $3,000
(C) $4,000
(D) $5,000

13. Under which circumstances at expiration would an investor experience the largest profit from selling, 1 ACI Sep 40 Call and buying 1 ACI Sep 50 Call?

(A) ACI is at $40.
(B) ACI is between $40 and $50.
(C) ACI is at $50.
(D) It cannot be determined.

14. At what expiration price would this investor experience the greatest loss?

(A) ACI is at $40.
(B) ACI is between $40 and $50.
(C) ACI is at $50.
(D) It cannot be determined.

15. Which of the following would not be considered "good delivery" in a municipal bond transaction?

(A) Callable bonds
(B) Bearer bonds in $1,000 denominations
(C) Bonds with an attached legal opinion
(D) None of the above

16. The MSRB regulates all of the following EXCEPT:

(A) banks that do municipal securities business
(B) brokers that do municipal securities business
(C) dealers that do municipal securities business
(D) issuers of municipal securities

17. A new issue of a municipal bond due to mature on July 1, 2009 is dated January 1, 1987. A customer purchases these with a settlement date of February 15. How many days of accrued interest must the customer pay?

(A) 43
(B) 44
(C) 45
(D) 46

18. All of the following are *direct* obligations of the United States Government EXCEPT:

(A) FNMA
(B) GNMA
(C) Series EE bonds
(D) flower bonds

19. The moment when taxable income begins to exceed cash distributions in a direct participation program is the:

(A) phantom income point
(B) cross-over point
(C) profit point
(D) cash-flow point

20. In a direct participation program, if there was depreciation of the asset, all of the following would be true EXCEPT:

(A) cash flow increases
(B) income increases
(C) taxes decrease
(D) net assets decrease

21. A municipal security issue of revenue bonds is being analyzed for "coverage." The appropriate ratio is:

(A) net revenue to total expenses
(B) gross revenue to operating expenses plus debt service
(C) net revenue to debt service
(D) gross revenue to debt service

22. A bull spread "breaks even" when the difference between the market price and the lower strike price is equal to the:

(A) higher premium minus the lower one
(B) higher premium minus the market price
(C) higher premium plus the lower one
(D) lower premium minus the market price

23. A put option is "in the money" if:

(A) the strike price is at market price
(B) the strike price is above market price
(C) the strike price is below market price
(D) the strike price is at exercise price

24. Federal funds are:

(A) obligations of the Federal Reserve Bank
(B) obligations to the Federal Reserve Bank
(C) obligations by one bank to another to meet Federal Reserve requirements
(D) very stable interest rates

25. All of the following are money market instruments EXCEPT:

    (A) commercial paper
    (B) banker's acceptances
    (C) federal funds
    (D) ADRs

26. All of the following are true of the pink sheets EXCEPT:

    (A) they show firm quotes for one round lot
    (B) they are wholesale quotes
    (C) they are published daily
    (D) they list market makers for the quoted securities

27. The order in which a transaction is processed is:

    I.   order department
    II. margin department
    III. purchase and sale
    IV. cashier

    (A) I, III, II, IV
    (B) III, I, IV, II
    (C) I, II, III, IV
    (D) III, IV, I, II

    Questions 28–30 refer to the following strategy:

    Buy 100 shares of CAI at $53. Sell one CAI Nov 50 Call at 7.

28. The investor will first experience a loss if CAI is:

    (A) below $48
    (B) below $46
    (C) below $50
    (D) below $60

29. If CAI is at $51 when the previously unexercised option expires, his profit (loss) will be:

    (A) $100
    (B) $100 (loss)
    (C) $400
    (D) $600

30. The maximum profit possible during the life of the option is:

    (A) $100
    (B) $300
    (C) $400
    (D) $700

The following information is useful for answering Questions 31 and 32:

A limited partner in a balanced oil and gas program has invested $50,000 and is responsible for a recourse loan of an additional $40,000

31. The investor's basis is:

    (A) $10,000
    (B) $40,000
    (C) $50,000
    (D) $90,000

32. If the investor had passive income of $70,000, the maximum loss he could claim would be:

    (A) $40,000
    (B) $50,000
    (C) $70,000
    (D) $90,000

33. The sponsor of a functional sharing arrangement oil- and gas-drilling program would pay:

    (A) all nondeductible expenses
    (B) all intangible expenses
    (C) a share of deductible expenses
    (D) a share of nondeductible expenses

34. A preliminary prospectus can do which of the following?

    (A) It can be used during the cooling-off period
    (B) It can be used to blue-sky an issue
    (C) It can be used to generate orders
    (D) It can be used to get indications of interest

Questions 35–38 refer to the following:

An investor with no other positions buys 1 ACI Mar 40 Put at $4\frac{1}{2}$ and buys 1 ACI Mar 40 Call at $1\frac{1}{2}$.

35. The market price at ACI is most likely to be:

    (A) below $40
    (B) at $40
    (C) above $40
    (D) it cannot be determined

36. The maximum loss this investor could experience is:

    (A) $300
    (B) $450
    (C) $600
    (D) unlimited

37. The maximum profit he could experience is:

    (A) $450
    (B) $600
    (C) $3,400
    (D) unlimited

38. At expiration, ACI was at $50. If he had not exercised up to then, he would experience:

    (A) $600 loss
    (B) $400 gain
    (C) $600 gain
    (D) $1,000 gain

39. Which of the following has the least volatile interest rate?

    (A) Federal funds rate
    (B) Prime rate
    (C) T-bill rate
    (D) Discount rate

40. Interest on new issues of municipal bonds accrues from the:

    (A) previous interest payment
    (B) dated date
    (C) settlement date
    (D) purchase date

41. All of the following provide information about proposed municipal bond issues EXCEPT:

    (A) *Munifacts*
    (B) *Daily Bond Buyer*
    (C) *Blue List*
    (D) newspapers

42. If all of the following municipal securities mature on the same date, which has the lowest price?

    (A) $7\frac{1}{4}$% coupon at $7\frac{1}{4}$%
    (B) 8% coupon at $8\frac{3}{8}$%
    (C) 8% coupon at $7\frac{3}{4}$%
    (D) $7\frac{1}{4}$% coupon at $7\frac{3}{8}$%

Questions 43–45 refer to the following strategy:

An investor buys 3 ACI Jun 50 Calls at 4.

43. At what price will the investor break even?

    (A) $46
    (B) $50
    (C) $54
    (D) $62

44. His maximum possible loss on this investment is:

    (A) $400
    (B) $1,200
    (C) $15,000
    (D) unlimited

45. If he exercises these when ACI is at $60 and wishes to purchase the stock in his margin account, how much will he be required to deposit in the margin account?

    (A) $7,500
    (B) $8,700
    (C) $9,000
    (D) $10,200

46. To analyze a general obligation bond, one would consider all of the following EXCEPT the:

    (A) size of the issue
    (B) size of the population base
    (C) denomination of the issue
    (D) income of the ratepayers

47. The name of the interest rate at which member banks may borrow from the Federal Reserve Bank is:

    (A) federal funds rate
    (B) discount rate
    (C) prime rate
    (D) money supply rate

Questions 48–50 refer to the following information:

A customer has the following accounts:

Account	Market Value	Balance
Cash (with marginable securities)	$20,000	$ 5,000
Long	$30,000	$16,000 (Debit)
Short	$10,000	$14,000 (Credit)
SMA	$ 4,000	

48. What is her total equity?

    (A) $43,000
    (B) $60,000
    (C) $65,000
    (D) $69,000

49. What is the total buying power in the two margin accounts?

    (A) $4,000
    (B) $6,000
    (C) $8,000
    (D) $10,000

50. What is the total buying power of all accounts?

    (A) $20,000
    (B) $27,000
    (C) $38,000
    (D) $40,000

51. The premium on a Value Line index option is $2\frac{1}{2}$. The total dollar price of this premium is:

    (A) $250
    (B) $500
    (C) $625
    (D) $1,250

Questions 52–54 refer to the following strategy:

An investor buys 100 shares of CAI at 45 and writes 1 CAI Apr 50 Call at 2.

52. At what price would she break even?

    (A) $43
    (B) $48
    (C) $50
    (D) $52

53. If the call is exercised when CAI is at $54, she has:

    (A) $200 loss
    (B) $200 gain
    (C) $500 gain
    (D) $700 gain

54. What is the most this investor could lose?

    (A) $200
    (B) $4,300
    (C) $4,500
    (D) Unlimited

    Questions 55 and 56 refer to the following information:

    ACI has issued a convertible bond with a conversion price of $100 per share.

55. The conversion rate is:

    (A) 5 to 1
    (B) 10 to 1
    (C) 20 to 1
    (D) 100 to 1

56. If the bond is selling at $1,150, the parity price for the stock is:

    (A) $100
    (B) $110
    (C) $115
    (D) $150

    Questions 57 and 58 refer to the following information:

    CAI has ten million shares authorized. A total of eight million shares have been issued, and there are currently one million shares of treasury stock. CAI has a market price of $50.

57. If the next common stock dividend is declared at $.75, the total amount to be distributed is:

    (A) $750,000
    (B) $5,250,000
    (C) $6,000,000
    (D) $7,500,000

58. If the annual dividend for CAI has been $3.00, CAI has a current yield of:

    (A) 3%
    (B) 6%
    (C) 7.5%
    (D) 15%

59. When an offering becomes effective under SEC rules, this means that the SEC has:

    (A) checked the accuracy of the registration statement
    (B) approved the offering
    (C) attested that the offering meets minimum investment standards
    (D) determined that the registration statement is complete

    Questions 60–62 refer to the following investments:

    Long 2 ACI Jun 50 Puts at $3\frac{1}{2}$

    Short 2 ACI Jun 45 Puts at $\frac{1}{2}$

60. If they have not been previously exercised, what is the maximum possible profit on this trade at expiration?

    (A) $200
    (B) $300
    (C) $400
    (D) $600

61. If they have not been previously exercised, what is the maximum possible loss from this trade at expiration?

    (A) $300
    (B) $400
    (C) $600
    (D) Unlimited

62. At what market price would this investment break even?

    (A) $45.50
    (B) $47.00
    (C) $48.00
    (D) $49.50

63. Another name for the nominal rate (yield) is:

    (A) yield to maturity
    (B) current yield
    (C) coupon rate
    (D) current yield-coupon rate

64. Regular way for United States treasury securities means:

    (A) next business day payment—five business day delivery
    (B) five business day payment—five business day delivery
    (C) next business day payment—next business day delivery
    (D) five business day payment—next business day delivery

65. An investor pays $70 in accrued interest on a 9% corporate bond bought at 90. If the bond has ten years to maturity, how much interest is reportable for this first tax year?

    (A) $10
    (B) $30
    (C) $90
    (D) $100

66. If a municipality solicits bids for an offering, the winning bid will be the one that offers to:

    (A) sell it at the lowest price
    (B) sell it at the highest price
    (C) sell it at the lowest cost to the municipality
    (D) raise the most money for the municipality

67. According to MSRB rules, a municipal securities principal must approve all of the following EXCEPT:

    (A) opening new accounts
    (B) handling of customer complaints
    (C) legal opinions
    (D) every transaction

68. According to MSRB rules, the total of gifts and gratuities that may be accepted from one person by a registered representative in one year may not exceed:

    (A) $25
    (B) $50
    (C) $75
    (D) $100

69. All of the following are true of full discretionary accounts EXCEPT:

    (A) they must be reviewed regularly by a supervisory person
    (B) they must have written authorization from the customer
    (C) a father can sell securities for a son's account with verbal authorization
    (D) a registered representative can remove cash from such an account

Questions 70–72 are based on the following:

Sell 1 CAI Apr 35 Put at 2 when CAI is at $39.

In all cases, assume that there has been no exercise prior to expiration.

70. This trade will break even if CAI is at:

    (A) $33
    (B) $35
    (C) $37
    (D) $41

71. The maximum possible profit is:

    (A) $200
    (B) $400
    (C) $3,700
    (D) $4,100

72. If CAI is at 25, the investor's profit (loss) is:

    (A) $800 profit
    (B) $800 loss
    (C) $1,200 profit
    (D) $1,200 loss

73. All of the following are true of T-bills EXCEPT:

    (A) they are issued in book-entry form
    (B) they are traded on a discount basis
    (C) they are less risky than T-bonds
    (D) they usually have a higher rate than the prime

74. For information on unlisted corporate bonds, one should examine the:

    (A) yellow sheets
    (B) *Blue List*
    (C) pink sheets
    (D) visible supply

75. All of the following are required by MSRB rules for customer confirmations EXCEPT:

    (A) the amount of any commission in any broker transaction
    (B) the source of any commission in any broker transaction
    (C) notification if the bonds are not in bearer form
    (D) the amount of any markup on a dealer transaction

76. The Securities Act of 1933 regulates which of the following?

    (A) Securities dealer operations
    (B) Registration of securities
    (C) Management of investment companies
    (D) Securities exchange operations

77. The Securities Exchange Act of 1934 regulates all of the following EXCEPT:

    (A) capital requirements for broker/dealers
    (B) financial reports by broker/dealers
    (C) hypothecation of customer securities
    (D) cooling-off period

Questions 78–80 refer to the following strategy:

Sell short 200 shares of ACI at 50.

Buy 2 ACI Sep 55 Calls at $1\frac{1}{2}$.

78. This strategy will break even if ACI is at:

    (A) $48.50
    (B) $51.50
    (C) $53.00
    (D) $56.50

79. The maximum possible profit would occur if ACI were at:

    (A) $0
    (B) $1.50
    (C) $50
    (D) $55

80. The maximum possible loss from this strategy is:

    (A) $700
    (B) $1,300
    (C) $9,700
    (D) $10,000

81. All of the following are true of GNMAs EXCEPT:

    (A) they are direct obligations of the United States Government
    (B) they usually pay a higher rate than T-bonds of comparable maturity
    (C) they often include some return of capital before maturity
    (D) they are exempt from state and local taxes

Questions 82–84 refer to the following income statement:

Consolidated Amalgamated Inc. Income Statement for year ending December 31, 1990.

Net Sales	$20,000,000
Cost of Goods	($12,000,000)
Administrative Costs	($3,000,000)
Operating Profits	$5,000,000
Other Income	$500,000
(EBIT) Total Income	$5,500,000
Fixed Interest	($1,000,000)
(EBT) Income before Taxes	$4,500,000
Income Tax	($1,500,000)
Net Income	$3,000,000
Common Stock Dividends	($1,200,000)
Retained Earnings	$1,800,000

CAI has 1.2 million shares issued of which 200,000 are treasury stock.

82. What are the earnings per share?

    (A) $1.00
    (B) $1.20
    (C) $2.50
    (D) $3.00

83. What is the profit margin on operations?

    (A) 15%
    (B) 22.5%
    (C) 25%
    (D) 27.5%

84. What is the times interest earned?

    (A) 5.5 to 1
    (B) 4.5 to 1
    (C) 3 to 1
    (D) 1.8 to 1

85. Which of the following choices represent the same class?

    (A) All ACI options
    (B) All ACI 50 options
    (C) All ACI Calls
    (D) All ACI Jun

86. The premium on an option that is "at the money" is made up of:

    (A) all intrinsic value
    (B) all time value
    (C) half intrinsic value plus half time value
    (D) some positive amounts of intrinsic and time value

87. Which of the following is a long straddle?

    (A) Buy 1 CAI Sep 45 Call; sell 1 CAI Sep 40 Call
    (B) Buy 1 CAI Sep 45 Put; sell 1 CAI Sep 40 Call
    (C) Buy 1 CAI Sep 45 Put; buy 1 CAI Sep 45 Call
    (D) Sell 1 CAI Sep 45 Call; sell 1 CAI Sep 45 Put

Questions 88–90 refer to the following choices:

(A) Banker's acceptances
(B) T-bills
(C) Repos
(D) Commercial paper

Choose the money market instrument best described in each of the following:

88. This instrument is limited to 270-day maturity.

89. This instrument is used to foster foreign trade.

90. This instrument is traded for a fixed length of time.

91. An account in which both owners have trading authority and in which the tenant's portion reverts to his estate is called:

(A) joint tenants with rights of survivorship
(B) tenants in entirety
(C) communal tenants
(D) joint tenants in common

92. A client account for an investment advisor requires all of the following EXCEPT a(n):

(A) full trading authorization
(B) new account forms for each account
(C) agreement to furnish any other forms dictated by house requirements
(D) disclosure form stating that the client knows that the advisor is trading other accounts

93. Which of the following is a good delivery for a transaction of 500 shares?

(A) Four 25-share certificates; ten 20-share certificates; one 200-share certificate
(B) Ten 40-share certificates; one 100-share certificate
(C) Four 50-share certificates; four 75-share certificates
(D) Five 40-share certificates; one 300-share certificate

94. For each listed options contract the issuer is the:

(A) exchange on which it is listed
(B) writer of the contract
(C) writer's brokerage firm
(D) Options Clearing Corporation

95. Exercise notices are assigned on the basis of:

(A) earliest written
(B) latest written
(C) largest holder
(D) random selection

96. Settlement for the purchase of OCC listed options is:

(A) same day
(B) next day
(C) five business days
(D) seven business days

97. The minimum denomination for T-notes and T-bonds is:

(A) $1,000
(B) $5,000
(C) $10,000
(D) $100,000

98. All of the following are acceptable collateral by a brokerage firm EXCEPT:

    (A) FNMA securities
    (B) AAA Corporates
    (C) EE bonds
    (D) T-bills

99. Four directors are to be elected at the ACI annual meeting under cumulative voting. Mr. P owns 200 shares. He may cast no more than:

    (A) 200 votes
    (B) 200 votes for any one director
    (C) 400 votes for any one director
    (D) 800 votes for any one director

100. If any employee of an insurance company provides a letter from an officer of the insurers saying that the employee may open a margin account and that the company does not wish to receive duplicate confirmations, the registered representative may:

    (A) not open the account
    (B) open the account
    (C) open the account but send duplicates anyway
    (D) open the account but inform the SEC that no duplicates are being sent

101. All of the following would result in an adjustment of the options contract EXCEPT:

    (A) 5% stock dividend
    (B) $1.0 dividend
    (C) 3/2 stock split
    (D) rights distribution

102. ACI has declared a 25% stock dividend. At the ex-dividend date, an ACI Dec 50 option will become (remain):

    (A) unchanged
    (B) ACI 50 for 125 shares
    (C) ACI 40 for 100 shares
    (D) ACI 40 for 125 shares

103. Listed options cease trading on the third Friday of expiration month at:

    (A) 3:00 P.M. Eastern Time
    (B) 3:00 P.M. Central Time
    (C) 4:30 P.M. Eastern Time
    (D) 4:30 P.M. Central Time

104. A corporation that earns no income in a particular year would not be required to pay interest on what type of bond?

    (A) Equipment trust certificate
    (B) Income bond
    (C) Convertible debenture
    (D) Subordinated debenture

105. The inclusion of a call protection provision for a bond means:

    (A) the investor must pay a premium for this protection
    (B) the issuer is protected if the bonds are called
    (C) the investor is insured against loss of principal in the event of a call
    (D) the issuer may not call the bond for some period of time

106. A 9% bond due to mature in one year trades at 10%. What is its approximate price?

    (A) $900
    (B) $990
    (C) $1,000
    (D) $1,100

107. The most risky oil and gas limited partnership is likely to be a(n):

    (A) exploratory program
    (B) balanced program
    (C) drilling program
    (D) income program

108. If a partnership borrows money from one of its limited partners, this partner:

    (A) becomes a general partner
    (B) loses his limited partner status
    (C) is in violation of the partnership agreement
    (D) becomes a general creditor of the partnership

109. To protect itself, a Japanese car manufacturer who is buying parts from the United States and is afraid that the yen will fall relative to the dollar is most likely to buy:

    (A) Japanese yen puts
    (B) Japanese yen calls
    (C) U.S. dollar puts
    (D) U.S. dollar calls

110. An investor sells 1 CAI Jul 50 Call at 7 and 1 CAI Jul 50 Put at 3. He will profit unless CAI is:

    (A) above 60 or below 40
    (B) above 57 or below 43
    (C) above 54 or below 47
    (D) above 53 or below 47

111. The writer of a put option on D-marks would like:

    (A) the D-mark to decline
    (B) the D-mark to appreciate relative to the dollar
    (C) the dollar to appreciate relative to the D-mark
    (D) United States interest rates to rise relative to German rates

112. The usual methods for underwriting municipal bonds are:

    I. negotiated for revenue bonds
    II. negotiated for general obligation bonds
    III. competitive for revenue bonds
    IV. competitive for general obligation bonds

    (A) I and II
    (B) II and IV
    (C) III and II
    (D) III and IV

113. According to MSRB, a potential customer must be told all of the following with respect to a negotiated municipal underwriting EXCEPT:

    (A) amount of any fee received from the issuer by the firm
    (B) initial offering price of each maturity
    (C) membership of the underwriting syndicate
    (D) amount of the underwriting spread

114. The advantage of writing a covered call is that it:

    (A) limits gain on the equity position
    (B) reduces possible loss on equity position
    (C) raises maximum possible gain on the equity position
    (D) prevents major loss on the equity position

115. Which of the following is a spread?

    (A) Long 1 ACI Sep 50 Call; short 1 ACI Sep 60 Call.
    (B) Long 1 ACI Sep 50 Call; short 1 ACI Sep 50 Put.
    (C) Long 1 ACI Sep 50 Call; long 1 ACI Sep 50 Put.
    (D) Long 1 ACI Sep 50 Call; long 1 ACI Dec 60 Call.

116. Variable annuities must be registered with the SEC and:

    (A) state insurance commissions
    (B) NASD
    (C) state banking commissions
    (D) ERISA governors

117. Arrange from first to last the order in which to allocate bonds in a new municipal bond issue.

    I.   Syndicate orders
    II. Pre-sale orders
    III. Designated orders
    IV. Member orders

    (A) II, I, III, IV
    (B) III, I, II, IV
    (C) II, IV, I, III
    (D) IV, II, III, I

118. An investor writes 1 CAI 40 Call at 12 when CAI is selling at $50. If this call is uncovered, how much must she deposit to meet margin requirements?

    (A) $750
    (B) $1,200
    (C) $1,950
    (D) $2,500

119. A customer must return a signed options agreement to the brokerage firm at which he is trading:

    (A) before trading begins
    (B) within five days of when trading begins
    (C) when trading begins
    (D) within 15 days of when trading begins

120. What type of risk is assumed by the purchaser of a fixed annuity contract?

    (A) Investment risk
    (B) Mortality risk
    (C) Purchasing power risk
    (D) All of the above

121. The ratio of net debt to assessed valuation would be considered for which type of municipal bonds?

    (A) Revenue bonds
    (B) General obligation bonds
    (C) Industrial development bonds
    (D) Double-barreled bonds

122. An investor makes fixed payments of $1,000 each to purchase shares of a mutual fund when the shares are selling at $50, $40, and $50 respectively. Her average cost per share is closest to:

    (A) $43.33
    (B) $46.15
    (C) $46.67
    (D) $50.00

123. The taxable portion of a variable annuity purchased for a lump sum payment five years earlier is taxed:

    (A) not at all
    (B) as ordinary income
    (C) as capital gains
    (D) as part ordinary and part capital gains

124. An open-end mutual fund with an NAV of $46.25 has a 7.5% load. An investor who bought these shares would pay:

    (A) $46.25 per share
    (B) $49.73 per share
    (C) $50.00 per share
    (D) $53.50 per share

125. Which of the following most closely resembles a REIT with respect to method of acquisitions?

    (A) Closed-end fund
    (B) Open-end fund
    (C) Load fund
    (D) No-load fund

PART TWO

Time   3 Hours

Questions   126–250

DIRECTIONS

Each of the questions or incomplete statements below is followed by four suggested answer options. Choose the best answer and then blacken the corresponding space on the answer sheet.

126. The 65 securities in the Dow Jones average are comprised of:

    (A) industrials
    (B) industrials, financials, and transportations
    (C) transportations and utilities
    (D) industrials, transportations, and utilities

127. A variable annuity has a "15-year certain" life annuity. If the annuitant lives beyond 15 years from the time payout begins:

    (A) payments stop
    (B) payments decrease but continue for the recomputed life expectancy period
    (C) payments continue as before
    (D) payments continue for the recomputed life expectancy period

128. In the secondary market, an investor buys $20,000 municipal bonds at 92 and holds them two years to maturity where he collects $20,000. His tax liability is based on:

    (A) $0
    (B) $800
    (C) $1,600
    (D) $9,200

129. In examining an income statement, an analyst could determine all of the following EXCEPT:

    (A) earnings per share
    (B) net working capital
    (C) dividend payout ratio
    (D) additions to retained earnings

130. In the absence of a discretionary account, a customer's order to "use your judgment" would allow a registered representative to do all of the following EXCEPT:

    (A) decide when to place the order
    (B) choose the security to be traded
    (C) choose the price at which a security is sold
    (D) decide not to place the order

131. With respect to an official statement, all of the following are true EXCEPT:

    (A) an official statement must be filed with the SEC
    (B) customers must get it no later than with confirmation
    (C) it contains financial information about the issue
    (D) it is not a requirement for a new municipal issue

132. Municipal bonds are insured by which of the following?

    I. SIPC
    II. MBIAC
    III. FDIC
    IV. FGIC

    (A) I only
    (B) II and IV
    (C) I and III
    (D) I, II, III, and IV

133. An investor has a $17,000 capital loss in 1990. If he has no other capital transactions except in 1991 when he has an $8,000 gain, he will be able to deduct losses until:

    (A) 1990
    (B) 1991
    (C) 1992
    (D) 1993

Use this information to answer Questions 134 and 135.

A section of the NYSE tape reads:

ACI pr $20\frac{1}{4}$ CAI wt 20s2

134. The transaction(s) in ACI was/were:

    (A) 100 ACI sold at $20\frac{1}{4}$
    (B) 100 ACI preferred sold at $20\frac{1}{4}$
    (C) 100 ACI preferred sold at 20, then 100 sold at $20\frac{1}{4}$
    (D) 100 ACI previously sold at $20\frac{1}{4}$

135. With respect to the CAI transactions, we are told:

    (A) 200 warrants sold at 20
    (B) 2,000 warrants sold at 20
    (C) there was a wait (hold) on 200 shares of CAI
    (D) there was a wait (hold) on 2,000 shares of CAI

136. $10,000 face value municipal bonds are purchased at 107.5 when there are 15 years to maturity. If they are sold in five years for 102.5, the tax consequences are:

    (A) $250 loss
    (B) $250 gain
    (C) $500 gain
    (D) $500 loss

137. The equivalent yield for an investor in the 33% bracket for a municipal bond paying $7\frac{1}{2}$% is approximately:

    (A) $7\frac{1}{2}$%
    (B) 10%
    (C) 11.10%
    (D) 11.19%

138. If a callable municipal security is partially recalled, which of the following is true?

    (A) The remaining bonds become less attractive
    (B) The remaining bonds become more attractive
    (C) The yield on the remaining bonds goes up
    (D) This cannot happen. The issue must be called in its entirety

139. One benefit of an oil and gas limited partnership is:

    (A) rental income
    (B) depletion allowance
    (C) mortgage interest deduction
    (D) perpetual income

140. All of the following should be considered in deciding the suitability of a limited partnership EXCEPT:

    (A) the customer's objectives
    (B) the size of the partnership
    (C) the customer's tax status
    (D) the program's managers

141. All of the following are considered insiders in a corporation under the Securities Act of 1934 EXCEPT:

   (A) a clerk who has access to nonpublic information
   (B) a corporate director
   (C) a corporate officer
   (D) an owner of at least $1\frac{1}{2}\%$ of stock

142. Which of the following would result from the Federal Reserve's causing a lowering of interest rates?

   (A) The dollar would rise in value relative to other currencies
   (B) The dollar would fall in value relative to other currencies
   (C) Business failures would increase
   (D) The stock market would fall

143. An investor buys $150,000 of a direct participation program. If the program generates a $30,000 loss for her share, the tax consequences for this investor are:

   (A) no loss is allowed
   (B) a $15,000 loss
   (C) a $30,000 loss
   (D) a $150,000 loss

144. ACI is about to sell 2,000,000 additional shares in a public offering. The issue is in the registration process. If a positive research report comes out, an account executive can send this report to potential customers:

   (A) under no circumstances
   (B) if the preliminary prospectus is out
   (C) if the final prospectus is out
   (D) at any time, since it is not an initial public offering

145. The sponsor of a direct participation program might be considered to have a conflict of interest if:

   (A) he managed adjacent property for himself
   (B) he exchanged partnership property at fair market value
   (C) he marketed partnership shares himself
   (D) he sought partnership approval to change objectives

146. A letter sent to syndicate members by the manager of a successful bid on a municipal bond issue contains all of the following information EXCEPT:

   (A) the amount of good faith deposit required
   (B) the exact date of settlement and delivery of the bonds
   (C) a list of each member's participation
   (D) how the bonds will be advertised

147. How many days are municipal syndicate accounts usually set up to run for?

   (A) 10 days
   (B) 20 days
   (C) 30 days
   (D) 60 days

148. The charges for services like collecting dividends and holding securities:

   (A) must be no more than $\frac{1}{2}\%$ of total assets
   (B) must be fair and nondiscriminatory
   (C) are governed by the 5% rule
   (D) are not limited

149. Who is entitled to the "take-down" in municipal bond under-writing?

    (A) A member of the syndicate
    (B) A member of the selling group
    (C) Any municipal securities dealer
    (D) Any trust department of a commercial bank

150. New issues of municipal securities are exempted from all but the:

    (A) Securities Act of 1933
    (B) Securities Exchange Act of 1934
    (C) Holding Company Act of 1935
    (D) Trust Indenture Act of 1939

151. Under the Securities Acts Amendments of 1975, MSRB rules are enforced by the:

    I. NYSE
    II. SEC
    III. Federal Reserve Board
    IV. NASD

    (A) II, III, and IV only
    (B) II and III only
    (C) I and II only
    (D) I, II, III, and IV

152. A "cash" transaction of municipal bonds would settle on:

    (A) the same day
    (B) the next day
    (C) five business days later
    (D) on a date to be agreed to

153. Which of the following are exempt from *all* Federal and local income taxes?

    (A) Virgin Islands
    (B) Puerto Rico
    (C) Guam
    (D) All of the above

154. The rate of return in a tombstone advertisement for a municipal serial bond is characterized as a(n):

    (A) after tax yield
    (B) effective yield
    (C) nominal yield
    (D) yield to maturity

155. The *most* significant factor in evaluating the safety of a sewer revenue bond is:

    (A) population
    (B) number of users of the sewers
    (C) property taxes
    (D) debt service coverage

156. An investor owns 4 ACI Jan 50 calls. If ACI distributes a 25% stock dividend, the investor would now hold:

    (A) 4 calls of 100 shares
    (B) 5 calls of 100 shares
    (C) 4 calls of 125 shares
    (D) 5 calls of 125 shares

157. An investor buys a Jun DM (deutsche mark) 68 call at $\frac{1}{2}$. The size of the contract is 62,500 DM. His premium would total:

    (A) $312.50
    (B) $625.00
    (C) $3,125.00
    (D) $6,250.00

158. Which of the following is exempt from compliance with Regulation T?

    (A) A broker or dealer who does not handle margin accounts
    (B) A broker or dealer who handles business only in fully registered securities
    (C) A broker or dealer who transacts less than 10% of his business through the medium of a member of a national securities exchange
    (D) None of the above

159. All of the following taxes are recognized as flat rate taxes EXCEPT:

    (A) a gift tax
    (B) an excise tax
    (C) a gasoline tax
    (D) a general tax

160. Under Regulation T of the Federal Reserve, which of the following may grant extensions of time for payment in a client's account?

    (A) The NASD
    (B) The New York Stock Exchange
    (C) The Midwest Stock Exchange
    (D) Any of the above

161. If T-note options are backed by $100,000 of face value securities, the purchase of four T-note options at 16 would require a premium of:

    (A) $640
    (B) $2,000
    (C) $2,560
    (D) $4,000

162. If an account is "frozen" a customer:

    (A) may sell but not buy securities
    (B) must have the necessary cash or securities in the account before the order can be executed
    (C) may not trade securities under any circumstances
    (D) must deposit sufficient cash for any transaction by the settlement date

Use the following income statement to answer Questions 163–165.

ACI INCOME STATEMENT

Net Sales	$10,000,000
Cost of Goods, Selling & Administrative Expenses	$7,000,000
Operating Income	$3,000,000
Interest Expense	$1,000,000
Income Before Taxes	$2,000,000
Income Taxes	$700,000
Income After Taxes	$1,300,000
Dividend Payout $1 (500,000 shares)	$500,000
Retained Earnings	$800,000

163. ACI earnings per share were:

    (A) $1.00
    (B) $1.60
    (C) $2.60
    (D) $4.00

164. The interest coverage (times interest earned) is:

    (A) 0.25
    (B) 0.80
    (C) 2.00
    (D) 3.00

165. ACI's dividend payout ratio is:

    (A) 19.2%
    (B) 20%
    (C) 38.5%
    (D) 62.5%

166. A "buy-in" of a customer occurs if he has failed to deliver securities:

    (A) 10 days after settlement date
    (B) 15 days after settlement date
    (C) 20 days after settlement date
    (D) 30 days after settlement date

167. Pledging customer securities as security for debit balances is called:

    (A) subordination
    (B) hypothecation
    (C) rehypothecation
    (D) intermediation

168. An investor seeking predictable tax-sheltered cash flow should probably choose:

    (A) cattle feeding programs
    (B) oil exploration programs
    (C) real estate triple net lease-back programs
    (D) undeveloped land programs

169. The United States balance of payments deficit goes down if:

    (A) foreign investment in United States companies increases
    (B) foreign investment in United States companies decreases
    (C) interest rates paid on domestic savings accounts decrease
    (D) yields on foreign deposits in the United States decrease

170. A tax shelter specifically designed for self-employed individuals is called a(n):

    (A) Individual Retirement Account
    (B) Keogh plan
    (C) variable annuity
    (D) limited partnership

171. To maintain a fair and orderly market and to act as a broker's broker are the two functions of the:

    (A) two-dollar broker
    (B) specialist
    (C) odd-lot broker
    (D) floor trader

172. A concession of one point on the sale of a new issue of municipals is equal to:

    (A) $.10
    (B) $1
    (C) $10
    (D) $100

173. In a trade of municipal bonds, the confirmation would include all of the following EXCEPT the:

    (A) bond rating
    (B) trade date
    (C) total dollar amount of the trade
    (D) description of the bond

174. The registered representative should maintain all of the following customer records EXCEPT a record of:

    (A) each customer's current holdings
    (B) all of his customer's securities in a cross-indexed file
    (C) his customer's capital gains and losses for the past three years
    (D) all of his customer's purchases and sales for the past three years

175. Under the UGMA, all of the following are true EXCEPT:

    (A) minors cannot make gifts to other minors
    (B) the maximum value of a gift to a minor is $10,000
    (C) gifts given to minors cannot be reclaimed
    (D) only one custodian for one minor at any one time

176. In a limited partnership, the subscription agreement contains all of the following EXCEPT:

    (A) the identity of the signatories
    (B) the recipient of the funds
    (C) suitability standards
    (D) the order of priority of payouts on liquidation

177. Which of the following NYSE orders are automatically reduced in value when the underlying stock begins trading ex-dividend?

    I. Buy stop
    II. Buy limit
    III. Sell stop
    IV. Sell limit

    (A) I and III
    (B) I and IV
    (C) II and III
    (D) II and IV

178. An entry in a customer account that said "opening sale" would refer to:

    (A) purchase of an option
    (B) purchase of common stock
    (C) sale of common stock
    (D) sale of an option

179. The bond counsel takes responsibility for all of the following EXCEPT judging:

    (A) the validity of an issue
    (B) its eligibility for federal tax exemption
    (C) the syndicate
    (D) the issuance procedures

180. A customer owns 100,000 shares of restricted stock. If there are 2,000,000 shares outstanding, what is the least number of shares he can be sure of selling under Rule 144?

    (A) 1,000 shares
    (B) 2,000 shares
    (C) 20,000 shares
    (D) There is no minimum.

181. The Balance Sheet Equation is:

    (A) Assets – Liabilities = Shareholders' Equity
    (B) Assets – Liabilities = Working Capital
    (C) Assets + Shareholders' Equity = Liabilities
    (D) Working Capital + Assets = Liabilities

182. Exchange-listed securities traded in the over-the-counter market are traded in the:

    (A) primary market
    (B) second market
    (C) third market
    (D) fourth market

183. All of the following can be used as collateral in a margin account EXCEPT:

    (A) FNMA stock
    (B) FNMA bonds
    (C) option contracts
    (D) T-notes

184. The flow-through principle applies to all of the following EXCEPT:

    (A) corporate earnings
    (B) mutual funds
    (C) REITs
    (D) limited partnerships

185. Which of the following represents ownership of a foreign company?

    (A) Banker's acceptances
    (B) ADRs
    (C) Japanese yen options
    (D) Eurobonds

186. Which of the following best describes the tax consequences of a 5% stock dividend from a U.S. corporation?

    (A) Dividend income in the year of the declaration
    (B) A capital gain in the year of the declaration
    (C) A 5% increase in the cost basis
    (D) A 5% decrease in the cost basis

187. An investor who is bullish on the stock market over the next two or three years is most likely to buy:

    (A) LEAPS
    (B) CMOs
    (C) TGRS
    (D) LYONS

188. If one brother gives an order to sell some securities from a joint account that he holds with his brother and asks that he be sent a check for the proceeds, the account executive:

    (A) cannot accept the order unless it is confirmed by the other brother
    (B) should comply with the request
    (C) should send the check made out to both brothers
    (D) should sell the securities but not send the check

189. All of the short positions described below are acceptable EXCEPT:

    (A) borrowing stock from another broker to go short
    (B) shorting stock while long the shares
    (C) borrowing stock to take advantage of a tender offer
    (D) shorting stock while owning bonds convertible to that stock

190. Investment companies must issue financial statements:

    (A) monthly
    (B) quarterly
    (C) semiannually
    (D) after each audit

191. The Securities Exchange Act of 1934 allows the SEC to regulate:

    (A) short selling
    (B) proxy solicitations
    (C) margin activities
    (D) all of the above

192. To qualify for listing on the NASDAQ system, a security must satisfy which of the following?

    I.   At least two market makers
    II. Assets of at least $2,000,000
    III. 100,000 shares publicly held
    IV. Must be owned by at least 300 investors

    (A) I and II
    (B) II and IV
    (C) I, II, and IV
    (D) I, II, III, and IV

193. Upon the formation of a municipal security syndicate account, the syndicate letter would indicate all of the following EXCEPT the:

    (A) proposed members' participation
    (B) type of issue
    (C) duration of the syndicate
    (D) yield to the public

194. ACI has 1 million shares outstanding and makes a rights offering of 200,000 shares. If the price of ACI cum rights is $52 and the subscription price is $50, then the theoretical value of a right is:

    (A) $.40
    (B) $.50
    (C) $1.00
    (D) $2.00

195. On Monday morning, an investor bought 400 shares of ACI at $30 per share on margin. By the close on Monday, shares of ACI were selling for $35. How much would have to be deposited to meet a 50% Reg T requirement?

    (A) $6,000
    (B) $7,000
    (C) It depends on the close at the end of five business days.
    (D) The average of $6,000 and $7,000

196. Property has a market valuation of $25,000,000 and is assessed uniformly at 50%. If the tax rate is 10 mills, the amount to be collected is:

    (A) $12,500
    (B) $25,000
    (C) $125,000
    (D) $250,000

197. An investor in a real estate direct participation program is least likely to benefit from:

    (A) depreciation
    (B) depletion
    (C) appreciation
    (D) rental income

198. When a new issue of stock is sold to a limited number of investors without any registration statement having been filed, this is called a:

    (A) secondary distribution
    (B) private placement
    (C) Rule 144 distribution
    (D) Regulation A offering

199. The NASD 5% markup policy could apply to which of the following?

    (A) Sale of open-end mutual fund shares
    (B) Sale of shares in a secondary distribution
    (C) Sale of over-the-counter securities
    (D) Sale of a new issue of nonexempt securities

200. All of the following are risks of participation in a limited partnership EXCEPT:

    (A) illiquidity of the investment
    (B) an unfavorable ruling on the tax status of the program
    (C) larger than anticipated losses
    (D) premature termination of the program

201. Transactions from all of the following markets appear on the consolidated tape EXCEPT those of the:

    (A) primary market
    (B) secondary market
    (C) third market
    (D) fourth market

202. All of the following are part of current assets EXCEPT:

    (A) inventory
    (B) receivables
    (C) payables
    (D) marketable securities

203. An investor in a real estate limited partnership that bought raw land would primarily be seeking:

    (A) current income
    (B) capital appreciation
    (C) deductions for operating expenses
    (D) intangible cost deductions

204. An investor buys a municipal bond "regular way" on September 16. Coupon dates for this security are June 15 and December 15. How many days of accrued interest would she have to add to the purchase price?

    (A) 88
    (B) 89
    (C) 93
    (D) 94

205. Which of the following trades appears on the tape only after the trade is completed?

    (A) Special offer
    (B) Exchange distribution
    (C) Specialist block purchase
    (D) Secondary distribution

206. An investor has no additional incentive to convert a bond in any of the following situations EXCEPT:

    (A) when the bond is at par and the stock is above parity
    (B) when the bond is at par and the stock is below parity
    (C) when the bond and stock are both at par
    (D) when the bond is callable

207. If a $10,000,000 junk bond issue has $4,000,000 redeemed early, the effect on the rest of the issue is:

    (A) to raise its quality
    (B) to lower its quality

    (C) to bring it to investment grade
    (D) to pay the total interest to the remaining bonds

208. A firm offer for "one hour and five minute recall" is followed 30 minutes later with "fill or kill." The offeree has:

    (A) 30 minutes to take all of the bonds
    (B) his offer automatically filled if he does not respond in five minutes
    (C) five minutes to take the offer
    (D) to take the bonds immediately or lose the offer

209. A bond that is purchased at a discount and is used for the payment of estate taxes is called a(n):

    (A) estate bond
    (B) deep-discount bond
    (C) tax-free bond
    (D) flower bond

210. A municipal bond with an 8% coupon which matures in 2010 to yield 8.5% is called at par in 1999. The yield to call is:

    (A) 8%
    (B) between 8% and 8.5%
    (C) 8.5%
    (D) greater than 8.5%

211. ACI has declared an $0.83 dividend. If ACI closes at $60 and opens tomorrow ex-dividend with no other changes, it will open at:

    (A) $59\frac{1}{8}$
    (B) $59\frac{1}{4}$
    (C) $60\frac{3}{4}$
    (D) $60\frac{7}{8}$

212. A bond is callable at 101 plus $\frac{5}{8}$ for each full year that it is called before maturity on 6-15-01, up to a maximum of 105. If the bond had been called 8-15-94, it would have been redeemed at:

    (A) $104\frac{3}{8}$

    (B) $104\frac{3}{4}$

    (C) 105

    (D) $105\frac{3}{8}$

213. To facilitate his efforts at explaining direct participation programs to his clients, an accountant asks to receive your offering literature automatically. Which of the following is true?

    (A) This is permitted for registered investment advisors.
    (B) This is always allowed.
    (C) The material must be marked "not for general public".
    (D) This is not permitted.

214. The margin requirement on a short sale of 2,000 shares of stock selling at $1.75 would be:

    (A) $1,750
    (B) $2,000
    (C) $3,500
    (D) $5,000

215. The legal opinion on a municipal bond does all of the following EXCEPT:

    (A) attest to its exemption from federal tax
    (B) describe the conditions of the bond
    (C) give assurance as to the payment of interest
    (D) attest to the validity of the issue

216. An investor's margin account is restricted by $500. If the account is credited with $1,500 of dividends, how much can the investor withdraw?

    (A) $0
    (B) $500
    (C) $1,000
    (D) $1,500

217. If the yield curve flattens, we can be certain that:

    (A) short-term rates have increased
    (B) long-term rates have decreased
    (C) the spread between short and long term has narrowed
    (D) the spread between short and long term has widened

218. If $20,000 of 6% municipals maturing 1-15-03 had been purchased to settle on 9-15-93, the purchaser would have been owed accrued interest of:

    (A) $100
    (B) $200
    (C) $600
    (D) $1,200

219. The discount on an original issue municipal that is held to maturity generates what tax consequence?

    (A) Some nontaxable interest income
    (B) An ordinary taxable income gain
    (C) A long-term capital gain
    (D) A short-term capital gain

220. A DPP in a drilling program would have large deductions in the first year from:

    (A) depletion allowance
    (B) depreciation
    (C) tangible drilling costs
    (D) intangible drilling costs

221. An order was entered as good for two months and placed as GTC. Who is responsible for canceling the order after two months?

    (A) The broker
    (B) The customer
    (C) The member firm
    (D) The specialist

222. An "insider" has filed a form 144 with the SEC. How long does he have to sell these securities under this notice?

    (A) 30 days
    (B) 60 days
    (C) 90 days
    (D) 180 days

223. If a municipal securities dealer acting for a client recommends a security, according to MSRB rules, he would have to notify the client in writing:

    (A) of the security's recent range of prices
    (B) of any financial interest he had in the underwriting
    (C) of the security's credit rating
    (D) none of the above

224. Which of the following is the lowest investment grade rating?

    (A) BBB
    (B) Ba
    (C) BB
    (D) B

225. The "Official Notice of Sale" would contain all of the following EXCEPT:

    (A) size of the issue
    (B) type of bond
    (C) amount of good faith deposit
    (D) bond rating

226. Which of the following describes the "dated date" on a bond?

    (A) The date on which trading begins
    (B) The date on which interest begins to accrue
    (C) The settlement date
    (D) The trade date

Questions 227–229 refer to the excerpt from the specialist's book listed below:

BUY	CAI	SELL
200 DWR	55	
100 Hutton	$\frac{1}{8}$	
300 Drexel	$\frac{1}{4}$	
	$\frac{3}{8}$	
	$\frac{1}{2}$	
	$\frac{5}{8}$	200 Drexel
		100 Schwab
	$\frac{3}{4}$	200 Merrill
	$\frac{7}{8}$	100 DWR

227. The size of the market in CAI is:

    (A) 300 by 100
    (B) 300 by 200
    (C) 300 by 300
    (D) 600 by 600

228. The specialist could bid for stock for his own account at:

    (A) $55\frac{1}{4}$
    (B) $55\frac{3}{8}$
    (C) $55\frac{1}{2}$
    (D) $55\frac{5}{8}$

229. If both entries at $55\frac{5}{8}$ were sell stops, the specialist could sell from his own account at:

    (A) $55\frac{3}{8}$

    (B) $55\frac{1}{2}$

    (C) $55\frac{5}{8}$

    (D) $55\frac{3}{4}$

230. Member firms must keep a written record of all speaking engagements for at least:

    (A) six months
    (B) one year
    (C) three years
    (D) five years

231. The type of variable annuity that will result in the largest monthly checks is:

    (A) lump sum
    (B) life annuity
    (C) life annuity with rights of survivorship
    (D) 10-year certain life

232. Selling stock under Rule 144 is regulated by the:

    (A) Securities Act of 1933
    (B) Securities Exchange Act of 1934
    (C) Holding Company Act of 1935
    (D) Maloney Act of 1938

233. Short sales on the over-the-counter market can take place:

    (A) never
    (B) without restriction
    (C) after a plus tick only
    (D) after a plus tick or a zero plus tick

234. Disintermediation is not likely to occur unless:

    (A) the Fed reduces the discount rate
    (B) the Fed reduces reserve requirements
    (C) the Fed does long term reverse repos
    (D) the Fed resorts to jawboning

235. All of the following are true of variable annuities EXCEPT:

    (A) annuity income is not taxed until payout begins
    (B) returns are based on portfolio performance
    (C) there is no minimum payout
    (D) performance is proportional to the movement of the Dow

236. An escrow account for pre-refunded municipals could contain:

    (A) only secured municipals
    (B) U.S. Treasury or agency securities
    (C) any revenue bond
    (D) AAA corporate bonds

237. When transacting a municipal bond swap, you are likely to incur a wash sale ruling if you vary only the:

    (A) rating
    (B) municipality
    (C) maturity
    (D) coupon

238. The portion of net revenues set aside for replacement of major equipment in a municipal revenue issue would be placed in a:

    (A) surplus fund
    (B) renewal fund
    (C) debt service fund
    (D) maintenance fund

239. The maximum amount that an investor could be due in a margin account without generating a margin call is:

    (A) $100
    (B) $500
    (C) $1,000
    (D) at the broker's discretion

240. The security that gives the investor the longest time within which to purchase a stock is:

    (A) calls
    (B) puts
    (C) rights
    (D) warrants

241. If an investor sells short a security that she already owns, she is said to have:

    (A) sold short
    (B) sold out the position
    (C) sold "short against the box"
    (D) done a wash sale

242. According to MSRB rules, copies of MSRB rules must be available at which of the following locations?

    (A) Each office of the firm
    (B) The main office of the firm
    (C) Any office where no principal of the firm is stationed
    (D) Any office where there are at least two salespersons

243. The opening of a numbered account under NYSE Rule 406:

    (A) is never allowed
    (B) is allowed for accounts not covered by SIPC
    (C) is allowed if the investor provides a "letter of credit"
    (D) requires a written voucher of responsibility

244. In a cash account, under NYSE rules, which of the following would require written consent by an employer?

    (A) An employee of a bank
    (B) An employee of an insurance company
    (C) An employee of a trust company
    (D) None of the above

245. An abusive tax shelter is one:

    (A) which has no legitimate profit-making purpose
    (B) which allows large tax write-offs
    (C) which takes advantage of investors
    (D) in which the general partner has a conflict of interest

246. The "nine-bond" rule applies to:

    (A) bonds with coupons below 9%
    (B) trades of nine bonds or less
    (C) trades of 90 bonds or less
    (D) markets that offer no more than nine types of bonds

247. Under Rule 147, the minimum time before securities from intrastate offerings can be sold outside the state is:

    (A) 3 months
    (B) 6 months
    (C) 9 months
    (D) 1 year

248. The maximum coverage of cash in any one account under SIPC is:

    (A) $100,000
    (B) $300,000
    (C) $500,000
    (D) unlimited

249. All of the following are true of convertible bonds EXCEPT:

    (A) they can be converted to common stock
    (B) they can be used as collateral
    (C) they can be used to hedge a short position
    (D) their coupon rate is higher than that of nonconvertible bonds

250. The random walk theory is related to:

    (A) the theory of variable returns
    (B) the diversifiability of risk
    (C) the efficient market hypothesis
    (D) the existence of negative betas

PRACTICE EXAMINATION TWO
Answer Key

PART ONE

1	B	37	D	73	D	109	A
2	B	38	B	74	A	110	A
3	C	39	D	75	D	111	B
4	C	40	B	76	B	112	C
5	C	41	C	77	D	113	C
6	A	42	B	78	A	114	B
7	B	43	C	79	A	115	A
8	C	44	B	80	B	116	A
9	A	45	A	81	D	117	A
10	D	46	C	82	D	118	A
11	B	47	B	83	C	119	D
12	D	48	A	84	A	120	C
13	A	49	C	85	C	121	B
14	C	50	C	86	B	122	B
15	A	51	D	87	C	123	B
16	D	52	A	88	D	124	C
17	B	53	D	89	A	125	A
18	A	54	B	90	C		
19	B	55	B	91	D		
20	B	56	C	92	D		
21	C	57	B	93	A		
22	A	58	B	94	D		
23	B	59	D	95	D		
24	C	60	C	96	B		
25	D	61	C	97	A		
26	A	62	B	98	C		
27	A	63	C	99	D		
28	B	64	C	100	B		
29	C	65	B	101	B		
30	C	66	C	102	D		
31	D	67	C	103	B		
32	C	68	D	104	B		
33	A	69	C	105	D		
34	D	70	A	106	B		
35	A	71	A	107	A		
36	C	72	B	108	D		

PRACTICE EXAMINATION TWO
Answer Key

PART TWO

126	D	**162**	B	**198**	B	**234**	D
127	C	**163**	C	**199**	C	**235**	D
128	C	**164**	D	**200**	C	**236**	B
129	B	**165**	C	**201**	A	**237**	A
130	B	**166**	A	**202**	C	**238**	B
131	A	**167**	C	**203**	B	**239**	B
132	B	**168**	C	**204**	D	**240**	D
133	C	**169**	A	**205**	B	**241**	C
134	C	**170**	B	**206**	A	**242**	A
135	B	**171**	B	**207**	A	**243**	D
136	A	**172**	C	**208**	C	**244**	D
137	D	**173**	A	**209**	D	**245**	A
138	B	**174**	C	**210**	D	**246**	B
139	B	**175**	B	**211**	A	**247**	C
140	B	**176**	D	**212**	B	**248**	A
141	D	**177**	C	**213**	D	**249**	D
142	B	**178**	D	**214**	D	**250**	C
143	C	**179**	C	**215**	C		
144	A	**180**	C	**216**	D		
145	A	**181**	A	**217**	C		
146	B	**182**	C	**218**	B		
147	C	**183**	C	**219**	A		
148	B	**184**	A	**220**	D		
149	A	**185**	B	**221**	A		
150	D	**186**	D	**222**	C		
151	A	**187**	A	**223**	B		
152	A	**188**	C	**224**	A		
153	D	**189**	C	**225**	D		
154	D	**190**	C	**226**	B		
155	D	**191**	D	**227**	C		
156	C	**192**	D	**228**	B		
157	A	**193**	D	**229**	B		
158	D	**194**	B	**230**	C		
159	A	**195**	A	**231**	B		
160	D	**196**	C	**232**	A		
161	B	**197**	B	**233**	B		

ANSWER EXPLANATIONS

PART ONE

1. ACI issued one million shares of convertible preferred (par $100). The shares are convertible at $45, and the common is currently selling at $36. If an investor paid $90 per share for 100 shares of preferred, which of the following is true?

   I. The conversion rate is 2.22.
   II. The conversion rate is 2.50.
   III. The preferred is selling below parity.
   IV. The preferred is selling above parity.

   (A) I and III
   (B) I and IV
   (C) II and III
   (D) II and IV

   (B) The conversion rate is $100 \div $45 = 2.22. If one can get 2.22 shares of common for one share of preferred and common is selling at $36, then the conversion is worth 2.22 × $36 = $79.92. So, at $90, the preferred is above parity.

2. Which act empowered the Federal Reserve Board to regulate credit in securities transactions?

   (A) The Securities Act of 1933
   (B) The Securities Exchange Act of 1934
   (C) The Maloney Act of 1938
   (D) The Investment Company Act of 1940

   (B) The Securities Exchange Act regulated the operations of the exchanges and the secondary markets in general. The Securities Act of 1933 was designed to regulate new issues.

3. CAI had earnings of $6 per share. If it paid quarterly dividends of $.60, its dividend payout ratio was:

   (A) 10%
   (B) 30%
   (C) 40%
   (D) 60%

   (C) Quarterly dividends of 60 give a $2.40 annual dividend. $2.40 is 40% of the $6 that was earned.

4. Which of the following strategies has the greatest potential risk?

   (A) Writing naked puts
   (B) Buying naked puts
   (C) Writing naked calls
   (D) Buying naked calls

(C) If the option is uncovered (naked), the potential loss to the writer is governed by the price change in the stock. This naturally is largest on the upside (calls) since it can never go below $0 but can go up without limit. Recall that the buyer's risk is limited to the premium.

5. An investor owns 100 shares of ACI at $45.00. If she writes a straddle on ACI with a $45.00 strike, which subsequent event will create the greatest potential loss for her?

   (A) ACI remains unchanged
   (B) ACI goes to 100
   (C) ACI goes to 0
   (D) Neither option is exercised

(C) If ACI goes to 100 (Choice B), the writer gives up potential gain but actually has a profit from the straddle premium collected. If it goes to $0, she actually loses $4,500 less premiums collected.

6. All of the following are on the same side EXCEPT:

   (A) long call-short stock.
   (B) long call-long stock.
   (C) short call-short stock.
   (D) short put-long stock.

(A) To be long a call means to buy a call, in which case you want the stock to rise. This is the opposite of being short stock.

7. In 1987, an investor purchased a T-note with a May 12 settlement date. If the most recent interest payment had been January 15, how many days of accrued interest must he add to the purchase price?

   (A) 116
   (B) 118
   (C) 120
   (D) 121

(B) Accrued interest is based on actual days up to and including settlement date. This gives 17 days in January, 28 days in February, 31 in March, 30 in April, and 12 in May for a total of 118.

8. An investor purchased a corporate bond with settlement on June 5. If the most recent payment had been on March 15, how many days of accrued interest must she add to the purchase price?

   (A) 78
   (B) 79
   (C) 80
   (D) 81

(C) For corporates, accrued interest is based on a 30-day month and does not include the settlement date. Hence, 16 days in March, 30 in April and May, and 4 in June for a total of 80.

9. ACI is trading at 50. What is the loan value of an ACI Jun 30 Call trading at 22?

   (A) $0
   (B) $1,000
   (C) $1,100
   (D) $2,000

(**A**) Options have no loan value.

Questions 10–12 are based on the following information:

Regulation T is at 50%, house maintenance margin at 30% and NYSE maintenance at 25%.

Market Value	30,000
Debit Balance	17,000
SMA	5,000

10. How much in marginable securities would Mrs. P need to deposit to remove the account from restricted status?

    (A) $0
    (B) $1,000
    (C) $2,000
    (D) $4,000

(**D**) A deposit of $4,000 in securities would bring the market value to $34,000, at which point a $17,000 debit balance would mean the account was at 50%.

11. At what market value will this account be at NYSE minimum maintenance?

    (A) $20,000
    (B) $22,667
    (C) $24,287
    (D) $25,000

(**B**) With maintenance margin at 25%, $\frac{4}{3}$ times the debit balance equals the market value. $\frac{4}{3} \times \$17,000 = \$22,667$.

12. How much cash can she currently withdraw from the account without any other transactions?

    (A) $0
    (B) $3,000
    (C) $4,000
    (D) $5,000

(**D**) With house maintenance at 30%, $\left(\frac{1}{1-.3}\right)$ times the debit record or $24,286 is maintenance margin. Hence, all $5,000 can be withdrawn from the SMA.

13. Under which circumstances at expiration would an investor experience the largest profit from selling, 1 ACI Sep 40 Call and buying 1 ACI Sep 50 Call?

(A) ACI is at $40
(B) ACI is between $40 and $50
(C) ACI is at $50
(D) It cannot be determined

(A) If ACI is $40, both options are worthless. The premium on the ACI Sept 40 Call is larger than the one on the ACI Sep 50 Call, so the investor pockets all of that difference.

14. At what expiration price would this investor experience the greatest loss?

(A) ACI is at $40
(B) ACI is between $40 and $50
(C) ACI is at $50
(D) It cannot be determined

(C) At $50, the ACI Sep 40 is worth $1,000, and the other one is worthless. Above $50, both options increase in value at the same rate, and the investor's loss is unchanged. Below $50, the option he sold loses value (he gains), and, since the one he bought remains worthless, his total loss decreases. Therefore, his maximum loss occurs if ACI expires at $50 (or higher).

15. Which of the following would not be considered "good delivery" in a municipal bond transaction?

(A) Callable bonds
(B) Bearer bonds in $1,000 denominations
(C) Bonds with an attached legal opinion
(D) None of the above

(A) Unless otherwise specified, good delivery requires noncallable bonds.

16. The MSRB regulates all of the following EXCEPT:

(A) banks that do municipal securities business
(B) brokers that do municipal securities business
(C) dealers that do municipal securities business
(D) issuers of municipal securities

(D) The MSRB has no jurisdiction over municipalities that are issuing securities.

17. A new issue of a municipal bond due to mature on July 1, 2009 is dated January 1, 1987. A customer purchases these with a settlement date of February 15. How many days of accrued interest must the customer pay?

    (A) 43
    (B) 44
    (C) 45
    (D) 46

(**B**) The municipal begins accruing interest from the dated date up to, but not including, settlement date on a 30-day month basis. Thus, we have 30 days for January plus 14 in February.

18. All of the following are *direct* obligations of the United States Government EXCEPT:

    (A) FNMA
    (B) GNMA
    (C) Series EE bonds
    (D) flower bonds

(**A**) Federal National Mortgage Association securities have an implied obligation from the federal government, but it is not direct. GNMA is owned by a department of the government (HUD) and is a direct obligation. The other two choices are treasury issues and, hence, are certainly direct obligations.

19. The moment when taxable income begins to exceed cash distributions in a direct participation program is the:

    (A) phantom income point
    (B) cross-over point
    (C) profit point
    (D) cash-flow point

(**A**) It is called phantom income because the investor has more taxable income than cash.

20. In a direct participation program, if there was depreciation of the asset, all of the following would be true EXCEPT:

    (A) cash flow increases
    (B) income increases
    (C) taxes decrease
    (D) net assets decrease

(**B**) Since depreciation reduces the value of assets, it represents an income loss.

21. A municipal security issue of revenue bonds is being analyzed for "coverage." The appropriate ratio is:

    (A) net revenue to total expenses
    (B) gross revenue to operating expenses plus debt service

(C) net revenue to debt service

(D) gross revenue to debt service

(C) The net revenue is that revenue available for debt service after expenses have been paid.

22. A bull spread "breaks even" when the difference between the market price and the lower strike price is equal to the:

(A) higher premium minus the lower one

(B) higher premium minus the market price

(C) higher premium plus the lower one

(D) lower premium minus the market price

(A) For example, if the premiums were 9 for the ACI Sep 40 and 3 for the ACI Sep 50, then with ACI at $46, the difference between $46 and $40 market price minus lower strike price exactly equals the difference between 9 and 3.

23. A put option is "in the money" if:

(A) the strike price is at market price

(B) the strike price is above market price

(C) the strike price is below market price

(D) the strike price is at exercise price

(B) A put is "in the money" if one can sell "put" stock at a higher price than one must pay for the stock. The latter is the market price and the former is the strike (or exercise) price.

24. Federal funds are:

(A) obligations of the Federal Reserve Bank

(B) obligations to the Federal Reserve Bank

(C) obligations by one bank to another to meet Federal Reserve requirements

(D) very stable interest rates

(C) They are, in fact, cash assets over and above the requirements for federal reserves. These are lent overnight to banks that do not have sufficient reserves to meet FRB reserve requirements.

25. All of the following are money market instruments EXCEPT:

(A) commercial paper

(B) banker's acceptances

(C) federal funds

(D) ADRs

(D) American Depository Receipts are receipts for shares of stock in foreign corporations.

26. All of the following are true of the pink sheets EXCEPT:

    (A) they show firm quotes for one round lot
    (B) they are wholesale quotes
    (C) they are published daily
    (D) they list market makers for the quoted securities

(A) They are not firm quotes, but rather yesterday's closing dealer-to-dealer quote.

27. The order in which a transaction is processed is:

    I. order department
    II. margin department
    III. purchase and sale
    IV. cashier

    (A) I, III, II, IV
    (B) III, I, IV, II
    (C) I, II, III, IV
    (D) III, IV, I, II

(A) The order is placed from the order room. It then goes to P&S, after which it is processed for margin (if necessary), and, finally, goes to the cashier for disbursements or collection.

Questions 28–30 refer to the following strategy:

Buy 100 shares of CAI at $53. Sell one CAI Nov 50 Call at 7.

28. The investor will first experience a loss if CAI is:

    (A) below $48
    (B) below $46
    (C) below $50
    (D) below $60

(B) At $46, the $700 premium exactly offsets the $700 loss in the value of CAI.

29. If CAI is at $51 when the previously unexercised option expires, his profit (loss) will be:

    (A) $100
    (B) $100 (loss)
    (C) $400
    (D) $600

(C) If CAI is at $51, the buyer exercises at $50, which means that our investor collects $5,000. He paid $5,300 for the shares and has pocketed a $700 premium. The net of these transactions is $400.

30. The maximum profit possible during the life of the option is:

(A) $100
(B) $300
(C) $400
(D) $700

(**C**) This is the most he can make during the life of the option since he can never get more than $5,000 plus $700 in premium no matter how high CAI goes. Of course, he can gain more after expiration if CAI was below $50 until then and rises afterwards.

The following information is useful for answering Questions 31 and 32:

A limited partner in a balanced oil and gas program has invested $50,000 and is responsible for a recourse loan of an additional $40,000.

31. The investor's basis is:

(A) $10,000
(B) $40,000
(C) $50,000
(D) $90,000

(**D**) The basis consists of the total liability of the investor, which would include the value of a recourse loan.

32. If the investor had passive income of $70,000, the maximum loss he could claim would be:

(A) $40,000
(B) $50,000
(C) $70,000
(D) $90,000

(**C**) Losses cannot exceed the value of any passive income for the year. Of course, the investor could carry forward as much as $20,000 if the entire oil program investment, including the recourse loan, were to be lost.

33. The sponsor of a functional sharing arrangement oil- and gas-drilling program would pay:

(A) all nondeductible expenses
(B) all intangible expenses
(C) a share of deductible expenses
(D) a share of nondeductible expenses

(**A**) The point of a functional sharing arrangement is to allow the limited partners all of the deductible expenses.

34. A preliminary prospectus can do which of the following?

   (A) It can be used during the cooling-off period
   (B) It can be used to blue-sky an issue
   (C) It can be used to generate orders
   (D) It can be used to get indications of interest

(D) All of the other choices describe events that occur later.

Questions 35–38 refer to the following:

An investor with no other positions buys 1 ACI Mar 40 Put at $4\frac{1}{2}$ and buys 1 ACI Mar 40 Call at $1\frac{1}{2}$.

35. The market price at ACI is most likely to be:

   (A) below $40
   (B) at $40
   (C) above $40
   (D) it cannot be determined

(A) The premium for the Put is much larger than that for the Call. This must reflect intrinsic value, *i.e.*, the Put is in the money. Therefore, the strike price of $40 for the Put is above the market price.

36. The maximum loss this investor could experience is:

   (A) $300
   (B) $450
   (C) $600
   (D) unlimited

(C) If ACI is at $40, both options expire worthless, and the investor loses both premiums or $600.

37. The maximum profit he could experience is:

   (A) $450
   (B) $600
   (C) $3,400
   (D) unlimited

(D) If ACI goes to $0, he earns $4,000 – $600, which is the most he can make from the Put. If ACI goes to $100, he earns $6,000 – $600, and the higher ACI goes, the higher is his profit. In principle, there is no upper bound on ACI's price, and, hence, his profit potential is also unlimited.

38. At expiration, ACI was at $50. If he had not exercised up to then, he would experience:

   (A) $600 loss
   (B) $400 gain

    (C) $600 gain

    (D) $1,000 gain

(B) At $50, he earns $1,000 on his call and has paid $600 in premiums for a net profit of $400.

39. Which of the following has the least volatile interest rate?

    (A) Federal funds rate

    (B) Prime rate

    (C) T-bill rate

    (D) Discount rate

(D) The discount rate is the least volatile of these rates as it represents a conscious choice by the Fed to affect rates. Of the others, the prime rate is least volatile, but it too is now automatically readjusted as other rates move.

40. Interest on new issues of municipal bonds accrues from the:

    (A) previous interest payment

    (B) dated date

    (C) settlement date

    (D) purchase date

(B) There is no previous payment date on a new issue. Thus, the dated date is when interest begins to accrue.

41. All of the following provide information about proposed municipal bond issues EXCEPT:

    (A) *Munifacts*

    (B) *Daily Bond Buyer*

    (C) *Blue List*

    (D) newspapers

(C) The *Blue List* describes already issued securities.

42. If all of the following municipal securities mature on the same date, which has the lowest price?

    (A) $7\frac{1}{4}\%$ coupon at $7\frac{1}{4}\%$

    (B) 8% coupon at $8\frac{3}{8}\%$

    (C) 8% coupon at $7\frac{3}{4}\%$

    (D) $7\frac{1}{4}\%$ coupon at $7\frac{3}{8}\%$

(B) The 8% coupon yielding $8\frac{3}{8}\%$ has a greater discount than the $7\frac{1}{4}\%$ coupon yielding $7\frac{3}{8}\%$. The other two are not at a discount. It is important to remember that this might not be true if the securities had different times to maturity.

Questions 43–45 refer to the following strategy:

An investor buys 3 ACI Jun 50 Calls at 4.

43. At what price will the investor break even?

(A) $46
(B) $50
(C) $54
(D) $62

(C) Break-even will occur when he can realize the same amount from exercising as he has paid in premiums — in this case, if he exercises (to buy at $50) when the market price is $54.

44. His maximum possible loss on this investment is:

(A) $400
(B) $1,200
(C) $15,000
(D) unlimited

(B) His maximum possible loss occurs if his investment is worthless. He paid three times $400 for this, so his loss can be as high as $1,200.

45. If he exercises these when ACI is at $60 and wishes to purchase the stock in his margin account, how much will he be required to deposit in the margin account?

(A) $7,500
(B) $8,700
(C) $9,000
(D) $10,200

(A) If he exercises, he buys at $50. The total on three calls is three times $5,000. With a 50% Regulation T, he must put up $7,500. The premiums paid earlier go to the writer and are irrelevant here.

46. To analyze a general obligation bond, one would consider all of the following EXCEPT the:

(A) size of the issue
(B) size of the population base
(C) denomination of the issue
(D) income of the ratepayers

(C) The denomination of the issue would not affect the ability of the municipality to service or repay the debt.

47. The name of the interest rate at which member banks may borrow from the Federal Reserve Bank is:

    (A) federal funds rate
    (B) discount rate
    (C) prime rate
    (D) money supply rate

(B) By definition. The federal funds rate is the rate on funds *between* banks. The prime is the rate at which banks lend to their best customers.

Questions 48–50 refer to the following information:

A customer has the following accounts:

Account	Market Value	Balance
Cash (with marginable securities)	$20,000	$ 5,000
Long	$30,000	$16,000 (Debit)
Short	$10,000	$14,000 (Credit)
SMA	$ 4,000	

48. What is her total equity?

    (A) $43,000
    (B) $60,000
    (C) $65,000
    (D) $69,000

(A) The total equity is $25,000 in the cash account + $14,000 in the long account ($30,000 − $16,000) + $4,000 in the short account ($14,000 − $10,000) for a total of $43,000.

49. What is the total buying power in the two margin accounts?

    (A) $4,000
    (B) $6,000
    (C) $8,000
    (D) $10,000

(C) The buying power in the margin accounts comes from the SMA. The $4,000 there gives $8,000 in buying power with Regulation T at 50%.

50. What is the total buying power of all accounts?

    (A) $20,000
    (B) $27,000
    (C) $38,000
    (D) $40,000

(C) The total buying power would consist of $9,000 in cash and $20,000 in marginable securities. This comes to $18,000 (two times cash) + $20,000 or $38,000.

51. The premium on a Value Line index option is $2\frac{1}{2}$. The total dollar price of this premium is:

    (A) $250
    (B) $500
    (C) $625
    (D) $1,250

(D) The Value Line index option has a multiple of 500 times the quoted value. $500 \times \$2.50 = \$1,250$.

Questions 52–54 refer to the following strategy:

An investor buys 100 shares of CAI at 45 and writes 1 CAI Apr 50 Call at 2.

52. At what price would she break even?

    (A) $43
    (B) $48
    (C) $50
    (D) $52

(A) She breaks even where the $200 premium exactly offsets her loss on the stock. This occurs when CAI is at $43 since she bought it at $45. Note: The option strike price is irrelevant here.

53. If the call is exercised when CAI is at $54, she has:

    (A) $200 loss
    (B) $200 gain
    (C) $500 gain
    (D) $700 gain

(D) Her profit is $500 from stock which she bought at $45 and sold at $50 plus $200 of premium.

54. What is the most this investor could lose?

    (A) $200
    (B) $4,300
    (C) $4,500
    (D) Unlimited

(B) Her loss is limited to $4,300. She loses $4,500 if the stock is worthless minus the $200 premium that she collected. Note: Her *potential profit* from owning the stock is unlimited and giving up this opportunity is *not a loss.*

Questions 55 and 56 refer to the following information:

ACI has issued a convertible bond with a conversion price of $100 per share.

55. The conversion rate is:

   (A) 5 to 1
   (B) 10 to 1
   (C) 20 to 1
   (D) 100 to 1

(B) If a bond (par value $1,000) can be converted into common stock at $100 per share, then the conversion ratio is 10 shares to one bond.

56. If the bond is selling at $1,150, the parity price for the stock is:

   (A) $100
   (B) $110
   (C) $115
   (D) $150

(C) If they are at parity, then 10 shares must be worth $1,150 or each share $115.

Questions 57 and 58 refer to the following information:

CAI has ten million shares authorized. A total of eight million shares have been issued, and there are currently one million shares of treasury stock. CAI has a market price of $50.

57. If the next common stock dividend is declared at $.75, the total amount to be distributed is:

   (A) $750,000
   (B) $5,250,000
   (C) $6,000,000
   (D) $7,500,000

(B) Only the shares that are issued (not including treasury stock) get dividends. Here 7,000,000 shares times $.75 per share = $5,250,000.

58. If the annual dividend for CAI has been $3.00, CAI has a current yield of:

   (A) 3%
   (B) 6%
   (C) 7.5%
   (D) 15%

(B) The current yield is $3.00 ÷ $50.00 = 6%.

59. When an offering becomes effective under SEC rules, this means that the SEC has:

(A) checked the accuracy of the registration statement
(B) approved the offering
(C) attested that the offering meets minimum investment standards
(D) determined that the registration statement is complete

(D) The SEC responsibility is to determine that the statement contains all of the required information and not to pass judgment on the accuracy of the statement or advisability of the investment.

Questions 60–62 refer to the following investments:

Long 2 ACI Jun 50 Puts at $3\frac{1}{2}$

Short 2 ACI Jun 45 Puts at $\frac{1}{2}$

60. If they have not been previously exercised, what is the maximum possible profit on this trade at expiration?

(A) $200
(B) $300
(C) $400
(D) $600

(C) The maximum possible profit would occur if ACI were at $45 where the 50 puts would be worth $500 each and the 45 puts would be worthless. Since the investor paid a *net* price of $300 for this opportunity for a net profit of $200 and there are two options, the maximum possible profit is two times $200 or $400.

61. If they have not been previously exercised, what is the maximum possible loss from this trade at expiration?

(A) $300
(B) $400
(C) $600
(D) Unlimited

(C) The maximum loss occurs if the investor loses all premiums, in this case ($350 – $50) times two. Note: There is no loss possible from exercise because the investor can exercise (at $50) if the option written is exercised (at $45).

62. At what market price would this investment break even?

(A) $45.50
(B) $47.00
(C) $48.00
(D) $49.50

(B) This investment breaks even if ACI is at $47 where being long a put with a $50 strike earns $300, which is the net premium ($350 paid, $50 collected) paid.

63. Another name for the nominal rate (yield) is:

    (A) yield to maturity
    (B) current yield
    (C) coupon rate
    (D) current yield-coupon rate

(C) By definition. The current yield is the coupon rate divided by the market price as a percentage of par. The yield to maturity is a combination of the current and any additional yield positive (or negative) if the bond is selling at a discount (or premium).

64. Regular way for United States treasury securities means:

    (A) next business day payment—five business day delivery
    (B) five business day payment—five business day delivery
    (C) next business day payment—next business day delivery
    (D) five business day payment—next business day delivery

(C) For United States treasuries, "regular way" is next business day payment and delivery.

65. An investor pays $70 in accrued interest on a 9% corporate bond bought at 90. If the bond has ten years to maturity, how much interest is reportable for this first tax year?

    (A) $10
    (B) $30
    (C) $90
    (D) $100

(B) The investor collects $90 (9% of $1,000) and must add $10 each year for the ten years as additional interest since the bond purchased at $900 pays $1,000 at maturity. In the first year, $70 of the $90 goes to the previous owner, leaving the investor with $20 plus $10 = $30.

66. If a municipality solicits bids for an offering, the winning bid will be the one that offers to:

    (A) sell it at the lowest price
    (B) sell it at the highest price
    (C) sell it at the lowest cost to the municipality
    (D) raise the most money for the municipality

(C) The winning bid is the one that results in the lowest cost to the municipality.

67. According to MSRB rules, a municipal securities principal must approve all of the following EXCEPT:

    (A) opening new accounts
    (B) handling of customer complaints
    (C) legal opinions
    (D) every transaction

(C) Legal opinions are the responsibility of bond attorneys.

68. According to MSRB rules, the total of gifts and gratuities that may be accepted from one person by a registered representative in one year may not exceed:

    (A) $25
    (B) $50
    (C) $75
    (D) $100

(D) This does not include expenses generated in the normal course of business like business dinners, etc.

69. All of the following are true of full discretionary accounts EXCEPT:

    (A) they must be reviewed regularly by a supervisory person
    (B) they must have written authorization from the customer
    (C) a father can sell securities for a son's account with verbal authorization
    (D) a registered representative can remove cash from such an account

(C) Discretionary accounts of all kinds require written authorization.

Questions 70–72 are based on the following:

Sell 1 CAI Apr 35 Put at 2 when CAI is at $39.

In all cases, assume that there has been no exercise prior to expiration.

70. This trade will break even if CAI is at:

    (A) $33
    (B) $35
    (C) $37
    (D) $41

(A) At $33, the $200 premium is offset by the $200 loss from having to buy 100 shares at $35 when their market value is $33.

71. The maximum possible profit is:

    (A) $200
    (B) $400
    (C) $3,700
    (D) $4,100

(A) The maximum possible profit for someone who has written an option with no other position occurs if the investor keeps the entire premium, in this case $200.

72. If CAI is at 25, the investor's profit (loss) is:

   (A) $800 profit
   (B) $800 loss
   (C) $1,200 profit
   (D) $1,200 loss

(B) If CAI is at $25, the writer forced to buy at $35 loses $1,000 minus the $200 that he collected.

73. All of the following are true of T-bills EXCEPT:

   (A) they are issued in book-entry form
   (B) they are traded on a discount basis
   (C) they are less risky than T-bonds
   (D) they usually have a higher rate than the prime

(D) The other statements are true. The fact that they mature quickly means that they have less principal risk than T-bonds.

74. For information on unlisted corporate bonds, one should examine the:

   (A) yellow sheets
   (B) *Blue List*
   (C) pink sheets
   (D) visible supply

(A) The yellow sheets have unlisted corporates and their market makers. Pink sheets are for securities, and the others are for municipal bonds.

75. All of the following are required by MSRB rules for customer confirmations EXCEPT:

   (A) the amount of any commission in any broker transaction
   (B) the source of any commission in any broker transaction
   (C) notification if the bonds are not in bearer form
   (D) the amount of any markup on a dealer transaction

(D) A dealer is not required to reveal the markup on a transaction but must list any commission that is charged.

76. The Securities Act of 1933 regulates which of the following?

   (A) Securities dealer operations
   (B) Registration of securities
   (C) Management of investment companies
   (D) Securities exchange operations

(B) This act was the first major attempt to regulate the securities industries and focused primarily on the issuance of new securities.

77. The Securities Exchange Act of 1934 regulates all of the following EXCEPT:

   (A) capital requirements for broker/dealers
   (B) financial reports by broker/dealers
   (C) hypothecation of customer securities
   (D) cooling-off period

(D) This act dealt with the secondary market and, in particular, the regulation of the exchanges. The cooling-off period refers to new issues and the time between the filing of a registration and its effective dates.

Questions 78–80 refer to the following strategy:

Sell short 200 shares of ACI at 50.
Buy 2 ACI Sep 55 Calls at $1\frac{1}{2}$.

78. This strategy will break even if ACI is at:

   (A) $48.50
   (B) $51.50
   (C) $53.00
   (D) $56.50

(A) Break-even occurs where the premium paid per share, $1.50, equals the amount realized per share on the stock position. Since it was sold short at $50, this occurs when ACI reads $48.50.

79. The maximum possible profit would occur if ACI were at:

   (A) $0
   (B) $1.50
   (C) $50
   (D) $55

(A) The maximum possible profit would occur when the short position was most profitable. This naturally is at $0. Note: Any profits made by exercising the call are lost on the short position.

80. The maximum possible loss from this strategy is:

   (A) $700
   (B) $1,300
   (C) $9,700
   (D) $10,000

(B) The maximum possible loss would occur if ACI were at $55: a loss of $1,000 on the short position plus a loss of $300 in premium for a total of $1,300.

81. All of the following are true of GNMAs EXCEPT:

   (A) they are direct obligations of the United States Government
   (B) they usually pay a higher rate than T-bonds of comparable maturity

(C) they often include some return of capital before maturity

(D) they are exempt from state and local taxes

(D) They are subject to all of these taxes. The GNMA pools of mortgages will include some mortgages which are refinanced when interest rates drop sharply. This is a return of capital.

Questions 82–84 refer to the following income statement:

Consolidated Amalgamated Inc.

Income Statement for year ending

December 31, 1990.

Net Sales	$20,000,000
Cost of Goods	($12,000,000)
Administrative Costs	($3,000,000)
Operating Profits	$5,000,000
Other Income	$500,000
(EBIT) Total Income	$5,500,000
Fixed Interest	($1,000,000)
(EBT) Income before Taxes	$4,500,000
Income Tax	($1,500,000)
Net Income	$3,000,000
Common Stock Dividends	($1,200,000)
Retained Earnings	$1,800,000

CAI has 1.2 million shares issued of which 200,000 are treasury stock.

82. What are the earnings per share?

(A) $1.00

(B) $1.20

(C) $2.50

(D) $3.00

(D) Earnings per share are net income divided by shares outstanding. In this case, $3 million divided by $1 million, since treasury stock is not part of outstanding shares.

83. What is the profit margin on operations?

(A) 15%

(B) 22.5%

(C) 25%

(D) 27.5%

(C) The profit margin on operations is operating profit divided by operating revenue (net sales here) or $5 million divided by $20 million.

84. What is the times interest earned?

 (A) 5.5 to 1
 (B) 4.5 to 1
 (C) 3 to 1
 (D) 1.8 to 1

(A) Times earned interest is earnings before interest and taxes, EBIT (the money available to pay interest with), divided by interest costs. In this case, $5.5 million divided by $1 million or 5.5.

85. Which of the following choices represent the same class?

 (A) All ACI options
 (B) All ACI 50 options
 (C) All ACI Calls
 (D) All ACI Jun

(C) The same class is all options of the same type (put or call) on the same security.

86. The premium on an option that is "at the money" is made up of:

 (A) all intrinsic value
 (B) all time value
 (C) half intrinsic value plus half time value
 (D) some positive amounts of intrinsic and time value

(B) An option "at the money" has no intrinsic value yet. It is at the point where it can begin to accumulate intrinsic value.

87. Which of the following is a long straddle?

 (A) Buy 1 CAI Sep 45 Call; sell 1 CAI Sep 40 Call
 (B) Buy 1 CAI Sep 45 Put; sell 1 CAI Sep 40 Call
 (C) Buy 1 CAI Sep 45 Put; buy 1 CAI Sep 45 Call
 (D) Sell 1 CAI Sep 45 Call; sell 1 CAI Sep 45 Put

(C) A straddle is a put and a call on the same equity with the same strike. A long straddle is owning or buying a straddle.

Questions 88–90 refer to the following choices:

 (A) banker's acceptances
 (B) T-bills
 (C) repos
 (D) commercial paper

Choose the money market instrument best described in each of the following:

88. This instrument is limited to 270-day maturity.

(D) Commercial paper matures in 270 days or less. This allows issuers to avoid registration of these securities.

89. This instrument is used to foster foreign trade.

(A) A major tool in foreign trade. It allows traders to arrange payment in other countries at later dates.

90. This instrument is traded for a fixed length of time.

(C) Repos are securities which are traded with an express agreement to repossess them at some specific future date.

91. An account in which both owners have trading authority and in which the tenant's portion reverts to his estate is called:

   (A) joint tenants with rights of survivorship
   (B) tenants in entirety
   (C) communal tenants
   (D) joint tenants in common

(D) Joint tenants with rights of survivorship, choice A, means that the surviving tenant retains the deceased's interest.

92. A client account for an investment advisor requires all of the following EXCEPT a(n):

   (A) full trading authorization
   (B) new account forms for each account
   (C) agreement to furnish any other forms dictated by house requirements
   (D) disclosure form stating that the client knows that the advisor is trading other accounts

(D) There is no such disclosure form.

93. Which of the following is a good delivery for a transaction of 500 shares?

   (A) Four 25-share certificates; ten 20-share certificates; one 200-share certificate
   (B) Ten 40-share certificates; one 100-share certificate
   (C) Four 50-share certificates; four 75-share certificates
   (D) Five 40-share certificates; one 300-share certificate

(A) None of the other choices meets the requirements that the delivery be in round lots or units which make up single round lots. Choice A does since $4 \times 25 = 100$ and $5 \times 20 = 100$.

94. For each listed options contract the issuer is the:

   (A) exchange on which it is listed
   (B) writer of the contract
   (C) writer's brokerage firm
   (D) Options Clearing Corporation

(D) The OCC is the issuer of all contracts. It is technically "on the other side" of each long or short.

95. Exercise notices are assigned on the basis of:

    (A) earliest written
    (B) latest written
    (C) largest holder
    (D) random selection

(D) This is the rule except under extraordinary circumstances.

96. Settlement for the purchase of OCC listed options is:

    (A) same day
    (B) next day
    (C) five business days
    (D) seven business days

(B) Note: This is the requirement of the OCC, not the Federal Reserve.

97. The minimum denomination for T-notes and T-bonds is:

    (A) $1,000
    (B) $5,000
    (C) $10,000
    (D) $100,000

(A) T-notes and T-bonds are issued in denominations of $1,000. The notes have maturity of one to 10 years while bonds have maturities of 10 to 30 years (or longer).

98. All of the following are acceptable collateral by a brokerage firm EXCEPT:

    (A) FNMA securities
    (B) AAA Corporates
    (C) EE bonds
    (D) T-bills

(C) These are nonnegotiable and so would be useless to the broker if he held them as forfeit on a loan.

99. Four directors are to be elected at the ACI annual meeting under cumulative voting. Mr. P owns 200 shares. He may cast no more than:

    (A) 200 votes
    (B) 200 votes for any one director
    (C) 400 votes for any one director
    (D) 800 votes for any one director

(D) As worded, choice D is correct since under cumulative voting he may cast up to 800 votes for a single director.

100. If any employee of an insurance company provides a letter from an officer of the insurers saying that the employee may open a margin account and that the company does not wish to receive duplicate confirmations, the registered representative may:

    (A) not open the account
    (B) open the account
    (C) open the account but send duplicates anyway
    (D) open the account but inform the SEC that no duplicates are being sent

    (B) If the employing firm acknowledges the fact of the account and does not want the confirmations, the representative may proceed as with every other customer.

101. All of the following would result in an adjustment of the options contract EXCEPT:

    (A) 5% stock dividend
    (B) $1.0 dividend
    (C) 3/2 stock split
    (D) rights distribution

    (B) No adjustments are made for cash dividends. All of the others result in a change in the number of shares represented. To keep the value constant, shares and strike prices are adjusted.

102. ACI has declared a 25% stock dividend. At the ex-dividend date, an ACI Dec 50 option will become (remain):

    (A) unchanged
    (B) ACI 50 for 125 shares
    (C) ACI 40 for 100 shares
    (D) ACI 40 for 125 shares

    (D) The stock dividend changes 100 shares to 125 shares. The strike is adjusted so that $125 \times \$40$ (new strike) $= 100 \times \$50$ (old strike).

103. Listed options cease trading on the third Friday of expiration month at:

    (A) 3:00 P.M. Eastern Time
    (B) 3:00 P.M. Central Time
    (C) 4:30 P.M. Eastern Time
    (D) 4:30 P.M. Central Time

    (B) Trading for expiration month ends at 3:00 P.M. Central Time (4:00 P.M. Eastern Time). Other options trade for ten minutes longer.

104. A corporation that earns no income in a particular year would not be required to pay interest on what type of bond?

    (A) Equipment trust certificate
    (B) Income bond
    (C) Convertible debenture
    (D) Subordinated debenture

    (B) An income or adjustment bond promises to repay principal in full at maturity but pays interest only if earnings are sufficient to meet the payment.

105. The inclusion of a call protection provision for a bond means:

    (A) the investor must pay a premium for this protection
    (B) the issuer is protected if the bonds are called
    (C) the investor is insured against loss of principal in the event of a call
    (D) the issuer may not call the bond for some period of time

    (D) The investor is protected from the possibility of the bond being called during some time after issuance. Since the bond is called by the issuer only if that is good for him, and, hence, bad for the investor, call protection is valuable to the investor.

106. A 9% bond due to mature in one year trades at 10%. What is its approximate price?

    (A) $900
    (B) $990
    (C) $1,000
    (D) $1,100

    (B) If it trades to yield 10 and matures in one year, then the interest ($90)—plus appreciation—represent a 10% yield to maturity. Using the approximation (interest plus appreciation) divided by (average of current price and price at maturity). Choice B gives ($90 + $10) ÷ $995 or approximately 10%. None of the others is close to this value.

107. The most risky oil and gas limited partnership is likely to be a(n):

    (A) exploratory program
    (B) balanced program
    (C) drilling program
    (D) income program

    (A) Each of the others has at least a component that consists of productive wells.

108. If a partnership borrows money from one of its limited partners, this partner:

    (A) becomes a general partner
    (B) loses his limited partner status
    (C) is in violation of the partnership agreement
    (D) becomes a general creditor of the partnership

(D) There is no change of status for such a limited partner.

109. To protect itself, a Japanese car manufacturer who is buying parts from the United States and is afraid that the yen will fall relative to the dollar is most likely to buy:

    (A) Japanese yen puts
    (B) Japanese yen calls
    (C) U.S. dollar puts
    (D) U.S. dollar calls

(A) There are no dollar options, so to protect against a falling yen, one would buy puts on the Japanese yen.

110. An investor sells 1 CAI Jul 50 Call at 7 and 1 CAI Jul 50 Put at 3. He will profit unless CAI is:

    (A) above 60 or below 40
    (B) above 57 or below 43
    (C) above 54 or below 47
    (D) above 53 or below 47

(A) He has collected $1,000 in premiums. He profits if exercise does not cost $1,000. Choice A is the only one in which he loses more than $1,000 from exercise.

111. The writer of a put option on D-marks would like:

    (A) the D-mark to decline
    (B) the D-mark to appreciate relative to the dollar
    (C) the dollar to appreciate relative to the D-mark
    (D) United States interest rates to rise relative to German rates

(B) The put writer does not want to be exercised. He does not want D-marks to decline. Note: If United States interest rates rise (choice D), the dollar is more attractive and D-marks less attractive, which the writer does not want.

112. The usual methods for underwriting municipal bonds are:

    I. negotiated for revenue bonds
    II. negotiated for general obligation bonds
    III. competitive for revenue bonds
    IV. competitive for general obligation bonds

    (A) I and II
    (B) II and IV
    (C) III and II
    (D) III and IV

  (C) Revenue bonds are usually awarded under competitive bidding and general obligation bonds are negotiated.

113. According to MSRB, a potential customer must be told all of the following with respect to a negotiated municipal underwriting EXCEPT:

    (A) amount of any fee received from the issuer by the firm
    (B) initial offering price of each maturity
    (C) membership of the underwriting syndicate
    (D) amount of the underwriting spread

  (C) This is not material to the investor's decision about the worth of the investment. It might steer him to a different broker.

114. The advantage of writing a covered call is that it:

    (A) limits gain on the equity position
    (B) reduces possible loss on equity position
    (C) raises maximum possible gain on the equity position
    (D) prevents major loss on the equity position

  (B) Writing a call, one collects a premium which effectively lowers the cost of the underlying stock. This reduces possible loss but does not prevent major loss. Naturally, there is no advantage to limiting gain (choice A).

115. Which of the following is a spread?

    (A) Long 1 ACI Sep 50 Call; short 1 ACI Sep 60 Call.
    (B) Long 1 ACI Sep 50 Call; short 1 ACI Sep 50 Put.
    (C) Long 1 ACI Sep 50 Call; long 1 ACI Sep 50 Put.
    (D) Long 1 ACI Sep 50 Call; long 1 ACI Dec 60 Call.

  (A) A spread is being long and short a call (or a put) at different strike prices.

116. Variable annuities must be registered with the SEC and:

    (A) state insurance commissions
    (B) NASD
    (C) state banking commissions
    (D) ERISA governors

   (A) Since annuities are a form of insurance, the securities are under the jurisdiction of state insurance commissions in any states in which they are sold.

117. Arrange from first to last the order in which to allocate bonds in a new municipal bond issue.

    I.   Syndicate orders
    II. Pre-sale orders
    III. Designated orders
    IV. Member orders

    (A) II, I, III, IV
    (B) III, I, II, IV
    (C) II, IV, I, III
    (D) IV, II, III, I

   (A) Orders received before the sale get priority. Then sales for the benefit of the entire syndicate, then designated orders, and, finally, orders from members.

118. An investor writes 1 CAI 40 Call at 12 when CAI is selling at $50. If this call is uncovered, how much must she deposit to meet margin requirements?

    (A) $750
    (B) $1,200
    (C) $1,950
    (D) $2,500

   (A) The requirement is 15% of market value plus premium (less any out of the money). Here, 15% of $5,000 plus $1,200 = $1,950. Since $1,200 has been collected in premiums, an additional $750 must be deposited.

119. A customer must return a signed options agreement to the brokerage firm at which he is trading:

    (A) before trading begins
    (B) within five days of when trading begins
    (C) when trading begins
    (D) within 15 days of when trading begins

   (D) This agreement must be returned within 15 days of the beginning of trading. If it is not, trading is restricted to closing out existing positions.

120. What type of risk is assumed by the purchaser of a fixed annuity contract?

     (A) Investment risk
     (B) Mortality risk
     (C) Purchasing power risk
     (D) All of the above

   (C) With a fixed annuity payment, he assumes the risk that the purchasing power of that payment will be inadequate.

121. The ratio of net debt to assessed valuation would be considered for which type of municipal bonds?

     (A) Revenue bonds
     (B) General obligation bonds
     (C) Industrial development bonds
     (D) Double-barreled bonds

   (B) A general obligation would be affected by the overall debt level relative to the base from which revenues (taxes) are generated. All of the other choices have specific revenues or another source of revenue.

122. An investor makes fixed payments of $1,000 each to purchase shares of a mutual fund when the shares are selling at $50, $40, and $50 respectively. Her average cost per share is closest to:

     (A) $43.33
     (B) $46.15
     (C) $46.67
     (D) $50.00

   (B) The $3,000 invested has purchased 20, 25, and 20 shares respectively. This gives an average cost of $3,000 divided by 65 or $46.15.

123. The taxable portion of a variable annuity purchased for a lump sum payment five years earlier is taxed:

     (A) not at all
     (B) as ordinary income
     (C) as capital gains
     (D) as part ordinary and part capital gains

   (B) Some of the payment is considered a return of capital, but the taxable portion is taxed as ordinary income.

124. An open-end mutual fund with an NAV of $46.25 has a 7.5% load. An investor who bought these shares would pay:

     (A) $46.25 per share
     (B) $49.73 per share
     (C) $50.00 per share
     (D) $53.50 per share

(C) The 7.5% is based on the selling price. Here, 7.5% of $50 = $3.75 which, when subtracted from $50, yields the NAV of $46.25.

125. Which of the following most closely resembles a REIT with respect to method of acquisitions?

(A) Closed-end fund
(B) Open-end fund
(C) Load fund
(D) No-load fund

(A) A REIT is bought and sold on the market. As such, it resembles a closed-end fund, which is not redeemed but rather is bought and sold in the market.

ANSWER EXPLANATIONS
PART TWO

126. The 65 securities in the Dow Jones average are comprised of:

(A) industrials
(B) industrials, financials, and transportations
(C) transportations and utilities
(D) industrials, transportations, and utilities

(D) The 65 securities in the Dow consist of 30 industrials, 20 transportations, and 15 utilities.

127. A variable annuity has a "15-year certain" life annuity. If the annuitant lives beyond 15 years from the time payout begins:

(A) payments stop
(B) payments decrease but continue for the recomputed life expectancy period
(C) payments continue as before
(D) payments continue for the recomputed life expectancy period

(C) The 15-year certain future guarantees a minimum payment to the annuitant or his estate. It does not affect the payment of a life annuity except that the existence of a minimum payment reduces the size of the payments.

128. In the secondary market, an investor buys $20,000 municipal bonds at 92 and holds them two years to maturity where he collects $20,000. His tax liability is based on:

(A) $0
(B) $800
(C) $1,600
(D) $9,200

(C) Municipals purchased in the market are treated as capital assets. If they are redeemed at face value, the investor realizes a $1,600 gain.

129. In examining an income statement, an analyst could determine all of the following EXCEPT:

    (A) earnings per share
    (B) net working capital
    (C) dividend payout ratio
    (D) additions to retained earnings

   (B) Net working capital is current assets minus current liabilities. This information appears in the balance sheet. The income statement would include earnings, dividends, and the number of shares outstanding. These entries would allow one to find the other three items.

130. In the absence of a discretionary account, a customer's order to "use your judgment" would allow a registered representative to do all of the following EXCEPT:

    (A) decide when to place the order
    (B) choose the security to be traded
    (C) choose the price at which a security is sold
    (D) decide not to place the order

   (B) Without the "power of attorney" of a discretionary account, he may not decide which security to trade. He could however make all of the other decisions at the customer's request.

131. With respect to an official statement, all of the following are true EXCEPT:

    (A) an official statement must be filed with the SEC
    (B) customers must get it no later than with confirmation
    (C) it contains financial information about the issue
    (D) it is not a requirement for a new municipal issue

   (A) Since municipal securities are exempt from the Securities Act of 1933, there is no requirement that an official statement be filed with the SEC.

132. Municipal bonds are insured by which of the following?

    I. SIPC
    II. MBIAC
    III. FDIC
    IV. FGIC

    (A) I only
    (B) II and IV
    (C) I and III
    (D) I, II, III, and IV

   (B) The Financial Guarantee and Insurance Company and the Municipal Bond Investors Assurance Company are two companies that insure municipal bond investors. Two others are AMBAC Indemnity Corporation and Bond Investors Guaranty Insurance Corporation. Neither the FDIC nor the SIPC directly insures municipal bonds.

133. An investor has a $17,000 capital loss in 1990. If he has no other capital transactions except in 1991 when he has an $8,000 gain, he will be able to deduct losses until:

   (A) 1990
   (B) 1991
   (C) 1992
   (D) 1993

   (C) The investor may deduct up to $3,000 of capital loss from ordinary income and carry the remainder forward. In this case, $3,000 for 1990, $11,000 for 1991, after netting out the $8,000 gain and $3,000 for 1992, exhausts the $17,000 capital loss.

   Use this information to answer Questions 134 and 135.

   A section of the NYSE tape reads:

   ACI pr $20\frac{1}{4}$ CAI wt 20s2

134. The transaction(s) in ACI was/were:

   (A) 100 ACI sold at $20\frac{1}{4}$

   (B) 100 ACI preferred sold at $20\frac{1}{4}$

   (C) 100 ACI preferred sold at 20, then 100 sold at $20\frac{1}{4}$

   (D) 100 ACI previously sold at $20\frac{1}{4}$

   (C) The pr stands for preferred and the $20\frac{1}{4}$ signifies two trades: one at 20 and the next one at $20\frac{1}{4}$.

135. With respect to the CAI transactions, we are told:

   (A) 200 warrants sold at 20
   (B) 2,000 warrants sold at 20
   (C) there was a wait (hold) on 200 shares of CAI
   (D) there was a wait (hold) on 2,000 shares of CAI

   (B) The "20s" stands for 20 round lots of 100 warrants each for a total of 2,000 warrants.

136. $10,000 face value municipal bonds are purchased at 107.5 when there are 15 years to maturity. If they are sold in five years for 102.5, the tax consequences are:

   (A) $250 loss
   (B) $250 gain
   (C) $500 gain
   (D) $500 loss

   (A) The premium on this bond can be amortized over the life of the bond. Over five years, this would bring the price to $105, and, hence, a sale for $102.50 would represent a loss of $250.

137. The equivalent yield for an investor in the 33% bracket for a municipal bond paying $7\frac{1}{2}$% is approximately:

    (A) $7\frac{1}{2}$%
    (B) 10%
    (C) 11.10%
    (D) 11.19%

(D) The equivalent yield is found by dividing the yield by 1 − tax bracket. Here $7\frac{1}{2}$% divided by (1 − .33) = 11.19%.

138. If a callable municipal security is partially recalled, which of the following is true?

    (A) The remaining bonds become less attractive
    (B) The remaining bonds become more attractive
    (C) The yield on the remaining bonds goes up
    (D) This cannot happen. The issue must be called in its entirety

(B) After a partial recall, the remaining bonds are more attractive since the total outstanding debt is now smaller, and the likelihood of default is less.

139. One benefit of an oil and gas limited partnership is:

    (A) rental income
    (B) depletion allowance
    (C) mortgage interest deduction
    (D) perpetual income

(B) The depletion allowance refers to oil sold. The other choices are more directly applicable to real estate partnership except for choice D, which does not pertain to anything in particular.

140. All of the following should be considered in deciding the suitability of a limited partnership EXCEPT:

    (A) the customer's objectives
    (B) the size of the partnership
    (C) the customer's tax status
    (D) the program's managers

(B) The size of a partnership does not directly or materially affect the suitability of the investment.

141. All of the following are considered insiders in a corporation under the Securities Act of 1934 EXCEPT:

    (A) a clerk who has access to nonpublic information
    (B) a corporate director
    (C) a corporate officer
    (D) an owner of at least $1\frac{1}{2}$% of stock

(D) To be considered an insider, one would have to own more than 10% of the stock.

142. Which of the following would result from the Federal Reserve's causing a lowering of interest rates?

    (A) The dollar would rise in value relative to other currencies
    (B) The dollar would fall in value relative to other currencies
    (C) Business failures would increase
    (D) The stock market would fall

 (B) If the Federal Reserve caused interest rates to drop, the dollar would become less attractive as an investment vehicle for foreigners. They would sell dollars to invest in other countries.

143. An investor buys $150,000 of a direct participation program. If the program generates a $30,000 loss for her share, the tax consequences for this investor are:

    (A) no loss is allowed
    (B) a $15,000 loss
    (C) a $30,000 loss
    (D) a $150,000 loss

 (C) A passive investment cannot generate losses beyond the size of the investment. Here, the $30,000 loss is less than the total investment.

144. ACI is about to sell 2,000,000 additional shares in a public offering. The issue is in the registration process. If a positive research report comes out, an account executive can send this report to potential customers:

    (A) under no circumstances
    (B) if the preliminary prospectus is out
    (C) if the final prospectus is out
    (D) at any time, since it is not an initial public offering

 (A) While the issue is in registration, only the preliminary prospectus may be sent. The account executive could take indications of interest from customers at this time.

145. The sponsor of a direct participation program might be considered to have a conflict of interest if:

    (A) he managed adjacent property for himself
    (B) he exchanged partnership property at fair market value
    (C) he marketed partnership shares himself
    (D) he sought partnership approval to change objectives

 (A) If he managed an adjacent property, he might be in a position to take advantage of that to the detriment of the partnership. The other choices do not inherently represent a conflict of interest.

590 Series 7: STOCKBROKER EXAM

146. A letter sent to syndicate members by the manager of a successful bid on a municipal bond issue contains all of the following information EXCEPT:

    (A) the amount of good faith deposit required
    (B) the exact date of settlement and delivery of the bonds
    (C) a list of each member's participation
    (D) how the bonds will be advertised

(B) The settlement date would not be known. The bonds would trade on a when-issued basis. Such a letter is called a "release letter."

147. How many days are municipal syndicate accounts usually set up to run for?

    (A) 10 days
    (B) 20 days
    (C) 30 days
    (D) 60 days

(C) The usual syndicate is set up for 30 days.

148. The charges for services like collecting dividends and holding securities:

    (A) must be no more than $\frac{1}{2}$% of total assets
    (B) must be fair and nondiscriminatory
    (C) are governed by the 5% rule
    (D) are not limited

(B) The NASD requirement is that all customers be treated fairly and equally.

149. Who is entitled to the "takedown" in municipal bond underwriting?

    (A) A member of the syndicate
    (B) A member of the selling group
    (C) Any municipal securities dealer
    (D) Any trust department of a commercial bank

(A) The syndicate members get the takedown or discount from the offering price.

150. New issues of municipal securities are exempted from all but the:

    (A) Securities Act of 1933
    (B) Securities Exchange Act of 1934
    (C) Holding Company Act of 1935
    (D) Trust Indenture Act of 1939

(D) All debt securities require an indenture and come under the provisions of the Trust Indenture Act of 1939.

151. Under the Securities Acts Amendments of 1975, MSRB rules are enforced by the:

      I.   NYSE
     II.   SEC
    III.   Federal Reserve Board
    IV.   NASD

    (A) II, III, and IV only
    (B) II and III only
    (C) I and II only
    (D) I, II, III, and IV

(A) The NYSE has no direct enforcement responsibility for the MSRB.

152. A "cash" transaction of municipal bonds would settle on:

    (A) the same day
    (B) the next day
    (C) five business days later
    (D) on a date to be agreed to

(A) By definition. MSRB Rule 12.

153. Which of the following are exempt from *all* Federal and local income taxes?

    (A) Virgin Islands
    (B) Puerto Rico
    (C) Guam
    (D) All of the above

(D) In general, bonds of all U.S. territories are triple tax exempt.

154. The rate of return in a tombstone advertisement for a municipal serial bond is characterized as a(n):

    (A) after tax yield
    (B) effective yield
    (C) nominal yield
    (D) yield to maturity

(D) Serial bonds are generally advertised on a yield to maturity basis. Term bonds are advertised on a dollar price basis.

155. The *most* significant factor in evaluating the safety of a sewer revenue bond is:

    (A) population
    (B) number of users of the sewers
    (C) property taxes
    (D) debt service coverage

(D) The most relevant factor would be the debt service coverage rather than the number of users since the latter does not specify anything about the rates that users pay.

156. An investor owns 4 ACI Jan 50 calls. If ACI distributes a 25% stock dividend, the investor would now hold:

    (A)   4 calls of 100 shares
    (B)   5 calls of 100 shares
    (C)   4 calls of 125 shares
    (D)   5 calls of 125 shares

  (C) The number of shares in each option would be adjusted as would the exercise price. In this case, the exercise price would be 400 shares × $50/500 shares = $40.

157. An investor buys a Jun DM (deutsche mark) 68 call at $\frac{1}{2}$. The size of the contract is 62,500 DM. His premium would total:

    (A) $312.50
    (B) $625.00
    (C) $3,125.00
    (D) $6,250.00

  (A) The premium would be 0.5 cents for each of 62,500 marks. This total is $312.50.

158. Which of the following is exempt from compliance with Regulation T?

    (A)   A broker or dealer who does not handle margin accounts
    (B)   A broker or dealer who handles business only in fully registered securities
    (C)   A broker or dealer who transacts less than 10% of his business through the medium of a member of a national securities exchange
    (D)   None of the above

  (D) Since Regulation T covers both cash and margin accounts, all of these come under it.

159. All of the following taxes are recognized as flat rate taxes EXCEPT:

    (A)   a gift tax
    (B)   an excise tax
    (C)   a gasoline tax
    (D)   a general tax

  (A) Since the gift tax does not apply to the first $10,000 in any one year, it is not a flat tax.

160. Under Regulation T of the Federal Reserve, which of the following may grant extensions of time for payment in a client's account?

    (A)   The NASD
    (B)   The New York Stock Exchange
    (C)   The Midwest Stock Exchange
    (D)   Any of the above

(D) All of them are empowered to grant extensions under appropriate circumstances.

161. If T-note options are backed by $100,000 of face value securities, the purchase of four T-note options at 16 would require a premium of:

(A) $640
(B) $2,000
(C) $2,560
(D) $4,000

(B) The existence of the backing is irrelevant since the investor is purchasing the options. The premium would be $\frac{16}{32}$ or $500 for each of the four options.

162. If an account is "frozen" a customer:

(A) may sell but not buy securities
(B) must have the necessary cash or securities in the account before the order can be executed
(C) may not trade securities under any circumstances
(D) must deposit sufficient cash for any transaction by the settlement date

(B) An account that is "frozen" can only transact on the basis of payment or delivery in advance.

Use the following income statement to answer Questions 163–165.

ACI INCOME STATEMENT

Net Sales	$10,000,000
Cost of Goods, Selling & Administrative Expenses	$7,000,000
Operating Income	$3,000,000
Interest Expense	$1,000,000
Income Before Taxes	$2,000,000
Income Taxes	$700,000
Income After Taxes	$1,300,000
Dividend Payout $1 (500,000 shares)	$500,000
Retained Earnings	$800,000

163. ACI earnings per share were:

(A) $1.00
(B) $1.60
(C) $2.60
(D) $4.00

(C) With 500,000 shares outstanding and after tax income of $1,300,000, EPS is $1,300,000 ÷ 500,000 = $2.60.

164. The interest coverage (times interest earned) is:

    (A) 0.25
    (B) 0.80
    (C) 2.00
    (D) 3.00

(D) Interest is paid from income before taxes. In this case $3,000,000 income ÷ $1,000,000 interest yields coverage of 3.

165. ACI's dividend payout ratio is:

    (A) 19.2%
    (B) 20%
    (C) 38.5%
    (D) 62.5%

(C) The dividend payout ratio is $1 ÷ $2.60 = 38.5%

166. A "buy-in" of a customer occurs if he has failed to deliver securities:

    (A) 10 days after settlement date
    (B) 15 days after settlement date
    (C) 20 days after settlement date
    (D) 30 days after settlement date

(A) Ten days' grace is all that is allowed before the securities are bought back.

167. Pledging customer securities as security for debit balances is called:

    (A) subordination
    (B) hypothecation
    (C) rehypothecation
    (D) intermediation

(C) By definition. Hypothecation is the pledging of his securities by the customer to the firm.

168. An investor seeking predictable tax-sheltered cash flow should probably choose:

    (A) cattle feeding programs
    (B) oil exploration programs
    (C) real estate triple net lease-back programs
    (D) undeveloped land programs

(C) Since the leasing arrangement provides a schedule of rent payments, the cash flow is most predictable.

169. The United States balance of payments deficit goes down if:

(A) foreign investment in United States companies increases
(B) foreign investment in United States companies decreases
(C) interest rates paid on domestic savings accounts decrease
(D) yields on foreign deposits in the United States decrease

(A) Foreign investment represents the purchase of U.S. goods even if they are capital goods. This decreases the balance of payments deficit.

170. A tax shelter specifically designed for self-employed individuals is called a(n):

(A) Individual Retirement Account
(B) Keogh plan
(C) variable annuity
(D) limited partnership

(B) Keogh plans are specifically designed for self-employed individuals. All of the other choices apply to a more general population.

171. To maintain a fair and orderly market and to act as a broker's broker are the two functions of the:

(A) two-dollar broker
(B) specialist
(C) odd-lot broker
(D) floor trader

(B) These are part of the specialist's responsibility.

172. A concession of one point on the sale of a new issue of municipals is equal to:

(A) $.10
(B) $1
(C) $10
(D) $100

(C) Since each point is 1% of par, one point of a $1,000 bond is $10.

173. In a trade of municipal bonds, the confirmation would include all of the following EXCEPT the:

(A) bond rating
(B) trade date
(C) total dollar amount of the trade
(D) description of the bond

(A) While some firms do include the bond rating, MSRB rules do not require it. They do require a complete description of the bonds and the transaction including: coupon, call features, principal amount, accrued interest, and whether the firm acted as broker or agent.

174. The registered representative should maintain all of the following customer records EXCEPT a record of:

    (A) each customer's current holdings
    (B) all of his customer's securities in a cross-indexed file
    (C) his customer's capital gains and losses for the past three years
    (D) all of his customer's purchases and sales for the past three years

(C) Recording his gains and losses is not required, nor are records of dividend payments required.

175. Under the UGMA, all of the following are true EXCEPT:

    (A) minors cannot make gifts to other minors
    (B) the maximum value of a gift to a minor is $10,000
    (C) gifts given to minors cannot be reclaimed
    (D) only one custodian for one minor at any one time

(B) There is no maximum; however, gifts of more than $10,000 per person per annum are subject to gift taxes.

176. In a limited partnership, the subscription agreement contains all of the following EXCEPT:

    (A) the identity of the signatories
    (B) the recipient of the funds
    (C) suitability standards
    (D) the order of priority of payouts on liquidation

(D) The order of priority of payouts would be in the partnership agreement.

177. Which of the following NYSE orders are automatically reduced in value when the underlying stock begins trading ex-dividend?

    I. Buy stop
    II. Buy limit
    III. Sell stop
    IV. Sell limit

    (A) I and III
    (B) I and IV
    (C) II and III
    (D) II and IV

(C) The acronym OBLOSS (Open Buy Limit, Open Sell Stop) describes orders that are automatically reduced.

178. An entry in a customer account that said "opening sale" would refer to:

    (A) purchase of an option
    (B) purchase of common stock
    (C) sale of common stock
    (D) sale of an option

(D) The designation is used for the writer (or seller) of an option.

179. The bond counsel takes responsibility for all of the following EXCEPT judging:

    (A) the validity of an issue
    (B) its eligibility for federal tax exemption
    (C) the syndicate
    (D) the issuance procedures

(C) The bond counsel is responsible for the issue and not for the underwriters.

180. A customer owns 100,000 shares of restricted stock. If there are 2,000,000 shares outstanding, what is the least number of shares he can be sure of selling under Rule 144?

    (A) 1,000 shares
    (B) 2,000 shares
    (C) 20,000 shares
    (D) There is no minimum.

(C) Rule 144 allows the greater of 1% of shares outstanding and the average number of shares traded over the previous four weeks. Thus, he could sell at least 1% of the 2,000,000 shares or 20,000 shares.

181. The Balance Sheet Equation is:

    (A) Assets – Liabilities = Shareholders' Equity
    (B) Assets – Liabilities = Working Capital
    (C) Assets + Shareholders' Equity = Liabilities
    (D) Working Capital + Assets = Liabilities

(A) The Balance Sheet has Assets on one side balanced by Liabilities and Stockholders' Equity on the other Therefore, Assets – Liabilities = Stockholders' Equity.

182. Exchange-listed securities traded in the over-the-counter market are traded in the:

    (A) primary market
    (B) second market
    (C) third market
    (D) fourth market

(C) The primary market is the new issue market, the second is the over-the-counter, and the fourth is the one between institutional traders.

183. All of the following can be used as collateral in a margin account EXCEPT:

    (A) FNMA stock
    (B) FNMA bonds
    (C) option contracts
    (D) T-notes

(C) There is no loan value on an option contract so such contracts cannot be used as collateral.

184. The flow-through principle applies to all of the following EXCEPT:

    (A) corporate earnings
    (B) mutual funds
    (C) REITs
    (D) limited partnerships

   (A) Corporate earnings do not flow through to investors; they are taxed at the corporate level first.

185. Which of the following represents ownership of a foreign company?

    (A) Banker's acceptances
    (B) ADRs
    (C) Japanese yen options
    (D) Eurobonds

   (B) American Depository Receipts are negotiable receipts for specified numbers of shares of stock in foreign corporations.

186. Which of the following best describes the tax consequences of a 5% stock dividend from a U.S. corporation?

    (A) Dividend income in the year of the declaration
    (B) A capital gain in the year of the declaration
    (C) A 5% increase in the cost basis
    (D) A 5% decrease in the cost basis

   (D) The stock dividend is treated as if the original purchase price was for all of the shares including those of the dividend. This effectively reduces the purchase price by 5%.

187. An investor who is bullish on the stock market over the next two or three years is most likely to buy:

    (A) LEAPS
    (B) CMOs
    (C) TGRS
    (D) LYONS

   (A) LEAPS, Long-term Equity Appreciation Securities, are options with maturity of up to two years. CMOs are Collateralized Mortgage Obligations and LYONS and TGRS are treasury backed securities.

188. If one brother gives an order to sell some securities from a joint account that he holds with his brother and asks that he be sent a check for the proceeds, the account executive:

    (A) cannot accept the order unless it is confirmed by the other brother
    (B) should comply with the request
    (C) should send the check made out to both brothers
    (D) should sell the securities but not send the check

   (C) In a joint account, either owner can execute trades, but disbursements must be made out to both owners.

189. All of the short positions described below are acceptable EXCEPT:

    (A) borrowing stock from another broker to go short
    (B) shorting stock while long the shares
    (C) borrowing stock to take advantage of a tender offer
    (D) shorting stock while owning bonds convertible to that stock

  (C) According to SEC rules, a customer may not sell short into a tender offer. A tender offer is made to take over a company and is usually at a higher price than the current market price.

190. Investment companies must issue financial statements:

    (A) monthly
    (B) quarterly
    (C) semiannually
    (D) after each audit

  (C) Some issue them more regularly.

191. The Securities Exchange Act of 1934 allows the SEC to regulate:

    (A) short selling
    (B) proxy solicitations
    (C) margin activities
    (D) all of the above

  (D) In general, the act regulates trading on the exchanges.

192. To qualify for listing on the NASDAQ system, a security must satisfy which of the following?

    I. At least two market makers
    II. Assets of at least $2,000,000
    III. 100,000 shares publicly held
    IV. Must be owned by at least 300 investors

    (A) I and II
    (B) II and IV
    (C) I, II, and IV
    (D) I, II, III, and IV

  (D) In addition, the stock must have a minimum bid price of $5.

193. Upon the formation of a municipal security syndicate account, the syndicate letter would indicate all of the following EXCEPT the:

    (A) proposed members' participation
    (B) type of issue
    (C) duration of the syndicate
    (D) yield to the public

  (D) The yield to the public would not be known until after a bid had been entered.

194. ACI has 1 million shares outstanding and makes a rights offering of 200,000 shares. If the price of ACI cum rights is $52 and the subscription price is $50, then the theoretical value of a right is:

    (A) $.40
    (B) $.50
    (C) $1.00
    (D) $2.00

(B) Each share gets one right so that five rights are necessary to acquire one new share. The theoretical value is computed as the difference between a share "cum" rights and a share "ex" rights divided by the number of rights minus one. Here, we have ($52 − $50) ÷ (5 − 1) = $.50.

195. On Monday morning, an investor bought 400 shares of ACI at $30 per share on margin. By the close on Monday, shares of ACI were selling for $35. How much would have to be deposited to meet a 50% Reg T requirement?

    (A) $6,000
    (B) $7,000
    (C) It depends on the close at the end of five business days.
    (D) The average of $6,000 and $7,000

(A) The margin requirement would be 50% of the $12,000 purchase price or $6,000.

196. Property has a market valuation of $25,000,000 and is assessed uniformly at 50%. If the tax rate is 10 mills, the amount to be collected is:

    (A) $12,500
    (B) $25,000
    (C) $125,000
    (D) $250,000

(C) A tax rate of 1 mill represents $1 per $1,000 of assessed value. In this case, we have an assessed value of $12,500,000 and a rate of 10 mills or 10 × 12,500.

197. An investor in a real estate direct participation program is least likely to benefit from:

    (A) depreciation
    (B) depletion
    (C) appreciation
    (D) rental income

(B) Depletion is generally available from oil and gas programs.

198. When a new issue of stock is sold to a limited number of investors without any registration statement having been filed, this is called a:

    (A) secondary distribution
    (B) private placement
    (C) Rule 144 distribution
    (D) Regulation A offering

(B) By definition.

199. The NASD 5% markup policy could apply to which of the following?

    (A) Sale of open-end mutual fund shares
    (B) Sale of shares in a secondary distribution
    (C) Sale of over-the-counter securities
    (D) Sale of a new issue of nonexempt securities

(C) All of the others are sold through a prospectus, and the rule does not apply.

200. All of the following are risks of participation in a limited partnership EXCEPT:

    (A) illiquidity of the investment
    (B) an unfavorable ruling on the tax status of the program
    (C) larger than anticipated losses
    (D) premature termination of the program

(C) The nature of a limited partnership is that the risk is limited usually, although not always, to the amount invested.

201. Transactions from all of the following markets appear on the consolidated tape EXCEPT those of the:

    (A) primary market
    (B) secondary market
    (C) third market
    (D) fourth market

(A) The primary market is the new issue market and does not appear on the tape.

202. All of the following are part of current assets EXCEPT:

    (A) inventory
    (B) receivables
    (C) payables
    (D) marketable securities

(C) In fact, accounts payable is part of current liabilities.

203. An investor in a real estate limited partnership that bought raw land would primarily be seeking:

    (A) current income
    (B) capital appreciation
    (C) deductions for operating expenses
    (D) intangible cost deductions

(B) None of the other choices make much sense with respect to raw land. The investor hopes that the value of the land will increase.

204. An investor buys a municipal bond "regular way" on September 16. Coupon dates for this security are June 15 and December 15. How many days of accrued interest would she have to add to the purchase price?

    (A) 88
    (B) 89
    (C) 93
    (D) 94

(D) Regular way would settle on the 19th, and accrued interest would be 16 days in June, 30 each for July and August, and 18 in September (up to but not including settlement day) for a total of 94 days.

205. Which of the following trades appears on the tape only after the trade is completed?

    (A) Special offer
    (B) Exchange distribution
    (C) Specialist block purchase
    (D) Secondary distribution

(B) A special offer and a secondary distribution both appear beforehand, and the specialist block purchase does not appear at all. Only the exchange distribution is announced after the fact.

206. An investor has no additional incentive to convert a bond in any of the following situations EXCEPT:

    (A) when the bond is at par and the stock is above parity
    (B) when the bond is at par and the stock is below parity
    (C) when the bond and stock are both at par
    (D) when the bond is callable

(A) If the stock is at parity, the number of shares one would receive on converting the bond times the stock price is equal to the price of the bond. Since these shares are above parity, an investor could convert to shares and sell the shares for more than the cost of the bond. The bond's being at par is irrelevant.

207. If a $10,000,000 junk bond issue has $4,000,000 redeemed early, the effect on the rest of the issue is:

   (A) to raise its quality
   (B) to lower its quality
   (C) to bring it to investment grade
   (D) to pay the total interest to the remaining bonds

 (A) With less debt outstanding, it should be easier to make interest payments. This makes the remaining bonds more secure or of higher quality.

208. A firm offer for "one hour and five minute recall" is followed 30 minutes later with "fill or kill." The offeree has:

   (A) 30 minutes to take all of the bonds
   (B) his offer automatically filled if he does not respond in five minutes
   (C) five minutes to take the offer
   (D) to take the bonds immediately or lose the offer

 (C) The expression means the offer is firm for one hour and that if another buyer appears during that time, the original prospective buyer has five minutes to complete the trade. Hence, the "fill or kill."

209. A bond that is purchased at a discount and is used for the payment of estate taxes is called a(n):

   (A) estate bond
   (B) deep-discount bond
   (C) tax-free bond
   (D) flower bond

 (D) By definition.

210. A municipal bond with an 8% coupon which matures in 2010 to yield 8.5% is called at par in 1999. The yield to call is:

   (A) 8%
   (B) between 8% and 8.5%
   (C) 8.5%
   (D) greater than 8.5%

 (D) The bond must have been sold at a discount to yield 8.5% on an 8% coupon. If it is called earlier *at par*, then the yield would increase even more.

604 Series 7: STOCKBROKER EXAM

211. ACI has declared an $0.83 dividend. If ACI closes at $60 and opens tomorrow ex-dividend with no other changes, it will open at:

    (A) $59\frac{1}{8}$
    (B) $59\frac{1}{4}$
    (C) $60\frac{3}{4}$
    (D) $60\frac{7}{8}$

(A) With no other changes, the ex-dividend price is lower by an amount sufficient to cover the dividend. In this case, the price is lower by $\frac{7}{8}$.

212. A bond is callable at 101 plus $\frac{5}{8}$ for each full year that it is called before maturity on 6-15-01, up to a maximum of 105. If the bond had been called 8-15-94, it would have been redeemed at:

    (A) $104\frac{3}{8}$
    (B) $104\frac{3}{4}$
    (C) 105
    (D) $105\frac{3}{8}$

(B) The bond has been called six years and ten months or six full years before maturity. The price is, therefore, computed by adding $6 \times \frac{5}{8}$ and 101 to give $104\frac{3}{4}$.

213. To facilitate his efforts at explaining direct participation programs to his clients, an accountant asks to receive your offering literature automatically. Which of the following is true?

    (A) This is permitted for registered investment advisors
    (B) This is always allowed
    (C) The material must be marked "not for general public"
    (D) This is not permitted

(D) This is not permitted. In providing this information to his clients, the accountant is, effectively, soliciting from the general public.

214. The margin requirement on a short sale of 2,000 shares of stock selling at $1.75 would be:

    (A) $1,750
    (B) $2,000
    (C) $3,500
    (D) $5,000

(D) The NYSE margin requirement for short sales of stock selling for less than $5 is the larger of $2.50 and the price of the stock, which is $1.75. Hence, $2.50 × 2,000 = $5,000.

215. The legal opinion on a municipal bond does all of the following EXCEPT:

    (A) attest to its exemption from federal tax
    (B) describe the conditions of the bond
    (C) give assurance as to the payment of interest
    (D) attest to the validity of the issue

   (C) The legal opinion does not guarantee interest payments.

216. An investor's margin account is restricted by $500. If the account is credited with $1,500 of dividends, how much can the investor withdraw?

    (A) $0
    (B) $500
    (C) $1,000
    (D) $1,500

   (D) The investor can always take all cash dividends credited to the account.

217. If the yield curve flattens, we can be certain that:

    (A) short-term rates have increased
    (B) long-term rates have decreased
    (C) the spread between short and long term has narrowed
    (D) the spread between short and long term has widened

   (C) The yield curve describes the relationship between yield and maturity. To say it flattens is to say that short and long term rates come closer together. It does not say anything about whether rates are going up or down.

218. If $20,000 of 6% municipals maturing 1-15-03 had been purchased to settle on 9-15-93, the purchaser would have been owed accrued interest of:

    (A) $100
    (B) $200
    (C) $600
    (D) $1,200

   (B) If maturity occurs on 1-15-03, the bond interest payments are on January 15th and July 15th. Interest on municipals is counted in 30 day months from the last payment date up to but not including the settlement date. In this case, from 7–15 to 9–15 or exactly 2 months. The rate 6% per annum comes to 1% for two months. Therefore, 1% of $20,000 or $200 has accrued.

219. The discount on an original issue municipal that is held to maturity generates what tax consequence?

   (A) Some nontaxable interest income
   (B) An ordinary taxable income gain
   (C) A long-term capital gain
   (D) A short-term capital gain

(A) The discount on original issue municipal bonds is considered part of the (nontaxable) interest that these bonds pay.

220. A DPP in a drilling program would have large deductions in the first year from:

   (A) depletion allowance
   (B) depreciation
   (C) tangible drilling costs
   (D) intangible drilling costs

(D) All of the other costs would not be large if they existed at all in the first year.

221. An order was entered as good for two months and placed as GTC. Who is responsible for canceling the order after two months?

   (A) The broker
   (B) The customer
   (C) The member firm
   (D) The specialist

(A) This is part of the broker's responsibility.

222. An "insider" has filed a form 144 with the SEC. How long does he have to sell these securities under this notice?

   (A) 30 days
   (B) 60 days
   (C) 90 days
   (D) 180 days

(C) As detailed in the act.

223. If a municipal securities dealer acting for a client recommends a security, according to MSRB rules, he would have to notify the client in writing:

   (A) of the security's recent range of prices
   (B) of any financial interest he had in the underwriting
   (C) of the security's credit rating
   (D) none of the above

(B) In general, he would notify the client of any relationship which might represent a conflict of interest.

224. Which of the following is the lowest investment grade rating?

    (A) BBB
    (B) Ba
    (C) BB
    (D) B

  (A) Alternatively Baa.

225. The "Official Notice of Sale" would contain all of the following EXCEPT:

    (A) size of the issue
    (B) type of bond
    (C) amount of good faith deposit
    (D) bond rating

  (D) The rating would not exist yet.

226. Which of the following describes the "dated date" on a bond?

    (A) The date on which trading begins
    (B) The date on which interest begins to accrue
    (C) The settlement date
    (D) The trade date

  (B) By definition.

Questions 227–229 refer to the excerpt from the specialist's book listed below:

BUY	CAI	SELL
200 DWR	55	
100 Hutton	$\frac{1}{8}$	
300 Drexel	$\frac{1}{4}$	
	$\frac{3}{8}$	
	$\frac{1}{2}$	
	$\frac{5}{8}$	200 Drexel
		100 Schwab
	$\frac{3}{4}$	200 Merrill
	$\frac{7}{8}$	100 DWR

227. The size of the market in CAI is:

    (A) 300 by 100
    (B) 300 by 200
    (C) 300 by 300
    (D) 600 by 600

  (C) The size is the number of shares of the highest bid and the lowest offer.

228. The specialist could bid for stock for his own account at:

(A) $55\frac{1}{4}$

(B) $55\frac{3}{8}$

(C) $55\frac{1}{2}$

(D) $55\frac{5}{8}$

(B) He would have to bid more than any of the customer bids.

229. If both entries at $55\frac{5}{8}$ were sell stops, the specialist could sell from his own account at:

(A) $55\frac{3}{8}$

(B) $55\frac{1}{2}$

(C) $55\frac{5}{8}$

(D) $55\frac{3}{4}$

(B) He would have to offer at a lower price than the customer offers. The stop offers would not be triggered by his action. Recall that his bid and offer may not trigger stops.

230. Member firms must keep a written record of all speaking engagements for at least:

(A) six months
(B) one year
(C) three years
(D) five years

(C) By NYSE rules.

231. The type of variable annuity that will result in the largest monthly checks is:

(A) lump sum
(B) life annuity
(C) life annuity with rights of survivorship
(D) 10-year certain life

(B) All of the others (except the lump sum, which has no monthly payment) have some fixed minimum. This forces the monthly payment to be lower than if it were not so encumbered.

232. Selling stock under Rule 144 is regulated by the:

(A) Securities Act of 1933
(B) Securities Exchange Act of 1934
(C) Holding Company Act of 1935
(D) Maloney Act of 1938

(A) This is a regulation dealing with the registration of securities.

233. Short sales on the over-the-counter market can take place:

    (A) never
    (B) without restriction
    (C) after a plus tick only
    (D) after a plus tick or a zero plus tick

 (B) Since there is no auction, but rather a negotiated market, there is no restriction on short sales.

234. Disintermediation is not likely to occur unless:

    (A) the Fed reduces the discount rate
    (B) the Fed reduces reserve requirements
    (C) the Fed does long term reverse repos
    (D) the Fed resorts to jawboning

 (D) Also called "moral suasion." This is one way that the Fed attempts to reduce borrowing. It undertakes such an effort when rates are getting high. This is the only choice that fits the definition of disintermediation, the removal of money from banks to earn higher rates elsewhere.

235. All of the following are true of variable annuities EXCEPT:

    (A) annuity income is not taxed until payout begins
    (B) returns are based on portfolio performance
    (C) there is no minimum payout
    (D) performance is proportional to the movement of the Dow

 (D) There is no direct link to the Dow even though payout is related to portfolio performance.

236. An escrow account for pre-refunded municipals could contain:

    (A) only secured municipals
    (B) U.S. Treasury or agency securities
    (C) any revenue bond
    (D) AAA corporate bonds

 (B) These funds must be secure, and they represent advanced refunding of the original issue. Technically, the refunded bonds are no longer considered part of the municipalities' indebtedness. This process is also called defeasement.

237. When transacting a municipal bond swap, you are likely to incur a wash sale ruling if you vary only the:

    (A) rating
    (B) municipality
    (C) maturity
    (D) coupon

 (A) Different issuers is the safest way of avoiding wash sale rulings. Otherwise, the coupon and the maturity should be substantially different. The rating has the least power to avoid a wash sale ruling.

238. The portion of net revenues set aside for replacement of major equipment in a municipal revenue issue would be placed in a:

    (A) surplus fund
    (B) renewal fund
    (C) debt service fund
    (D) maintenance fund

    (B) Choice D, maintenance funds, comes from gross revenues. The other funds come from net revenues. The order of disbursement would be: debt service, renewal, and then surplus, which might be used for redemption or for expanding the facility.

239. The maximum amount that an investor could be due in a margin account without generating a margin call is:

    (A) $100
    (B) $500
    (C) $1,000
    (D) at the broker's discretion

    (B) This is a Regulation T requirement.

240. The security that gives the investor the longest time within which to purchase a stock is:

    (A) calls
    (B) puts
    (C) rights
    (D) warrants

    (D) Warrants have a long life and may even be perpetual. The calls and rights are both short lived and the Puts, of course, cannot be used to purchase stock.

241. If an investor sells short a security that she already owns, she is said to have:

    (A) sold short
    (B) sold out the position
    (C) sold "short against the box"
    (D) done a wash sale

    (C) The point is that there are now two positions, one long and one short.

242. According to MSRB rules, copies of MSRB rules must be available at which of the following locations?

    (A) Each office of the firm
    (B) The main office of the firm
    (C) Any office where no principal of the firm is stationed
    (D) Any office where there are at least two salespersons

    (A) By MSRB rules.

243. The opening of a numbered account under NYSE Rule 406:

(A) is never allowed
(B) is allowed for accounts not covered by SIPC
(C) is allowed if the investor provides a "letter of credit"
(D) requires a written voucher of responsibility

(D) Numbered accounts are allowed as long as the owner of the account has given written testimony that he is responsible for it.

244. In a cash account, under NYSE rules, which of the following would require written consent by an employer?

(A) An employee of a bank
(B) An employee of an insurance company
(C) An employee of a trust company
(D) None of the above

(D) These are cash accounts. For margin accounts, they would be required to obtain the consent of (and to have duplicate copies of statements sent to) their employers.

245. An abusive tax shelter is one:

(A) which has no legitimate profit-making purpose
(B) which allows large tax write-offs
(C) which takes advantage of investors
(D) in which the general partner has a conflict of interest

(A) The definition of an abusive tax shelter. None of the other choices defines an abusive shelter.

246. The "nine-bond" rule applies to:

(A) bonds with coupons below 9%
(B) trades of nine bonds or less
(C) trades of 90 bonds or less
(D) markets that offer no more than nine types of bonds

(B) By definition. The rule states that orders for nine bonds or less must ordinarily be brought to the floor of the exchange.

247. Under Rule 147, the minimum time before securities from intrastate offerings can be sold outside the state is:

(A) 3 months
(B) 6 months
(C) 9 months
(D) 1 year

(C) The minimum time is 9 months.

248. The maximum coverage of cash in any one account under SIPC is:

    (A) $100,000
    (B) $300,000
    (C) $500,000
    (D) unlimited

(**A**) The total coverage for any one account has a maximum of $500,000, but only $100,000 of that can be for cash in the account.

249. All of the following are true of convertible bonds EXCEPT:

    (A) they can be converted to common stock
    (B) they can be used as collateral
    (C) they can be used to hedge a short position
    (D) their coupon rate is higher than that of nonconvertible bonds

(**D**) The conversion feature is a sweetener that allows them to be offered with a lower coupon.

250. The random walk theory is related to:

    (A) the theory of variable returns
    (B) the diversifiability of risk
    (C) the efficient market hypothesis
    (D) the existence of negative betas

(**C**) The efficient market hypothesis comes in three forms: weak, semi-strong, and strong. All of them say, with differing degrees of qualification, that one cannot trade markets profitably. The theory of random walk roughly states that future price movements are random in size and direction. Hence, one should not be able to predict the future direction of the market (or of any single security, for that matter).

Practice
Examination
Three

PRACTICE EXAMINATION THREE
Answer Sheet

PART ONE

1 Ⓐ Ⓑ Ⓒ Ⓓ	37 Ⓐ Ⓑ Ⓒ Ⓓ	73 Ⓐ Ⓑ Ⓒ Ⓓ	109 Ⓐ Ⓑ Ⓒ Ⓓ
2 Ⓐ Ⓑ Ⓒ Ⓓ	38 Ⓐ Ⓑ Ⓒ Ⓓ	74 Ⓐ Ⓑ Ⓒ Ⓓ	110 Ⓐ Ⓑ Ⓒ Ⓓ
3 Ⓐ Ⓑ Ⓒ Ⓓ	39 Ⓐ Ⓑ Ⓒ Ⓓ	75 Ⓐ Ⓑ Ⓒ Ⓓ	111 Ⓐ Ⓑ Ⓒ Ⓓ
4 Ⓐ Ⓑ Ⓒ Ⓓ	40 Ⓐ Ⓑ Ⓒ Ⓓ	76 Ⓐ Ⓑ Ⓒ Ⓓ	112 Ⓐ Ⓑ Ⓒ Ⓓ
5 Ⓐ Ⓑ Ⓒ Ⓓ	41 Ⓐ Ⓑ Ⓒ Ⓓ	77 Ⓐ Ⓑ Ⓒ Ⓓ	113 Ⓐ Ⓑ Ⓒ Ⓓ
6 Ⓐ Ⓑ Ⓒ Ⓓ	42 Ⓐ Ⓑ Ⓒ Ⓓ	78 Ⓐ Ⓑ Ⓒ Ⓓ	114 Ⓐ Ⓑ Ⓒ Ⓓ
7 Ⓐ Ⓑ Ⓒ Ⓓ	43 Ⓐ Ⓑ Ⓒ Ⓓ	79 Ⓐ Ⓑ Ⓒ Ⓓ	115 Ⓐ Ⓑ Ⓒ Ⓓ
8 Ⓐ Ⓑ Ⓒ Ⓓ	44 Ⓐ Ⓑ Ⓒ Ⓓ	80 Ⓐ Ⓑ Ⓒ Ⓓ	116 Ⓐ Ⓑ Ⓒ Ⓓ
9 Ⓐ Ⓑ Ⓒ Ⓓ	45 Ⓐ Ⓑ Ⓒ Ⓓ	81 Ⓐ Ⓑ Ⓒ Ⓓ	117 Ⓐ Ⓑ Ⓒ Ⓓ
10 Ⓐ Ⓑ Ⓒ Ⓓ	46 Ⓐ Ⓑ Ⓒ Ⓓ	82 Ⓐ Ⓑ Ⓒ Ⓓ	118 Ⓐ Ⓑ Ⓒ Ⓓ
11 Ⓐ Ⓑ Ⓒ Ⓓ	47 Ⓐ Ⓑ Ⓒ Ⓓ	83 Ⓐ Ⓑ Ⓒ Ⓓ	119 Ⓐ Ⓑ Ⓒ Ⓓ
12 Ⓐ Ⓑ Ⓒ Ⓓ	48 Ⓐ Ⓑ Ⓒ Ⓓ	84 Ⓐ Ⓑ Ⓒ Ⓓ	120 Ⓐ Ⓑ Ⓒ Ⓓ
13 Ⓐ Ⓑ Ⓒ Ⓓ	49 Ⓐ Ⓑ Ⓒ Ⓓ	85 Ⓐ Ⓑ Ⓒ Ⓓ	121 Ⓐ Ⓑ Ⓒ Ⓓ
14 Ⓐ Ⓑ Ⓒ Ⓓ	50 Ⓐ Ⓑ Ⓒ Ⓓ	86 Ⓐ Ⓑ Ⓒ Ⓓ	122 Ⓐ Ⓑ Ⓒ Ⓓ
15 Ⓐ Ⓑ Ⓒ Ⓓ	51 Ⓐ Ⓑ Ⓒ Ⓓ	87 Ⓐ Ⓑ Ⓒ Ⓓ	123 Ⓐ Ⓑ Ⓒ Ⓓ
16 Ⓐ Ⓑ Ⓒ Ⓓ	52 Ⓐ Ⓑ Ⓒ Ⓓ	88 Ⓐ Ⓑ Ⓒ Ⓓ	124 Ⓐ Ⓑ Ⓒ Ⓓ
17 Ⓐ Ⓑ Ⓒ Ⓓ	53 Ⓐ Ⓑ Ⓒ Ⓓ	89 Ⓐ Ⓑ Ⓒ Ⓓ	125 Ⓐ Ⓑ Ⓒ Ⓓ
18 Ⓐ Ⓑ Ⓒ Ⓓ	54 Ⓐ Ⓑ Ⓒ Ⓓ	90 Ⓐ Ⓑ Ⓒ Ⓓ	
19 Ⓐ Ⓑ Ⓒ Ⓓ	55 Ⓐ Ⓑ Ⓒ Ⓓ	91 Ⓐ Ⓑ Ⓒ Ⓓ	
20 Ⓐ Ⓑ Ⓒ Ⓓ	56 Ⓐ Ⓑ Ⓒ Ⓓ	92 Ⓐ Ⓑ Ⓒ Ⓓ	
21 Ⓐ Ⓑ Ⓒ Ⓓ	57 Ⓐ Ⓑ Ⓒ Ⓓ	93 Ⓐ Ⓑ Ⓒ Ⓓ	
22 Ⓐ Ⓑ Ⓒ Ⓓ	58 Ⓐ Ⓑ Ⓒ Ⓓ	94 Ⓐ Ⓑ Ⓒ Ⓓ	
23 Ⓐ Ⓑ Ⓒ Ⓓ	59 Ⓐ Ⓑ Ⓒ Ⓓ	95 Ⓐ Ⓑ Ⓒ Ⓓ	
24 Ⓐ Ⓑ Ⓒ Ⓓ	60 Ⓐ Ⓑ Ⓒ Ⓓ	96 Ⓐ Ⓑ Ⓒ Ⓓ	
25 Ⓐ Ⓑ Ⓒ Ⓓ	61 Ⓐ Ⓑ Ⓒ Ⓓ	97 Ⓐ Ⓑ Ⓒ Ⓓ	
26 Ⓐ Ⓑ Ⓒ Ⓓ	62 Ⓐ Ⓑ Ⓒ Ⓓ	98 Ⓐ Ⓑ Ⓒ Ⓓ	
27 Ⓐ Ⓑ Ⓒ Ⓓ	63 Ⓐ Ⓑ Ⓒ Ⓓ	99 Ⓐ Ⓑ Ⓒ Ⓓ	
28 Ⓐ Ⓑ Ⓒ Ⓓ	64 Ⓐ Ⓑ Ⓒ Ⓓ	100 Ⓐ Ⓑ Ⓒ Ⓓ	
29 Ⓐ Ⓑ Ⓒ Ⓓ	65 Ⓐ Ⓑ Ⓒ Ⓓ	101 Ⓐ Ⓑ Ⓒ Ⓓ	
30 Ⓐ Ⓑ Ⓒ Ⓓ	66 Ⓐ Ⓑ Ⓒ Ⓓ	102 Ⓐ Ⓑ Ⓒ Ⓓ	
31 Ⓐ Ⓑ Ⓒ Ⓓ	67 Ⓐ Ⓑ Ⓒ Ⓓ	103 Ⓐ Ⓑ Ⓒ Ⓓ	
32 Ⓐ Ⓑ Ⓒ Ⓓ	68 Ⓐ Ⓑ Ⓒ Ⓓ	104 Ⓐ Ⓑ Ⓒ Ⓓ	
33 Ⓐ Ⓑ Ⓒ Ⓓ	69 Ⓐ Ⓑ Ⓒ Ⓓ	105 Ⓐ Ⓑ Ⓒ Ⓓ	
34 Ⓐ Ⓑ Ⓒ Ⓓ	70 Ⓐ Ⓑ Ⓒ Ⓓ	106 Ⓐ Ⓑ Ⓒ Ⓓ	
35 Ⓐ Ⓑ Ⓒ Ⓓ	71 Ⓐ Ⓑ Ⓒ Ⓓ	107 Ⓐ Ⓑ Ⓒ Ⓓ	
36 Ⓐ Ⓑ Ⓒ Ⓓ	72 Ⓐ Ⓑ Ⓒ Ⓓ	108 Ⓐ Ⓑ Ⓒ Ⓓ	

PRACTICE EXAMINATION THREE
Answer Sheet

PART TWO

126 Ⓐ Ⓑ Ⓒ Ⓓ	162 Ⓐ Ⓑ Ⓒ Ⓓ	198 Ⓐ Ⓑ Ⓒ Ⓓ	234 Ⓐ Ⓑ Ⓒ Ⓓ
127 Ⓐ Ⓑ Ⓒ Ⓓ	163 Ⓐ Ⓑ Ⓒ Ⓓ	199 Ⓐ Ⓑ Ⓒ Ⓓ	235 Ⓐ Ⓑ Ⓒ Ⓓ
128 Ⓐ Ⓑ Ⓒ Ⓓ	164 Ⓐ Ⓑ Ⓒ Ⓓ	200 Ⓐ Ⓑ Ⓒ Ⓓ	236 Ⓐ Ⓑ Ⓒ Ⓓ
129 Ⓐ Ⓑ Ⓒ Ⓓ	165 Ⓐ Ⓑ Ⓒ Ⓓ	201 Ⓐ Ⓑ Ⓒ Ⓓ	237 Ⓐ Ⓑ Ⓒ Ⓓ
130 Ⓐ Ⓑ Ⓒ Ⓓ	166 Ⓐ Ⓑ Ⓒ Ⓓ	202 Ⓐ Ⓑ Ⓒ Ⓓ	238 Ⓐ Ⓑ Ⓒ Ⓓ
131 Ⓐ Ⓑ Ⓒ Ⓓ	167 Ⓐ Ⓑ Ⓒ Ⓓ	203 Ⓐ Ⓑ Ⓒ Ⓓ	239 Ⓐ Ⓑ Ⓒ Ⓓ
132 Ⓐ Ⓑ Ⓒ Ⓓ	168 Ⓐ Ⓑ Ⓒ Ⓓ	204 Ⓐ Ⓑ Ⓒ Ⓓ	240 Ⓐ Ⓑ Ⓒ Ⓓ
133 Ⓐ Ⓑ Ⓒ Ⓓ	169 Ⓐ Ⓑ Ⓒ Ⓓ	205 Ⓐ Ⓑ Ⓒ Ⓓ	241 Ⓐ Ⓑ Ⓒ Ⓓ
134 Ⓐ Ⓑ Ⓒ Ⓓ	170 Ⓐ Ⓑ Ⓒ Ⓓ	206 Ⓐ Ⓑ Ⓒ Ⓓ	242 Ⓐ Ⓑ Ⓒ Ⓓ
135 Ⓐ Ⓑ Ⓒ Ⓓ	171 Ⓐ Ⓑ Ⓒ Ⓓ	207 Ⓐ Ⓑ Ⓒ Ⓓ	243 Ⓐ Ⓑ Ⓒ Ⓓ
136 Ⓐ Ⓑ Ⓒ Ⓓ	172 Ⓐ Ⓑ Ⓒ Ⓓ	208 Ⓐ Ⓑ Ⓒ Ⓓ	244 Ⓐ Ⓑ Ⓒ Ⓓ
137 Ⓐ Ⓑ Ⓒ Ⓓ	173 Ⓐ Ⓑ Ⓒ Ⓓ	209 Ⓐ Ⓑ Ⓒ Ⓓ	245 Ⓐ Ⓑ Ⓒ Ⓓ
138 Ⓐ Ⓑ Ⓒ Ⓓ	174 Ⓐ Ⓑ Ⓒ Ⓓ	210 Ⓐ Ⓑ Ⓒ Ⓓ	246 Ⓐ Ⓑ Ⓒ Ⓓ
139 Ⓐ Ⓑ Ⓒ Ⓓ	175 Ⓐ Ⓑ Ⓒ Ⓓ	211 Ⓐ Ⓑ Ⓒ Ⓓ	247 Ⓐ Ⓑ Ⓒ Ⓓ
140 Ⓐ Ⓑ Ⓒ Ⓓ	176 Ⓐ Ⓑ Ⓒ Ⓓ	212 Ⓐ Ⓑ Ⓒ Ⓓ	248 Ⓐ Ⓑ Ⓒ Ⓓ
141 Ⓐ Ⓑ Ⓒ Ⓓ	177 Ⓐ Ⓑ Ⓒ Ⓓ	213 Ⓐ Ⓑ Ⓒ Ⓓ	249 Ⓐ Ⓑ Ⓒ Ⓓ
142 Ⓐ Ⓑ Ⓒ Ⓓ	178 Ⓐ Ⓑ Ⓒ Ⓓ	214 Ⓐ Ⓑ Ⓒ Ⓓ	250 Ⓐ Ⓑ Ⓒ Ⓓ
143 Ⓐ Ⓑ Ⓒ Ⓓ	179 Ⓐ Ⓑ Ⓒ Ⓓ	215 Ⓐ Ⓑ Ⓒ Ⓓ	
144 Ⓐ Ⓑ Ⓒ Ⓓ	180 Ⓐ Ⓑ Ⓒ Ⓓ	216 Ⓐ Ⓑ Ⓒ Ⓓ	
145 Ⓐ Ⓑ Ⓒ Ⓓ	181 Ⓐ Ⓑ Ⓒ Ⓓ	217 Ⓐ Ⓑ Ⓒ Ⓓ	
146 Ⓐ Ⓑ Ⓒ Ⓓ	182 Ⓐ Ⓑ Ⓒ Ⓓ	218 Ⓐ Ⓑ Ⓒ Ⓓ	
147 Ⓐ Ⓑ Ⓒ Ⓓ	183 Ⓐ Ⓑ Ⓒ Ⓓ	219 Ⓐ Ⓑ Ⓒ Ⓓ	
148 Ⓐ Ⓑ Ⓒ Ⓓ	184 Ⓐ Ⓑ Ⓒ Ⓓ	220 Ⓐ Ⓑ Ⓒ Ⓓ	
149 Ⓐ Ⓑ Ⓒ Ⓓ	185 Ⓐ Ⓑ Ⓒ Ⓓ	221 Ⓐ Ⓑ Ⓒ Ⓓ	
150 Ⓐ Ⓑ Ⓒ Ⓓ	186 Ⓐ Ⓑ Ⓒ Ⓓ	222 Ⓐ Ⓑ Ⓒ Ⓓ	
151 Ⓐ Ⓑ Ⓒ Ⓓ	187 Ⓐ Ⓑ Ⓒ Ⓓ	223 Ⓐ Ⓑ Ⓒ Ⓓ	
152 Ⓐ Ⓑ Ⓒ Ⓓ	188 Ⓐ Ⓑ Ⓒ Ⓓ	224 Ⓐ Ⓑ Ⓒ Ⓓ	
153 Ⓐ Ⓑ Ⓒ Ⓓ	189 Ⓐ Ⓑ Ⓒ Ⓓ	225 Ⓐ Ⓑ Ⓒ Ⓓ	
154 Ⓐ Ⓑ Ⓒ Ⓓ	190 Ⓐ Ⓑ Ⓒ Ⓓ	226 Ⓐ Ⓑ Ⓒ Ⓓ	
155 Ⓐ Ⓑ Ⓒ Ⓓ	191 Ⓐ Ⓑ Ⓒ Ⓓ	227 Ⓐ Ⓑ Ⓒ Ⓓ	
156 Ⓐ Ⓑ Ⓒ Ⓓ	192 Ⓐ Ⓑ Ⓒ Ⓓ	228 Ⓐ Ⓑ Ⓒ Ⓓ	
157 Ⓐ Ⓑ Ⓒ Ⓓ	193 Ⓐ Ⓑ Ⓒ Ⓓ	229 Ⓐ Ⓑ Ⓒ Ⓓ	
158 Ⓐ Ⓑ Ⓒ Ⓓ	194 Ⓐ Ⓑ Ⓒ Ⓓ	230 Ⓐ Ⓑ Ⓒ Ⓓ	
159 Ⓐ Ⓑ Ⓒ Ⓓ	195 Ⓐ Ⓑ Ⓒ Ⓓ	231 Ⓐ Ⓑ Ⓒ Ⓓ	
160 Ⓐ Ⓑ Ⓒ Ⓓ	196 Ⓐ Ⓑ Ⓒ Ⓓ	232 Ⓐ Ⓑ Ⓒ Ⓓ	
161 Ⓐ Ⓑ Ⓒ Ⓓ	197 Ⓐ Ⓑ Ⓒ Ⓓ	233 Ⓐ Ⓑ Ⓒ Ⓓ	

PART ONE

Time   3 Hours

Questions   1–125

DIRECTIONS

Each of the questions or incomplete statements below is followed by four suggested answer options. Choose the best answer and then blacken the corresponding space on the answer sheet.

1. During the cooling off period, every one of the following occurs EXCEPT:

   (A) stabilizing the issue
   (B) blue-skying the issue
   (C) the due diligence meeting
   (D) the issuance of a red herring

2. An options investor wishes to enter into a spread position. This would be done:

   (A) in the margin account
   (B) in the cash account
   (C) in two separate transactions: the long in the margin account, the short in the cash account
   (D) in two separate transactions, the long in the cash account, the short in the margin account

3. The agreement on a new municipal issue between the issuer and the trustee is written by whom?

   (A) Bond attorney
   (B) Trustee
   (C) Underwriter's attorney
   (D) Syndicate manager

4. By its charter, LoTec Co., may issue 5 million shares. Three million shares have been issued, of which 1 million are treasury stock. LoTec Co., now has how many shares outstanding?

   (A) 1 million
   (B) 2 million
   (C) 3 million
   (D) 5 million

Questions 5–7 refer to the following settlement date requirements.

   (A) Same business day
   (B) Next business day
   (C) Three business days
   (D) Five business days

Which choice applies in the following questions? (Remember that a choice might be used more than once.)

5. Regular-way settlement for a municipal securities transaction.

6. Regular-way settlement for an option transaction.

7. Payment date for a stock transaction.

8. Approval of an over-the-counter stock for purchase on margin is done by the:

   (A) Federal Reserve Board
   (B) state securities commission
   (C) Securities Exchange Commission
   (D) New York Stock Exchange or the NASD

9. If under statutory voting six directors are to be elected, a stockholder with 50 shares of stock could cast:

   I. 50 votes for each director
   II. 300 votes to one director
   III. 300 votes freely distributed among the six

   (A) I only
   (B) II only
   (C) I or II only
   (D) I, II, or III

10. Which of the following yields to maturity would the investor expect to get if he purchases a 4.5% bond at a discount and holds it to maturity?

    (A) 5%
    (B) 4.5%
    (C) 4%
    (D) 3.5%

11. If an investor is in the 28% tax bracket, which of the following would offer the best after-tax yield?

    (A) A $6\frac{3}{4}$% convertible bond
    (B) A $6\frac{1}{2}$% preferred stock
    (C) A $5\frac{3}{4}$% corporate bond
    (D) A 5% municipal bond

12. Convertible debentures of BOOP are convertible into 20 shares of BOOP Corp. common stock. If the bonds were selling in the market at $980, what would the common stock price have to be in order to be at parity?

    (A) $50
    (B) $49
    (C) $45
    (D) $20

13. A "covered writer" is someone who has:

    (A) sold a call option but does not own the underlying stock
    (B) sold a call option and owns the underlying stock
    (C) purchased a call option but does not own the underlying stock
    (D) purchased a call option and owns the underlying stock

14. Which is true of a progressive tax?

    I. The rates are higher for those with low incomes.
    II. It has a flat rate.
    III. It has graduated rates.
    IV. The rates are higher for those with large incomes.

    (A) II and IV
    (B) I and II
    (C) III and IV
    (D) I and III

15. All of the following financial information can be found in a corporation's balance sheet EXCEPT:

    (A) expense ratios of the corporation
    (B) book value of the corporation
    (C) assets of the corporation
    (D) long-term funds received from all sources

16. In the analysis of a company's stock, a technical analyst would be LEAST worried about:

    (A) debt-to-equity ratio
    (B) chart pattern
    (C) short interest
    (D) trading volume

17. The Federal Reserve Board could stimulate a slow economy by:

    I. lowering reserve requirements
    II. reducing margin requirements
    III. buying U.S. government securities in the open market

    (A) II and III only
    (B) I and II only
    (C) I and III only
    (D) I, II, and III

18. What do you call a security that depends completely on current earnings for payment of interest?

    (A) A warranted bond
    (B) An income bond
    (C) A convertible bond
    (D) A noncumulative preferred stock

19. In the context of limited partnerships, what does "flow-through" mean?

    (A) Title to the properties purchased by the business flows through to the limited partners.
    (B) Business profits are passed along to the limited partners untaxed.
    (C) Both business profits and losses are passed through to limited partners in proportion to their individual ownership.
    (D) The general business debts flow through to the limited partners.

20. When a municipal bond is to be issued, who hires the attorney responsible for the legal opinion?

    (A) The syndicate manager
    (B) The underwriter
    (C) The municipality
    (D) The corporation

21. A conversion privilege is offered by some open-end investment firms permitting:

    (A) the owner of the shares to convert his bonds or preferred stock to common stock of the fund at a predesignated ratio
    (B) conversion of securities to cash at the option of the shareholder
    (C) conversion from the shares of one fund or class of fund to the shares of another fund under the same sponsorship at a nominal cost or at a reduced sales charge
    (D) liquidation of shareholdings with an option to buy the shares back at the current market price

22. All of the following are leading economic indicators EXCEPT:

    (A) prime rate
    (B) stock prices
    (C) building permits
    (D) money supply

23. Regarding "dollar bonds," none of the following statements is generally true EXCEPT:

    (A) they are revenue bonds
    (B) they are quoted as a percentage of par
    (C) they are term bonds
    (D) they are serial bonds

24. A registered representative wants shares of a hot issue his firm is underwriting. By the NASD Rules of Fair Practice, the rep may:

    I. NOT do so for his own account, but may purchase shares for members of his immediate family

II. do so if his allotment is modest, is not disproportionate to public orders, and is within his investment practice

III. NOT do so under any circumstances

IV. do so if he has a history of buying hot issues

(A) III only
(B) I only
(C) II only
(D) II and IV only

25. Interest income from which of the following investments is free from state income tax in ALL states?

  I. General obligation bonds of the State of Wyoming.
  II. U.S. Treasury Bills
  III. U.S. Series EE savings bonds
  IV. Bonds issued by the Commonwealth of Puerto Rico

(A) I only
(B) I and IV only
(C) II and III only
(D) II, III, and IV only

26. You get an open order to buy 50 XRX at 110 Stop. The following are all true EXCEPT:

(A) this order is good, but only if it can be executed at 110
(B) this order becomes a market order if XRX sells at 110
(C) the order is good until canceled
(D) the order may be left with the specialist in XRX.

27. At age 50, the client comes into a sum and deposits it in a single payment deferred annuity. At age 65, he chooses a straight life settlement option and, unfortunately, dies six months later.

(A) Payments cease upon his death; no further money is received.
(B) His estate will get back the value of his account.
(C) His estate will receive a lump sum equal to his original investment less the amount already withdrawn.
(D) His beneficiary may select a settlement option to be used with the remaining balance in his account.

28. If the underlying common stock sells ex-dividend, a GTC buy-limit order will:

(A) be reduced
(B) be increased
(C) change at the discretion of the specialist
(D) remain unchanged

29. For the sale of restricted securities under SEC Rule 144, which of the following are true?

  I. The sale can be made on an agency or principal basis.
  II. A form 144 notice of sale must be filed with the SEC not later than 30 days after the sale.
  III. The securities must be owned for two years.
  IV. The securities must be fully paid.

(A) IV only
(B) I and IV only
(C) I, II, and IV only
(D) I, III, and IV only

Questions 30–32 refer to the following types of offerings:

(A) A contingency offering
(B) A firm commitment
(C) A best efforts
(D) An all or none

Which type of offering is best described in the following questions? (Remember that a choice might be used more than once.)

30. A type of offering in which whatever is not sold is returned to the issuing corporation.

31. A type of offering in which the issuing corporation is assured of receiving the whole amount of the offering, and whatever is not sold is retained by the underwriter.

32. A type of offering which is canceled if the entire lot is not sold.

33. The legal opinion regarding a new municipal issue:

    (A) attests to the validity of the issue
    (B) is approved by the MSRB
    (C) attests to the issuer's ability to meet debt service
    (D) ensures the legality of the syndicate

34. Mr. Hashimoto's wife calls to purchase 150 shares of ZIP Corp. in her husband's personal account. The account executive for the account knows that a favorable earnings report is about to be issued. She:

    (A) cannot enter the order because the earnings report has not been released
    (B) cannot accept the order because Mrs. Hashimoto does not have trading authorization to enter orders for Mr. Hashimoto's personal account
    (C) can enter the order because Mr. Hashimoto had previously mentioned he would like to establish a position in ZIP Corp.

    (D) can enter the order because Mrs. Hashimoto has a joint account with Mr. Hashimoto

35. ABC closes at $37 and the following day sells ex-dividend at $0.68 per share. At what price should the stock open the next day if it opens at the same level at which it closed the day before?

    (A) 37
    (B) $36\frac{1}{2}$
    (C) $36\frac{3}{8}$
    (D) $36\frac{1}{4}$

36. The customer buys a stock in a margin account not listed with the Federal Reserve Board's marginable securities. He purchases 100 shares over the counter at $50 each. The FRB's initial margin requirement is 50%. He would get a margin call for:

    (A) $7,500
    (B) $5,000
    (C) $2,500
    (D) $1,250

37. Should a broker/dealer go bankrupt, the Securities Investors Protection Corp., requires the appointment of a trustee who would be responsible for:

    I. making sure the distribution of cash and securities is administered properly
    II. informing the firm's customers that the firm is being liquidated
    III. distributing the customers' securities that the firm holds

    (A) II and III
    (B) I and II
    (C) I and III
    (D) I, II, and III

38. When he evaluates the common stock of a corporation, a fundamental analyst must examine all that follows EXCEPT:

    (A) current amount of earnings paid out as dividends to shareholders
    (B) current amount of short-interest positions for the stock
    (C) the corporation's sales
    (D) the corporation's management

39. A war veteran, age 55, has some money problems and wants to make a withdrawal from his IRA. This would:

    (A) not be permitted
    (B) involve a 10% penalty and would be taxable income
    (C) would be taxable, but without penalty
    (D) result in a 50% penalty

40. With respect to bearer bonds, which would not be rejected?

    (A) A certificate without a seal
    (B) A mutilated coupon
    (C) The absence of a legal opinion
    (D) Lack of the owner's endorsement

41. Mr. Ross purchased 500 shares of ARIA at $12 on February 3 and presented them to his nephew for a birthday present on July 8. If on July 8 the market price of ARIA was up to $17, the nephew's cost basis would be:

    (A) $7
    (B) $8
    (C) $12
    (D) $17

42. Foreign currency transactions in the Interbank Market:

    (A) occur on exchanges throughout the world
    (B) are regulated by the SEC
    (C) are reported on the NASDAQ system
    (D) may settle on a spot or forward basis

43. The Securities Exchange Act of 1934 on rules of manipulation refers to transactions involving:

    I. municipal bonds.
    II. U.S. Government bonds.
    III. common stock.
    IV. corporate bonds.

    (A) III and IV
    (B) I and II
    (C) I, III, and IV
    (D) all the above

44. The following appears on the NYSE ticker tape:

    YYY.SLD 103 $\frac{1}{2}$

    This means:

    (A) trading in YYY was stopped
    (B) the trade is being reported out of sequence
    (C) 100 shares of YYY were sold short at 103 $\frac{1}{2}$
    (D) the opening for YYY stock was delayed

45. All of these are subject to the 5% policy EXCEPT:

    (A) a riskless or simultaneous action
    (B) transactions in which the broker acts as principal
    (C) transactions requiring a prospectus
    (D) transactions in which the broker acts as agent

46. According to the "know your customer rule," a registered representative opening a new account should determine the customer's:

   I. objectives
   II. ability to assume risk
   III. financial condition and needs

   (A) I, II, and III
   (B) I and III
   (C) II and III
   (D) I and II

47. The combined long and short margin account of the customer follows:

   Debit Balance = $8,000

   Credit Balance = $15,000

   Short Market Value = $13,000

   Long Market Value = $25,000

   What would his combined equity be?

   (A) $15,000
   (B) $19,000
   (C) $22,000
   (D) $35,000

48. A stockholder has a noncumulative preferred stock paying a $7 dividend per year. If dividends on the preferred stock were not paid last year, but will be paid this year, how much should he receive?

   (A) $20
   (B) $14
   (C) $10
   (D) $7

49. For investment-grade bonds, which is the most speculative rating?

   (A) Aaa
   (B) Aa

   (C) Baa
   (D) Ba

50. This Moody's rating would mark a bond as speculative:

   (A) Aaa
   (B) Aa
   (C) Baa
   (D) Ba

51. Regarding the Eurodollar bond, which of the following is NOT true?

   (A) It is not registered in the U.S.
   (B) It is issued overseas by multinational corporations.
   (C) It pays interest and principal in dollars.
   (D) It may never trade in the U.S. markets.

52. Which of the following characterize EE bonds?

   I. They have no call feature.
   II. Debt may or may not be in bearer form.
   III. They have no credit risk.
   IV. They are transferable.

   (A) III and IV only
   (B) I and III only
   (C) I, III, and IV only
   (D) all the above

53. A municipal security of the kind known as a double-barreled security is:

   (A) a general obligation of the U.S. government that can be paid from revenues of a project
   (B) a general obligation of a municipal government that can be paid from revenues of a project
   (C) exempt from state and federal taxes
   (D) exempt from local and state taxes

54. Which one of the following is NOT subject to MSRB rules?

    (A) Dealer-banks doing secondary market municipal securities transactions
    (B) Issuers of municipal securities
    (C) Underwriters of municipal securities
    (D) Broker/dealers who act as financial advisor to an issuer

55. A grandmother, age 78, wants to buy an annuity for her son, age 40, and his 10-year-old daughter. Of the following annuities, which would be most suitable?

    (A) A joint annuity in the name of the son and granddaughter
    (B) A joint and last survivor annuity
    (C) Life income with 10-year period certain
    (D) None of these

56. The proper order for settling accounts when a limited partnership dissolves would be which sequence of the following parties?

    I. Limited partners
    II. General partners
    III. Secured lenders
    IV. General creditors

    (A) III, IV, I, II
    (B) IV, III, II, I
    (C) IV, III, I, II
    (D) III, II, IV, I

57. Who issues listed options?

    (A) The Options Clearing Corporation
    (B) The writer of the option
    (C) The buyer of the option
    (D) Exchanges where the option trades

58. With option contracts, the riskiest form of speculation would be:

    (A) not to sell short, but to buy a put
    (B) sell short, then purchase a call
    (C) to write naked call options
    (D) to sell calls against a large portfolio

59. An investor gets a $2,000 dividend distribution from shares in an open-end investment company. The distribution is reinvested back into the fund. The investor is in the 15% tax bracket. How much tax must he pay on this dividend?

    (A) $300
    (B) $210
    (C) $90
    (D) Zero because the dividend was reinvested

Questions 60–62 refer to the following descriptions of the state of the economy:

    (A) expansion
    (B) recession
    (C) inflation
    (D) deflation

Which choice applies in the following questions? (Remember that a choice might be used more than once.)

60. After a GNP decrease for two consecutive quarters, this is a normal indication.

61. Prices and interest rates down; bond prices up.

62. The FRB sells securities to control this.

63. One issues a debenture based upon:

    (A) ability to levy taxes
    (B) a pledge of real estate
    (C) the credit of the corporation
    (D) a pledge of equipment

64. For limited partnerships, which is true?

    I. They are a kind of ownership free of income taxes in which profits and losses are passed on to the partners.
    II. The limited partner's right to be involved in the daily operations, as regards centralized management, is proportional to his ownership.
    III. The limited partner is liable only to the extent of his investment.

    (A) I and II only
    (B) I and III only
    (C) III only
    (D) I, II, and III

65. When municipal bonds are purchased by an investment banker for resale to the public, her action would be described as:

    (A) subscribing the issue
    (B) underwriting the issue
    (C) managing the issue
    (D) distributing the issue

66. Which type of voting will help minority stockholders to elect a director?

    (A) Statutory voting
    (B) Cumulative voting
    (C) Preemptive voting
    (D) Directed voting

67. Which municipal security is often issued with different rates for different parts of the issue?

    (A) Serial bond
    (B) Term bond
    (C) Revenue bond
    (D) General obligation bond

68. If a put holder exercises her option, she will:

    (A) buy the security at the strike price
    (B) sell the security at the strike price
    (C) buy the security at the market price
    (D) sell the security at the market price

69. To best hedge a position holding 300 ACI against a possible decline in price, an investor would:

    (A) sell 3 ACI calls
    (B) buy 3 ACI puts
    (C) buy 3 ACI calls
    (D) sell 3 ACI puts

70. Taxes that are based on assessed value of property are called:

    (A) *ad valorem* taxes
    (B) sales taxes
    (C) capital gains taxes
    (D) income taxes

Use the following information in connection with Questions 71–74.

A client buys 200 shares of ACI at $36 per share in August and proceeds to write two ACI Nov 40 calls. He collects a $4 premium for each option.

71. The order ticket for the options would be marked:

    (A) opening sale, uncovered
    (B) opening buy, uncovered
    (C) opening sale, covered
    (D) opening buy, covered

72. The writer's break-even point is:

    (A) $28
    (B) $32
    (C) $36
    (D) $44

73. The options would expire on the:

    (A) third Thursday of November
    (B) third Friday of November
    (C) Saturday following the third Friday of November
    (D) Friday following the third Saturday in November

74. If the options are exercised, the writer will have a:

    (A) $1,600 loss
    (B) $800 loss
    (C) $800 gain
    (D) $1,600 gain

75. An investor buys $50,000 of municipals in the secondary market for $45,000. The bonds still have ten years to maturity. If he sells them two years later for $47,000, the taxable gain is:

    (A) $0
    (B) $1,000
    (C) $2,000
    (D) determined by economic accrual

76. The vesting in a newly opened IRA begins:

    (A) immediately
    (B) after five years
    (C) at age 59
    (D) at age 70

77. The Security Investor Protection Corporation will protect investors against:

    (A) market risk
    (B) inflation risk
    (C) broker bankruptcy
    (D) issuer bankruptcy

78. If a mutual fund charges the maximum $8\frac{1}{2}$% sales commission, it must provide all of the following EXCEPT:

    (A) breakpoints
    (B) rights of accumulation
    (C) free fund transfer
    (D) dividend reinvestment at NAV

79. If a dividend is to be paid to stockholders of record of Friday, March 13, the stock trades ex-dividend on:

    (A) March 9
    (B) March 10
    (C) March 11
    (D) March 12

80. Penalties for violations of NASD rules can be assessed, and suspensions from NASD membership can be issued by:

    I. SEC
    II. NASD Board of Governors
    III. District Business Conduct Committee

    (A) I and II
    (B) I and III
    (C) I, II, and III
    (D) II and III

81. A convertible corporate bond has a conversion price of $25 per share. If the bond is now selling at 110, what is the parity price for the stock?

    (A) $25
    (B) $27.50
    (C) $30
    (D) $40

82. An investor seeking monthly income would do best to invest in:

    (A) T-bills
    (B) mutual funds
    (C) high dividend stocks
    (D) GNMAs

83. An investor has a long-term capital loss of $8,000 for the year 1998. With no other capital gains or losses, how much can he deduct from ordinary income in the year 2000?

    (A) $0
    (B) $2,000
    (C) $3,000
    (D) $8,000

84. Call protection in a bond saves an investor from the risk of:

    (A) rising interest rates
    (B) fluctuating interest rates
    (C) falling interest rates
    (D) rising stock prices

Use the following information for Questions 85–87:

An investor buys 400 shares of ACI on margin when the shares are selling for $30. Assume that Regulation T is at 50%.

85. If the investor makes an initial deposit of $5,000 in cash, how much must he deposit in fully paid marginable securities?

    (A) $0
    (B) $1,000
    (C) $2,000
    (D) $7,000

86. If the price rises to $40 per share, what will the SMA hold?

    (A) $0
    (B) $2,000
    (C) $3,000
    (D) $4,000

87. The shares drop from $40 to $25. What is the debit record?

    (A) $3,000
    (B) $4,000
    (C) $6,000
    (D) $7,000

Use the following information for Questions 88–90:

ACI is trading at 43

Feb 40 calls in ACI are trading at 5

Feb 50 calls in ACI are trading at 1

88. The time value of these two options totals:

    (A) $0
    (B) $1
    (C) $2
    (D) $3

89. The maximum profit available to a buyer of a bull spread is:

    (A) $400
    (B) $600
    (C) $800
    (D) $1,000

90. The maximum loss for a buyer of a bear spread is:

    (A) $600
    (B) $800
    (C) $1,000
    (D) unlimited

91. In a Keogh Plan, a self-employed individual can contribute up to:

    (A) $2,000
    (B) 20% of total income with a maximum of $4,000
    (C) 20% of total income with a maximum of $7,000
    (D) 20% of total income with a maximum of $30,000

92. A new open-ended investment company issues and then sells shares to the public. In doing so, it must comply with the regulations of:

    (A) Securities Act of 1933
    (B) Securities Exchange Act of 1934
    (C) Investment Company Act of 1940
    (D) all of the above

93. No-load mutual funds are most likely to be sold:

    (A) directly to the public
    (B) through a distributor
    (C) using a network of brokers
    (D) through a bank

94. A U.S. company that sold equipment in Germany and was to receive payment in Deutsche marks could best hedge its currency exposure by:

    (A) buying D-mark calls
    (B) buying D-mark puts
    (C) selling D-mark calls
    (D) selling D-mark puts

95. A premature withdrawal of $30,000 from a Keogh plan for a person in the 15% tax bracket would result in a tax bill of:

    (A) $3,000
    (B) $4,500
    (C) $7,500
    (D) cannot be determined

96. A company that grows rapidly and pays no dividends will show:

    (A) an increase in paid-in capital
    (B) an increase in shareholders' equity
    (C) an increase in par value
    (D) none of the above

97. There are adjustments in the strike price of listed options for all of the following EXCEPT:

    (A) cash dividends
    (B) stock dividends
    (C) stock splits
    (D) rights offerings

98. None of the following is an employee of an options exchange EXCEPT the:

    (A) order book official
    (B) market maker

    (C) floor broker
    (D) $2 broker

99. If T-bill quotes go from 3.62% to 3.81%:

    (A) prices are increasing
    (B) prices are decreasing
    (C) yields are decreasing
    (D) par value has changed

100. Quotes on corporate bonds can be found in:

    (A) yellow sheets
    (B) pink sheets
    (C) the *Blue List*
    (D) the yield book

Use the following information to answer Questions 101 and 102:

An investor puts up $40,000 in a limited partnership. The next year, he gets a distribution of $10,000, and his share of partnership losses is $32,000.

101. What is his basis?

    (A) $0
    (B) $8,000
    (C) $30,000
    (D) $40,000

102. What is the maximum loss he can claim on his income tax that year?

    (A) $0
    (B) $2,000
    (C) $22,000
    (D) $30,000

103. Which of the following is known when a customer buys a bond when, as, and if issued?

    (A) The price
    (B) The accrued interest
    (C) The settlement date
    (D) The issue date

104. In a competitive bid underwriting, priority for accepting new orders would be found in the:

    (A) official statement
    (B) agreement among underwriters
    (C) notice of sale
    (D) syndicate letter

105. All of the following are part of per capita debt for the city of Pluto EXCEPT:

    (A) revenue bonds for a Pluto toll road
    (B) double-barreled bonds issued by Pluto county and the city
    (C) county general obligation bonds
    (D) city general obligation bonds

106. If the yield to maturity for a 10-year bond is higher than the coupon yield, then:

    (A) the bond is selling at a discount
    (B) the bond is selling at a premium
    (C) the current yield is higher than the yield to maturity
    (D) the current yield is lower than the coupon yield

Use the following information to answer Questions 107–109:

An investor sells short 300 shares of ACI at 26 and writes 3 ACI Jun 30 puts at 7.

107. Where is her break-even point?

    (A) 26
    (B) 30
    (C) 33
    (D) 37

108. What is her maximum possible loss?

    (A) $300
    (B) $900
    (C) $2,100
    (D) Unlimited

109. What is her maximum possible gain?

    (A) $300
    (B) $900
    (C) $2,100
    (D) Unlimited

110. As a first transaction, a customer writes some at-the-money calls. How much must he place on deposit?

    (A) Initial margin
    (B) Initial margin plus the premium
    (C) Initial margin minus the premium
    (D) Just the premium

111. How large is the spread on a Treasury-note quote of 110:12 bid, 110:28 asked?

    (A) $1.50
    (B) $1.60
    (C) $5.00
    (D) $8.00

112. Being long a straddle would be profitable whenever the market price:

    (A) exceeds the sum of the two strike prices
    (B) differs from the strike price by more than the sum of the two premiums
    (C) is less than the sum of the strike prices
    (D) differs from the strike price by less than the sum of the two premiums

113. A 7% bond is trading at 105. To the nearest 0.1%, what is the current yield?

    (A) 6.2%
    (B) 6.4%
    (C) 6.7%
    (D) 7%

114. The concession on a municipal offering is the discount available to:

    (A) a syndicate member
    (B) a member of the selling group
    (C) the syndicate manager
    (D) a large customer

115. The offer price for a mutual fund is $12.50. If the load is 8%, what is the NAV?

    (A) $13.50
    (B) $12.50
    (C) $11.50
    (D) $11.00

116. A fund with an NAV of $11 sells for $10.50. It is a(n):

    (A) no-load fund
    (B) closed-end fund
    (C) front-load fund
    (D) open-end fund

Answer Questions 117–119 on the basis of the following trades:

Buy 2 ACI Dec 70 calls at 5 and 2 ACI Dec 70 puts at 2.

117. What is the maximum possible loss on these trades?

    (A) Unlimited
    (B) $300
    (C) $700
    (D) $1,400

118. What is the maximum possible gain?

    (A) Unlimited
    (B) $300

(C) $700
(D) $1,400

119. If ACI goes to 100 at expiration and there is no previous execution, what will be the gain (or loss)?

    (A) $4,600
    (B) $6,000
    (C) $7,400
    (D) $10,000

120. An investor sells 1 SF Oct 70 put at 2.1. If the Swiss franc contract is for 125,000 SF and the option is exercised when the SF is at 69, the investor will realize a:

    (A) $1,375 loss
    (B) $1,250 loss
    (C) $1,250 gain
    (D) $1,375 gain

121. A fundamental trader would use all of the following EXCEPT:

    (A) earnings per share
    (B) double bottom
    (C) leading indicators
    (D) the current ratio

122. All of the following are considerations in avoiding a wash sale EXCEPT:

    (A) coupon
    (B) riskiness
    (C) maturity
    (D) accrued interest

123. An investor buys a 6% out-of-state revenue bond. If she pays $10 in accrued interest and collects that year's coupon payments, her federal tax liability is:

    (A) $0
    (B) $10
    (C) $50
    (D) $60

124. If the Fed raises the target for the fed funds rate:

    (A) the Fed is loosening
    (B) the Fed is tightening
    (C) the Fed wants to speed up the economy
    (D) the prime rate will decrease

125. Under NASD Uniform Practice Code, all of the following are good deliveries on a 400-share trade EXCEPT:

    (A) six certificates of 60 shares and one 40-share certificate
    (B) one 400-share certificate
    (C) two 200-share certificates
    (D) four 60s and eight 20s

PART TWO

Time 3 Hours

Questions 126–250

DIRECTIONS

Each of the questions or incomplete statements below is followed by four suggested answer options. Choose the best answer and then blacken the corresponding space on the answer sheet.

Questions 126 and 127 use the following information:

A Direct Participation Program (DPP) statement contains the following:

Revenue	$400,000
Expense	$250,000
Depreciation	$150,000
Interest	$50,000

126. The income for this DPP is:

(A) $50,000 loss
(B) $0
(C) $100,000 gain
(D) $150,000 gain

127. The cash flow for this DPP is:

(A) $50,000
(B) $0
(C) $100,000
(D) $150,000

128. Which of the following is not a liquidity measure?

(A) Current ratio
(B) Net working capital
(C) Quick ratio
(D) Debt ratio

129. Under the UGMA:

(A) each parent may give a minor up to $10,000 per year
(B) gifts may be reclaimed within the first year

(C) each minor may have only one custodian for any one gift
(D) twins may have joint custodians

130. If the four-week average number of shares traded is 25,000 and an investor owns 10% of the 12,000,000 shares outstanding, the most he can sell under Rule 144 is:

(A) no shares
(B) 12,000 shares
(C) 25,000 shares
(D) 120,000 shares

The following Balance Sheet is the basis for Questions 131–134:

Cash $200,000	Accounts Payable $200,000
Accounts Receivable $200,000	Interest Payable $100,000
Inventory $400,000	Declared Annual Dividend $100,000
Current Assets $800,000	Current Liabilities $400,000
Fixed Assets $1,200,000	Long-Term Debt $600,000
Total Assets $2,000,000	Total Liabilities $1,000,000

Common Stock ($2 par) $200,000

Paid in Excess $300,000

Retained Earnings $500,000

Total Shareholders' Equity $1,000,000

131. The current ratio is:

    (A) .5
    (B) 1
    (C) 1.5
    (D) 2

132. The dividend is:

    (A) $.50 per share
    (B) $1.00 per share
    (C) $1.50 per share
    (D) cannot be determined

133. If the dividend payout ratio is .25, then earnings per share are:

    (A) $1
    (B) $2
    (C) $3
    (D) $4

134. If ACI is currently selling for $60, the P/E is:

    (A) 15
    (B) 20
    (C) 30
    (D) 60

135. For an investor in the 28% bracket, a 6% municipal has an after-tax yield equivalent to that of a:

    (A) 6% T-bond
    (B) 6.6% corporate
    (C) 7.3% T-note
    (D) 8% corporate

136. ACI makes a rights offering of 500,000 shares. There are currently 2,500,000 shares outstanding. The number of rights necessary to buy 10 shares is:

    (A) 5
    (B) 10
    (C) 50
    (D) 100

137. If the subscription price in the above rights offering is $40 and the shares trade at $41 cum rights, the value of a right is:

    (A) .05
    (B) .25
    (C) .50
    (D) 1.00

138. The highest noninvestment grade bond rating is:

    (A) BBB
    (B) BB
    (C) B1
    (D) B

139. A margin account has $30,000 of securities long and $20,000 of securities short. The debit balance is $16,000, and the credit balance is $35,000. What is the margin requirement?

    (A) $15,000
    (B) $20,000
    (C) $25,000
    (D) $40,000

140. For the account of the previous question, what is the SMA?

    (A) $0
    (B) $2,000
    (C) $4,000
    (D) $9,000

141. If the long account went to $20,000 and the short account went to $30,000, what would the margin call be?

    (A) $0
    (B) $2,000
    (C) $4,000
    (D) $5,000

142. Instinet is a trading system in the:

    (A) fourth market
    (B) third market
    (C) second market
    (D) first market

143. Convertible securities afford the investor the advantage of:

    (A) higher yields
    (B) lower yields
    (C) possible participation in future growth
    (D) none of the above

144. The spread in an initial public offering depends on:

    (A) the financial track record of the issuer
    (B) the issuer's industry
    (C) the size of the issue
    (D) all of the above

145. For a municipal with interest payments on March 15 and September 15, how many days of accrued interest will be paid by a buyer on July 10 for regular settlement?

    (A) 117 days
    (B) 118 days
    (C) 119 days
    (D) 120 days

146. In a 3 for 2 stock split of a stock selling for $60, the adjusted price would be:

    (A) $90
    (B) $40
    (C) $30
    (D) $20

147. A firm would use an investment banker for all of the following services EXCEPT:

    (A) maintaining a secondary market for the first few weeks after an IPO
    (B) securing financing
    (C) underwriting a secondary issuance
    (D) distributing a large block held for two years by an insider

148. Auctions for one-year T-bills are held:

    (A) daily
    (B) weekly
    (C) monthly
    (D) quarterly

149. Refunding of a corporate bond could do all of the following EXCEPT:

    (A) change the corporate debt-to-equity ratio
    (B) change the maturity of the debt structure
    (C) lower interest costs
    (D) remove restrictive covenants

The following table is for Questions 150–152:

	ACI	CAI	ABC	CBA
Dividend payment	$.40	$.05	$.80	$1.00
Earnings/share	$1.20	$3.00	$1.20	$2.00
Price/Earnings	15	25	13.25	17

150. The firm that is most likely to be a growth firm is:

    (A) ACI
    (B) CAI
    (C) ABC
    (D) CBA

151. The firm with the highest market price is:

    (A) ACI
    (B) CAI
    (C) ABC
    (D) CBA

152. The firm that is most likely to be a utility is:

    (A) ACI
    (B) CAI
    (C) ABC
    (D) CBA

153. The balance sheet equation is best stated as:

    (A) total assets plus shareholders' equity equals total liabilities
    (B) total liabilities equals total assets plus shareholders' equity
    (C) total assets plus total liabilities equals shareholders' equity
    (D) total assets minus total liabilities equals shareholders' equity

154. A corporation's 3,000,000 authorized shares include 2,500,000 issued and 500,000 treasury stock. If the corporation earns $1,000,000, its earnings per share are:

    (A) $.33
    (B) $.40
    (C) $.50
    (D) $2.00

155. A bond secured by marketable securities is called a(n):

    (A) collateral trust bond
    (B) revenue bond
    (C) mortgage bond
    (D) equipment trust certificate

156. The yield to maturity of an 8% 20-year bond selling at 80 is approximately:

    (A) 8%
    (B) 8.4%
    (C) 9%
    (D) 10%

157. A "cash" settlement of a municipal bond purchase settles:

    (A) the same day
    (B) the next day
    (C) three days later
    (D) depends on the size of the transaction

158. Firms that make a market OTC are:

    (A) brokers
    (B) dealers
    (C) specialists
    (D) OTC brokers

159. Initial margin requirements are determined by:

    (A) NYSE
    (B) Federal Reserve Board
    (C) SEC
    (D) NYSE and FRB

160. A limited partner's liability is limited to:

    (A) cash outlay
    (B) cash outlay plus any recourse loans
    (C) cash outlay plus nonrecourse loans
    (D) cash outlay plus any profits

161. A corporation would ordinarily get the highest yield from:

    (A) 6% preferred dividend
    (B) 6% government bond
    (C) 7% corporate bond
    (D) 7% commercial paper

162. To retain the tax exempt status for an IRA which has been closed, a client must roll it into a new one within:

    (A) immediately
    (B) 30 days
    (C) 60 days
    (D) the current quarter

163. Which of the following groups do not have enforcement responsibility for MSRB rules?

    (A) NYSE and NASD
    (B) FRB and Comptroller of the Currency
    (C) FDIC and FRB
    (D) NASD and FDIC

164. Under normal conditions on the yield curve, the order for securities ranked by decreasing yield is:

    (A) T-bonds, corporate bonds, T-notes, T-bills
    (B) corporate bonds, T-bonds, T-notes, T-bills
    (C) T-bills, T-notes, T-bonds, corporate bonds
    (D) depends on the prime rate

165. An underwriting agreement in which members are responsible only for their own portion is called a(n):

    (A) Western agreement
    (B) Eastern agreement
    (C) undivided account
    (D) severally and jointly account

166. An investor has an account with $300,000 in cash and $200,000 in securities. The maximum he could receive from the SIPC is:

    (A) all $500,000
    (B) $300,000 cash and $100,000 securities
    (C) $100,000 cash and $200,000 securities
    (D) $100,000 cash and $100,000 securities

167. Options expire on the:

    (A) third Friday of the month
    (B) Friday following the third Saturday
    (C) third Saturday following the third Friday
    (D) third Saturday of the month

168. An investor buys shares in a mutual fund in August. In October, the fund distributes long-term capital gains. For this investor, these are taxed as:

    (A) ordinary income
    (B) short-term capital gains
    (C) long-term capital gains.
    (D) part long-term and part short-term gains

169. The investment company that has the least active management of the portfolio is likely to be:

    (A) an index fund
    (B) a closed-end fund
    (C) an open-end fund
    (D) a unit investment trust

170. A spread that includes 1 ACI Mar 60 call and 1 ACI Jul 60 call is called a:

    (A) vertical spread
    (B) bull spread
    (C) horizontal spread
    (D) bear spread

171. If a municipal bond has been prerefunded, the bonds are:

    (A) paid off immediately
    (B) paid off when they mature
    (C) held in escrow
    (D) still the responsibility of the issuer even though they are secured

172. The type of bond that is most price sensitive to changes in interest rates is a:

    (A) junk bond
    (B) zero
    (C) T-bill
    (D) noninvestment-grade bond

173. All of the following are not direct obligations of the U.S. government EXCEPT:

    (A) GNMA
    (B) FNMA
    (C) Freddie Mac
    (D) Sallie Mae

174. With respect to customer accounts, member firms are required to do all of the following EXCEPT:

(A) maintain current records
(B) keep all customer complaints on file
(C) safeguard all customer securities
(D) have a new account form

175. The tool that the Fed uses most frequently in controlling interest rates is:

(A) moral suasion
(B) changing the discount rate
(C) changing the reserve requirement
(D) open-market operations

176. In a "plain vanilla" CMO, repayment of principal occurs:

(A) uniformly to all tranches
(B) proportionately to the order of the tranches
(C) based on the Public Securities Association formula
(D) completely to one tranche before the next one receives any

177. For income tax purposes, the CMO is considered to:

(A) be like a bond
(B) have only interest income
(C) represent residual interests
(D) be a limited partnership

178. Which of the following sequences contains trades that allow a short sale?

(A) 9; 9; $8\frac{7}{8}$
(B) 12; $12\frac{1}{8}$; $12\frac{1}{8}$
(C) 8; 8; 8
(D) $7\frac{1}{8}$; 7; 7

179. Bearer bonds have which characteristics?

I. They require proof of ownership.
II. They are highly marketable.
III. They are in book-entry form.

(A) I and II
(B) II and III
(C) I only
(D) II only

180. A convertible preferred is convertible at 25. If the preferred is called at 107 and the common is at 26, what is the best course of action?

(A) Tender the stock.
(B) Convert to common.
(C) Hold the preferred.
(D) It cannot be determined.

181. A margin call is not mandatory if the call is for less than:

(A) there is no minimum
(B) $100
(C) $500
(D) 10% of the equity

182. For out-of-state residents, State of Virginia bonds are:

(A) exempt from Virginia taxes
(B) exempt from all taxes
(C) exempt from federal taxes
(D) exempt from federal and Virginia taxes

183. An NASD member may retain part of a "hot issue":

(A) under no circumstances
(B) if it is part of its regular trading policy
(C) if it is an insignificant amount
(D) if it was previously agreed to

184. Writers of call options get the dividend on the underlying stock:

(A) never
(B) always
(C) if the option is exercised before the ex-div date
(D) if it is a covered call

The following page from a specialist's book is to be used for Questions 185–187:

BUY	ACI	SELL
200 Prudential	36	
500 Merrill	$36\frac{1}{8}$	
300 Stop Schwab	$36\frac{1}{4}$	
	$36\frac{3}{8}$	
	$36\frac{1}{2}$	400 Merrill
	$36\frac{5}{8}$	300 DWR
	$36\frac{3}{4}$	300 Schwab
		200 Prudential
	$36\frac{7}{8}$	100 Stop DWR

185. The specialist may sell for his own account at no lower than:

(A) $36\frac{1}{4}$
(B) $36\frac{3}{8}$
(C) $36\frac{1}{2}$
(D) $36\frac{5}{8}$

186. The current quote and size is:

(A) $36\frac{1}{4}$–$36\frac{1}{2}$ 1000–1100
(B) $36\frac{1}{4}$–$36\frac{1}{2}$ 300–400
(C) $36\frac{1}{8}$–$36\frac{1}{2}$ 300–400
(D) $36\frac{1}{8}$–$36\frac{1}{2}$ 500–400

187. If the sequence of trades were $36\frac{1}{4}$; $36\frac{3}{8}$; $36\frac{1}{8}$, the Schwab Stop would be filled at:

(A) $36\frac{1}{8}$
(B) $36\frac{1}{4}$
(C) $36\frac{3}{8}$
(D) it would not be filled

188. An OTC order for 140 shares must be executed as:

(A) a single order
(B) orders of 100 shares and 40 shares
(C) any two orders that total 140
(D) orders of 100 shares and 40 shares with no odd-lot premium

Questions 189–191 are based on Buy 3 ACI Mar 50 calls at 3 when ACI is $50.50.

189. This trade will break even when ACI is at:

(A) 47
(B) 50
(C) 53
(D) $53\frac{1}{2}$

190. The time value of these options totals:

(A) $250
(B) $300
(C) $750
(D) $900

191. If ACI goes to 48, the investor's gain (loss) will be:

(A) $900 loss
(B) $600 loss
(C) $600 gain
(D) $900 gain

192. If settlement of $50,000 of 4% municipals maturing on 2-1-08 occurs on 5-1-98, the accrued interest is:

(A) $250
(B) $500
(C) $1,000
(D) $2,000

193. An index option is settled by delivery of:

    (A) a market basket of securities
    (B) cash
    (C) an index certificate
    (D) any of these

194. The type of security that is likely to do best if the economy weakens is called:

    (A) blue chip
    (B) growth
    (C) counter cyclical
    (D) income

Questions 195–197 are based on the following margin account:

Long Market $40,000   Short Market $25,000

Debit Record $24,000   Credit Record $40,000

SMA $4,000

195. The equity in this account is currently:

    (A) $4,000
    (B) $16,000
    (C) $31,000
    (D) $35,000

196. The purchasing power of this account is:

    (A) none; the account is restricted
    (B) equal to half of the equity
    (C) $4,000
    (D) $8,000

197. If the long market value goes to $35,000 and the short market value goes to $15,000, the margin requirement will become:

    (A) $15,000
    (B) $25,000
    (C) $30,000
    (D) $40,000

198. Even if an account is inactive, customers must still receive statements:

    (A) monthly
    (B) quarterly
    (C) semiannually
    (D) annually

199. Changing an accounting system from FIFO to LIFO in an inflationary environment will result in:

    (A) lower profits, lower taxes
    (B) lower profits, higher taxes
    (C) higher profits, lower taxes
    (D) higher profits, higher taxes

200. The payment method that yields the lowest monthly annuity payments is:

    (A) life annuity
    (B) life annuity plus survivors
    (C) 10-year certain
    (D) lump sum

201. The 8% bonds of ACI, Amalgamated Consolidated Incorporated, mature in 12 years. They are currently trading at 82. An investor owning five of these bonds would get semiannual interest of:

    (A) $200
    (B) $100
    (C) $40
    (D) $20

202. The current yield, to the nearest 0.1%, on these bonds is:

    (A) 8%
    (B) 8.2%
    (C) 9.8%
    (D) 10%

203. In increasing order, the yields are:

    (A) nominal, current, YTM
    (B) current, YTM, nominal
    (C) YTM, current, nominal
    (D) nominal, YTM, current

204. The security that represents ownership of overseas companies engaged in foreign trade is a(n):

    (A) banker's acceptance
    (B) ADR
    (C) commercial paper
    (D) Eurobond

205. ACI's balance sheet shows $20,000,000 of convertible bonds with a conversion price of 50 and 2,000,000 shares outstanding. The income statement shows earnings of $2,400,000. If the bonds are all called, the earnings per share will be:

    (A) $1.00
    (B) $1.20
    (C) $2.00
    (D) $2.40

206. In the previous problem, if half of the bonds are converted before they are called and ACI declares a dividend of $1,100,000, the dividend per share will be:

    (A) $.46
    (B) $.50
    (C) $.92
    (D) $1.00

207. An index which is based on 65 common stocks is:
    (A) Value Line
    (B) Dow Jones Industrials
    (C) S&P
    (D) Dow Jones Composite

208. The nine-bond rule states that:

    (A) orders for fewer than 10 bonds must be sent to the floor of NYSE
    (B) orders for fewer than 10 bonds go OTC
    (C) orders for six bonds go to the cabinet
    (D) orders for six bonds go to the NYSE unless the customer orders them elsewhere

209. If a stock is held in "street name," it:

    (A) may not be used in a short sale
    (B) lists the broker as the beneficial owner but not the owner of record
    (C) can be borrowed for a short sale
    (D) belongs to a customer beneficially and as a matter of record

210. The order in which the departments of a brokerage firm process a transaction is:

    (A) order, P&S, margin, cashier
    (B) order, margin, P&S, cashier
    (C) P&S, order, cashier, margin
    (D) P&S, cashier, order, margin

211. An investor in the 15% bracket has a single short-term capital gain. The tax rate on this transaction is:

    (A) 28%
    (B) 20%
    (C) 15%
    (D) cannot be determined

212. An investor has $100,000 in earnings and $10,000 in investment income. If he also has $12,000 in passive income losses from a DPP, the income subject to taxes that year is:

    (A) $110,000
    (B) $100,000
    (C) $98,000
    (D) $88,000

213. An investment letter is most often required in conjunction with a(n):

    (A) intrastate offering
    (B) new issue
    (C) closed-end mutual fund
    (D) private placement

214. A bond that has no specific asset as its security is called a:

    (A) general obligation bond
    (B) junior security
    (C) collateral trust certificate
    (D) debenture

215. The document laying out all of the terms of a bond issue is called the:

    (A) indenture
    (B) legal opinion
    (C) covenant of loan
    (D) trust agreement

216. The options strategy with the least risk is:

    (A) write a call, sell the stock short
    (B) write a call, buy the stock
    (C) write a put, sell the stock short
    (D) write a put, buy the stock

217. "Rehypothecation" is the term used to describe:

    (A) the right of the broker to use the customer's shares as collateral
    (B) the right to lend the customer's shares
    (C) the right of the broker to pledge the customer's shares to a lender
    (D) the right of the customer to avoid having his shares used as collateral

218. The maintenance margin requirement for the purchase of $50,000 par value municipals selling at 80 is:

    (A) $2,800
    (B) $3,500
    (C) $6,000
    (D) $7,500

219. An investor opens a margin account with an initial purchase of 200 shares at $9. He must deposit:

    (A) $900
    (B) $1,800
    (C) $2,000
    (D) $3,000

220. The premium on a T-bond option is 1.04. A buyer of this option would pay:

    (A) $1,040
    (B) $1,125
    (C) $10,400
    (D) $11,125

221. When interest rates rise, the premiums on debt put options will:

    (A) rise
    (B) fall
    (C) move toward out of the money
    (D) not change

222. When issuing a BAN, a municipality expects to pay it off with:

    (A) general tax revenues
    (B) anticipated tax increases
    (C) anticipated sales of municipal property
    (D) revenues from an upcoming bond sale

223. Cash flow is calculated by:

    (A) adding depreciation to after-tax earnings
    (B) subtracting depreciation from after-tax earnings
    (C) adding depreciation to before-tax earnings
    (D) subtracting depreciation from before-tax earnings

224. A portfolio with a beta of 1.2 would:

    (A) grow at 20% under normal market conditions
    (B) be less risky than an S&P index fund
    (C) would grow by 1.2% when the whole market was flat
    (D) would shrink by 6% if the market dropped 5%

225. A portfolio with $10,000,000 and a beta of 1.8 is to be completely hedged by S&P 500 options. If the index is at 900, one would buy:

    (A) 22 puts
    (B) 22 calls
    (C) 40 puts
    (D) 40 calls

226. An investor writing a T-bill call to hedge his portfolio of $1,000,000 of T-bills would deposit:

    (A) 15% of face minus the premium
    (B) 20% of market value minus the premium
    (C) nothing at all
    (D) the greater of A or B

227. An underwriter may not send any of the following to a prospective customer EXCEPT:

    (A) a reprint of an article which has already appeared in a magazine
    (B) a preliminary prospectus
    (C) Moody's credit evaluation
    (D) a newspaper story

228. The only one of the following not considered a "control person" is:

    (A) an outside director
    (B) an owner of 5% of the shares
    (C) the son of a principal
    (D) the treasurer of the firm who owns no shares

229. A customer who bought 1 ACI Jun 50 call and sold 1 ACI Jun 60 call would have put on a(n):

    (A) horizontal spread
    (B) straddle
    (C) bear spread
    (D) bull spread

230. If the investor of the previous question had paid $4 and collected $1:

    (A) his maximum gain could be $700 and his maximum loss $300
    (B) his maximum gain could be $300 and his maximum loss $700
    (C) his maximum gain could be unlimited and his maximum loss $300
    (D) his maximum gain could be unlimited and his maximum loss $700

231. The writer of an ACI Jun 60 put is covered by:

    (A) owning an ACI Mar 60 put
    (B) being long 100 shares of ACI
    (C) writing an ACI Jun 60 call
    (D) owning an ACI Aug 60 put

232. Which of the following is not an advantage of issuing convertible debt?

    (A) Stock price at conversion
    (B) The interest rate of the debt
    (C) Tax consequences of conversion
    (D) These are all advantages

233. In general, the maturity of a GNMA is:

    (A) always shorter than that of a CMO
    (B) always longer than that of a CMO

(C) varies more than that of a CMO

(D) less dependent on prepayments than that of a CMO

234. A T-bond which last paid interest on March 15 was bought for cash on June 12. How many days of accrued interest are there?

(A) 87 days
(B) 88 days
(C) 89 days
(D) 90 days

235. A municipal bond issue from an "overlapping" tax jurisdiction:

(A) is riskier than an issue from a non-overlapping one
(B) has two sources of revenue
(C) is exempt from both federal and state taxes
(D) is none of the above

236. The management company that manages a mutual fund can be:

(A) compensated based on performance of the fund
(B) made up of the directors of the fund
(C) compensated by a percentage of the assets under management
(D) all of the above

237. An investor enters an order to sell 100 ACI short on a stop limit of $25\frac{3}{4}$. The last recorded round lot sale was at 26. Subsequently, there are round lot sales at $25\frac{5}{8}$, $25\frac{5}{8}$, $25\frac{7}{8}$, and $25\frac{3}{4}$. The sale that triggers the order is:

(A) $25\frac{5}{8}$
(B) $25\frac{3}{4}$
(C) $25\frac{7}{8}$
(D) 26

238. The order is executed at:

(A) $25\frac{5}{8}$
(B) $25\frac{3}{4}$
(C) $25\frac{7}{8}$
(D) 26

239. The securities used as collateral in a rehypothecation are limited in value to:

(A) 50% of the loan
(B) 70% of the loan
(C) 100% of the loan
(D) 140% of the loan

240. None of the following are available to an exploratory drilling program EXCEPT:

(A) current income
(B) low risk
(C) investment tax credit
(D) depletion

Questions 241–243 are based on the following information:

A syndicate underwrites an offering of 8 million shares to be sold at $22. Of the 8 million shares, 2 million are allocated to the selling group. The issuer is to receive $21 per share, the selling concession is $.55, and the management fee is $.10.

241. The total spread is:

(A) $.55
(B) $.90
(C) $1.00
(D) $1.10

242. How much money will the managing underwriter get for his management services?

(A) $600,000
(B) $800,000
(C) $1,000,000
(D) Depends on how many the selling group actually sells

243. How much will a syndicate member realize for shares sold by the selling group?

    (A) $.35
    (B) $.55
    (C) $.65
    (D) $.90

    Questions 244 and 245 are based on the following excerpt from the ticker:

    ACI Pr 45s 98 CAI. SLD 55 ACI 3s 25

244. The CAI trade shows:

    (A) 100 shares of CAI sold short
    (B) 100 shares of CAI at 45 reported out of sequence
    (C) 100 shares CAI at 45
    (D) 100 shares CAI at 45 in a delayed opening

245. The total number of ACI preferred reported is:

    (A) 45 shares
    (B) 450 shares
    (C) 4,500 shares
    (D) 1,020 shares

246. A custodial account for a three-year-old must have a social security or tax I.D. number for the:

    (A) custodian
    (B) guardian
    (C) child
    (D) child or the custodian

247. The efficient market hypothesis claims that certain information is not helpful for predicting prices. In the strong form, it claims that:

    (A) technical analysis is not helpful
    (B) fundamental analysis is not helpful
    (C) insider information is not helpful
    (D) none of these is helpful

248. In an OTC transaction, the spread refers to the:

    (A) difference between the bid and the asked
    (B) markup from cost
    (C) 5% rule
    (D) fair and reasonable commissions which are NASD policy

249. A covered-call writer of German-mark options must have available to him:

    (A) U.S. dollars
    (B) German marks
    (C) either one since settlement is in cash
    (D) Eurodollars

250. Limited trading authority allows one to:

    (A) enter orders without further authorization
    (B) withdraw securities from an account
    (C) withdraw cash from the account only to pay for a transaction
    (D) none of the above

PRACTICE EXAMINATION THREE
Answer Key
PART ONE

#	Ans	#	Ans	#	Ans	#	Ans
1	A	37	D	73	C	109	B
2	A	38	B	74	D	110	B
3	A	39	B	75	C	111	C
4	B	40	D	76	A	112	B
5	C	41	C	77	C	113	C
6	B	42	D	78	C	114	B
7	D	43	D	79	C	115	C
8	A	44	B	80	D	116	B
9	A	45	C	81	B	117	D
10	A	46	A	82	D	118	A
11	D	47	B	83	B	119	A
12	B	48	D	84	C	120	D
13	B	49	C	85	C	121	B
14	C	50	D	86	B	122	D
15	A	51	D	87	C	123	A
16	A	52	B	88	D	124	B
17	D	53	B	89	B	125	A
18	B	54	B	90	A		
19	D	55	B	91	D		
20	C	56	A	92	D		
21	C	57	A	93	A		
22	A	58	C	94	B		
23	D	59	A	95	C		
24	A	60	B	96	B		
25	D	61	D	97	A		
26	A	62	C	98	A		
27	A	63	C	99	B		
28	A	64	B	100	A		
29	D	65	B	101	C		
30	C	66	B	102	D		
31	B	67	A	103	A		
32	D	68	B	104	D		
33	A	69	B	105	A		
34	B	70	A	106	A		
35	D	71	C	107	C		
36	B	72	B	108	D		

PRACTICE EXAMINATION THREE
Answer Key
PART TWO

126	A	162	C	198	B	234	C
127	C	163	A	199	A	235	A
128	D	164	B	200	D	236	C
129	C	165	A	201	A	237	A
130	D	166	C	202	C	238	B
131	D	167	C	203	A	239	D
132	B	168	C	204	B	240	D
133	D	169	D	205	B	241	C
134	A	170	C	206	B	242	B
135	C	171	B	207	D	243	A
136	C	172	B	208	D	244	B
137	B	173	A	209	C	245	C
138	B	174	C	210	A	246	C
139	C	175	D	211	C	247	D
140	C	176	D	212	A	248	A
141	D	177	A	213	D	249	B
142	A	178	B	214	D	250	A
143	C	179	D	215	A		
144	D	180	A	216	B		
145	B	181	C	217	C		
146	B	182	C	218	C		
147	A	183	A	219	B		
148	C	184	D	220	B		
149	A	185	B	221	A		
150	B	186	D	222	D		
151	B	187	C	223	A		
152	C	188	A	224	D		
153	D	189	C	225	C		
154	C	190	C	226	C		
155	A	191	A	227	B		
156	D	192	B	228	B		
157	A	193	B	229	D		
158	B	194	C	230	A		
159	B	195	C	231	D		
160	B	196	D	232	C		
161	A	197	B	233	C		

ANSWER EXPLANATIONS

PART ONE

1. During the cooling off period, every one of the following occurs EXCEPT:

    (A) stabilizing the issue
    (B) blue-skying the issue
    (C) the due diligence meeting
    (D) the issuance of a red herring

(**A**) Stabilizing the issue (if needed) happens after the new security is selling in the market. A registration statement must be filed with the SEC when a new stock issue is to be sold. A period of time is needed after filing for the SEC to review the information to make sure there is full disclosure. In this cooling off period, a preliminary prospectus (red herring) is served up to see if there's public interest. In whichever state it's sold, the issue must be registered to accord with that state's Blue Sky Laws. A due diligence meeting is held before the completion of the final prospectus. Here, all concerned parties, including underwriter and issuer, meet to confirm that everything is in order.

2. An options investor wishes to enter into a spread position. This would be done:

    (A) in the margin account
    (B) in the cash account
    (C) in two separate transactions: the long in the margin account, the short in the cash account
    (D) in two separate transactions, the long in the cash account, the short in the margin account

(**A**) The margin account is where spread positions are made. The difference between the premium collected and the premium paid would have to be deposited.

3. The agreement on a new municipal issue between the issuer and the trustee is written by whom?

    (A) Bond attorney
    (B) Trustee
    (C) Underwriter's attorney
    (D) Syndicate manager

(**A**) The interest of the bondholders is pursued by the bond attorney (counsel) who, in addition to writing the legal opinion, also writes the agreement (the indenture) between the trustee and the issuer.

4. By its charter, LoTec Co., may issue 5 million shares. Three million shares have been issued, of which 1 million are treasury stock. LoTec Co., now has how many shares outstanding?

(A) 1 million
(B) 2 million
(C) 3 million
(D) 5 million

(B) Two million shares are outstanding since 1 million is treasury stock. Issue stock minus treasury stock equals outstanding stock. LoTec Co., issued 3 million shares.

Questions 5–7 refer to the following settlement date requirements.

(A) Same business day
(B) Next business day
(C) Three business days
(D) Five business days

Which choice applies in the following questions? (Remember that a choice might be used more than once.)

5. Regular-way settlement for a municipal securities transaction.

(C) Transactions involving municipal securities settle regular-way three business days from trade date.

6. Regular-way settlement for an option transaction.

(B) Transactions involving option contracts settle regular-way on the next business day.

7. Payment date for a stock transaction.

(D) According to Regulation T, securities transactions settle five business days following the trade date.

8. Approval of an over-the-counter stock for purchase on margin is done by the:

(A) Federal Reserve Board
(B) state securities commission
(C) Securities Exchange Commission
(D) New York Stock Exchange or the NASD

(A) The Federal Reserve Board lists the OTC stocks approved for purchase on margin. These are higher quality stocks traded over-the-counter.

9. If under statutory voting six directors are to be elected, a stockholder with 50 shares of stock could cast:

I. 50 votes for each director
II. 300 votes to one director
III. 300 votes freely distributed among the six

(A) I only
(B) II only

(C) I or II only

(D) I, II, or III

(A) A stockholder with 50 shares can, under statutory voting, cast 50 votes for each director.

10. Which of the following yields to maturity would the investor expect to get if he purchases a 4.5% bond at a discount and holds it to maturity?

(A) 5%

(B) 4.5%

(C) 4%

(D) 3.5%

(A) The investor purchased the bond at a discount so the yield-to-maturity must be more than the nominal 4.5%, which leaves 5% as the only choice.

11. If an investor is in the 28% tax bracket, which of the following would offer the best after-tax yield?

(A) A $6\frac{3}{4}$% convertible bond

(B) A $6\frac{1}{2}$% preferred stock

(C) A $5\frac{3}{4}$% corporate bond

(D) A 5% municipal bond

(D) The interest income on the 5% municipal bond is completely free from U.S. government taxes. It is best because the other investments are subject to U.S. taxes and 28% of the income received would be taxable. The taxable equivalent yield of the 5% municipal bond is 6.94% (5% municipal yield divided by 72% complement of tax bracket) which is greater than the other choices.

12. Convertible debentures of BOOP are convertible into 20 shares of BOOP Corp. common stock. If the bonds were selling in the market at $980, what would the common stock price have to be in order to be at parity?

(A) $50

(B) $49

(C) $45

(D) $20

(B) To find the parity, divide the bond's market price by the conversion rate. $980 divided by 20 equals $49.

13. A "covered writer" is someone who has:

(A) sold a call option but does not own the underlying stock

(B) sold a call option and owns the underlying stock

(C) purchased a call option but does not own the underlying stock

(D) purchased a call option and owns the underlying stock

(B) A "covered call writer" is a person who has sold a call option and owns the underlying stock.

14. Which is true of a progressive tax?

   I.   The rates are higher for those with low incomes.
   II. It has a flat rate.
   III. It has graduated rates.
   IV. The rates are higher for those with large incomes.

   (A) II and IV
   (B) I and II
   (C) III and IV
   (D) I and III

(C) In a progressive tax, the rate increases with income. High income persons pay more proportionately than do those with low incomes. Taxes on incomes, estates, and gifts are progressive.

15. All of the following financial information can be found in a corporation's balance sheet EXCEPT:

   (A) expense ratios of the corporation
   (B) book value of the corporation
   (C) assets of the corporation
   (D) long-term funds received from all sources

(A) Expense ratios cannot be derived from the balance sheet. Expenses are found in the profit-and-loss statement. The other items mentioned are determined from the balance sheet.

16. In the analysis of a company's stock, a technical analyst would be LEAST worried about:

   (A) debt-to-equity ratio
   (B) chart pattern
   (C) short interest
   (D) trading volume

(A) The debt-to-equity ratio would be the least concern to a technical analyst. The debt-to-equity ratio is used to analyze a company's capitalization.

17. The Federal Reserve Board could stimulate a slow economy by:

   I.   lowering reserve requirements
   II. reducing margin requirements
   III. buying U.S. government securities in the open market

   (A) II and III only
   (B) I and II only
   (C) I and III only
   (D) I, II, and III

(**D**) Buying securities in the open market adds money to the system to ease credit. A lower reserve requirement makes more money available for loans and also eases credit. A slow economy is also stimulated by reducing margins, which allows investors to purchase securities on credit.

18. What do you call a security that depends completely on current earnings for payment of interest?

    (A) A warranted bond
    (B) An income bond
    (C) A convertible bond
    (D) A noncumulative preferred stock

(**B**) Companies that have recently had financial difficulties use income bonds. They must pay interest only when they've earned enough money. Such bonds are sometimes called *adjustment* bonds.

19. In the context of limited partnerships, what does "flow-through" mean?

    (A) Title to the properties purchased by the business flows through to the limited partners.
    (B) Business profits are passed along to the limited partners untaxed.
    (C) Both business profits and losses are passed through to limited partners in proportion to their individual ownership.
    (D) The general business debts flow through to the limited partners.

(D) By definition. This is a major reason why limited partnership is popular for tax-advantaged investments.

20. When a municipal bond is to be issued, who hires the attorney responsible for the legal opinion?

    (A) The syndicate manager
    (B) The underwriter
    (C) The municipality
    (D) The corporation

(**C**) An independent law firm hired by the municipality writes the legal opinion. No such bond can be issued without a legal opinion.

21. A conversion privilege is offered by some open-end investment firms permitting:

    (A) the owner of the shares to convert his bonds or preferred stock to common stock of the fund at a predesignated ratio
    (B) conversion of securities to cash at the option of the shareholder
    (C) conversion from the shares of one fund or class of fund to the shares of another fund under the same sponsorship at a nominal cost or at a reduced sales charge
    (D) liquidation of shareholdings with an option to buy the shares back at the current market price

(C) Often the conversion privilege is referred to as the exchange privilege. You must know that, unlike conversion of a bond or preferred stock to common stock, which is not a taxable event, converting from a growth fund to an income fund (or similar conversion) is considered to be a sale or new purchase. A capital gain could result upon the sale of the old fund shares if they have appreciated in value.

22. All of the following are leading economic indicators EXCEPT:

    (A) prime rate
    (B) stock prices
    (C) building permits
    (D) money supply

(A) The prime rate is a lagging economic indicator.

23. Regarding "dollar bonds," none of the following statements is generally true EXCEPT:

    (A) they are revenue bonds
    (B) they are quoted as a percentage of par
    (C) they are term bonds
    (D) they are serial bonds

(D) Dollar bonds are actively traded term bonds which are quoted by price rather than by yield.

24. A registered representative wants shares of a hot issue his firm is underwriting. By the NASD Rules of Fair Practice, the rep may:

    I. NOT do so for his own account, but may purchase shares for members of his immediate family
    II. do so if his allotment is modest, is not disproportionate to public orders, and is within his investment practice
    III. NOT do so under any circumstances
    IV. do so if he has a history of buying hot issues

    (A) III only
    (B) I only
    (C) II only
    (D) II and IV only

(A) A representative must never sell shares of a "hot issue" to himself. Conditions for sale to family are so stringent most firms simply forbid it.

25. Interest income from which of the following investments is free from state income tax in ALL states?

    I. General obligation bonds of the State of Wyoming
    II. U.S. Treasury Bills
    III. U.S. Series EE savings bonds
    IV. Bonds issued by the Commonwealth of Puerto Rico

(A) I only
(B) I and IV only
(C) II and III only
(D) II, III, and IV only

(D) Interest on any U.S. Treasury issue, most U.S. Agency issues (except FNMA and GNMA), and savings bonds are free from income tax in all state and local jurisdictions. The interest is subject to federal income tax, however. Interest paid on the debt obligations of any of the U.S. Protectorates, such as Puerto Rico, are free of income tax on state, local, and federal levels. The interest on Wyoming bonds would be tax free to a resident of the state, not otherwise.

26. You get an open order to buy 50 XRX at 110 Stop. The following are all true EXCEPT:

(A) this order is good, but only if it can be executed at 110
(B) this order becomes a market order if XRX sells at 110
(C) the order is good until canceled
(D) the order may be left with the specialist in XRX

(A) When we reach the stop price, the stock order becomes a market order. Since a market order will be placed as soon as the stock trades at 110 (or more), we don't know what the actual trade will be.

27. At age 50, the client comes into a sum and deposits it in a single payment deferred annuity. At age 65, he chooses a straight life settlement option and, unfortunately, dies six months later.

(A) Payments cease upon his death; no further money is received.
(B) His estate will get back the value of his account.
(C) His estate will receive a lump sum equal to his original investment less the amount already withdrawn.
(D) His beneficiary may select a settlement option to be used with the remaining balance in his account.

(A) The only thing sure about a life annuity settlement option is that you will receive payments as long as you live.

28. If the underlying common stock sells ex-dividend, a GTC buy-limit order will:

(A) be reduced
(B) be increased
(C) change at the discretion of the specialist
(D) remain unchanged

(A) Good-until-canceled orders (GTC) entered below the current market are automatically reduced by the amount of the dividend on the ex-dividend date unless they are marked DNR (Do Not Reduce). A buy-limit order is entered below the current market at the time it is entered and would be reduced.

29. For the sale of restricted securities under SEC Rule 144, which of the following are true?

    I. The sale can be made on an agency or principal basis.
    II. A form 144 notice of sale must be filed with the SEC not later than 30 days after the sale.
    III. The securities must be owned for two years.
    IV. The securities must be fully paid.

    (A) IV only
    (B) I and IV only
    (C) I, II, and IV only
    (D) I, III, and IV only

(D) The securities must be owned for two years and must be fully paid. They can be sold on an agency or principal basis. At the time of the sale, a 144 notice of sale, which is good for 90 days, must be filed with the SEC.

Questions 30–32 refer to the following types of offerings:

(A) A contingency offering
(B) A firm commitment
(C) A best efforts
(D) An all or none

Which type of offering is best described in the following questions? (Remember that a choice might be used more than once.)

30. A type of offering in which whatever is not sold is returned to the issuing corporation.

(C) A best efforts underwriting is the type of offering in which whatever is not sold is returned to the issuing corporation.

31. A type of offering in which the issuing corporation is assured of receiving the whole amount of the offering, and whatever is not sold is retained by the underwriter.

(B) A firm commitment is the offering in which the issuing corporation is assured of receiving the full amount of the offering, and whatever is not sold is retained by the underwriter.

32. A type of offering which is canceled if the entire lot is not sold.

(D) If the offering is canceled unless the entire amount of shares is sold, it is an all or none offering.

33. The legal opinion regarding a new municipal issue:

    (A) attests to the validity of the issue
    (B) is approved by the MSRB
    (C) attests to the issuer's ability to meet debt service
    (D) ensures the legality of the syndicate

(**A**) Municipal issues must have a legal opinion written by a qualified bond counsel stating that interest is free from federal tax and that the issue is valid and legal.

34. Mr. Hashimoto's wife calls to purchase 150 shares of ZIP Corp. in her husband's personal account. The account executive for the account knows that a favorable earnings report is about to be issued. She:

    (A) cannot enter the order because the earnings report has not been released
    (B) cannot accept the order because Mrs. Hashimoto does not have trading authorization to enter orders for Mr. Hashimoto's personal account
    (C) can enter the order because Mr. Hashimoto had previously mentioned he would like to establish a position in ZIP Corp.
    (D) can enter the order because Mrs. Hashimoto has a joint account with Mr. Hashimoto

(**B**) The order cannot be accepted. Mrs. Hashimoto doesn't have trading authorization to enter orders for her husband's personal account. A personal account is just that—personal.

35. ABC closes at $37 and the following day sells ex-dividend $0.68 per share. At what price should the stock open the next day if it opens at the same level at which it closed the day before?

    (A) 37
    (B) $36\frac{1}{2}$
    (C) $36\frac{3}{8}$
    (D) $36\frac{1}{4}$

(**D**) The stock's price is reduced sufficiently to cover the dividend. Therefore, it will be reduced by $\frac{3}{4}$ ($0.75) since $\frac{5}{8}$ ($0.625) would not be sufficient to cover the $0.68 dividend. $37 - \frac{3}{4} = $36\frac{1}{4}$.

36. The customer buys a stock in a margin account not listed with the Federal Reserve Board's marginable securities. He purchases 100 shares over the counter at $50 each. The FRB's initial margin requirement is 50%. He would get a margin call for:

    (A) $7,500
    (B) $5,000
    (C) $2,500
    (D) $1,250

(**B**) If it's an over-the-counter not listed with the FRB as marginable, the full price must be paid. The customer would receive a margin call for 100% of the purchase price, $5,000.

37. Should a broker/dealer go bankrupt, the Securities Investors Protection Corp,. requires the appointment of a trustee who would be responsible for:

    I.   making sure the distribution of cash and securities is administered properly
    II. informing the firm's customers that the firm is being liquidated
    III. distributing the customers' securities that the firm holds

    (A) II and III
    (B) I and II
    (C) I and III
    (D) I, II, and, III

(D) When a company goes bankrupt, the SIPC trustee is responsible for all of the three.

38. When he evaluates the common stock of a corporation, a fundamental analyst must examine all that follows EXCEPT:

    (A) current amount of earnings paid out as dividends to shareholders
    (B) current amount of short-interest positions for the stock
    (C) the corporation's sales
    (D) the corporation's management

(B) The current amount of short-interest positions would not be examined. A technical analyst examines this statistic, which represents the total amount of shares sold short that will be covered in the future.

39. A war veteran, age 55, has some money problems and wants to make a withdrawal from his IRA. This would:

    (A) not be permitted
    (B) involve a 10% penalty and would be taxable income
    (C) would be taxable, but without penalty
    (D) result in a 50% penalty

(B) There is a 10% penalty for withdrawal before age $59\frac{1}{2}$, and the withdrawal would be taxable income. This penalty does not apply where physical disability or death is involved nor where there are extraordinary medical expenses, including medical insurance premiums.

40. With respect to bearer bonds, which would not be rejected?

    (A) A certificate without a seal
    (B) A mutilated coupon
    (C) The absence of a legal opinion
    (D) Lack of the owner's endorsement

(D) The owner's signature isn't needed on a bearer bond.

41. Mr. Ross purchased 500 shares of ARIA at $12 on February 3 and presented them to his nephew for a birthday present on July 8. If on July 8 the market price of ARIA was up to $17, the nephew's cost basis would be:

(A) $7
(B) $8
(C) $12
(D) $17

(C) In the case of gifts of securities, the recipient assumes the cost at time of purchase for tax purposes; in this case, $12.

42. Foreign currency transactions in the Interbank Market:

(A)   occur on exchanges throughout the world
(B)   are regulated by the SEC
(C)   are reported on the NASDAQ system
(D)   may settle on a spot or forward basis

(D) Foreign currency transactions may settle on a spot or forward basis. Currencies of different countries are bought and sold on the Interbank Market, which is an unregulated over-the-counter market. Spot transactions settle in two business days from the trade date. In a forward transaction, the exchange rate is established on the trade date, but settlement occurs in more than two business days. While foreign currency transactions are not reported on NASDAQ, spot quotes are available from information vendors such as Knight-Ridder Financial Information Systems, Reuters, and Telerate.

43. The Securities Exchange Act of 1934 on rules of manipulation refers to transactions involving:

   I. municipal bonds
   II. U.S. Government bonds
   III. common stock
   IV. corporate bonds

(A)   III and IV
(B)   I and II
(C)   I, III, and IV
(D)   all the above

(D) The SEC Act of 1934 rules of manipulation apply to all types of securities.

44. The following appears on the NYSE ticker tape:

YYY.SLD $103\frac{1}{2}$

This means:

(A)   trading in YYY was stopped
(B)   the trade is being reported out of sequence
(C)   100 shares of YYY were sold short at $103\frac{1}{2}$
(D)   the opening for YYY stock was delayed

(B) SLD means the trade is being reported out of sequence.

45. All of these are subject to the 5% policy EXCEPT:

    (A) a riskless or simultaneous action
    (B) transactions in which the broker acts as principal
    (C) transactions requiring a prospectus
    (D) transactions in which the broker acts as agent

(C) The 5% policy doesn't apply to transactions requiring a prospectus. It applies when a broker acts as an agent (broker) or principal (dealer) and also applies to riskless or simultaneous transactions.

46. According to the "know your customer rule," a registered representative opening a new account should determine the customer's:

    I.   objectives
    II. ability to assume risk
    III. financial condition and needs

    (A) I, II, and III
    (B) I and III
    (C) II and III
    (D) I and II

(A) All three should be considered for your customer.

47. The combined long and short margin account of the customer follows:

    Debit Balance = $8,000

    Credit Balance = $15,000

    Short Market Value = $13,000

    Long Market Value = $25,000

    What would his combined equity be?

    (A) $15,000
    (B) $19,000
    (C) $22,000
    (D) $35,000

(B) For a combined long and short margin account, the equity equals the long market value plus the credit balance minus the debit balance minus the short market value: $25,000 + $15,000 − $8,000 − $13,000 = $19,000.

48. A stockholder has a noncumulative preferred stock paying a $7 dividend per year. If dividends on the preferred stock were not paid last year, but will be paid this year, how much should he receive?

    (A) $20
    (B) $14
    (C) $10
    (D) $7

(D) For a noncumulative preferred stock, an unpaid dividend does not accumulate. The preferred stockholder will receive only the $7 for the current year.

49. For investment-grade bonds, which is the most speculative rating?

(A) Aaa
(B) Aa
(C) Baa
(D) Ba

(C) Moody's top four ratings, meaning "investment grade" or "bank quality," in declining order are: Aaa, Aa, A, Baa. Decreased rating means increased risk, so Baa is most speculative.

50. This Moody's rating would mark a bond as speculative:

(A) Aaa
(B) Aa
(C) Baa
(D) Ba

(D) A rating below investment grade such as Ba is speculative.

51. Regarding the Eurodollar bond, which of the following is NOT true?

(A) It is not registered in the U.S.
(B) It is issued overseas by multinational corporations.
(C) It pays interest and principal in dollars.
(D) It may never trade in the U.S. markets.

(D) Although the securities are not registered in the U.S. under the Securities Act of 1933, they may trade in the U.S. three months after issuance. The Eurodollar bond pays interest and principal in dollars on deposit in banks outside the U.S.

52. Which of the following characterize EE bonds?

   I. They have no call feature.
  II. Debt may or may not be in bearer form.
 III. They have no credit risk.
  IV. They are transferable.

(A) III and IV only
(B) I and III only
(C) I, III, and IV only
(D) all the above

(B) EE bonds, which are a type of U.S. government savings bond, are noncallable, nontransferable, and without credit risk. They must always be in registered form; therefore, they will not be issued as bearer bonds.

53. A municipal security of the kind known as a double-barreled security is:

    (A) a general obligation of the U.S. government that can be paid from revenues of a project
    (B) a general obligation of a municipal government that can be paid from revenues of a project
    (C) exempt from state and federal taxes
    (D) exempt from local and state taxes

(B) A municipal security is double barreled when is can be paid from revenues of a project and is also a general obligation of a municipal government. It might be subject to state tax, but not federal.

54. Which one of the following is NOT subject to MSRB rules?

    (A) Dealer-banks doing secondary market municipal securities transactions
    (B) Issuers of municipal securities
    (C) Underwriters of municipal securities
    (D) Broker/dealers who act as financial advisor to an issuer

(B) Issuers of municipal securities are not subject to MSRB rules, but they are subject to the antifraud provisions of the federal securities acts. The rules do, however, apply to all broker/dealers and dealer-banks engaged in municipal securities activities.

55. A grandmother, age 78, wants to buy an annuity for her son, age 40, and his 10-year-old daughter. Of the following annuities, which would be most suitable?

    (A) A joint annuity in the name of the son and granddaughter
    (B) A joint and last survivor annuity
    (C) Life income with 10-year period certain
    (D) None of these

(B) A joint and last survivor annuity provides benefit payments to both persons in the joint account and then to the survivor for life. This would best fulfill the grandmother's wishes.

56. The proper order for settling accounts when a limited partnership dissolves would be which sequence of the following parties?

    I.   Limited partners
    II. General partners
    III. Secured lenders
    IV. General creditors

    (A) III, IV, I, II
    (B) IV, III, II, I
    (C) IV, III, I, II
    (D) III, II, IV, I

(A) The priority of claims for assets in this situation is: secured lenders, general creditors, limited partners, general partners.

57. Who issues listed options?

    (A) The Options Clearing Corporation
    (B) The writer of the option
    (C) The buyer of the option
    (D) Exchanges where the option trades

(A) The Options Clearing Corporation issues options listed on exchanges.

58. With option contracts, the riskiest form of speculation would be:

    (A) not to sell short, but to buy a put
    (B) sell short, then purchase a call
    (C) to write naked call options
    (D) to sell calls against a large portfolio

(C) With option contracts, the greatest risk is to write naked (uncovered) call options. This means selling a call option without owning the underlying stock. If the buyer of the option exercises it, the seller must go to the market to buy and deliver the stock, which may have risen steeply.

59. An investor gets a $2,000 dividend distribution from shares in an open-end investment company. The distribution is reinvested back into the fund. The investor is in the 15% tax bracket. How much tax must he pay on this dividend?

    (A) $300
    (B) $210
    (C) $90
    (D) Zero because the dividend was reinvested

(A) The investor must pay 15% of the full $2,000 dividend. Tax on dividends must be paid on all stocks or shares of mutual funds regardless of subsequent use for reinvestment.

Questions 60–62 refer to the following descriptions of the state of the economy:

    (A) expansion
    (B) recession
    (C) inflation
    (D) deflation

Which choice applies in the following questions? (Remember that a choice might be used more than once.)

60. After a GNP decrease for two consecutive quarters, this is a normal indication.

(B) Economists consider that a two-consecutive-quarter-GNP decline points to recession.

61. Prices and interest rates down; bond prices up.

(**D**) These characterize deflation, the result of a sluggish economy. The FRB might try to stimulate the economy by feeding money into it, possibly through the purchase of securities.

62. The FRB sells securities to control this.

(**C**) In inflation, too much money chases the goods and services of an economy causing prices to rise. By selling securities, the FRB sops up some of this excess money.

63. One issues a debenture based upon:

    (A) ability to levy taxes
    (B) a pledge of real estate
    (C) the credit of the corporation
    (D) a pledge of equipment

(**C**) A debenture is just a corporate IOU. It has no support but the credit standing of the company.

64. For limited partnerships, which is true?

    I. They are a kind of ownership free of income taxes in which profits and losses are passed on to the partners.
    II. The limited partner's right to be involved in the daily operations, as regards centralized management, is proportional to his ownership.
    III. The limited partner is liable only to the extent of his investment.

    (A) I and II only
    (B) I and III only
    (C) III only
    (D) I, II, and III

(**B**) The general partner controls the daily operation of the firm. If a limited partner intrudes, he could be reclassified and lose flow-through benefits.

65. When municipal bonds are purchased by an investment banker for resale to the public, her action would be described as:

    (A) subscribing the issue
    (B) underwriting the issue
    (C) managing the issue
    (D) distributing the issue

(**B**) This is underwriting, whether the issue is municipal or otherwise. Managing the issue refers to the duties of the lead underwriter.

66. Which type of voting will help minority stockholders to elect a director?

    (A) Statutory voting
    (B) Cumulative voting

(C) Preemptive voting

(D) Directed voting

(B) In cumulative voting, the stockholders may pool all of their votes for a single director, and thus, make it easier to elect one.

67. Which municipal security is often issued with different rates for different parts of the issue?

(A) Serial bond

(B) Term bond

(C) Revenue bond

(D) General obligation bond

(A) A serial bond is issued in a single offering with varying maturities. The later maturing bonds will have a higher coupon rate or be issued at a discount to par.

68. If a put holder exercises her option, she will:

(A) buy the security at the strike price

(B) sell the security at the strike price

(C) buy the security at the market price

(D) sell the security at the market price

(B) Holding a put gives one the right to sell the security at the strike price.

69. To best hedge a position holding 300 ACI against a possible decline in price, an investor would:

(A) sell 3 ACI calls

(B) buy 3 ACI puts

(C) buy 3 ACI calls

(D) sell 3 ACI puts

(B) Owning a put protects when the stock price goes down. Selling a call gives some protection, but only up to the level of the premium.

70. Taxes that are based on assessed value of property are called:

(A) *ad valorem* taxes

(B) sales taxes

(C) capital gains taxes

(D) income taxes

(A) The definition of *ad valorem* is "based on the value of."

Use the following information in connection with Questions 71–74.

A client buys 200 shares of ACI at $36 per share in August and proceeds to write two ACI Nov 40 calls. He collects a $4 premium for each option.

71. The order ticket for the options would be marked:

    (A) opening sale, uncovered
    (B) opening buy, uncovered
    (C) opening sale, covered
    (D) opening buy, covered

(C) The writer is the seller of the option. Since he already owns the shares, he is covered.

72. The writer's break-even point is:

    (A) $28
    (B) $32
    (C) $36
    (D) $44

(B) If ACI goes to $32, he will offset the $800 loss in the stock with the two $400 premiums.

73. The options would expire on the:

    (A) third Thursday of November
    (B) third Friday of November
    (C) Saturday following the third Friday of November
    (D) Friday following the third Saturday in November

(C) Options stop trading on the third Friday of the month but can be exercised until the next day.

74. If the options are exercised, the writer will have a:

    (A) $1,600 loss
    (B) $800 loss
    (C) $800 gain
    (D) $1,600 gain

(D) The option will be exercised if the price goes to $40 or more. He will sell the stock at $40 for $800 and keep the $800 premium.

75. An investor buys $50,000 of municipals in the secondary market for $45,000. The bonds still have ten years to maturity. If he sells them two years later for $47,000, the taxable gain is:

    (A) $0
    (B) $1,000
    (C) $2,000
    (D) determined by economic accrual

(C) There is no accretion for secondary market gains, so all $2,000 is taxable.

76. The vesting in a newly opened IRA begins:

    (A) immediately
    (B) after five years

(C) at age 59

(D) at age 70

(A) The investor puts up his own money, and it is vested immediately.

77. The Security Investor Protection Corporation will protect investors against:

(A) market risk

(B) inflation risk

(C) broker bankruptcy

(D) issuer bankruptcy

(C) SIPC does not provide insurance against any kind of market risk.

78. If a mutual fund charges the maximum $8\frac{1}{2}\%$ sales commission, it must provide all of the following EXCEPT:

(A) breakpoints

(B) rights of accumulation

(C) free fund transfer

(D) dividend reinvestment at NAV

(C) All of the others must be provided if the maximum sales charge is levied.

79. If a dividend is to be paid to stockholders of record of Friday, March 13, the stock trades ex-dividend on:

(A) March 9

(B) March 10

(C) March 11

(D) March 12

(C) The ex-dividend date is two business days before the record date.

80. Penalties for violations of NASD rules can be assessed, and suspensions from NASD membership can be issued by:

  I. SEC

  II. NASD Board of Governors

  III. District Business Conduct Committee

(A) I and II

(B) I and III

(C) I, II, and III

(D) II and III

(D) The SEC does not perform those regulatory functions.

81. A convertible corporate bond has a conversion price of $25 per share. If the bond is now selling at 110, what is the parity price for the stock?

(A) $25

(B) $27.50

666 **Series 7:** STOCKBROKER EXAM

(C) $30
(D) $40

(B) The conversion rate is $1,000 ÷ $25 = 40. If the bond is selling for $1,100, then the parity price is now $1,100 ÷ 40 = $27.50

82. An investor seeking monthly income would do best to invest in:

(A) T-bills
(B) mutual funds
(C) high dividend stocks
(D) GNMAs

(D) GNMA income comes from monthly mortgage payments, which are passed through to the holders of the GNMA certificates.

83. An investor has a long-term capital loss of $8,000 for the year 1998. With no other capital gains or losses, how much can he deduct from ordinary income in the year 2000?

(A) $0
(B) $2,000
(C) $3,000
(D) $8,000

(B) He can deduct a maximum of $3,000 against ordinary income in any year and may roll the rest of the loss forward. Therefore, he may deduct $3,000 in 1998, $3,000 in 1999, and the remaining $2,000 in the year 2000.

84. Call protection in a bond saves an investor from the risk of:

(A) rising interest rates
(B) fluctuating interest rates
(C) falling interest rates
(D) rising stock prices

(C) An issuer is likely to call a bond if interest rates fall, hence call protection is useful to the investor under those circumstances.

Use the following information for Questions 85–87:

An investor buys 400 shares of ACI on margin when the shares are selling for $30. Assume that Regulation T is at 50%.

85. If the investor makes an initial deposit of $5,000 in cash, how much must he deposit in fully paid marginable securities?

(A) $0
(B) $1,000
(C) $2,000
(D) $7,000

(C) The $5,000 in cash covers $10,000 of purchase. The other $2,000 of purchase is covered by the $2,000 of marginable securities. The debit record is $7,000.

86. If the price rises to $40 per share, what will the SMA hold?

    (A) $0
    (B) $2,000
    (C) $3,000
    (D) $4,000

(B) With the stock at $40, the total stock holding is $16,000 and the required margin is $8,000. Since the debit record is still $6,000, the investor could take $2,000 out of the account. This is his SMA.

87. The shares drop from $40 to $25. What is the debit record?

    (A) $3,000
    (B) $4,000
    (C) $6,000
    (D) $7,000

(C) The debit record doesn't change, and the investor still owes the broker $6,000.

Use the following information for Questions 88–90:

ACI is trading at 43

Feb 40 calls in ACI are trading at 5

Feb 50 calls in ACI are trading at 1

88. The time value of these two options totals:

    (A) $0
    (B) $1
    (C) $2
    (D) $3

(D) Since the Feb 40 call is $3 in the money, its time value is $2. The Feb 50 call has only time value, so the total is $3.

89. The maximum profit available to a buyer of a bull spread is:

    (A) $400
    (B) $600
    (C) $800
    (D) $1,000

(B) A bull spread would be buying the Feb 40 and selling the Feb 50. The maximum profit would occur if ACI went to 50. The buyer would make $5 on the Feb 40 call and would keep the $1 premium on the Feb 50 call.

90. The maximum loss for a buyer of a bear spread is:

    (A) $600
    (B) $800
    (C) $1,000
    (D) unlimited

(A) The bear spread, buying the 50 and selling the 40, would be taking the opposite side from the bull spread. Therefore, if the stock goes up to 50, the bear spread has a maximum loss of $600.

91. In a Keogh Plan, a self-employed individual can contribute up to:

    (A) $2,000
    (B) 20% of total income with a maximum of $4,000
    (C) 20% of total income with a maximum of $7,000
    (D) 20% of total income with a maximum of $30,000

(D) The plan must also be available to all eligible employees. Note that 20% of total compensation is the same as 25% of net compensation after the Keogh deduction.

92. A new open-ended investment company issues and then sells shares to the public. In doing so, it must comply with the regulations of:

    (A) Securities Act of 1933
    (B) Securities Exchange Act of 1934
    (C) Investment Company Act of 1940
    (D) all of the above

(D) The Securities Exchange Act of 1934 has antifraud regulations that also apply to investment companies.

93. No-load mutual funds are most likely to be sold:

    (A) directly to the public
    (B) through a distributor
    (C) using a network of brokers
    (D) through a bank

(A) A no-load fund has no sales commissions and, hence, is most likely to be sold directly to the public.

94. A U.S. company that sold equipment in Germany and was to receive payment in Deutsche marks could best hedge its currency exposure by:

    (A) buying D-mark calls
    (B) buying D-mark puts
    (C) selling D-mark calls
    (D) selling D-mark puts

(B) The fear is that the D-mark will go down. The best hedge would be to buy a put.

95. A premature withdrawal of $30,000 from a Keogh plan for a person in the 15% tax bracket would result in a tax bill of:

    (A) $3,000
    (B) $4,500
    (C) $7,500
    (D) cannot be determined

(C) A premature withdrawal would incur a 10% penalty along with a 15% tax on the withdrawal or $3,000 + $4,500 = $7,500.

96. A company that grows rapidly and pays no dividends will show:

    (A) an increase in paid-in capital
    (B) an increase in shareholders' equity
    (C) an increase in par value
    (D) none of the above

(B) If the company is growing rapidly and does not pay dividends, it is retaining earnings. This will show as an increase in stockholders' equity.

97. There are adjustments in the strike price of listed options for all of the following EXCEPT:

    (A) cash dividends
    (B) stock dividends
    (C) stock splits
    (D) rights offerings

(A) All of the others change the number of shares outstanding and require an adjustment in the strike price.

98. None of the following is an employee of an options exchange EXCEPT the:

    (A) order book official
    (B) market maker
    (C) floor broker
    (D) $2 broker

(A) An order book official is the employee on an options exchange who performs part of the role played by the specialist on the NYSE.

99. If T-bill quotes go from 3.62% to 3.81%:

    (A) prices are increasing
    (B) prices are decreasing
    (C) yields are decreasing
    (D) par value has changed

(B) The quote represents the discount from par that a buyer would pay. Thus, if the quote is increasing, the price is decreasing.

100. Quotes on corporate bonds can be found in:

    (A) yellow sheets
    (B) pink sheets
    (C) the *Blue List*
    (D) the yield book

(A) Pink sheets give OTC stock quotes. The *Blue List* lists bonds for sale in the secondary market but has no quotes.

Use the following information to answer Questions 101 and 102:

An investor puts up $40,000 in a limited partnership. The next year, he gets a distribution of $10,000, and his share of partnership losses is $32,000.

101. What is his basis?

    (A) $0
    (B) $8,000
    (C) $30,000
    (D) $40,000

(C) The basis is the original investment minus the $10,000 distribution.

102. What is the maximum loss he can claim on his income tax that year?

    (A) $0
    (B) $2,000
    (C) $22,000
    (D) $30,000

(D) Since his basis is now $30,000, this is the most he can now deduct, and this only from other passive income.

103. Which of the following is known when a customer buys a bond when, as, and if issued?

    (A) The price
    (B) The accrued interest
    (C) The settlement date
    (D) The issue date

(A) Since the issue date is in question and the settlement date will only be known after the bond is printed, accrued interest cannot be determined; only the price is known at this point.

104. In a competitive bid underwriting, priority for accepting new orders would be found in the:

    (A) official statement
    (B) agreement among underwriters
    (C) notice of sale
    (D) syndicate letter

(D) In a negotiated underwriting, this would appear in the agreement among underwriters, but in a competitive underwriting, it appears in the syndicate letter.

105. All of the following are part of per capita debt for the city of Pluto EXCEPT:

   (A) revenue bonds for a Pluto toll road
   (B) double-barreled bonds issued by Pluto county and the city
   (C) county general obligation bonds
   (D) city general obligation bonds

  (A) The revenue bonds are to be paid off by the proceeds of the tolls and, hence, do not count as part of per capita debt.

106. If the yield to maturity for a 10-year bond is higher than the coupon yield, then:

   (A) the bond is selling at a discount
   (B) the bond is selling at a premium
   (C) the current yield is higher than the yield to maturity
   (D) the current yield is lower than the coupon yield

  (A) If the yield to maturity is higher than the coupon, then the bond is at a discount. In that case, the coupon yield is less than the current yield, which is less than the YTM.

   Use the following information to answer Questions 107–109:

   An investor sells short 300 shares of ACI at 26 and writes 3 ACI Jun 30 puts at 7.

107. Where is her break-even point?

   (A) 26
   (B) 30
   (C) 33
   (D) 37

  (C) Her break-even occurs when the stock rises to 33 for a loss of $2,100, which exactly offsets the premium she collected.

108. What is her maximum possible loss?

   (A) $300
   (B) $900
   (C) $2,100
   (D) Unlimited

  (D) Her maximum possible loss is unlimited since, if the stock price keeps rising, so does her loss on the short sale.

109. What is her maximum possible gain?

   (A) $300
   (B) $900
   (C) $2,100
   (D) Unlimited

(B) The maximum gain is just three times the $300 in time value on the option. If the stock is anywhere below 30, the put holder will exercise and the writer buys at 30. This leaves her with $3 of the premium after covering the short of 26.

110. As a first transaction, a customer writes some at-the-money calls. How much must he place on deposit?

   (A) Initial margin
   (B) Initial margin plus the premium
   (C) Initial margin minus the premium
   (D) Just the premium

(B) Since the premium is collected, the money he must deposit is reduced by that amount.

111. How large is the spread on a Treasury-note quote of 110:12 bid, 110:28 asked?

   (A) $1.50
   (B) $1.60
   (C) $5.00
   (D) $8.00

(C) The spread is $\frac{16}{32}$ of a point, which is $5.

112. Being long a straddle would be profitable whenever the market price:

   (A) exceeds the sum of the two strike prices
   (B) differs from the strike price by more than the sum of the two premiums
   (C) is less than the sum of the strike prices
   (D) differs from the strike price by less than the sum of the two premiums

(B) Being long means buying the call and the put; hence, it is profitable when the market price moves away from the strike price by more than the sum of the premiums.

113. A 7% bond is trading at 105. To the nearest 0.1%, what is the current yield?

   (A) 6.2%
   (B) 6.4%
   (C) 6.7%
   (D) 7%

(C) The current yield is $70 ÷ $1050 = 6.66%

114. The concession on a municipal offering is the discount available to:

   (A) a syndicate member
   (B) a member of the selling group
   (C) the syndicate manager
   (D) a large customer

   (B) The concession is that discount which the syndicate gives a member of the selling group.

115. The offer price for a mutual fund is $12.50. If the load is 8%, what is the NAV?

   (A) $13.50
   (B) $12.50
   (C) $11.50
   (D) $11.00

   (C) 8% of $12.50 is $1, so the NAV is $11.50.

116. A fund with an NAV of $11 sells for $10.50. It is a(n):

   (A) no-load fund
   (B) closed-end fund
   (C) front-load fund
   (D) open-end fund

   (B) Since it is selling at a discount to NAV, it can only be a closed-end fund.

   Answer Questions 117–119 on the basis of the following trades:

   Buy 2 ACI Dec 70 calls at 5 and 2 ACI Dec 70 puts at 2.

117. What is the maximum possible loss on these trades?

   (A) Unlimited
   (B) $300
   (C) $700
   (D) $1,400

   (D) The maximum loss will occur if both options expire unexercised, and he loses both premiums.

118. What is the maximum possible gain?

   (A) Unlimited
   (B) $300
   (C) $700
   (D) $1,400

   (A) The maximum gain is unlimited since the stock could go up indefinitely, and he owns some calls.

119. If ACI goes to 100 at expiration and there is no previous execution, what will be the gain (or loss)?

(A) $4,600
(B) $6,000
(C) $7,400
(D) $10,000

(A) If it goes to 100, the calls are $30 in the money, which is $6,000 less the premiums of $1,400.

120. An investor sells 1 SF Oct 70 put at 2.1. If the Swiss franc contract is for 125,000 SF and the option is exercised when the SF is at 69, the investor will realize a:

(A) $1,375 loss
(B) $1,250 loss
(C) $1,250 gain
(D) $1,375 gain

(D) The premium of 2.1 is reduced by the one penny that the SF is in the money leaving 1.1 times 125,000 cents, or $1,375.

121. A fundamental trader would use all of the following EXCEPT:

(A) earnings per share
(B) double bottom
(C) leading indicators
(D) the current ratio

(B) Double bottoms are a chart pattern used by technical traders. All of the others are fundamental information.

122. All of the following are considerations in avoiding a wash sale EXCEPT:

(A) coupon
(B) riskiness
(C) maturity
(D) accrued interest

(D) The accrued interest merely counts income since the last coupon payment and does not affect "wash" sales.

123. An investor buys a 6% out-of-state revenue bond. If she pays $10 in accrued interest and collects that year's coupon payments, her federal tax liability is:

(A) $0
(B) $10
(C) $50
(D) $60

(A) Since it is a municipal bond, there is no federal tax liability.

124. If the Fed raises the target for the fed funds rate:

    (A) the Fed is loosening
    (B) the Fed is tightening
    (C) the Fed wants to speed up the economy
    (D) the prime rate will decrease

  (B) Raising rates makes it harder to borrow money.

125. Under NASD Uniform Practice Code, all of the following are good deliveries on a 400-share trade EXCEPT:

    (A) six certificates of 60 shares and one 40-share certificate
    (B) one 400-share certificate
    (C) two 200-share certificates
    (D) four 60s and eight 20s

  (A) Certificates must be summable into round lots of 100 or multiples of 100 shares.

ANSWER EXPLANATIONS

PART TWO

Questions 126 and 127 use the following information:

A Direct Participation Program (DPP) statement contains the following:

Revenue	$400,000
Expense	$250,000
Depreciation	$150,000
Interest	$50,000

126. The income for this DPP is:

    (A) $50,000 loss
    (B) $0
    (C) $100,000 gain
    (D) $150,000 gain

  (A) The income is revenue minus all of the other items.

127. The cash flow for this DPP is:

    (A) $50,000
    (B) $0
    (C) $100,000
    (D) $150,000

  (C) The cash flow ignores depreciation. There is $400,000 of cash in and $300,000 of cash out for a cash flow of $100,000.

128. Which of the following is not a liquidity measure?

   (A) Current ratio
   (B) Net working capital
   (C) Quick ratio
   (D) Debt ratio

   (D) The debt ratio measures equity to debt; all of the others compare current assets to current liabilities, which is a way of measuring liquidity.

129. Under the UGMA:

   (A) each parent may give a minor up to $10,000 per year
   (B) gifts may be reclaimed within the first year
   (C) each minor may have only one custodian for any one gift
   (D) twins may have joint custodians

   (C) All of the others are false. Remember that gift size is unlimited, but gifts over $10,000 are taxable.

130. If the four-week average number of shares traded is 25,000 and an investor owns 10% of the 12,000,000 shares outstanding, the most he can sell under Rule 144 is:

   (A) no shares
   (B) 12,000 shares
   (C) 25,000 shares
   (D) 120,000 shares

   (D) He can sell the larger of 1% of the outstanding shares or the average number traded over a four-week period.

The following Balance Sheet is the basis for Questions 131–134:

Cash $200,000	Accounts Payable $200,000
Accounts Receivable $200,000	Interest Payable $100,000
Inventory $400,000	Declared Annual Dividend $100,000
Current Assets $800,000	Current Liabilities $400,000
Fixed Assets $1,200,000	Long-Term Debt $600,000
Total Assets $2,000,000	Total Liabilities $1,000,000
	Common Stock ($2 par) $200,000
	Paid in Excess $300,000
	Retained Earnings $500,000
	Total Shareholders' Equity $1,000,000

131. The current ratio is:

    (A) .5
    (B) 1
    (C) 1.5
    (D) 2

 (D) The current ratio is current assets divided by current liabilities.

132. The dividend is:

    (A) $.50 per share
    (B) $1.00 per share
    (C) $1.50 per share
    (D) cannot be determined

 (B) The $2 par value implies that there are 100,000 shares outstanding, which means that the dividend is $1 per share.

133. If the dividend payout ratio is .25, then earnings per share are:

    (A) $1
    (B) $2
    (C) $3
    (D) $4

 (D) A payout ratio of .25 means that EPS are four times the dividend or $4.

134. If ACI is currently selling for $60, the P/E is:

    (A) 15
    (B) 20
    (C) 30
    (D) 60

 (A) With a price of $60 and earnings of $4 the P/E is 15.

135. For an investor in the 28% bracket, a 6% municipal has an after-tax yield equivalent to that of a:

    (A) 6% T-bond
    (B) 6.6% corporate
    (C) 7.3% T-note
    (D) 8% corporate

 (C) The equivalent yield is 6% ÷ (1 − .28) = 7.3%.

136. ACI makes a rights offering of 500,000 shares. There are currently 2,500,000 shares outstanding. The number of rights necessary to buy 10 shares is:

    (A) 5
    (B) 10
    (C) 50
    (D) 100

(C) With 2,500,000 shares outstanding, it takes five rights to buy one share. Therefore, 10 shares require 50 rights.

137. If the subscription price in the above rights offering is $40 and the shares trade at $41 cum rights, the value of a right is:

    (A) .05
    (B) .25
    (C) .50
    (D) 1.00

(B) Since it takes five rights for one share, the theoretical value is $1 \div (5-1)$ rights, or .25.

138. The highest noninvestment grade bond rating is:

    (A) BBB
    (B) BB
    (C) B1
    (D) B

(B) Investment grade begins at BBB or Baa.

139. A margin account has $30,000 of securities long and $20,000 of securities short. The debit balance is $16,000, and the credit balance is $35,000. What is the margin requirement?

    (A) $15,000
    (B) $20,000
    (C) $25,000
    (D) $40,000

(C) The margin requirement is $\frac{1}{2}$ of the market value for each account; so for the long account, it is $15,000 and for the short account, it is $10,000 for a total of $25,000.

140. For the account of the previous question, what is the SMA?

    (A) $0
    (B) $2,000
    (C) $4,000
    (D) $9,000

(C) The equity in the account is $30,000–$16,000 long and $35,000 – $20,000 short for a total of $29,000. Hence, the SMA is $4,000.

141. If the long account went to $20,000 and the short account went to $30,000, what would the margin call be?

    (A) $0
    (B) $2,000

(C) $4,000
(D) $5,000

(D) If the long account is at $20,000, the minimum is 25% of that or $5,000. For the short account, it is 30% of $30,000 or $9,000 for a total of $14,000. Since his current equity is $20,000 – $16,000 + $35,000 – $30,000 or $9,000, the margin call is for $5,000.

142. Instinet is a trading system in the:

(A) fourth market
(B) third market
(C) second market
(D) first market

(A) It is a trading system used by institutions to trade amongst themselves.

143. Convertible securities afford the investor the advantage of:

(A) higher yields
(B) lower yields
(C) possible participation in future growth
(D) none of the above

(C) The issuer can offer lower yields with a convertible security because the investor gets the advantage of possible participation in future growth.

144. The spread in an initial public offering depends on:

(A) the financial track record of the issuer
(B) the issuer's industry
(C) the size of the issue
(D) all of the above

(D) All of these affect the riskiness of the issue and, hence, the cost of under-writing, which is the spread.

145. For a municipal with interest payments on March 15 and September 15, how many days of accrued interest will be paid by a buyer on July 10 for regular settlement?

(A) 117 days
(B) 118 days
(C) 119 days
(D) 120 days

(B) Accrued interest is based on a 30-day month beginning on the last pay-ment day and up to the day before settlement. In this case: 16 days in March; 30 in April, May, and June; and 12 in July up to settlement day on July 13, for a total of 118 days.

146. In a 3 for 2 stock split of a stock selling for $60, the adjusted price would be:

    (A) $90
    (B) $40
    (C) $30
    (D) $20

(B) The adjustment must keep the total value constant. Before the split, 100 shares was worth $6,000, so afterwards 150 shares is worth the same, or $40 per share.

147. A firm would use an investment banker for all of the following services EXCEPT:

    (A) maintaining a secondary market for the first few weeks after an IPO
    (B) securing financing
    (C) underwriting a secondary issuance
    (D) distributing a large block held for two years by an insider

(A) All of the others are services that an investment banker does provide; an investment banker does not maintain a secondary market.

148. Auctions for one-year T-bills are held:

    (A) daily
    (B) weekly
    (C) monthly
    (D) quarterly

(C) Three- and six-month bills are auctioned weekly, but one-year bills are auctioned monthly.

149. Refunding of a corporate bond could do all of the following EXCEPT:

    (A) change the corporate debt-to-equity ratio
    (B) change the maturity of the debt structure
    (C) lower interest costs
    (D) remove restrictive covenants

(A) Refunding will not change the amount of debt outstanding, so the debt-to-equity ratio remains unchanged. All of the others are possible benefits of the refunding.

The following table is for Questions 150–152:

	ACI	CAI	ABC	CBA
Dividend payment	$.40	$.05	$.80	$1.00
Earnings/share	$1.20	$3.00	$1.20	$2.00
Price/Earnings	15	25	13.25	17

150. The firm that is most likely to be a growth firm is:

    (A) ACI
    (B) CAI
    (C) ABC
    (D) CBA

(B) CAI's dividend payout ratio is very low, which means it needs most of its earnings for reinvestment. In addition, it has the highest PE, which is another sign of a growth company.

151. The firm with the highest market price is:

    (A) ACI
    (B) CAI
    (C) ABC
    (D) CBA

(B) With earnings of $3 and a PE of 25, CAI's market price is $75, which is the highest by far of all of these.

152. The firm that is most likely to be a utility is:

    (A) ACI
    (B) CAI
    (C) ABC
    (D) CBA

(C) ABC has a dividend payout of 66%, which is high and is the highest among these companies.

153. The balance sheet equation is best stated as:

    (A) total assets plus shareholders' equity equals total liabilities
    (B) total liabilities equals total assets plus shareholders' equity
    (C) total assets plus total liabilities equals shareholders' equity
    (D) total assets minus total liabilities equals shareholders' equity

(D) The left side of the balance sheet is total assets. These have been paid for partly with debt, that is, total liabilities; the rest is shareholders' equity.

154. A corporation's 3,000,000 authorized shares include 2,500,000 issued and 500,000 treasury stock. If the corporation earns $1,000,000, its earnings per share are:

    (A) $.33
    (B) $.40
    (C) $.50
    (D) $2.00

(C) Only shares that have been issued and remain in public hands are used to compute EPS. In this case, there are 2,000,000 such shares.

155. A bond secured by marketable securities is called a(n):

    (A) collateral trust bond
    (B) revenue bond
    (C) mortgage bond
    (D) equipment trust certificate

(A) The securities are deposited with the trustee. They may not be the securities of the issuer, but could be those of a subsidiary of the issuer.

156. The yield to maturity of an 8% 20-year bond selling at 80 is approximately:

    (A) 8%
    (B) 8.4%
    (C) 9%
    (D) 10%

(D) Using the approximation for YTM coupon plus annual accretion divided by average of market and maturity price we get $\left(\$80 + \frac{\$200}{20}\right) \div \$900 = 10\%$.

157. A "cash" settlement of a municipal bond purchase settles:

    (A) the same day
    (B) the next day
    (C) three days later
    (D) depends on the size of the transaction

(A) Cash settlement is always on the trade date.

158. Firms that make a market OTC are:

    (A) brokers
    (B) dealers
    (C) specialists
    (D) OTC brokers

(B) As market makers, they are dealers, although such firms also act as brokers.

159. Initial margin requirements are determined by:

    (A) NYSE
    (B) Federal Reserve Board
    (C) SEC
    (D) NYSE and FRB

(B) The FRB has sole responsibility to set initial margin requirements. The NYSE sets maintenance requirements, and member firms can choose to have higher maintenance requirements.

160. A limited partner's liability is limited to:

    (A) cash outlay
    (B) cash outlay plus any recourse loans
    (C) cash outlay plus nonrecourse loans
    (D) cash outlay plus any profits

 (B) The limits of his liability are his investment and any loans for which he is
    responsible, *i.e.,* recourse loans.

161. A corporation would ordinarily get the highest yield from:

    (A) 6% preferred dividend
    (B) 6% government bond
    (C) 7% corporate bond
    (D) 7% commercial paper

 (A) Stock dividends are usually 70% tax exempt for corporations. Thus, a
    corporation which has to pay corporate taxes would usually do best with
    the preferred stock.

162. To retain the tax exempt status for an IRA which has been closed, a
    client must roll it into a new one within:

    (A) immediately
    (B) 30 days
    (C) 60 days
    (D) the current quarter

 (C) The 60-day rule also applies to lump sum payments from qualified pen-
    sion plans.

163. Which of the following groups do not have enforcement responsibility
    for MSRB rules?

    (A) NYSE and NASD
    (B) FRB and Comptroller of the Currency
    (C) FDIC and FRB
    (D) NASD and FDIC

 (A) Of the groups named in all of the choices, only the NYSE does not have
    this responsibility, although NASD does.

164. Under normal conditions on the yield curve, the order for securities
    ranked by decreasing yield is:

    (A) T-bonds, corporate bonds, T-notes, T-bills
    (B) corporate bonds, T-bonds, T-notes, T-bills
    (C) T-bills, T-notes, T-bonds, corporate bonds
    (D) depends on the prime rate

 (B) Ordinarily the yield curve increases with maturity, and corporate bonds
    would be riskier than T-bonds and have the highest yield.

165. An underwriting agreement in which members are responsible only for their own portion is called a(n):

    (A) Western agreement
    (B) Eastern agreement
    (C) undivided account
    (D) severally and jointly account

    (A) All of the other terms are used in connection with agreements where all of the members are jointly responsible for any unsold amounts.

166. An investor has an account with $300,000 in cash and $200,000 in securities. The maximum he could receive from the SIPC is:

    (A) all $500,000
    (B) $300,000 cash and $100,000 securities
    (C) $100,000 cash and $200,000 securities
    (D) $100,000 cash and $100,000 securities

    (C) While the SIPC affords up to $500,000 in coverage, the limit on cash coverage is $100,000.

167. Options expire on the:

    (A) third Friday of the month
    (B) Friday following the third Saturday
    (C) third Saturday following the third Friday
    (D) third Saturday of the month

    (C) The key is that they stop trading on the third Friday and expire the next day.

168. An investor buys shares in a mutual fund in August. In October, the fund distributes long-term capital gains. For this investor, these are taxed as:

    (A) ordinary income
    (B) short-term capital gains
    (C) long-term capital gains
    (D) part-long term and part short-term gains

    (C) The fund acts as a conduit for the investors, and hence, any gains are passed through as they exist.

169. The investment company that has the least active management of the portfolio is likely to be:

    (A) an index fund
    (B) a closed-end fund
    (C) an open-end fund
    (D) a unit investment trust

    (D) While parts of the original portfolio of such a fund may be sold, they cannot be reinvested; so after the initial purchases, there is no more active management of the account.

170. A spread that includes 1 ACI Mar 60 call and 1 ACI Jul 60 call is called a:

   (A) vertical spread
   (B) bull spread
   (C) horizontal spread
   (D) bear spread

(C) Vertical spreads have varying prices, while horizontal or time spreads have the same price and different expiration months.

171. If a municipal bond has been prerefunded, the bonds are:

   (A) paid off immediately
   (B) paid off when they mature
   (C) held in escrow
   (D) still the responsibility of the issuer even though they are secured

(B) The proceeds of a new issue are used to buy treasury securities, which are held in escrow. The old bonds are paid off at maturity, and the responsibility for these bonds is now with the escrow agent.

172. The type of bond that is most price sensitive to changes in interest rates is a:

   (A) junk bond
   (B) zero
   (C) T-bill
   (D) noninvestment-grade bond

(B) While junk or noninvestment-grade bonds are price sensitive, a zero, which makes no interest payments until maturity, has the most price volatility with respect to changing interest rates.

173. All of the following are not direct obligations of the U.S. government EXCEPT:

   (A) GNMA
   (B) FNMA
   (C) Freddie Mac
   (D) Sallie Mae

(A) Only GNMAs are directly backed by the government. The others are backed by agencies sponsored by the government and are also very safe.

174. With respect to customer accounts, member firms are required to do all of the following EXCEPT:

   (A) maintain current records
   (B) keep all customer complaints on file
   (C) safeguard all customer securities
   (D) have a new account form

(C) Only those securities which are left in street name must be safeguarded. Securities sent directly to the customer are obviously not the firm's responsibility.

175. The tool that the Fed uses most frequently in controlling interest rates is:

    (A) moral suasion
    (B) changing the discount rate
    (C) changing the reserve requirement
    (D) open-market operations

(D) The Fed Open Market Committee meets monthly and often makes daily adjustments to the money supply through its open-market operations.

176. In a "plain vanilla" CMO, repayment of principal occurs:

    (A) uniformly to all tranches
    (B) proportionately to the order of the tranches
    (C) based on the Public Securities Association formula
    (D) completely to one tranche before the next one receives any

(D) This is the simplest form of these securities. All repayments of principal go to the next maturing tranche. Interest payments, however, are distributed to other tranches as well.

177. For income tax purposes, the CMO is considered to:

    (A) be like a bond
    (B) have only interest income
    (C) represent residual interests
    (D) be a limited partnership

(A) They are treated as debt instruments. For CMOs, which are REMICs, residual interests are treated like partners in a partnership.

178. Which of the following sequences contains trades that allow a short sale?

    (A) $9; 9; 8\frac{7}{8}$
    (B) $12; 12\frac{1}{8}; 12\frac{1}{8}$
    (C) $8; 8; 8$
    (D) $7\frac{1}{8}; 7; 7$

(B) This is the only one that has the up tick necessary for a short sale.

179. Bearer bonds have which characteristics?

    I.   They require proof of ownership.
    II. They are highly marketable.
    III. They are in book-entry form.

    (A) I and II
    (B) II and III
    (C) I only
    (D) II only

(D) It is just because possession represents ownership that they are highly marketable.

180. A convertible preferred is convertible at 25. If the preferred is called at 107 and the common is at 26, what is the best course of action?

    (A) Tender the stock
    (B) Convert to common
    (C) Hold the preferred
    (D) It cannot be determined

(A) If it is convertible at 25, the conversion rate is four. Thus, converting would give the holder four shares at 26 for a value of 104, which is less than the 107 call.

181. A margin call is not mandatory if the call is for less than:

    (A) there is no minimum
    (B) $100
    (C) $500
    (D) 10% of the equity

(C) The broker has the option of issuing the call if the amount is less than $500, but she is not required to issue it.

182. For out-of-state residents, State of Virginia bonds are:

    (A) exempt from Virginia taxes
    (B) exempt from all taxes
    (C) exempt from federal taxes
    (D) exempt from federal and Virginia taxes

(C) In-state residents would be exempt from Virginia taxes, but out-of-staters are exempt only from federal taxes.

183. An NASD member may retain part of a "hot issue":

    (A) under no circumstances
    (B) if it is part of its regular trading policy
    (C) if it is an insignificant amount
    (D) if it was previously agreed to

(A) This is never permissible.

184. Writers of call options get the dividend on the underlying stock:

    (A) never
    (B) always
    (C) if the option is exercised before the ex-div date
    (D) if it is a covered call

(D) If the call is covered, they own the underlying stock and, hence, collect the dividend.

The following page from a specialist's book is to be used for Questions 185–187:

BUY	ACI	SELL
200 Prudential	36	
500 Merrill	$36\frac{1}{8}$	
300 Stop Schwab	$36\frac{1}{4}$	
	$36\frac{3}{8}$	
	$36\frac{1}{2}$	400 Merrill
	$36\frac{5}{8}$	300 DWR
	$36\frac{3}{4}$	300 Schwab
		200 Prudential
	$36\frac{7}{8}$	100 Stop DWR

185. The specialist may sell for his own account at no lower than:

   (A) $36\frac{1}{4}$

   (B) $36\frac{3}{8}$

   (C) $36\frac{1}{2}$

   (D) $36\frac{5}{8}$

(B) The specialist must offer at a lower price than any other customer.

186. The current quote and size is:

   (A) $36\frac{1}{4}$–$36\frac{1}{2}$ 1000–1100

   (B) $36\frac{1}{4}$–$36\frac{1}{2}$ 300–400

   (C) $36\frac{1}{8}$–$36\frac{1}{2}$ 300–400

   (D) $36\frac{1}{8}$–$36\frac{1}{2}$ 500–400

(D) The highest bid and the lowest offer excluding stop orders.

187. If the sequence of trades were $36\frac{1}{4}$; $36\frac{3}{8}$; $36\frac{1}{8}$, the Schwab Stop would be filled at:

   (A) $36\frac{1}{8}$

   (B) $36\frac{1}{4}$

   (C) $36\frac{3}{8}$

   (D) it would not be filled

(C) The stop is not a limit but rather a trigger. Once the stop price is met, it becomes a market order.

188. An OTC order for 140 shares must be executed as:

   (A) a single order.
   (B) orders of 100 shares and 40 shares.
   (C) any two orders that total 140.
   (D) orders of 100 shares and 40 shares with no odd-lot premium.

   (A) As long as the order is for more than 100 shares, it is entered as a single order.

   Questions 189–191 are based on Buy 3 ACI Mar 50 calls at 3 when ACI is $50.50.

189. This trade will break even when ACI is at:

   (A) 47
   (B) 50
   (C) 53
   (D) $53\frac{1}{2}$

   (C) The breakeven occurs when the intrinsic value (the in-the-money amount) is equal to the premium.

190. The time value of these options totals:

   (A) $250
   (B) $300
   (C) $750
   (D) $900

   (C) The time value is that part of the premium which is not intrinsic. In this case, ACI, is $.50 in the money, so the time value is three times $2.50.

191. If ACI goes to 48, the investor's gain (loss) will be:

   (A) $900 loss
   (B) $600 loss
   (C) $600 gain
   (D) $900 gain

   (A) With ACI at 48, there is no point to exercising at 50; the investor loses his entire premium.

192. If settlement of $50,000 of 4% municipals maturing on 2-1-08 occurs on 5-1-98, the accrued interest is:

   (A) $250
   (B) $500
   (C) $1,000
   (D) $2,000

   (B) Municipals accrue interest at 30 days per month from the last interest payment up to the day before settlement. In this case, that is exactly 90 days or $\frac{1}{4}$ of a year. Hence, the accrued interest is $\frac{1}{4}$ of the $2,000 in annual interest.

193. An index option is settled by delivery of:

    (A) a market basket of securities
    (B) cash
    (C) an index certificate
    (D) any of these

  (B) It is precisely because it would be difficult to deliver an appropriate basket of stocks that settlement is in cash.

194. The type of security that is likely to do best if the economy weakens is called:

    (A) blue chip
    (B) growth
    (C) counter cyclical
    (D) income

  (C) The name is intended to indicate that its fortunes are counter to the business cycle.

Questions 195–197 are based on the following margin account:

Long Market	$40,000	Short Market	$25,000
Debit Record	$24,000	Credit Record	$40,000
SMA	$4,000		

195. The equity in this account is currently:

    (A) $4,000
    (B) $16,000
    (C) $31,000
    (D) $35,000

  (C) Both the debit balance (record) and the credit balance never change. The equity is the difference between the long market value and the debit record plus the difference between credit record and market value. In this case, that is $16,000 + $15,000 = $31,000.

196. The purchasing power of this account is:

    (A) none; the account is restricted
    (B) equal to half of the equity
    (C) $4,000
    (D) $8,000

  (D) Even if the account is restricted, the SMA is available to the investor, and purchasing power is twice the SMA.

197. If the long market value goes to $35,000 and the short market value goes to $15,000, the margin requirement will become:

    (A) $15,000
    (B) $25,000

    (C) $30,000
    (D) $40,000

(B) The margin requirement is 50% of $35,000 + $15,000, or $25,000.

198. Even if an account is inactive, customers must still receive statements:

    (A) monthly
    (B) quarterly
    (C) semiannually
    (D) annually

(B) Most brokers will send monthly statements unless the account is inactive for a very long time.

199. Changing an accounting system from FIFO to LIFO in an inflationary environment will result in:

    (A) lower profits, lower taxes
    (B) lower profits, higher taxes
    (C) higher profits, lower taxes
    (D) higher profits, higher taxes

(A) The switch to Last In, First Out causes the most expensive inventory to be charged against sales, reducing profits. Reduced profits yield reduced taxes.

200. The payment method that yields the lowest monthly annuity payments is:

    (A) life annuity
    (B) life annuity plus survivors
    (C) 10-year certain
    (D) lump sum

(D) This question is something of a trick since a lump sum means there are no monthly payments.

201. The 8% bonds of ACI, Amalgamated Consolidated Incorporated, mature in 12 years. They are currently trading at 82. An investor owning five of these bonds would get semiannual interest of:

    (A) $200
    (B) $100
    (C) $40
    (D) $20

(A) An 8% bond pays $40 semiannually. Five bonds pay $200.

202. The current yield, to the nearest 0.1%, on these bonds is:

    (A) 8%
    (B) 8.2%

(C) 9.8%

(D) 10%

(C) The current yield is the coupon payment ÷ current price = $80 ÷ $820 = 9.8%.

203. In increasing order, the yields are:

    (A) nominal, current, YTM

    (B) current, YTM, nominal

    (C) YTM, current, nominal

    (D) nominal, YTM, current

(A) A bond at a discount to par has a current yield above the nominal yield. The YTM adds to the income the annual accretion between the discount and par, thereby increasing the yield.

204. The security that represents ownership of overseas companies engaged in foreign trade is a(n):

    (A) banker's acceptance

    (B) ADR

    (C) commercial paper

    (D) Eurobond

(B) American Depository Receipts are the ownership security. Banker's Acceptances facilitate foreign trade but are not ownership certificates. Similarly, Euros are debt instruments.

205. ACI's balance sheet shows $20,000,000 of convertible bonds with a conversion price of 50 and 2,000,000 shares outstanding. The income statement shows earnings of $2,400,000. If the bonds are all called, the earnings per share will be:

    (A) $1.00

    (B) $1.20

    (C) $2.00

    (D) $2.40

(B) If all of the bonds are called, then there are still 2,000,000 shares outstanding; this leads to EPS of $2,400,000 ÷ 2,000,000 = $1.20

206. In the previous problem, if half of the bonds are converted before they are called and ACI declares a dividend of $1,100,000, the dividend per share will be:

    (A) $.46

    (B) $.50

    (C) $.92

    (D) $1.00

(B) A conversion price of $50 means that each bond is converted into 20 shares. Thus, $10,000,000 of bonds are converted into 200,000 shares, and the dividend per share is $1,100,000 ÷ 2,200,000 shares = $.50 per share.

207. An index which is based on 65 common stocks is:

    (A) Value Line
    (B) Dow Jones Industrials
    (C) S&P
    (D) Dow Jones Composite

  (D) It is a composite of 30 industrial, 20 transportation, and 15 utility stocks.

208. The nine-bond rule states that:

    (A) orders for fewer than 10 bonds must be sent to the floor of NYSE
    (B) orders for fewer than 10 bonds go OTC
    (C) orders for six bonds go to the cabinet
    (D) orders for six bonds go to the NYSE unless the customer orders them elsewhere

  (D) The rule says that these orders go to the NYSE, but the customer has the last word.

209. If a stock is held in "street name," it:

    (A) may not be used in a short sale
    (B) lists the broker as the beneficial owner but not the owner of record
    (C) can be borrowed for a short sale
    (D) belongs to a customer beneficially and as a matter of record

  (C) To be held in "street name" means the broker is the owner of record even though the customer is the beneficial owner. These are exactly the shares that may be borrowed for a short sale.

210. The order in which the departments of a brokerage firm process a transaction is:

    (A) order, P&S, margin, cashier
    (B) order, margin, P&S, cashier
    (C) P&S, order, cashier, margin
    (D) P&S, cashier, order, margin

  (A) The logic of this is that, after an order is given, it goes to Purchase and Sale; the margin department checks for margin, and then it goes to the cashier.

211. An investor in the 15% bracket has a single short-term capital gain. The tax rate on this transaction is:

(A) 28%
(B) 20%
(C) 15%
(D) cannot be determined

(C) Short-term capital gains are taxed at the ordinary income rate, in this case 15%.

212. An investor has $100,000 in earnings and $10,000 in investment income. If he also has $12,000 in passive income losses from a DPP, the income subject to taxes that year is:

(A) $110,000
(B) $100,000
(C) $98,000
(D) $88,000

(A) Passive losses can be deducted only against passive income gains, of which there are none here. Thus, all $110,000 of his income is subject to tax.

213. An investment letter is most often required in conjunction with a(n):

(A) intrastate offering
(B) new issue
(C) closed-end mutual fund
(D) private placement

(D) The purpose of the letter is to attest that the investor intends to keep the security and not, resell it to the general public, thereby avoiding the registration requirements of public offerings, hence a "private placement."

214. A bond that has no specific asset as its security is called a:

(A) general obligation bond
(B) junior security
(C) collateral trust certificate
(D) debenture

(D) The term "debenture" is specifically used for these bonds.

215. The document laying out all of the terms of a bond issue is called the:

(A) indenture
(B) legal opinion
(C) covenant of loan
(D) trust agreement

(A) It is also called the "deed of trust."

216. The options strategy with the least risk is:

(A) write a call, sell the stock short
(B) write a call, buy the stock

(C) write a put, sell the stock short
(D) write a put, buy the stock

(B) Buying the stock risks the price of the shares; writing a call reduces that risk by the amount of the premium. Selling the stock short has an unlimited risk which, even if reduced by the collecting of a premium, is still a higher risk.

217. "Rehypothecation" is the term used to describe:

(A) the right of the broker to use the customer's shares as collateral
(B) the right to lend the customer's shares
(C) the right of the broker to pledge the customer's shares to a lender
(D) the right of the customer to avoid having his shares used as collateral

(C) The customer "hypothecates" his shares as security for the broker's loan of margin. The broker rehypothecates these to a bank to secure the loan, which he then gives to the customer.

218. The maintenance margin requirement for the purchase of $50,000 par value municipals selling at 80 is:

(A) $2,800
(B) $3,500
(C) $6,000
(D) $7,500

(C) The maintenance requirement is the larger of 7% of par = $3,500 and 15% of market = .15 × $40,000 = $6,000.

219. An investor opens a margin account with an initial purchase of 200 shares at $9. He must deposit:

(A) $900
(B) $1,800
(C) $2,000
(D) $3,000

(B) While a minimum deposit of $2,000 is normally required in a margin account, in this case, $1,800 pays for the shares completely and is all that is required.

220. The premium on a T-bond option is 1.04. A buyer of this option would pay:

(A) $1,040
(B) $1,125
(C) $10,400
(D) $11,125

(B) The option is for $100,000 of bonds, and the premium is $1\frac{4}{32}$, or $11.25 per $1,000 for a total of $1,125.

221. When interest rates rise, the premiums on debt put options will:

    (A) rise
    (B) fall
    (C) move toward out-of-the-money
    (D) not change

(A) If rates rise, prices fall, and existing put options become more valuable.

222. When issuing a BAN, a municipality expects to pay it off with:

    (A) general tax revenues
    (B) anticipated tax increases
    (C) anticipated sales of municipal property
    (D) revenues from an upcoming bond sale

(D) BAN stands for bond anticipation note.

223. Cash flow is calculated by:

    (A) adding depreciation to after-tax earnings
    (B) subtracting depreciation from after-tax earnings
    (C) adding depreciation to before-tax earnings
    (D) subtracting depreciation from before-tax earnings

(A) Depreciation is subtracted from revenues but does not represent actual cash outlays. Hence, the cash flow is the after-tax income plus the depreciation.

224. A portfolio with a beta of 1.2 would:

    (A) grow at 20% under normal market conditions
    (B) be less risky than an S&P index fund
    (C) would grow by 1.2% when the whole market was flat
    (D) would shrink by 6% if the market dropped 5%

(D) Beta represents the volatility of a stock or a portfolio. It is assumed that the market as a whole has a volatility of one, so if the market dropped 5%, the portfolio would drop 1.2 of 5%, or 6%.

225. A portfolio with $10,000,000 and a beta of 1.8 is to be completely hedged by S&P 500 options. If the index is at 900, one would buy:

    (A) 22 puts
    (B) 22 calls
    (C) 40 puts
    (D) 40 calls

(C) Each option represents $500 \times 900 = \$450,000$. With a beta of 1.8, the portfolio moves the equivalent of $18,000,000 of the S&P. Hence, 40 options have the same value as the portfolio. To hedge the portfolio is to protect it against dropping prices. Buying puts is such a hedge.

226. An investor writing a T-bill call to hedge his portfolio of $1,000,000 of T-bills would deposit:

    (A) 15% of face minus the premium
    (B) 20% of market value minus the premium
    (C) nothing at all
    (D) the greater of A or B

   (C) This is a covered call and needs no margin deposit.

227. An underwriter may not send any of the following to a prospective customer EXCEPT:

    (A) a reprint of an article which has already appeared in a magazine
    (B) a preliminary prospectus
    (C) Moody's credit evaluation
    (D) a newspaper story

   (B) While all of the others may be public information, they are forms of solicitation, which are not allowed.

228. The only one of the following not considered a "control person" is:

    (A) an outside director
    (B) an owner of 5% of the shares
    (C) the son of a principal
    (D) the treasurer of the firm who owns no shares

   (B) A stockholder must own 10% of the shares to be considered a "control person."

229. A customer who bought 1 ACI Jun 50 call and sold 1 ACI Jun 60 call would have put on a(n):

    (A) horizontal spread
    (B) straddle
    (C) bear spread
    (D) bull spread

   (D) The investor hopes the price rises to 60 or more.

230. If the investor of the previous question had paid $4 and collected $1:

    (A) his maximum gain could be $700 and his maximum loss $300
    (B) his maximum gain could be $300 and his maximum loss $700
    (C) his maximum gain could be unlimited and his maximum loss $300
    (D) his maximum gain could be unlimited and his maximum loss $700

   (A) If the stock goes to 60, he gains $10 minus the difference in premiums: $3 × 100. If it goes to 50, both options are worthless, and he loses the difference in premiums, which is $300.

231. The writer of an ACI Jun 60 put is covered by:

    (A) owning an ACI Mar 60 put
    (B) being long 100 shares of ACI
    (C) writing an ACI Jun 60 call
    (D) owning an ACI Aug 60 put

    (D) Owning the later put means that the owner could offset any exercise of the put she wrote by exercising her own put.

232. Which of the following is not an advantage of issuing convertible debt?

    (A) Stock price at conversion
    (B) The interest rate of the debt
    (C) Tax consequences of conversion
    (D) These are all advantages

    (C) Since debt payments are deductible and dividends are not, the tax consequences of conversion are a disadvantage.

233. In general, the maturity of a GNMA is:

    (A) always shorter than that of a CMO
    (B) always longer than that of a CMO
    (C) varies more than that of a CMO
    (D) less dependent on prepayments than that of a CMO

    (C) GNMAs mature when all of the mortgages have been paid off. This is affected by the prepayment rate. CMO tranches have more narrowly defined maturities, some of which are short and some long. Only the last tranches have maturities that can be as variable as those of GNMAs.

234. A T-bond which last paid interest on March 15 was bought for cash on June 12. How many days of accrued interest are there?

    (A) 87 days
    (B) 88 days
    (C) 89 days
    (D) 90 days

    (C) Treasuries accrue interest on a 365-day basis from the last day interest was paid. In this case, we have 17 days in March, 30 in April, 31 in May, and 11 in June since the transaction was cash settlement, for a total of 89 days.

235. A municipal bond issue from an "overlapping" tax jurisdiction:

    (A) is riskier than an issue from a non-overlapping one
    (B) has two sources of revenue
    (C) is exempt from both federal and state taxes
    (D) is none of the above

(A) Overlapping jurisdiction means that there are two sources of taxes for the same jurisdiction, *e.g.*, a city and a county. This lessens the ability of the taxpayers to pay and makes the issue riskier.

236. The management company that manages a mutual fund can be:

    (A) compensated based on performance of the fund
    (B) made up of the directors of the fund
    (C) compensated by a percentage of the assets under management
    (D) all of the above

(C) It is expressly forbidden to be compensated on the basis of performance, and at least 40% of the directors of the fund must be unaffiliated with the managers.

237. An investor enters an order to sell 100 ACI short on a stop limit of $25\frac{3}{4}$. The last recorded round lot sale was at 26. Subsequently, there are round lot sales at $25\frac{5}{8}$, $25\frac{5}{8}$, $25\frac{7}{8}$, and $25\frac{3}{4}$. The sale that triggers the order is:

    (A) $25\frac{5}{8}$
    (B) $25\frac{3}{4}$
    (C) $25\frac{7}{8}$
    (D) 26

(A) A sell stop is an order to sell if the market goes at or below the stop point. In this case, the first transaction does that.

238. The order is executed at:

    (A) $25\frac{5}{8}$
    (B) $25\frac{3}{4}$
    (C) $25\frac{7}{8}$
    (D) 26

(B) To sell short, you need an up tick. $25\frac{7}{8}$ is an up tick so the sale takes place at the next transaction.

239. The securities used as collateral in a rehypothecation are limited in value to:

    (A) 50% of the loan
    (B) 70% of the loan
    (C) 100% of the loan
    (D) 140% of the loan

(D) A bank will typically lend up to 70% of the value of the collateral. Since 70% of 140% is 98%, the bank will lend essentially the full amount of the loan.

240. None of the following are available to an exploratory drilling program EXCEPT:

    (A) current income
    (B) low risk
    (C) investment tax credit
    (D) depletion

  (D) These programs are very risky, offer no current income, and are not eligible for an investment tax credit. They do, however, offer the possibility of offsetting income through the depletion allowance.

  Questions 241–243 are based on the following information:

  A syndicate underwrites an offering of 8 million shares to be sold at $22. Of the 8 million shares, 2 million are allocated to the selling group. The issuer is to receive $21 per share, the selling concession is $.55, and the management fee is $.10.

241. The total spread is:

    (A) $.55
    (B) $.90
    (C) $1.00
    (D) $1.10

  (C) The shares are sold to the public for $22, and the issuer is to realize $21, so the total spread is $1.

242. How much money will the managing underwriter get for his management services?

    (A) $600,000
    (B) $800,000
    (C) $1,000,000
    (D) Depends on how many the selling group actually sells

  (B) The managing underwriter gets $.10 for every share sold regardless of who sells it. Since there are 8 million shares, he gets $800,000.

243. How much will a syndicate member realize for shares sold by the selling group?

    (A) $.35
    (B) $.55
    (C) $.65
    (D) $.90

  (A) If the concession is $.55 and the manager gets $.10, the syndicate member gets $.35.

  Questions 244 and 245 are based on the following excerpt from the ticker:

  ACI Pr 45s 98 CAI. SLD 55 ACI 3s 25

244. The CAI trade shows:

    (A) 100 shares of CAI sold short
    (B) 100 shares of CAI at 45 reported out of sequence
    (C) 100 shares CAI at 45
    (D) 100 shares CAI at 45 in a delayed opening

(B) SLD is the symbol for trades reported out of sequence.

245. The total number of ACI preferred reported is:

    (A) 45 shares
    (B) 450 shares
    (C) 4,500 shares
    (D) 1,020 shares

(C) The *s* refers to the number of round lots, so 4,500 shares were traded.

246. A custodial account for a three-year-old must have a social security or tax I.D. number for the:

    (A) custodian
    (B) guardian
    (C) child
    (D) child or the custodian

(C) The tax liability belongs to the child, so his number is on the account.

247. The efficient market hypothesis claims that certain information is not helpful for predicting prices. In the strong form, it claims that:

    (A) technical analysis is not helpful
    (B) fundamental analysis is not helpful
    (C) insider information is not helpful
    (D) none of these is helpful

(D) It is called the strong form because it makes the strongest claim. Most now think that there is good evidence for the weak form, especially for widely followed stocks, and some for the semi-strong form. However, most people believe that insider information is useful for predicting stock price movements.

248. In an OTC transaction, the spread refers to the:

    (A) difference between the bid and the asked
    (B) markup from cost
    (C) 5% rule
    (D) fair and reasonable commissions which are NASD policy

(A) The spread is just the difference between bid and asked.

702 **Series 7:** STOCKBROKER EXAM

249. A covered-call writer of German-mark options must have available to him:

    (A) U.S. dollars
    (B) German marks
    (C) either one since settlement is in cash
    (D) Eurodollars

(B) A call writer must be able to deliver the asset (DM in this case) if the option is exercised.

250. Limited trading authority allows one to:

    (A) enter orders without further authorization
    (B) withdraw securities from an account
    (C) withdraw cash from the account only to pay for a transaction
    (D) none of the above

(A) The authority is limited to trading. Assets may not be removed from the account.

index

Symbols

5% Markup, 173-176
365-Day High-Low, 362
401(k) plans, 134

A

abbreviated quotes, 196
Accelerated Cost Recovery System (ACRS),
    125-126
accounts. *See also* margin accounts
  bookkeeping, 260, 262
  cashiering, 260, 262
  client confirmations, 259
  controller, 261
  corporate, 252-253, 262
  credit agreement, 252
  custodial, 254-255, 262
  death of account holder, 257-258, 262
  discretionary, 256
  dividends, 261-262
  fiduciary, 253-254, 262
  hypothecation agreement, 252, 386-387
  individual, 252, 257, 261
  investment advisors', 254, 262
  joint, 252, 258, 262
  loan consent agreement, 252
  new account form, 221, 250-251, 261
  numbered, 257, 262
  opening, 249-250
  options agreement, 252
  ordering departments, 260-262
  partnership, 253, 258, 262
  power of attorney, 252, 257-258
  proxies, 262-262
  purchase and sales (P&S), 260, 262
  "refusal to receive duplicate information," 257
  registered representative, 260
  reorganization, 261
  restrictions, 256
  rights of survivorship, 258
  second, 257
  tenants in common, 258
  tickets, 258-259, 262
  transaction reports, 259-260
  unincorporated associations, 253, 262
accrued interest
  bonds, 44, 54-55, 65, 70, 73
  debt instruments, 354

accumulation, mutual funds breakpoints, 95, 107
active trading of bonds, 194, 199
adjustment (income) bonds, 40, 69
ADRs (American Depository Receipts), 21-22
advanced-decline (breadth of market) theory,
      315-316, 340
aliens, 256
All or None order, 186, 198
alpha, market returns, 341
American Depository Receipts (ADRs), 21-22
annuities
    contracts, 131, 138
    fixed, 126-127, 137
    income taxes, 131, 138
    payouts, 130, 138
    purchasing options, 129-130, 138
    sales charges, 131, 138
    variables, 127-129, 138
arbitrage, bond conversion, 43
Articles of Incorporation, 11
ask price (mutual funds), 93, 106
assets
    REITs, 123
    utilization ratio, 330
assignment of stocks, 15, 22
at the money option, 239
auction rules, exchange markets, 183-184, 197
automatic response, fiscal policy, 311, 339
authorized stock (authorized shares), 12, 21
automating exchange market orders, 186, 198
averages, 313, 340

B

balance sheets (securities), 320, 341
    assets, 321
    equity (net worth), 322
    liabilities, 321-322
balanced mutual funds, 92
balloon bonds
    maturity, 32, 68
    serials, 61
banker's acceptances, 82-84
bankruptcy, 196, 253
basis book, 37
bearer (coupon) bonds, 30-31, 59, 68, 73
below investment grade bonds, 41, 70
benefit plans, 132-133
beta, characteristic line slope, 341
bidding
    mutual funds, 93, 106
    over-the-counter (OTC) quotes, 170, 176
    securities, 156-157
    special, 187, 198
block transactions
    exchange distribution, 188, 198
    secondary distribution, 189-190
    special offer/special bid, 187-188, 198
    specialist, 188, 198
blue chips, 13
The Blue List, 64, 156, 160, 369
blue-skying, securities, 151, 160
bondholders' rights, 69
Bond Buyer Index, 156, 160, 372
bonds, 67
    active trading, 194, 199
    basics, 29-30

bearer (coupon), 30-31, 59, 68, 73
below investment grade, 41, 70
bondholders' rights, 69
book-entry, 31, 68
cabinet trading, 194, 199
call procedures/provisions, 33, 61, 69
certificates, 68
conversion, 41, 70
    arbitrage, 43
    conditions, 70
    duration, 43
    forced, 44
    parity, 43, 70
    prices, 42-43, 70
    ratio, 42, 70
    rights, 43
corporate, 37-38, 69
debt securities, 69
defeasance, 32
Eurobonds, 46, 70
funded debt, 30, 67
government issue
    collateralized mortgage obligations (CMOs),
      52-54, 72
    CMS structure, 72
    delivery, 55, 72-73
    exempt, 70
    Federal Farm Credit Bank, 50, 71
    Federal Home Loan Bank, 51, 71
    Federal Home Loan Mortgage Corporation
      (Freddie Mac), 51, 71
    Federal National Mortgage Association
      (FNMA/Fannie Mae), 51, 71
    financial news, 365
    "flower," 71
    Government National Mortgage Association
      (GNMA/Ginnie Mae), 52, 71
    Inter-American Development Bank, 54, 72
    negotiable, 70
    non-negotiable, 71
    Series EE, 49-50, 71
    Series HH, 50, 71
    strips (Treasury receipts), 49, 71
    Student Loan Marketing Association (SLMA/
      Sallie Mae), 52
    Treasury bills, 46-48, 70-71
    Treasury bonds, 48, 71
    Treasury notes, 48, 71
    World Bank, 54, 72
    zero-coupon, 41, 49, 70
guaranteed, 41, 70
income (adjustment), 40, 69
interest, 59-61
    accrued, 44, 54-55, 65, 70, 73
    rates, 34, 69
maturity dates, 30, 32, 68
members, 182, 197
municipal, 55, 64, 92
    concessions, 65, 73
    debt obligations, 72
    default, 67
    double-barreled, 57-58, 72
    flow of funds, 73
    general obligation (G.O.), 56, 66-67, 72
    income taxes, 62
    indenture, 60, 73
    industrial revenue, 58, 72

insurance, 62, 73
legal opinion, 59-60, 73
moral obligation, 58, 72
New Housing Authority (NHA), 72
notes, 72
over-the-counter, 73
owner, 59
payment, 73
pollution control, 58, 72
principal, 59-61
revenue, 57, 67, 72
short-term, 59
special tax, 57, 72-73
tender offers, 61, 73
workable quotes, 65, 73
mutual funds, 92
nine bond rule, 194-195, 199
par value, 30, 67, 353
points, 69
prerefunding (advanced), 32, 69
pricing, 33-34, 69, 194, 199
put procedures/provisions, 33, 61, 69
quotations, 36-37, 195, 199
ratings, 45, 66-68, 73
redeeming, 33
refunding, 32, 69
registered, 31, 68, 73
secured
    closed-end, 39
    collateral trust, 39, 69
    Equipment Trust Certificates (ETCs), 40, 69
    first mortgage (senior lien), 39
    open-end, 39
    second mortgage (junior lien), 39
serial, 31, 61, 68, 73
series, 31, 68
sinking fund (call), 32-33, 68-69
swaps, 66
terms, 61, 73
transactions, 64
    buyer's option, 45, 70
    cash, 45, 70
    ratings, 70
    regular way, 45, 70
    seller's options, 45, 70
    when issued, 45
transfers, 31
trust indenture, 38-39, 69
unregistered, 59
unsecured, 40, 69
warrants, 21
yields, 34, 47-48
    current, 35, 69-71
    equivalent, 62-63, 73
    nominal, 35, 69
    quotations, 69
    yield to call/put, 36, 63-64, 69
    yield to maturity, 35-36, 63, 69, 73
zero-coupon, 41, 49, 70-71
book value, 12
book-entry bonds, 31, 68
breakpoints, 95-96, 107
brokers
    allied members, 182
    bond members, 182
    commission house, 182, 196
    floor, 182

loans (call loans), 84
market makers, 182
over-the-counter (OTC), 169, 176
business cycles
    Consumer Price Index (CPI), 338
    controlling, 307-310
    cyclical industries, 338, 341
    expansion, 304, 338
    growth industries, 341
    inflation
        cost-push theory, 306, 338
        demand-pull theory, 306, 338
        effects, 305-306
    leading indicators, 305, 338
    noncyclical industries, 338, 341
    recession, 305, 338
    stagflation, 338
buyer's option transactions
    bonds, 45, 70

C

cabinet trading of bonds, 194, 199
calls, 206, 238
    bonds
        preferred stock, 20, 22
        prerefunding, 32
        procedures, 33
        refunding, 32
        sinking fund call, 32-33
    loan rates, 310, 339
    options
        break-even, 239
        holder (buyer), 208, 213, 226, 238
        in the money, 239
        out of the money, 239
        writer (seller), 208-209, 212-213, 226, 238-240
    procedures/provisions, 61, 69
    risks, 334
capital
    account, 312, 340
    gains income tax, 350-352
capitalization ratio, 329-330
capped options, 229
cash
    dividends, 17
    flow ratio, 331
    margin account, 268-269
    transaction, bonds, 45, 70
certificates, 21
    bonds, 68
    CDs (Certificates of Deposit), 83
    ownership
        assignment, 15
        registrars, 14
        tranfer agents, 14
    stock, 16
characteristic line, market returns, 341
charters. *See* Articles of Incorporation
charting stock market, 316, 340
    levels, 317
    patterns, 318
classes
    options, 207, 238
    stocks, 20
clearing agreement (options), 221, 241

closed-end
  bonds, 39
  companies, 89-90, 99, 106
CMOs (collateralized mortgage obligations),
  52-54
CMS structure, 72
collateral trust bonds, 39, 69
collateralized mortgage obligations (CMOs), 52
  income taxes, 54
  REMICs, 53-54, 72
combinations (options), 215, 240
commercial paper, 83, 84
commission house brokers, 182, 196
common stock, 11, 91
Computer-Aided Execution System (CAES),
  172-173, 176
concession, 65, 73
  selling, 154
  underwriters, 154, 160
confidence index, 316, 340
conservator for an incompetent, 253
Consolidated Quote Service (CQS), 173
Consumer Price Index (CPI), 338
contracts
  mutual funds, 100-101, 108
  options, 219
    cash dividends, 223, 242
    issuing, 241
    size, 242
    stock dividends, 223, 242
    stock splits, 223, 242
control person, 256
conversion
  bonds, 41-42
    arbitrage, 43
    conditions, 70
    duration, 43
    forced, 44
    parity, 43
    price, 70
    pricing, 42-43
    ratio, 42, 70
    rights, 43
  preferred stock, 20, 22
cooling-off period, securities, 151, 159
corporations
  accounts, 252-253
  Articles of Incorporation, 11
  bonds, 37-38
    bondholders' rights, 69
    debt securities, 69
    trust indenture, 69
  dividend reports, 351, 369
  financial tables, 367-368
  securities, 326-327
  units of ownership, 11
cost basis, debt instruments, 353
cost-push theory, 306, 338
coupon (bearer) bonds, 30-31, 59
  nominal rates, 68
covered options, 235, 239-240
CPI (Consumer Price Index), 338
cumulative preferred stock, 20, 22
cumulative voting rights, 16
current yield, 35, 69-70
custodian accounts for minors. *See* uniform gifts
  to minors
cyclical industries, 13, 318, 338, 341

D

Daily Bond Buyer, 64, 156, 160
day order, 185, 197
dealers, over-the-counter transactions, 169, 175
debentures, 40, 69
debt. *See also* bonds
  instruments
    accrued interest, 354
    cost basis, 353
    ratio, 329
deceased person's accounts, 257-258
deed of trust. *See* Trust Indenture Act of 1939
default municipal bonds, 67
defeasance of bonds, 32
defensive stock, 13
delivery of bonds, government issue, 55, 72-73
demand-pull theory, 306, 338
depletion allowance, 124
Direct Participation Programs (DPPs)
  limited partnerships, 116-117, 136
    dissolving, 126
    evaluation, 118
    funding, 119
  managed offerings, 119, 136
  non-managed offerings, 119-120, 136
  subscription agreement, 120, 137
disclosure, 158
discount rate (money supply), 308-309
Disposable Income (DI), 304
dissolution rights, 19
diversifiable risks, 341
diversified common stock, 91
dividends
  cash, 17
  corporate, 351, 356
  income, 351, 356
  mutual funds, 90, 106
  property, 18
  stocks, 17-18
Do Not Reduce (DNR)/Do Not Increase (DNI)
    order, 186, 198
dollar cost averaging, 96
double-barreled municipal bonds, 57-58, 72
Dow Jones Averages, 313-314, 340
Dow theory, 315, 340
drilling costs, 124
dual-purpose mutual funds, 92
due diligence meeting, securities, 151, 160
duration, bond conversion, 43

E

earnings ratio, 332-333
economy
  averages, 340
  business cycles
    Consumer Price Index (CPI), 338
    controlling, 307-310
    cyclical industries, 318, 338, 341
    expansion, 304, 338
    growth industries, 318, 341
    inflation, 306-307, 338
    leading indicators, 305, 338
    noncyclical industries, 318, 338, 341
    recession, 305, 338
    stagflation, 338
  call loan rate, 339

discount rate, 339
Dow Jones Averages, 313-314, 340
federal funds rate, 339
Federal Reserve System, 339
fiscal policies, 339
fundamental analysts, 318-319, 340
Gross National Product (GNP), 304, 338
indexes, 313-314, 340
industry life cycles, 318-319
interest rates, 310
international factors, 311-312, 339-340
margin requirements, 339
markets, 314-316, 339-340
monetary supply, 308-309, 339
moral suasion, 339
NASDAQ-OTC Price Indexes, 314, 340
NYSE Index, 314, 340
open market operations, 339
portfolios, 335-338, 341
prime rate, 339
reserve requirements, 339
risks, 333-335
securities, 319, 339-340
    balance sheets, 320-322
    corporation changes, 326-327
    income statements, 322-324
    Statement of Changes in Financial Condition,
        324-325
    valuation practices, 325-326
Standard & Poor's (S&P) 500, 314, 340
technical analysts, 340
Wilshire 5000 Stock Index, 314, 340
Efficient Market Hypothesis (EMH), 341
Equipment Trust Certificates (ETCs), 40, 69
equipment-leasing programs, 125, 137
equity securities. *See* ownership
equivalent yields of bonds, 62-63
ETCs (equipment trust certificates), 40
Eurobonds, 46, 70
Eurodollars, 84
exchange markets. *See also* New York Stock
        Exchange (NYSE); over-the-counter (OTC)
        transactions
    allied members, 182, 197
    at the close order, 186
    auction rules, 183-184, 197
    automating, 186
    block transactions
        exchange distribution, 188, 198
        secondary distribution, 189-190, 198
        special offer/special bid, 187-188, 198
        specialist, 188, 198
    bonds
        active trading, 194, 199
        cabinet trading, 194, 199
        members, 182, 197
        nine bond rule, 194-195, 199
        pricing, 194, 199
        quotations, 195, 199
    commission house brokers, 182, 196
    day orders, 185, 197
    delisting, 183
    Fill or Kill, 186, 197
    floor brokers, 182, 196
    Good-Till-Canceled (GTC), 185, 197
    immediate or cancel, 186, 197
    limit order, 184, 197
    listing requirements, 182-183

markets
    makers, 182, 197
    orders, 184, 197
Not held order (market not held), 186, 197
at the opening order, 186
over-the-counter transactions, 168
registered traders, 182, 196
specialists
    arranging the opening, 192, 198
    block purchase (sale), 188, 198
    ex-sales, 92, 198
    odd-lot trading, 192-194, 198
    regulations, 189-190
    shopping stock, 191-192, 198
stop order, 185, 197
stop-limit order, 185-197
tape
    errors, 195
    messages, 196
    symbols, 195
executors of estates, 253
exempt
    bonds, 70
    securities, 150-151
exercising, 241-242
    price, 21, 207, 220, 226, 238
    notice, 207, 220, 223
expansion business cycle, 304, 308
expiration date (options), 207, 222-223, 225, 238,
        241-242

F

face value. *See* par value
face-amount certificate companies, 88, 102, 106,
        108
Federal Farm Credit Bank, 50, 71
federal funds, 82, 84, 310, 339
Federal Home Loan Bank, 51, 71
Federal Home Loan Mortgage Corporation
        (Freddie Mac), 51, 71
Federal National Mortgage Association (FNMA/
        Fannie Mae), 51, 71
Federal Reserve Board, 268, 293, 307-309, 391-392
fiduciary accounts, 253-254
Fill or Kill order, 186, 197
financial news
    risks, 333
    tables, 362
firm quotes, 170, 176
first mortgage (senior lien) bonds, 39
fiscal policies
    automatic responses, 311, 339
    government, 311, 339
fixed annuities, 126-127, 137
floor brokers, 182, 196
flow of funds, 73
"flower bonds," 71
forced conversion
    bonds, 44
foreign currency (options)
    capped, 237
    European terms, 232, 242
    exercise, 233
    expirations, 233
    Interbank, 232
    International Monetary Market (IMM), 233
    LEAPs, 237

limits, 236
objectives, 236-237
quotes, 234-235
rules, 233
settlement, 233, 242
specifications, 233-234
spreads, 235-236
straddles, 236
U.S. terms, 232-233, 242
fourth market. *See* transactions
Freddie Mac (Federal Home Loan Mortgage
    Corporation), 51, 71
front-end load, 101
frozen margin accounts, 269
fundamental analysts, 340
funded debt (bonds), 30, 67

G

gains, mutual funds, 91
general obligation (G.O.) municipal bonds, 56,
    66-67, 72
gifts, income, 354
GNP. *See* Gross National Product
Good-Till-Canceled (GTC) order, 185, 197
government issue bonds
  accrued interest, 72
  collateralized mortgage obligations (CMOs), 52
    income taxes, 54
    REMICs, 53-54, 72
  CMS structure, 72
  delivery, 55, 72
  Federal Farm Credit Bank, 50, 71
  Federal Home Loan Bank, 51, 71
  Federal Home Loan Mortgage Corporation
    (Freddie Mac), 51, 71
  Federal National Mortgage Association (FNMA/
    Fannie Mae), 51, 71
  financial news, 365
  Government National Mortgage Association
    (GNMA/Ginnie Mae), 52, 71
  Inter-American Development Bank, 54, 72
  Series EE, 49-50
  Series HH, 50
  strips (Treasury receipts), 49
  Student Loan Marketing Association (SLMA/
    Sallie Mae), 52
  Tennessee Valley Authority (TVA), 72
  Treasury bills, 46
    return, 47
    yields, 47-48
  Treasury bonds, 48
  Treasury notes, 48
  World Bank, 54, 72
  zero-coupon, 49
Government National Mortgage Association
    (GNMA/Ginnie Mae), 52, 71
Gross National Product (GNP)
  Disposable Income (DI), 304, 338
  National Income (NI), 304, 338
  Net National Product (NNP), 304, 338
  Personal Income (PI), 304, 338
gross spread, securities 154, 157-158, 160
growth
  industries, 318, 341
  stock, 13, 21
guaranteed bonds, 41, 70
guardians. *See* uniform gifts to minors

H

hedges funds, 213
  long call/short stock, 214, 239
  long put/long stock, 214, 239
  mutual funds, 92
information form, 220-221, 241
hypothecation, 252, 268, 387-387

I

Immediated or Cancel order, 186, 197
income
  bonds, 40, 44, 54-55, 65, 69-70, 73
  capital gains, 350-352, 355
  debt instruments, 354
  dividends, 351-352
  expenses, 352
  gifts of securities, 352
  inheritance, 352
  interest, 351, 356
  net capital losses, 351-352, 356
  REITs, 123
  statements, 322-324, 341
  stock, 13, 21
  taxes
    CMOs, 54
    gifts and estates, 354
    minors, 354
    municipal bonds, 62, 73
    mutual funds, 91, 98-99, 107, 354
    options, 225-226, 242, 354
    progressive, 349-350, 355
    regressive, 349-350, 355
    shelters, 354-355
  wash sales, 353
indenture, municipal bonds, 60, 73
indexes, 313-314, 316, 340
indicators, business, 305
individual accounts, 252, 257
industries
  life cycles, 318-319
  revenue municipal bonds, 58, 72
inflation
  cost-push theory, 306, 338
  demand-pull theory, 306, 338
  effects, 306-307
  inflation, 310
information form (options), 220-221, 241
inspection rights, 19
insurance, municipal bonds, 62, 73
Inter-American Development Bank, 54, 72
interest
  bonds, 34
    accrued, 44, 54-55
    municipal, 59-61, 65
    rates, 69
  expenses, 352, 356
  income, 351, 356
  inflation, 310
  options, 229-231, 242
  REMICs, 53-54
  reversionary, 124
  risks, 333
  royalty, 124
intrinsic value (options), 210-211, 239

international economy. *See also* foreign currency;
    World Bank
  balance of payments, 312, 339
  capital account, 312, 340
  current account, 312, 340
  value, 311
Investment Company Act of 1940, 102-104, 107,
    391
investments. *See also* securities
  advisors' accounts, 254
  annuities
    contracts, 131, 138
    fixed, 126-127, 137
    income taxes, 131, 138
    payouts, 130, 138
    purchasing options, 129-130, 138
    sales charges, 131, 138
    variables, 127-128, 138
  Direct Participation Programs (DPPs)
    limited partnerships, 116-119, 136
    managed offerings, 119, 136
    non-managed offerings, 119-120, 136
    subscription agreement, 120, 137
  equipment-leasing programs, 125
  oil and gas programs 123-125, 137
  portfolios, 334-335
  real estate, 121-123
  retirement, 131
    401(k) plans, 134, 138
    deferred compensation, 136
    IRAs (Individual Retirement Accounts),
      134-135, 138
    Keogh plans, 133-134, 138
    pension plans, 132-133, 138
    Roth IRA, 135
    SEP plans, 134, 138
  risks, 333-334
  tax shelters, 116, 125-126, 136, 354-355
IRAs (Individual Retirement Accounts), 134-135,
    138
reissued stock, 12, 21

J-K

joint accounts, 252
  with righs of survivorship, 258
junior lien (second mortgage) bonds, 39
Keogh plans, 133-134

L

law of agency, 394
leading indicators, 305
legal issues
  lists, 254, 393
  opinion, municipal bonds, 59-60, 73
letter of intent, breakpoints, 95-96, 107
life annuities, 130
limited partnerships, 116-117, 136
  dissolving, 126
  evaluation, 118
  funding, 119
limits
  options, 229
  orders, 170, 176
liquidation
  margin accounts, 277, 281, 283
  ratio, 328-329

rights, 19
  risks, 333
listed securities. *See* securities; transactions
load funds, 94, 106
loan values, 268
lone rates, calls, 310
long margin accounts, 269, 294
long-term options, 229

M

margin accounts, 260-262
  additional purchases, 275, 284
  approval, 270, 294
  cash, 268-269
  debit balance, 271, 294
  equity, 271-274, 282, 294
  hypothecation, 268, 293
  inactive, 284-285
  ineligible, 270, 294
  liquidation, 277, 281, 283
  loan values, 268, 272, 294
  long market value, 271, 292, 294
  maintenance calls, 278
    calculations, 279-280
    deposits, 280-281
    meeting, 280, 295-296
  NASD, 277-278, 295
  NYSE, 277-278, 289, 295
  opening, 269-270
  Reg T calls, 271, 277-279, 293-295
  regulations, 268, 271, 293
  rehypothecation, 268, 293
  requirements, 273
  restricted, 274-277, 295
  short sales, 285, 292, 296
    against the box, 286-287
    calculations, 290
    closing, 288, 297
    future delivery, 287
    hedging, 286, 297
    market arbitage, 287
    regulation, 289-290
    requirements, 288
    rights of lenders, 287
    speculation, 286, 297
  securities
    buying power, 272-273, 294
    deposits, 281, 296
    eligible, 270, 294
    equivalent, 287, 297
    exempt, 270-271, 294
    marginable, 282
    selling, 275-276
    transactions of unequal value, 277
  simultaneous purchase, 277
  Special Memorandum Account (SMA), 281
    balances, 282, 296
    cash additions, 282, 291
    dividends, 282
    equity, 282
  withdrawals, 276-277, 283-284
margins (options), 228-231
  deposits, 218
  Federal Reserve System, 307-309
  marked to market, 240
  naked equity options, 240
  on calls, 217, 240

on puts, 218, 240
  spreads, 219
markets
  makers, 169, 175, 182, 197
  orders, 170-171, 176, 184, 197
  risks, 333, 341
  theories, 314-316, 340
  value, 13
markup policy, over-the-counter (OTC)
    transactions, 173-176
maturity dates, bonds, 30, 68
membership, exchange markets
  allied members, 182, 197
  bond members, 182, 197
  commission house brokers, 182, 196
  delisting, 183
  floor brokers, 182, 196
  listing requirements, 182-183
  market makers, 182, 197
  registered traders, 182, 196
minors. *See* uniform gifts to minors
monetary supply
  call loan rate, 310, 339
  discount rate, 308-309, 339
  federal funds rate, 310, 339
  Federal Reserve System, 308-310, 339
  margin requirements, 309, 339
  monetarist theory (business cycle), 307-310
  moral suasion, 309, 339
  open market operations, 308, 339
  policies, 339
  prime rate, 310, 339
  reserve requirements, 309, 339
  securities, 309-310, 339
money markets, 81
  banker's acceptances, 82-84
  broker's loans (call loans), 84
  Certificates of Deposit (CDs), 83
  commercial paper, 83, 84
  Eurodollars, 84
  federal funds, 82, 84
  mutual funds, 92
  repurchase agreements ("repos"), 82, 84
Moody's Manual, 64
  bond ratings, 45
moral obligation municipal bond, 58, 72
mortgage backed securities. *See* government issue
  bonds
mortgage bonds, 69
  first, 39
  second, 39
municipal bonds, 55
  bearer, 59, 73
  bidding, 156-157
  call procedures, 61
  concessions, 65, 73
  coupon, 59
  debt obligation, 72
  default, 67
  delivery, 73
  disclosure, 158
  double-barreled, 57-58, 72
  exempt securities, 271
  flow of funds, 73
  general obligation (G.O.), 56, 66-67, 72
  income taxes, 62
  indenture, 60, 73
  industrial revenue, 58, 72

  insurance, 62, 73
  interest, 59-61, 73
  legal opinion, 59-60, 73
  moral obligation, 58, 72
  mutual funds, 92
  MSRB regulations, 413
    advertising, 416
    board rules, 417
    commissions, 417
    confirmations, 415
    control relationships, 416
    CUSIP numbers, 418
    customer treatment, 416
    discretionary accounts, 417
    disputes, 418
    examinations, 415
    fiduciary status, 416
    financial advisors, 416
    gifts, 416
    improper use of assets, 417
    Know Your Customer, 416
    outside employees, 417
    prices, 417
    reciprocal dealings, 417
    rules, 414
    standards, 414
    brokers, 414
    quotations, 415
    recordkeeping, 414-415
    settlement and delivery, 415
    supervision, 417
    underwriting, 415
  New Housing Authority (NHA), 72
  notes, 72
  official notice of sale, 370
  over-the-counter (OTC), 73, 175
  owner, 59
  payment, 73
  pollution-control, 58, 72
  principal, 59-61
  put procedure, 61
  ratings, 66-67, 73
  registered, 31, 68, 73
  revenue, 57, 67, 72
  securities, 155, 160
  selling, 156-157
  serial, 61, 73
  short-term, 59
  special tax, 57, 72
  spreads, 157-158
  swaps, 66
  table listings, 369-374
  taxation, 73
  tender offers, 61, 73
  term, 61, 73
  tombstones, 371
  transactions, 64
  unregistered, 59
  workable quotes, 65, 73
  yields, 62
    equivalent, 62, 73
    yield to maturity, 63, 73
    yield to call/put, 63
Municipal Securities Rulemaking Board. *See*
  municipal bonds, MSRB regulations
mutual funds
  balanced funds, 92
  bond and preferred stock, 92

breakpoints, 95-96, 107
closed-end companies, 89-90, 99, 106
contractual plans, 100-101, 108
diversified common stock, 91
dividends, 90, 106
dollar cost averaging, 96
dual-purpose, 92
face-amount certificate companies, 88, 102, 106, 108
gains, 91
hedge funds, 92
income taxes, 91, 98-99, 107, 354
Investment Company Act of 1940, 102-104, 107
letter of intent, 95-96, 107
load, 94, 106
management companies, 92-93, 102-103, 106
money markets, 92
municipal bonds, 92
NASD regulations, 104-105, 108
net asset value (NAV), 94, 106
no load, 94, 106
open-end companies, 90, 106
   advantages, 99
   custodians, 97, 107
   registration requirements, 97, 107
   shareholders' rights, 97, 107
ownership, 98, 107
periodic payment plan, 100, 107
pricing, 93-94, 106
redemption
   fees, 94-95, 107
   shares, 96-97, 107
regular (open) accounts, 100, 107
rights of accumulation, 95, 107
sales charges, 94, 100-101, 107
specialized funds, 91
tables, 365-366
unit investment trusts, 88, 102, 106, 108
U.S. government securities, 92
voluntary accumulation plan, 100, 107
withdrawals, 102, 108
yields, 93

N

NASDAQ National Market
   OTC Price Indexes, 171-172, 176, 314, 340
   quotations, 363-364
National Association of Securities Dealers
   (NASD)
   arbitration, 407
   District Business Conduct Committee, 407
   margin accounts, 277-278, 295
   markup policy, 173-176
   regulations, 395
      membership, 396-397
      mutual funds, 104-105, 108
   Rules of Fair Practice
      commissions, 401
      concessions, 405
      disclosure, 403, 405
      discretionary accounts, 403
      fair dealing, 400
      favoring, 406
      fiduciary status, 402
      fraudulent devices, 404
      "free riding and withholding," 398-399
      gifts, 402-403
      improper use of funds, 404
      influencing market prices, 403
      installments, 404
      margin accounts, 406
      nonmembers, 405
      offerings, "at the market," 404
      partial payments, 404
      pricing, 398, 401-402, 405
      proxies, 398
      purchases, 398
      quotations, 402
      recommendations, 400
      records, 405
      sales charges, 398, 400, 405
      solicitation, 404
      supervision, 406
      taken in trade, 402
      transactions, 402, 406
      underwriters, 405
      variable contracts, 406
   Securities Act of 1933, 395-396
   shelters, 354-355
   Uniform Practice Code, 406
National Income (NI), 304, 338
National Market System (NMS), 172
negotiable securities. *See* government issue bonds
net asset value (NAV), 94, 106
net capital losses, 351-352, 356
Net National Product (NNP), 304, 338
new account form, 221, 250-251, 261
New Housing Authority (NHA) bonds, 72
New York Stock Exchange (NYSE). *See also*
   Exchange Markets
   accounts
      audits, 412
      bookkeeping, 260, 262
      cashiering, 260, 262
      client confirmations, 259
      controller, 261
      corporate, 252-253, 262
      credit agreement, 252
      custodial, 254-255, 262
      death of account holder, 257-258, 262
      designation, 410-411
      discretionary, 256, 411
      dividends, 261-262
      errors, 412
      fiduciary, 253-254, 262
      hypothecation agreement, 252
      individual, 252, 257, 261
      investment advisors', 254, 262
      joint, 252, 258, 262
      loan consent agreement, 252
      margin, 260, 262, 277-278, 295
      members, 411
      new account form, 221, 250-251, 261
      nonmembers, 411
      numbered, 257, 262
      opening, 249-250
      options agreement, 252
      ordering departments, 260-262
      partnership, 253, 258, 262
      power of attorney, 252, 257-258
      proxies, 262-262
      purchase and sales (P&S), 260, 262
      records, 412
      "refusal to receive duplicate information," 257
      registered representative, 260

reorganization, 261
restrictions, 256
rights of survivorship, 258
second, 257
statements, 411
street names, 410
tenants in common, 258
tickets, 258-259, 262
transaction reports, 259-260
unincorporated associations, 253, 262
Index, 314, 340
listing requirements, 182
membership, 196
financial tables, 361-363
listings, 412-413
regulations
discipline, 412
disputes, 412
duties, 408-409
qualifications, 408
public speaking, 409
registered representatives, 407
Rule 405 (Know Your Customer), 249-250, 261, 410
NI (National Income), 304, 338
nine bond rule, 194-195, 199
NNP (Net National Product), 304, 338
no load funds, 94, 106
nominal yield
bonds, 35, 69
coupons, 68
non-cumulative preferred stock, 20, 22
non-cyclical industries, 318, 338, 341
non-negotiable securities. *See* government issue bonds
Not held order (market not held), 186
notes (options), 239
NYSE. *See* New York Stock Exchange

O

objectives (options), 216-217, 231-232
OCC (Options Clearing Corporation), 206
odd-lot theory, 316, 340
oil and gas programs, 123-125, 137
OID (Original Issue Discount), 353
offerings
primary, 146
secondary, 146
shares, 90
open-end
investment companies, 90, 106
advantages, 99
custodians, 97, 107
registration requirements, 97
shareholders' rights, 97, 107
secured bonds, 39
open market operations (money supply), 308
options, 237
at the money, 239
call, 206, 238
break-even, 239
holder (buyer), 208, 213, 226, 238
in the money, 239
out of the money, 239
writer (seller), 208-209, 212-213, 226, 238-240
capped, 229
class, 207, 238

clearing agreement, 221, 241
combinations, 215, 240
contracts, 219
cash dividends, 223, 242
issuing, 241
size, 242
stock dividends, 223, 242
stock splits, 223, 242
covered, 235, 239-240
exercising, 241-242
price, 207, 220, 226, 238
notice, 207, 220, 223
expiration date, 207, 222-223, 225, 238, 241-242
foreign currency
capped, 237
European terms, 232, 242
exercise, 233
expirations, 233
Interbank, 232
International Monetary Market (IMM), 233
LEAPs, 237
limits, 236
objectives, 236-237
quotes, 234-235
rules, 233
settlement, 233, 242
specifications, 233-234
spreads, 235-236
straddles, 236
U.S. terms, 232-233, 242
hedges, 213
long call/short stock, 214, 239
long put/long stock, 214, 239
income taxes, 225-226, 242, 354
information form, 220-221, 241
interest rates, 229-231, 242
limits, 229, 242
long-term, 229
margins, 228-231
deposits, 218
marked to market, 240
naked equity options, 240
on calls, 217, 240
on puts, 218, 240
spreads, 219
new account form, 221
notes, 239
objectives, 216-217, 231-232
ordering, 219-220, 241
premiums, 207-208, 238
intrinsic value, 210-211, 239
time value, 211
volatility, 211
pricing, 222, 241
prospectus (disclosure document), 221, 241
put, 206-207
break-even, 239
holder (buyer), 209, 213, 226, 238-239
in the money, 239
out of the money, 239
short the underlying stock, 239
writer (seller), 209-210, 212-213, 226, 238-240
series, 207, 238
spreads, 215, 226, 242
credit, 216, 240
debit, 216, 240
standard agreement, 221, 241
stock indexes, 365

exercise and expiration, 228
settlement, 227-228
size, 227
straddles
long, 214-215, 240
short, 215, 240
strike price, 207, 238
time value, 239
transactions, 206, 222, 225, 238, 241
Treasury bills/bonds/notes, 230
type, 207, 238
uncovered, 235, 239
Options Clearing Corporation (OCC), 206
contracts, 223
exchanges, 224, 238
exercise notice, 223
expirations, 222-223
limits, 224
ordering (options), 219-220, 241
Original Issue Discount (OID), 353
outstanding stock, 12, 21
over-the-counter (OTC) transactions
additional lists, 173
bank companies, 168
brokers, 169, 176
Computer-Aided Execution System (CAES),
172-173
confirmation, 169
Consolidated Quote Service (CQS), 173
dealers, 169, 175
exchange markets, 168
insurance companies, 168
local lists, 173
market makers, 169, 175
markup policy, 173-175
municipal bonds, 73, 175
NASDAQ, 171-173, 176
National Market System (NMS), 172
orders, 170-171, 176
pink sheets, 173
quotes, 170, 176
retail, 171
Small Order Execution System (SOES), 172
trust companies, 168
wholesale, 171
yellow sheets, 173
overriding royalty interest, 124
ownership
certificates
assignment, 15
registrars, 14
stocks, 14
transfer, 14
dividend rights
cash, 17
property, 18
stocks, 17-18
municipal bonds, 59
mutual funds, 98, 107
pre-emptive rights, 19
proxies, 16-17
REITs, 123
rights
dissolution, 19
inspection, 19
liquidation, 19
pre-emptive, 18

reverse splits, 18
stock splits, 18
voting rights, 15
cumulative, 16
regulatory (statutory), 16

P

par value, 12, 21
bonds, 30, 67, 353
parity price, 20
bonds, 43, 70
exchange markets, 184, 197
participating preferred stock, 20, 22
partnership accounts, 253, 258
payments
municipal bonds, 73
periodic, 100, 107
Personal Income (PI), 304, 338
pink sheets, 173
points, bonds, 69
pollution control municipal bonds, 58, 72
portfolios
investment risks, 333-335
selling parts of a position, 353
theory, 341
power of attorney, 258
pre-emptive rights, 18
value of rights, 19
precedence, exchange markets, 184, 197
preferred stock
callable, 20, 22
convertible, 20, 22
cumulative, 20, 22
non-cumulative, 20, 22
participating, 20, 22
warrants, 21
preliminary prospectus, securities, 151, 159
premiums (options), 207-208, 238
intrinsic value, 210-211
time value, 211
volatility, 211
prerefunding (advanced) bonds, 32, 69
pricing
bonds, 33-34, 42-43, 69, 194
mutual funds, 93-94, 106, 222, 241
shares, 89-90
prime rate (Federal Reserve System), 310, 339
principal, municipal bonds, 59-61
profitability ratio, 330
progressive taxes, 349-350, 355
property dividends, 18
prospectus (disclosure document for options),
221, 241
prudent man rule, 254, 393
purchasing-power risks, 333
puts, 206-207
bonds, 33, 61, 69
options
break-even, 239
holder (buyer), 209, 213, 226, 238-239
in the money, 239
out of the money, 239
short the underlying stock, 239
writer (seller), 209-210, 212-213, 226, 238-240
proxies
ownership rights, 16-17

Q

quotations
  abbreviated, 196
  basis book, 37
  bonds, 36-37, 47-48, 69, 195, 199
  Consolidated Quote Service (CQS), 173
  NASDAQ National Market, 363-364
  over-the-counter (OTC) transactions, 170, 176
  workable, 65

R

random walk, market returns, 341
ratings
  bonds, 45
    interest, 69
    municipal, 66-67, 73
    nominal (coupon), 68
  transactions, 70
ratios
  asset utilization, 330
  bond conversion, 42
  capitalization, 329-330
  cash flow, 331
  debt, 329
  earnings, 332-333
  liquidity, 328-329
  profitability, 330
  valuation, 331-332
real estate investments
  condominimum securities, 122
  existing properties, 121, 137
  government-aided housing, 121, 137
  incentives, 120, 137
  land, 122
  new construction, 121, 137
  REITs, 122-123
Real Estate Mortgage Investment Conduit
    (REMICs), 53-54
reallowance, securities, 155, 160
recession, 305, 338
redemption
  bonds, 33
  mutual funds fees, 94-95, 107
  shares, 96, 97, 107
refunding bonds, 32, 69
registration
  bonds, 31, 68
  representatives, 407-409
  securities, 150, 159
registrars, 14
Reg T calls, 271, 277-279, 293-295
regressive taxes, 349-350, 355
regular transactions
  bonds, 45, 70
  mutual funds accounts, 100, 107
regulations, 395
  Federal Reserve Board, 268, 293, 307-309,
    391-392
  Investment Company Act of 1940, 102-104, 107,
    391
  law of agency, 394
  legal lists, 394
  MSRB, 413
    advertising, 416
    board rules, 417

commissions, 417
confirmations, 415
control relationships, 416
CUSIP numbers, 418
customer treatment, 416
discretionary accounts, 417
disputes, 418
examinations, 415
fiduciary status, 416
financial advisors, 416
gifts, 416
improper use of assets, 417
Know Your Customer, 416
outside employees, 417
prices, 417
reciprocal dealings, 417
rules, 414
standards, 414
brokers, 414
quotations, 415
recordkeeping, 414-415
settlement and delivery, 415
supervision, 417
underwriting, 415
NASD
  arbitration, 407
  District Business Conduct Committee, 407
  margin accounts, 277-278, 295
  markup policy, 173-176
  membership, 396-397
  mutual funds, 104-105, 108
NYSE
  account designation, 410
  cash accounts, 411
  discretionary, 411
  duties, 408-409
  employee restrictions, 256
  listings, 412-413
  margin accounts, 411
  members, 411
  order designation, 411-412
  nonmembers, 411
  qualifications, 408
  public speaking, 409
  registered representatives, 407
  Rule 405 (Know Your Customer), 249-250,
    261, 410
  statements, 411
  street name accounts, 410
prudent man rule, 393
Rules of Fair Practice
  commissions, 401
  concessions, 405
  disclosure, 403, 405
  discretionary accounts, 403
  fair dealing, 400
  favoring, 406
  fiduciary status, 402
  fraudulent devices, 404
  "free riding and withholding," 398-399
  gifts, 402-403
  improper use of funds, 404
  influencing market prices, 403
  installments, 404
  nonmembers, 405
  offerings, "at the market," 404
  partial payments, 404

pricing, 398, 401-402, 405
proxies, 398
purchases, 398
quotations, 402
recommendations, 400
records, 405
sales charges, 398, 400, 405
solicitation, 404
supervision, 406
taken in trade, 402
transactions, 402, 406
underwriters, 405
variable contracts, 406
Securities Act of 1933, 38, 378, 395-396
  advertising, 384-385
  exempt securities, 380
  exempt transactions, 381
  intrastate transactions, 383-384
  nonaffiliated persons, 383
  penalties for misleading statements, 378-379
  preliminary prospectus, 379-380
  registration requirements, 378
  restricted securities, 382-383
  Regulation A offerings, 384
  Rule 501, 381-382
  S-1 statement, 378
  SEC review process, 379
  selling new issues, 380
Securities Exchange Act of 1934, 268, 385
  credit, 386
  customer protection, 391
  disclosure, 388
  false information, 387
  free credit balance, 390
  hypothecation, 386-387
  insider trading, 388-389
  matching orders, 387
  net capital requirements, 390
  over-the-counter (OTC) transactions, 389-390
  proxies, 389
  registration, 386
  short sales, 387
  solicitation, 387-388
  stabilization, 388
  tenders, 388
  wash sales, 387
Securities Investor Protection corporation
  (SIPC), 392-393
shelters, 354-355
Trust Indenture Act of 1939, 38-39, 69, 393
uniform gifts to minors, 393
voting rights, 16
rehypothecation, 268
REMICs (Real Estate Mortgage Investment
  Conduit), 53-54
repurchase agreements ("repos"), 82, 84
reserve requirements (money supply), 309
restricted stocks, 14
retail transactions, 171
retirement, 131
  401(k) plans, 134, 138
  deferred compensation, 136
  IRAs (Individual Retirement Accounts),
    134-135, 138
  Keogh plans, 133-134, 138
  pension plans, 132-133, 138
  Roth IRA, 135
  SEP plans, 134, 138

returns
  analyses, 341
  bonds
    Treasury bills, 47
revenue municipal bonds, 57, 67, 72
reverse splits, 18
reversionay (subordinate) working interest, 124
rights of ownership
  bonds
    conversion, 43
    cumulative, 22
    dissolution, 19
    dividends
      cash, 17
      property, 18
      rights, 22
      stocks, 17-18
    inspection, 19
    liquidation, 19
    pre-emptive rights, 18-19, 22
    preferred stock, 22
    proxies, 16-17, 22
    regulatory (statutory), 22
    reverse splits, 18
    rights, 22
    stock splits, 18, 22
    voting, 15
      cumulative, 16
      regulatory (statutory), 16
risks
  calls, 334
  diversifiable, 341
  financial, 333
  interest-rate, 333
  liquidity, 333
  markets, 333, 341
  portfolios, 334-335
  purchasing-power, 333
Roth IRAs, 135

S

S&P. *See* Standard & Poor's
sale charges, mutual funds, 94, 100-101, 107
savings bonds. *See* Series EE bonds; Series HH
    bonds
second mortgage (junior lien) bonds, 39
secondary market. *See* transactions
secured bonds
  closed-end, 39
  collateral trust, 39, 69
  Equipment Trust Certificates (ETCs), 40, 69
  first mortgage (senior lien), 39
  open-end, 39
  second mortgage (junior lien), 39
securities. *See also* mutual funds; stocks
  American Depository Receipts (ADRs), 21-22
  balance sheet, 320, 341
    assets, 321
    equity (net worth), 322
    liabilities, 321-322
  bidding, 156-157
  closing the books, 152, 160
  cooling-off period, 151, 159
  due diligence meeting, 151, 160
  exempt, 150-151
  gifts, 352
  gross spread, 154, 157-158, 160

hot issues, 153-154, 160
income statements, 322-324
liquidation, 277, 281, 283
municipal, 155-156, 160
negotiated offerings, 146-147
opening the books, 152, 160
primary offerings, 146, 158
private placements, 146, 159
reallowance, 155, 160
registration, 150, 159
secondary offerings, 146, 159
selling parts of a position, 353
stabilizing the issue, 152-153, 160
Statement of Changes in Financial Condition, 324-325
tombstone announcements, 152, 160
underwriting, 146, 158
  as agent, 148
  agreements, 147
  concessions, 154, 160
  divided accounts, 149, 159
  market-out clause, 148
  as principal, 148
  selling group, 150, 156, 159
  syndicates, 149, 159
  undivided accounts, 150, 154, 159
valuation practices, 325-326
warrants, 21, 23
Securities Act of 1933, 38, 378
  advertising, 384-385
  exempt securities, 380
  exempt transactions, 381
  intrastate transactions, 3830384
  nonaffiliated persons, 383
  private palcement (regulation D)
  registration requirements, 378
    S-1 statement, 378
    penalties for misleading statements, 378-379
    SEC review process, 379
    preliminary prospectus, 379-380
    selling new issues, 380
  Regulation A offerings, 384
  restricted securities, 382-383
  Rule 501, 381-382
Securities Exchange Act of 1934, 268, 385
  credit, 386
  customer protection, 391
  disclosure, 388
  false information, 387
  free credit balance, 390
  hypothecation, 386-387
  insider trading, 388-389
  matching orders, 387
  net capital requirements, 390
  over-the-counter (OTC) transactions, 389-390
  proxies, 389
  registration, 386
  short sales, 387
  solicitation, 387-388
  stabilization, 388
  tenders, 388
  wash sales, 387
Securities Investor Protection Corporation (SIPC), 392-393
self-employed retirement plans. See retirement
seller's option transactions, 45, 70
senior lien (first mortgage) bonds, 39
serial bonds, 31, 61, 68, 73

series bonds, 31, 68, 207, 238
  EE bonds, 49-50, 71
  HH bonds, 50, 71
shares, 29
  authorized
    See also mutual funds; ownership; stocks
short interest theory, 316
short sales, 285, 296
  against the box, 286-287
  calculations, 290-291
  closing, 288
  dividends, 288
  equivalent securities, 287, 297
  future delivery, 287
  hedging, 286, 297
  maintenance, 289
  mark to the market, 288
  market arbitage, 287
  NYSE, 29
  plus tick rule, 289-290
  requirements, 288-289
  return of stock, 288
  rights of lenders, 287
  speculation, 286, 297
short-term municipal bonds, 59
single payment annuities, 129
sinking fund bonds, 68
  callable, 32-33, 69
Small Order Execution System (SOES), 172
Special Memorandum Account (SMA), 281
  additional purchases, 284
  balances, 282, 296
  buying power, 291
  cash additions, 282
  dividends, 282
  equity, 282
  inactive, 284-285
  long accounts, 292
  marginable securities, 282
  short market values, 291-292
  withdrawals, 283-284
special offer/special bid block transaction, 187, 198
special tax municipal bonds, 57, 72
specialists
  arranging the opening, 192, 198
  block purchase (sale), 188, 198
  ex-sales, 92, 198
  odd-lot trading, 192-194, 198
  regulations, 189-190
  shopping stock, 191-192, 198
specialized mutual funds, 91
speculative stocks, 14
splits
  reverse, 18
  stocks, 18
spreads, 215, 226, 242
  credit, 216, 240
  debit, 216, 240
  load plan, 101
  securities 154, 157-158, 160
stabilizing the issue, 152-153, 160
stagflation, 338
Standard & Poor's (S&P) 500, 340
  bonds ratings, 45
  Stock Guide, 374-375
standard agreement (options), 221, 241

Statement of Changes in Financial Condition, 324-325, 341
statutory (regulatory) voting rights, 16
"stock power," 15
stocks
  assignment, 22
  authorized, 12, 21
  blue chips, 13
  book value, 12
  certificates, 14, 16, 21
  charting, 316-318
  classes, 20
  common, 11
  cyclical, 13
  defensive, 13
  dividends, 17-18, 352, 356
  gifts of securities, 352, 356
  growth, 13, 21
  income, 13, 21
  indexes
    exercise and expiration, 228
    settlement, 227-228
    size, 227
  inheritance, 352
  issued, 12, 21
  market value, 13
  options, 365
  outstanding, 12, 21
  par value, 12, 21
  preferred
    callable, 20, 22
    convertible, 20, 22
    cumulative, 20, 22
    non-cumulative, 20, 22
    participating, 20, 22
  restricted, 14
  rights, 352
  speculative, 14
  splits, 18
  transfers, 21
  treasury, 12, 21
  types, 21
  unissued, 12, 21
stop order, 170, 176, 185, 197
stop-limit orders, 185, 197
straddles
  long, 214-215, 240
  short, 215, 240
strike price, 207, 238
strips (Treasury receipts) bonds, 49, 71
Student Loan Marketing Association (SLMA/ Sallie Mae), 52
subject quotes, 170, 176
subordinated debentures, 40
swaps
  bonds
    municipal, 66

T

T-bills. *See* Treasury bills, 47
  tape
    errors, 195
    messages, 196
    symbols, 195
Tax Reform Act of 1986, 58, 350
taxes. *See* income taxes; investments
technical analysts, 340

tender offers, municipal bonds, 61, 73
tenants in common accounts, 258
Tennessee Valley Authority (TVA), 54, 72
term bonds, 61, 73
time
  options values, 239
  qualification of orders, 185
tombstone announcements
  financial tables, 369, 373
  securities, 152, 160
trading. *See* transactions
transactions
  bonds
    active trading, 194, 199
    buyer's option, 45, 70
    cabinet trading, 194, 199
    cash, 45, 70
    Eurobonds, 70
    members, 182, 197
    municipal, 64, 72
    nine bond rule, 194-195, 199
    pricing, 194, 199
    quotations, 195, 199
    ratings, 70
    regular way, 45, 70
    seller's option, 45, 70
    when issued, 45
  exchange markets, 168
  options, 206, 222, 225, 238, 241
  over-the-counter (OTC), 168, 175
    additional lists, 173
    bank companies, 168
    brokers, 169, 176
    Computer-Aided Execution System (CAES), 172
    confirmation, 169
    Consolidated Quote Service (CQS), 173
    dealers, 169, 175
    insurance companies, 168
    local lists, 173
    market makers, 169, 175
    markup policy, 173-176
    municipal bonds, 73, 175
    NASDAQ, 171-172, 176
    national lists, 173
    National Market System (NMS), 172
    orders, 170, 176
    pink sheets, 173, 176
    quotes, 170, 176
    retail, 171
    Small Order Execution System (SOES), 172
    trust companies, 168
    wholesale, 171
    yellow sheets, 173, 176
transfers of ownership, 21
  bonds, 31
  certificates
    assignment, 15
    registrars, 14
    tranfer agents, 14
Treasury
  bills, 46
    options, 230
    returns, 47
    yields, 47-48
  bonds/notes, 48, 230
  financial reports, 364
  receipts (strips), 49
  stock, 12, 21

Trust Indenture Act of 1939, 38-39, 69, 393
trustees, 253
TVA (Tennessee Valley Authority), 54, 72
type of options, 207, 238

U

U.S. government issues. *See* government issue
    bonds; mutual funds
uncovered options, 235, 239
underwriting securities, 146, 158
  as agent, 148
  as principal, 148
  agreements, 147
  bidding, 156-157
  concessions, 154, 160
  divided accounts, 149, 159
  market-out clause, 148
  municipal, 155-156, 160
  selling group, 150, 156, 159
  syndicates, 149, 159
  undivided account, 150, 159
unincorporated associations, 253
uniform gifts to minors, 253-255, 393
unissued stock, 12, 21
units
  investment trusts, 88, 102, 106, 108
  of ownership, 11
unlisted securities. *See* securities; transactions
unregistered bonds, 59
unsecured bonds, 40, 69

V

valuation
  book, 12
  market, 13
  par, 12
  practices, 325-326
  pre-emptive rights, 19
  ratio, 331-332
  shares, 89

variable annuities, 127-129, 138
vesting, 132
Visible Bond Supply, 156, 160
volume of trading, 316, 340
voluntary accumulation plan (mutual funds), 100,
    107
voting rights
  ownership, 15
    cumulative, 16
    regulatory (statutory), 16

W

warrants, 21, 23
wash sales, 353
when-issued transactions, 45, 196
wholesale transactions, 171
Wilshire 5000 Stock Index, 314, 340
withdrawals
  margin accounts, 276-277
  mutual funds, 102, 108
workable quotes, 65, 73
World Bank, 54, 72

Y

yellow sheets, 173, 176
yields
  bonds, 34
    current, 35, 69
    equivalent, 62-63, 73
    municipal, 62
    nominal, 35, 69
    quotations, 69
    Treasury bills, 47-48
    yield to call/put, 36, 63-64, 69
    yield to maturity, 35-36, 63, 69, 73
  mutual funds, 93, 106

Z

zero-coupon bonds, 41, 49, 70-71